UTAH
HANDBOOK

UTAH
Welcomes You

UTAH
HANDBOOK

BILL WEIR & ROBERT BLAKE

MOON
PUBLICATIONS INC.

UTAH HANDBOOK
4TH EDITION

Published by
Moon Publications, Inc.
P.O. Box 3040
Chico, California 95927-3040, USA

Printed by
Colorcraft Ltd., Hong Kong

ISBN: 1-56691-068-4
ISSN: 1078-5280

Editor: Charles Mohnike
Copy Editors: Sharon Brown, Asha Johnson
Production & Design: Carey Wilson
Cartographers: Bob Race, Brian Bardwell, Jason Sadler
Index: Deana Corbitt, Valerie Sellers

Front cover photo: David Houser
All photos by Bill Weir unless otherwise noted.

Distributed in the U.S.A. by Publishers Group West
Printed in Hong Kong

Please send all comments,
corrections, additions,
amendments, and critiques to:

**UTAH HANDBOOK
MOON PUBLICATIONS, INC.
P.O. BOX 3040
CHICO, CA 95927-3040, USA
e-mail: travel@moon.com**

Printing History
1st edition — 1988
2nd edition — Feb. 1991
3rd edition — Feb. 1993
4th edition — June 1995

CONTENTS

MAPS

MAP SYMBOLS

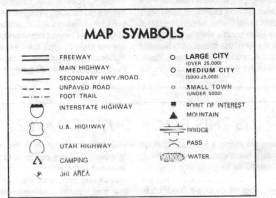

FREEWAY
MAIN HIGHWAY
SECONDARY HWY./ROAD
UNPAVED ROAD
FOOT TRAIL
INTERSTATE HIGHWAY
U.S. HIGHWAY
UTAH HIGHWAY
CAMPING
SKI AREA

○ **LARGE CITY** (OVER 25,000)
○ **MEDIUM CITY** (5000-25,000)
○ SMALL TOWN (UNDER 5000)
■ POINT OF INTEREST
▲ MOUNTAIN
BRIDGE
PASS
WATER

ABBREVIATIONS

ATV—all-terrain vehicle
AZ—Arizona
BLM—Bureau of Land
   Management
CA—California
CO—Colorado
d—double
elev.—elevation
F—Fahrenheit
4WD—four-wheel drive

h.p.—horsepower
mph—miles per hour
N.R.A.—National Recreation
   Area
NM—New Mexico
NV—Nevada
ORV—off-road vehicle
OW—one way
pop.—population
RV—recreational vehicle

s—single
tel.—telephone
2WD—two-wheel drive
USFS—United States
   Forest Service
USGS—United States
   Geological Survey
UT—Utah
w/—with
WY—Wyoming

CHARTS AND SPECIAL TOPICS

ACKNOWLEDGMENTS

Many thanks go to the hundreds of people who assisted in making *Utah Handbook* as complete and accurate as it is. I am especially indebted to people of the National Park Service, U.S. Forest Service, Bureau of Land Management, and Utah State Parks, whose high standards help make Utah such a wonderful place to visit. Tourist offices, from the tiniest communities to the largest cities, supplied valuable maps, ideas, and advice. Most of the wonderful historic photos appear with the assistance of friendly librarians Bill Slaughter of the LDS Historical Department and Susan Whetstone of the Utah State Historical Society, both in Salt Lake City. Extra special thanks go to John Williams of NAVTEC Expeditions for showing the author some of the wonders of Cataract Canyon from his sportboats. And last, but not least . . . the hard working crew at Moon Publications deserves a round of applause for their patience in dealing with a fussy author!

IS THIS BOOK OUT OF DATE?

Nothing stays the same, it seems. Although this book has been carefully researched, Utah will continue to grow and change. New sights and places to stay and eat will open, while other change hands or close. Your comments and ideas for improving *Utah Handbook* will be highly valued. If you find something new or discontinued or changed, or perhaps a map or worthwhile place to visit has been overlooked, please let me know so that I can include it in the next edition. All contributions (letters, maps, and photos) will be carefully saved, checked, and acknowledged. If we use your photos or artwork, you will be mentioned in the credits. Be aware, however, that the author and publisher are not responsible for unsolicited manuscripts, photos, or artwork and, in most cases, cannot return them unless you include a self-addressed, stamped envelope. Address your letters to:

UTAH HANDBOOK
c/o Moon Publications
P.O. Box 3040
Chico, CA 95927, USA
e-mail: travel@moon.com

ILLUSTRATION CREDITS

INTRODUCTION

Few places in the world combine such spectacular terrain and unusual history as does Utah. Lying in the heart of the American West, the state hosts the majestic splendor of the Rocky Mountains, the colorful canyonlands of the Colorado Plateau, and the remote desert ranges of the Great Basin. This region beckoned as the "Promised Land" to members of the struggling Mormon church in the 1800s—a place where the faithful could survive and prosper. Today you can comfortably enjoy the scenic splendor of Utah, much of it little changed since the first pioneers arrived in 1847.

Salt Lake City in the north and the five national parks in the south rank at the top of most visitors' lists, but many other beautiful and intriguing places remain undiscovered. Incredibly varied canyon country, rugged mountain ranges, glistening salt flats, Indian reservations, old mining towns—this handbook will help you discover these and many more attractions.

THE LAND

Utah's 84,990 square miles place it 11th in size among the 50 states. You could fit Maine, Vermont, New Hampshire, Connecticut, Massachusetts, New Jersey, and Maryland within its borders and still have room to squeeze in Rhode Island. The varied landscape is divided into three major physiographic provinces: the **Basin and Range Province** to the west; the **Middle Rocky Mountain Province** of the soaring Uinta, Wasatch, and Bear River ranges to the north and northeast; and the **Colorado Plateau Province** of canyons, mountains, and plateaus in the southeast. Some physiographers argue for a fourth province, the **Basin and Range-Colorado Plateau Transition**. This area, also known as the "High Plateaus," stretches from the Wasatch Range south into Arizona. Mountains and plateaus in this area share structural features with both neighboring provinces.

Basin And Range Province
Rows of fault-block mountain ranges follow a north-south alignment in this province, located in the Great Basin west of the Wasatch Range and the High Plateaus. Most of the land lies between 4,000 and 5,000 feet. Peaks in the Stansbury and Deep Creek mountains rise more than 11,000 feet above sea level, creating "biological islands" inhabited by cool-climate plants and animals.

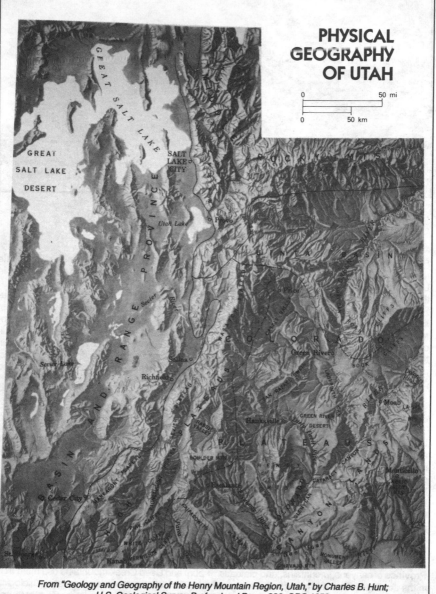

PHYSICAL
GEOGRAPHY
OF UTAH

From "Geology and Geography of the Henry Mountain Region, Utah," by Charles B. Hunt;
U.S. Geological Survey Professional Paper 228, GPO 1953.

UTAH PHYSIOGRAPHIC PROVINCES

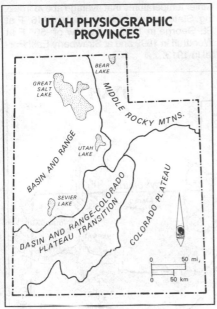

BEAR LAKE

GREAT SALT LAKE

MIDDLE ROCKY MTNS.

BASIN AND RANGE

UTAH LAKE

SEVIER LAKE

COLORADO PLATEAU

BASIN AND RANGE-COLORADO PLATEAU TRANSITION

0   50 mi
0   50 km

© MOON PUBLICATIONS, INC.

Utah's ski resorts lie in this area. The Uinta Mountains in the northeast corner of the state present a broad rise about 150 miles long from west to east and 30 miles across. Twenty-four peaks exceed 13,000 feet, with Kings Peak (elev. 13,528 feet) the highest mountain in Utah. An estimated 1,400 tiny lakes dot glacial moraines of the Uintas.

Colorado Plateau Province
World-famous for its scenery and geology, the Colorado Plateau covers nearly half of Utah. Elevations lie mostly between 3,000 and 6,000 feet; some mountain peaks reach nearly 13,000 feet. The Uinta Basin forms the northern part of this vast complex of plateaus; it's bordered on the north by the Uinta Mountains and on the south by the Roan Cliffs. Although most of the basin terrain is gently rolling, the Green River and its tributaries have carved some spectacular canyons into the Roan and Book cliffs. Farther south, the Green and Colorado rivers have sculpted remarkable canyons, buttes, mesas, arches, and badlands. Uplifts and foldings have formed such features as the San Rafael Swell, Waterpocket Fold, and Circle Cliffs. The rounded Abajo, Henry, La Sal, and Navajo mountains are examples of intrusive rock, an igneous layer that is formed below the earth's surface and later exposed by erosion. The High Plateaus in south-central Utah drop in a series of steps known as the "Grand Staircase." Exposed layers range from the relatively young rocks of the Black Cliffs (lava flows) in the north to the increasingly older Pink Cliffs (Wasatch Formation), Gray Cliffs (Mancos Shale), White Cliffs (Navajo Sandstone), and Vermilion Cliffs (Chinle and Wingate formations) toward the south.

CLIMATE

The hot summer sun awakens wildflowers in the mountains and turns desert areas brown. Autumn brings pleasant weather to all elevations until the snow line begins to creep down the mountain slopes. Winter snowfalls provide excellent skiing and add beauty to the landscape, but many mountain roads close and you'll need chains or snow tires on those that don't. Spring tends to be unpredictable—wet and windy one

Erosion has worn down many of the ranges, forming large alluvial fans in adjacent basins. Many of these broad valleys lack effective drainage; none have outlets to the ocean. Terraces mark the hills along the shore of prehistoric Lake Bonneville, which once covered most of this province. Few perennial streams originate in these rocky mountains, but rivers from eastern ranges end their voyages in the Great Salt Lake, Sevier Lake, or barren silt-filled valleys.

Middle Rocky Mountains Province
The Wasatch Range and the Uinta Mountains that form this province provide some of the most dramatic alpine scenery in the state. In both mountainous areas, you'll find cirques, arêtes, horns, and glacial troughs carved by massive rivers of ice during periods of glaciation. Structurally, however, the ranges have little in common. The narrow Wasatch, one of the most rugged ranges in the country, runs north-south for about 200 miles between the Idaho border and central Utah. Slippage along the still-active Wasatch Fault has resulted in a towering western face with few foothills. Most of

day, sunny and calm the next—but it's then you'll find the deserts at their greenest.

Utah's mid-continent location brings wide temperature variations between the seasons. Only a small part of the south experiences winter temperatures that average above freezing. State records include a high of 116° F at St. George in 1892 and a low of -50° F at Woodruff in 1899 and at Strawberry East Portal in 1913.

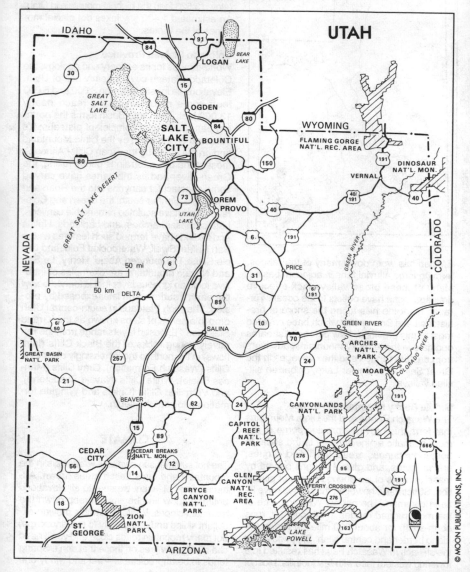

Precipitation

Most of Utah is dry—evaporation exceeds precipitation. In fact, of the 50 states, only Nevada receives less moisture annually than Utah's 13 inches. Precipitation varies greatly from place to place due to local topography and the irregularities of storm patterns. Deserts cover about 33% of the state; the driest areas are in the Great Basin, the Uinta Basin, and on the Colorado Plateau, where annual precipitation is around 5-10 inches.

At the other extreme, the highest peaks of the Wasatch Range receive more than 50 inches of annual precipitation, most of it as snow; approximately 24% of Utah has a highland climate. About 40% of the state, classified as steppe, receives 8-14 inches of annual precipitation and supports grasslands suitable for ranching. Three percent of the state's land is humid continental, ideal for agriculture. This heavily populated strip lies along the Wasatch Front. Utah enjoys lots of sunshine, but storm systems briefly darken the skies at anytime.

Winter And Spring Weather Patterns (October to April)

Periods of high-pressure systems broken by Pacific storm fronts shape most of Utah's winter weather. The high-pressure systems cause inversions when cold, dense air flows down the snow-covered mountain slopes into the valleys, where it traps moisture and smoke. The blanket of fog or smog maintains even temperatures, but is the bane of the Salt Lake City area. Skiers, however, enjoy bright, sunny days and cold nights in the clear air of the mountain peaks. The blankets of stagnant air in the valleys are cleaned out when cold fronts roll in from the Pacific. When skies clear, the daily temperature range is much greater until the inversion process sets in again.

Most winter precipitation arrives as snow, which all regions of the state expect. Fronts originating over the Gulf of Alaska typically arrive every six to seven days and trigger most of Utah's snowfall.

Summer And Autumn Weather Patterns (May to September)

During summer, the valleys still experience inversions of cold air on clear, dry nights, but with a much less pronounced effect than in winter. The canyon country in the south has higher daytime temperatures than do equivalent mountain elevations, because there's no source of cold air in the canyons to replace the rising heated air. Also, canyon walls act as an oven, reflecting and trapping heat. Thunderstorms are most common in summer, when warm, moist air rises in billowing clouds. The storms, though they can produce heavy rains and hail, tend to be erratic and concentrated in small areas less than three miles across. Southeastern Utah sees the first thunderstorms of the season, often in mid-June; by mid-July, these storms have spread across the entire state. They lose energy as autumn approaches, and by October they're supplanted by lows aloft (low-pressure systems at high altitudes) and Pacific storm fronts. Lows aloft move in erratic patterns, but can cause long periods of heavy precipitation. They're often the main source of weather disturbances during October, late April, and May. Surprisingly, most of Utah's moisture originates in the Gulf of California or the Gulf of Mexico. The Pacific fronts often lose most of their moisture by the time they reach Utah, yet their cold air can produce heavy precipitation when it meets warm moist air from the south. Hikers need to be aware that the highest mountain peaks can receive snow even in midsummer.

Storm Hazards

Rainwater runs quickly off the rocky desert surfaces and into gullies and canyons. Flash floods can sweep away anything in their path, including boulders, cars, and campsites. Do not camp or park in potential flash-flood areas. If you come to a section of flooded roadway, a common occurrence on desert roads after storms, wait until the water goes down before crossing—it shouldn't take long. Summer lightning causes forest and brush fires, posing a danger to hikers foolish enough to climb mountains when storms threaten.

FLORA AND FAUNA

A wide variety of plants and animals find a home within Utah's great range of elevations (more than 11,000 feet). To help simplify and understand the different environments, some scientists use the Merriam system of life zones, which offers a concise way to get an overview of Utah's vegetation and animal life. Because plants subsist on rainfall, which is determined largely by elevation, each life zone can be identified with an elevation range. These ranges are not exact, however—due to the different rainfall patterns and evaporation rates.

Lower Sonoran Life Zone (Below 3,500 Feet)

This zone is found in the Mojave Desert, which extends into the southwest corner of the state. Annual precipitation here is usually less than eight inches. Creosote bush dominates the plantlife, though you're also likely to see grasses, rabbitbrush, snakeweed, blackbrush, saltbush, yucca, and cacti. Joshua trees grow on some of the higher gravel benches. Flowering plants tend to bloom after either the winter rains (the Sonoran or Mexican species) or the summer rains (the Mojave or Californian species).

Most desert animals retreat to a den or burrow during the heat of the day, when ground temperatures can reach 130° F! Look for wildlife in early morning, late afternoon, or at night. You may see kangaroo rat, desert cottontail, black-tailed jackrabbit, striped and spotted skunks, kit fox, ringtail cat, coyote, bobcat, mountain lion, and several kinds of squirrels and mice. Birds include the native Gambel's quail, roadrunner, red-tailed hawk, great horned owl, cactus wren, black-chinned and broad-tailed hummingbirds, and rufous-sided towhee. The endangered desert tortoise lives here too, but faces extinction in a losing battle with livestock, which trample and graze on the tortoise's precious environment. The rare Gila monster, identified by beadlike skin with black and yellow patterns, is the only poisonous lizard in the United States. In Utah, it is found only in the state's southwest corner. Although slow and nonaggressive, it has powerful jaws and excretes a potentially lethal venom from a gland in its lower jaw. Once the reptile gets a grip, it does not like to let go and the jaws must be pried loose—even if the head has been cut off. Sidewinder, Great Basin, and other western rattlesnakes are occasionally seen. Also watch for other poisonous creatures; scorpions, spiders, and centipedes can inflict painful stings or bites. It's a good idea when camping to check for these unwanted guests in shoes and other items left outside. Be careful, too, not to reach under rocks or into places you can't see.

Upper Sonoran Life Zone (3,500-5,500 Feet)

Most of Utah's land lies in this zone. Shadscale, a plant resistant to both salt and drought, grows on the valley floors and lower slopes of the Great Basin, Uinta Basin, and Canyonlands. Commonly growing with shadscale are grasses, annuals, Mormon tea, budsage, gray molley, and winterfat. In salty soils, more likely companions are greasewood, salt grass, and iodine bush. Nonalkaline soils, on the other hand, may have blackbrush as the dominant plant. Sagebrush, the most common shrub in Utah, thrives on higher terraces and in alluvial fans of nonalkaline soil. Grasses are commonly found mixed with sagebrush and may even dominate the landscape. Piñon pine and juniper, small trees often found together, can grow only if there are 12 inches or more of annual precipitation; the lower limit of their growth is sometimes called the "arid timberline." In the Wasatch Range, scrub oaks often grow near junipers.

Many of the same animals live here as in the Lower Sonoran Zone. You might also see Utah prairie dog, beaver, muskrat, black bear, desert bighorn sheep, desert mule deer, and the antelope-like pronghorn. Marshes of the Great Basin have an abundance of food and cover that attract waterfowl; species include whistling swan, Great Basin Canada goose, lesser snow goose, great blue heron, seagull (Utah's state bird), common mallard, gadwall, and American common merganser. Chukar partridge (from similar desert lands in Asia) and Hungarian partridge (from eastern Europe and western Asia) thrive under the cover of sagebrush in dry-farm areas. Sage and sharp-tailed grouse also prefer the open country. Rattlesnakes and other reptiles like the Upper Sonoran Zone best.

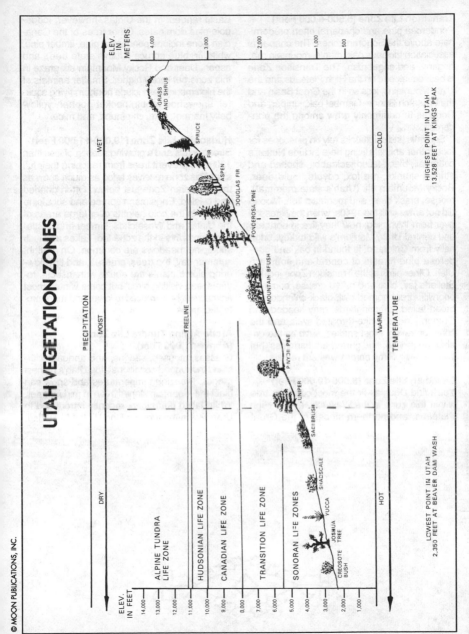

© MOON PUBLICATIONS, INC.

UTAH VEGETATION ZONES

ELEV. IN METERS

4,000

3,000

2,000

1,000

500

PRECIPITATION

DRY   MOIST   WET

GRASS AND SHRUB

SPRUCE

FIR

ASPEN

DOUGLAS FIR

PONDEROSA PINE

MOUNTAIN B'USH

PINYON PINE

JUNIPER

SAGEBRUSH

SHADSCALE

YUCCA

JOSHUA TREE

CREOSOTE BUSH

TREELINE

Alpine Tundra Life Zone

Hudsonian Life Zone

Canadian Life Zone

Transition Life Zone

Sonoran Life Zones

ELEV. IN FEET

14,000
13,000
12,000
11,000
10,000
9,000
8,000
7,000
6,000
5,000
4,000
3,000
2,000
1,000

TEMPERATURE

HOT   WARM   COLD

LOWEST POINT IN UTAH
2,350 FEET AT BEAVER DAM WASH

HIGHEST POINT IN UTAH
13,528 FEET AT KINGS PEAK

Transition Life Zone (5,500-8,000 Feet)

Ponderosa pine and chaparral often predominate above the Sonoran zones. The chaparral association includes oak, maple, mountain mahogany, and sagebrush. The Transition Zone is best developed on the High Plateaus and the Uinta Mountains, less so in the Great Basin and the Wasatch Range. Gambel oak, juniper, and Douglas fir commonly grow among the ponderosa.

Squirrels and chipmunks rely on pinecones for food; other animals living here include Nuttall's cottontail, black-tailed jackrabbit, spotted and striped skunks, red fox, coyote, mule deer, Rocky Mountain elk (Utah's state mammal), moose, black bear, and mountain lion. Moose did not arrive until the 1940s, when they crossed over from Wyoming; now they live in northern and central Utah. Merriam's wild turkey, originally from Colorado, is found in oak and ponderosa pine forests of central and southern Utah. Other birds of the Transition Zone include Steller's jay, blue and ruffed grouse, common poorwill, great horned owl, black-chinned and broad-tailed hummingbirds, gray-headed and Oregon juncos, white-throated swift, and the common raven. Most snakes, such as the gopher, hognosed, and garter, are harmless, but you can also come across western rattlers.

Canadian Life Zone (8,000-10,000 Feet)

You'll find Douglas fir the most common tree within this zone in the Wasatch Range, High Plateaus, and northern slopes of the Great Basin ranges. In the Uintas, however, lodgepole pine dominates. Other trees of the Canadian Zone include ponderosa pine, limber pine, white fir, blue spruce (Utah's state tree), and aspen. Deer and Rocky Mountain elk graze in this zone but rarely higher. Smaller animals of the high mountains include northern flying squirrel, snowshoe rabbit, pocket gopher, yellow belly marmot, pika, chipmunk, and mice.

Hudsonian Life Zone (10,000-11,000 Feet)

Strong winds and a growing season of less than 120 days prevent trees from reaching their full size. This zone receives twice as much snow as the Canadian Zone just below. Often gnarled and twisted, Engelmann spruce and subalpine fir grow in the cold heights over large areas of the Uintas and Wasatches. Limber and bristlecone pines live in the zone too. Lakes and lush subalpine meadows are common. On a bright summer day, the trees, grasses, and tiny flowering alpine plants are abuzz with insects, rodents, and visiting birds, but come winter, most animals will have moved to lower and more protected areas.

Arctic-Alpine Tundra Life Zone (Above 11,000 Feet)

Grasses, mosses, sedges, and annuals withstand the rugged conditions atop Utah's highest ranges. Freezing temperatures and snow can blast the mountain slopes even in midsummer. White-tailed ptarmigan, recently introduced to Utah, live in the tundra of the Uinta Mountains.

THE PEOPLE

Eighty percent of Utah's 1,775,000 citizens live along the Wasatch Front, a magnificent backdrop formed by the Wasatch Range in the northern part of the state. The Mormon pioneers who arrived here in 1847 left their descendants a strong heritage of industriousness, self-reliance, and religious faith. A relatively young population, combined with the Mormons' emphasis on family life and clean living, has resulted in Utah having one of the highest birth rates and lowest death rates in the country. Racially, the state largely reflects the British and northern European origins of Mormon pioneers; smaller numbers of southern and eastern Europeans, many attracted by mining industries, also arrived during Utah's early years. Minorities form less than 7% of the state's population and include Hispanics (3.9%), Native Americans (1.3%), Asians (0.9%), and African-Americans (0.6%). Agriculture, pioneered by the Mormons, and mining, pioneered by the non-Mormons, remain important to the state's economy. Manufacturing, however, has become the most economically significant. Tourism has increased in importance as more people discover the state's exceptional scenery and outdoor recreation.

UTAH'S NATIVE AMERICANS

The size of prehistoric Indian populations has varied greatly in Utah. There were probably few inhabitants during the Archaic period (before A.D. 500), but many more during the time of the Anasazi and Fremont cultures (A.D. 500-1250), rising to a peak of perhaps 500,000. New tribes moving into Utah before the historic period may have contributed to the disappearance of the Fremont and the departure of the Anasazi. Numic (Shoshoni-speaking) tribes likely came from the southwestern Great Basin; they settled in much of western and northern Utah between A.D. 1100 and 1300. Navajo, probably from the northern Great Plains, are thought to have entered Utah from the Four Corners area in about 1600. Numic and Navajo tribes first had a nomadic hunting-and-gathering lifestyle. Only later did they begin to cultivate corn and other crops to supplement wild foods. Except for the Athapascan-speaking Navajo, all of Utah's historic tribes spoke Shoshonian languages and had similar cultures.

Shoshoni

Nomadic bands of Shoshoni occupied much of northern Utah, southern Idaho, and western Wyoming for thousands of years. Horses obtained from the Spanish via Plains Indians allowed hunting parties to cover a large range. The great Chief Washakie led his people for 30 years and negotiated the tribe's treaties with the federal government. The Washakie Indian Reservation in far northern Utah, near Plymouth, belongs to the Northwestern Band of Shoshoni, though few Indians live there now. Tribal headquarters are in Rock Springs, Wyoming, south of the large Wind River Indian Reservation.

Handcart Immigration of 1851

KAREN MCKINLEY

Goshute (or Gosiute)

This branch of the Western Shoshoni, more isolated than other Utah tribes, lived in the harsh Great Basin. They survived through intricate knowledge of the land and use of temporary shelters. These peaceful hunters and gatherers ate almost everything that they found—plants, birds, rodents, crickets, and other insects. Because the Indians had to dig for much of their food, early explorers called the tribe "Digger Indians." White men couldn't believe these Indians survived in such a barren land of alkaline flats and sagebrush. Also known as the Newe, the tribe now lives on the Skull Valley Indian Reservation in Tooele County and on the Goshute Indian Reservation along the Utah-Nevada border.

Ute

Several bands of Utes, or Núuci, ranged over large areas of central and eastern Utah and adjacent Colorado. Originally hunter-gatherers, they acquired horses in about 1800 and became skilled raiders. Customs adopted from Plains Indians included the use of rawhide, teepees, and the travois (a sled used to carry goods). The discovery of gold in southern Colorado and the pressures of farmers there and in Utah forced the Utes to move and renegotiate treaties many times. They now have the large Uintah and Ouray Indian Reservation in northeast Utah, the small White Mesa Indian Reservation in southeast Utah, and the Ute Mountain Indian Reservation in southwest Colorado and northwest New Mexico.

Southern Paiute

Six of the 19 major bands of the Southern Paiute, or Nuwuvi, lived along the Santa Clara, Beaver, and Virgin rivers and in other parts of southwest Utah. Extended families hunted and gathered food together. Fishing and cultivation of corn, beans, squash, and sunflowers supplemented the diet of most of the bands. Today, Utah's Paiutes have a tribal headquarters in Cedar City and scattered small parcels of reservation land. Southern Paiutes also live in southern Nevada and northern Arizona.

Navajo

Calling themselves "Diné," the Navajo moved into the San Juan River area about 1600. The tribe has proved exceptionally adaptable in learning new skills from other cultures: many Navajo crafts, clothing, and religious practices have come from Indian, Spanish, and Anglo neighbors. They were the first tribe in the area to move away from a hunting and gathering lifestyle; instead they relied on the farming and shepherding techniques they had learned from the Spanish. The Navajo have become one of the largest Native American groups in the country, occupying 16 million acres of exceptionally scenic land in southeast Utah and adjacent Arizona and New Mexico. Tribal headquarters is at Window Rock in Arizona.

MEET THE MORMONS

If you're new to the "Beehive State," you'll find plenty of opportunities to learn about Mormon history and religion. At least half of Utah's population actively participates in the Mormon church. Temple Square in Salt Lake City offers excellent tours and exhibits about the church. You'll also find many other visitor centers and historic sites scattered around the state.

The Church of Jesus Christ of Latter-day Saints, headquartered in Salt Lake City, has a

CHURCH OF JESUS CHRIST OF LATTER-DAY SAINTS

Ute mother and papoose

Joseph Smith preaching to Indians in the Midwest

worldwide membership of nearly nine million, due largely to a vigorous missionary program. Members usually call themselves "Latter-day Saints" (LDS). Nonmembers commonly use the nickname "Mormon" because of the emphasis the church puts on the Book of Mormon.

Members believe that God's prophets have restored teachings of the true Christian church to the world "in these latter days." Although the LDS church considers itself a Christian denomination, Mormons don't classify themselves as either Catholic or Protestant. They believe their church presidents, starting with Joseph Smith, to be prophets of God, and they hold both the Bible and the Book of Mormon as the sacred word of God. The latter, they believe, was revealed to Joseph Smith from 1823 to 1830. The text tells of three migrations from the Eastern Hemisphere to the New World and the history of the people who lived in the Americas from about 2200 B.C. to A.D. 421. The book contains 239 chapters that include teachings Christ supposedly gave in the Americas, prophecy, doctrines, and epic tales of the rise and fall of nations. It's regarded by the church as a valuable addition to the Bible—but not a replacement.

Membership in the Mormon church requires faith, a willingness to serve, tithing, and obedience to church authorities. The church emphasizes healthful living, moral conduct, secure family relationships, and a thoughtful approach to social services.

The Early Church

At the time of his revelations, Joseph Smith worked as a farmer in New York State. In 1830, he and his followers founded the new church and published the first edition of the Book of Mormon. But Smith's revelations evoked fear and anger in many of his neighbors, and in 1831 he and his new church moved to Kirtland, Ohio. They set to work building a temple for sacred ordinances, developing a missionary program, and recruiting new followers. Mormons also settled farther west in Missouri, where they made plans for a temple and a community of Zion. Persecution by nonbelievers continued to mount in both Ohio and Missouri, fueled largely by the church's polygamist views, the prosperity of its members, and the LDS claim that it was the "true" church. Many perceived the Mormons as a dire threat to existing political, economic, and religious systems; Missourians disliked the Mormons' anti-slavery views. Violence by gangs of armed men eventually forced church members to flee for their lives.

The dark winter of 1838-39 saw Joseph Smith in jail on treason charges and many church members without homes or legal protection. The Missouri Mormons made their way east to Illinois, not knowing where else to go. Brigham Young, a member of the Council of the Twelve Apostles, directed this exodus, foreshadowing the much longer migration he would lead eight years later.

KAREN McKINLEY

Nauvoo The Beautiful

The Mormons managed to purchase a large tract of swampy land along the Mississippi River in Illinois, then set to work draining swamps and building a city. Joseph Smith, allowed to escape from the Missouri jail, named the Mormons' new home Nauvoo—a Hebrew word for "the beautiful location." Despite extreme poverty and the inability to secure reparations for losses suffered in Missouri, the Mormons managed to build an attractive city that would one day rival any in the United States. A magnificent temple, begun in 1841, rose above Nauvoo. Despite their success, the Mormons continued to face virulent opposition from those who objected to their religion.

Smith, who had withstood tarring and feathering among other punishments, met his death in 1844 at Carthage, Illinois. He had voluntarily surrendered to the authorities to stand trial for treason, but a mob stormed the jail and killed both Smith and his brother Hyrum in a hail of bullets. Opponents thought that the Mormons would disband on the death of their leader. When they did not, their crops and houses were destroyed and their livestock was driven off. Brigham Young, who succeeded Smith, realized the Mormons would never find peace in Illinois. He and other leaders began looking toward the vastness of the West. They hoped the remote Rocky Mountains would provide a sanctuary from mobs and politicians. Plans for departure from Nauvoo began in the autumn of 1845.

The Mormon Exodus

Attacks against Nauvoo's citizens made life so difficult that they had to evacuate the following February, despite severe winter weather. Homes, businesses, the temple, and most personal possessions were left behind as the Mormons crossed the Mississippi into Iowa. (Mobs later took over the town and desecrated the temple; not a single stone of the structure is in its original position today.) The group slowly pushed westward through the snow and mud. Faith, a spirit of sharing, and competent leadership enabled them to survive. Brigham Young thought it best not to press on all the way to the Rocky Mountains in that first year, so the group spent a second winter on the plains. Dugouts and log cabins housed more than 3,500 people at Winter Quarters, near present-day Omaha. By early spring of 1847, the leaders had worked out plans for the rest of the journey. The Salt Lake Valley, an uninhabited and isolated region, would be its goal. Mountain men encountered on the journey gave discouraging descriptions of this place as a site for a major settlement. Samuel Brannan, a Mormon who had settled on the West Coast, rode east to meet Brigham Young and to present glowing reports of California. But Young wouldn't be swayed from his original goal. On July 24, 1847, Young arrived at the edge of the Salt Lake Valley and announced, "This is the right place."

BOB RACE

OUT AND ABOUT
TRANSPORTATION

TOURS

See your travel agent for the latest on package tours to Utah. Within the state, local operators offer everything from tours of city sights to rafting trips. You can also take "flightseeing" trips from many airports; the five national parks are the most popular destinations. "Transportation" sections in each chapter list tour operators; also ask local chambers of commerce.

BY CAR

Public transportation serves cities and some towns but very few of the scenic, historic, and recreational areas. Unless you're on a tour, you'll really need your own transportation. Cars are easily rented in any large town; Salt Lake City offers by far the largest selection. Four-wheel-drive vehicles can be rented too, and they'll be very handy if you plan extensive travel on back roads. Most tourist offices carry the Utah road map published by the Utah Department of Trans-

portation; it's one of the best available and is free. Most regular grade unleaded gasoline is only 85 octane. If your automobile owner's manual calls for a higher grade of octane you might consider a higher grade of gasoline.

Driveaways
These are autos that need to be delivered to another city. If it's a place you're headed for, a driveaway can be like a free car rental. To sign up, you must be at least 21 years old and make a refundable deposit of $75-150. There are time and mileage limits. Ask for an economy car if money's a consideration. Check the *Yellow Pages* under "Automobile Transporters & Driveaway Companies."

Hitchhiking
Opinions and experiences vary on hitching. It can be a great way to meet people despite the dangers and long waits. Offer to buy lunch or help with gas money to repay the driver's favor. Highway police tolerate hitchhiking as long as it doesn't create a hazard or take place on an interstate or freeway. They do routinely check

THE GREAT WESTERN TRAIL

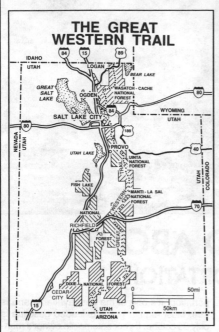

the Manti-La Sal National Forest, the trail ascends the lofty Wasatch Plateau and extends for 75 miles through rolling meadows and forest country. Uinta National Forest features lush forests beneath the jagged peaks of the Wasatch Range's Mt. Timpanogos and Lone Peak. The ups and downs of the Wasatch Range continue as the trail winds through the Wasatch-Cache National Forest high above Salt Lake City and the Great Salt Lake. The northernmost trail section in Utah climbs into the Bear River Range and meets the Idaho border near Beaver Mountain.

Note that some trail sections are open for vehicles and pets, and some aren't. Obtain the latest trail info from the respective agencies below. The **Great Western Trail Association** needs volunteers for trail construction and maintenance. If you'd like to help, contact the Association at Box 1428, Provo, UT 84602.

Cedar District Office
Bureau of Land Management
176 East DL Sargent Dr.
Cedar City, UT 84720
Tel. (801) 586-2401

Dixie National Forest
Box 580
82 N. 100 East
Cedar City, UT 84720
Tel. (801) 865-3700

Fishlake National Forest
115 E. 900 North
Richfield, UT 84701
Tel. (801) 896-9233

Manti-La Sal National Forest
599 West Price River Dr.
Price, UT 84501
Tel. (801) 637-2817

Uinta National Forest
88 W. 100 North
Provo, UT 84601
Tel. (801) 377-5780

Wasatch-Cache National Forest
8230 Federal Bldg.
125 S. State St.
Salt Lake City, UT 84138
Tel. (801) 524-5030

As its name implies, the Great Western Trail, when completed, will traverse some of the West's most spectacular country. The Utah stretch, approximately 350 miles of trail, will link trails in Arizona and Idaho with those in New Mexico, Wyoming, and Montana. Planners envision a trail network stretching all the way from Mexico to Canada, providing travel possibilities for bicycles, horses, and motorized vehicles as well as hikers. About 90% of the finished network will employ existing roads and trails.

The southernmost Utah section follows washes and canyons across land administered by the Bureau of Land Management; elevations drop as low as 4,800 feet. The Dixie National Forest section skirts the west edge of Bryce Canyon National Park and continues across high plateaus to Boulder Top, where it reaches elevations topping 11,000 feet. Fishlake National Forest has more fine alpine country and expansive views from Thousand Lake Mountain, Windstorm Peak, and UM Plateau areas. In

IDs, however. Rides can often be arranged with fellow travelers at youth hostels. Bulletin boards at universities and college ride lists are also good sources.

BY BUS

The **Greyhound** bus line offers frequent service to Utah on its transcontinental routes along I-15. Greyhound often features special deals on bus passes and one-way "anywhere" tickets. Outside the U.S., residents may purchase a Greyhound **Ameripass** at additional discounts.

Local bus services come in handy at Salt Lake City, Provo, Park City, and Ogden. Service in other towns is usually nonexistent or too infrequent to be useful. When taking local buses, always have exact change ready.

BY TRAIN

Amtrak has three luxury train lines across Utah; all stop in Salt Lake City. The California Zephyr runs between Oakland and Chicago; the Desert Wind goes southwest from Salt Lake City through Las Vegas to Los Angeles; and the Pioneer connects Salt Lake City with Portland and Seattle. Amtrak charges more than Greyhound for one-way tickets but has far roomier seating, as well as lounge cars and sleepers. Special fares and roundtrip discounts often make train travel a good value that is fairly competitive with bus rates. For information and reservations, see a travel agent or call Amtrak, tel. (800) 872-7245. A **USA Railpass** is sold by travel agents outside the United States.

BY AIR

More than a dozen major airlines connect with Salt Lake City, which has the only major airport in the state. Fares and schedules tend to change frequently—a travel agent can help find the best flights. Big-city newspapers usually have advertisements for discount fares and tours in their Sunday travel sections. You'll have the best chance of getting low fares by planning at least a week ahead. Regional airlines connect Salt Lake City with other communities in the state; see

"Air" under "Transportation" in the "Salt Lake City" chapter for sample destinations and fares. The cost per mile of these short hops is high, but you'll often have excellent views!

BY BICYCLE

Touring on a bicycle is to be fully alive to the land, skies, sounds, plants, and birds of Utah. The experience of gliding across the desert or topping out on a mountain pass go beyond words. Some effort, a lightweight touring or mountain bicycle, touring gear, and awareness of what's going on around you are all that's needed. Start with short rides if you're new to bicycle touring, then work up to longer cross-country trips. By learning to maintain and repair your steed, you'll seldom have trouble on the road. An extra-low gear of 30 inches or less will take the strain out of long mountain grades. Utah has almost every kind of terrain and road condition imaginable; mountain bicyclists find the Moab area in the southeast especially challenging and scenic. Note that designated wilderness areas are closed to cycling.

Most bookstores and bicycle shops have good publications on bicycle touring. *Bicycle Touring in Utah* and *The Mountain Bike Manual*, both by Dennis Coello, contain general information and details on various rides within the state. As when hiking, always have rain and wind gear and carry plenty of water. Also, don't forget to wear a bicycling helmet. Cyclists with a competitive spirit can test themselves in a series of U.S. Cycling Federation-sanctioned races in the northern part of the state; local bicycle shops have schedules of races and training events. Unlike other states, Utah as yet has no helmet law for cyclists.

BOB RACE

INFORMATION AND SERVICES

MONEY

Prices of all services mentioned in this book were current at press time. Whenever possible, taxes have been included in the cost given in the text. (Chart listings, however, don't include Utah's sales tax, which is 6.5 percent. Some cities may also add a city tax to purchases.) You're sure to find seasonal and long-term price changes, so *please* don't use what's listed here to argue with staff at a motel, campground, museum, airline, or other office!

TIME ZONES

Travelers in Utah should remember that the state is in the mountain time zone and goes on daylight saving time (advanced one hour) May-October. Nevada is in the Pacific time zone (one hour earlier); all other bordering states are in the mountain time zone. An odd exception is Arizona, which stays on mountain standard time all year, except for the Navajo Reservation, which goes on daylight saving time to keep up with its Utah and New Mexico sections.

FREE INFORMATION

General tourist literature and maps are available from the **Utah Travel Council,** Council Hall/Capitol Hill, Salt Lake City, UT 84114-7420, tel. 538-1030, fax 538-1399. Utah's many chambers of commerce also have free material and are happy to help with travel suggestions in their areas; see "Information" under each community described in this book. Also listed are national forest offices and other government agencies that have information on outdoor recreation in their areas.

POSTAL AND TELEPHONE SERVICES

Normal post office hours are Mon.-Fri. 8:30 a.m.-5 p.m. and sometimes Saturday 8:30 a.m.-

EVENTS

Utah has a full schedule of rodeos, parades, art festivals, historical celebrations, gem and mineral shows, and sporting events. Stop at a tourist office or chamber of commerce to see what's coming up. The offices should also have the annual *Utah! Travel Guide,* which lists major events.

Major Holidays

Many museums, recreation areas, and other tourist attractions close on Thanksgiving, Christmas, New Year's, and other holidays. These closings are not always mentioned in the text, so call ahead to check.

New Year's Day: January 1

Martin Luther King, Jr.'s Birthday (Civil Rights Day): January 15; usually observed the third Monday in January

Presidents' Day (honors Washington and Lincoln): third Monday in February

Easter Sunday: late March or early April

Memorial Day (honors veterans of all wars): last Monday in May

Independence Day: July 4

Pioneer Day: July 24

Labor Day: first Monday in September

Columbus Day: second Monday in October

Veterans Day: November 11

Thanksgiving Day: fourth Thursday in November

Christmas Day: December 25

noon. U.S. post offices sell stamps and postal money orders. If you need to ship a package they can also offer overnight express service.

All telephone numbers within Utah have an **801** area code (use only when calling from outside Utah). Toll-free numbers in the U.S. have an **800** area code. To obtain a number within the state, dial 1-411; for another state, dial 1, the area code, then 555-1212. Many airlines and motel chains offer a toll-free 800 number; if you don't have it, dial 1-800-555-1212 for information.

HEALTH AND WELL-BEING

MEDICAL SERVICES

In emergencies, dial 911 (most communities in Utah), use the emergency number listed on most telephones, or dial a zero for an operator. Hospital emergency rooms offer the quickest help, but cost more than a visit to a doctor's office or clinic. Hospital care is very expensive—medical insurance is recommended.

WILDERNESS TRAVEL

Keeping The "Wild" In Wilderness

As more people seek relief from the stress of urban life, the use of wilderness areas increases. Fortunately, Utah has an abundance of this fragile and precious resource. The many designated wilderness areas have been closed to mechanized vehicles (including mountain bicycles) to protect both the environment and the experience of solitude. Most designated areas lie within national forests or Bureau of Land Management lands, and are normally free to visit without a permit. The national parks and monuments require backcountry permits for overnight stays.

Some of the most spectacular and memorable hiking and camping await the prepared outdoorsperson. If you are new to hiking, start with easy trips, then work up gradually. The following are suggestions for backcountry travel and camping:

Before heading into the backcountry, check with a ranger about weather, water sources, fire danger, trail conditions, and regulations. Backpacking stores are good sources of information too.

Tell a ranger or other reliable person where you are going and when you expect to return.

Travel in small groups for the best experience (group size may also be regulated).

Try not to camp on meadows, as the grass is easily damaged.

Use a portable stove to avoid leaving fire scars.

Resist the temptation to shortcut switchbacks. This causes erosion and can be dangerous.

Avoid digging tent trenches or cutting vegetation.

Help preserve old Indian and historic ruins.

Camp at least 300 feet away from springs, creeks, and trails. Camp at least a quarter mile from a sole water source to avoid scaring away wildlife and livestock.

GIARDIA

It can be tough to resist: Picture yourself hiking in a beautiful area by the banks of a crystal clear stream. The water in your canteen tastes stale, hot, and plastic; the nearby stream looks so inviting that you can't resist a cautious sip. It tastes delicious, clean, and cold, and for the rest of your hike you refresh youself with water straight from the stream.

Days pass and you forget about drinking untreated water. Suddenly one evening after your meal you are terribly sick to your stomach. You develop an awful case of cramps, and feel diarrhea beginning to set in. Food poisoning?

Nope—it's the effects of giardia, a protozoan that has become common in even the remotest of mountain streams. Giardia is carried in animal or human waste that is deposited or washed into natural waters.

When ingested, it begins reproducing, causing a sickness in the host that can become very serious and may not be cured without medical attention.

You can take precautions against giardia with a variety of chemicals and filtering methods, or by boiling water before drinking it. The various chemical solutions on the market work in some applications, but because they need to be safe for human consumption, they are weak and ineffective against the protozan in its cyst stage of life, when it encases itself in a hard shell. Filtering may eliminate giardia, but there are other water pests too small to be caught by most filters. The most effective way to eliminate such threats is to boil all suspect water. A few minutes at a rolling boil will kill giardia even in the cyst stage of life.

Avoid camping in washes at any time; hikers need to be alert to thunderstorms.

Take care not to throw or kick rocks off trails—someone might be below.

Don't drink water directly from streams or lakes, no matter how clean the water appears; it may contain the parasitic protozoan *Giardia lamblia,* which causes giardiasis. Boiling water for several minutes will kill giardia as well as most other bacterial or viral pathogens. Chemical treatments and water filters usually work too, although they're not as reliable as boiling (giardia spends part of its life in a hard shell that protects it from most chemicals).

Bathe away from lakes, streams, and springs.

Bring a trowel for personal sanitation; dig four to six inches deep.

Bring plenty of feed for your horses and mules.

Leave dogs at home if possible; they may disturb wildlife and other hikers and foul campsites. If you do bring a dog, please keep it under control at all times.

Take home all your trash.

If you realize you're lost, find shelter. If you're sure of a way to civilization and plan to walk out, leave a note with your departure time and planned route.

Hypothermia

The greatest danger outdoors is one that can sneak up and kill with very little warning. Hypothermia, a lowering of the body's temperature below 95° F, causes disorientation, uncontrollable shivering, slurred speech, and drowsiness. The victim may not even realize what's wrong. Unless corrective action is taken immediately, hypothermia can lead to death. This is why hikers should travel with companions and always carry wind and rain protection. (Close-fitting rain gear works far better than ponchos.) Also, space blankets are lightweight and cheap, and offer protection against the cold in emergencies. Remember that temperatures can plummet rapidly in Utah's dry climate—a drop of 40° F between day and night is common. Be especially careful at high elevations, where summer sunshine can quickly change into freezing

rain or a blizzard. Simply falling into a mountain stream while fishing can also lead to hypothermia and death unless proper action is taken. If cold and tired, don't waste time! Seek shelter and build a fire; also change into dry clothes and drink warm liquids. If a victim isn't fully conscious, warm him or her by skin-to-skin contact in a sleeping bag. Try to keep the victim awake and offer plenty of warm liquids.

DRIVING HAZARDS

Summer heat in the desert puts an extra strain on both cars and drivers. It's worth double-checking the cooling system, engine oil, transmission fluid, fan belts, and tires to make sure they are in top condition. Carry several gallons of water in case of a breakdown or radiator trouble. Never leave children or pets in a parked car during warm weather—temperatures inside can cause fatal heatstroke in just minutes. At times the desert has *too much* water, when late-summer storms frequently flood low spots in the road. Wait for the water level to subside before crossing. Dust storms also tend to be short-lived but can completely block visibility. During such storms, pull completely off the road and stop; turn off your lights so as not to confuse other drivers. Radio stations carry frequent weather updates when weather hazards exist. Continuous weather forecasts can be received on a VHF radio (162.4 or 162.55 MHz) in the Salt Lake City area (Wasatch Front), Logan (Cache Valley), Vernal (Uinta Basin), Cedar City, Glen Canyon N.R.A., and Las Vegas (NV) areas.

If stranded, whether on the desert or in the mountains, stay with your vehicle unless you're *positive* of where to go for help, then leave a note explaining your route and departure time. Airplanes can easily spot a stranded car (tie a piece of cloth to your antenna), but a person walking out is more difficult to see. It's best to carry emergency supplies: blankets or sleeping bags, first-aid kit, tools, jumper cables, shovel, traction mats or chains, flashlight, rain gear, water, food, and a can opener.

Great Salt Lake Desert

NORTHERN UTAH

INTRODUCTION

Northern Utah offers a great diversity of sights, recreation, terrain, little-known mountain ranges, and the Western Hemisphere's largest inland body of salt water. Its cities boast art exhibits, concerts, festivals, museums, and amusement parks. You can leave civilization behind and head east into the Wasatch Range for skiing and hiking among splendid peaks. Camping, fishing, and boating also bring many visitors into the higher country.

THE LAND

Even by Utah standards, contrasts between barren and luxuriant are especially great in the north. A collision of the earth's plates has pushed up rugged mountains and plateaus in the northeast portion of the state while leaving vast expanses of lower-lying valleys and desert ranges to the west. The Great Salt Lake dominates the low country, casting its spell across the sterile salt flats and rocky ranges west toward Nevada. To the east, the northern Wasatch Range towers in verdant splendor. Though other mountains rise higher into Utah skies, none match the sheer beauty of these glacier-carved peaks and their sharp drops to the valleys far below. The highest summits reach over 10,000 feet, with Mt. Nebo crowning

the range at 11,928 feet. (In the Great Basin area, "summit" means the high point of a road or trail, while "peak" denotes the actual mountaintop.) The mountains bring life to northern Utah; rivers course down their slopes, turning desert valleys into lush pastures and productive farmland. Salt Lake City and its populous suburbs hug the base of the Wasatches in a long north-south line known as the Wasatch Front.

In the north state, you'll see large terraces or benches left behind by prehistoric Lake Bonneville. Two terrace levels stand out most clearly, the Bonneville and the Provo, 400 feet lower. Massive Lake Bonneville has dwindled to only a few remnants of its former expanse, but the largest of these, the Great Salt Lake, is still immense—up to 92 miles long and 48 miles wide. Much of the water comes from the Bear River, originating on the north slopes of the Uinta Mountains and making a long loop through Wyoming, Idaho, and northern Utah. Waterfowl and other wildlife thrive in marshes and lakes where the Bear River meets the lake. Other rivers, such as the Weber, Ogden, Provo, and Spanish Fork, have cut through the Wasatch Range to empty into the Great Salt Lake or upstream into Utah Lake, a large freshwater body connected to the Great Salt Lake by the Jordan River.

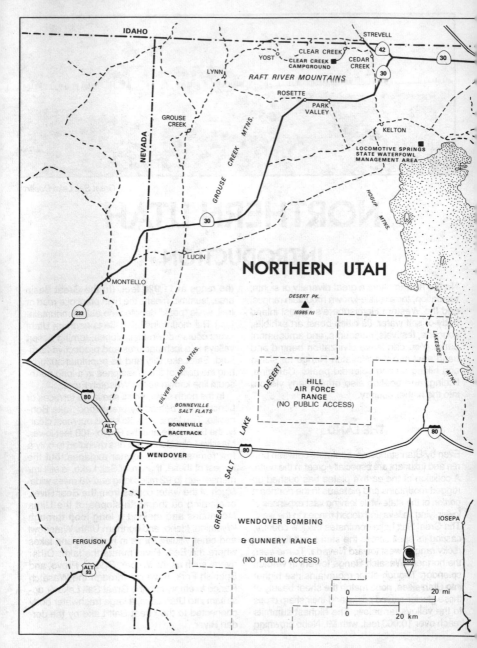

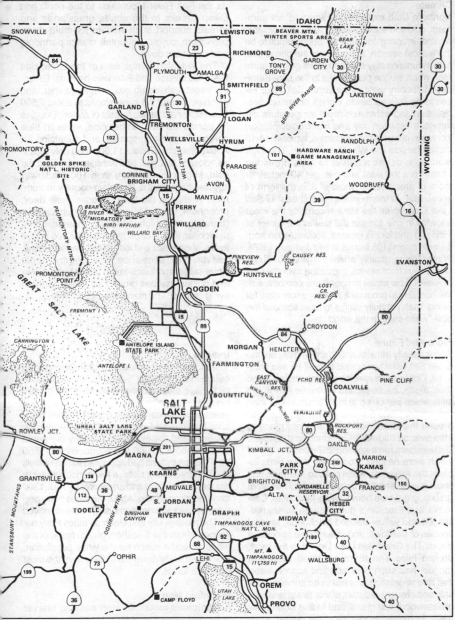

Climate

Northern Utah experiences warm to hot summers, cold and snowy winters, and unpredictable weather in spring and autumn. Spring tends to be the wettest season, and summer the driest. The high mountains stay cool and moist even in summer, when the the plains bake in the sun. Semi-desert country west of the Great Salt Lake receives as little as seven inches of annual precipitation and withstands great temperature differences between day and night. Precipitation increases closer to the mountains, typically 14-15 inches beside the Wasatch Range. The high mountains act as a barrier to moisture-laden winds from the west and can get 40 inches or more of precipitation, most of it in the form of snow. Alta, in the mountains southeast of Salt Lake City, holds the state record for the most snowfall in one season (52 feet in the winter of 1951-52) and for the greatest accumulation from a single storm (105 inches in late January 1965). Winter fronts usually arrive in cycles of six to seven days from storms originating over the Gulf of Alaska. Low winter temperatures combine with low humidity to produce a powder snow ideal for skiing. Utah rightfully claims to have some of the best "white stuff" in the world.

Flora And Fauna

Water usually attracts abundant wildlife, but the Great Salt Lake has limited appeal for sea creatures. Only certain species of brine shrimp, brine flies, algae, bacteria, and protozoa live in the lake, which can be up to eight times saltier than the ocean. Birds find the freshwater marshes around the Great Salt Lake an ideal place to stop over on migrations in spring and autumn. Birdwatchers have spotted 257 species, 117 of which were nesting. Commonly seen birds include the American white pelican, Canada and snow geese, whistling swan, eared and western grebes, great blue heron, white-faced ibis, California and Franklin's gulls, marsh wren, red-winged and yellow-headed blackbirds, several species of swallows, and at least nine species of ducks. The Great Salt Lake Desert to the west, broken here and there by small mountain ranges, has such poor soil and scarce water that little vegetation or wildlife can survive. Only salt- and drought-resistant plants like shadscale, greasewood, salt grass, and iodine bush grow there. In higher ranges near the desert, such

as the Raft River Mountains to the north and Deep Creeks to the south, grasslands and forests support such wildlife as mule deer, pronghorn, coyote, cottontail, chukar partridge, and mourning dove.

The Wasatch Range east of the Great Salt Lake has diverse and extensive habitats. Grasses, sagebrush, scrub oak, maple, juniper, and piñon pine cover the lower slopes to about 7,500 feet. Higher are dense forests of aspen, Douglas fir, ponderosa pine, limber pine, white fir, blue spruce, Engelmann spruce, and subalpine fir. Above timberline (about 11,000 feet) only grasses, mosses, sedges, and annuals withstand the cold, strong winds. More than 100 wildflower species brighten the mountain country in summer. Wildlife in the area includes mule deer, pronghorn, Rocky Mountain elk, mountain goat (transplanted), bighorn sheep, mountain lion, black bear, ringtail cat, coyote, badger, red and kit foxes, short-tailed and long-tailed weasels, mink, beaver, pika, snowshoe hare, pygmy rabbit, white-tailed and black-tailed jackrabbits, Uinta and golden-mantled ground squirrels, northern flying squirrel, and many species of birds.

HISTORY

Indians

The story of man in northern Utah begins long before the founding of Salt Lake City. Archaeologists have evidence that Paleo-Indians hunted big game and gathered plant foods about 15,000 years ago. The early tribes continued their primitive hunting and gathering, despite climate changes and the extinction of many big-game species about 10,000 years ago. By A.D. 550 the Fremont Indians had appeared with new tools and pottery-making skills, a few agriculture techniques, and the bow and arrow. Yet by A.D. 1300 they had disappeared. About the same time, perhaps by coincidence, nomadic Shoshoni moved in. The modern Ute and Goshute tribes likely descended from this Shoshoni group. None of the tribes proved a match for the white population, which eventually drove the Indians from the most desirable lands.

Mountain Men

Adventurous mountain men seeking beaver pelts and other furs entered northern Utah in

Shoshoni village

the mid-1820s. They explored the mountain ranges, rivers, and the Great Salt Lake, and blazed most of the trails later used by wagon trains, Pony Express, telegraph lines, and railroads. By 1830 most of the mountain men had moved on to better trapping areas and left the land to the Indians; some, however, did return to guide government explorers and groups of pioneer settlers. The names of several mountain men are remembered on maps today. Peter Skene Ogden (city of Ogden), Etienne Provost (city of Provo), Jim Bridger (Bridgerland is the nickname of Cache and Rich counties), John H. Weber (Weber River and County), and William Ashley (Ashley National Forest).

Explorers

Joseph Walker, under Captain Benjamin Bonneville, crossed the northwest corner of Utah in 1833 on a trip to California. He reported such difficult conditions that no one else attempted the route for the rest of the decade. California-bound wagon trains took heed and followed a more northerly path through Idaho on the Oregon Trail. An exception was the Bartleson-Bidwell wagon train, which turned south into Utah in 1841 and skirted the northern edges of the Great Salt Lake and Great Salt Lake Desert. Though members suffered immense hardships and later had to abandon their wagons, they eventually made it across. The group was the first to take wagons across Utah and included the first white women known to have crossed Utah and Nevada to California.

In 1843, John C. Frémont led one of his several government-sponsored scientific expeditions into Utah. Frémont determined the salinity of the Great Salt Lake and laid to rest speculation that a river drained the lake into the Pacific Ocean. Two years later, he led a well-prepared group across the heart of the dreaded Great Salt Lake Desert, despite warnings from the local Indians that no one had crossed it and survived. His accounts of the region described not only the salty lake and barren deserts, but also the fertile valleys near the Wasatch Range. Mormon leaders planning a westward migration from Nauvoo, Illinois, carefully studied Frémont's reports.

Langsford Hastings, an ambitious politician, seized the opportunity to promote Frémont's desert route as a shortcut to California. Hastings had made the trip on horseback but failed to anticipate the problems of a wagon train. On this route in 1846, the Donner-Reed wagon train became so bogged down in the salt mud that many wagons were abandoned. Moreover, an 80-mile stretch between waterholes proved too far for many of the oxen, which died from dehydration. Today motorists can cruise in comfort along I-80 on a similar route between Salt Lake City and Wendover.

SALT LAKE CITY

In 1847 the Mormon prophet Brigham Young proclaimed this site the "right place" for a new settlement. Today many residents and visitors would still agree. Salt Lake City now offers an appealing mix of cultural activities, historic sites, varied architecture, shopping, sophisticated hotels, and elegant restaurants. About 173,000 citizens live in the city, by far the largest and most important in Utah. More than half a million more people reside close by in sprawling suburbs. Utah's political life centers on the stately Capitol, which overlooks the city from a hill just north of downtown. The University of Utah serves a major role in education and research on its 1,500-acre campus in the foothills east of the city. Some 8.6 million members of the Church of Jesus Christ of Latter-day Saints (Mormons) look to Salt Lake City as their world headquarters. You can't miss seeing the Mormons' temple and soaring office tower in the heart of downtown. Free tours of Temple Square provide a look at the vigorous faith of the "Saints" and their unique history.

The Setting
Salt Lake City lies on the broad valley floor and terraces once occupied by prehistoric Lake Bonneville. The Great Salt Lake, the largest remnant of that ancient inland sea, has state parks on its southern shore and on Antelope Island. The Jordan River winds through the valley, connecting Utah Lake with the Great Salt Lake. Rugged mountain ranges, snowcapped much of the year, nearly surround Salt Lake City. In the Wasatch Range, beginning on the eastern edge of the city, many peaks exceed 11,000 feet. In just minutes, you can be skiing on some of the world's best powder in winter or hiking among wildflowers in summer. On the other side of the valley, Lewiston Peak (elev. 10,626 feet) crowns the Oquirrh Mountains. No ski resorts are here yet, but workings of the world's largest open-pit copper mine can be seen on the mountainside.

Climate
The city experiences a full range of seasons at its 4,300-foot elevation. Rapidly moving storms can bring rain or snow one day and sunshine the next. Average temperatures range from highs in the upper 30s F in January to the lower 90s in July. Total precipitation averages 15.3 inches for the year. Most of the winter moisture arrives as fluffy white flakes; average annual snowfall is 54 inches in town and considerably more in the mountains.

HISTORY

The Vision
Salt Lake City began as a dream—a Utopia in which the persecuted Mormons would have the freedom to create a Kingdom of God on earth. Their prophet, Brigham Young, led the first group of 143 men, three women, and two children to the valley of the Great Salt Lake in July 1847. Only great faith could have supported the followers when they saw the wasteland that Young pronounced as "the right place." The bleak valley, covered with sagebrush and inhabited mainly by lizards, could best be described as the land nobody wanted. Even the Indians seldom camped in the area. Many Mor-

Brigham Young

BOB RACE

bird's-eye view of Salt Lake City, looking southeast, 1875

mon settlers wanted to continue under Young's leadership to the rich lands of California. But Young saw the value in staying; the land's remoteness would protect them from enemies.

Settlement

The pioneers put their doubts aside and immediately set to work digging irrigation canals, planting crops, constructing a small fort, and laying out a city. Nearly 2,000 more immigrants arrived that same summer of 1847. After having endured 17 years of mob attacks and other hardships in the Midwest, the Mormons had reached their promised land. Brigham Young and other leaders designated a temple site and determined land use. Church members shared their resources and eagerly took up tasks assigned by committees. Married men received city lots and farmlands, which were recalled if the land was not productively used. Similarly, the community shared streams, forests, and canyons.

By necessity, early citizens had to be self-sufficient—the nearest outposts of civilization lay 1,000 miles away. Also, Brigham Young had declared that the Kingdom of God should be independent of the gentile (non-Mormon) nations. Through trial and error, farmers learned techniques of irrigating and farming the desert land. Tanneries, flour mills, blacksmith shops, stores, and other enterprises sprang up under church direction. Then disaster struck. A plague of "crickets" (actually a flightless grasshopper, *Anabrus simplex*) descended from the hills to the east and began devouring the crops of the 1848 harvest, nearly ending chances for the community's survival. But flocks of California seagulls appeared out of the west to feed on the insects. Thought a miracle, the seagull intervention saved part of the crops and gave the pioneers hope that life in the Great Salt Lake Valley would eventually be fruitful.

Success

The "city of Zion" came close to its goal of being a community devoted to God. Nearly all aspects of political, economic, and family life came under the influence of the church during the first 20 years. Immigrants from Europe and the eastern U.S. poured in, many under the sponsor-

THE UNITED ORDER OF ENOCH

The United Order of Enoch was an attempt by Brigham Young to remedy several ills caused by an economic boom in the church community. The arrival of the railroad had brought some forms of prosperity to the Mormons, especially in allowing the development of mining. But the railroad also brought in a rougher class of folk that had no intention of emulating the quiet, industrious lifestyle of the Mormons, and it allowed the import of commercially produced goods at cheaper prices than could be had locally. Both factors spelled trouble for a church seeking self-sufficiency.

As Joseph Smith had envisioned in his Law of Consecration, The United Order was proposed as a policy of communal living in which members would commit all their privately owned goods toward a common end. Many members had surrendered their property in the early days of the church, but the troubled times the church found in the east had thwarted the success of true communal villages. In the 1870s, church leaders felt the time had come.

When Brigham Young reactivated the United Order, it took life in several forms. The earliest and one of the most successful was the Brigham City Cooperative, started by Lorenzo Snow in 1864. BCC was a cooperative general store that met with great success, expanding over the years to 40 departments. The store was run on investments by voluntary members who received dividends based on their contributions. So successful was this venture that its business was barely touched by the Panic of 1873.

Branches of the order offered full communal living in which members ate in a communal dining hall, wore uniform clothing, and worked in community owned facilities. In such a commune, all private possessions were surrendered upon membership. The most successful commune of this type may have been Orderville, where travel-weary settlers went about living the United Order in its most idealistic form.

Orderville's effort was largely a success, but citizens from surrounding communities openly scoffed at the spartan life of the commune. Mormon children were gradually swayed by the taunts of their peers, which led to a "trouser rebellion." One story tells of a Mormon youth who sought permission and money to buy pants more fashionable than the standard communal issue. When he was denied on the grounds that his present pair was still serviceable, he took to work, earned the money himself, and promptly purchased a pair in the fashionable store-bought style. He was taken before the commune's elected board, which lauded his enterprise, but decreed that every youth had to have the new pants or no one would. It was considered wasteful to replace pants that were still wearable, so youngsters were soon busy at the community grindstone wearing out the seats of their britches.

Younger members of the Orderville commune also suffered in that, unlike their elders, they didn't receive shares in the community when relinquishing their property. They were paid only a wage with no dividends—75 cents a day until they reached 18, $1.50 thereafter. Eventually, the younger population trickled away, seeking higher-paying jobs in the surrounding area.

Most communal attempts, though, lasted less than a year, crippled primarily by human nature. Wealthy residents didn't wish to relinquish their property, dissatisfaction with the distribution of goods was common, and residents were often lured away by employment and business opportunities outside the commune. The Orderville community lasted 11 years, during which time its communal property nearly quadrupled in value. In that, it can be considered something of a success.

ship of the Perpetual Emigrating Fund Company. Colonization of the surrounding country proceeded at a rapid pace. Of all the social experiments ever tried in the United States, the Mormon settlements had the greatest success.

The Utah War

Mistrust and suspicion from outside Utah flared up just 10 years after the city's founding. The Utah War never really happened, but rumors of a Mormon rebellion caused President James Buchanan to dispatch the largest peacetime army ever assembled in the United States. Mormon "guerrillas" managed to delay the troops by driving off livestock and cutting supply lines. Meanwhile, nearly the entire population of the city staged an orderly evacuation southward. When columns of soldiers marched down the deserted streets in June 1858, they found only a handful of men ready to torch the houses and buildings in case the U.S. Army chose to occupy the city. Peace prevailed and residents soon returned.

CHURCH OF JESUS CHRIST OF LATTER-DAY SAINTS

Zion's Co-operative Mercantile Institution, ca. 1888

Coming Of The Gentiles

The isolation that had shielded Salt Lake City from outside influence began to fade about 1870. Completion of the transcontinental railroad through Utah in the previous year encouraged non-Mormon politicians and businessmen to seek opportunity in the territory. Also, with cheap transportation close at hand, mining became highly profitable.

Even in this new social climate, Mormons and gentiles remained largely segregated. Each group developed its own social and political organizations and its own schools. Political life had been very dull during the first decades, when only a single set of church-appointed candidates appeared on the ballots. Voters had a choice of voting "no," but they knew that their numbered ballots could be traced. The church discouraged political parties, believing they would lead to corruption and disharmony and that civil government should simply be a branch of the church. With the rising power of the gentile population in the 1870s, the church founded the People's Party to counter the anti-church Liberal Party. Salt Lake City's two major newspapers date from this time, with the *Deseret News* stating Mormon views, and the *Salt Lake Tribune* representing the Gentiles. Such fine shades of the

political spectrum as the Republican or Democratic parties rarely entered the picture. The Mormons steadily lost control of their city; from a 93% majority population in 1867, they slipped to only 50% by 1891. In 1889 the first non-Mormons were elected to city offices.

An American City

The church leadership lost its grasp on Salt Lake City during the legal battles over polygamy in the 1880s. Embarking on a new course, the church ended the practice of multiple marriages, dissolved its People's Party, and sold off most of its businesses. Even the famed ZCMI—a Mormon co-op that is thought to be the first department store in America—became a private profit-making concern. The end of the 19th century saw Salt Lake making the transition from a Mormon village to an American city.

The 20th Century

Wealth from successful mining operations fueled much of the development in Salt Lake City's business district, located in the blocks south of Temple Square. As a rule, the blocks nearest the temple had affiliations with the church and those farther south belonged to non-Mormons. In the early 1900s, skyscrapers began sprouting high above East Temple Street—rechristened Main Street. Exchange Place became the non-Mormon financial center, much like New York City's Wall Street. Though growth in the city has been modest since WW II, a profusion of surrounding towns and expressways has sprung up. Like any major metropolitan area, Salt Lake City suffers its share of air pollution and traffic congestion. On the brighter side, a new interest in historical conservation has preserved many graceful mansions, ornate churches, and stately office towers. A drive or walk through downtown will reveal the city's unique heritage.

SALT LAKE CITY SIGHTS

TEMPLE SQUARE

Easily Salt Lake City's most famous attraction, this complex has a special meaning for Mormons. Brigham Young chose this spot for a temple in July 1847, just four days after arriving in the valley. You're welcome to see these buildings, along with the Assembly Hall, exhibits in the North and South visitor centers, and historic monuments—all of which provide an excellent introduction to the Mormon religion and Utah's early history. Only members who meet church requirements of good standing may enter the sacred temple itself; others can learn about temple activities and see photos of interior rooms in the South Visitor Center.

Enthusiastic guides offer several tours in Temple Square, which covers an entire block in the heart of Salt Lake City. It would take more than a day to see all the Mormon exhibits in Temple Square and adjacent blocks. A 15-foot wall surrounds the square's 10 acres; you can enter through wrought-iron gates on the south, west, or north sides. Across the street to the east are the LDS Office and Brigham Young's restored Beehive House, both offering tours. Head west across the street from the square to see the Museum of Church History and Art and the Family History Library. Temple Square is open daily 9 a.m.-9 p.m., extended in summer to 8 a.m.-10 p.m.; all tours, exhibits, and concerts are free. Foreign-language tours are available too—ask at the North Visitor Center. Smoking is prohibited on the grounds.

For additional activities check the bulletin boards as you enter Temple Square, ask any of the guides, or call 240-2534/2535 for programs and times. Organists demonstrate the sounds and versatility of the tabernacle's famous instrument in 25-minute recitals, held once or twice daily. The reknowned Tabernacle Choir sings on Sunday mornings and rehearses on Thursday evenings and early Sunday mornings. Occasionally, when the choir is on tour, a youth choir, youth symphony, or other group replaces it. A concert series presents programs on Friday and Saturday evenings through the year in Assembly Hall or in the tabernacle featuring soloists, small ensembles, or full orchestras. Except for a few special events, you won't need tickets to attend Temple Square performances.

The square lies just north of the downtown business district and close to the bus and train station. It's bounded by Main, North Temple, West Temple, and South Temple streets. Park at meters around the square, at pay lots on North Temple Street, or for free on streets farther north.

Temple Square Historical Tour
Guides will approach you near the flagpole in the center of the square to offer an introduction to Salt Lake City's Mormon pioneers, temple, tabernacle, Assembly Hall, and historic monuments. The 40-minute tours begin every 10 minutes during the summer season and every 15 minutes the rest of the year. Custom group tours can be scheduled in advance. Points of interest, which you may also see on your own, include the Seagull Monument (commemorating the seagulls that devoured the plague of "crickets" in 1848); a bell from the abandoned Nauvoo Temple; sculptures of Christ, church leaders, and handcart pioneers; an astronomy observation site; and a meridian marker (outside the walls at Main and South Temple streets) from which surveyors mapped out Utah.

The Salt Lake Temple
Mormons believe that they must have temples within which to hold sacred rites and fulfill God's

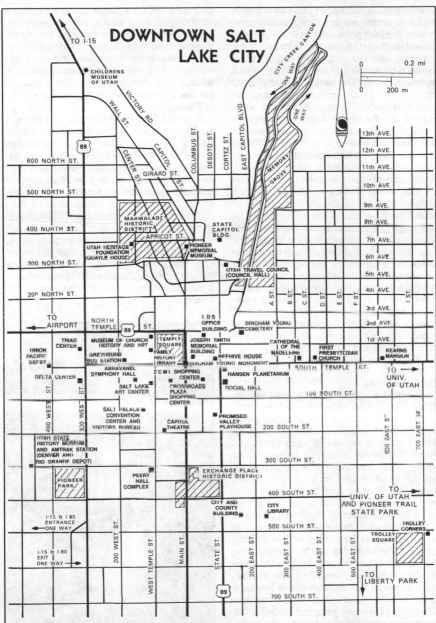

DOWNTOWN SALT LAKE CITY

TO I-15

CHILDRENS MUSEUM OF UTAH

CITY CREEK CANYON

ONE WAY

ONE WAY

0   0.2 mi
0   200 m

VICTORY RD.

WALL ST.

CENTER ST.

CAPITOL ST.

COLUMBUS ST.

DESOTO ST.

CORTEZ ST.

EAST CAPITOL BLVD.

MEMORY GROVE

13th AVE.
12th AVE.
11th AVE.
10th AVE.
9th AVE.
8th AVE.
7th AVE.
6th AVE.
5th AVE.
4th AVE.
3rd AVE.
2nd AVE.
1st AVE.

600 NORTH ST.
500 NORTH ST.
400 NORTH ST.
300 NORTH ST.
200 NORTH ST.

GIRARD ST.

MARMALADE HISTORIC DISTRICT

APRICOT ST.

STATE CAPITOL BLDG.

UTAH HERITAGE FOUNDATION (QUAYLE HOUSE)

PIONEER MEMORIAL MUSEUM

UTAH TRAVEL COUNCIL (COUNCIL HALL)

A ST.
B ST.
C ST.
D ST.
E ST.
F ST.
I ST.

TO AIRPORT

NORTH TEMPLE ST.

LDS OFFICE BUILDING

BRIGHAM YOUNG CEMETERY

UNION PACIFIC DEPOT

TRIAD CENTER

MUSEUM OF CHURCH HISTORY AND ART

GREYHOUND BUS STATION

TEMPLE SQUARE

FAMILY HISTORY LIBRARY

JOSEPH SMITH MEMORIAL BUILDING

BEEHIVE HOUSE

BRIGHAM YOUNG MONUMENT

CATHEDRAL OF THE MADELEINE

FIRST PRESBYTERIAN CHURCH

KEARNS MANSION

DELTA CENTER

ABRAVANEL SYMPHONY HALL

SALT LAKE ART CENTER

ZCMI SHOPPING CENTER

CROSSROADS PLAZA SHOPPING CENTER

HANSEN PLANETARIUM

SOCIAL HALL

SOUTH TEMPLE ST.

TO UNIV. OF UTAH

100 SOUTH ST.

400 WEST ST.

300 WEST ST.

200 WEST ST.

WEST TEMPLE ST.

MAIN ST.

STATE ST.

200 EAST ST.

300 EAST ST.

400 EAST ST.

500 EAST ST.

600 EAST ST.

700 EAST ST.

SALT PALACE CONVENTION CENTER AND VISITORS BUREAU

CAPITOL THEATRE

PROMISED VALLEY PLAYHOUSE

200 SOUTH ST.

UTAH STATE HISTORY MUSEUM AND AMTRAK STATION (DENVER AND RIO GRANDE DEPOT)

300 SOUTH ST.

PIONEER PARK

PEERY HALL COMPLEX

EXCHANGE PLACE HISTORIC DISTRICT

400 SOUTH ST.

TO UNIV. OF UTAH AND PIONEER TRAIL STATE PARK

I-15 & I-80 ENTRANCE ONE WAY

CITY AND COUNTY BUILDING

CITY LIBRARY

500 SOUTH ST.

TROLLEY CORNERS

I-15 & I-80 EXIT ONE WAY

TROLLEY SQUARE

TO LIBERTY PARK

US 89

700 SOUTH ST.

commandments. According to the Mormon faith, baptisms, marriages, and family-sealing ceremonies that take place inside a temple will last beyond death and into eternity. Prior to entering a temple, members prepare for a spiritual experience by dressing in white clothing, which represents purity. The temple is used only for these special functions; normal Sunday services take place in local stake or ward buildings—in fact, the temple is closed on Sundays.

The plan of Salt Lake City's temple came first as a vision to Brigham Young when he still lived in Illinois. Later, Young's concept became a reality with help from church architect Truman O. Angell; construction began in 1853. Workers chiseled granite blocks from Little Cottonwood Canyon, 20 miles southeast of the city, then hauled them by oxen and later by railroad for final shaping at the temple site. The foundation alone required 7,478 tons of stone. Walls measure nine feet thick at the base and taper to six feet on the second story. The highest of the six slender spires stands 210 feet, topped by a glittering statue of the angel Moroni with trumpet in hand. The 12.5-foot statue is made of hammered copper covered with gold leaf. As with all Mormon temples, the interior was open to the public for a short time after completion. Dedication took place on April 6, 1893, 40 years to the day after the work began.

The Tabernacle

Pioneers labored from 1863 to 1867 to construct this unique dome-shaped building. Brigham Young desired a meeting hall capable of holding thousands of people in an interior free of supports that would block vision and sound. His design, drawn by bridge-builder Henry Grow, took shape in massive latticed wooden beams resting on 44 supports of red sandstone. Because Utah lacked many common building supplies, the workers often had to make substitutions. Wooden pegs and rawhide strips hold the structure together. The large organ pipes resemble metal, balcony pillars appear to be marble, and the benches look like oak, yet all are pine wood painted to simulate these materials. The tabernacle has become known for both the phenomenal acoustics of the smooth arched ceiling and the massive tabernacle pipe organ, regarded as one of the finest ever built. From 700 pipes when constructed in 1867, the organ has grown to about 12,000 pipes, five manuals, and one pedal keyboard. Daily recitals demonstrate the instrument's capabilities. Temple Square tours include a stop in the tabernacle for a short presentation on the history of the famed building; an acoustic demonstration shows that a dropped pin can be heard even in the back rows 170 feet away!

Important church conferences take place in the tabernacle every spring and autumn, but the seating capacity of about 6,500—considered huge when it was built—is now far too small, despite the addition of a balcony. Hundreds of thousands watch the proceedings on TV via a church satellite network. The renowned Mormon Tabernacle Choir, 320 voices strong, sings on Sunday mornings over national radio (CBS) and regional TV network. The choir's radio broadcast, which dates back to 1929, is the longest-running broadcast in the world. Visitors may also attend choir rehearsals Thursday evenings and early Sunday mornings. Families with infants can sit in a glassed-in room at the rear without fear of disturbing other listeners.

Assembly Hall

Thrifty craftspeople built this smaller Gothic-revival structure in 1877-82, using granite left over from the temple construction. The truncated spires, reaching as high as 130 feet, once functioned as chimneys. Inside the hall, there's seating for 1,500 people and a choir of 100. The baroque-style organ, installed in 1983, has 3,500 pipes and three manuals; of particular note are the organ's horizontal pipes, called trumpets. Initially, the Salt Lake Stake congregation met here; now the building serves as a concert hall and hosts a variety of church functions.

North Visitor Center

Wander around on your own, or ask the ever-present tour guides for help. Beautiful murals on the lower floor show Old Testament prophets; head upstairs to see paintings of the life of Christ. A spiraling ramp leads to the upper level where *Christus,* an 11-foot replica of a sculpture by Bertel Thorvaldsen, stands in a circular room whose wall mural depicts the universe. The Resource Center, near the bottom of the ramp, offers touch-screen video programs. Downstairs display areas and theaters have other offerings, which change periodically.

South Visitor Center

Two 30-minute tours begin here: **Book of Mormon** and **Purpose of Temples.** Things to see on the main level include paintings of prophets and church history, a baptismal font supported by 12 life-size oxen (representing the 12 tribes of

Tabernacle under construction, ca. 1867

CHURCH OF JESUS CHRIST OF LATTER-DAY SAINTS

Israel) as used in temples, photos of the Salt Lake Temple interior, and a scale model of Solomon's Temple. Head downstairs to see replicas of the metal plates inscribed with the Book of Mormon, which Mormons believe were revealed to Joseph Smith in 1823. Ancient plates of Old World civilizations and stone boxes from the Americas are exhibited to support the claim that the plates are genuine. Mormon literature can be obtained at a desk near the entrance.

VICINITY OF TEMPLE SQUARE

Museum Of Church History And Art

Brigham Young encouraged the preservation of church history, especially when he saw that Salt Lake City's pioneering era was drawing to a close. The collection of church artifacts, begun by the Deseret Museum in 1869, includes the plow that cut the first furrows in the Salt Lake Valley. Exhibits document each of the past church presidents—from Joseph Smith to the present—with paintings, photos, documents, and personal belongings. Art exhibits illustrate many styles of 19th- and 20th-century paintings and sculpture. Perhaps the most striking piece is the gilded 11.5-foot statue of Moroni, which crowned a Washington, D.C., chapel from 1933 to 1976. Temporary exhibits also display Mormon artistry and themes in photography, abstract art, textiles, furniture, and woodworking. Work by Native Americans and foreign artists shows the diversity of church members. A theater downstairs presents programs about the museum's work and other topics. The museum store sells prints, books, recordings, postcards, and other souvenirs.

Step outside to see the 1847 log cabin, one of only two surviving from Salt Lake City's beginnings. The interior has been furnished as it might have been during the first winter here. The Museum of Church History and Art is open (April-Dec.) Mon.-Fri. 9 a.m.-9 p.m. and Saturday, Sunday, and holidays 10 a.m.-7 p.m.; winter hours (Jan.-March) are daily 10 a.m.-7 p.m. (extended until 9 p.m. Monday and Wednesday); free. It's located just west of Temple Square at 45 N. West Temple, tel. 240-3310.

Family History Library

This new building houses the largest collection of genealogical information in the world. Library workers have made extensive travels to many countries to microfilm documents and books. More than 500 employees, assisted by over 400 volunteers, keep track of the records. The Mormon Church has gone to this effort to enable members to trace their ancestors, who can then be baptized by proxy. In this way, according to Mormon belief, the ancestors will be sealed in the family and church for eternity. However, the spirits for whom these baptisms are performed have a choice of accepting or rejecting the baptism.

The library is open to the public. If you'd like to research your family tree, bring what information you have and get the library's *A Guide to Research* booklet. A brief slide presentation explains what types of records are kept and how to get started. Staff will answer questions. In most cases the files won't have information about living persons because of rights to privacy. The Mormon Church leaves nothing to chance in preserving its genealogical records and history—master copies on microfilm rest in vaults deep within the mountains southeast of Salt Lake City. The Family History Library is open Mon.-Sat. at 7:30 a.m., closing Mondays at 6 p.m., Tues.-Fri. at 10 p.m., and Saturdays at 5 p.m.; closed Sundays and some holidays. Located just west of Temple Square at 35 N. West Temple, tel. 240-2331.

LDS Office Building
Day-to-day running of the massive church organization focuses on the 28-story tower east of Temple Square. On any weekday you'll see church workers engaged in leadership, educational, and missionary roles. Such a volume of correspondence takes place that the building has its own zip code. Free tours that begin in the main lobby explain a bit about the work here, but the big attraction is a visit to the 26th-floor observation deck. You'll see Temple Square and all the city spread out below like a map. Weather permitting, the valley, Great Salt Lake, and surrounding mountains stand out clearly. Tours last about 30 minutes, depending on how long you want to take in the panorama. The main lobby has some noteworthy artwork, including a giant 66-by-16-foot mural of Christ appearing to his apostles just prior to his ascension. Gardens and fountains grace a small park behind the building. You can take tours Mon.-Fri. (and

Saturday April-Oct.) 9 a.m.-4:15 p.m.; closed Sunday and holidays. The address is 50 E. North Temple.

Beehive House
This former house of Brigham Young was built in 1854 and occupied by him until his death in 1877. The adobe and brick structure stood out as one of the most ornate houses of early Salt Lake City. Free tours lasting 30-40 minutes take visitors through the house and tell of family life within the walls. The interior has been meticulously restored with many original furnishings. A beehive symbol, representing industry, caps the top of the house and appears in decorative motifs inside. Brigham Young had about 27 wives, but only one stayed in this house at a time. Downstairs, Young's children gathered in the sitting room for evenings of prayer, talks, and music. Upstairs, he entertained guests and dignitaries in a lavish reception room called the Long Hall. Other rooms to see include the kitchen, family store, bedrooms, playroom, and the "fairy castle," where small children could peer through a window at grown-ups in the hallway below. Tours leave Mon.-Sat. 9:30 a.m.-4:30 p.m. (until 6:30 p.m. Mon.-Fri. in summer) and Sunday 10 a.m.-1 p.m.; closed on Thanksgiving, Christmas, and New Year's Day; open other holidays but usually closes at 1 p.m. Beehive House is on the corner of South Temple and State, in the same block as the LDS Office Building, tel. 240-2671. The **Lion House** next door was built in 1855-56 of stuccoed adobe; a stone lion guards the entrance. Brigham Young used the dwelling as a supplementary house for his large family. No tours are offered.

Brigham Young Cemetery
Church president, founder of Utah, colonizer, and territorial governor, Brigham Young rests here with five of his wives and his eldest son. Several monuments on the grounds honor the pioneers and Young's family. From State Street near Beehive House, go one-half block east on First Avenue.

Eagle Gate
This modern replacement of the original 1859 gate spans State St. just north of South Temple Street. It once marked the entrance to Brigham Young's property, which included City Creek

*Beehive House and
Eagle Gate, ca. 1869*

Canyon. The bronze eagle has a 20-foot wing-span and weighs two tons. The present gate, designed by Brigham Young's grandson, architect George Cannon Young, was dedicated in 1963.

Hansen Planetarium

The heavens come to earth in multimedia star shows using a sophisticated Digistar computer projection system. Laser/music shows, science shows, and children's programs are also scheduled regularly. Museum exhibits include the planetarium's original Spitz star projector, meteorites, Apollo displays, a rock from the moon, a Foucault pendulum, and hands-on displays. Exhibit halls have free admission; open Mon.-Sat. about 9 a.m.-9 p.m. and Sunday 1-5 p.m. Shows cost $4-5.50 adult ($3-4 for children 12 and under and seniors) depending on the program. For upcoming astronomical events and telescope viewings, call 532-STAR. Hansen Planetarium is in a historic building at 15 S. State St. (just east of ZCMI Shopping Center) downtown, tel. 538-2098 (recording), 363-0559 (laser concerts), or 538-2104 (office).

Social Hall

Early settlers built Utah's first theater in 1852-53 under the direction of Brigham Young. Recent excavations have unearthed the foundation and sandstone walls of the venerable building, torn down and buried in 1921. The ruins and historic exhibits lie within a glass enclosure south of Hansen Planetarium and directly across State Street from ZCMI Center; an underground passage connects Social Hall with ZCMI Shopping Center; both are open daily.

Brigham Young Monument

You'll want to be sure not to miss this monument—it stands right in the middle of the busy intersection at Main and South Temple streets! Brigham Young, in bronze, stands atop a granite pedestal with figures below representing an Indian, a fur trapper, and a pioneer family. Unveiled on July 24, 1897, it celebrates the first 50 years of settlement in Salt Lake City. A plaque lists the names of the first group of 148 Mormon pioneers.

Joseph Smith Memorial Building/Hotel Utah

Step inside the lobby to admire the ornate interior. Built of white terra-cotta brick in a Modern Italian Renaissance style, this building was opened in 1911 as a first-class hotel for church and business leaders. Massive marble columns, chandeliers, and a stained glass ceiling create an opulent atmosphere. The LDS church, owners of the hotel, converted the venerable structure into an office building and a memorial to the LDS founding father, Joseph Smith. On the ground floor the Family Search Center has 200 computers available to trace family ancestry; tel. 240-4085. Also on the ground floor is a large-screen theater showing the 53-minute film, *Legacy*, which traces a Mormon family's experiences from conversion through years of persecution, relocation, war, and settlement in Utah; admission is free; tel. 240-2205. The tenth floor offers observation areas, the formal **Roof Restaurant,** and the less formal **Garden Restaurant,** tel. 539-1911. The building is open Mon.-Sat. but is closed on Sunday except to those attending worship services.

Symphony Hall

Abravanel (Symphony) Hall

Easily the most striking modern building in Salt Lake City, Abravanel Hall glitters with gold leaf, crystal chandeliers, and more than a mile of brass railing. Careful attention to acoustic design has paid off: the concert hall is one of the best in the world. The Utah Symphony Orchestra inaugurated its new home in 1979 after $12 million and three years of construction. An illuminated fountain flows outside on the plaza during concerts. Tours lasting about 30 minutes take you through the building and explain details of its construction. Call the box office for tour times and concert dates, tel. 533-6407/6683. On the southwest corner of South Temple and West Temple streets.

Salt Lake Art Center

Several exhibitions usually take place simultaneously at this busy place. Paintings, photographs, sculptures, ceramics, and some very hard-to-categorize art forms may be shown. Diverse art classes and workshops are scheduled along with films, lectures, poetry readings, music

concerts, and theater. A shop offers art books, posters, crafts, and artwork. Open Tues.-Sat. 10 a.m.-5 p.m. and Sun. 1-5 p.m.; donation. Located at 20 S. West Temple between Abravanel (Symphony) Hall and the Salt Palace Convention Center, tel. 328-4201; parking validation is sold for Crossroads Plaza across the street.

Utah State History Museum

The Denver and Rio Grande Railroad built this grand terminal in 1910 while in keen competition with Union Pacific, which kept a depot two blocks to the north. Steam whistles no longer blow outside, but Amtrak trains now stop here. The spacious lobby is worth a visit to see changing exhibits on Utah's history; the museum is open Mon.-Fri. 8 a.m.-5 p.m. and Sat. 10 a.m.-2 p.m.; free. The Utah State Historical Society has a bookstore just off the lobby with an excellent selection of Utah history and travel books. Upstairs, the society offers a research library containing thousands of books and photos about Utah's past. Located at the west end of 300 South at 455 West, tel. 533-3500.

NORTH OF DOWNTOWN

Pioneer Memorial Museum

Descendants of Utah's Mormon pioneers have packed all four levels of the museum with a huge collection of pioneer portraits and memorabilia. These artifacts tell the story of persecuted families who fled Nauvoo, Illinois, and trekked 2,000 miles west to Utah to build their city of Zion. It helps to have some knowledge of Mormon history to fully appreciate the exhibits. A video program, shown on request, introduces the collection.

The present museum, built in 1950, is a replica of the old Salt Lake Theatre, used from 1862 until torn down in 1928. Theatrical exhibits on the main floor include printed programs, props, musical instruments, and seats. The main floor also has paintings, photos, and personal effects of Brigham Young and his First Counselor, Heber C. Kimball. A manuscript room in the back is full of proclamations, religious books, maps, scrapbooks, and photos. A family tree shows Samuel Rose Parkinson (1831-1919), his three wives, and a total of 221 children, grandchildren, and great-grandchildren during

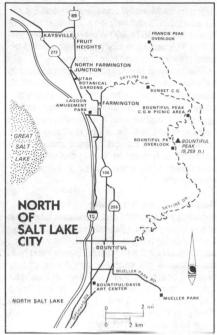

NORTH OF SALT LAKE CITY

his lifetime. Indian exhibits scattered around the museum contain exotic items like an Inca god and a Maori bride's skirt. The second floor has a medical/midwifery display, a pioneer kitchen, clothing, a large doll collection, and chinaware. The third floor has displays of clocks, Utah silk production, furniture, quilts, and lots of bric-a-brac. Go downstairs to the basement for exhibits of spinning and weaving, railroading, mining, and guns. The two-story Carriage House, connected to the basement by a short tunnel, has saddles and harnesses, a mule-drawn streetcar, stagecoaches, a steam fire pumper, a blacksmith shop, and the wagon in which Brigham Young is believed to have arrived in the Salt Lake Valley. A small gift shop just inside the museum's entrance sells books, postcards, slides, and other souvenirs of Utah's history. The Pioneer Memorial Museum, 300 N. Main St. (near the State Capitol), tel. 538-1050, is open Mon.-Sat. 9 a.m.-5 p.m., also Sun. 1-5 p.m. in summer, closed major holidays, donation appreciated. There's free parking at a lot between the museum and the State Capitol.

The State Capitol
Utah's Capitol building occupies a prominent spot on a hill just north of downtown. Fund shortages during the state's early years left the legislators without a permanent home from 1896 until completion of this building in 1915. If the architectural style looks familiar, that's because the building was patterned after the national Capitol. Utah granite makes up the outside. The interior, with its Ionic columns, is of polished marble from Georgia. Murals depict early explorers and pioneers. Smaller paintings show all the territorial and state governors. Statues, busts, and plaques also honor prominent Utah figures of the past. The Gold Room, used for receiving dignitaries, has a formal setting graced by chandeliers, wall tapestries, elegant furniture, and cherubs on the ceiling. The chambers of the House of Representatives, Senate, and Supreme Court are entered from the mezzanine. Hallways on the lowest floor have photo exhibits of the state's scenic and historic spots, beehive memorabilia, mining, and agriculture.

Forty acres of park lands with historic statues and monuments surround the Capitol. The statue of the heroic Indian *Massasoit* in front of the Capitol is a bronze replica by Utah sculptor Cyrus E. Dallin. From this spot you can look out over Salt Lake City and straight down State Street, which runs south about 28 miles without a curve. The Mormon Battalion Monument, a large bronze and granite memorial in the southeast corner of the capitol grounds, commemorates the 549 Mormon soldiers who marched 2,000 miles from Council Bluffs, Iowa, to San Diego, California, to assist in the Mexican War of 1846. Except for an attack by wild animals in the "Battle of the Bulls," the group saw no action. Steps lead down into a small canyon east of the capitol to **Memory Grove.** Monuments and relics honor Utah's war dead from WW I to the present.

The Capitol is open 8 a.m.-6 p.m., extended in summer to daily 8 a.m.-8 p.m. Free tours in summer depart every half hour Mon.-Fri. 9 a.m.-3 p.m.; meet in front of the large map located on the first floor; tel. 538-3000. Visitors are welcome to dine at the circular cafeteria (open Mon.-Fri. 7 a.m.-4 p.m.) behind the Capitol. Annual legislative sessions begin in January and last about 45 days. The Utah State Capitol is at 300 North and State streets.

Council Hall

Across the street from the Capitol lies the venerable Council Hall. Dedicated in 1866, the brick building served as city hall and a meeting place for the territorial and early state legislatures. Many historic decisions were made within its walls. Council Hall used to be downtown at 120 E. 100 South before being moved here in 1963. Drop in to see staff of the **Utah Travel Council** for information on sights, services, and events in the state. You'll also find literature and advice on visiting national parks and monuments, national forests, Bureau of Land Management areas, and state parks. Council Hall and the Utah Travel Council are open Mon.-Fri. 8 a.m.-5 p.m. (also weekends and holidays 10 a.m.-5 p.m.); tel. 538-1030. The 1883 Gothic-Revival building just to the east was also moved here. Formerly the 18th Ward Chapel of the LDS church, it's now the **White Memorial Chapel** and is used for community events.

Historic Houses

Streets in the **Marmalade District** on the hillside west of the Capitol have names of fruit trees—hence the term "marmalade." Many residences date from the 19th century. The **Utah Heritage Foundation,** located at 355 Quince St. in the 1880s Quayle House, has information and self-guided tour brochures about Salt Lake City's historic districts. Group walking tours can be arranged with at least one week's notice. The **McCune Mansion** at 200 N. Main, tel. 533-0858, is one of the city's most eye-catching old houses. The turn-of-the-century turreted structure has a tiled roof and exceptional interior woodwork; it's now used for offices and wedding receptions.

Children's Museum Of Utah

None of the exhibits here have "do not touch" signs. Kids get to explore by "excavating" a saber-toothed tiger skeleton, piloting a 727 jet trainer, implanting an artificial heart in a dummy, "shopping," "banking," creating art projects, and using computer exhibits. Everything is great fun; just don't say anything to the kids about the exhibits being educational. Handicap-awareness simulations let a youngster experience what life is like for others by entering a blind room or by taking a wheelchair through an obstacle course. The museum is open Mon.-Sat. 9:30 a.m.-5 p.m.

(til 9 p.m. on Monday) and Sunday noon-5 p.m.; $3 adult, $2.75 children 2-13. Located north of downtown at 840 N. 300 West (US 89), tel. 328-3383. The adjacent city park offers picnic tables, playground, and tennis courts.

The building housing the museum used to be known as the Wasatch Plunge or Wasatch Springs Municipal Baths. Mormon pioneers discovered the sulfurous springs soon after arriving and built a bathhouse. The spot served as a bathing resort until the early 1970s, when the baths closed and the springs were capped. People had lost interest in "taking the waters" for their health and turned instead to jogging and other sports.

Bountiful-Davis Art Center

Exhibits by Utah artists and art classes take place at this gallery eight miles north of Salt Lake City. Open Monday 5-9 p.m., Tues.-Fri. 10 a.m.-6 p.m., and Saturday 2-5 p.m.; closed Sunday and holidays; free. A gift shop is open during gallery hours. Located at 2175 S. Main in Bountiful (84010); take I-15 North Salt Lake/Woods Cross Exit 318, go east 0.3 mile on 2600 South to 500 West (which becomes Main Street), then turn left (north) 0.2 mile; tel. 292-0367.

Lagoon Amusement Park
And Pioneer Village

History, recreation, and thrilling rides come together in this attractively landscaped park, 16 miles north of Salt Lake City (or 16 miles south of Ogden), tel. 451-8000. Lagoon traces its own history back to 1887, when bathers came to Lake Park on the shores of the Great Salt Lake, two miles to the west of its present location. The vast **Lagoon Amusement Park** area includes roller coaster rides, a giant Ferris wheel, Tilt-a-Whirl, Flying Carpet, Mother Goose Land, Dracula's Castle, Sky Fighter, a log flume ride, a steam train ride, and many arcade games. Musical events you might see include Music USA (song and dance), Summer Rhythm (pop), and performances by the marching Show Band. Other things to do include picnicking and playing miniature golf (extra charge). **Lagoon A Beach** provides thrilling water slides and landscaped pools.

Pioneer Village brings the past to life with authentic 19th century buildings, stagecoach and steam train rides, a Ute Indian museum, a carriage museum, a gun collection, and many other exhibits. Almost every kind of shop or office you'd expect to find in a Utah town of 100 years ago will be here (no saloon—sorry!). Wild West shootouts take place several times daily. Food booths are scattered throughout the park or you can dine at the Gaslight Restaurant near the Opera House. Lagoon Amusement Park, Lagoon A Beach, and Pioneer Village open at 11 a.m. Sun.-Fri., 10 a.m. Saturday, and close 11 p.m.-midnight (depending on weather and day of week): Saturday and Sunday from early April to Memorial Day weekend, daily from Memorial to Labor day weekends, then Saturday and Sunday through September. An all-day ride pass (the best deal as individual rides cost $1.50-2.50) is $21 adult, less for children and seniors. The all-day pass includes Lagoon A Beach privileges. An additional $3.50 is charged for parking. Take I-15 to the Lagoon Exit and follow signs.

Pioneer Village Campground, on the south side of the amusement park, tel. 451-8100, offers showers, a store, laundry, and discounts for rides; sites for tents or RVs cost $15.30 without hookups, $16.93-20.76 w/hookups; open mid-April to mid-October.

Utah Botanical Gardens
Thousands of brightly colored flowers make this a lovely spot in season. The grounds include a rose garden, groups of annuals and perennials, herbs, lilies, lilacs, an iris walk, garden vegetables, a native landscape garden, shrubs, and trees. Labels identify the plants, which come from Utah and other temperate regions of the world. Utah State University (Logan) uses the gardens for research and as a demonstration area. The gardens offer a pleasant place for a stroll and an opportunity for local gardeners to see what will grow well in this area. Demonstration home greenhouses show a variety of construction styles and materials. Staff schedule flower shows, workshops, gardening classes, and answer questions. Public tours are offered Wednesday at 10 a.m. May-September. The grounds are open daily during daylight hours all year; office hours are Mon.-Fri. 8:30 a.m.-4:30 p.m. Located at 1817 N. Main in Farmington (at the junction of US 89 and UT 273), tel. 451-3204. Take I-15 Exit 327 and go north two miles on US 89, then turn right just past the gardens to the entrance.

Kearns Mansion

EAST OF DOWNTOWN

South Temple Street
South Temple was probably the most prestigious street address in all of early Utah. Many religious and business leaders had stately mansions along South Temple, once known as Brigham Street. The book *Brigham Street* by Margaret Lester details the history of the people who lived here and their magnificent buildings. The Utah Heritage Foundation sells booklets outlining a self-guided tour called *Historic Buildings Along South Temple Street.* Several buildings dating from the early 1900s are open to the public.

Twin towers and gargoyles embellish the imposing Catholic **Cathedral of the Madeleine,** 331 E. South Temple, tel. 328-8941, constructed of sandstone in a Roman Gothic style; open daily all year. The **First Presbyterian Church,** 347 E. South Temple, tel. 363-3889, is in an English Gothic Revival style; open daily (check at office if front doors are closed). The palatial **Kearns Mansion,** 603 E. South Temple, tel.

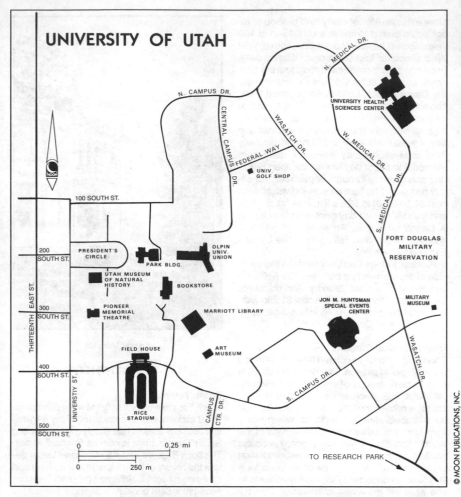

UNIVERSITY OF UTAH

538-1005, now serves as the official governor's residence. Thomas Kearns, noted for his silver-mining wealth, became a U.S. senator and publisher of the *Salt Lake Tribune*. He spared no expense to make the 28 rooms as elegant and lavish as possible. Tours have been temporarily stopped because of damage caused by a fire but will resume sometime in 1996.

University Of Utah

Mormon pioneers established a university in their short-lived town of Nauvoo, Illinois, and brought its books with them to Utah. The University of Deseret opened in 1850, just two and one half years after the first colonizers reached the Salt Lake Valley. Lack of funds forced the school to close after two years, as church educators concentrated their efforts on primary classes. Doctor John R. Park brought the university back to life as a business academy in 1867. It was renamed the University of Utah in 1892 and moved to its present site on a terrace east of town in 1900. The state-assisted institution now sprawls across a 1,500-acre campus. A giant "U" on the hillside lights up during sporting events; if the university team wins, the lights flash.

About 28,000 students and a faculty of 3,700 take part in a wide range of fields, including the liberal arts, business, medicine, science, engineering, and architecture—some 16 colleges and schools in all. The adjacent Research Park is a partnership of university and private enterprise involving many students and faculty. A center of culture, the University of Utah offers the Utah Museum of Natural History, Utah Museum of Fine Arts, symphony, bands, dance, theater, and choral groups. Visitors are welcome at the cultural and sporting events, libraries, bookstore, movie theater, and Olpin Union food services. You'll have to accompany someone with a university card to get into most recreational facilities, however. For a campus map, list of scheduled events, and other information, drop by the Park Building, at the top of President's Circle, tel. 581-6515, or the Olpin Union, tel. 581-5888. On-campus parking is available at metered spaces around the grounds and pay lots next to the Olpin Union and the Marriott Library; free parking can be found off campus on residential streets.

Utah Museum Of Natural History

This large and varied collection of geology, biology, and anthropology exhibits tells the story of Utah before the pioneers arrived. A reproduction of the huge Barrier Canyon Mural pictograph shows the art of prehistoric Indians. Exhibits display artifacts and trace the development of early cultures and their replacement by modern tribes, such as the Ute and Navajo. Other exhibits illustrate Utah's mining history and feature beautiful specimens of the state's more than 600 minerals. Impressive natural history models include dinosaurs and early mammals, as well as the varied wildlife of the present day. Look for the exhibit of California gulls *(Larus californicus)* devouring the plague of grasshoppers. Visiting exhibits may be on display too. A gift shop sells animal souvenirs for the kids, fossil and mineral specimens, Utah and natural history books, and posters. The museum is open Mon.-Sat. 9:30 a.m.-5:30 p.m., Sunday and holidays noon-5 p.m.; $3 adult, $1.50 children 3-14 and seniors 65 and up (special exhibits may cost more). Located on the University of Utah campus on President's Circle; turn in off University St. (1350 East) between 200 and 300 South streets, tel. 581-4303 (recording). Free validated parking is available in front.

Utah Museum Of Fine Arts

Though of modest size, the museum displays a little of everything, from 5,000-year-old Egyptian art to works by contemporary artists. Permanent exhibits include art of China, India, Southeast Asia, Europe, Africa, pre-Columbia, and the early American West. Three large galleries host visiting exhibitions. Open Mon.-Fri. 10 a.m.-5 p.m., Saturday and Sunday 2-5 p.m.; free. Located just south of the Marriott Library on the university campus, tel. 581-7049. Metered parking is available near the museum or at the library; both are off South Campus Drive, an extension of 400 South Street.

Red Butte Garden And Arboretum

This is Utah's largest botanical garden complete with floral displays, ponds, waterfalls, and four miles of mountain nature trails. The Garden Visitor Center features botanical gifts and books. The Courtyard Garden is an excellent place for a family picnic. To reach the garden from I-15, take the Sixth South exit, which will take you east, then turn north two blocks to Fourth South and head east past where Fourth merges into Fifth South. After rising up a hill, take the left turn onto Wakara Way and continue east to the Garden exit. The garden is open all year with irregular hours and days. For times, call 581-4747 (recording) or 581-5322. Entrance fees are $3 adults and $2 children under 16.

Fort Douglas Military Museum

Artifacts and many historical photos take the visitor back to the days of the Nauvoo Legion, the Mormon Battalion, and U.S. Army life in Utah from its beginnings. In late 1862, Colonel Patrick Connor marched to this site with his California-Nevada volunteers and built Camp Douglas. Officially the post defended the mail route and kept check on the Indians. Connor also felt it necessary to keep an eye (and cannon) on the Mormons, whom he and other federal officials distrusted. The colonel wasted no time in seeking Indians to fight. In January 1863, just months after his arrival, Connor's troops killed several hundred Shoshoni on the Bear River in northern

Cache Valley. The event advanced Connor's career, but historians have criticized the action because of the many women and children slaughtered. Later, in a more peaceable mood, the colonel and some of his soldiers pioneered the development of Utah's minerals near Park City and elsewhere in the territory.

Fort Douglas Museum's exhibits show the unique histories of Fort Douglas and other military bases in Utah. The most unusual may have been Fort Rawlins, whose only battle was with the townspeople of Provo. Soldiers staged a rambunctious raid on the town after a payday, but Provo's citizens didn't see the humor and had the troops and fort promptly removed. A WW I room includes photos of German POWs once interned here. Other exhibits illustrate the big military buildup during WW II, when Utah had a naval base! Newer exhibits have artifacts from Desert Storm. Groups can schedule tours. Military history buffs can learn more in the museum's library. Fort Douglas Museum is open Tues.-Sat. 10 a.m.-5 p.m.; free.

The museum building, officers' row, and some of the other structures at Fort Douglas date from the 1870s and 1880s in an architectural style termed Quartermaster Victorian. Pick up a walking-tour leaflet of the fort at the museum; a map shows the nearby post cemetery, where Colonel Connor, soldiers, and German POWs are buried. Fort Douglas, formerly used by the military for administration and recruitment offices, is now part of the University of Utah; turn north on Wasatch Drive from 500 South and travel one-half mile to the museum, tel. 588-5188.

Pioneer Trail State Park

Brigham Young gazed onto the Salt Lake Valley for the first time from this spot, it's believed, and spoke the famous words, "This is the right place. Drive on." Exactly 100 years later, on July 24, 1947, a crowd gathered to dedicate the massive *This Is the Place* monument. Twelve-foot bronze statues of Brigham Young flanked by Heber C. Kimball and Wilford Woodruff stand atop a central pylon. The monument honors not only the Mormon pioneers but also the missionaries from Spain, fur trappers and traders, government explorers, and California immigrants who contributed to the founding of an empire in "the top of the mountains." Sculptures, bas-reliefs, and plaques around the base of the

monument illustrate Utah's beginnings. A visitor center contains a mural depicting major events on the migration of the "Saints" from Nauvoo, Illinois, to their promised land. An eight-minute narration recounts the journey; narration in a foreign language can be requested too. The visitor center is open daily 11 a.m.-5 p.m. year-round; the entry fee of $1.50 adult, $1 ages 6-15 includes admission to Old Deseret. The park has a pleasant picnic area.

Old Deseret, near the monument, re-creates a Utah pioneer village. During the summer it comes alive with farming and craft demonstrations and wagon rides. Most of the dozen buildings that were moved here are original—some of the first in the valley. Some notable structures include Brigham Young's forest farmhouse, the 1847 Levi Riter cabin, and the Charles Rich house, designed in the 1850s for polygamous family living. Brigham Young's forest farmhouse stays open year-round, but the rest of Old Deseret is open daily from Memorial Day to Labor Day weekends 11 a.m.-5 p.m.; tel. 584-8391 (recording). At other times you can walk around on your own to see the exteriors. Pioneer Trail State Park is southeast of the University of Utah near the mouth of Emigration Canyon; from Wasatch Dr., turn east one-half mile on Sunnyside Ave. (850 South), tel. 584-8391 (recording).

Hogle Zoo

Utah's state zoo, an especially popular spot with the kids, is on the eastern edge of town and across from Pioneer Trail State Park. Children like to ride the miniature train (75 cents; closed in winter) and see exhibits in the Discovery Center. Many of the large-animal enclosures have natural settings; here you'll see the familiar elephants, rhinos, and hippos. The apes and monkeys carry on almost all the time, though mornings are best to hear the songs of the white-handed gibbons of Southeast Asia. Also meet Dan the gorilla, Pongo the orangutan, and admire the mandrill—most colorful of all primates. Exhibits of tropical, temperate, and desert zones contain deadly cobras and vipers, aardvarks, Australian kookaburras, brightly colored birds in a walk-in aviary, and dozens of other exotic species. The cats include lions, leopards, tigers, and ocelots. Though zoos don't normally display stuffed animals, Hogle Zoo's unusual "liger" can be seen in the cat area. Shasta the Liger was born of a Bengal tigress and an African lion father, the result of a mating that wouldn't happen in nature because the animal's territories don't overlap. Hogle Zoo is open daily in summer 9 a.m.-7:30 p.m. (gates close at 6 p.m.) and daily in winter 9 a.m.-4 p.m. Entrance fees are $5 adult, $3 children 4-14 and seniors 65 and over. Snack bars and strollers are available. Located at 2600 Sunnyside Ave. (one-half mile east from Wasatch Drive), tel. 582-1631.

Westminster College

The Salt Lake Collegiate Institute, founded in 1875 by the Presbyterian Church as a boys' preparatory school, became Westminster College about the turn of the century. By 1944 it had grown to be a four-year college, and in 1974 it became independent. Converse Hall, constructed in 1906 as the first building on the present campus, is a registered national historic site.

This private four-year college provides a liberal arts background with training in such careers as business, computer science, education, and nursing. Post-graduate programs are offered in business and education. Westminster College has approximately 2,200 students and 90 faculty members. Shaw Center in the middle of the campus serves as a student meeting place with snack bar, cafeteria, and a small bookstore. Concerts, theater performances, poetry series, lectures by prominent people, art exhibits, and other cultural activities are open to the public. Westminster College is at 1840 S. 1300 East, tel. 484-7651.

SOUTH OF DOWNTOWN

Tracy Aviary

Birds have taken over the southwest corner of Liberty Park. Step into their domain to see majestic golden and bald eagles, showy flamingos and peacocks, the hyacinthine macaw (world's largest parrot), the golden pheasant of China, and hundreds of other feathered friends. Emus from Australia prance across fields while ducks, geese, swans, and other waterfowl keep to the ponds. You'll also get to meet Utah's only native vulture, the turkey vulture. Hundreds of trained birds are turned loose to give an open air flying show (most return) at 1 p.m. and 3 p.m. Wed.-Fri. and at 1 p.m., 3 p.m., and 5 p.m. Saturday, Sunday and holidays. Tracy Aviary is open daily 9 a.m.-6 p.m. in summer (daylight saving time) and 9 a.m.-4:30 p.m. the rest of the year; adults $2, children 6-12 and seniors $1. Located in Liberty Park at 589 E. 1300 South, tel. 596-5034; enter the aviary from the east side.

Chase Home Museum Of Utah Folk Art

See contemporary Utah folk art including quilts, rugs, woodcarvings, ethnic arts, and Indian art in this museum located in the center of Liberty Park, tel. 533-5760. Open noon-5 p.m. daily in summer, weekends only the rest of the year; free.

Wheeler Historic Farm

Kids enjoy a visit to this working farm to experience rural life of milking cows, gathering eggs, churning butter, and feeding the animals. Hay rides (sleigh rides in winter) take visitors around the farm. Henry and Sariah Wheeler started the farm in 1887 and developed it into a prosperous dairy and ice-making operation. Tour guides take you through the Wheeler's restored Victorian house, built 1896-98, the first in the county to have an indoor bathroom. Signs on other farm buildings recount their history and use. The "Ice House" now sells crafts and snacks. The Salt Lake County Recreation Department operates the farm and offers special programs for both youngsters and adults; call or write for a schedule, 6351 S. 900 East, Salt Lake City, UT 84121, tel. 264-2212. Admission costs just $1 adult, 50 cents children 3-11 and seniors 65 and up; hay rides are an additional $1. Birthday parties and family picnics are popular (make advance reservations). The Family Garden Program has garden plots and classes available to the community. Though once on the outskirts of town, suburbs now surround Wheeler Historic Farm.

Bingham Canyon Copper Mine

An overlook within the world's largest and oldest open-pit copper mine provides a close look at the nonstop excavation work taking place on the terraced slopes. Signs and exhibits explain the mining process. Prospectors discovered the mineral wealth in 1863, though the Mormon rancher

Utah Copper Mill, Bingham Canyon, ca. 1905

UTAH STATE HISTORICAL SOCIETY

for whom the canyon was named never took part in the mining. Most of the early production concentrated on gold, silver, and lead. Attention shifted to copper in 1906 as mining companies began excavation of an open-pit mine. Today, five billion tons of rock later, the pit measures 2.5 miles in diameter at its top and one-half mile deep. The "richest hole on earth" has yielded 12 million tons of copper and significant amounts of gold, silver, and molybdenum. Efficient mining, smelting, and refining techniques can make a profit even though Bingham Canyon ore now averages only 0.7% copper. Miners once lived in the town of Bingham Canyon, famed for being one street wide and seven miles long! Expanding operations gradually destroyed the town in the 1950s; by 1961 nothing remained. Company officials lived in the attractive town of Copperton, which survives today.

The mine overlook and visitor center are in the Oquirrh Mountains 25 miles southwest of Salt Lake City. Because of the distance, it's a good idea to call ahead before coming out, tel. 322-7300 (recording). Open daily from 8 a.m. until dusk from mid-April to October 31; admission is $2 car, $1 motorcycle. Take I-15 Midvale Exit 301 and follow UT 48 west through Copperton to the mine. Stop at the mine gate for a pass,

then follow signs to the overlook. For a bird's-eye view of the mine from the crest of the Oquirrh Mountains, follow the winding unpaved roads from Tooele or the Salt Lake Valley (see "Oquirrh Overlook" under "Sights" in the "Toole" section of the West-Central Utah chapter).

Jordan River Temple

One of the largest Mormon temples, this striking building has an exterior covered with white marble chips. A gilded statue of the angel Moroni stands atop a 200-foot central tower. In 1981, when opened to the public just prior to its dedication, the temple was toured by 570,000 visitors in 35 days. You're welcome to visit the temple grounds, though no tours are offered. Jordan River Temple is in the town of South Jordan, 18 miles southwest of downtown Salt Lake City, at 10200 S. 1300 West.

WEST OF DOWNTOWN

Welfare Square

This large operation is an effort by the Mormon church to tackle social problems among its members. Started during the Great Depression, Welfare Square consists of a dairy plant, cannery, grain elevator, warehouses, Deseret Industries (repair and sales of used clothing and household items), and social services (counseling, adoption, foster homes). A bishop's storehouse, one of 390 around the world, stocks a full range of groceries and clothing—yet nothing is sold or given away free. Welfare recipients require a bishop's requisition order before anything can leave the shelves. Church members volunteer their time at Welfare Square, farms, or other work projects. Tours, lasting about an hour,

begin with a short film, *Welfare—Another Perspective.* You're welcome to visit Mon.-Fri. 10 a.m.-4 p.m. (last tour begins at 3 p.m.); free. You may be able to take a shuttle bus from Temple Square; ask at either visitor center there. Welfare Square is at 751 W. 700 South, tel. 579-1332. Driving here is a bit tricky because the freeway and railroad tracks block 700 South and other streets; two suggested routes are west on North Temple, then south on 900 West; or south on West Temple, then west on 800 South.

SALT LAKE CITY ACCOMMODATIONS

Youth Hostel
The **Avenues Residential Center,** one mile east of Temple Square, has dorm rooms with use of a kitchen, TV room, and laundry. Information-packed bulletin boards list city sights and goings-on, and you'll meet travelers from all over the world. Year-round rates for the dorm are $13 (cost includes sheets). Rooms are $28 s or d, but only half have private baths. Reservations (with first night's deposit) are advised in the busy summer travel and winter ski seasons. The hostel is on the corner of 107 F St. and Second Ave., Salt Lake City, UT 84103, tel. 363-3855; open 8 a.m.-10 p.m. all year. From downtown, head east on South Temple St. to F St., then turn north two blocks.

Bed And Breakfasts
These are mostly private homes open to travelers. The degree of luxury varies, but the hosts offer a personal touch not found in motels. Most discourage smoking and pets. Advance reservations are requested. Add 10.75% tax to room rates.

Brigham Street Inn, a restored mansion at 1135 E. South Temple, tel. 364-4461, has rooms from $75 s, $105 d. **Anton Boxrud Bed and Breakfast** offers lodging in an eclectic 1901 Victorian brick house at 57 S. 600 East, tel. 363-8035; $38-109 s, $55-109 d. **Saltair Bed & Breakfast,** the oldest continuously operating bed and breakfast in Utah, at 164 S. 900 East, tel. 533-8184, costs $38-79 s, $55-109 d. **The Spruces Bed & Breakfast Inn** is a 1903 Gothic Victorian house at 6151 S. 900 East (just north of Wheeler Historic Farm), tel. 268-8762; rooms run $55-135 s or d. **Pinecrest Bed &**

Breakfast Inn is on the eastern edge of the city at 6211 Emigration Canyon Rd., tel. 583-6663; rooms are $70-175 s or d.

MOTELS AND HOTELS

Salt Lake City has the best selection of accommodations in Utah. An estimated 100 motels and hotels offer more than 10,000 rooms ranging from spartan to posh. Downtown Salt Lake City has the advantage of being close to Temple Square and most other visitor attractions; from here the airport, University of Utah, and ski areas are just a short drive away. Rates listed apply in summer and may be slightly lower the rest of the year. Reservations are most likely to be needed in the summer tourist and winter ski seasons. The listing in the following chart is just a sample. You'll also find many motels and hotels listed in free publications from the Salt Lake Convention & Visitors Bureau, 180 S. West Temple, tel. 521-2868; and at their booth in Terminal 2 of the airport. The Visitors Bureau has plans to relocate to the new Salt Palace Convention Center.

COMMERCIAL CAMPGROUNDS

Camp VIP offers tent and RV sites year-round with showers, swimming pool, game room, playground, store, and laundry. Rates are $17.45 tent or RV without hookups, $22.99 w/hookups. The campground is between downtown and the airport at 1350 W. North Temple, tel. 328-0224. From I-15 northbound, take Exit 311 for I-80, go west 1.3 miles on I-80, exit north one-half

SALT LAKE CITY ACCOMMODATIONS
Add 10.75% tax to all prices; rates listed are for 1-2 persons

DOWNTOWN

Carlton Hotel; 140 E. South Temple; $64-69; tel. 355-3418 or (800) 633-3500; 1935 hotel

Crystal Inn; 230 W. 500 South; $99-175; tel. 328-4466 or (800) 366-4466; pool, exercise room

Inn at Temple Square; 71 W. South Temple; $73-95; tel. 531-1000 or (800) 843-4668; free breakfast, central location

Howard Johnson Hotel; 122 W. South Temple; $79-89; tel. 521-0130 or (800) 366-3684; pool

Doubletree Hotel; 215 W. South Temple; $92-139; tel. 531-7500 or (800) 528-0444; pool

Travelodge at Temple Square; 144 W. North Temple; $48-58; tel. 533-8200 or (800) 255-3050

Covered Wagon Motel; 230 W. North Temple; $28-30; tel. 533-9100

Royal Executive Inn; 121 N. 300 West (US 89); $44.50-49.50; tel. 521-3450 or (800) 541-7639; pool

Temple View Motel; 325 N. 300 West (US 89); $35; tel. 521-9525; kitchenettes

Ken-Dell Motel; 667 N. 300 West (US 89); $35-40 or $15 dorm; tel. 355-0293; kitchenettes, youth hostel

Marriott Hotel; 75 S. West Temple; $69-119; tel. 531-0800 or (800) 228-9290; pool, sauna

Shilo Inn; 206 S. West Temple; $89-95; tel. 521-9500 or (800) 222-2244; pool, sauna

Red Lion Hotel; 255 S. West Temple; $79-115; tel. 328-2000 or (800) 547-8010; pool, sauna

Peery Hotel; 110 W. 300 South; $59-79; tel. 521-4300; historic 1910 hotel

Stratford Hotel; 169 E. 200 South; $15-20; tel. 328-4089; old-style hotel

Emerald Inn; 476 S. State; $44-49; tel. 533-9300; pool

Little America Hotel & Towers; 500 S. Main St.; $63-73; tel. 363-6781 or (800) 453-9450; pools, sauna

Deseret Inn; 50 W. 500 South; $37-41; tel. 532-2900 or (800) 359-2170; spa

Salt Lake Hilton; 150 W. 500 South; $90-130; tel. 532-3344 or (800) 421-7602; pool

Travelodge Downtown; 524 S. West Temple; $50-54; tel. 531-7100 or (800) 578-7878; pool

Embassy Suites; 600 S. West Temple; $70-129; tel. 359-7800 or (800) 362-2779; all suites, pool, sauna

Quality Inn City Center; 154 W. 600 South; $78-88; tel. 521-2930 or (800) 221-2222; pool

Olympus Hotel (Best Western); 161 W. 600 South; $75-85; tel. 521-7373 or (800) 528-1234; pool, spa

Motel 6 Downtown; 176 W. 600 South; $36-42; tel. 531-1252; pool

Holiday Inn Downtown; 230 W. 600 South; $79-89; tel. 359-8600 or (800) 465-4329; pool, sauna

Super 8 Motel; 616 S. 200 West; $46-53; tel. 534-0808 or (800) 800-8000

Clarion Hotel and Suites; 999 South Main; $79-119; tel. 359-8600 or (800) 933-9678; pool, spa, tennis, weight room

The Residence Inn by Marriott; 765 E. 400 South; $89-132; tel. 532-5511 or (800) 331-3131; kitchens, pool, near University of Utah

Scenic Motel; 1345 Foothill Dr.; $34-36; tel. 582-1527; east edge of Salt Lake City

WEST DOWNTOWN TO AIRPORT

Se Rancho Motor Hotel; 640 W. North Temple; $27.22; tel. 532-3300; kitchenettes, pool

Econo Lodge; 715 W. North Temple; $46-50; tel. 363-0062 or (800) 424-4777; pool

Allstar Travel Inn; 754 W. North Temple; $24.50-32.50; tel. 531-7300; kitchenettes, pool

Continental Motel; 819 W. North Temple; $28-40; tel. 363-4546; pool

Regal Inn; 1025 N. 900 West; $22-30; tel. 364-6591 or (800) 524-9999; kitchenettes

Overniter Motor Inn; 1500 W. North Temple; $36-40; tel. 533-8300; pool

Holiday Inn Airport; 1659 W. North Temple; $79-84; tel. 533-9000 or (800) 465-4329; pool, spa

Days Inn; 1900 W. North Temple; $49-56; tel. 539-8538 or (800) 329-7466

Motel 6 Airport; 1990 W. North Temple; $32-38; tel. 364-1053; pool

Nendel's Inn Airport; 2080 W. North Temple; $47-53; 355-0088 or (800) 626-2824; pool

Radison Hotel Airport; 2177 W. North Temple; $69-79; tel. 364-5800 or (800) 333-3333; pool, spa, fitness room

Airport Inn; 2333 W. North Temple; $45-50; tel. 539-0438; pool

Airport Hilton; 5151 Wiley Post Way; $89-195; 539-1515 or (800) 999-3736; pool, spa

Quality Inn Airport; 5575 W. Amelia Earhart Dr.; $68-69; 537-7020 or (800) 522-5575; pool, spa

mile on Redwood Rd. (UT 68), then turn right one-half mile on North Temple; from I-15 southbound, take Exit 313 and turn south one and one half miles on 900 West, then turn right 0.8 mile on North Temple; from I-80 either take the North Temple exit or exit on Redwood Rd. (UT 68) and go north one-half mile, then right one-half mile on North Temple.

Salt Lake City KOA features tent and RV sites open all year with showers, swimming pool, miniature golf, store, and laundry. Rates are $18.60 tent or RV without hookups, $22.94 w/hookups. The campground is between downtown and the airport at 1400 W. North Temple, tel. 355-1192; follow same directions as for Camp VIP, above.

Oquirrh Motor Inn, 21 miles west of Salt Lake City, tel. 250-0118, offers inexpensive RV spaces (no tents); March-late Oct.; $10.75 w/hookups but no showers; located just south of I-80 Tooele Exit 99.

Hidden Haven Campground, 18 miles east of Salt Lake City, tel. 649-8935, has showers, store, laundry, and a trout stream. Tent and RV sites are open all year; $13.35 no hookups, $16.62 w/hookups. Take I-80 Exit 143, then go east 1.6 miles on the north frontage road (or take Park City Exit 145 and go west one mile on the north frontage road).

Pioneer Village Campground, 16 miles north of Salt Lake City, at Lagoon Amusement Park, tel. 451-8100, is open mid-April to mid-October with showers, store, laundry, and discounts for rides; tent and RV sites cost $15.30 no hookups, $16.93-20.76 w/hookups. Take I-15 Lagoon Exit and follow signs.

Cherry Hill Recreation Park, 18 miles north of Salt Lake City, tel. 451-5379, features a water slide, inner tube ride, swimming pool, Pirates Cove (for young children), restaurant, miniature golf, and a variety of games, as well as a large campground with showers, store, and laundry. The season lasts from about mid-April to mid-October, though some activities operate only from Memorial to Labor day weekends. Tent or RV sites cost $15.30 no hookups, $19.67 w/hookups. Take I-15 Lagoon/Farmington Exit 327 and go north two miles on US 89.

FOREST SERVICE CAMPGROUNDS

There are three campgrounds in Big Cottonwood Canyon, located about 15 miles southeast of downtown Salt Lake City. All have drinking water. Groups can reserve **Jordan Pines Campground** (elev. 7,400 feet) by calling (800) 280-CAMP; it's 8.8 miles up the canyon. **Spruces Campground** (elev. 7,400 feet, 9.1 miles up the canyon) is open from early June to mid-Oct.; $9. Some sites can be reserved by calling (800) 280-CAMP. The season at **Redman Campground** (elev. 8,300 feet) lasts from mid-June to early October; $9. It's located between Solitude and Brighton, 13 miles up the canyon.

Little Cottonwood Canyon, about 19 miles southeast of downtown Salt Lake City, has two campgrounds with drinking water. **Tanners Flat Campground** (elev. 7,200 feet, 4.3 miles up the canyon) is open from mid-May to mid-Oct.; $8. Some sites can be reserved by calling (800) 280-CAMP. **Albion Basin Campground** lies high in the mountains (elev. 9,500 feet) and opens from early July to late Sept.; $8; go 11 miles up the canyon (the last two and one half miles are gravel).

SALT LAKE CITY RESTAURANTS

Nowhere else in Utah will you find so many places to eat and so varied a selection. The following are just some of the possibilities. The free *Salt Lake Visitors Guide* and the magazine *Utah Holiday* also list dining establishments. Restaurants in private clubs require purchase of a temporary membership (even if you're not drinking) unless the club is in the hotel where you're staying. Dinner reservations are advisable at the more expensive restaurants; also check to see if coat and tie are required for men.

Restaurant prices (for dinner) are marked $: Inexpensive (to $8); $$: Moderate ($8-15); $$$: Expensive ($15 and up).

AMERICAN

$ **Bill and Nada's Cafe,** 479 S. 600 East, tel. 359-6984, is an especially good place for breakfast, served anytime. Open daily 24 hours.

$ **Chuck-A-Rama Buffet,** 744 E. 400 South; tel. 531-1123, is a great value with limitless servings of mostly meat and potato selections plus daily special ethnic offerings. Open daily for lunch and dinner.

$ **Dee's Family Restaurants,** 143 W. North Temple, tel. 359-4414; 855 W. North Temple, tel. 359-3916; 515 E. 400 South, tel. 322-3811, are open daily for breakfast, lunch, and dinner.

$ to $$ **The Dodo,** 680 S. 900 East, tel. 328-9348, a popular cafe known for paintings of giant dodos is open Mon.-Fri. for lunch and dinner, Sunday for brunch.

$ to $$ **E.I.B.O.'s Famous for Nothing,** Trolley Square, 500 South and 700 East; tel. 531-7788, serves chef's grill steak, chicken, shrimp, oysters, and fish over mesquite charcoal fires. The menu also offers sandwiches, salads, and soups. Open daily for lunch and dinner.

$ **JB's,** at the Howard Johnson Hotel, 122 W. South Temple, tel. 328-8344; and in Crossroads Plaza, South Temple, tel. 355-2100, is open daily for breakfast, lunch, and dinner.

$$ **Lamb's,** downtown at 169 S. Main, tel. 364-7166, claims to be Utah's oldest restaurant; it started in Logan in 1919 and moved to Salt Lake City in 1939. You can still enjoy the 1930s atmosphere as well as the fine food. The menu offers seafood, steak, chops, chicken, and sandwiches. Open daily except Sunday for breakfast, lunch, and dinner.

$$ **Little America,** south of downtown at 500 South Main, tel. 363-6781, is especially noted for its lavish Sunday brunch. Open Sunday for brunch, Mon.-Sat. for breakfast, Mon.-Fri. for lunch, and daily for dinner.

$$ to $$$ **Mullboon's,** in Trolley Corners across from Trolley Square at 515 S. 700 East, tel. 363-9653; in the Olympus Hotel's 13th floor at 161 W. 600 South, tel. 530-1313; and in Midvale at 6930 S. State, tel. 562-5147, has elegant dining with steak, prime rib, and seafood. Open Mon.-Fri. for lunch, daily for dinner, and Sunday for brunch.

$$ **Old Salt City Jail Restaurant,** two blocks east of Trolley Square near the University of Utah at 460 S. 1000 East, tel. 355-2422, offers steak, prime rib, and seafood in an authentic Old West jailhouse. Open daily for dinner.

$$ to $$$ Enjoy panoramic views of the city at the **Room at the Top,** the Salt Lake Hilton at 150 W. 500 South, tel. 532-3344, while dining on steak, prime rib, or seafood. Live piano music provides entertainment nightly. Open Sun.-Fri. for lunch and daily for dinner.

$$ **The Shed,** 1063 E. 2100 South behind the Pine Cone Restaurant, tel. 467-1442, offers Texas-style steak, jumbo Gulf prawns, Alaskan halibut, and chicken. Informal Western atmosphere (entertainment on weekends). Open daily for dinner only.

$$ **Shenanigans Restaurant,** in the Peery Hotel at 274 S. West Temple, tel. 364-3663, has an excellent selection of American, Mexican, and Continental fare—seafood, steak, chicken, sandwiches, and salads. Cartoon-filled menus start the dining off on a humorous note. Open daily for lunch and dinner.

$ **Training Table Restaurant,** 809 E. 400 South, tel. 355-7523, is a great place to come for hamburgers (17 different kinds), sandwiches, salads, and soups. Open daily for lunch and dinner.

MEXICAN

$$ to $$$ Cordova's El Rancho, 543 W. 400 North, tel. 355-1914, offers authentic food in the city's oldest Mexican restaurant. Open Wed.-Sat. for dinner only.

$ La Frontera Cafe, 1236 W. 400 South, tel. 532-3158; and 1434 S. 700 West, tel. 974-0172, serves burritos, enchiladas, tacos, huevos rancheros, and other Mexican favorites here. Open daily for breakfast, lunch, and dinner.

$ Miquelita, 49 E. 900 South, tel. 531-6331, is not much on atmosphere but has good, freshly prepared food at low prices. Open Mon.-Sat. for lunch and dinner.

$ Rio Grande Cafe is located in the nostalgic old Rio Grande train station downtown at 455 W. 300 South, tel. 364-3302. Open Mon.-Sat. for lunch and daily for dinner.

SEAFOOD

$$ to $$$ Market Street Broiler, 258 S. 1300 East, tel. 583-8808, specializes in fresh seafood, which you can enjoy in the dining room, pick up at the take-out counter, or purchase at the fresh fish market. An in-house bakery creates tempting pastries. Open Mon.-Sat. for lunch (daily in summer), daily for dinner.

$$ to $$$ Market Street Grill, downtown at 54 Market St., near Main and Broadway, tel. 322-4668, features fresh seafood plus steak, prime rib, chops, chicken, and pasta. The Market Street Oyster Bar (private club) is next door with a similar menu and prices. Open daily for breakfast, lunch, and dinner; brunch on Sunday.

$$ Oceans Restaurant and Oyster Cafe, 4760 S. 900 East, tel. 261-0115, on the banks of Big Cottonwood Creek, has an excellent selection of seafood including trout from Utah's mountain streams and fish from the Atlantic, Gulf, and Pacific. The Oyster Cafe offers appetizers and lighter meals. The restaurant and cafe are open Mon.-Fri. for lunch and dinner; the restaurant is also open Saturday and Sunday for dinner only.

CONTINENTAL

$$ to $$$ Finn's, southeast of downtown at 2675 Parley's Way, tel. 466-4682, gives generous servings of Continental and American food served in an elegant setting. Selections include New York steak, prime rib, lamb chops, Wiener schnitzel, lobster, and halibut. Enjoy live piano music Friday and Saturday evenings. Open daily except Sunday for dinner only.

$$ to $$$ L'Abeille, in the Marriott Hotel, 75 S. West Temple, tel. 531-0800, provides gourmet dining with meat and seafood prepared in French and other European styles. Open daily for dinner.

$$$ La Caille at Quail Run, near Little Cottonwood Canyon at 9565 Wasatch Blvd., tel. 942-1751, offers superb pastry, crepe, egg, seafood, and meat dishes in an 18th century rural France atmosphere. Vineyards, gardens, ponds, and manicured lawns surround the re-created French chateau. Antique furnishings grace the dining rooms and halls. Expect to pay

LA CAILLE AT QUAIL RUN

$30-40 per person for dinner. Dress is semiformal; reservations advised. Dinner is served daily; brunch and a Basque-style dinner are served on Sunday.

$ to $$ **Le Parisien,** 417 S. 300 East, tel. 364-5223, offers a choice of French and Italian specialties at modest prices. Open Mon.-Sat. for lunch and dinner, Sunday for dinner only.

$ to $$ **Peery Pub and Cafe,** downtown in Peery Hotel at 110 W. 300 South, tel. 521-8919, has fine Continental and other cuisines at cafe prices. Open Mon.-Sat. for lunch, and Saturday for dinner.

$ to $$ **Ristorante Della Fontana,** 336 S. 400 East, tel. 328-4243, serves fine Italian food, available as six-course dinners or a la carte, in an old church building. Specialties include spaghetti, lasagna, fettuccine, chicken cacciatore, and tenderloin *alla griglia.* Open Mon.-Sat. for lunch and dinner.

GREEK

$ to $$ **Dionysus,** 369 S. 400 East, tel. 355-6688, is a family restaurant with Greek and American food; try gyros (grilled meat), shish kabob, dolma (stuffed grape leaves), steaks, or seafood. Open daily for breakfast, lunch, and dinner.

INDIAN

$ to $$ **Royal Taj,** downtown in Arrow Press Square at 165 S. West Temple, behind the Bank of Utah, tel. 355-3617, offers flavorful *biriyani,* tandoori, and other styles of vegetarian and meat dishes. You can order a la carte or set dinners *(thali)* or sample from the lunch buffet. Open Mon.-Sat. for lunch, daily for dinner.

MIDDLE EASTERN

$$ to $$$ **Cedars of Lebanon,** downtown at 152 E. 200 South, tel. 364-4096, has exotic Mediterranean flavors from Lebanon, Morocco, Armenia, Greece, and Israel. Many vegetarian items too. Belly dancers enliven the scene on Friday and Saturday nights. Open Mon.-Sat. for lunch and dinner.

CHINESE

$$ **Fong Ling,** near Big Cottonwood Canyon at 3698 E. 7000 South; tel. 943-8199, is one of the city's finest restaurants for Mandarin, Szechuan, and some Cantonese dining. Open Mon.-Fri. for lunch and daily for dinner.

$ to $$ **Golden Dragon Restaurant,** south of downtown at 1518 S. Main, tel. 486-3991, offers Cantonese, Szechuan, and vegetarian dishes. Open daily for lunch and dinner.

$ to $$ **Hunan Restaurant,** downtown in Arrow Press Square at 165 S. West Temple, tel. 531-6677, serves Mandarin and Szechuan cuisine. Open Mon.-Fri. for lunch, daily for dinner.

$$ **Panda Restaurant,** south of downtown at 1701 S. State, tel. 485-3226, offers grilled Mongolian style meats and vegetables. Or order from the list of Mandarin and American foods. Open daily for lunch and dinner.

JAPANESE

$$ to $$$ **Benihana of Tokyo,** downtown in Arrow Press Square at 165 S. West Temple, behind the Bank of Utah, tel. 322-2421, serves seafood, steak, and chicken cooked at your hibachi table. Open Mon.-Fri. for lunch and daily for dinner.

$$ to $$$ **47 Samurai,** in Trolley Square at 500 South and 700 East, tel. 363-7294, offers meat and seafood in teppanyaki, sukiyaki, tempura, and other styles. Open Mon.-Fri. for lunch and daily for dinner.

$$ to $$$ **Hibachi,** downtown at 238 E. South Temple, tel. 364-5456, serves sukiyaki, sashimi, tempura, and teriyaki steak or seafood. Open Mon.-Sat. for lunch and dinner.

$$ **Kyoto,** 1080 E. 1300 South, tel. 487-3525, chefs and waitresses take pride in the authentic food and atmosphere. Try their sukiyaki, teriyaki, and other styles. Dinner reservations requested. Open Mon.-Sat. for lunch and daily for dinner.

$$ **Mikado,** 67 W. 100 South, tel. 328-0929, specialties include *shabu shabu,* steak teriyaki, and shrimp tempura. Has a sushi bar. Open Mon.-Sat. for dinner only; reservations recommended.

VIETNAMESE

$ **Cafe Trang,** south of downtown at 818 S. Main, tel. 539-1638, is a top-rated restaurant with wonderful food, though don't expect much in the way of decor. Open daily for lunch and dinner.

$ to $$ **The Orient,** southwest of downtown at 4768 Redwood Rd., tel. 966-3659, has expertly prepared and seasoned Vietnamese food. Open Tues.-Sat. for lunch and Tues.-Sun. for dinner.

PIZZA

$ **Gepetto's,** near the University of Utah at 230 S. 1300 East, tel. 583-1013, presents pizza, lasagna, sandwiches, and salads. Live entertainment is offered Thurs.-Saturday. Open Mon.-Sat. for lunch and dinner.

$ **The Pie Pizzeria,** downstairs of the University Pharmacy, 1320 E. 200 South, tel. 582-0193, offers New York-style hand-thrown pizza. Live music Monday and Tuesday evenings. Open daily for lunch and dinner.

DELIS

$ **Marianne's Delicatessen,** downtown at 149 W. 200 South, tel. 364-0513, has many tempting German foods: sausage, cold cuts, sauerkraut, cheese, breads, and chocolates. Open Tues.-Saturday.

$ **New Frontiers Market and Cafe,** 1026 E. Second Ave., tel. 355-7401; 2454 S. 700 East, tel. 359-7913, serves whole-foods cuisine using only the freshest ingredients. A health-food store offers meats, seafood, produce, deli items, and bulk foods. Open daily.

$ **Robert's Deli and Market,** 1071 E. 900 South, tel. 355-8141, has falafel, tabouli, gyro, and many other tasty items from Greek, Armenian, and Lebanese cuisines. The deli specializes in vegetarian foods, though meat items are offered too. Open Mon.-Saturday.

$ **Siegfried's Delicatessen,** downtown at 69 W. 300 South, tel. 355-3891, has a great selection of German sausages, cold cuts, breads, pastries, and cheese. Open Mon.-Saturday.

SALT LAKE CITY ENTERTAINMENT

Check local publications to find out what's going on in town. *The Event* newspaper, published every two weeks, gives the most detailed coverage of local films, concerts, theater, dance, art exhibits, art classes, and nightspots. Other good sources include *Salt Lake Visitors Guide* (available free at the Salt Lake Convention & Visitors Bureau) and *Utah Holiday* magazine (monthly). The daily papers, *Deseret News* and *Salt Lake Tribune,* each have listings in their Friday "weekend" and Sunday "art and entertainment" sections.

CONCERTS

Temple Square
The **Concert Series** at Temple Square presents hundreds of performances a year for the public; all are free. The LDS church sponsors the varied musical fare to provide a common meeting ground of great music for people of all faiths. You might hear chamber music, a symphony, operatic selections, religious choral works, piano solos, organ works, a brass band, or a percussion ensemble. Programs last about an hour and usually take place Friday and Saturday evenings at 7:30 p.m. in either the Assembly Hall or the Tabernacle. Organists present 25-minute **Organ Recitals** in the Tabernacle Mon.-Sat. at noon (also at 2 p.m. in summer) and Saturday and Sunday at 4 p.m. The **Mormon Tabernacle Choir** sings in the Tabernacle on Sunday mornings at 9:30 a.m. (be seated 15 minutes before) for a 30-minute radio broadcast. You're also welcome to attend rehearsals by the Mormon Tabernacle Choir and the Mormon Symphony Chorus. Schedules are posted in Temple Square; tel. 240-2534/2535.

Utah Symphony Orchestra
From its modest beginnings in 1940, the Utah Symphony has grown to be one of the best in the country. Each season, the symphony performs in the glittering Symphony Hall at the Salt Palace in Salt Lake City, and travels to Snowbird, Deer Valley, Ogden, Provo, Logan, and other cities. Symphony Hall and ticket offices are at 123 W. South Temple, tel. 533-6407/6683.

Utah Opera Company
The company, founded in 1978, stages several operas during its Oct.-May season. Ticket offices and performances are in the restored Capitol Theatre, downtown at 50 W. 200 South, tel. 534-0842. The Capitol Theatre opened in 1913 as the Orpheum, one of Salt Lake City's most

Lightning Express,
Salt Lake City Theatre,
ca. 1900

CHURCH OF JESUS CHRIST OF LATTER-DAY SAINTS

flamboyant movie houses. The Italian Renaissance facade has a host of cherubs, theatrical masks, and floral designs.

University Of Utah
The University Symphony Orchestra, University Chamber Orchestra, jazz ensembles, opera, bands, ballet, dance, and choral groups present regular concerts on and off campus; the season runs Sept.-May. Call the university's Public Relations office, tel. 581-6773.

THEATER

Promised Valley Playhouse
Originally, vaudeville troupes performed here after the theater was completed in 1905. Later it became a movie palace, and finally a playhouse in 1972. Musicals and dramas entertain during summer and the Christmas season. Promised Valley Playhouse is downtown at 132 S. State, tel. 364-5696.

Pioneer Memorial Theatre
A wide variety of theatrical performances takes place at this theater on the University of Utah campus. Professional and amateur actors present musicals and plays on Lees Main Stage. University students and faculty stage productions in the Babcock Theatre downstairs. Plays by students in the Young People's Theatre group entertain children. Pioneer Memorial Theatre is near the corner of 300 South and University St., tel. 581-6961.

In September and October the university sponsors the Classic Theatre Festival, a program of Greek dramas at various locations, tel. 581-6448.

DANCE

Ballet West
Ballet West began in Salt Lake City in 1963 as the Utah Civic Ballet, but as the group gained fame and began traveling widely, it chose its present name to reflect its regional status. This versatile group's repertoire includes classical, modern, and foreign works. Most Utah performances take place at the Capitol Theatre Sept.-April. Capitol Theatre and box office are at 50 W. 200 South, tel. 363-9318 (box office) or 524-8300 (business office).

Ririe-Woodbury Dance Company
This professional company has one of the most active programs outside New York City. The varied repertoire includes mixed media, eye-catching choreography, and humor. The group also shares its expertise in teaching production and dance skills to students and professionals. Ririe-Woodbury Dance Company is based at the Capitol Theatre, 50 W. 200 South; tel. 328-1062.

Repertory Dance Theatre
A professional company focusing on classical American and contemporary dance. Performances take place year-round in the Capitol Theatre and other locations, tel. 534-6345.

MOVIES

Newspapers list the latest flicks. For old movie classics, foreign films, and other special films, plus also video rentals of classics call: **Avalon Theatre,** 3605 S. State (five and one half miles south of downtown), tel. 266-0258; and **Utah Film and Video Center,** 20 S. West Temple (Salt Lake Art Center), tel. 534-1158.

SPORTS

Pro Sports
Utah sports fans cheer on their **Utah Jazz** NBA basketball and **Salt Lake Trappers** minor league baseball teams. Basketball takes place at the Delta Center, one block west of the Salt Palace in downtown Salt Lake City, 301 W. South Temple, tel. 355-DUNK. Other sporting events, concerts, and special events are held at the Delta Center too, tel. 325-SEAT or (800) 358-SEAT. Dierks Field hosts baseball games at 1301 S. West Temple; for the Trappers call 484-9901 (ticket office) or 484-9900 (business office).

University Of Utah
University athletic teams compete in football, basketball, baseball, softball, tennis, track and field, gymnastics, swimming, golf, skiing, and other sports. Contact the Jon M. Huntsman Special Events Center, on campus near 400 South

*bareback riding
at the Utah State Fair*

and 2000 East, tel. 581-6641 (recording) or 581-3510 (office).

Bonneville Raceway Park
For roaring engines, smoking tires, and checkered flags, visit the raceway during its April-Oct. season. Located in West Valley City at 6555 W. 2100 South, tel. 250-2600.

EVENTS

Concerts, festivals, shows, and other special events happen nearly every day, and the Salt Lake Convention & Visitors Bureau can tell you what's going on, 180 S. West Temple, tel. 521-2822. Also check the Visitors Bureau *Salt Lake Visitors Guide.* Some of the best-known annual happenings:

January: The **Utah Winter Games** bring amateur athletes to the Wasatch Front for alpine and nordic ski events, hockey, and figure skating.

March: Citizens deck out in green for the **St. Patrick's Day Parade** downtown on the Saturday nearest March 17.

April: Semi-annual **Conference of the Church of Jesus Christ of Latter-day Saints** is held during a weekend at Temple Square. The church president, believed to be a prophet of God, and other church leaders give guidance to members throughout the world. Non-Mormons are welcome to attend too; expect large crowds. Contact the Temple Square visitor cen-

ters for more information, tel. 240-2534/2535.

May: The Mexican-American community leads the **Cinco de Mayo** celebration the week of May 5th. Enjoy dances, food, and entertainment of many different cultures during **Living Traditions Festival** in Washington Square (City and County Building yard), tel. 533-5760.

June: Utah Pageant of the Arts brings the world's art masterpieces to life—literally—using actors to stage the scene; this amazing spectacle takes place in the Capitol Theatre. The **Utah Scottish Association Highland Games** has lively contests, bagpipe music and dancing, and ethnic food; held in Salt Lake City. **Utah Arts Festival** features artists' and craftspeople's booths, video art, music concerts, and dance performances; in Salt Lake City. **Strawberry Days** is a community celebration with rodeos, games, and entertainment in Pleasant Grove, 35 miles south of Salt Lake City. Cowboys show their skills at the **Lehi Round-up and Rodeo** in Lehi, 30 miles south of Salt Lake City.

July: Western Stampede and Rodeo (near the Fourth of July) takes place in West Jordan, 12 miles southwest of Salt Lake City. Many towns celebrate **the Fourth of July** with entertainment and fireworks; **Oakley,** a tiny village 42 miles east of Salt Lake City, has a PRCA rodeo. **Steel Days** is a community celebration in American Fork, 32 miles south of Salt Lake City. **Days of '47 Celebration** commemorates pioneers arriving here on July 24, 1847; Salt Lake City has a big rodeo at the Delta Center, parades, fireworks, and other festivities.

August: The town of Magna celebrates **Magna Copper Days** with entertainment, crafts, and arts. **Salt Lake County Fair** has exhibits and entertainment in Murray, seven miles south of Salt Lake City. Middle Eastern dancers gyrate in the **Utah Belly Dance Festival** at Liberty Park.

September: Pioneer Harvest Days recreates early farm life at Pioneer Trail State Park. The **Greek Festival** celebrates Greek culture with food, music, folk dancing, and tours of the historic Holy Trinity Greek Orthodox Cathedral. **Utah State Fair** features entertainment, rodeo, horse show, contests, art and craft exhibits, and livestock judging at the fairgrounds, North Temple and 1000 West. **Oktoberfest** takes place

weekends during September and October at the Snowbird resort in Little Cottonwood Canyon, southeast of Salt Lake City.

October: Second part of semi-annual **Conference of the Church of Jesus Christ of Latter-day Saints;** see April description above.

December: Temple Square Christmas Lighting illuminates the square with more than 250,000 lights from late November through New Year's Day. **Festival of Trees** has more than 300 decorated Christmas trees, entertainment, and gift sales as a fund-raiser early in the month. Visit the **Dickens Christmas Festival** at the Utah State Fairpark for entertainment, food, and crafts in a re-created 19th-century London.

SALT LAKE CITY RECREATION

PARKS

The many parks in Salt Lake City offer golf, tennis, swimming, picnicking, and space to enjoy the outdoors. Special attractions include Tracy Aviary in Liberty Park, the International Peace Gardens, and the canoe trip down the Jordan River. Contact the Salt Lake City Parks and Recreation Department for details on facilities and programs at 1965 W. 500 South, Salt Lake City, UT 84104, tel. 972-7800. For information on touring the Jordan River by canoe, ask at the Jordan River State Park, 1084 N. Redwood Rd., Salt Lake City, UT 84116, tel. 533-4496.

Liberty Park

Tracy Aviary, historic buildings, children's play areas, a small amusement park, a swimming pool, a tennis center, and acres of grass and shady trees make this large park a popular destination for residents and visitors. Tracy Aviary, with its hundreds of birds, lies in the southwest corner (see "South of Downtown" under "Salt Lake City Sights" earlier in this chapter). The Children's Garden playground, amusement park, snack bar, and a large pond with rental boats are in the southeast corner of the park (all closed in winter). The Chase Mill, just north of the aviary entrance, was built by Isaac Chase in 1852. It's one of the oldest buildings in the valley. Free flour from the mill saved many families during the famine of 1856-57. The interior is closed to the public, but you can view the exterior and an old millstone. Formal gardens lie north of the mill. Chase's adobe brick house (built 1853-54), farther to the north, has been restored. Go inside to see exhibits of the Folk Arts Program, sponsored by the Utah Arts Council; open noon-5 p.m. weekends from mid-April to mid-Oct. and daily Memorial Day to Labor Day weekends, free, tel. 533-5760. You'll find horseshoe pits to the north of the Chase house. The tennis center on the western side of the park offers 16 lighted courts and instruction, tel. 596-5036. The outdoor swimming pool adjacent to the tennis center is open in summer.

Liberty Park is southeast of downtown and bordered by 900 and 1300 South and by 500 and 700 East.

Sugarhouse Park

Mormon pioneers manufactured beet sugar here beginning in 1851; the venture later proved unprofitable and was abandoned. Today's expanses of rolling grassland in the 113-acre park are ideal for picnics, strolling, and jogging. A lake attracts seagulls and other birds. Sweet smells rise from the Memorial Rose Garden in the northeast corner. The park has a playground and fields for baseball, soccer, and football. In winter, the rolling hills provide good sledding and tubing. Sugarhouse Park is on the southeast edge of Salt Lake City at 1300 East and 2100 South (access is from 2100 South).

International Peace Gardens

With wishes for world peace, the Salt Lake Council of Women created this unusual garden next to Jordan Park. Landscaping, vegetation, and monuments represent 18 nations of the world. Located near 900 West and 1000 South.

Jordan River State Park

A canoe trip down the Jordan reveals birds and other wildlife in a peaceful setting that you wouldn't expect so close to downtown Salt Lake City. A green canopy of willow, Russian olive, and Siberian elm overhangs the river for much of its length. Canoeists can stop at the International Peace Gardens and other parks along the way. The state park office can advise on boating conditions and places to rent canoes, paddles, and life jackets. Park rangers enforce the rule that each boater must wear a Coast Guard-approved life jacket. You'll need two cars or someone to pick you up at trip's end. Put-in is at 1200 W. 1700 South (across from Raging Waters) and take-out at 1000 N. 1525 West; allow at least two and one half hours (without stops) for the six-mile route. This is the only section of river open to boats. Jordan River State Park office is at 1084 N. Redwood Rd., Salt Lake City, UT 84116, tel. 533-4496 (open Mon.-Fri. 8 a.m.-5 p.m.). It's a good idea to call the park before a trip to check on possible river obstructions. Off-season boating isn't recommended because of the greater likelihood of hazards blocking the way.

Attractions along the Jordan River include Raging Waters (a private water park with wave pool at 1200 W. 1700 South, tel. 973-9900), International Peace Gardens, jogging and exercise areas, four golf courses, an equestrian trail, a wheelchair exercise course (take bridge across river from 350 N. Redwood Rd.), a model airplane field ($3 per vehicle, $1 adult walk-in day-use fee), and various parks. A map available from the state park office shows the locations.

SKIING

Utah's "Greatest Snow on Earth" lies close at hand. Within an hour's drive from Salt Lake City you can be at one of seven downhill areas in the Wasatch Range, each with its own character and distinctive skiing terrains. Cross-country skiers can ski on maintained trails in Big Cottonwood Canyon and at Park City. The snow season runs from about mid-Nov. to April or May; call 521-8102 for Utah snow conditions. Be sure to get the free Utah Ski Vacation Planner publication from Ski Utah, Inc., 150 W. 500 South, Salt Lake City, UT 84101, tel. 534-1779 or 800-SKI-UTAH; fax 521-3722, or from many tourist offices in Utah. The Planner lists most Utah resorts with diagrams of the lifts and runs, lift ticket rates, and detailed information on lodging. Public buses (UTA) will take you to the four resorts on the west side of the Wasatch Range: Solitude and Brighton in Big Cottonwood Canyon and Snowbird and Alta in Little Cottonwood Canyon. You can get on the buses at the airport, downtown, University of Utah, or at the bottoms of the canyons, tel. 287-4636. Lewis Brothers Stages offers a "Ski Express" from Salt Lake City to the same four resorts; its "Red Horse Express" connects the airport and downtown with the three resorts on the other side of the range—Wolf Mountain, Park City, and Deer Valley. Lewis Brothers Stages also has a shuttle between Park City and the resorts of Snowbird, Alta, Brighton, Solitude, and Sundance; optional ski packages include transportation and lifts, tel. 359-8677 (Salt Lake City), 649-2256 (Park City), or (800) 826-5844.

The ski areas near Salt Lake City actually lie close together as the crow flies. **Interconnect Adventure Tours** provides a guide service for extensive touring among them. Skiers should be experienced and in good condition because of the high elevations (around 10,000 feet) and the need for some walking and traversing. Touring is with downhill equipment. Trips include Snowbird-Alta-Brighton-Solitude ($95) and Park City-Brighton-Solitude-Alta-Snowbird ($95). For details, contact Ski Utah, Inc., 150 W. 500 South, Salt Lake City, UT 84101, tel. 534-1907.

Solitude Ski Area

Skiers come here for the wide variety of runs—some highly challenging for experts, others ideal for beginners and intermediate skiers. Honeycomb Canyon, on the back side of the resort, contains over 400 acres of ungroomed powder skiing. Seven lifts (one quad, two triple chair, and four double chair) service the 63 named runs and bowls. Skiers enjoy a vertical drop of 2,030 feet from the top of the highest lift. One run makes a loop with nearby Brighton Ski Area for even more skiing. Solitude has a ski school, Moonbeam Learning Center, rentals, ski shops, nordic center (see below), and six restaurants. Adult lift tickets cost $28 ($22 afternoon) and $38 for skiing both Solitude and Brighton. Lift tickets for children (12 and under) and beginners cost $16. Kids under 48 inches tall can use the Link Lift for the Easy Street run free of charge. Contact Solitude at Box 21350, Salt Lake City, UT 84121-0350, tel. 534-1400 or (800) 748-4754. The ski area is 12 miles up Big Cottonwood Canyon and only a 23-mile drive southeast of downtown Salt Lake City. Nearest accommodations are in Brighton (see below) two miles up the canyon or at Silver Fork Lodge, one and one half miles down the canyon, tel. 649-9551. Solitude Ski Area plans to open a series of hotels beginning in the 1995-96 season.

Solitude Nordic Center

Plenty of snow and groomed tracks make this one of the best places in Utah for cross-country skiers. The 21 km of groomed trails range from easy level loops to varied rolling terrain. Most trails have both compacted snow for skating and set tracks. The center is based in the Silver Lake Day Lodge (immediately after the highway joins the Brighton loop); open daily 9 a.m.-

4:30 p.m. from mid-November to mid-April. Trail fee is $8 ($6 after 12:30 p.m.), $4 children 8-12, and free for children under 8 and seniors 65 and over. Staff at the shop offer rentals (touring, racing, telemark, and snowshoes), sales, instruction, day tours, and advice on backcountry touring and avalanche hazards. Tickets can also be purchased at Solitude Ski Area. For more information, contact Box 21350, Salt Lake City, UT 84121-0350, tel. 536-5774 or (800) 748-4754.

Brighton Ski Area

This is a favorite with local families for the excellent skiing and friendly, unpretentious atmosphere. While 21% of the runs are beginner and 40% intermediate, Brighton does offer some difficult powder-bowl skiing and steep runs as well. Two quads, two triple chairlifts and three double chairs climb as high as 10,500 feet for a 1,745-foot vertical descent to the base. In addition to the more than 60 runs and trails at Brighton, you can hop on the Sol Bright run to visit Solitude Ski Area; a lift there will put you back on a trail to Brighton. Night skiing is offered Mon.-Sat., too. Brighton has a ski school with a learn-to-ski package, rentals, two shops, and three cafeterias. Adults ski for $25 day, $23 afternoon, $10 night, and $38 for skiing both Brighton and Solitude. Children 10 and under go free with a paying adult. The adjacent **Brighton Lodge** offers accommodations with a heated outdoor pool and spa at $50 dorm, $85 s or d (winter rates). Contact the ski area and lodge at Brighton, UT 84121, tel. 532-4731 or (800) 873-5512. Brighton is at road's end, two miles past Solitude, in Big Cottonwood Canyon.

Cabins can be arranged through **Brighton Chalets,** 2750 E. 9800 South, Sandy, UT 84092, tel. 942-8824, and the **Brighton Village Store,** Brighton, UT 84121, tel. 649-9156. The Brighton Village Store also has a small cafe serving American food open daily for breakfast, lunch, and dinner.

Snowbird Ski Area

This highly developed resort lies in Little Cottonwood Canyon on the west side of the Wasatch Range. Snowbird had a difficult time getting started back in the early '70s—not everyone wanted to see high-rise hotels among the mountains. Today, the complete resort facili-

skiing on Hidden Peak, at Snowbird Ski Resort

ties, excellent snow conditions, varied terrain, and large lift capacity (9,200 people per hour) entice many skiers. Twenty percent of the runs are classed beginner, 30% intermediate, and 50% advanced. Plenty of ungroomed areas lie in the backcountry too. Snowbird's ski school and separate "bunny hill" make it a good place to learn, too. Seven double chairlifts and a large aerial tram serve the 47 named runs. The longest run is three and one half miles and drops 3,100 feet.

Nonskiers can enjoy the heights aboard the tram as it climbs 2,900 vertical feet to the summit of Hidden Peak (elev. 11,000 feet) for a fantastic panorama of the Wasatches, surrounding valleys, and the distant Uinta Mountains. Wear a warm jacket and hat for this roundtrip; $8 adult, $6 children under 12 and seniors 62 and up.

The exceptionally long season at Snowbird continues to mid-May, though most lifts close by May 1st. Adult lift tickets cost $40 ($33 half day) including tram and $33 ($27 half day) chairlifts only. Seniors (ages 62-69) and children (12 and under) ski for $26 ($21 half day) including tram and $21 ($18 half day) chairlifts only. All skiers can use the beginners' Chickadee Chairlift free of charge. Guided ski tours of about two hours (free with lift purchase) introduce new customers to the resort's skiing; groups divide up according to ability. Advanced skiers may take the Snowbird Mountain Experience, a five-hour guided tour on steeper, more challenging terrain, including powder and off-trail skiing (extra cost).

In addition to its ski school, Snowbird offers rentals, a wide selection of shops, restaurants, snack bars, four lodges, swimming pools, health spa, and child-care services. Accommodation costs vary according to early/late, value, and peak seasons. Some sample nightly rates: dormitory ($58.30), hotel room ($229.90), studio w/fireplace and kitchen ($174.90), and condo w/fireplace and kitchen ($213.40). For reservations and information on the skiing and year-round resort facilities, contact Snowbird Ski Resort, Snowbird, UT 84092, tel. 742-2222 (snow conditions), 532-1700, or (800) 453-3000 (reservations). Snowbird is six miles up Little Cottonwood Canyon and 25 miles southeast of downtown Salt Lake City.

Alta Ski Area

Famed for its deep powder, wide-open terrain, and charming accommodations, Alta is probably the best known of Utah's ski resorts. In 1937, when some skiers decided to try the revolutionary concept of using ski lifts, detractors complained that the $1.50 per day lift tickets reserved the sport just for the rich. Some of the original Collins single chairs are still around; look for them at the bus stop beside Goldminer's Daughter Lodge and in the Shallow Shaft Steak House. Today Alta offers two triple and six double chairlifts serving 35 named runs of which 25% are rated beginner, 40% intermediate, and 35% advanced. The longest run is three and one half miles and drops 2,500 feet. Beginners can use the free rope tows beside Alta Lodge and Snowpine Lodge or the three beginners' lifts. Lift tickets cost $23 ($17 half day) or $17 ($11 half day) for the beginners' lifts. Skier Services offers a ski school, rentals, shops, childcare services, and restaurants (two are on the slopes). For more information, contact Alta Ski Lifts Co., Box 8007, Alta, UT 84092, tel. 359-1078 (office) or 572-3939 (snow conditions).

Alta is eight miles up Little Cottonwood Canyon in an old silver mining area.

You can choose from five lodges and three condominiums in Alta, but all are expensive—even for dormitory space. The lodges operate only on the modified American plan or full American plan, with two or three meals included or added to the price. Expect to pay $88 dorm, $138-232 s, $100-147.50 per person d, depending on season and room. **Alta Reservation Service** represents the lodges and can arrange accommodation, transportation, and ski packages, tel. 942-0404. The *Utah Ski Vacation Planner* lists facilities, prices, and package plans. Skiers on a lower budget can base themselves in Salt Lake City.

Alta Cross-Country Skiing

Both beginning and experienced skiers enjoy cross-country skiing at Alta. No groomed tracks, but you can head up the unplowed summer road to Albion Basin. Sno-Cats often pack the snow. The road begins from the upper end of the Albion parking lot, then climbs gently to the top of Albion Lift, where skiers can continue to Albion Basin. Intermediate and advanced skiers can also ski to Catherine Pass and Twin Lakes Pass. Cross-country skiers may ski the beginner (green) Alta trails. Those heading for the backcountry should have proper equipment and experience; the Alta ski school office at the Albion ticket building can advise on avalanche hazards. There's no charge for skiing at Alta unless you use the lifts. Rent track and telemark cross-country skis at the Albion Day Lodge near the trailhead.

Wolf Mountain Ski Area

One of three ski areas near Park City, Wolf Mountain is the first one you'll reach if coming from Salt Lake City. The slopes look deceptively easy from the lodge at the base, but tucked into three mountains lie machine-groomed slopes, open bowls, and challenging moguls. Seven double chairs serve 50 designated runs. Ski trails are rated 22% beginner and lower intermediate, 30% intermediate, 48% advanced and expert. Longest run is two and one half miles and drops 2,200 feet. Adult lift tickets cost $25 ($15 half day) or $15 for full-day beginner lifts. Children 12 and under pay $15 full day, $8 half day, or $8 full-day beginner lifts. The Kids

Central facility offers day care, supervised lunches, ski lessons, and rentals for the younger set. Wolf Mountain includes a ski school, rental and sales shop, four restaurants (two mid-slope), and a free shuttle service from lodges in Park City. For skiing information, contact Wolf Mountain at 4000 Park West Dr., Park City, UT 84060, tel. 649-5400. Wolf Mountain is 27 miles east of Salt Lake City via I-80 and UT 224.

Park City Ski Area
Utah's biggest ski area is located in the historic silver mining town of Park City. A gondola, three quad chairs, five triple chairs, and five double chairs carry skiers high onto the eastern slope of the Wasatch Range. The 88 trails range in length from one-quarter to three and one half miles (17% easier, 45% more difficult, 38% most difficult). Also, experienced skiers can enjoy the powder in five open bowls near the top of the mountain—a total of 650 acres. The total drop is 3,100 feet in elevation from the top of Jupiter Bowl to the Resort Center. Park City Ski Area and the adjacent village offer night skiing, a ski school, rentals, ski shops, ice-skating, and restaurants (three are on the slopes). A Town Lift and two runs allow skiers staying in downtown Park City to connect directly with the ski area. Visitors without skis can enjoy the mountains on a 23-minute ride in the gondola to the Summit House, which has a restaurant; $9. Adult lift tickets cost $44 all day, $30 afternoon, or $9 night skiing. Children 12 and under go for $18 all day, $15 afternoon, or $5 night. Contact Park City at Box 39, Park City, UT 84060, tel. 649-8111 (office), 649-9571 (snow report), or 649-0493 or (800) 222-PARK (lodging reservations). You'll find accommodations right at the ski center and many more places close by in town; see the *Utah Ski Vacation Planner* or *Park City Winter Vacation Planner* for details. Park City is 31 miles east of Salt Lake City via I-80 and UT 224.

Deer Valley Ski Resort
The crème de la crème of Utah ski areas. Here you'll find good uncrowded skiing with all the extras of posh accommodations, gourmet dining, attentive service, and polished brass everywhere. Attendants meet you in the parking lot to assist in unloading your skis and guide you; help is never far away. Video programs in the ski rental shop show how to put on and use your gear. Don't look for "men's" or "women's" restrooms at Deer Valley—here it's "Gentlemen's Lounge" and "Ladies' Lounge." Two quad chairs, nine triple chairs, and two double chairs carry skiers to the top of Bald Eagle Mountain, Bald Mountain, and Flagstaff Mountain, providing 66 runs, three bowls, and a vertical drop of 2,200 feet. Longest run is two miles. Fifteen percent of the skiing is rated easier, 50% more difficult, and 35% most difficult. The majestic Snow Park Lodge (elev. 7,200 feet) contains the ticket office, ski school, rentals, ski shop, child-care service, gift shop, and restaurant. You can drive 1,000 feet higher to Silver Lake Lodge, which offers two more restaurants. Adult lift tickets cost $47 full day or $34 afternoon. Deer Valley will reserve accommodations, lift tickets, restaurants, flights, and local transportation for you. Contact Deer Valley Central Reservations, Box 3149, Park City, UT 84060, tel. 649-1000 or (800) 424-3337 (skiing information and reservations) or 649-2000 (snow report). Deer Valley is one and one half miles south of downtown Park City (33 miles east of Salt Lake City).

White Pine Touring
Park City's cross-country ski center offers rentals, instruction, and guided tours. It has a touring center and 20 km of groomed trails at the **Park City Golf Course,** Park Ave. and Thaynes Canyon Dr., tel. 649-8701, during the winter. The season runs from about mid-Nov. to early April. Trail fee is $6 adult ($4 after 4 p.m.); kids under 12 and seniors 65 and up ski free. Year-round office is on Main St. at Heber Ave. in Park City, tel. 649-8710 (Park City) or 521-2135 (Salt Lake).

OTHER SPORTS

Swimming Pools And Gymnasiums
For an outdoor swim, try **Liberty Park,** 1300 South and 700 East, or **Fairmont Park,** 2361 S. 900 East. For a bigger splash, **Raging Waters,** 1200 W. 1700 South, tel. 973-9900, features many aquatic attractions, including water slides and the Wild Wave pool. The children's area has waterfalls, geysers, and a small wave pool.

Deseret Gymnasium, located a half block north of Temple Square at 161 N. Main St., Salt Lake City, UT 84103, tel. 359-3911, has a variety of facilities for both men and women, including two indoor swimming pools, indoor track, weight and exercise rooms, basketball, racquetball, handball, squash, volleyball, badminton, table tennis, and a golf practice range. The gymnasium, run by the LDS church, is open to the public for a daily fee or by membership. Classes are offered in swimming, racquetball, squash, handball, and exercise.

Tennis

Seventeen city parks have courts; call the Salt Lake City Parks and Recreation Department, tel. 972-7800, for the one nearest you. **Liberty Park,** 1300 South and 500 East., tel. 596-5036, offers a pro shop, instruction, and 16 courts.

Golf

Salt Lake City has plenty of places to tee off. The following lie close to town and are open to the public. (See the telephone *Yellow Pages* for golf courses in neighboring towns.) **Bonneville** is an 18-hole/72-par course east of downtown at 954 Connor St. (2130 East off Sunnyside Ave. near the Hogle Zoo), tel. 583-9513. **University** is a nine-hole/33-par executive course on the University of Utah campus at 100 S. 1900 East, tel. 581-6511. **Mountain Dell** is a 36-hole/72- and 71-par course east in Parleys Canyon; take I-80 East Canyon/Emigration Canyon Exit 134, tel. 582-3812. **Forest Dale** is a nine-hole/36-par

course at 2375 S. 900 East (near Sugarhouse Park), tel. 483-5420. **Nibley Park** is a nine-hole/34-par course at 2780 S. 700 East, tel. 483-5418. **Glendale** is an 18-hole/72-par course at 1630 W. 2100 South, tel. 974-2403. **Rose Park** is an 18-hole/72-par course northwest of downtown at 1386 N. Redwood Rd., tel. 596-5030.

Horseback Riding

Valley View Riding Stables offers instruction and trail rides in the Wasatch Range at 13800 S. 1300 East in Draper (20 miles south of Salt Lake City), tel. 572-9088. **East Canyon Outfitters** lead hourly, day, breakfast, sunset, and overnight rides on the Mormon Pioneer Trail and other areas in the Wasatch Range east of Salt Lake City; located 20 miles from Salt Lake City via I-80 and UT 65 (one-half mile south of East Canyon Reservoir), tel. 355-3460.

Skating

Cottonwood Heights Recreation Center, 7500 S. 2700 East, tel. 943-3190, offers year-round ice-skating and lessons, indoor and outdoor pools, racquetball courts, and weight room. Roll with **Roller Towne USA,** the 49th Street Galleria, 4998 S. 360 West in Murray, tel. 263-2987, and **Classic Roller Skating Centers,** 2774 S. 625 West in Bountiful, tel. 295-8301; and at 9151 S. 255 West in Sandy, tel. 561-1791.

OTHER PRACTICALITIES IN SALT LAKE CITY

SHOPPING

Trolley Square

Salt Lake City's most unusual shopping center came about when developers cleverly converted the old trolley barn. Railroad magnate E.H. Harriman built the barn in 1908 as a center for the city's extensive trolley system. The vehicles stopped rolling in 1945, but their memory lives on in Trolley Square. Inside you'll see several trolleys, a large stained-glass dome, salvaged sections of old mansions and churches, and many antiques. More than 100 shops and restaurants call this gigantic barn their home. Watch movies at Cineplex-Odeon Theatres (four screens, tel. 355-5047) and Mann's Flick (two screens, tel. 466-6266). Trolley Square is open daily, including Sunday afternoons, at the corner of 500 South and 700 East, tel. 521-9877. **Trolley Corners** across the street at 515 S. 700 East is a smaller shopping area with shops, restaurants, and Trolley Corners Theatres, tel. 364-6183.

Crossroads Plaza

Located at 50 S. Main across from Temple Square in the heart of downtown, tel. 531-1799, this modern shopping center on four levels has more than 100 shops, fast-food restaurants, banks, and Crossroads Cinemas (three screens, tel. 355-3883). Waldenbooks on the main floor and B. Dalton Bookseller on the second level have good selections of Utah books. Crossroads Plaza is open daily, including Sunday afternoons

ZCMI Mall

What may be America's oldest department store, Zion's Cooperative Mercantile Institution, downtown at the corner of South Temple and State streets, tel. 321-8743, began in 1869 as a church-owned operation. The old facade graces the Main St. side, but the more than 90 shops and restaurants inside are new. Deseret Book Co. specializes in LDS literature and has many books on Utah's history. ZCMI Mall is open Mon.-Saturday.

Arrow Press Square

Restaurants and shops have taken over the picturesque old buildings in what used to be Salt Lake City's printing district. Downtown at 165 S. West Temple, tel. 531-9700.

Mormon Handicrafts

Purchase lovingly made quilts, teddy bears, Raggedy Anns, dollhouses, baby apparel, dresses, lace, porcelain figures, and other creations. Or, if you'd rather do it yourself, buy supplies and patterns for making quilts, counted cross-stitch, and other crafts. Open Mon.-Saturday. Located across from Temple Square at the corner of Main and North Temple streets, tel. 355-2141.

TP Gallery

Crafts and art by Native Americans are featured here. Look for beadwork and leather items (Ute Indians), jewelry (Navajo, Hopi, and Zuni tribes), pottery (Hopi and New Mexico Pueblo tribes), kachina dolls (Hopi), baskets (Papago), sandpaintings, books, and cassettes. Open Mon.-Saturday. Located downtown at 252 S. Main Street, tel. 364-2961.

Recreational Equipment, Inc. (REI)

This large store has an outstanding array of outdoor recreation gear for hiking, camping, bicycling, skiing, river running, rock-climbing, and travel. Gear can be rented too. The book section is a good place to look for regional outdoor guides. Topo maps sold cover the most popular hiking areas of Utah. REI memberships (optional) allow you to receive annual dividends on your purchases. Open daily. Located at 3285 East 3300 South, tel. 486-2100.

Gardner Historic Village

This attractive shopping village offers a restaurant and craft shops in the restored Gardner Mill, built in 1877. Old houses and cabins have been moved to the grounds and restored for additional shops. Step into the silo to dine at **Archibald's Restaurant**, tel. 566-6940 (American and Continental food), open daily for lunch and dinner (and breakfast on Saturday and Sunday). The village also has a small museum of historic exhibits. Located in West Jordan, 12 miles south of downtown Salt Lake City; take I-15 Midvale Exit 301 (7200 South), turn west and follow signs to the Gardner Mill at 1095 W. 7800 South, tel. 566-8903 (village and museum).

SERVICES

The main **downtown post office** is at 230 W. 200 South in the Expo Mart, tel. 974-2200. Pioneer branch is on the first floor of the Federal Bldg., 125 S. State. The University of Utah has a post office in the bookstore.

Change foreign currency at Zions First National Bank downtown at Main and South Temple, tel. 524-4873, or at the airport, tel. 524-8879.

Minor medical emergencies can be treated by **InstaCare,** just west of downtown at 55 N. Redwood Rd., and at six other area locations, tel. 321-2490. Hospitals with 24-hour emergency care include: **Holy Cross Hospital,** 1050 E. South Temple, tel. 350-4111; **LDS Hospital,** Eighth Ave. and C St., tel. 321-1100; **HCA St. Mark's Hospital,** 1200 E. 3900 South, tel. 268-7074; and **University Hospital,** 50 N. Medical Dr. (1800 East), tel. 581-2121. For a physician referral, contact one of the hospitals or the Utah State Medical Association, tel. 355-7477.

The **Salt Lake Art Center School,** 20 S. West Temple, Salt Lake City, UT 84101, tel. 328-4201, offers classes in ceramics, drawing, painting, sculpture, photography, and crafts.

Low on dough? **Job Service Center** offers free services at 720 S. 200 East, tel. 536-7000, and at 5735 S. Redwood Rd., tel. 269-4700.

PHONE NUMBERS

Emergencies (fire, police, medical): 911.
Police (Salt Lake City): 799-3000.
Sheriff (Salt Lake County): 535-5441.
Road Conditions: 964-6000 (local); (800) 492-2400 (statewide).
Weather Forecast: 575-7669.
Salt Lake Convention & Visitors Bureau (local travel information): 521-2868.
Utah Travel Council (statewide travel information): 538-1030.
Utah Recreation/Ski Report: 521-8102.

Utah State Parks: 538-7221.
Utah Division of Wildlife Resources: 538-4700.
Community Information & Referral Service: 487-4716.
Lawyer Referral Service (Utah State Bar Association): 531-9075.
Physician Referral Service (Utah State Medical Association): 355-7477.
Utah Transit Authority (UTA): 287-4636.

INFORMATION

Tourist Offices
Salt Lake Convention & Visitors Bureau, downtown at the corner of West Temple and 200 South (180 S. West Temple, Salt Lake City, UT 84101-1493), tel. 521-2868, will tell you about the sights, facilities, and goings-on in town. The office also has many helpful magazines and brochures. Open Mon.-Fri. 8 a.m.-5 p.m. (to 6 p.m. in summer) and Saturday 9 a.m.-4 p.m.; you can park in spaces behind the office. This office will relocate to the new Salt Palace Convention Center when that building is finished. The Visitors Bureau has branches in Terminal 2 at the airport (Concourse D is open 24 hours daily and staffed only during the day; an information kiosk near the baggage claim area is also staffed only during the day) and near the Great Salt Lake beaches just off the I-80 Magna Exit 104 (open daily 9 a.m.-4 p.m.). The chamber of commerce downtown has little visitor information; its main work is business promotion.

The **Utah Travel Council** publishes a well-illustrated *Utah Travel Guide,* travel maps (series of five covering the state), and other helpful publications. (You can also find these publications at the Salt Lake Convention & Visitors Bureau and at local chambers of commerce.) The staff at the information desk provides advice and literature for Utah's national parks and monuments, national forests, Bureau of Land Management areas, and state parks as well as general travel in the state. You can stop by the Utah Travel Council offices in historic Council Hall, across the street from the Capitol, or write Council Hall/Capitol Hill, Salt Lake City, UT 84114. Open Mon.-Fri. 8 a.m.-5 p.m. (also weekends and holidays 10 a.m.-5 p.m.), tel. 538-1030, fax 538-1399.

Wasatch-Cache National Forest
The **Supervisor's office**, downtown on the eighth floor of the Federal Bldg., 125 S. State St., Salt Lake City, UT 84138, tel. 524-5030, has general information and forest maps for all the national forests in Utah; some forest and wilderness maps of Nevada, Idaho, and Wyoming; and regional books. Open Mon.-Fri. 7:30 a.m.-4:30 p.m. (til 5 p.m. in summer).

For detailed information on hiking and camping in the nearby Wasatch Range, visit the **Salt Lake Ranger District office.** The office is a few blocks west of the mouth of Big Cottonwood Canyon at 6944 S. 3000 East, Salt Lake City, UT 84121, tel. 524-5042. The district includes the popular Mill Creek, Big Cottonwood, and Little Cottonwood canyons in the Wasatch Range, the Wasatch Range east of Bountiful and Farmington, and the Stansbury Mountains west of Tooele. Large reference books cover nearly every recreational activity and trail. The foresters here will likely have personal knowledge of the area you're heading to. Open Mon.-Fri. 8 a.m.-5 p.m

U.S. Geological Survey
Topo maps for Utah and other states can be purchased here. Other publications include geologic maps, national park maps, a satellite photo of the Great Salt Lake, specialized books of regional geology, and free brochures on earth science topics. Open Mon.-Fri. 8 a.m.-4 p.m. Located in the second floor at 2222 W. 2300 South, Salt Lake City, UT 84119, tel. 975-3742.

Bureau Of Land Management
The state office has general information on BLM areas in Utah and sells recreation and land status maps of the state. Open Mon.-Fri. 8 a.m.-4 p.m. Downtown on the fourth floor at 324 S. State St., Salt Lake City, UT 84111-2303, tel. 539-4001.

Utah Division Of Parks And Recreation
Obtain literature and the latest information for all of Utah's state parks. If you're planning a lot of state park visits, ask about the $50 annual park pass or $25 annual pass for a specific park; these cover only day-use fees. Open Mon.-Fri. 8 a.m.-5 p.m. Located west of downtown at 1636 W. North Temple, Salt Lake City, UT 84116, tel. 538-7221 (information line). Reservations for campgrounds and some other services can be made by calling 322-3770 or (800) 322-3770; a reservation fee of $5 family or $10 group applies.

Utah Division Of Wildlife Resources
The staff issues fishing and hunting licenses and information. Fishermen and hikers may want to purchase a series of 10 booklets, *Lakes of the High Uintas.* Open Mon.-Fri. 8 a.m.-5 p.m. Located at 1596 W. North Temple, Salt Lake City, UT 84116, tel. 538-4700.

Libraries
The large **City Library** contains a wealth of reading material, a children's library, records, and audio and video tapes. Special collections include Western Americana and Mormon history. The Atrium Gallery hosts art exhibits. Puppet shows and story hours entertain the kids. Large bulletin boards on the main floor list upcoming art shows, entertainment, local events, classes, volunteer opportunities, and bus routes. Open Mon.-Thurs. 9 a.m.-9 p.m., Friday and Saturday 9 a.m.-6 p.m. The main library is at 209 E. 500 South, tel. 363-5733. See the telephone blue pages or call for locations of the five branch libraries.

The **Marriott Library** at the University of Utah ranks as one of the leading research libraries of the region. You'll find more than two million volumes and over 14,000 periodical titles inside. Special collections include the Middle East, United Nations, Western Americana, and Utah manuscripts. The large map collection has topo maps of all 50 states as well as maps and atlases of distant lands. Hikers can photocopy maps of areas they plan to visit. The public is welcome to use the library; a Library Permit Card can be purchased to use materials outside of the library. Open Mon.-Thurs. 7 a.m.- 10 p.m., Friday 7 a.m.-5 p.m., and Saturday 9 a.m.-5 p.m.; shorter hours during summer and breaks; tel. 581-6085 (hours) or 581-6273 (information).

Newspapers And Magazines
The *Salt Lake Tribune* morning daily reflects the liberal views of the city. The *Deseret News* comes out daily in the afternoon with a conservative viewpoint and greater coverage of Mormon church news. The monthly *Utah Holiday*

magazine reports on the politics, personalities, recreation, cultural events, restaurants, and other aspects of life in Utah. *The Event* (every two weeks) describes the latest on art, entertainment, events, and social spots. *Sports Guide* appears monthly or bimonthly with articles and event listings for bicycling, running, kayaking, rafting, canoeing, and other sports; available free at sporting goods stores and newsstands.

Book Stores

Sam Weller's Zion Book Store, 254 S. Main, tel. 328-2586, claims to be one of the West's largest, with more than half a million new and used books covering many topics. **Waldenbooks,** in the Crossroads Plaza, 50 S. Main, tel. 363-1271, has a good selection of general reading and Utah books. The **B. Dalton Bookseller** stores are also a good source for general reading and Utah books, in the Crossroads Plaza, 50 S. Main, tel. 355-7906; in Trolley Square, 500 South and 700 East, tel. 532-7107, and other locations. **Deseret Book Co.** specializes in LDS literature, but it also has many general reading and Utah books; 36 S. State (ZCMI Mall), tel. 328-8191 and other locations. **Waking Owl Books,** 208 S. 1300 East, tel. 582-7323, features literature and fiction. The **University of Utah's Bookstore,** tel. 581-6326, has a varied selection of books on many subjects. **The Magazine Shop,** 207 S. Main, tel. 359-3295, claims to have "something for every one" among its paperbacks, magazines, and newspapers (out-of-state and foreign too).

TRANSPORTATION

Tours

Old Salty operated by Lewis Brothers Stages, tel. 359-8677 or (800) 826-5844, will take you on a 90-minute historical city tour. The season runs Memorial Day weekend into October; $7 adult, $6 senior, and $4 children under 12.

The **Gray Line,** 553 W. 100 South, Salt Lake City, UT 84101, tel. 521-7060, offers a two-and-a-half-hour city tour in the morning (afternoons too in summer) for $14 adult, $7 ages 5-12. A four-hour Utah Copper Mine and Great Salt Lake tour visits the Bingham Canyon open-pit mine and a beach on the Great Salt Lake for $22 adult, $11 ages 5-12. Both tours can be combined for $34 adult, $17 ages 5-12. Three-day tours head south to Bryce, Zion, and Grand Canyon national parks or northeast to Yellowstone and Grand Teton national parks.

Great Western Aviation, Salt Lake Air Service, 369 N. 2370 West, Salt Lake City, UT 84116, tel. 359-4840 or 800-748-5454, will show you any part of this scenic state. Tours are as follows: Salt Lake City area (one hour, 25 minutes); the Uinta Range, Flaming Gorge, and Dinosaur National Monument (two hours, 20 minutes); Canyonlands and Arches national parks (three hours); Capitol Reef, Bryce Canyon, Lake Powell, and Monument Valley (four hours, 20 minutes); and Zion, Grand Canyon, and Bryce Canyon (four hours, 30 minutes). Flights operate from Salt Lake City, Ogden, and Logan.

Classic Helicopter Service, tel. 580-1694 or (800) 444-9220, has flights to and between ski areas, helicopter skiing, and tours of the Salt Lake City area.

Local Bus

Utah Transit Authority (UTA) provides inexpensive bus service in town and to the airport, University of Utah, and surrounding communities. Buses go as far north as Ogden, as far south as Provo and Springville, and as far west as Tooele. No charge is made for travel downtown within the "Free-Fare Square" (area bounded by North Temple and 400 South and from West Temple to 200 East). During the winter ski season, skiers can hop on the Ski Bus Service to Solitude, Brighton, Snowbird, and Alta ski areas from the airport, downtown, University of Utah, and other locations. A bus route map and individual schedules are available from the ground transportation information desk at the airport, the Salt Lake Convention and Visitors Bureau downtown, Temple Square visitor centers, Crossroads Mall, and ZCMI Mall, or call UTA at 287-4636 (BUS-INFO) Mon.-Sat. 6 a.m.-7 p.m. Free transfers are given when the fare is paid, if asked for. On Sunday, only the airport, Ogden, Provo, and a few other destinations are served. UTA shuts down on holidays.

Lewis Brothers Stages has a "Red Horse Express" service during ski season to Park City from the Salt Lake City airport ($14 one way, $26 roundtrip); a limited service operates in summer for $20 each way. The "Ski Express" from Salt Lake City serves Solitude, Brighton, Snowbird, and Alta ski areas ($13 roundtrip). The "Canyon Jumper" shuttle operates during the ski season connecting the Park City ski areas with Snowbird, Alta, and Sundance ($10 one way, $18 roundtrip). Ski packages with transportation and lift tickets can be purchased too. Reservations 12 hours in advance are advised for these trips, tel. 359-8677 (Salt Lake City), 649-2256 (Park City), or toll-free (800) 826-5844.

Park City Transportation provides year-round services to Park City from downtown Salt Lake City and the airport for $18 one way; ski shuttles depart from Salt Lake City and Park City in winter to Solitude, Brighton, Snowbird, Alta, Sundance, Snowbasin, and Powder Mountain ski areas; call two days in advance for reservations and to check if a passenger minimum applies, tel. 364-8472 (Salt Lake City), 649-8567 (Park City), or (800) 637-3803.

Long-Distance Bus
Greyhound goes to the Utah towns of Brigham City (four daily, $10), Logan (two daily, $13), Provo (three daily, $10.50), Cedar City (two daily, $42.24), St. George (two daily, $54.19), and other places along I-15. Out-of-state destinations include Portland (three daily, $99), Seattle (two daily, $123), Vancouver (two daily, $145), San Francisco (three daily, $69), Los Angeles (two daily, $79), Las Vegas (two daily, $49), Yellowstone (summer only, one daily, $47), and Denver (three daily, $59). The Greyhound station is downtown at 160 W. South Temple, tel. 355-9579 or (800) 231-2222.

Auto Rentals
You'll find all the major companies and many local outfits eager to rent a set of wheels. See the telephone *Yellow Pages* for names. In winter you can find "skierized" vehicles with snow tires and ski racks ready to head for the slopes. Many agencies have an office or delivery service at the airport.

Taxis
Rates for all the companies in Salt Lake City are fixed at about 95 cents flag up, then $1.40 per mile. The following have 24-hour service: City Cab, tel. 363-5014, Ute Cab, tel. 359-7788, and Yellow Cab, tel. 521-2100.

Train
Three **Amtrak** trains stop daily at the cavernous Denver and Rio Grande Depot. Trains with some destinations and one-way fares: The California Zephyr heads west to Reno ($111) and Oakland ($111) and east to Denver ($109) and Chicago ($217); The Desert Wind goes southwest to Las Vegas ($89) and Los Angeles ($111); and *The Pioneer* rolls west to Portland ($119) and Seattle ($119). Amtrak has many special discount fares for regional roundtrips, families, and to certain destinations; call for details. Amtrak office hours (timed to meet the trains) are irregular, so call first, tel. (800) 872-7245 (information and reservations). The station lobby is worth a visit to see the changing exhibits of the Utah State History Museum. Located near downtown at 320 S. Rio Grande (300 South and 455 West).

stained-glass window in the Union Pacific Station

Air

Salt Lake City International Airport is conveniently located seven miles west of downtown; take North Temple or I-80 to reach it. Many airlines fly here; in fact, this is the only Utah airport served by the major carriers. Two regional airlines serve other towns in the state with the following destinations and one-way fares (ask about roundtrip discounts and other special fares):

SkyWest Airlines, tel. (800) 453-9417, flies at least once daily to Vernal ($49), Cedar City ($75-103), St. George ($74-104), and towns in adjacent states; the lower prices apply with advance purchase.

Alpine Air, tel. 575-2839, flies once or twice daily to Moab ($69 Saturday and Sunday, $109 weekdays).

The **airport** has two terminals; in each you'll find a ground transportation information desk, cafeteria, motel/hotel courtesy phones, auto rentals (Hertz, Avis, National, Budget, and Dollar), Morris Travel office, and a ski rental shop. Terminal 1 also houses Zions First National Bank (has currency exchange), an ice-cream parlor, and gift shops. The Utah Information Center (Salt Lake Convention & Visitors Bureau) is upstairs in Terminal 2; open 24 hours daily (staffed during the day), tel. 575-2800. Staff at the ground transportation information desks will know the bus schedules into town and limousine services direct to Park City, Sundance, Provo, Ogden, Brigham City, Logan, and other communities. UTA Bus #50 is the cheapest way into town. It leaves the airport daily except holidays every hour about 6:30 a.m.-11:30 p.m. (less frequently and only to about 5:30 p.m. on Sundays).

Saltaire Resort, ca. 1900

CHURCH OF JESUS CHRIST OF LATTER-DAY SAINTS

VICINITY OF SALT LAKE CITY

THE GREAT SALT LAKE

Since its discovery by fur trappers in the 1820s, the lake has both mystified and entranced visitors. Early explorers guessed that it must be connected to the ocean, not realizing that they had come across a body of water far saltier. Only the Dead Sea has a higher salt content. When Mormon pioneers first tried evaporating the lake water, they found the residue bitter tasting, because it's only 84% sodium chloride (table salt); the remaining 16% is sulfates and chlorides of magnesium, calcium, and potassium. Mining companies have extracted salt, magnesium, lithium, chlorine, gypsum, potassium sulfate, and sodium sulfate from the water, which yields up to 27% solids. The lake's northern arm, isolated by a railroad causeway, contains the highest mineral concentrations—about twice those of the southern arm. Lowest salt levels occur on the south and east sides at river inlets. Bacteria grow in such numbers that they sometimes give a red tint to water in the northern arm, as do reddish-orange algae *(Dunaliella salina)*. The blue-green algae *(Dunaliella viridis)* occasionally give their own hue to the lake's southern arm. A tiny brine shrimp *(Artemia salina)*, and two species of brine fly

(Ephydra sp.) live in the lake too. The harmless flies emerge from the lake near the end of their life cycle to lay eggs, then die several days later. Until recently, no fish had ever been found alive in the Great Salt Lake. By the spring of 1986, however, unusually heavy runoff from tributaries had diluted the lake so that small rainwater killifish could survive.

The lake has always been changing—rising with spring snowmelt, then falling due to evaporation that peaks in late summer and autumn. These annual variations result in differences in lake levels of six to as much as 18 inches. Long-term changes have affected the lake too: climate variations and diversion of river water for irrigation have caused a 21-foot difference between record low and high levels. Because the lake lies in a very shallow basin, its area has varied dramatically between 900 square miles at the lowest water level to 2,500 square miles at the highest. The record low surface elevation of 4,191 feet was reached in 1963, and the "experts" thought the lake might shrink to nothing. Unfortunately, at that time much construction was going on near the shore without thought that the waters could rise. The lake's previous record high had occurred in 1873, causing concern to Brigham Young and other church leaders. They devised a plan to pump lake water into the desert to the west, but receding levels eliminated the need for the pumping project.

Present-day Utahans haven't been so lucky. In just five years, from 1982 to 1987, the lake rose 12 feet to record-setting elevations. The spreading waters threatened to inundate parts of Salt Lake City, nearby towns and farms, the airport, rail lines, and I-80. High levels also upset the lake's ecology and ruined much of the surrounding marshland. Seven of the state's nine bird refuges were flooded, including world-famous Bear River Migratory Bird Refuge. An emergency session of the Utah Legislature in May 1986 authorized a pumping project with an initial price tag of $60 million to transfer water to the West Pond site, located in the Great Salt Lake Desert. From a peak elevation of 4,212 feet in January 1987, the lake level subsided, soon eliminating the need for pumping. The Great Salt Lake continues to confound the experts.

Antelope Island State Park
Though just a short distance offshore from Salt Lake City, Antelope Island seems a world away. Its rocky slopes, rolling grasslands, marshes, sand dunes, and lake views instill a sense of remoteness and rugged beauty. An extension of the Oquirrh Mountains, Antelope Island is the largest of the lake's eight islands. It measures 15 miles long and five miles wide, Frary Peak (elev. 6,596 feet) rises in the center. Archaeologists have found prehistoric sites showing that Indians came here long ago, perhaps on a land bridge during times of low lake level. In 1843, explorers John Frémont and Kit Carson rode their horses across a sand bar to the island and named it after the antelope (pronghorn) herds that the party hunted for food. In 1849, Brigham Young established a ranch here for church herds of cattle, sheep, and horses. Ranching has continued to be a major activity, though the Mormons lost ownership of the island in 1884. Today the entire island is a state park. Buffalo, deer, and other wildlife live here. You drive to the island on a seven-mile paved causeway (county toll $2, plus $3 per vehicle day-use). Park trails for hiking, bicycling, and horseback riding allow access to much of the island. Campsites run $9 (including the toll and day-use fee) with an extra $1 charge for Saturday, Sunday, and holidays. Showers and restrooms are available in the swimming area in the northwest corner of the island. Take I-15 Exit 335 (two thirds of the way north to Ogden), then nine miles west to the start of the causeway and the entrance booth; 4528 W. 1700 South, Syracuse, UT 84075, tel. 773-2941.

Great Salt Lake State Park
Bathers have enjoyed hopping into the lake ever since the 1847 arrival of Mormon pioneers. Extreme buoyancy in the dense water makes it impossible for a bather to sink—no swimming ability is needed! But anyone who puts his head underwater quickly realizes that the salty water causes great irritation to the eyes, throat, and nose.

Beginning in the 1880s, several resorts popped up along the lake's east and south shores. Besides bathing, guests could enjoy lake cruises, dances, concerts, bowling, arcade games, and roller-coaster rides. Saltair Resort stood as the last and grandest of the old resorts. Completed in 1893, the Moorish structure rose five stories and contained a huge dance floor where as many as 1,000 couples could enjoy the orchestra's rhythms. A rail line from Salt Lake City ran out on a 4,000-foot pier to the resort, which stood on pilings over the water. After 1930, low water levels, the Great Depression, fires, and fewer visitors gradually brought an end to Saltair. Its buildings burned for the second time in 1970 and nothing remains today. A developer built a smaller replica of the Saltair Resort on the southern shore near I-80, but rising lake waters soon flooded the first floor. After reopening, this Saltair was also destroyed by fire. Saltair has been rebuilt again and, despite having been closed by wind damage, is now open. Many rides and shops are run by concessionaires with individual rates; general admission is $2 per car ($3 for special events), tel. 250-4400.

The adjacent **Great Salt Lake State Park beaches,** tel. 533-4081, suffered a similar fate, but have since been restored; $3 vehicle entry. Concessions near Saltair Resort sell snacks and souvenirs; open daily in summer and possibly off season too. Stop in at the nearby **Great Salt Lake Visitor Center,** tel. 533-4083, to see a video and exhibits about the lake; free. A good selection of local travel information is available too. Open daily 9 a.m.-4 p.m. year-round. From

Salt Lake City, drive west nine miles on I-80, take Exit 111 (7200 West), and follow the north frontage road west to the beaches; or take I-80 Exit 104 (Magna) and turn east on the north frontage road. If water levels permit, beaches west of Exit 104 will also be restored.

WASATCH RANGE AND CANYONS

Spectacular mountains and canyons of the Wasatch Range begin right at the edge of Salt Lake City. The name Wasatch comes from an Indian word meaning "high mountain pass," of which the range has a great abundance. The range is about 200 miles long, extending from Mount Nebo in central Utah to the Bear River in southern Idaho. Geologic forces over the last 20 million years have uplifted and twisted these block-faulted mountains into a confusing jumble of rock layers. Intrusions of molten granitic rock and volcanic eruptions then added to the complexity. Massive rivers of ice carved knife-edge ridges and U-shaped valleys during at least three major periods of glaciation in the last 500,000 years. None of the glaciers remain, though some snowfields persist through years of heavy precipitation.

City Creek, Mill Creek, Big Cottonwood, and Little Cottonwood canyons beginning on the edge of Salt Lake City have a special attraction for visitors. Paved roads lead up each canyon to idyllic picnic spots and trailheads for dozens of hiking paths. Brilliant autumn colors of maple, aspen, and oak trees decorate hillsides from mid-September to early October. Big and Little Cottonwood canyons also have campgrounds, lodges, and ski resorts (see "Salt Lake City Recreation" earlier in this chapter for descriptions of ski areas). Canyon streams and alpine lakes harbor elusive trout. Hikers will find detailed trail descriptions in *Hiking the Wasatch* by John Veranth (trails and major routes) and in two pocket-sized books published by the Wasatch Hiking Club: *Wasatch Trails, Volume One* describes 37 trips for beginner to intermediate hikers; *Wasatch Trails, Volume Two* has 32 trails and routes, most for intermediate to advanced hikers. Other good books with Wasatch hikes include *The Hiker's Guide to Utah* by Dave Hall and *Utah Mountaineering Guide* by Michael Kelsey. For first-hand information on recreation

in the range, contact the **Salt Lake Ranger District Office** of the Wasatch-Cache National Forest. The office is near the mouth of Big Cottonwood Canyon at 6944 S. 3000 East, tel. 524-5042, open Mon.-Fri. 8 a.m.-4 p.m. Camping is allowed only at designated sites or in the back-country. Camps must be at least 200 feet from trails and water sources and one-half mile from any road, but because of the steep terrain, nearly all camping is near the top of the trail. Dogs are prohibited in City Creek, Big Cottonwood, and Little Cottonwood canyons to protect drinking-water sources. Don't forget to bring wind and rain gear in case a sudden storm appears; hypothermia is a serious danger in the mountains. Poison ivy, with its shiny leaves in groups of three, grows along streams at lower elevations. Rattlesnakes live in many areas as high as 8,000 feet; look for them before reaching or stepping over rocks and logs.

SKYLINE DRIVE

This 28-mile scenic drive north of Salt Lake City climbs nearly 5,000 feet for impressive views west across the Great Salt Lake and east over the Weber River Valley; allow two to three hours. **Bountiful Peak Overlook,** just below the peak's 9,259-foot summit, has the most sweeping panorama. The forest road is narrow and mostly unpaved; it's not recommended for trailers or those who fear heights. Begin the drive either in Bountiful or Farmington; see the Wasatch-Cache National Forest map. From Bountiful (I-15 Exit 321), go east two miles on 400 North, turn left (north) two blocks on 1300 East, turn right (east) on 600 North, then take 1375 East (Skyline Drive) to Ward Canyon; look closely for the switchback below the giant "B"— don't take the road past a large gravel pit. From Farmington (I-15 Exit 327), go east one mile on State, then turn left (north) on 100 East into Farmington Canyon.

Bountiful Peak Campground (elev. 7,500 feet) is north of the overlook and eight and one half miles up Farmington Canyon; open mid-June to early October with drinking water; free. **Sunset Campground** (elev. 6,400 feet) is 5.3 miles up Farmington Canyon; open early May to mid-October; no water or charge; a hiking trail climbs to Sunset Point. The Francis Peak Rd.

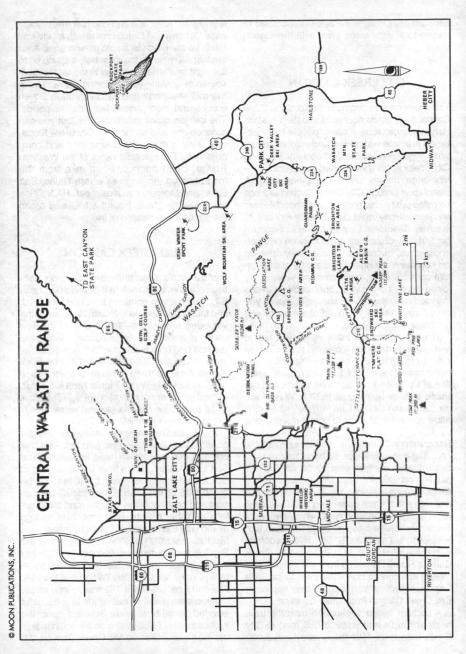

CENTRAL WASATCH RANGE

© MOON PUBLICATIONS, INC.

turns off near Bountiful Peak Campground to an overlook eight miles away with more good views.

CITY CREEK CANYON

This pretty canyon begins just east of the State Capitol, then winds northeast into the Wasatch Range. Since pioneer days, people have obtained precious water here and enjoyed the diverse vegetation, wildlife, and scenery. Because City Creek is still a watershed, regulations prohibit dogs, horses, and overnight camping. A paved road through City Creek Canyon extends six miles past picnic areas to a trailhead. Hikers and joggers may travel on the road every day. In summer (Memorial Day weekend to September 30), bicyclists may enter only on odd calendar days, motorized vehicles may drive up only on even calendar days; a gate at the bottom controls entry. No motorized vehicles allowed the rest of the year, but bicycles can use the road daily then. A $2 charge applies if you drive through to the trailhead at the upper end (no reservation needed).

The big attraction for many visitors is a stop at one of the picnic areas along the road. Picnickers can reserve sites with the Water Department; obtain the required receipt at least a day ahead by visiting the accounting office in the Public Utilities Building at 1530 S. West Temple (Salt Lake City, UT 84115), tel. 483-6797. Allow one week or more to obtain reservations by mail and mark envelope "Attn. City Creek Reservations." Sites are sometimes available on a first-come, first-served basis (midweek is best). Picnic permits cost $2.50 and up depending on size of group. The entrance to City Creek Canyon is reached by Bonneville Blvd., a one-way road. From downtown Salt Lake City, head east on North Temple (which becomes Second Ave. after crossing State St.), then turn left (north) 1.3 miles on "B" St. (which becomes Bonneville Blvd. after 11th Ave.) to City Creek Canyon Road. Returning from the canyon, you have to turn right on Bonneville Blvd. to the State Capitol. Bicyclists and joggers may approach City Creek Canyon from either direction.

A popular hiking destination from the trailhead at road's end (elev. 6,050 feet) is City Creek Meadows, four miles away and 2,000

feet higher. After one and one half miles, you'll pass Cottonwood Gulch on the left; a side trail leads up the gulch to an old mining area. After another half mile on the main trail, a spring off to the right in a small meadow is the last reliable source of drinking water. During the next mile, the trail steepens and winds through aspen groves and then passes two shallow ponds. The trail becomes indistinct here, but you can continue one mile northeast to City Creek Meadows (elev. 8,000 feet); a topo map and compass help. For splendid views of the Wasatch Range, climb north one-half mile from the meadows up the ridge to where Davis, Salt Lake, and Morgan counties meet. Hikers also enjoy shorter strolls from the trailhead along the gentle lower section of trail.

MILL CREEK CANYON

Plentiful picnic areas and many hiking possibilities lie along Mill Creek just outside Salt Lake City. The canyon entrance is at Wasatch Blvd. and Mill Creek Rd. (3800 South). You may bring your dog along too—this is one of the few canyons where pets are welcome. Picnic sites are free and on a first-come, first-served basis; most lack water. The first one, **Church Fork Picnic Area,** is three miles in at an elevation of 5,700 feet; **Big Water Picnic Area** is the last, 8.8 miles up at an elevation of 7,500 feet. A small usage fee applies (except winter weekdays) to visitors in Mill Creek Canyon.

Salt Lake Overlook on Desolation Trail is a good hiking destination for families. The trail climbs 1,200 feet in two miles for views of the Salt Lake Valley. Begin from the lower end of Box Elder Picnic Area (elev. 5,760 feet) on the south side of the road. Energetic hikers can continue on Desolation Trail beyond the overlook to higher country near timberline and go all the way to Desolation Lake (19 miles). The trail runs near the ridgeline separating Mill and Big Cottonwood canyons, connecting with many trails from both canyons. Much of this high country lies in the Mt. Olympus Wilderness. See Mt. Aire and Park City West 7½-minute topo maps.

Alexander Basin Trail winds to a beautiful wooded glacial bowl below Gobblers Knob; the trailhead (elev. 7,080 feet) is on the south side of the road eight miles up Mill Creek Canyon, 0.8

mile beyond Clover Springs Picnic Area. The moderately difficult trail begins by paralleling the road to the northwest for a few hundred feet, then turns southwest and switchbacks one mile to the beginning of Alexander Basin (elev. 8,400 feet). The trail to Bowman and Porter forks turns right here, but continue straight one-half mile for the meadows of the upper basin (elev. 9,000 feet). The limestone rock here has many fossils, mostly of shellfish. From the basin it's possible to rockscramble to the summit of Gobblers Knob (elev. 10,246 feet). The name comes from an attempt by mine owners to raise turkeys after their ores played out; the venture ended when bobcats ate all the birds. See the Mt. Aire 7 1/2-minute topo map.

BIG COTTONWOOD CANYON

Cliffs towering thousands of feet form the gateway to Big Cottonwood Canyon. Skiers come in season to try the downhill slopes at Solitude and Brighton and to cross-country ski at the Solitude Nordic Center. Enter the canyon from Wasatch Blvd. and 7000 South, about 15 miles southeast of downtown Salt Lake City. The 14-mile drive to Brighton Basin reveals splendid vistas at each turn while climbing to an elevation of 8,700 feet. Guardsman Pass Rd. turns off just before Brighton and winds up to Guardsman Pass (elev. 9,800 ft.) at the crest of the Wasatches, then drops down into either Park City or Heber City on the other side; the mostly unpaved road is usually open late June to mid-October. Eight picnic areas lie along Big Cottonwood Creek. You'll come first to **Oak Ridge Picnic Area,** one mile from the entrance, followed by **Dogwood Picnic Area** (elev. 5,200 feet), 1.1 miles from the entrance, and finally to **Silver Lake Picnic Area** (elev. 8,720 feet) near road's end, 14.5 miles up the canyon. Silver Lake has handicapped access to fishing and picnic sites. All picnic areas are first-come, first-served except the **Jordan Pines** group area (8.8 miles from the canyon entrance; has water), with picnic and campsites by reservation only, tel. (800) 280-CAMP. **Spruces Campground** has family sites 9.1 miles up the canyon at an elevation of 7,400 feet. The campground is open with water and a $9 fee from early June to mid-October. Some sites can be reserved, tel.

(800) 280-CAMP. **Redman Campground** lies 13 miles up between Solitude and Brighton at an elevation of 8,300 feet; family sites cost $9. Open from mid-June to early October with water.

You can find fancier accommodations at **Silver Fork Lodge,** 11.3 miles up the canyon, tel. 649-9551, $54.62 s, $71 d; and at **Brighton Lodge** in Brighton, tel. 649-2999, summer: $21.80-27.25 dorm, $32.70-65.40 rooms; heated pool and spa. Restaurants at Silver Fork Lodge (closed Monday) and Brighton Village Store (open daily) serve breakfast, lunch, and dinner. Visit the **Alpinist** in Brighton for hiking supplies, rentals, and information on exploring the backcountry.

Mineral Fork Trail follows an old mining road past abandoned mines, cabins, and rusting equipment to a high glacial cirque. Waterfalls, alpine meadows, wildflowers, and abundant birdlife make the steep climb worthwhile. The signed trailhead is on the south side of the road six miles up the canyon (0.8 mile past Moss Ledge Picnic Area). You'll climb 2,000 feet in three miles to Wasatch Mine, whose mineralized water makes up much of the flow of Mineral Fork Creek. Another two miles and 1,400 feet of climbing lead to Regulator Johnson Mine. A loop trip can be made by climbing the ridge west of Regulator Johnson (no trail) and descending Mill B South Fork Trail to Lake Blanche and the main road, coming out one and one half miles west of the Mineral Fork Trailhead. See Mt. Aire and Dromedary Peak 7 1/2-minute topo maps.

Brighton Lakes Trail winds through some of the prettiest lake country in the range. Families enjoy outings on this easy trail, which begins in Brighton behind the Brighton Lodge. Silver Lake has a boardwalk giving handicap access to fishing docks. The first section follows Big Cottonwood Creek through stands of aspen and evergreens. The trail continues south across meadows filled with wildflowers, then climbs more steeply to Brighton Overlook, one mile from the start. Dog Lake, surrounded by old mine dumps, lies 200 yards to the south. Continue on the main trail one-half mile to Lake Mary, a large, deep lake below Mt. Millicent. Lake Martha is another half mile up the trail. Another mile of climbing takes you to Lake Catherine, bordered by a pretty alpine mead-

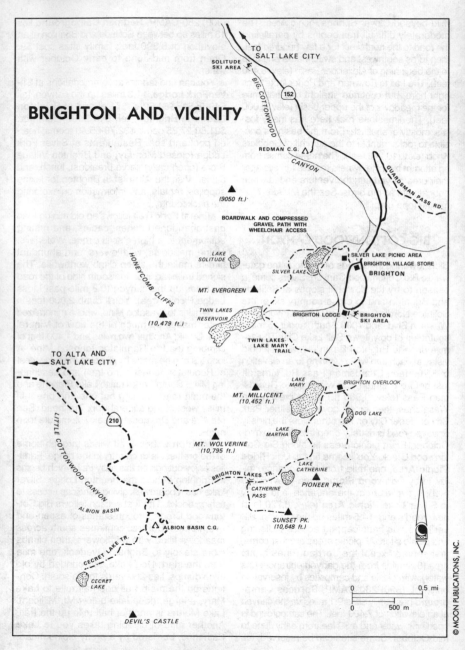

BRIGHTON AND VICINITY

TO SALT LAKE CITY

SOLITUDE SKI AREA

152

BIG COTTONWOOD CANYON

REDMAN C.G.

GUARDSMAN PASS RD.

▲ (9050 ft.)

BOARDWALK AND COMPRESSED GRAVEL PATH WITH WHEELCHAIR ACCESS

HONEYCOMB CLIFFS

LAKE SOLITUDE

SILVER LAKE

SILVER LAKE PICNIC AREA

BRIGHTON VILLAGE STORE

BRIGHTON

▲ MT. EVERGREEN

TWIN LAKES RESERVOIR

▲ (10,479 ft.)

BRIGHTON LODGE

BRIGHTON SKI AREA

TWIN LAKES LAKE MARY TRAIL

TO ALTA AND SALT LAKE CITY

210

LITTLE COTTONWOOD CANYON

LAKE MARY

BRIGHTON OVERLOOK

▲ MT. MILLICENT (10,452 ft.)

DOG LAKE

LAKE MARTHA

▲ MT. WOLVERINE (10,795 ft.)

BRIGHTON LAKES TR.

LAKE CATHERINE

PIONEER PK.

CATHERINE PASS

ALBION BASIN

SUNSET PK. (10,648 ft.)

ALBION BASIN C.G.

CECRET LAKE TR.

CECRET LAKE

0   0.5 mi

0   500 m

DEVIL'S CASTLE

ow on the north and by steep talus slopes of Sunset and Pioneer peaks on the south. Total elevation gain for the three-mile hike to Lake Catherine is 1,200 feet. Hikers can also go another half mile to Catherine Pass and descend one and one half miles to Albion Basin in Little Cottonwood Canyon. Sunset Peak (elev. 10,648 feet) can be climbed by following a one-half-mile trail from the pass. See the Brighton 7 1/2-minute topo map.

LITTLE COTTONWOOD CANYON

The road through this nearly straight glacial valley ascends 5,500 feet in 11 miles. Splendid peaks rise to more than 11,000 feet on both sides. In winter and spring, challenging terrain attracts skiers to Snowbird and Alta ski areas. Enter Little Cottonwood Canyon from the junction of UT 209 and UT 210, four miles south of the entrance to Big Cottonwood Canyon. Granite rock for the Salt Lake Temple came from quarries one mile up the canyon on the left. Here too are the Granite Mountain Record Vaults, containing genealogical and historical records of the LDS church, stored on millions of rolls of microfilm. Neither site is open to the public. There aren't any picnic areas in the canyon, but the U.S. Forest Service offers two places to camp. **Tanners Flat Campground** is 4.3 miles up the canyon at an elevation of 7,200 feet; sites cost $8 and have water from mid-May to early September, then no water or fee to mid-October. Some sites can be reserved, tel. (800) 280-CAMP. **Albion Basin Campground** lies 11 miles up near the head of the canyon at an elevation of 9,500 feet (the last two and one half miles are gravel road); sites cost $8 and have water from early July to early September, then no water or fee to late September/early October.

Snowbird Resort, seven miles up the canyon on the right, offers luxury accommodations, a good selection of restaurants, a varied calendar of concert and dance performances, sports facilities, and a tram ride to the heights. Lodging rates in summer run $28.50 dorm, $100.86 hotel, $83.32 studio, and $63.58-238.98 condo. The tram ride to the 11,000-foot summit of Hidden Peak gives you sweeping panoramas from the crest of the Wasatch Range; the tram operates 11 a.m.-8 p.m. from mid-May to mid-Octo-

Red Pine Trail in Little Cottonwood Canyon

ber; $8 adult, $6 children ages 6-16 and seniors 62-69, over age 70 ski free, or $22 family up to four kids. The Activity Center (near tennis courts) rents mountain bicycles and offers tours for hiking, climbing, backpacking, and mountain bicycling, tel. ext. 4147. A hiking map available at the Activity Center shows local trails and jogging loops. A spa is located atop the Cliff Lodge, tel. ext. 5900. Contact the resort at Snowbird, UT 84092, tel. 742-2222 (local), 521-6040 (Salt Lake City), or (800) 453-3000 (lodging reservations).

Alta's original reputation lay in the rich silver veins of the hills and the rip-roaring saloon life in town. Mining started in 1865 with the opening of the great Emma Mine and peaked in 1872, when Alta had a population of 5,000 served by 26 saloons and six breweries. Crashing silver prices the following year and a succession of deadly avalanches ended the boom. A few diehards continued to work the hills but the town faded away. Little remains from the old days except abandoned mine shafts, a few shacks,

Alta City during its early years

and the cemetery. Ski enthusiasts brought Alta to life again with ski jumping in 1930 and the introduction of ski lifts in 1937. **Alta Lodge** offers summer accommodations at $61.95 s, $69.69-94.03 d, and limited restaurant service; special packages include dinner or brunch with room, tel. 742-3500 (Alta) or 322-4631 (Salt Lake City). **Alta Peruvian Lodge** offers rooms at $39-75 s or d, and a restaurant (dinner Thurs.-Sat. and breakfast Sunday; reservations required), tel. 742-3000 (Alta), 328-8589 (Salt Lake City), or (800) 453-8488. Alta lies eight miles up the canyon (one mile beyond Snowbird).

White Pine, Red Pine, and **Maybird Gulch trails** lead to pretty alpine lakes. Red Pine and Maybird Gulch lie in the Lone Peak Wilderness. All three trails begin from the same trailhead, then diverge into separate valleys. On any one, you'll enjoy wildflowers and superb high-country scenery. Start from White Pine Trailhead (elev. 7,700 feet), 5.3 miles up the canyon and one mile beyond Tanners Flat Campground. The trail crosses a bridge over Little Cottonwood

Creek and contours west, then southwest to White Pine Fork. The effects of several avalanches can be seen along this section. The trails divide after one mile, just before crossing White Pine Fork; turn sharply left for White Pine Lake or continue straight across the stream for Red Pine Lake and Maybird Gulch. Red Pine Trail contours around a ridge, then parallels Red Pine Fork to the lake (elev. 9,680 feet), a beautiful deep pool ringed by conifers and alpine meadows. Energetic hikers can rockscramble along the stream another half mile (no trail) to Upper Red Pine Lake. The upper lake sits in a glacial cirque devoid of trees. Trout lurk in the waters, though the lake may remain frozen until late June. Maybird Gulch Trail begins two miles up Red Pine Trail from White Pine Fork and leads to tiny Maybird Lakes. From the trailhead, White Pine Lake is three and one half miles (2,300-foot elevation gain), Red Pine Lake is three and one half miles (1,920-foot elevation gain), and Maybird Lakes are four and one half miles (2,060-foot elevation gain). See the

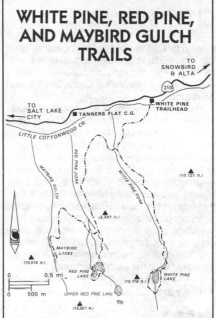

WHITE PINE, RED PINE, AND MAYBIRD GULCH TRAILS

Dromedary Peak 7¹/₂-minute topo map. This whole area is heavily used by hikers, so great care with the environment is needed. Please follow the Forest Service regulation that prohibits wood fires within one mile of the lakes.

Peruvian Gulch-Hidden Peak Trail gives you the advantage of hiking just one-way from either the top or bottom by using the Snowbird tram. From the top of Hidden Peak (elev. 11,000 feet), the trail crosses open rocky country on the upper slopes, spruce- and aspen-covered ridges lower down, then follows an old mining road down Peruvian Gulch. Elevation change along the three and one half-mile trail is 2,900 feet. Dromedary Peak 7¹/₂-minute topo map covers this area.

Cecret Lake Trail begins from the west side of Albion Basin Campground and climbs glacier-scarred granite slopes to a pretty alpine lake (elev. 9,880 feet) below Sugarloaf Mountain. Wildflowers put on colorful summer displays along the way. The trail is just one mile long and makes a good family hike; elevation gain is 360 feet. Continue another mile for fine views south to Mt. Timpanogos from Germania Pass. It's no secret that early miners had trouble spelling Cecret Lake; you'll see both versions on maps!

PARK CITY

Approaching this old silver-mining town, you might think the name should be changed to "Condo City," but keep going to the picturesque downtown area. Turn-of-the-century buildings along Main Street and on the hillsides recall Park City's colorful and energetic past. Here you'll find a historic museum, art galleries, specialty shops, and fine restaurants. A busy year-round schedule of festivals, concerts, and sporting events help make Park City a lively place. Instead of digging for silver, today's visitors head for the slopes to mine the light and dry powder snow in winter and to enjoy the verdant mountain scenery in summer. Three ski areas—Wolf Mountain, Park City, and Deer Valley—offer varied terrain and luxurious accommodations; see "Skiing" under "Salt Lake City Recreation" earlier in this chapter. The U.S. Ski Team liked the town so well that it based its headquarters here. Park City lies in a mountain valley at an elevation of 7,000 feet on the eastern side of the Wasatch Range. From Salt Lake City, drive 31 miles east via I-80 and UT 224.

History

In October 1868, with winter fast approaching, three off-duty soldiers from Fort Douglas discovered a promising outcrop of ore on a hillside two miles south of the present townsite. Their sample assayed at 96 ounces of silver per ton, with lesser values of lead and gold. Two years later, the Flagstaff Mine began operations at that first discovery and development of one of the West's richest mining districts took off. What had been a peaceful valley with grazing cattle now swarmed with hordes of fortune hunters and rang to the sound of pick axes. The famed Ontario Mine and dozens of other strikes soon followed. Silver from the Ontario, as much as 400 ounces in a ton, started the fortunes of U.S. Senator Thomas J. Kearns of Salt Lake City and George Hearst, father of publisher William Randolph Hearst. By 1880, Park City had grown to be a substantial town with a population of 10,000 of many nationalities. The *Park Mining Record,* later the *Park Record,* began weekly publication that continues today. Scandinavian miners introduced skiing to the com-

munity, though the heavy 10-foot boards used then have little in common with today's equipment. A lively red-light entertainment district sprang up in Deer Valley Gulch, but it's long gone today.

The great hotel fire of 1898 nearly brought an end to the young city. The fire raced along Main Street, reducing 200 businesses and houses to ashes and leaving much of the population homeless. Determined citizens immediately set to work rebuilding and had a new downtown within three months. Many of the businesses you see along Main Street date from that time. In the early 1900s, Park City's mining economy began seeing more depressions than upswings. Mine flooding, labor troubles, and a big drop in metal prices during the Great Depression caused many residents to leave. By the early 1960s the town looked ready to fold up, but then the big skiing and resort boom brought it to life again!

The Future

Salt Lake City is a candidate for the Olympic Winter Games of February 2002. Facilities have been built just south of Park City for ski jumping including 18- to 90-meter ski jumps, a ski-jump training area, and summer/winter freestyle jumps with a splashdown pool. Future facilities will include a bobsled and luge course with a 1,300-meter track and a 120-meter ski jump. These facilities will help train winter athletes but will not be open to the general public except as spectators. The facility is reached via a turnoff drive two miles north of the I-80 exit to Park City. Call for spectator hours and admission rates, tel. 649-5447.

SIGHTS

Park City Museum

Drop in to see the walk-in mine and other historic exhibits of Park City's colorful past. The museum is at 528 Main St. in the old City Hall Building, built in 1885 and rebuilt after the 1898 fire, tel. 649-6104. Go downstairs to see the original jail, known as the "dungeon." Open

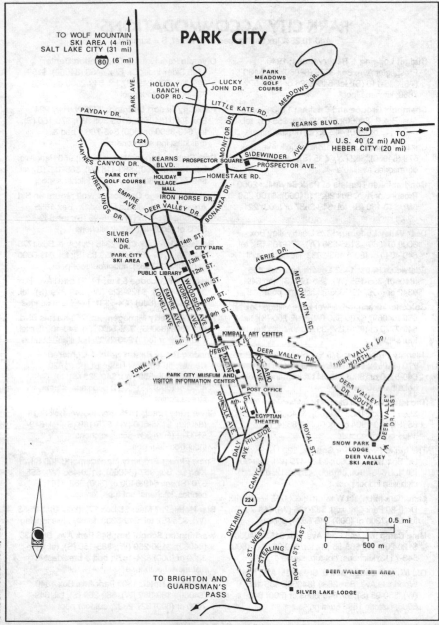

PARK CITY

TO WOLF MOUNTAIN
SKI AREA (4 mi)
SALT LAKE CITY (31 mi)
80 (6 mi)

PARK AVE.

HOLIDAY
RANCH
LOOP RD.

LUCKY
JOHN DR.

PARK
MEADOWS
GOLF
COURSE

MEADOWS DR.

LITTLE KATE RD.

PAYDAY DR.

224

KEARNS BLVD.

248

TO
U.S. 40 (2 mi) AND
HEBER CITY (20 mi)

MONITOR DR.

SIDEWINDER AVE.

THAYNES CANYON DR.

KEARNS
BLVD.

PROSPECTOR SQUARE

PROSPECTOR AVE.

PARK CITY
GOLF COURSE

HOLIDAY
VILLAGE
MALL

HOMESTAKE RD.

EMPIRE
AVE.

IRON HORSE DR.

THREE KINGS DR.

DEER VALLEY DR.

BONANZA DR.

SILVER
KING
DR.

14th ST.

CITY PARK

PARK CITY
SKI AREA

13th ST.

AERIE DR.

PUBLIC LIBRARY

12th ST.

11th ST.

WOODSIDE AVE.

EMPIRE AVE.

NORFOLK AVE.

LOWELL AVE.

10th ST.

9th ST.

8th ST.

MELLOW MTN. RD.

KIMBALL ART CENTER

HEBER AVE.

MAIN ST.

DEER VALLEY DR.

DEER VALLEY DR. NORTH

TOWN LIFT

ONTARIO AVE.

PARK CITY MUSEUM AND
VISITOR INFORMATION CENTER

DEER VALLEY
DR. SOUTH

DEER VALLEY DR. EAST

POST OFFICE

4th ST.

NORFOLK AVE.

EGYPTIAN
THEATER

DALY AVE.

HILLSIDE AVE.

ROYAL ST.

SNOW PARK
LODGE
DEER VALLEY
SKI AREA

ONTARIO CANYON

224

ROYAL ST.

0   0.5 mi
0   500 m

TO BRIGHTON AND
GUARDSMAN'S
PASS

ROYAL ST. WEST

STERLING

ROYAL ST. EAST

DEER VALLEY SKI AREA

SILVER LAKE LODGE

MOON

PARK CITY ACCOMMODATIONS
Add 10.25% tax to all prices; W = winter, S = summer

Budget Lodging & Reservations; 1940 Prospector Ave. Box 3868 (84060); $66-130 (W), $45-110 (S); tel. 649-2526 or (800) 522-7669; kitchens, pool

Chamonix Groupe and Chalets; 1183 Empire Ave. Box 9 (84060); $85-95 (W), $55 (S); tel. 649-8443 or (800) 443-8630; hot tub, sauna

Chateau Aprés Lodge; 1299 Norfolk Ave. Box 579 (84060); $62 (W), $35 (S); tel. 649-9372; dormitories available

Condominium Rentals of Park City/IML; 2000 Prospector Ave. Box 2909 (84060); $100-250 (W), $40-180 (S); tel. 649-2687 or (800) 221-0933; kitchens

Deer Valley Lodging; 1375 Deer Valley Box 3000 (84060); $185-335 (W), $70-195 (S); tel. 649-4040 or (800) 453-3833; kitchens, pool

Edelweiss Haus; 1482 Empire Ave. Box 495 (84060); $95-195 (W), $50-100 (S); tel. 649-9342 or (800) 438-3855; kitchens, pool

Goldener Hirsch Inn; Silver Lake Village Box 859 (84060); $285-550 (W), $95-200 (S); tel. 649-7770 or (800) 252-3373; Austrian Inn, hot tub, sauna

Identity Properties; 375 Saddle View Way Box 779 (84060); $160-385 (W), $75-160 (S); tel. 649-5100 or (800) 245-6417; kitchens, pools, hot tubs, saunas

The Imperial Hotel (bed & breakfast inn); 231 Main St. Box 1628 (84060); $145-230 (W), $60-85 (S); 649-1904 or (800) 669-8824; historic 1904 boardinghouse

The Inn at Prospector Square; 2200 Sidewinder Dr. Box 1698 (84060); $129-479 (W), $69-300 (S); tel. 649-7100 or (800) 453-3812; athletic club with indoor pool

Landmark Inn (Best Western); 6560 N. Landmark Dr. (I-80 Park City exit); $83-135 (W), $69-75 (S); tel. 649-7300 or (800) 548-8824; pool

Mine Camp Inn; 245 Park Ave. Box 3151 (84060); $120-205 (W), $65-95 (S); tel. 649-2577 or (800) 543-7113; kitchens, hot tub, sauna

Old Miners' Lodge Bed & Breakfast Inn; 615 Woodside Ave. Box 2639 (84060); $85-155 (W), $50-95 (S); tel. 645-8068 or (800) 648-8068; historic 1893 building

Olympia Park Hotel & Convention Center; 1895 Sidewinder Dr. Box 4439 (84060); $159-399 (W), $99-249 (S); tel. 649-2900 or (800) 234-9003; indoor pool

Park City Resort Lodging; 3770 N. Hwy 224 Box 3000 (84060); $105-305 (W), $70-160 (S); tel. 649-8200 or (800) 545-7669; bed & breakfast inn and condos

Park Station Condominium Hotel; 950 Park Ave. Box 1360 (84060); $80-415 (W), $65-125 (S); tel. 649-7717 or (800) 367-1056; kitchens, pool

ParkWest Village Condos at Wolf Mountain Ski Area; 3819 W. Village Round Dr. Box 1655 (84060); $45-215 (W), $45-95 (S); tel. 649-8023 or (800) 421-5056; kitchens

Radisson Inn Park City; 2346 Park Ave. Box 1778 (84060); $159-169 (W), $59-85 (S); tel. 649-5000 or (800) 333-3333; indoor/outdoor pool

Resort Center Lodge & Inn; 1415 Lowell Ave. Box 3449 (84060); $129-829 (W), $49-329 (S); tel. 649-0800 or (800) 824-5331; hotel and condos

Resort Property Management; 750 Kearns Blvd. Box 3808 (84060); $79-1400 (W), $40-400 (S); tel. 649-6606 or (800) 243-2932; hotel and condos

Shadow Ridge Resort Hotel & Conference Center; 50 Shadow Ridge St. Box 1820 (84060); $69-580 (W), $49-225 (S); tel. 649-4300 or (800) 451-3031; pool, spa, sauna, fitness center

Silver King Hotel; 1485 Empire Ave. Box 2818 (84060); $135-600 (W), $75-189 (S); tel. 649-5500 or (800) 331-8652; kitchens, indoor/outdoor pool

Snow Flower Property Management; 400 Silver King Dr. Box 957 (84060); $120-485 (W), $55-370 (S); tel. 649-6400 or (800) 852-3101; condos, kitchens, hot tubs, tennis

Star Hotel; 227 Main St. Box 777 (84060); $45-55 (W), $35 (S); tel. 649-8333; family style lodging

Washington School Inn; 543 Park Ave. Box 536 (84060); $190-250 (W), $85-150 (S); tel. 649-3800 or (800) 824-1672; bed & breakfast in historic schoolhouse

The Yarrow Hotel; 1800 Park Ave. Box 1840 (84060); $99-389 (W), $89-269 (S); tel. 649-7000 or (800) 327-2332; outdoor pool

Mon.-Sat. 10 a.m.-7 p.m., Sunday noon-6 p.m.; hours in May and October change to daily noon-5 p.m.; free admission. The **Visitor Information Center** is here too during the same hours; staff can answer your questions and provide literature on the area. Ask for a historic walking tour leaflet. Groups can arrange guided walking tours.

Kimball Art Center

This large art gallery exhibits works of noted artists and sponsors classes and workshops. Galleries on the main floor and downstairs display paintings, prints, sculptures, ceramics, photography, and other media. Exhibits change every four weeks. The gift shop has many items for sale. Open Mon.-Sat. 10 a.m.-6 p.m., Sunday noon-6 p.m. Located at the corner of Heber and Park near the bottom of Main Street, tel. 649-8882. Look for other art galleries along Main Street too.

ACCOMMODATIONS

Park City offers more than 70 places to stay. Guest capacity far exceeds the town's permanent population! Rates peak during the ski season, when accommodations may be hard to find. Off season, prices can drop as much as 50% at the more expensive places. See the *Vacation Planner* published by the Park City Area Chamber/Bureau for additional listings of accommodations (Box 1630, Park City UT 84060). Skiers will also want to check accommodation and ski package listings in the *Utah Ski Vacation Planner*, Ski Utah, Inc., 150 W. 500 South, Salt Lake City, UT 84101. Lodging reservations services include **ABC Reservations,** tel. 649-2223 or 800-820-ABCD; **A-Vermeers Reservations,** tel. 649-1103; **Deer Valley Central Reservations,** also includes Park City, tel. 649-1000 or 800-424-3337; **Park City Ski Holidays,** tel. 649-0493 or 800-222-7275; **Park City Travel and Lodging,** tel. 645-8200 or 800-421-9741; and **Reservations Network,** tel. 649-1592.

Campgrounds

Hidden Haven offers tent and RV sites all year with showers and laundry; guests may cast for trout in a stream running beside the campground; $13.35 no hookups, $16.62 w/hookups; drive to I-80 Park City Exit 145 (five miles north of town on UT 224) and turn west one mile on the north frontage road, tel. 649-8935.

RESTAURANTS

American

Barking Frog Grill, 368 Main St., tel. 649-6222, features contemporary Southwest cuisine; open daily for dinner. **The Riverhorse Cafe,** in the old Masonic building at 540 Main St., tel. 649-3536, has a variety of seafood and pasta dishes; open daily for dinner. **The Claimjumper,** 573 Main St., tel. 649-8051, features steaks, prime rib, and seafood; open Thurs.-Sun. (daily in ski season) for breakfast and daily for dinner. **Morning Ray,** 268 Main, tel. 649-5686, prepares gourmet vegetarian, seafood, and chicken dishes; open daily for lunch and dinner, Thurs.-Sun. for dinner. **The Eating Establishment,** 317 Main St., tel. 649-8284, is a favorite place for breakfast, served until 4:30 p.m.; dinner is served too; open daily. **Grub Steak Restaurant,** Prospector Square Hotel, Kearns Blvd. and Sidewinder Ave., tel. 649-8060, rustles up steak, prime rib, seafood, and has a large salad bar; open Sunday for brunch, Mon.-Fri. for lunch, and daily for dinner. **The Stew Pot,** Deer Valley Plaza, tel. 645-STEW, serves stews, chicken, seafood, sandwiches, and salads; open daily for lunch and dinner. **Texas Red's Pit Barbecue,** 440 Main St., tel. 649-7337, dishes out ribs, beef, pork, chicken, two-alarm chili, and catfish in a Western setting; open daily for lunch, dinner, and takeout.

During the ski season, **Brand X Cattle Company,** 1064 Park Ave., tel. 649-2346, serves up steaks, prime rib, local trout, and seafood with a large salad bar; open daily for dinner. Also just in the ski season, the **Mariposa,** Deer Valley Resort, Silver Lake Lodge, mid-mountain, tel. 645-6715, prepares "classic and current" cuisine; open daily (winter only) for dinner (reservations suggested). The **Snow Park Restaurant,** Snow Park Lodge in Deer Valley Resort, tel. 645-6632, creates outstanding buffets during the ski season; open daily for breakfast and lunch and Mon.-Sat. for dinner (seafood buffet). **McHenry's Grill,** Silver Lake Lodge, tel. 645-6724, serves grilled sandwiches, appetizers, and salads for lunch and dinner (ski season only).

Mexican

The **Baja Cantina,** the Resort Center, Park City Ski Area, tol. 610 2260, serves favorite south-of-the-border items plus steaks and seafood; open daily for lunch and dinner. Despite its name, **The Irish Camel,** 434 Main St., tel. 649-6645, serves good Mexican food; open daily for lunch and dinner.

Continental

Adolph's, Park City Golf Course, corner Park Ave. and Thaynes Canyon Dr., tel. 649-7177, varied international menu features lamb, veal, chicken, and seafood dishes; open daily for dinner (reservations suggested). **Cisero's Italian Ristorante,** 306 Main St., tel. 649-6800, serves pasta, veal, chicken, and seafood; open daily for lunch and dinner. **Mid-Mountain Restaurant,** in an old miners' mess hall on the Webster run, Pioneer lift, in the Park City Ski Area, tel. 649-3044, offers such Continental delights as Swiss-style veal bratwurst, chicken Wellington, and roast loin of lamb; open daily during the ski season for lunch. **Mileti's,** 412 Main St., tel. 649-8211, Italian restaurant uses homemade pasta in its traditional and modern dishes; open daily for dinner. **The Tapestry,** Stag Lodge in Deer Valley, 8200 Royal St. East, tel. 649-2421, offers a variety of European cuisines; open daily for dinner, also breakfast and lunch during the ski season (reservations recommended). Chefs prepare German, Austrian, and other specialties at **The Grill at the Depot,** 660 Main, bottom of hill, tel. 649-2102; open Sunday for breakfast and Thurs.-Mon. for lunch and dinner. The **Glitretind,** in the Stein Eriksen Lodge at Deer Valley Resort, tel. 649-3700, offers fine European cuisine in elegant surroundings; open daily for breakfast, lunch, and dinner (reservations recommended for dinner and Sunday brunch).

Chinese

Szechuan Chinese Restaurant, 438 Main St., tel. 649-0957, offers spicy and mild dishes; open daily for lunch and dinner. **Yen-Jing Restaurant,** next to the ice rink in the Resort Center at the Park City Ski Area, tel. 649-7800, features Mandarin and Szechuan cuisines; open daily for lunch and dinner.

Japanese

Ichiban Sushi, 586 Main St., tel. 649-2865, prepares sushi, sashimi, tempura, teriyaki, and other styles; open Mon.-Sat. for lunch and dinner.

Pizza

Davanza's Pizza, Holiday Village Mall, tel. 649-9700, fixes pizza, subs, burgers, and salads; open Mon.-Sat. (daily in ski season) for lunch, dinner, and takeout too. **Park City Pizza Company,** 430 Main St., tel. 649-1591, prepares pizza, hot sandwiches, pasta dishes, and salads for sit-down or takeout; open daily for lunch and dinner. **Red Banjo Pizza Parlour,** 322 Main St., tel. 649-9901, offers pizza, spaghetti, sandwiches, and salads; open daily for lunch and dinner. **Olive Barrel Food Co.,** 444 Main St., tel. 647-7777, serves authentic rustic Italian cuisine including pizza baked in wood-fired ovens and meat and fish grilled over cherrywood coals; open daily for breakfast, lunch, and dinner (reservations required).

OTHER PRACTICALITIES

Entertainment And Events

Catch movies at **Holiday Village Cinemas III** in Holiday Village Mall, 1776 Park Ave. (north edge of town), tel. 649-6541. **Park City Performances** puts on plays, musicals, and children's programs in the historic Egyptian Theatre, 328 Main St., tel. 649-9371. Contact the Park City Area Chamber/Bureau for the latest news on happenings around town, tel. 649-6100/6104. Major annual events include:

January: Sundance Film Festival presents screenings and seminars of the best cinema projects by independent producers. U.S. senators compete in the **Senators' Ski Cup,** a charity fundraiser. **Utah Winter Games** features alpine and nordic skiing and ice-skating.

February: Park City High School sponsors the **Snow Sculpture Contest and Winterfest.**

March: Snowshine Festival features two weeks of family races, snow softball, and other sports in the snow at Park City Ski Area (late March to early April).

April: Kids enjoy the **Easter Egg Hunt** at Park City Ski Area.

June: Wolf Mountain Summer Concert Series presents big-name rock, country, and jazz

Park City, looking south, ca. 1900

bands. Area restaurants prepare **Savor the Summit,** a food festival at the Resort Center. **Writers at Work** offers readings and seminars by nationally known writers and poets. Fishermen enter the **Coalville Fishing Derby** at Echo Reservoir. Cyclists speed toward the finish line in the **Park City Pedalfest,** a major bicycle event with road race, criterium, and time-trial stages.

July: Wolf Mountain Summer Concert Series continues. Citizens put on an **Old-Fashioned Fourth of July Celebration** with a parade and fireworks. **Utah Symphony Summer Series** plays weekly concerts at Deer Valley in July and August. Cowboys and cowgirls compete in the **Oakley Rodeo,** Thurs.-Sat. on the Fourth of July weekend; 15 miles east of Park City.

August: Utah Symphony Summer Series continues. **Wolf Mountain Summer Concert Series** continues. **Park City International Music Festival** brings more good music. About 200 artists exhibit their work on Main Street for the **Art Festival. Summit County Fair** in nearby Coalville has a parade, rodeo, horse show, roping, demolition derby, entertainment, and exhibits. Golfers meet for the **Franklin Quest Championship,** a senior PGA tournament held at Park Meadows Golf Club.

September: Wolf Mountain Summer Concert Series concludes early in month. **Deer Valley Bluegrass Festival** features lively music. **Miners' Day Celebration** has a parade and mucking and drilling contests on Labor Day weekend. Dozens of balloons take flight over Park City for the **Autumn Aloft Hot-Air Balloon Festival.** Players fight it out in the **Rugby Challenge Cup.**

November: Ski areas open! A big **street dance** has dancing, ski racing, and fireworks near Thanksgiving.

December: Christmas in the Park presents carols, lighting of a community tree, and a visit by Santa. Skiers descend the slopes with torches at Park City Ski Area for the **Christmas Eve Torchlight Parade.** In **Santa Claus on the Mountain,** Santa takes to skis to give treats to kids at Park City Ski Area. Well-known personalities compete in the **Celebrity Ski Classic** and **Tournament of Champions** at Deer Valley in mid-December.

Recreation

Winter sports draw the most visitors to Park City. Because the ski areas near Salt Lake City and here are so close together; all have been listed in "Skiing" under "Salt Lake City Recreation" earlier in this chapter.

Mountain Bicycling is a favorite summer activity in the Park City area. Some of the local landowners, including ski resorts and mining companies, have offered access to their land and have even built trail sections at their own expense. The Chamber of Commerce publishes an annual summer booklet, *Park City Mountain Bike Trails,* that gives descriptions and maps of the trails open for that summer. In addition, Park City is at one end of the new **Historic Union Pacific Rail Trail State Park,** which runs 27 miles to Echo Reservoir and will connect with other planned trails (including a 26-mile Jordanelle Trail that will circle the Jordanelle Reservoir).

The **Alpine Slide** gives the thrill of a toboggan ride for summer visitors. A chairlift takes you to the start of a 3,000-foot track that twists and winds down the hillside. No special skills are needed to ride the sled. Open late May to late September: weekdays noon-10 p.m., weekends 10 a.m.-10 p.m. (shorter hours after Labor Day); located at Park City Ski Area, tel. 649-7150. Play the **Silver Putt Miniature Golf Course** at Park City Ski Area, tel. 649-7150; open same hours as the Alpine Slide.

Golfers have a choice of three 18-hole courses. **Park City Municipal Golf Course** is at Park Ave. and Thaynes Canyon Dr., tel. 649-8701. **Park Meadows Golf Club's** course, designed by Jack Nicklaus, is one of the longest in the state at 7,338 yards; 2000 Meadows Dr., tel. 649-2460. Arnold Palmer designed **Jeremy Ranch Golf Course,** private; located eight miles north of Park City on the I-80 frontage road, tel. 649-2700.

Though expensive, a flight aboard a hot-air balloon is an exhilarating experience. Balloons take off in the early morning year-round, weather permitting. Typical costs are $75 for 30 minutes, $135 for one hour with **Balloon the Rockies,** tel. 645-7433, **Balloon Adventures,** tel. 645-8787, **Balloon Affaire,** tel. 649-3343, **Park City Balloon Escape,** tel. 645-9400, **Park City Balloons,** tel. 645-7999, and **Sunrise Fantasy Ballooning,** tel. 649-9009 or (800) 658-9191. Reservations can be made with several of the balloon companies by calling **ABC Reservations;** tel. (800) 820-ABCD.

The **city park** next to the former miners' hospital (1904) has picnic tables, playground, volleyball, basketball, and ball fields. **Park City Recreation Department,** tel. 645-5112, organizes classes in art, music, folk dancing, gymnastics, aerobics, karate, and a variety of sports. The **Norwegian School of Nature Life,** tel. 649-5322, is a nonprofit organization offering cross-country ski tours and instruction, snowshoeing, hiking, backpacking, canoeing, and mountain-bike treks for people of all ages.

Prospector Athletic Club, at the Prospector Square Hotel, 2200 Sidewinder Dr., tel. 649-6670, has an indoor pool, racquetball and tennis courts, gym, weight room, saunas, jacuzzi, classes, and massage and physical therapies; open daily. **Park City Racquet Club,** 1200 Little Kate Rd., tel. 645-5100, features an outdoor pool, tennis, racquetball, basketball, volleyball, and saunas.

Services
For **emergencies** (police, fire, or medical), dial 911. **Park City Family Health and Emergency Center** provides care 24 hours a day; located at 1665 Bonanza Dr., tel. 649-7640. The **post office** is downtown at 450 Main St., tel. 649-9191.

Many shoppers enjoy a visit to the new **Factory Stores,** which has about 50 factory outlets at 6699 Landmark Dr., just south of I-80 Park City Exit 145, tel. 645-7078. Bicycles (mountain and road), camping gear, and cross-country skis can be purchased and rented at **White Pine Touring,** 201 Heber Ave., tel. 649-8710; tours on cross-country skis and mountain bicycles can be arranged too. **Gart Brothers Sporting Goods,** in Holiday Village Mall, 1780 Park Ave., tel. 649-6922, has skiing (also downhill and cross-country rentals), hiking, camping, fishing, and other outdoor gear. **Recreation Rental** offers rafting trips on the Provo River in summer and rents snowmobiles in winter; located near Guardsman Pass (a shuttle service is provided from town in winter), tel. 649-FUNN.

Information
Park City Area Chamber/Bureau has excellent vacation planners and other free literature; the staff knows of upcoming events and will answer your questions. Stop by the Visitor Information Center at the Park City Museum, 528 Main St., tel. 649-6100/6104 or (800) 453-1360. Open Mon.-Sat. 10 a.m.-7 p.m., Sunday noon-6 p.m.; hours in May and October change to daily noon-5 p.m.; Box 1630, Park City, UT 84060. The main office is in Prospector Square at 1910 Prospector Ave.; the staff here provides help for convention planning and for new residents; open Mon.-Fri. 8 a.m.-5 p.m. (same phone numbers and mailing address as above). Park City's **public library,** 1255 Park Ave., tel. 645-5140, has a good collection of regional

books and maps; open Sunday 1-5 p.m., Mon.-Thurs. 10 a.m.-9 p.m, and Friday and Saturday 10 a.m.-6 p.m.

Transportation

Park City Transit operates a trolley bus up and down Main St. (about every 10 minutes daily) and has several bus routes to other parts of town, including Park City and Deer Valley ski areas (about every 10-20 minutes daily). All buses are free; pick up a transit guide from the Visitor Information Center or any of the buses or call Park City Transit, tel. 645-5130 (recording). **Wolf Mountain,** tel. 649-5400, runs a free shuttle to its ski area during the ski season from lodges at the other ski resorts. **Park City Transportation** provides year-round services with Salt Lake City downtown and airport for $20 one-way; ski shuttles depart from Park City and Salt Lake City in winter to Brighton, Solitude, Snowbird, Alta, Sundance, Snowbasin, and Powder Mountain ski areas; call two days in advance for reservations and to check if a passenger minimum applies, tel. 649-8567 (Park City), 364-8472 (Salt Lake City), (800) 356-7384 in Utah, or (800) 637-3803 out of state. **Lewis Brothers Stages** has a "Red Horse Express" service during the ski season between Park City and Salt Lake City airport or downtown ($15 one-way, $28 roundtrip); a limited service operates in summer for $22 each way. A shuttle during the ski season connects the Park City ski areas with Solitude, Brighton, Snowbird, Alta, and Sundance ($11 one-way, $20 roundtrip). Ski packages with transportation and lift tickets can be purchased too. Reservations two days in advance are advised for these trips, tel. 359-8677 (Salt Lake City), 649-2256 (Park City), or (800) 826-5844.

Auto rentals and **taxi** companies are listed in the Vacation Planner and telephone *Yellow Pages.*

VICINITY OF PARK CITY

Enjoying the outdoors comes naturally to visitors and residents of Park City. The invigorating climate and surrounding mountains encourage exploration of the high forests and tundra, with wildflowers in summer and endless views in any season. Relics of the mining past lie scattered about. You're likely to come across miners'

cabins in all states of decay, hoist buildings, aerial tramway towers, rusting machinery, and great piles of mine tailings. Unlike other parts of the Wasatch Range, most of the land here belongs to mining companies and other private owners. Visitors need to keep a distance from mine shafts, which can be hundreds of feet deep, and respect No Trespassing signs. *Park City Trails* by Raye Ringholz describes many hiking and ski touring possibilities in the area, along with a history and walking tour of Park City.

COALVILLE AND VICINITY

In 1858, when William Smith noticed that wheat that had spilled from wagons here had grown to maturity, he decided that this area would be a good place to settle. Smith returned the following spring with several families to begin farming. Coal mines discovered by the pioneers provided additional income and gave the community its name. Today coal has lost importance, but a large oil and gas field discovered in the 1970s holds future promise. Coalville (pop. 1,100), the

LOUISE FOOTE

yellow belly marmot (Marmota flaviventris)

Summit County seat, lies 40 miles east of Salt Lake City on I-80 near the confluence of Chalk Creek and the Weber (pronounced "WEE-ber") River. The nearby Rockport and Echo reservoirs attract fishermen and boaters.

Practicalities

Stay at **A Country Place,** 99 S. Main, tel. 336-2451 or (800) 371-2451, $25-50 s or d; or **Moore's Motel,** 90 S. Main, tel. 336-5991, $32.89 s, $41.06 d. **Holiday Hills RV Park** offers tent ($10.60) and RV ($16.35) sites, showers, and a store; located just off I-80 Coalville Exit 164, tel. 336-4421. **Dean's Coffee Shop,** 53 S. Main, and a couple of fast-food places offer meals. The big **Coalville Fishing Derby** is held in June at Echo Reservoir, three and one half miles to the north. In August, the **Summit County Fair** features a parade, rodeo, horse show, roping, demolition derby, entertainment, and exhibits. The **city park** has picnicking, playground, and tennis courts, four blocks east of the junction of Main and Center. For visitor information, stop by the **city hall** at 10 N. Main, tel. 336-5981. **Coalville Health Center** provides medical care, 82 N. 50 East, tel. 336-4403.

Rockport State Park

Rockport Reservoir (1,189 surface acres) is tucked in the Weber River Valley 13 miles south of Coalville. Visitors enjoy fishing, water-skiing, sailing, windsurfing, and swimming. Fishermen come to reel in rainbow, cutthroat, and German brown trout and smallmouth bass. The Weber River above and below the lake also has good fishing for trout and whitefish. During freeze-up, Dec.-April, fishermen try their luck through the lake ice. Like most high-country lakes, Rockport (elev. 6,100 feet) is usually calm in the mornings and evenings, but windy in the afternoons. The state park facilities are along the eastern shore with a paved boat ramp, docks, three picnic areas with covered tables, eight primitive campgrounds, and the modern Juniper Campground (with showers). Reservations are recommended for Juniper Campground on summer weekends, though there's usually plenty of space in the primitive campgrounds. The main season runs April-Oct., but a camping area (no water) is kept open for winter visitors. Entrance fees are $3 day use, $5 primitive camping, and $9 ($10 Friday, Saturday, and holidays) for Ju-

niper Campground. Fishermen may park in highway pullouts on the lake's west side without charge. Contact the park at 9040 N. State Hwy. 302, Peoa, UT 84061, tel. 336-2241 (ranger), 538-7221 (Salt Lake City), or (800) 322-3770 (reservations). Rockport State Park is 46 miles east of Salt Lake City; take I-80 Wanship Exit 156 and go south five miles on US 189.

Echo Reservoir

This privately owned reservoir between Coalville and Echo averages about 1,000 surface acres. **Echo Resort,** tel. 336-9894/2247, in a grove of large cottonwood trees on the eastern shore, has a paved boat ramp, picnicking, camping, and a snack bar. The resort has a second camping area two miles south. Fishing, mostly for rainbow and brown trout and channel catfish, is fair to good. Water-skiing and sailing are the most popular lake activities. Open early May through Sept.; fees are $3.50 parking, $4.50 boat launch, $7.50 tent or RV camping w/hookups. Take I-80 Coalville Exit 164 and go north three and one half miles (or take I-80 Echo Exit 169 and go south two miles).

Echo

This old railroad town at the junction of I-80 and I-84, five miles north of Coalville, serves travelers with the **Kozy Cafe and Motel,** tel. 336-5641, open 24 hours, $23.98-30.52 rooms; and the **Echo Cafe/gas station,** tel. 336-5642. I-80 enters Echo Canyon east of here, following the route used by Indians, fur trappers, Mormon pioneers, Pony Express, and the first transcontinental railroad. A museum display commemorates the railroad in the restored **Old Church and Schoolhouse,** one block off the highway, tel. 336-5641, open Saturday (in summer) 10 a.m.-4 p.m.

MORGAN AND VICINITY

Mormons settled here along the Weber River in 1852 and named their community after one of its members. The town (pop. 2,100) is the Morgan County seat and a center for farming, livestock raising, and dairying. Morgan lies 21 miles southeast of Ogden and just a few miles east of the Wasatch Range. Nearby attractions include Devil's Slide, Lost Creek Reservoir, and East Canyon Reservoir. Look for **Devil's Slide** seven and one half miles east of Morgan on the south side of I-84; the natural rock formation resembles a giant playground slide. Allow a stop for a better look at view areas.

Practicalities

The old **Como Springs Resort,** tel. 829-3489, has a motel ($40 s or d), an RV Park ($10, self-contained only), and a restaurant (open daily for lunch and dinner); follow Commercial St. east past the fairgrounds and across a bridge. Morgan also has the **Spring Chicken Inn Cafe,** 4 N. State, tel. 829-6062, open daily for breakfast, lunch, and dinner; and several fast-food places. Rodeo action takes place during **Morgala Days** in late June and at the **Morgan County Fair** in August. **Round Valley Golf & Country Club,** 1875 E. Round Valley Rd. (go east 2.8 miles on 100 South), tel. 829-3796, maintains an 18-hole golf course, tennis courts, and a campground ($5; showers available) from mid-March to early November. The **county clerk's office** knows about events and services of the area, 48 W. Young St. (across from the Spring Chicken Inn Cafe), tel. 829-6811.

Lost Creek State Park

Steep hillsides covered with grass, sage, and groves of evergreens surround the 365-acre reservoir. Fishermen catch mostly rainbow trout; winter visitors come to ice fish. The east arm has a paved boat ramp. Picnicking and camping are primitive; there are outhouses but no established sites, tables, drinking water, or fees. Elevation is 6,000 feet. For information, contact East Canyon State Park, tel. 829-6866 (538-7221 in Salt Lake City). The road is paved to the dam, then turns to gravel. Take I-84 Devil's Slide/Croydon Exit 111, go northeast two miles past a cement plant to the small farming town of Croydon, then turn left 13 miles to Lost Creek Reservoir. Or take I-84 Henefer Exit 115 and turn northwest four and one half miles to Croydon, then right 13 miles to the reservoir.

East Canyon State Park

East Canyon Reservoir is one of the closest mountain lakes to Salt Lake City (38 miles). It's also close to Ogden (33 miles) and Morgan (12 miles). The 600-acre lake is about six miles long and one and one half miles wide; elevation is 5,700 feet. Power boating, water-skiing, and angling are the most popular activities. Fishing is good for rainbow trout in the lake and in East Canyon Creek. You'll find a marina and most of the state park facilities at the lake's north end. The marina is open from late May to mid-September with a store, snack bar, boat storage, slips, and boat rentals (fishing boats with or without motors, canoes, jet skis, paddle boats, and ski boats), tel. 829-6157. A beach east of the marina is popular with swimmers and picnickers. The state park is open all year; facilities at the north end of the lake include a paved boat ramp, picnic area, and campground (water and showers). Parking areas with outhouses are along the east side and at the south end. Camping reservations are recommended for summer weekends. The **park office** can be reached at 5535 S. Hwy. 66, Morgan, UT 84050, tel. 829-6866 (538-7221 in Salt Lake City) or (800) 322-3770 (reservations). Entrance fees are $3 for day use at the recreation area and at the south end of the lake, $5 for camping at the five primitive areas, and $9 ($10 Friday, Saturday, and holidays) for developed camping at the north end. **East Canyon Resort,** a quarter mile south of the reservoir, has a restaurant open to the public. For the most scenic way in from Salt Lake City, go east on the road through Emigration Canyon, then turn left on UT 65 over the Wasatch Range at Big Mountain Pass (elev. 7,420 feet, closed in winter); forests of aspen, maple, and oak near the pass blaze with colors in autumn. A faster route is east on I-80 to Exit 134, then UT 65 over Big Mountain Pass. Drivers with trailers or large rigs prefer the northern approaches from I-84 Morgan Exit 103 or 104, then south on UT 66 (best route in winter) or I-84 Henefer Exit 113 or 115, then south on UT 65.

East Canyon Outfitters offers a variety of horseback rides along the Mormon Trail and other areas in the Wasatch Range. The stables are one half mile south of East Canyon State Park on UT 65, tel. 355-3460.

OGDEN

Travelers enjoy a stop here to see the museums, historic sites, and scenic spots. Ogden Canyon, beginning on the east edge of town, is the gateway to lakes, campgrounds, hiking trails, and three downhill ski areas in the Wasatch Range. Ogden lies 35 miles north of Salt Lake City at the foot of the Wasatch Range.

History

Tribes of nomadic Shoshoni Indians chose the confluence of the Weber and Ogden rivers as a winter camp because of the relatively mild climate, good fishing and hunting, and plentiful grass for their horses. This same location, the site of present-day Ogden, was also used in the winter of 1825-26 by a group of American fur trappers with their Indian wives and children. The Shoshoni maintained friendly relations with the new Americans and continued to camp in the area. Peter Skene Ogden of the British Hudson's Bay Co. explored and trapped in the upper reaches of the Ogden and Weber valleys, but he never descended to the site of the city that bears his name. In 1846, Miles Goodyear established an out-of-the-way trading post and stockade here, one of the first permanent settlements in Utah, and named it Fort Buenaventura. When Mormons arrived at the site of Salt Lake City in

1847, Goodyear, a former mountain man, felt too crowded. He sold out to the Mormons and left for California. Captain James Brown of the Mormon Battalion, who negotiated the purchase, moved in with his family. In 1849, Brigham Young visited the site, then known as Brownsville, and thought it favorable for settlement. The following year he sent 100 families to found the town of Ogden. The pioneer community suffered floods, drought, early frosts, insects, cholera, and Indian attacks, but managed to get by. At times residents had to supplement their meager harvests with roots of sego lilies, thistles, and other wild plants. Arrival of the transcontinental railroad in 1869 changed Ogden forever. Although the Golden Spike had been driven at Promontory Summit, 55 miles northwest, Ogden earned the title "Junction City" as lines branched from it through Utah and into surrounding states. New industries and an expanding non-Mormon population transformed the sleepy farm town into a bustling city. Today, Ogden (pop. 69,000) serves as a major administrative, manufacturing, and livestock center for the intermountain West.

Mormon pioneers laid out the city in their typically neat fashion, but adopted a different street-naming system. Streets running east-west are numbered beginning with 1st St. in the north of town to 47th St. in the south; streets running north-south commemorate U.S. presidents and other historical figures. The intersection of 25th St. and Washington Blvd. is usually considered the city's center.

SIGHTS

Union Station Museums

Travelers thronged into the cavernous Union Station building during the grand old days of railroading. Completed in 1924, it saw more than 120 trains stopping daily during the peak WW II years. Now, though, Union Station echoes mostly with memories. Visit the main lobby to see murals done in 1978 when the city restored the station to its former glory. The South Mural shows workers of the Central Pacific building the first transcontinental railroad from Sacramento (note the many Chinese laborers); the North Mural pictures the Union Pacific laying their line from Omaha. Special shows and performances occasionally take place in the lobby or at the M.S. Browning Theatre. The **Ogden-Weber Convention & Visitors Bureau Information Center** office supplies local travel information; open from Memorial Day weekend to Labor Day weekend Mon.-Sat. 8 a.m.-8 p.m. and Sunday 10 a.m.-7 p.m., then Mon.-Fri. 8 a.m.-5 p.m., the rest of the year; tel. 627-8288 or (800) ALL-UTAH. In the same office, the **Forest Service Information Center**, tel. 625-5306, has recreation information for its areas in the Wasatch Range; open Mon.-Fri. 8 a.m.-4:30 p.m. (and Saturday in summer). Union Station also houses the Union Grill Restaurant, a model train store, and a gift shop. The museums and small art gallery in the station are well worth a visit. A single ticket gives admission to all exhibits; purchase it from the gift shop in the lobby: $2 adult, $1 children 12 and under, and $1.50 ages 65 and over. Open Mon.-Sat. 10 a.m.-6 p.m. (also Sunday 1-5 p.m. in summer). Union Station is at 25th St. and Wall Ave., tel. 629-8444.

Browning-Kimball Car Museum displays a glittering collection of about a dozen antique autos, ranging from a one-cylinder 1901 Oldsmobile to a 16-cylinder 1930 Cadillac sports sedan. Chicago gangsters once owned the 1931 Pierce Arrow—probably the museum's most famous car; note the built-in gun holster. Car exhibits rotate about three times a year. The Utah license plate exhibit shows every tag from 1915, when they were first issued, to the present.

Wattis-Dumke Railroad Museum uses highly detailed dioramas to illustrate railroad scenes and construction feats. Eight model trains (HO scale) roll through the Ogden rail yard, wind through the Sierra and Humboldt Palisades, cross the Great Salt Lake on the Lucin Cutoff, and descend Weber Canyon. Exhibits and photos show railroading history and great trains, such as the "Big Boys" that weighed more than one million pounds and pulled heavy freights up the mountain ranges. A documentary film about the first transcontinental railroad is shown on request. Outside, just to the south of the station, you can visit giant diesel locomotives and some cabooses; ask for tour times.

The **Natural History Museum** displays beautiful rocks, minerals, and gemstones. Fossils reveal dinosaurs and other life forms of long ago. Indian artifacts and crafts can be seen too. A smoky quartz weighing 19 pounds—over 44,000 carats—is said to be the world's largest faceted stone.

Browning Firearms Museum (upstairs) contains the gun shop and many examples of firearms invented by the Browning family. John M. Browning (1855-1926), a genius in his field, held 75 major gun patents. He developed the world's first successful automatic firearms, which used gases from the bullet to expel the old shell, load a new one, and cock the mechanism. The skillfully done exhibits have both military and civilian handguns, automatic weapons, rifles, and shotguns. A 17-minute slide show illustrates the Browning family's story and their advancement of firearms design.

Myra Powell Art Gallery (also upstairs) displays paintings, sculpture, and photography in a former pigeon roost. Exhibits rotate monthly.

Historic 25th Street

The two blocks of 25th Street in front of Union Station still have many buildings from Ogden's early years. The Mormons, followed by new immigrants of many nationalities, built their grocery and hardware stores, blacksmith shops, livery stables, hotels, and restaurants here. The historic district is slowly being restored. Pick up

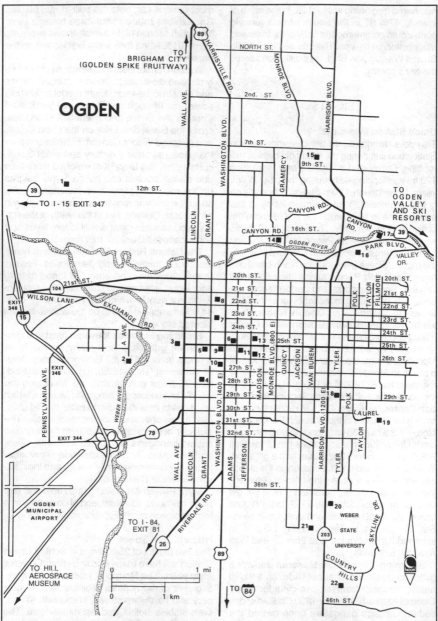

OGDEN

TO
BRIGHAM CITY
(GOLDEN SPIKE FRUITWAY)

89

HARRISVILLE RD.

NORTH ST.

2nd. ST.

7th. ST.

9th. ST.

15

WALL AVE.

WASHINGTON BLVD.

MONROE BLVD.

GRAMERCY

HARRISON BLVD.

1

39

TO I-15 EXIT 347

12th. ST.

TO
OGDEN
VALLEY
AND SKI
RESORTS

CANYON RD.

CANYON RD.

CANYON RD.

16th. ST.

14

OGDEN RIVER

PARK BLVD.

VALLEY
DR.

17

39

16

104

EXIT
346

15

21st. ST.

WILSON LANE

EXCHANGE RD.

A AVE.

LINCOLN

GRANT

WEBER RIVER

20th. ST.
21st. ST.
22nd. ST.
23rd. ST.
24th. ST.
25th. ST.

8
7
3
6
5 9
11
10
13
12

WASHINGTON BLVD. (400 E)

MADISON

MONROE BLVD. (800 E)

QUINCY

JACKSON

VAN BUREN

TYLER

POLK
TAYLOR
FILLMORE

20th. ST.
21st. ST.
22nd. ST.
23rd. ST.
24th. ST.
25th. ST.
26th. ST.

2

EXIT
345

4

27th. ST.
28th. ST.
29th. ST.
30th. ST.
31st. ST.
32nd. ST.

HARRISON BLVD. (1200 E)

POLK

TYLER

18

LAUREL

TAYLOR

29th. ST.

19

79

EXIT 344

PENNSYLVANIA AVE.

WALL AVE.

LINCOLN

GRANT

ADAMS

JEFFERSON

RIVERDALE RD.

36th. ST.

OGDEN
MUNICIPAL
AIRPORT

TO I-84,
EXIT 81

26

89

20

WEBER
STATE
UNIVERSITY

SKYLINE DR.

21

203

COUNTRY
HILLS

TO HILL
AEROSPACE
MUSEUM

0   1 mi

0   1 km

TO
84

22

46th. ST.

MOON

OGDEN

1. Ogden Nature Center
2. Fort Buenaventura
3. Union Station (museums and tourist office)
4. Marshall White Center (pool)
5. bus station (Greyhound)
6. Egyptian Theatre
7. Ogden City Mall
8. Tabernacle Square (Ogden Temple and Tabernacle, Pioneer Museum, and Miles Goodyear Cabin)
9. Municipal Gardens and local bus information booth
10. post office (downtown branch)
11. U.S. Forest Service (Ogden Ranger District)
12. Eccles Community Art Center
13. Weber County Library
14. Lorin Farr Park (pool)
15. Ben Lomond Community Pool
16. El Monte Golf Course
17. Eccles Dinosaur Park
18. Ogden Community Pool
19. Mount Ogden Park and Golf Course
20. Weber State University (entrance and information booth)
21. McKay-Dee Hospital
22. Dee Events Center

a brochure detailing histories of many of these buildings from the Golden Spike Empire tourist office in Union Station.

Egyptian Theatre

You can't miss the unusual facade of this venerable building! The interior of this "atmospheric theater" has a sun that moves across the ceiling, floating clouds, and glittering stars. Restoration is currently taking place. When done, it will be open as a performing arts theater. Contact the Information Center for opening dates.

Pioneer Museum And The Miles Goodyear Cabin

Drop in to examine the furnishings, clothes, and crafts of the Mormon pioneers. Walk behind the museum to see the Goodyear cabin, probably the oldest non-Indian structure in Utah. It was built in about 1845 of cottonwood logs and was later moved here from its original site near the

Weber River. The cabin can be seen even when the museum is closed. Pioneer Museum is open Mon.-Sat. 10 a.m.-5 p.m. from May 15 to September 15; free. The former Weber Stake Relief Society building (1902) that houses the museum is on Grant Ave. between 21st and 22nd in Tabernacle Square, tel. 393-4460.

Ogden Temple And Tabernacle

The modern temple of white cast stone and reflective glass has a central gold spire much like the Provo Temple. In fact, both temples were designed by the same architect and completed about the same time. Dedicated in January 1972, the Ogden Temple contains 283 rooms on four levels, efficiently accommodating many people while retaining a reverent atmosphere. Only Mormons engaged in sacred ordinance work may enter. The white-steepled Ogden Tabernacle, completed in 1956, sits just to the north. Visitors are welcome inside the tabernacle, when it's open; 2133 Washington Blvd. on Tabernacle Square.

Fort Buenaventura State Park

Miles Goodyear built the original Fort Buenaventura in 1846 to serve as a trading post and way station for travelers crossing the remote Great Basin region. Now a replica of the tiny fort provides a link with Utah's mountainman past. Researchers excavated the original site and pored through historical documents so that reconstruction would be authentic. The location, dimensions, and materials used for the stockade and three cabins inside closely follow the originals. Volunteers often have displays and presentations inside the cabins daily in the summer and on weekends in spring and autumn. Special programs are scheduled too. You might also catch the mountain-man rendezvous on Easter and Labor Day weekends or the pioneer skill show held on July 24. Check program schedules with the park office (tel. 621-4808) or Ogden-Weber Convention & Visitors Bureau office (tel. 627-8288). Trees and grass surrounding the fort provide a peaceful setting near downtown. The park has a picnic area and a pond, popular for canoeing in summer (rentals are available). Groups of 20 or more can reserve a campsite by calling (800) 322-3770. Open daily 8 a.m.-dark except in winter; $3 per vehicle or $1 per person walk in. From downtown Ogden, take 24th St. west across the rail yard and Weber River, turn left on "A" Ave., and follow signs to 2450 A Ave. (Ogden, UT 84401).

Eccles Community Art Center

Exhibits display the best regional paintings, sculpture, photography, and other media. Shows change monthly. The ornate mansion that houses the art center is an attraction in itself. Turrets, cut glass, and carved woodwork decorate the brick and sandstone structure, built in 1893 in a Richardsonian Romanesque style. The carriage house in back contains a sales gallery. Open Mon.-Fri. 9 a.m.-5 p.m. and Saturday 10 a.m.-4 p.m.; 2580 Jefferson Ave., tel. 392-6935.

Ogden Nature Center

The 127 acres of wildlife sanctuary on the outskirts of Ogden provide a place for children and adults to learn about nature. Trails lead through woods, wetlands, and open fields. Deer, porcupines, muskrats, rabbits, snakes, and about 130 species of birds have been spotted here. Ecology exhibits in the pioneer farmhouse include a see-through beehive and displays of local creatures and plants. Animals not ready to be released into the wild can be seen in cages outside. Visitors are welcome to use the picnic area. Call for information on summer camps and other children's programs or to arrange a tour. Open Mon.-Sat. 10 a.m.-4 p.m.; $1 ages 4

and up. Located northwest of downtown at 966 W. 12th St. (Ogden, UT 84404), tel. 621-7595.

Eccles Dinosaur Park

Life-size statues of dinosaurs make this park a favorite with many children. Exhibits are based on the most up-to-date studies of paleontologists. Real fossils are on display at the park entrance and casts of fossils are used in a children's study area where even the youngest can enjoy brushing dirt off "fossils" or participating in programs for children of all ages. Open Mon.-Sat. 10 a.m.-6 p.m. and Sunday noon-6 p.m.; $3 adult, $2 senior (62 and older), and $1 youth (5-17). Located near the entrance to Ogden Canyon at 1544 E. Park Blvd., tel. 393-DINO.

Hill Aerospace Museum

Construction of Hill Field began in 1940, just in time to serve the aircraft maintenance and storage needs of the military during the hectic WW II years. The decades since have seen a parade of nearly every type of bomber, fighter, helicopter, trainer, and missile belonging to the U.S. Air Force. About 50 of these can be seen close up in outdoor and indoor exhibits at Hill Aerospace Museum. The Stearman bi-wing trainer helped many servicemen and -women learn to fly during the late 1930s and early 1940s. The Boeing B-17 and B-29, Douglas C-47B "Skytrain," and the P-51 represent distinguished aircraft of WW II. Korean MASH units

B-29 at Hill Aerospace Museum

once relied on helicopters like the Bell TH-13T "Sioux" on display. Jet aircraft trace the development of modern aircraft right up to the superfast (Mach 3.5) SR-71 "Blackbird" strategic reconnaissance plane. The Engine Room has cutaway models of a 28-cylinder Pratt & Whitney R-4360 and several jet engines. Other exhibits inside include flight simulators, missiles, a Norden bombsight, uniforms, aircraft art, and models. The gift shop sells posters, books, T-shirts, models, and other souvenirs. Groups can arrange tours by calling in advance. Chances are you'll see jets from the adjacent air force base streaking overhead on training missions. Open all year Tues.-Fri. 9 a.m.-4:30 p.m., Saturday and Sunday 9 a.m.-5:30 p.m.; donation; tel. 777-6868/6818. Located five miles south of Ogden on I-15; take Roy Exit 341 and follow signs east 0.2 mile.

WEBER STATE UNIVERSITY

Weber (WEE-ber) State University emphasizes undergraduate education, though the four-year school also has a few graduate programs in education and business. The school began in 1889 as Weber Stake Academy under the Mormon church, then became a state-supported junior college in 1933, Weber State College in 1963, and Weber State University in 1991. It now operates on a four-quarter system with a student population of about 15,000 and faculty and staff of 1,200. The institution serves largely as a commuter university for Weber and Davis counties. Visitors are welcome on campus for the natural history museum, art gallery, library, recreational facilities, and a variety of cultural and sporting events. Obtain a free parking permit and map at the information booth along the main entrance road off 3750 Harrison Blvd. (Ogden, UT 84408), tel. 626-6975. Tours can be arranged too; tel. 626-6844. A clock tower at the center of campus makes a handy landmark, so it's hard to get lost. Weber State University is southeast of downtown on a bench of prehistoric Lake Bonneville; the Wasatch Range rises steeply behind.

Natural History Museum

This small museum has a little of everything: dioramas of native wildlife in realistic habitats, a fierce allosaurus skeleton, geology exhibits, and more. A Foucault pendulum swings in a hallway. Open weekdays 8 a.m.-5 p.m. during school terms; free. Located on the main floor of the circular Lind Lecture Hall, tel. 626-6653. The **Layton Ott Planetarium**, tel. 626-6855, presents star shows on Wednesday evenings Sept.-May.

Collett Art Gallery

Almost anything could be on display in the Collett Art Building during the late September to early June season. Open Mon.-Thurs. 8 a.m.-10 p.m. and Friday 8 a.m.-4 p.m., tel. 626-6455.

Shepherd Union Building

The social center of campus. On the first floor are the post office and bookstore (good selection of general reading, art supplies, WSU clothing and souvenirs, and topo maps of the area). On the second floor you'll find an information desk, movie theater, bowling alley, game room, and snack bar. Head to the third floor for the cafeteria and another level up for fine dining in the Sky Room (lunch and dinner).

Recreation, Sports, And Events

Swenson Gymnasium, on the south end of campus, tel. 626-6466, offers swimming, racquetball, tennis, basketball, indoor track, and weight room facilities to the public. **Wilderness Recreation Center** rents bicycles, whitewater kayaks, rafts, cross-country skis, camping gear, and other sports equipment; located next to Swenson Gymnasium, tel. 626-6373; open year-round Mon.-Fri. 9 a.m.-5 p.m., Saturday 8 a.m.-5 p.m., and Sunday 2-5 p.m. Weber State University belongs to the Big Sky Athletic Conference for men's athletics and the Mountain West Athletic Conference for women. Basketball, football, and popular concerts take place in the 12,000-seat **Dee Events Center**, tel. 626-8500. Concerts, theater, opera, and ballet performances usually take place in the **Val A. Browning Center,** tel. 626-7000.

ACCOMMODATIONS

For motels and hotels, see the chart "Ogden Accommodations."

Century Mobile Home and RV Park, 1399 W. 21st St. (I-15 Exit 346, then one block west

OGDEN ACCOMMODATIONS

Add 9.25% tax to all prices;
rates listed are for 1-2 persons

Big Z Motel; 1123 W. 21st St.; $29-31; tel. 394-6632; kitchenettes

Budget Inn; 1956 Washington Blvd.; $28-40; tel. 393-8667; kitchenettes, pool

Colonial Motel; 1269 Washington Blvd.; $27-32; tel. 399-5851

Flying J Motel; 1206 W. 21st St.; $44; tel. 393-8644 or (800) 343-8644; pool, 24-hour restaurant, store

High Country Inn (Best Western); 1335 W. 12th St.; $48-51; tel. 394-9474 or (800) 528-1234; suites, pool, spa, fitness room

Holiday Inn Ogden; 3306 Washington Blvd.; $65-71; tel. 399-5671 or (800) 999-6841; indoor pool, spa, fitness room

Millstream Motel; 1450 Washington Blvd.; $28-34; tel. 394-9425; kitchenettes

Motel Orleans; 1825 Washington Blvd.; $27-31; tel. 621-8350; kitchenettes, pool

Motel 6 Ogden; 1455 Washington Blvd.; $28-34; tel. 627-4560; pool

Motel 6 Riverdale; 5000 S. 1500 West; $34-40; tel. 627-2880; pool, tennis

Mt. Lomond Motel; 755 N. Harrisville Rd.; $66; tel. 782-7477; kitchenettes

Ogden Park Hotel (Best Western); 247 24th St.; $74-86; tel. 627-1190 or (800) 421-7599; suites, indoor pool, hot tub

Radisson Suite Hotel; 2510 Washington Blvd.; $99-109; tel. 627-1900 or (800) 333-3333; suites, health club

Sunchase Apartments; 425 Park Blvd.; $45-65; tel. 621-5744; kitchens, pool, spa, sauna, weight room

Super 8 Motel of Ogden; 1508 W. 21st St.; $33.88-36.88; tel. 731-7100 or (800) 800-8000

Travelodge Ogden; 2110 Washington Blvd.; $45-50; tel. 394-4563 or (800) 255-3050; pool

Western Colony Inn; 234 24th St.; $43-46; tel. 627-1332; kitchenettes

on Wilson Lane), tel. 731-3800, has showers, swimming pool, game room, store, and laundry. Sites are open all year: $15.84 tent or RV without hookups, $22 w/hookups. Nearby camp-

grounds are described under "Salt Lake City Accommodations," above, and in "East of Ogden" and "North of Ogden" under "Vicinity of Ogden" later in this chapter.

FOOD

American
Chick's Cafe, 319 24th St., tel. 621-9159, is a favorite breakfast spot; open Mon.-Sat. for breakfast and lunch. **Graycliff Lodge,** 508 Ogden Canyon, five miles up Ogden Canyon on the left, tel. 392-6775, serves steak and seafood in a romantic setting; open Sunday brunch and Tues.-Sun. for dinner. **Prairie Schooner,** 445 Park Blvd., tel. 392-2712, fixes steak, prime rib, and seafood in an informal Western atmosphere (dine in a covered wagon!); open daily for dinner. **Tamarack Restaurant,** 1254 W. 21st St., near I-15 21st St. Exit, tel. 393-8691, is open 24 hours daily. **Timber Mine,** 1701 Park Blvd., tel. 393-2155, serves steak and seafood in a rustic mine decor; open daily for dinner. **Ye Lion's Den,** 3607 Washington Blvd., tel. 399-5804, has steak, prime rib, and seafood in an old English atmosphere; open Mon.-Fri. for lunch and daily for dinner. **Zito's Fireside Supper Club & Steak House,** 7695 S. US 89 in South Weber, mouth of Weber Canyon at Uinta, tel. 479-4640, features steak and seafood in an elegant setting; open Mon.-Sat. for dinner. **Andy's Chuck Wagon,** 3684 Wall Ave., tel. 393-2911, offers buffet dining with over 40 entrees for lunch and dinner.

Continental
Bavarian Chalet, 4387 Harrison Blvd., across from Dee Event Center, tel. 479-7561, features German gourmet cooking; open Tues.-Sat. for dinner. **The Victorian at the Millcreek,** 1417 Washington Blvd., tel. 392-8597, serves American and continental cuisine in an elegant Victorian house; open Mon.-Fri. for lunch, and Mon.-Sat. for dinner. The **Radisson Hotel Restaurant,** 2510 Washington Blvd., tel. 627-1900, offers veal Oscar, prime rib, and other specialties; open daily for lunch and dinner. **La Ferrovia Ristorante,** 210 Historic 25th St., tel. 394-8628, presents pasta, pizza, sandwiches, and other items; open Tues.-Sat. for lunch and

dinner. **Berconi's Pasta House,** 4850 Harrison Blvd., tel. 479-4414, has a long menu of veal, seafood, and chicken specialties, pasta dishes, and pizza; open Mon.-Sat. for lunch and daily for dinner. **Piccolo Brothers Pizza and Italian Foods,** 1303 Washington Blvd., tel. 399-0618, fixes home-style Italian pasta dishes and hand-tossed pizza; open daily for dinner and takeout.

Mexican

Casa Diego, 4387 Harrison Blvd., across from Dee Event Center, tel. 479-8620, is open Mon.-Sat. for lunch and dinner. **El Matador,** 2564 Ogden Ave., tel. 393-3151, is open daily for lunch and dinner. **Fiesta Mexicana,** 236 24th St., tel. 394-3310, is open Mon.-Sat. for lunch and dinner.

Chinese

Bamboo Noodle Parlor, 2426 Grant Ave., tel. 394-6091, features steak, seafood, and noodle dishes; open Mon.-Sat. for lunch and dinner. **Ho Wah's Restaurant,** 633 Washington Blvd., tel. 627-1668, serves Chinese and American favorites; open daily for lunch and dinner. **Kim Wah's,** 350 37th St., tel. 392-7761, offers Cantonese and American dining; open daily (dinner only on Sunday, closed Tuesday. **Lee's Mongolian Barbecue,** 2866 Washington Blvd., tel. 621-9120, prepares Mongolian and Mandarin dishes; open Mon.-Sat. for lunch and dinner. **Eastern Winds Restaurant,** 3740 Washington Blvd., tel. 627-2739, serves Mandarin and Cantonese styles; open Mon.-Sat. for lunch and daily for dinner. **Star Noodle Parlor,** 225 Historic 25th St., tel. 394-0301, has popular Chinese and American dishes; open daily except Monday for dinner.

Japanese

Windy's Suki-Yaki, 3809 Riverdale Rd., tel. 621-4505, has a varied Japanese menu including teppanyaki, tempura, and sushi; open Mon.-Sat. for dinner.

OTHER PRACTICALITIES

Entertainment And Events

Ogden has a busy calendar of theater, dance, festivals, shows, and sporting events. To find out what's going on, contact the Ogden-Weber Convention & Visitors Bureau office in Union Station, tel. 627-8288.

January: Winterfest/Hof Sister City Festival celebrates winter and Ogden's German sister city Hof with ski and dogsled races and German food, music, and dancing.

February: President's Day Ski Races at Powder Mountain and Nordic Valley ski areas.

March: Golden Spike Gem and Mineral Show. Utah Gun Collectors Show. Home and Garden Show at Dee Events Center. **Para-Ski Competition** (a day of parachuting followed by a day of skiing) at Nordic Valley Ski Area.

April: Antique Show.

May: May Tenth Golden Spike Anniversary Celebration at Golden Spike National Historic Site.

June: Utah State Railroad Festival in mid-June opens with "Junction Function," a sampling of food from area restaurants, followed by handcar races, entertainment, and a model railroad fair at Union Station. **Morgala Days** (rodeo and livestock shows) in Morgan. **Utah Musical Theatre.**

July: Utah Musical Theatre continues. **Pioneer Days** (parade, rodeo, and crowning of Miss Rodeo Utah; held 19th-24th excluding Sunday). **Corps Encore** features competitions among top drum-and-bugle groups. **Vintage Car Show and Swap Meet** takes place at Liberty Park. **Ogden Street Festival and Chili Cook Off** has a 10K run, dog-trick contests, sales booths, and chili. **North Ogden Cherry Days** celebrates North Ogden's favorite crop with a parade, food booths, and contests.

August: Utah Musical Theatre continues. **Davis County Fair** puts on a horse show, horse racing, livestock sale, and exhibits. **Morgan County Fair and Rodeo** has competing cowboys and cowgirls, horse show, horse racing, livestock sale, and exhibits. **Weber County Fair** has similar activities but is one of the largest in the entire state. **Roy Days** celebrates with a parade, rodeo, and carnival. **Railroaders' Festival** at Promontory stages a reenactment of the transcontinental railroad completion with a spike-driving contest, steam engine demonstrations, and speeches at Golden Spike National Historic Site.

September: Autumnfest enlivens the month with entertainment, contests, craft exhibits, and food on the weekend after Labor Day at Union Station. **Peach Days** celebrates the harvest at Brigham City on the weekend after Labor Day. **Golden Spike Bicycle Classic** is a road race of about 85 miles from Promontory Summit to Ogden, also on the weekend after Labor Day.

Late September or early October: Greek Festival celebrates Ogden's Greek heritage with food, dancing, and entertainment at the Greek Orthodox Church of the Transfiguration (674 42nd Street).

November to December: Christmas Village Lighting Ceremony and Parade enchant kids and adults with visiting Santas, animated figures, and lighted trees at Ogden Municipal Park. **Christmas Tree Express** has exhibits and charity sales of decorated Christmas trees, holiday foods, and handicrafts at Union Station.

Recreation

Year-round swimming is offered at **Ben Lomond Community Pool,** 1049 7th St., tel. 625-1100; **Ogden Community Pool,** 2875 Tyler Ave., tel. 625-1101; and **Marshall White Center Pool,** 222 28th St., tel. 629-8346. The outdoor **Lorin Farr Community Pool,** 1691 Gramercy Ave., tel. 629-8691, is open in summer. **Wild Waters Water Slide Park,** 1750 S. 1350 West, tel. 627-3525, has still more ways to get wet in summer. **Tennis courts** are located at many parks around the city; call the Ogden Parks Dept. for the one nearest you; tel. 629-8284. The **Ogden City Recreation Dept.,** tel. 629-8253, organizes many sports and crafts programs for children and adults. **Deseret Gym,** 550 25th St., tel. 399-5861, features an indoor pool, track, weight room, basketball, racquetball, handball, and volleyball; by daily admission or membership. **Classic Skating Center Waterpark,** 4181 Riverdale Rd.; tel. 394-0822, has a roller-skating rink and water slides.

Enjoy golfing at any of these courses: 18-hole **Ben Lomond,** 1800 N. Hwy. 89, tel. 782-7754; nine-hole **El Monte,** 1300 Valley Dr. at the mouth of Ogden Canyon, tel. 629-8333; nine-hole **Golf City Family Fun Center,** 1400 E. 5600 South, tel. 479-3410 (also has a lighted 18-hole miniature golf course); 18-hole **Mt. Ogden,** 30th and Taylor, tel. 629-8700; nine-hole **Nordic Valley,** 15 miles east at 3567 Nordic Valley Way in Eden, tel. 745-3511; 18-hole **Schneiter's Riverside,** 5460 S. Weber Dr., tel. 399-4636; 18-hole **Valley View,** 2501 E. Gentile in Layton, tel. 546-1630; 18-hole **The Barn,** 305 W. Pleasant View Dr. in North Ogden, tel. 782-7320; and 18-hole **Wolf Creek,** 15 miles east at 3900 N. Wolf Creek Dr. in Eden, tel. 745-3365.

You'll find good downhill skiing in the Wasatch Range 15-19 miles east of Ogden at Nordic Valley, Snowbasin, and Powder Mountain; see "East Of Ogden," below. **Cross-country skiers** can use the easy set tracks in Mt. Ogden Park and Golf Course at 30th and Taylor or head into the mountains for more challenging terrain. The **Ogden Ranger District** office of the U.S. Forest Service, 25th and Adams Ave., tel. 625-5112 has a list of popular cross-country and snowshoeing areas. The *Wasatch Ski Touring and Hiking Map #3* by Alpentech details routes near Ogden.

Shopping

Ogden City Mall, downtown at 24th and Washington Blvd., tel. 399-1314, is a giant indoor shopping area with five department stores and about 60 smaller shops and restaurants; open daily including Sunday afternoons. The **Newgate Mall** has more than 60 stores and restaurants; open daily including Sunday afternoons in the southwest part of town at Wall Ave. and Riverdale Rd., tel. 621-1161. Outdoor supplies for camping, backpacking, mountain biking, and skiing (and rentals for both downhill and cross-country) can be obtained at **Alpine Sports,** 1165 Patterson, tel. 393-0066.

Services

In **emergencies** (police, fire, ambulance/paramedic) dial 911. Hospital care and physician referrals are provided by **McKay-Dee Hospital Center,** 3939 Harrison Blvd., tel. 627-2800, and **St. Benedict's Hospital,** 5475 S. 500 East, tel. 479-2111. Minor medical problems can be handled at **NowCare,** 335 12th St., tel. 394-7753. The downtown **post office** is at 2641 Washington Blvd., tel. 627-4184.

Information

The **Ogden-Weber Convention & Visitors Bureau Information Center** in Union Station at Wall Ave. and 25th St. (Ogden, UT 84401), tel. 627-8288 or (800) ALL-UTAH, can tell you about the sights, facilities, and goings-on for

Ogden and surrounding communities, including Davis, Morgan, and Box Elder Counties; open from Memorial Day weekend to Labor Day weekend Mon.-Sat. 8 a.m.-8 p.m. and Sunday 10 a.m.-7 p.m., then Mon.-Fri. 8 a.m.-5 p.m. the rest of the year.

Visit the **Forest Service Information Center** (Union Station) or the **Ogden Ranger District** office of the U.S. Forest Service to find out about local road conditions (or call 800-492-2400), camping, hiking, horseback riding, ski touring, snowshoeing, and snowmobiling. The district covers the Wasatch Range from Kaysville to just south of Brigham City; both offices have maps and books for sale. They are open Mon.-Fri. 8 a.m.-4:30 p.m. (and Saturday in summer at Union Station). The Forest Service Information Center is with the Visitors Bureau in Union Station at Wall Ave. and 25th St., tel. 625-5306. The district office is at 507 25th St. and Adams Ave. (Ogden, UT 84401), tel. 625-5112.

Weber County's **main library,** 2464 Jefferson Ave., has good reading; open Mon.-Thurs. 10 a.m.-9 p.m., Fri.-Sat. 10 a.m.-6 p.m., and Sunday (Oct.-May) 1-5 p.m. Call for information on the county's two branch libraries; tel. 627-6913. Weber State University has the large **Stewart Library,** tel. 626-6415/6403; hikers can make photocopies of topo maps; open Mon.-Thurs. 7:30 a.m.-midnight, Friday 7:30 a.m.-8 p.m., Saturday 9 a.m.-5 p.m., and Sunday noon-8 p.m.; open in summer and school breaks Mon.-Thurs. 7:30 a.m.-8 p.m., Friday 7:30 a.m.-6 p.m., and Saturday and Sunday 2-5 p.m.

Transportation
Utah Transit Authority (UTA) buses serve many areas of Ogden and head east to Huntsville and south to Salt Lake City and Provo; schedules operate Mon.-Sat. and have some late-night runs; one route goes several times to Salt Lake City on Sunday. UTA has an information booth at its main downtown bus stop in the city park at the corner of 25th and Washington Blvd., open weekdays noon-5 p.m., tel. 621-4636. **Greyhound** has long-distance service from the terminal at 25th and Grant Ave., tel. 394-5573.

Amtrak trains depart from Union Station east to Denver and Chicago and northwest to Portland and Seattle; other trains connect in Salt Lake City for San Francisco, Las Vegas, and Los Angeles, tel. (800) 872-7245 (information and reservations) or 627-3330 (Ogden office). Air travelers use the Salt Lake City International Airport, just 35 miles away.

Ogden has many auto rental agencies, both local and national; see the telephone Yellow Pages. **Yellow Cab,** tel. 394-9411, provides 24-hour taxi service.

VICINITY OF OGDEN

EAST OF OGDEN

Ogden Canyon

Precipitous cliffs rise thousands of feet above the narrow canyon, just barely allowing the highway and Ogden River to squeeze through. Fiery reds of maples and golden hues of oaks add color in autumn. This scenic drive deep within the Wasatch Range begins on the eastern edge of Ogden and, about six miles farther, comes out at Pineview Reservoir in the broad Ogden Valley. In winter, skiers turn south from the reservoir to Snowbasin Ski Area and north to Nordic Valley and Powder Mountain ski areas. Summer visitors have a choice of staying at swimming beaches and campgrounds on the shore of Pineview Reservoir or heading to canyons and mountain peaks of the Wasatch. For recreation and road information, contact the Forest Service Information Center, Union Station at Wall Ave. and 25th St., tel. 625-5306; or the Ogden Ranger District office, 507 25th St. and Adams Ave., tel. 625-5112, in Ogden. The canyon is reached from Ogden by heading east on 12th St. (take I-15 Exit 347).

Pineview Reservoir

This many-armed lake on the Ogden River provides excellent boating, fishing, water-skiing, and swimming. At an elevation of 4,900 feet, it is about four miles long and wide and has a surface area of 2,000 acres. Campgrounds, picnic areas, and marinas ring the shore. **Anderson Cove,** a large campground with a swimming beach on the southern shore, is eight miles east of Ogden. Camping costs $10; open Memorial Day to Labor Day weekends; sites have drinking water but no showers. Reservations can be made for family and group sites by calling (800) 280-CAMP. **Jefferson Hunt Campground** is on the South Fork of the Ogden River where it meets Pineview Reservoir, one mile east of Anderson Cove; all sites and facilities are wheelchair accessible, have drinking water, and cost $8 during the Memorial Day to Labor Day weekends season. **Bluffs Swim Area** offers sandy beaches and shaded picnic areas at Cemetery

Point on the lake's east side ($3 per vehicle, $1 per pedestrian, day-use only); a marina with boat ramp, docks, and snack bar is nearby ($3 boat launch); follow UT 39 to the Huntsville turnoff (10.5 miles east of Ogden), then turn west two miles. **Middle Inlet** is another beach area one and one half miles north of Huntsville ($3 vehicle). **Port Ramp,** tel. 745-8089, on the lake's western shore has a boat ramp, small store, dock, slips, fuel, and storage ($3 to launch or park); open daily late April to September 30. **North Arm Wildlife Viewing Trail** makes a 0.4-mile loop at the north end of the reservoir, where the North Fork of the Ogden River joins; the trail, built especially for wildlife viewing, has interpretive signs; it's off UT 162.

Abbey Of Our Lady Of The Holy Trinity

This community of 30-40 Trappist monks welcomes visitors to its chapel and reception room. The monks explain the monastery's work and sell locally produced bread, honey, and farm products. Although no tours are given, a slide show illustrates the religious life and work of the community. You may attend the Mass and chants held daily in the chapel. Quonset buildings, originally just temporary, have proved both practical and unique for nearly all the monastery's needs. The founders chose this location for its seclusion and beautiful setting. The reception room is open Mon.-Sat. 8 a.m.-noon and 1-5 p.m.; tel. 745-3784. Located four miles southeast of Huntsville at 1250 S. 9500 East; follow signs for "Monastery" from UT 39.

Ogden Valley
Accommodations And Food

Jackson Fork Inn, on UT 39 at Milepost 18 (7345 E. 900 South), tel. 745-0051, has motel rooms ($54.63-98.33), a restaurant open for Sunday brunch and daily for dinner, and a convenience store. Huntsville has a couple of places to eat and Utah's oldest bar—in business since 1879—the **Shootin' Star Saloon,** at 7350 E. 200 South. **Vue de Valhulla Bed & Breakfast,** 2787 Nordic Valley Rd., northwest of Pineview Reservoir in Liberty, UT 84310, tel. 745-2558, offers rooms for $40-45. **Wolf Lodge**

Father David Kinney at Abbey of Our Lady of the Holy Trinity

Condos/Skinner's Inc., 3720 N. Wolf Creek Dr., Eden, UT 84310, tel. 745-2621 or (800) 345-8824, offers luxury accommodations ($82-136.56) with miniature golf, tennis, swimming pools and water slide, and horseback riding. Nearby **Wolf Creek Village,** 3900 N. Wolf Creek Dr., Eden, UT 84310, tel. 745-0222 or (800) 933-9653, has condos ($87.40-125 63) and an 18-hole golf course. Several restaurants are in the Wolf Creek area. Wolf Creek is north of Pineview Reservoir on the road to Powder Mountain Ski Area.

Other Camping And Picnic Areas
The **Maples Campground** (elev. 6,200 feet) is nestled among maples and aspen in the mountains near Snowbasin Ski Area; the season lasts from late May to early September; no drinking water or charge. Drive to the ski area's lower parking lot (signed "Lower Shop"), then turn west one and one half miles on a gravel road.

Magpie Campground (elev. 5,200 feet) is the first of a series of eight recreation areas along the South Fork of the Ogden River. Magpie's sites are open from about mid-May to late October with drinking water; $7; located five and one half miles east of Huntsville on UT 39. **Botts Campground** has been a popular stopping place since pioneer days; open from about mid-May to late October with drinking water; $7; six and one half miles east of Huntsville on UT 39. **Hobble Campground** has only four sites; open from about mid-May to late October; no drinking water or charge; six and one

half miles east of Huntsville on UT 39. **South Fork Campground** is open from about mid-May to late September with drinking water; $7; seven miles east of Huntsville on UT 39. **Perception Park** offers a campground with family and group sites and a separate picnic area; open from about mid-May to late September with drinking water; $10 (picnic area is free); three group sites can be reserved (800-280-CAMP). Perception was specially built to accommodate handicapped people; seven and one half miles east of Huntsville on UT 39. **Upper and Lower Meadows and Willows** campgrounds are open mid-May to late September with drinking water; $7. All three campgrounds lie along the South Fork of the Ogden River (elev. 5,300 feet), eight miles east of Huntsville on UT 39.

Weber County Memorial Park, tel. 399-8491, is one mile down the paved road to Causey Reservoir, a narrow crescent-shaped lake in upper South Fork of the Ogden River. A paved road in the park crosses the river to individual sites (first-come, first-served; free); three group sites can be reserved with Weber County Parks and Recreation. Water is available from late May to late September. Turnoff for Causey Reservoir is one mile east of Willows Campground on UT 39. **Monte Cristo Campground** sits high in mountain forests of spruce, fir, and aspen at an elevation of 8,400 feet (between Mileposts 48 and 49, 40 miles east of Ogden, 21 miles west of Woodruff on UT 39); sites are open early July to late September with drinking water ($8). Two group sites can be reserved (800-283-CAMP). The highway summit (elev. 9,008 feet) near the campground has great panoramas. Snowmobilers find the terrain and snow in the Monte Cristo area excellent for their sport; a snowmobile trail guide can be obtained from most tourist and state park offices. **Birch Creek Campground** is a primitive BLM camping area between upper and lower Birch Creek reservoirs; no drinking water or charge. The turnoff is between Mileposts 61 and 62, 13 miles east of Monte Cristo Campground (eight miles west of Woodruff) on UT 39; go north one mile on a gravel road past the lower reservoir to the campground. Hike up the earth dam for rainbow trout fishing in the larger upper Birch Creek Reservoir (can be low in late summer).

OGDEN AREA SKIING

Snowbasin Ski Area
Skiers have been gliding down the varied terrain here since the early 1940s. Four triple and one double chairlifts serve more than 40 runs, of which 20% are rated beginner, 50% intermediate, and 30% expert. The longest run is three miles and drops 2,400 feet in elevation. Snowbasin's season usually lasts from Thanksgiving until mid-April. Adult lift tickets cost $24 full day, $20 afternoon. Snowbasin offers a ski school, ski shop, rentals, and a day lodge. Snowbasin is 17 miles southeast of Ogden; go through Ogden Canyon, continue two and one half miles past Pineview Dam, then turn right on Snowbasin Road. From the Salt Lake City area, take I-15 and US 89 to I-84, then UT 167; Box 460, Huntsville, UT 84317, tel. 399-1135/1136 (main office), 399-0198 (snow report), 399-4611 (ski school), and 399-0197 (ski shop).

Nordic Valley Ski Area
This downhill ski area is the closest to Ogden and is especially popular with families (Monday is family night). Two double chairlifts serve 16 named runs, of which 30% are beginner, 50% intermediate, and 20% expert. Elevation drop is 1,000 feet. You can ski at night too—all runs are under lights Mon.-Sat. until 10 p.m. Day skiing takes place Fri.-Sun. and all school holidays. Nordic Valley's season runs early December to late March. Adult lift tickets cost $15 full day, $13 half day, and $11 night. Nordic Valley has a ski school, ski shop, and a day lodge. Located 15 miles northeast of Ogden; go through Ogden Canyon, turn left at Pineview Dam, and follow signs; Box 478, Eden, UT 84310, tel. 745-3511.

Powder Mountain Ski Area
Two double and one triple chairlifts, each to a different peak, serve more than 30 interconnected runs; 10% are beginner, 60% intermediate, and 30% expert. Three surface tows supplement the chairlifts. High elevations of 7,600-8,900 feet catch plentiful powder snow. You can ski at night from the Sundown Lift until 10 p.m. Powder Mountain's season lasts from mid-November to late April. Adult lift tickets cost $22 all day, $17.50 half day, and $10.50 night. Facilities include a ski school, ski shops, rentals, and three day lodges. Located 19 miles northeast of Ogden; go through Ogden Canyon, turn left at Pineview Dam, and follow signs; Box 450, Eden, UT 84310, tel. 745-3771 (recording) or 745-3772 (office).

NORTH OF OGDEN

Golden Spike Fruitway
Following the old US 89 highway north to Brigham City, you'll pass many orchards. Fruit stands, open during the July to mid-September season, offer a bountiful supply of cherries, apples, peaches, pears, apricots, plums, berries, and vegetables.

Willard
This small community (pop. 1,600) is known for its fine pioneer houses. The city park has picnic tables and a playground. Willard lies at the foot of the Wasatch Range, 11 miles north of Ogden on US 89 (take I-15 Exit 360).

Willard Bay State Park
Two separate recreation areas along the eastern shore of Willard Bay provide a variety of water sports, camping, and opportunities for nature study. More than 200 species of birds have been observed near the park; common ones include the white pelican, California gull, snowy egret, western grebe, killdeer, black-

necked stilt, and American avocet; eagles visit in winter. Conditions are great for water-skiing and power boating, but only fair for sailing. Anglers catch channel catfish, smallmouth bass, bluegill, crappie, and walleye. Winter visitors find good ice fishing in the bay from mid-December to late February. Only two miles of Willard Bay's 15-mile circumference are natural shoreline. Dikes enclose nearly all of the bay to keep out salt-water from the Great Salt Lake, just to the west. Canals carry water into the bay during winter and spring, then out for irrigation during the growing season. Park fees are $3 day use, $9 camping ($10 Friday, Saturday, and holidays). Contact Willard Bay State Park at 900 W. 650 North, Box A, Willard, UT 84340, tel. 734-9494 (ranger) or (800) 322-3770 (reservations).

North Marina features a sandy swimming beach, campground with showers, boat ramp, and dock. The developed campground's season is normally April 1 (Easter if in March) to October 31, but an overflow area on the shore stays open all year. Reservations are recommended on summer weekends and holidays. North Marina is just west of I-15 Willard Exit 360.

South Marina has a boat ramp, docks, and campground with showers. The area is set up mostly for day use, as the open grassy areas used for camping lack designated sites. The dikes on this part of the bay prevent beaches and lake views, but you won't be so crowded here on summer weekends and the camp-ground nearly always has room. South Marina is open April 1 (Easter if in March) to October 31,

no reservations are taken here. Access is from I-15 Exit 354, then follow signs west two and one half miles.

BRIGHAM CITY

Peaks of the Wasatch Range exceeding 9,000 feet form the backdrop to this city of 22,400 people, 21 miles north of Ogden. Pioneers set-tled along Box Elder Creek in 1851, naming both the creek and town for the trees growing here. Five years later they renamed their com-munity to honor Mormon church president Brigham Young. Brigham City serves as Box Elder County seat and a center for surround-ing fruit orchards, truck farms, and ranches. Historic displays in the **Brigham City Museum-Gallery** show how residents lived in the 19th century. The art gallery, 24 N. 300 West, tel. 723-6769, features changing shows by Utah and local artists; open Tues.-Fri. 11 a.m.-6 p.m. and Saturday 1-5 p.m.; free. The **Brigham City Depot**, 833 W. Forest, tel. 723-2989, a turn-of-the-century railroad station, is being lovingly re-stored to its original condition, with separate waiting rooms for each gender and many an-tiques from railroading in the old days. The goal is to have a steam-powered passenger train running from Ogden to the Golden Spike His-toric Site with depots at Brigham City and Corinne by May 10, 1996, an ambitious project with existing track wide gauge and available lo-comotives narrow guage, but the same people

Box Elder Tabernacle

horse pull (pony class) at the Box Elder County Fair

are involved that pushed the historic site into being. Many people think the Mormon **Box Elder Tabernacle,** 251 S. Main St, tel. 723-5376, to be Utah's most beautiful building. Construction took place from 1865 to 1890. Six years later the tabernacle burned; the present structure dates from 1897. Gothic arched windows and doors, a soaring white steeple, and 16 smaller spires make the stone and brick structure distinctive. Tours are conducted in the tabernacle daily 9 a.m.-9 p.m. from May 1 to October 31.

Practicalities
Main Street, which runs north-south through Brigham City, has eight motels and a variety of restaurants. **Golden Spike RV Park,** 905 W. 1075 South, tel. 723-8858, has camping sites at $14.17 for tents, vans, or campers and $18.53-19.62 for RVs w/hookups. Grounds include showers, store, and laundry; may close in winter. **Brigham City KOA,** four miles south of Brigham City on US 89 (near I-15 Willard Exit 360), tel. 723-5503, offers sites for tents and RVs ($14.75 no hookups, $17.75 w/hookups) with showers, pool, store, and laundry; open March 1 to November 15. Other nearby places to camp are at Willard Bay State Park (see above) and Mantua Reservoir (see below). **Maddox Ranch House,** one and one half miles south on US 89, tel. 723-8545, is a popular dining spot south of town for steak, chicken, and trout; open Tues.-Sat. for lunch and dinner. During **Golden Spike Days** in May the city has historic art exhibits in the museum, the Golden Spike Parade, and other festivities. **Box Elder**

County Fair and Rodeo in late August at nearby Tremonton features a parade, rodeo, horse pulling, livestock judging, and varied exhibits. Brigham City celebrates the harvest during **Peach Days** on the weekend after Labor Day with a parade, entertainment, carnival, art show, Peach Queen Pageant, and a footrace. From May-Sept. Hwy. 89 from Brigham City to Ogden is known as the **Box Elder Fruitway** because of all the fruit stands selling peaches, cherries, blackberries, corn, pumpkins, and melons, to name just a few.

Box Elder Natatorium has an indoor pool, basketball court, and weight room at Box Elder High School, 380 S. 600 West, tel. 723-2622. An outdoor swimming pool is in **Pioneer Park** at 800 W. Forest, tel. 723-2711. **John Adams Park** has picnicking, playground, and tennis courts at 100 North and 500 East. The 18-hole **Eagle Mountain Golf Course** is at 960 East 700 South, tel. 723-3212. **Brigham City Community Hospital** is at 950 S. 500 West, tel. 734-9471. The **Chamber of Commerce,** 6 N. Main St., tel. 723-3931, will answer your questions about the area and offer a three hour tour of the historic city and surrounding area; open Mon.-Fri. 9 a.m.-noon and 1-4 p.m. The **city library,** 26 E. Forest, tel. 723-5850, is open Mon.-Saturday.

VICINITY OF BRIGHAM CITY

Bear River Migratory Bird Refuge
Millions of birds drop in to feed or nest in the freshwater marshes created by the intersection of the Bear River and the Great Salt Lake.

About 60 species nest in the refuge. In pioneer days, reports told of flocks of waterfowl that blackened the sky. Flooding in the late 1980s closed the area and displaced many birds until receding waters allowed it to reopen in 1990. At press time a four-mile loop gravel road was open to visitors. Head west 15 miles on Forest St. from Brigham City on a partly paved road. The refuge office in town has a bird list, a short video shown on request, and information at 866 S. Main in Breitenbeker's Plaza (Brigham City, UT 84302), tel. 723-5887; open Mon.-Fri. 8 a.m.-4:30 p.m.

Mantua Reservoir

This 554-acre reservoir beside the town of Mantua is popular for fishing, boating, and picnicking. From Brigham City, follow US 89/91 east four miles up Box Elder Canyon. **Box Elder Campground** (U.S. Forest Service) is just west of the reservoir; open with drinking water from mid-May to late September ($8); some sites can be reserved, tel. 800-280-CAMP. The adjacent picnic areas are free. **Mount Haven RV Park,** in Mantua at 130 N. Main St., tel. 723-7615/1292, has tent ($9.75) and RV ($12 w/hookups) spaces with showers and a store; open early April to late September. Visitors are welcome to view the native cutthroat and lake trout at **Mantua Fish Hatchery,** one mile southeast of Mantua; open daily 8 a.m.-5 p.m. Exhibits show how the trout are obtained as eggs at Bear Lake and returned a year later after growing to a five-inch length. All of the one million trout produced annually go to Bear Lake.

Inspiration Point

Beginning as Main Street in Mantua, unpaved Forest Route 084 leads south 14 miles to Inspiration Point (elev. 9,422 feet) and dizzying views across the Great Salt Lake and much of northern Utah; mountains in Nevada, Idaho, and Wyoming can be spotted on a clear day. Limber pine grow near the summit and subalpine fir lower down. The road is rough in spots, though cars with good clearance can make it to the top in dry weather. Keep left at the three-way fork two and one half miles from Mantua; see the Wasatch-Cache National Forest map. **Willard Basin Campground** (elev. 9,000 feet) is two miles before Inspiration Point; open about early June to mid-September; no water or fee.

Skyline Trail begins from Willard Basin and winds south to the summit of Ben Lomond (elev. 9,712 feet) and other peaks, then to North Ogden Pass and finally Pineview Reservoir, 22 miles away. Or you could start hiking from Inspiration Point. Other trails branch off Skyline too; see the Mantua, North Ogden, and Huntsville 7½-minute topo maps. For more information, contact the **Ogden Ranger District** office at 507 25th St. and Adams Ave. in Ogden, tel. 625-5112.

Crystal Springs

The water park features hot mineral baths, water slide rides, and a freshwater swimming pool. You can visit the snack bar (summer weekends only) or bring your own picnic. Crystal Springs stays open all year: in summer, Mon.-Thurs. 10 a.m.-9 p.m., Friday and Saturday 10 a.m.-10 p.m., and Sunday 10 a.m.-7 p.m.; in winter, Sunday noon-7 p.m., Mon.-Thurs. 1-9 p.m., Friday 1-10 p.m., and Saturday 10 a.m.-10 p.m. Admission is $4.50 adult ($3.50 children 3-12 and seniors) or $8 with the water slide; tel. 279-8104. A campground with showers has tent spaces ($9) and RV sites ($9 no hookups, $13 w/hookups); open early May to late September. Crystal Springs is one mile north of Honeyville, so named because this spot reminded settlers of a biblical land flowing with milk and honey. From Brigham City, go north 10 miles on UT 69 or take I-15/84 Honeyville Exit 375.

Tremonton

This agricultural center 15 miles northwest of Brigham City was settled in 1888 and named for Tremont, Illinois. **North Box Elder County Museum,** 150 S. Tremont, tel. 257-3371, has historic exhibits and Indian artifacts; open in summer Mon.-Fri. 8 a.m.-4 p.m., then Mon.-Fri. 9 a.m.-5 p.m. the rest of the year; free admission. Three motels are in town: **Marble Motel,** 116 N. Tremont, tel. 257-3524, $29.42 s, $33.79 d; **Sandman Motel,** 585 W. Main, tel. 257-5675, $31.61 s, $38.15 d; and **Western Inn,** 2301 W. Main at I-84 Exit 40, tel. 257-3399, $42.51 s, $45.78 d. A selection of restaurants is scattered around town too. **Box Elder County Fair and Rodeo** in late August features a parade, rodeo, horse pulling, livestock judging, and varied exhibits. **Bear River Valley Hospital** provides medical services at 440 W. 600 North, tel. 257-

7441. For information about the area, visit the **information desk** in the Tremonton Community Center, 150 S. Tremont (Tremonton, UT 84337), tel. 257-3371. The **public library** is open Mon.-Sat. at 200 N. Tremonton.

Belmont Springs

Hot springs have been developed into a swimming pool and hot tubs, a nine-hole golf course, and a campground. Volleyball and horseshoe equipment are available too. Belmont Springs is 10 miles north of Tremonton and one mile south of Plymouth, tel. 458-3200. The season at this small resort runs early May to early October. Open 9 a.m.-9 p.m.; golf hours are 8:30 a.m. until dark. Admission to the pool and hot tubs is $4 adult, $2.50 children; camping costs $8 no hookups and $14 w/hookups (ask about tent rates).

Corinne

The location beside the Bear River and along the transcontinental railroad seemed ideal in 1869, when Corinne's founders laid out the town. Banks, freight companies, and mining concerns based themselves at the promising new site. A steamboat service began ferrying ore across the Great Salt Lake to a mill and smelter at Corinne. The population swiftly rose to the 2,000 mark as business boomed. Saloons, dance halls, and "soiled doves" entertained the largely non-Mormon population and prompted Brigham

Young to declare the town off limits to his followers. Corinne became the Gentile capital of Utah and a hotbed of political opposition to the Mormon church. Yet the "curse of Corinne" kept the town from realizing its dreams. Lowering lake levels grounded the steamboat business, a diphtheria epidemic killed many citizens, appeals for political support from the U.S. Congress failed, and, finally, the railroads chose the Mormon city of Ogden as their junction point. Today Corinne is a sleepy farm town with a few old buildings from its past. The Methodist church, corner of S. Sixth St. and Colorado, dates from 1870 and is believed to be the first non-Mormon church built in Utah. Corinne is five miles west of Brigham City on the way to Golden Spike National Historic Site.

GOLDEN SPIKE NATIONAL HISTORIC SITE

At 12:47 p.m. on May 10, 1869, rails from the East and West met for the first time. People across the country closely followed telegraph reports as dignitaries and railway officials made their speeches and drove the last spikes, then everyone broke out in wild celebration. The joining of rails at this windswept pass in Utah's Promontory Mountains marked a new chapter in the growth of the United States. A transcontinental railroad at last linked both sides of the nation. The far western frontier would be a fron-

119 and Jupiter at Golden Spike N.H.S.

GOLDEN SPIKE NATIONAL HISTORIC SITE

Bottled spirits help celebrate the laying of the Golden Spike.

tier no more. Swift-moving Army troops would soon put an end to Indian troubles. Vast resources of timber, mineral wealth, and farmland lay open to development.

History

The Central Pacific and Union Pacific railroads, eager for land grants and bonuses, had been laying track at a furious pace and grading the lines far ahead. So great was the momentum that the grader crews didn't even stop when they met, but laid parallel grades for 250 miles across Utah. Finally Congress decided to join the rails at Promontory Summit and stop the wasteful duplication of effort. A ragged town of tents, box cars, and hastily built wooden shacks sprang up along a single muddy street. Outlaws and crooked gambling houses earned Promontory Summit an awful reputation as a real "hell-on-wheels town." That ended six months later when the railroads moved the terminal operations to Ogden. Soon only a depot, roundhouse, helper engines, and other rail facilities remained. The Lucin Cutoff across the

Great Salt Lake in 1904 bypassed the long twisting grades of Promontory Summit and dramatically reduced traffic along the old route. The final blow came in 1942 when the rails were torn up for scrap to feed wartime industries.

Visitor Center

The Golden Spike National Historic Site, authorized by Congress in 1965, re-creates the momentous period of railroad history that took place here. The visitor center has excellent exhibits and programs that illustrate the difficulties of building the railroad and portray the officials and workers who made it possible. A short slide show introduces Promontory Summit's history. The 20-minute program, *The Golden Spike,* presents a more detailed account of building the transcontinental railroad. Other related films are shown too. Rangers give talks several times a day in summer. An exhibit room has changing displays on railroading. Historic markers behind the visitor center indicate the spot where the last spike was driven.

The annual Last Spike Ceremony reenacts

GOLDEN SPIKE CEREMONY

In grade school, many of us learned that when the Union Pacific and Central Pacific railroads met, a solid-gold ceremonial stake was driven to mark the spot. One yearns to go to Promontory and pry out that golden spike. But the real story tells us the event was marked with no less than two golden spikes, both from California; a silver spike contributed by the state of Nevada; and an iron spike with its body plated silver and cap plated gold, courtesy of the state of Arizona.

A polished myrtle-wood tie was placed at the site to receive the spikes, protecting the precious metals from the damage of driving them into the earth. At the ceremony, Central Pacific President Leland Stanford (founder of Stanford University) took the first swing at the final spike, missing it entirely—but hitting the tie. Union Pacific vice president and general manager Thomas C. Durant next tried his hand, missing not only the spike but the rail and tie as well. A bystander was finally summoned from the crowd to tap the stake home.

Shortly after the formal ceremony concluded, the valuable spike and tie were removed and standard fittings were substituted to link the nation by rail.

the original celebration every May 10th with great fanfare. The Railroaders' Festival on a Saturday in August has special exhibits, a spike-driving contest, reenactments, handcar races, and entertainment. The visitor center is open daily 8 a.m.-6 p.m. Memorial Day to Labor Day weekends and 8 a.m.-4:30 p.m. the rest of the year; closed Thanksgiving, Christmas, and New Year's Day. Admission is $4 vehicle or $2 adult, whichever is less. A sales counter offers a good selection of books on railroading, Utah history, and natural history, as well as postcards and souvenirs. Motels and restaurants are in Brigham City and Tremonton. From the I-15 Brigham City Exit 368, head west on UT 13 and UT 83 and follow signs 29 miles. (Mailing address: Box 897, Brigham City, UT 84302, tel. 471-2209.)

The Locomotives

The two locomotives that met here in 1869, Central Pacific's Jupiter and Union Pacific's 119, succumbed to scrapyards around the turn of the

century. However, they have been born again as authentic replicas. Every day in summer the trains steam along a short section of track from the Engine House to the historic spot.

Promontory Trail Auto Tour

Imagine you're riding the rails across Utah a century ago. This scenic drive follows the old grades past many construction feats of hardworking railway men. You'll see the parallel grades laid by the competing Union Pacific and Central Pacific, clearings for sidings, original rock culverts, and many cuts and fills. Wildflowers, grass-covered hills, and views over the blue Great Salt Lake appear much the same as they did to early train travelers. A booklet available at the visitor center describes the features and history at numbered stops on the drive. Allow about one and a quarter hours for the complete tour. If time is short, drive along just the west section (45 minutes) or the east section (30 minutes).

Big Fill Walk

An easy one and one half mile roundtrip at the east end of the driving tour leads farther down a railroad grade to the famous Big Fill and Big Trestle sites. Rugged terrain on this side of the Promontory Mountains posed some of the greatest construction challenges to either line. The Central Pacific tackled an especially deep ravine here with a massive fill, 170 feet deep and 500 feet long, requiring about two months of work by 500 men and 250 teams of animals. The Union Pacific, pressed for time, threw together a temporary trestle over the gorge, paralleling the Big Fill.

VICINITY OF GOLDEN SPIKE NATIONAL HISTORIC SITE

Promontory Point

This peninsula that juts into the Great Salt Lake has no connection with the first transcontinental railroad, but it does make a pleasant scenic drive. A paved road follows the eastern shore of the peninsula below the Promontory Mountains for 22.5 miles, then becomes gravel for the last 17.5 miles around to the west side. There are good views of the Great Salt Lake,

Wasatch Range, and the Lucin Cutoff railroad causeway. Lake Crystal Salt Co. at road's end was a salt extraction plant (no longer in operation). There's no hiking or camping on Promontory Point as the land has been fenced and signed No Trespassing. The Promontory Point road turnoff is six miles east of the Golden Spike Visitor Center.

Thiokol

Many buildings of this giant aerospace corporation lie scattered across the countryside about six miles northeast of the historic site. You're not likely to be allowed to tour the facility, but you can see a group of missiles, rocket engines, and a space shuttle booster casing in front of administrative offices. Turn north two miles on UT 83 at the junction with the Golden Spike National Historic Site road (eight miles east of the visitor center).

Promontory Branch
Of The Central Pacific Railroad

Adventurous motorists, mountain bikers, and hikers can follow sections of the historic railroad grade west 89 miles from Golden Spike National Historic Site to Lucin, near the Nevada border. Signs along the way describe histories of townsites, sidings, and natural features in this austerely beautiful land. You may see small herds of pronghorn. Only cemeteries, foundations, and debris remain at such former towns as Kelton (1869-1942), Terrace (1869-1910), and historic Lucin (1875-1907).

Cars can do the 11-mile section of county road (gravel) between the junction near Locomotive Springs (20 miles southwest of Snowville) and Kelton. You'll need dry weather and a 4WD, high-clearance vehicle for other sections of the railroad grade. The grade west of Kelton into the Peplin Mountains has a hazardous section that may be closed to motor vehicles. A trestle between East Lake and West Lake historic sites, about 10 miles west of Golden Spike National Historic Site may be difficult; one driver got across by laying down boards in front of his tires! Many of the other old bridges have washed out, so you'll need to take the dirt tracks that bypass them. Hazards to watch out for include wet conditions (mud or quicksand), washouts, flat tires from nails (two spare tires

are recommended), and unmaintained bridges.

Only a few junctions have signs, but the railroad grade is always distinct. Drivers need to be experienced at backroad travel and have emergency supplies for this remote region. County roads connect with the railroad grade at many places. Roads to Kelton and Lucin branch south off UT 30, for example. A 47-mile gravel road also connects Lucin with I-80 Exit 4 near Wendover (from Wendover, head north 1.2 miles on the paved road, then turn left toward Lebby Pass). The Northern Utah map of the Utah Travel Council series has fair coverage of the area. Better yet are the USGS 1:100,000 series maps. The Bureau of Land Management's Salt Lake District office, tel. 977-4300, has information on the railroad grade. Staff at Golden Spike National Historic Site may know of road conditions too.

THE NORTHWEST CORNER

Raft River Mountains
(Sawtooth National Forest)

Few Utahans know about these mountains in the northwest corner of the state, despite their pretty alpine scenery. Panoramic views from the top take in the Great Salt Lake, barren desert, farmlands, and many mountains of Utah, Nevada, and Idaho. The range runs east-west, something of a rarity in the region. The summit ridge isn't what you'd expect either—it's a long ridge of gently rolling grasslands. Bull Mountain (elev. 9,931 feet) crowns the range, though it's hard to pick out from all the other grassy knolls! Hikers haven't discovered the range—you'll find pristine forests and canyons but no real trails. Aspen, Douglas fir, subalpine fir, and limber pine thrive in the canyons and northern slopes below the summit ridge. Ranchers run cattle on the top and other meadow areas. A 4WD road climbs the mountains from Yost. For information, contact the **Burley Ranger District** of the Sawtooth National Forest, 2621 S. Overland Ave., Burley, ID 83318, tel. (208) 678-0430.

Clear Creek Campground (elev. 6,400 feet) has sites in a beautiful setting below the north slope of the Raft River Range. Aspen and alders grow in the campground and deer aren't at all shy about dropping in to browse. Hand pumps and springs are in the campground, but it's best to bring your own drinking water; open early June to mid-October; free. Located 35 miles west of Snowville; take I-84 Exit 5 and go west 25 miles on UT 42 to Strevell (just into Idaho), turn left three and one half miles on the gravel road signed "Yost," then turn left (south) six miles on a gravel road to the campground.

Hikers will see the best scenery and forests on the Lake Fork route from the north. Drive to Clear Creek Campground, follow a jeep road

from the gate at the end of the campground south about one and one quarter miles to a stream ford, then turn right two and one half miles up Lake Fork Canyon. Use a map to make sure you're in the correct canyon; the Park Valley 15 minute topo map is best. Walk along the stream or follow deer trails to a marshy area with some small ponds. Bull Basin Lake lies a short distance upstream in a rugged cirque. To reach Bull Mountain, return to the marsh and look for a small trail climbing the

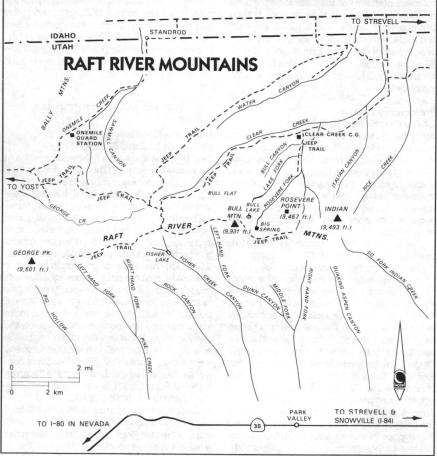

© MOON PUBLICATIONS, INC.

rocky slope to the west. You'll come out on the grassy ridge and meet the jeep road; Bull Mountain is about one-half mile to the southwest. Many other climbing routes are possible too. Nearly all hiking is done from the north; land south of the summit belongs to ranchers who prohibit hikers because the cattle are easily spooked.

Park Valley

Travelers can easily cross the lonely country of Utah's northwest corner on paved highways UT 42 and UT 30. Park Valley, south of the Raft River Mountains, has a small store and gas station (closed Sunday), the **Overland Trail Motel,** tel. 871-4755 (open all year; $30-35), and a cafe (closed Sunday).

LOGAN AND VICINITY

Logan (pop. 32,500) lies surrounded by lush farmlands of the Cache Valley to the west and lofty peaks of the Bear River Range to the east. Terraces mark ancient shorelines of Lake Bonneville in Logan and other places around Cache Valley. Plentiful water from the Logan River, named for the early trapper Ephraim Logan, made this site a good choice for the valley's largest settlement. Travelers enjoy the city because of its many trees, parks, and historic buildings. Utah State University adds considerably to the culture, sports, spirit, and population of the community. The mountains provide abundant year-round recreation, including scenic drives, camping, fishing, hiking, cross-country ski touring, and downhill skiing.

History

Mountain men tramped through Utah's northernmost lands in search of beaver and other fur-bearing animals as early as 1819. They found good trapping near Cache Valley and stayed for several seasons, holding one rendezvous here and two at nearby Bear Lake. The fur trappers often stored their valuable pelts in a cache (French for hiding place), for which the valley was later named. Cold winters and hostile Indians dis-

couraged permanent settlement in the area until 1856, when a small group of Mormons established Maughan's Fort (now Wellsville). Uncertainties caused by the Utah War delayed the founding of Logan and other communities another three years. Farms, dairy industries, and livestock raising begun in the early years continue to be an important part of Logan's economy today.

SIGHTS

Mormon Temple And Tabernacle

The distinctive castellated temple rises from a prominent hill just east of downtown. After Brigham Young chose this location in 1877, church members labored seven years to complete the temple. Architect Truman O. Angell, designer of the Salt Lake Temple, oversaw construction. Timber and blocks of limestone came from nearby Logan Canyon. Only Mormons engaged in sacred work may enter the temple, but visitors are welcome on the grounds to view the exterior. Located two blocks east of Main St. at 175 N. 300 East.

The tabernacle also stands as a fine example of early Mormon architecture. Construction of the stone structure began in 1865, but other priorities—building the temple and ward meetinghouses—delayed dedication until 1891. The public may enter when it's open; downtown at Main and Center streets.

Cache Valley Historical Museum (Daughters Of The Utah Pioneers Museum)

Exhibits show how Logan's early settlers lived. You'll see their tools, household furnishings, clothing, art, and photographs. Free admission; open Tues.-Fri. 10 a.m.-4 p.m. in summer and by appointment the rest of the year. The museum and Bridgerland office are both downtown at 160 N. Main, tel. 752-5139. More of Logan's history can be seen on a walking tour; ask for the self-guided, 45-minute *Logan's Historic Main Street* from the Bridgerland office.

Willow Park Zoo

This small zoo displays exotic birds such as the Andean condor, golden pheasant, mitered

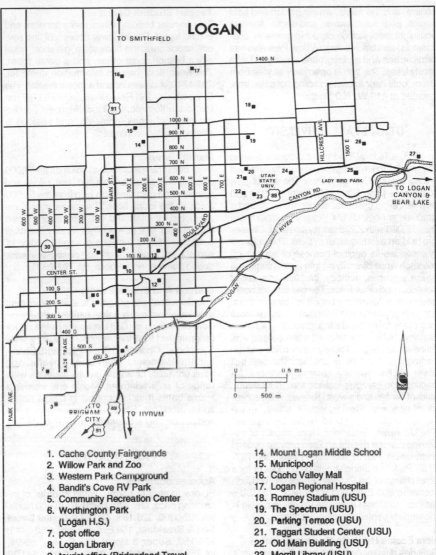

LOGAN

TO SMITHFIELD

1400 N

1000 N
900 N
800 N
700 N
600 N
500 N
400 N
300 N
200 N
100 N

CENTER ST.
100 S
200 S
300 S
400 S
500 S
600 S

BASE TRACK

UTAH STATE UNIV.
LADY BIRD PARK
CANYON RD.
LOGAN RIVER
BOULEVARD

TO LOGAN CANYON & BEAR LAKE

TO BRIGHAM CITY
TO HYRUM

PARK AVE.

0   0.5 mi
0   500 m

1. Cache County Fairgrounds
2. Willow Park and Zoo
3. Western Park Campground
4. Bandit's Cove RV Park
5. Community Recreation Center
6. Worthington Park (Logan H.S.)
7. post office
8. Logan Library
9. tourist office (Bridgerland Travel Region/Cache-Rich Tourist Council)
10. Mormon Tabernacle
11. Bicentennial Park
12. Central Park
13. Mormon Temple
14. Mount Logan Middle School
15. Municipool
16. Cache Valley Mall
17. Logan Regional Hospital
18. Romney Stadium (USU)
19. The Spectrum (USU)
20. Parking Terrace (USU)
21. Taggart Student Center (USU)
22. Old Main Building (USU)
23. Merrill Library (USU)
24. Harrison Museum of Art (USU)
25. Logan Ranger District (U.S. Forest Service)
26. Logan Golf and Country Club
27. Canyon Entrance Park

© MOON PUBLICATIONS, INC.

conure, and the more familiar golden and bald eagles, peacocks, swans, and ducks. Animals you might meet include capuchin monkeys, coatimundis, and black bears. Willow Park also has picnic areas and a playground among its large shady trees. The zoo is open daily all year from 8 a.m. until dark except on some holidays; free. Located at 419 W. 700 South.

UTAH STATE UNIVERSITY

In 1888, a federal land-grant program opened the way for the territorial legislature to establish the Agricultural College of Utah. The school grew to become Utah State University in 1957 and now has eight colleges, 45 departments, and a graduate school. USU's "Aggies" number more than 17,000 with 2,275 faculty and staff. Classes are held on a four-quarter system. The university continues its original purpose of agricultural research while diversifying into atmospheric and space sciences, ecology, creative arts, social sciences, and other fields. The campus sits northeast of downtown on a bench left by a northern arm of prehistoric Lake Bonneville. Large maples and other trees shade the grounds. Old Main Building, begun one year after the college was founded, has housed nearly every office and department at one time or another. The high bell tower of Old Main is a campus landmark. Attractions on campus include the art museum, student center, and several libraries. A full schedule of concerts, theater, lecture series, art exhibits, and sports competitions fills the calendar. The University Relations Dept. knows of upcoming cultural events and can provide general information; Room 102 in Old Main, tel. 797-1158. Park free along streets off campus or for a small charge at the Parking Terrace on 700 North (between 800 East and 900 East). Try USU's famous Traditional Aggie Ice Cream, available in the student center and other locations.

Nora Eccles Harrison Museum Of Art

Galleries display ceramics from the museum's permanent collection and changing exhibitions of paintings, sculpture, ceramics, prints, drawings, and photography. Open Tues.-Fri. 10:30 a.m.-4:30 p.m. (to 9 p.m. Wed.), Sat.-Sun. 2-5 p.m.; free. On campus at 650 N. 1100 East, tel. 797-1412.

Taggart Student Center

This popular building offers many services and places to eat. On the lower floor you'll find several snack bars, the book store, gift shop, ticket office branch, post office, and a game room. The main floor has an information desk, tel. 797-1710, a cafeteria, and a movie theater. The Skyroom Garden Restaurant, tel. 797-1767, on the fourth floor serves lunch Mon.-Fri.; a dinner menu of steak, prime rib, and seafood is offered Friday evenings.

Merrill Library

More than one million bound volumes and 7,000 different periodicals are housed here. Hikers and travelers can plan trips with help from the 51,000 maps on the fourth floor. The special collections are noted for Utah and Western history. Open Mon.-Thurs. 7 a.m.-midnight, Friday 7 a.m.-9 p.m., Saturday 9 a.m.-9 p.m., and Sunday 11 a.m.-9 p.m.; shorter hours and closed weekends during summer and breaks; tel. 797-2633.

Cultural And Sports Events

The Convocations program features prominent speakers from many fields; usually held Thursdays at 12:30 p.m. Call University Relations for program and location; tel. 797-1158. The USU Symphony, Chorale, Symphonic Band, Chamber Music Society, Utah State Theatre, and other university or visiting groups present a wide range of entertainment. Men's and women's teams battle their opponents in USU's active sports programs. For ticket information to sports and performing arts events, call 797-0305.

PRACTICALITIES

Accommodations

Places to stay in Logan, listed in order of increasing price, are: **Alta Motel,** 51 E. 500 North, tel. 752-6300, $26.16 s, $30.52 d; **Center Street Bed & Breakfast,** 169 E. Center, tel. 752-3443, $25-158; **Super 8 Motel,** 865 S. Hwy. 89-91, tel. 753-8883 or 800-800-8000, $35.92 s, $41.38 d; **Days Inn,** 364 S. Main, tel. 753-5623 or 800-325-2525, $39.33 s, $43.70 d; **Baugh Motel (Best Western),** 153 S. Main, tel. 752-5220 or 800-462-4154, $41.52 s, $45.89 d; **Comfort Inn,** 447 N. Main, tel. 752-9141 or 800-221-2222, $41.52 s, $45.89 d; and **Weston Inn**

(Best Western), 250 N. Main, tel. 752-5700 or (800) 528-1234, $43.70 s, $50.26 d.

Campgrounds

Riverside RV Park, turn east on 1700 South from US 89/91, tel. 752-9830, is open year-round just south of town with showers and laundry; $9.81 tent or RV no hookups, $16.35 RV w/hookups. **Western Park Campground,** 350 W. 800 South (signs point the way from S. Main), tel. 752-6424, offers basic facilities year-round including showers; $10 tents and RVs no hookups, $12 RVs w/hookups. **Bandit's Cove RV Park,** 590 1/2 S. Main, tel. 753-0508, has sites year-round for tents and RVs ($7 no hookups, $15 w/hookups); showers and a pizza restaurant. **Country Cuzzins RV Park,** 1936 N. Main, tel. 752-1025, is open all year with campsites, a laundromat, convenience store, and hot showers; $6 tent or RV no hookups, $14 w/hookups. **Hyrum State Park** offers camping, swimming, fishing, and boating seven miles south near the town of Hyrum; see "Hyrum State Park" under "Vicinity of Logan," below. The U.S. Forest Service has many campgrounds beginning six miles east of town on US 89 in Logan Canyon; see "Logan Canyon," below.

Food

Like any college town, Logan has a full array of pizza and fast-food places, you'll find most of them along N. Main. Restaurants serving American fare include: **Angie's Restaurant,** 690 N. Main, tel. 752-9252, open daily for breakfast, lunch, and dinner; **Blue Goose,** 1 N. Main, tel. 752-0619, open Mon.-Sat. for lunch and dinner; **Cottage Restaurant,** 51 W. 200 South, tel. 752-5260, open daily for breakfast and lunch, Mon.-Sat. for dinner; **Frontier Pies Restaurant,** 43 E. 1400 North, tel. 752-9280, open daily for breakfast, lunch, and dinner; and **Glauser's Restaurant,** 25 W. Center, tel. 752-1681, open Mon.-Sat. for breakfast, lunch, and dinner.

Steak and seafood top the menu at **The Bluebird,** 19 N. Main, tel. 752-3155, open Mon.-Sat. for breakfast, lunch, and dinner; **DeVerle's Juniper Inn,** 4088 N. Main, tel. 563-3622, open Tues.-Sat. for lunch and dinner; the **Sizzler,** 1065 N. Main, tel. 752-2771, open daily for lunch and dinner; the **Golden Corral,** 1114 N. Main, tel. 753-2611, open daily for lunch and dinner;

and the **Zanavoo Lodge Restaurant,** 4880 E. Hwy. 89 in Logan Canyon, tel. 752-0085, open Mon.-Sat. for dinner. A **JJ North's Grand Buffet** will open in Pinecrest Village Shopping Center at the northeast corner of Main at 1400 North.

Gia's Restaurant, 119 S. Main, tel. 752-8384, open Mon.-Sat. for lunch and dinner, specializes in fine Italian cuisine. Dine Chinese at **China House,** 1079 N. Main, tel. 752-9969, open Mon.-Sat. for breakfast, lunch, and dinner, Sunday for brunch and dinner; and **Mandarin Garden,** 432 N. Main, tel. 753-5789, open Mon.-Fri. for lunch and daily for dinner. At **Amy's Mongolian BBQ,** 1537 N. Main, tel. 753-3338, you can enjoy Mongolian barbecue, Chinese buffet, or order from the menu; open Mon.-Sat. for lunch and dinner. For Mexican food, try **Garcia's,** 130 S. Main, tel. 753-0777, open daily for lunch and dinner; and **El Sol,** 871 N. Main, tel. 752-5743, open daily for lunch and dinner. The **Shangri-La,** 438 1/2 N. Main, tel. 752-1315, sells a full range of health foods.

Entertainment

The old **Lyric Theatre** (known as the New Lyric when it opened in 1913) presents musicals and plays in summer; 28 W. Center, tel. 797-0305 (ticket office) or 797-1500 (business office). The **Capitol (Ellen Eccles) Theatre,** 43 S. Main, tel. 753-6518, presents opera, theater, ballet, and concerts; it first opened in 1920, patterned after the Capitol Theatre in Salt Lake City, and has now been restored to its original glory as an opera house. Watch the movies at **Excellence Theatres,** Cache Valley Mall, 1300 N. Main, tel. 753-3112 recording or 752-7762 office; **Cinema Theatre,** 60 W. 100 North, tel. 753-1900; or the **Utah Theatre,** 18 W. Center, tel. 752-3072.

Events

The Bridgerland Travel Region/Cache-Rich Tourist Council, tel. 752-2161, can fill you in on what's happening in the area. Major annual events include:

May: Mendon May Day Festival has a Maypole dance and other festivities (11 miles west). **Cache Dairy Festival Pageant** in Logan. **Richmond Black and White Days** is a Holstein cattle show (13 miles north). University students compete in the **USU Intercollegiate Rodeo** at Cache County Fairgrounds in Logan. **Smithfield Health Days** presents a parade, historic tour, crafts, and games (seven miles north).

June: Summerfest Art Faire in downtown Logan features works by local artists, concerts, food, and a home tour. **Clarkston Pony Express Days** is a community celebration (21 miles northwest).

July: A big **fireworks show** takes place around July 4 at the USU Romney Stadium. Hyrum puts on a **Fourth of July rodeo and parade** (seven miles south). Lewiston observes **Fourth of July** with horse racing, games, and fireworks (19 miles north). Musical festivities include the **Utah Festival Opera** and **Utah Music Festival. Festival of the American West** celebrates Western heritage with a historical pageant and Great West Fair: the multimedia pageant presented each evening has a cast of 200 actors, dancers, and musicians; fair exhibits feature traditional pioneer and Indian food, fiddle and banjo music, square dancing, medicine man shows, a mountain man camp, and Indian and pioneer craft demonstrations; events take place on the Utah State University campus and last 10 days, usually starting on the last Friday in July.

August: Festival of the American West continues. **Cache County Fair and Rodeo** has agricultural and craft exhibits along with PRCA rodeo action at the fairgrounds in Logan. The **Martin Harris Pageant** re-creates pioneer and Mormon history at the Clarkston Amphitheater (21 miles northwest).

September: Wellsville Founders Day Celebration on Labor Day commemorates the first pioneers to settle in Cache Valley (seven miles southwest).

November: A **Christmas Parade** starts off the holiday season.

Recreation

Willow Park, 450 W. 700 South, is a good place for a picnic and has the added attractions of a small zoo, playground, volleyball courts, and a softball field. **Bicentennial Park** offers picnic spots downtown at 100 S. Main. Swim year-round at the indoor **Municipool,** 114 E. 1000 North, tel. 750-9890. The **Community Recreation Center,** 195 S. 100 West, tel. 750-9877, features tennis and handball/racquetball courts, basketball, volleyball, weight room, indoor track, table tennis, sauna, and whirlpool. **Tennis courts** are also at Mount Logan Middle School, 875 N. 200 East; Central Park, 85 S. 300 East; and Worthington Park, Logan High School, 162 W. 100 South. **Golf** at the 18-hole **Logan Golf and Country Club,** 710 N. 1500 East, tel. 753-6020; the **Logan River Golf Club,** 550 W. 1000 South, tel. 753-0123; the 18-hole **Birch Creek Golf Course,** 600 E. Center in Smithfield, seven miles north, tel. 563-6825; or the nine-hole **Sherwood Hills,** in Sardine Canyon, 13 miles southwest on US 89/91, tel. 245-6055. Sherwood Hills also offers a hotel, tel. 245-6424, one indoor and two outdoor pools, horseback riding, cross-country ski trails, racquetball, and tennis. **Beaver Creek Lodge** not only offers rooms daily ($73.60 s or d) but also has horseback trail rides and mountain bike rentals in summer, then snowmobile rentals plus cross-country ski trails in winter; recreation facilities are closed Sunday. Located in the Bear River Mountains about 28 miles northeast on US 89, just past the turnoff for

rousing finale of the Martin Harris Pageant

Beaver Mountain Ski Area; tel. 753-1707/1076. **Ice-skating** is popular in winter at Central Park, 85 S. 300 East. The Logan Ranger District, tel. 753-3620, has lists of hikes and cross-country ski tours in the area.

Beaver Mountain Ski Area operates three double chairlifts serving 16 runs, longest of which is two and one quarter miles and drops 1,600 vertical feet. A cafeteria, ski shop, rentals, and lessons are available at the day lodge. Adult lift tickets cost $18 full day, $14 half day; children under 12 and seniors over 65 ski for $14 full day, $11 half day. Open daily 9 a.m.-4 p.m. from early December to late March; tel. 753-4822 (snow and road conditions), 753-0921 (office, ski school, and lift tickets). Go northeast 28 miles on US 89, then north one and one half miles on UT 243.

Services
In an **emergency** (police, fire, or medical), dial 911. **Logan Regional Hospital** provides 24-hour emergency care at 1400 N. 500 East, tel. 752-2050. The **post office** is at 151 N. 100 West, tel. 752-7246.

Trailhead Sports, 117 N. Main, tel. 753-1541, has hiking and camping gear, cross-country ski rentals and sales, canoes/kayak rentals and sales, and topo maps. Outdoor sporting goods are also sold at **Surplus Savers,** 140 S. Main, tel. 752-5745; **The Sportsman,** 129 N. Main, tel. 752-0211; and **Gart's Sporting Goods,** 585 N. Main, tel. 752-4287.

Information
The **Bridgerland Travel Region/Cache-Rich Tourist Council,** downtown at 160 N. Main (Logan, UT 84321), tel. 752-2161 or (800) 657-4433, has maps and travel information for Cache and Rich counties, including Logan and Bear Lake; open Mon.-Fri. 8 a.m.-5 p.m. (and sometimes Saturday in summer). To learn more of local history and architecture, ask for *Logan's Historic Main Street,* a self-guided, 45-minute walking tour. For recreation information and maps of the surrounding mountain country, visit the **Logan Ranger District office,** on US 89 at the east edge of town (1500 E. Hwy. 89, Logan, UT 84321), tel. 753-2772; open Mon.-Fri. 8 a.m.-4:30 p.m. (until 5 p.m. in summer and some Saturdays). The district covers Logan

Canyon, the Bear River Range, and the Wellsville Mountains. Logan's **public library,** 255 N. Main, tel. 750-9870, is open Mon.-Thurs. 10 a.m.-9 p.m., Fri.-Sat. 10 a.m.-6 p.m. Good places for regional and general reading include **A Bookstore,** 130 N. 100 East, tel. 752-9089; and **The Book Table,** 29 S. Main, tel. 752-3055.

Transportation
Greyhound buses, 2500 N. West., tel. 752-4921, run daily south to Ogden and Salt Lake City and northeast to Idaho Falls (and West Yellowstone in summer). **Logan Cab,** tel. 753-3663, provides taxi service. See the telephone *Yellow Pages* for auto rentals. No scheduled airlines serve Logan.

VICINITY OF LOGAN

Ronald V. Jensen Living Historical Farm
This outdoor museum re-creates life on a Cache Valley family farm in 1917. Workers dress in period clothing to plow soil, thresh grain, milk cows, shear sheep, and butcher hogs much as the early 20th century farmers did. The men mostly work in the fields, while women stay closer to home to cook, can, quilt, gather eggs from the hen house, and pick vegetables from the garden. You'll see breeds of animals representative of early farms, a lineup of steam tractors, a giant early gasoline tractor, and many other pieces of farm machinery. Buildings here include an 1875 farmhouse, summer kitchen, root cellar, smoke house, blacksmith shop, horse barn, sheep shed, and a privy or two. Special demonstrations take place all through the year, usually on Saturday; call to have a schedule sent. The farm is open Tues.-Sat. 10 a.m.-4 p.m. June-Aug.; $2 adult, 50 cents children, $5 family, $1 high-school student or senior. Utah State University operates the historical farm, located six miles southwest of Logan on US 89/91, tel. 245-4064.

Hyrum City Museum
The attractive small town of Hyrum has exhibits on local history, gems and minerals, and dinosaurs. Open Tuesday, Thursday, and Saturday 2-6 p.m. in the city offices at 83 W. Main, tel. 245-6033.

cutting alfalfa at the Ronald V. Jensen Farm

Hyrum State Park

The Little Bear River feeds this popular 450-acre reservoir beside the town of Hyrum. Boaters come to water-ski, sail, or paddle across the waters. There are sandy beaches at several places along the shore (no lifeguards). Fishing for bluegill, perch, and largemouth bass tends to be only fair while trout fishing can be excellent. Anglers sometimes have good luck in the river just below the spillway during spring runoff. Winter visitors fish through the ice, ice skate, and sail ice boats during freeze-up from about mid-December to late March. The state park has two developed areas on the north shore. The launch and campground area has picnic grounds, beach, boat ramp, docks, and the ranger office. Most park visitors head for the day-use area farther east along the shore for picnicking, lying on the beach, and swimming. It's reached by a one-half-mile drive (follow signs) or by a one-half-mile foot trail from the campground. The main season at Hyrum Lake (elev. 4,700 feet) runs mid-April to late September; water and outhouses are available off-season at the campground. Day use costs $3, camping $9 ($10 Friday, Saturday, and holi-

days). Campground reservations are advised on summer weekends. The park makes a good base for exploring the Cache Valley area; rangers can suggest places to go. They also have snowmobiling information. The ranger office, at the main entrance, is open daily 8 a.m.-5 p.m. during the warmer months and 8 a.m.-noon the rest of the year; 405 W. 300 South, Hyrum, UT 84319, tel. 245-6866 (ranger) or (800) 322-3770 (reservations). From Logan, drive south seven miles on the Hyrum Road (UT 165), which branches off US 89/91 on the south edge of town, or go southwest six miles on US 89/91, then turn east three miles on UT 101 and follow signs.

Hardware Ranch And Blacksmith Fork Canyon

The Utah Division of Wildlife Resources operates this ranch in the midst of the northern Wasatch Range to provide winter feed for herds of elk. In winter, staff offer sleigh rides for a closer look at the large animals; wagon rides run if there's not enough snow. A visitor center with displays and a cafe are also open in winter; tel. 245-3131 (recording). You're not likely to

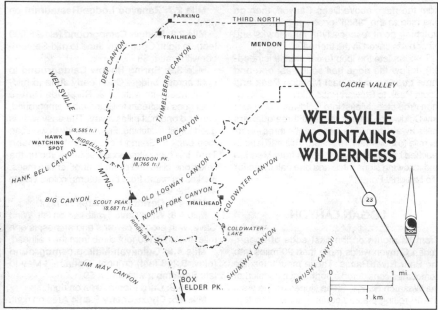

see elk here in the warmer months, though the drive in is still pretty. The 16-mile paved road from Hyrum east to Hardware Ranch follows the scenic Blacksmith Fork Canyon past fishing spots (for trout and whitefish), **Shenoah Picnic Area,** and **Pioneer Campground**. Pioneer's sites are open late May to late September with water; $8. Two small campgrounds, **Friendship** and **Spring,** are to the north along the Left Hand Fork of Blacksmith Canyon; they're open mid-May to late October (no water, $5 fee). An extensive snowmobile trail system extends from Hardware Ranch as far as Logan Canyon to the north and the Monte Cristo area to the south, with many side trails.

Wellsville Mountains Wilderness

Rarely do mountain ranges rise so high from so narrow a base. Steep slopes on each side tower 5,000 feet above the Cache Valley to the east and the Great Salt Lake to the west. Box Elder Peak tops the range at 9,372 feet. A loop hike to the Mendon Peak area offers outstanding views and birdwatching. Carry water as it's a long climb up. Also bring wind and rain gear; the breeze on the ridge is far cooler than tem-

peratures in the valley. See the Honeyville and Wellsville 7½-minute topo maps. Few people backpack here because of the steep terrain on the way up, exposed ridges on top, and scarcity of water.

From the farm community of Mendon (11 miles west of Logan), head west two miles on Third North to a parking area on the right. Follow a dirt road, too rough for most vehicles, about one-third of a mile (keep left at the fork) to the trailhead in Deep Canyon. The trail is easy to follow and well graded. Even so, expect a strenuous hike because of the relentless climb. From the trailhead (elev. 5,400 feet) in woods of oak and box elder, you'll climb 2,700 feet in three miles through groves of aspen, mountain ash, and white fir to the ridgeline. Panoramic views take in the Cache Valley, Great Salt Lake, Meanders and Oxbow lakes of the Bear River, and many mountains of northern Utah and southern Idaho. Mendon Peak (elev. 8,766 feet) is just to the east, one-half mile away and 660 feet higher; the trail contours to a saddle just past the peak, then switchbacks up the ridge to the summit. Limber pine and wildflowers cling to the slopes. Birdwatchers can turn northwest from the ridge above Deep Canyon, then go one mile to the "8585" peak—a prime hawk-watching point, especially in fall. Hawks and other birds cavort in the thermals.

To complete the loop (a car shuttle is needed), follow the ridge trail southeast one and three quarters miles past Mendon Peak and Scout Peak to Stewart Pass (elev. 8,376 feet), then drop steeply east into Coldwater Canyon; tiny Coldwater Lake is one and three quarters miles away, then it's a more gentle three-quarter mile to Coldwater Trailhead. This trailhead is reached by taking Main St. south from Mendon and following signs three and one half miles for "To National Forest."

LOGAN CANYON

From its mouth on the east edge of Logan, Logan Canyon winds more than 20 miles into the Bear River Range. These mountains are sometimes considered a northeast extension of the Wasatch Range. Steep slopes on the west rise to rolling plateau country across the top, and moderate slopes descend to Bear Lake on the east. Paved US 89 follows the canyon floor past picnic areas, campgrounds, fishing spots, and trailheads before turning away from the Logan River and topping out at an elevation of 7,800 feet at Bear Lake Summit. Beaver Mountain Ski Area offers downhill action near the upper end of Logan Canyon. In autumn, maples of the lower canyon turn a brilliant crimson while aspen of the higher country are transformed to gold. Roadside geologic signs explain features in Logan Canyon. Picnicking is free at picnic areas, though you have to pay to picnic at some campgrounds. Contact the Logan Ranger District office for information on picnicking, camping, fishing, hiking, cross-country skiing, snowmobiling, and road conditions; open Mon.-Fri. 8 a.m.-5 p.m.; near 1500 East and US 89 in Logan, tel. 753-2772. Some campsites can be reserved by calling (800) 283-CAMP.

Logan Canyon Scenic Drive
Mile 0: Entering Logan Canyon (two and one half miles east of downtown Logan on US 89). Ragged cliffs rise steeply on each side, allowing just enough room for the river and highway to squeeze through.

Mile 2.7: Zanavoo Lodge Restaurant on right.

Mile 2.9: Bridger Campground (elev. 5,000 feet) on right. Open early June to mid-September with water; $8.

Mile 3.9: Spring Hollow Campground to right across bridge. Open early June to mid-September with water; $8. **Riverside Nature Trail** goes upstream to Guinavah Campground, one and one half miles away. The easy walk is good for birdwatching. From Guinavah, you can loop back to Spring Hollow via the **Crimson Trail**; this more strenuous trail takes you up the limestone cliffs and down in another two miles. It takes its name from the autumn colors visible along the way.

Mile 4.4: Dewitt Picnic Area on right.

Mile 4.8: Wind Cave Trailhead on left. Wind Cave, with eroded caverns and arches, is one mile and an 1,100-foot climb from the trailhead.

Mile 4.9: Guinavah-Malibu campground (elev. 5,200 feet) on right. Open mid-May to late September with water; $9.

Mile 6.8: Card Picnic Area on right.

Mile 7.5: Choke Cherry Picnic Area on right.

Mile 7.8: Preston Valley Campground (elev. 5,500 feet) on right. Open mid-May to late September with water; $8.

Mile 9.0: Lodge Campground (elev. 5,600 feet) one mile to right on Forest Route 047. Open late May to mid-September with water; $7.

Mile 9.8: China Row Picnic Area on right.

Mile 10.0: Wood Camp Campground (elev. 5,600 feet) on left. Open mid-May to late October; no water, $5 charge. The **Jardine Juniper Trail** begins nearby, climbing 1,900 feet in 4.4 miles to Old Jardine, a venerable Rocky Mountain juniper tree. Still alive after 1,500 years, it measures about 27 feet in circumference and 45 feet high. The name honors a USU alumnus.

Mile 11.7: Logan Cave on left. This wild cave, about 2,000 feet long, can easily be explored (take at least two lights). Though dissolved from limestone, the cave lacks elaborate formations.

Mile 15.3: Rick's Spring on left. Crystal-clear water flows out of a small cave. This water has tested positive for giardia so don't drink it without treating it first.

Mile 19.2: Tony Grove Lake Recreation Area to left. **Lewis Turner Campground** (elev. 6,300 feet) is one-half mile in from the highway; open

Tony Grove Lake

early June to late September with water; $7. Tony Grove Lake Campground (elev. 8,100 feet) is seven miles in beside an alpine lake; open mid-July to late September with water; $10. Fishermen try for the lake's trout; no boat motors allowed. An easy self-guided **nature trail** circles clockwise around Tony Grove Lake; brochures should be in a box at the end of the road. This is also the trailhead for **White Pine and Naomi Peak trails.** Naomi Peak (elev. 9,980 feet) crowns the Mount Naomi Wilderness.

Mile 20.2: Red Banks Campground (elev. 6,500 feet) on left. Open early June to mid-October with water; $7.

Mile 22.5: Highway leaves Logan Canyon and climbs along Beaver Creek.

Mile 25.3: Beaver Mountain Ski Area one and one half miles to left on paved UT 243. **Sink Hollow Cross-Country Ski Trail** begins near the turnoff; open about mid-December to late March, depending on snow. **Beaver Mountain Ski Area** offers three double chairlifts serving 16 runs, the longest of which is two and one quarter miles with a 1,600-foot vertical drop. Adult lift tickets cost $18 full day, $14 half day; children under 12 and seniors over 65 ski for $14 full day, $11 half day. A cafeteria, ski shop, rentals, and lessons are available at the day lodge. Open daily 9 a.m.-4 p.m. from early December to late March; tel. 753-4822 (snow and road conditions), 753-0921 (office, ski school, and lift tickets).

Mile 25.7: Beaver Creek Lodge, tel. 753-1707/1076, has rooms ($73.60 s or d), horseback trail rides and mountain bike rentals in summer, then snowmobile rentals in winter; closed Sunday except for lodging.

Mile 30.3: Bear Lake Summit (elev. 7,800 feet). **Limber Pine Nature Trail** begins from the parking area on the right and goes to a massive limber pine 25 feet in circumference and 44 feet high. At one time this tree was thought to be the world's oldest and largest limber pine, but a forestry professor at USU discovered that it is really five trees grown together and "only" about 560 years old. The easy self-guided walk takes about an hour; Bear Lake can be seen to the east.

Mile 31.1: Sunrise Campground (elev. 7,000 feet) on right. Open mid-June to mid-September with water; $10.

Mile 31.3: Bear Lake Overlook on right. This viewpoint has a sweeping panorama of Bear Lake and surrounding mountains. Signs tell about this unique lake. The Sawtooth Mountains on the northeast horizon belong to the Salt River Range, a southern extension of the Grand Tetons. The Uinta Mountains to the southeast are the only major range in the "lower 48" states that run east-west; Kings Peak, Utah's highest summit, tops the range at 13,528 feet.

Mile 37.4: Garden City on the shore of Bear Lake.

BEAR LAKE

More than 28,000 years ago, faulting of massive blocks of the earth's crust created a basin

BEAR LAKE MONSTER

When white settlers first arrived in the Bear Lake area, the local Indians warned them that a monster lived in Bear Lake. The beast was described as being of the "legged serpent" variety and was said to have carried humans away. Few Indians of the area would bathe in the lake or camp nearby, but settlers scoffed even after a few sightings by whites.

In 1868, no fewer than 20 people reported seeing the monster, all within a period of a few weeks. These included a few citizens of local repute and a wagonload of eight travelers. The monster gained fame and many believers, both in the area and beyond. Soon monsters were "spotted" in other lakes, including a 45-foot-long alligator that came out of Great Salt Lake and smashed a campsite as the residents fled. This proliferation of tall tales began to cast doubts on the existence of Bear Lake's monster, and fewer sightings were reported.

There were even a few legends explaining the monster's demise. One farmer told of a huge creature from the lake that hungrily devoured part of his flock of sheep. As the surviving animals fled, the monster's eye caught a coil of barbed wire about the size and shape of huddled prey and swallowed it whole. By the farmer's account, the resulting pain drove the beast back into the lake and it was never seen again.

Rangers at Minnetonka Cave offer another story. They maintain the monster was intimidated by the surrounding human population and sought refuge in Minnetonka Cave, where the creature survived on cave popcorn and coral. In this version, the monster was felled by a collapsing cave wall, with all but a clenched claw buried under rubble. The existing trail was built over that rockfall, and rangers today still point out a piece of flowstone just under the trail that strangely resembles a large dragon claw.

here 50 miles long and 12 miles wide. Bear Lake filled the entire valley during the last ice age, but it now has receded to cover an area 20 miles long and eight miles wide, at an elevation of 5,900 feet. About half the lake lies in Utah and half in Idaho. The turquoise color is thought to be caused by limestone particles suspended in the water. The ecology of Bear Lake has been upset somewhat by canals that divert water from the Bear River into the lake in times of surplus and drain water when needed downstream for irrigation. Eight thousand years ago the lake and river were connected, then changing conditions separated the two bodies of water until man intervened. Bear Lake National Wildlife Refuge occupies 17,600 acres of marshlands north of the lake, a favored stopping place for sandhill cranes, herons, white pelicans, egrets, and many species of ducks. Four species of fish evolved in Bear Lake that are not found any other place in the world. One of these, the Bonneville cisco, attracts fishermen by the thousands. During spawning in January, nets are used to dip the small (six to eight inches long) and tasty fish from the icy water. Fish sought year-round by anglers include the native Bear Lake cutthroat and Bonneville whitefish and the introduced rainbow trout, mackinaw trout, and yellow perch. Keep an eye out for the Bear Lake Monster, a dark dragonlike creature 90 feet long that spouts water!

David McKenzie, an early fur trapper, named the lake after the many black bear once found here. Nomadic Indian tribes and groups of trappers frequented the shores during the 1820s and held two large rendezvous here. Mormons arrived beginning in 1863 to start farms and ranches. Thousands of summer cabins have sprouted along the shore and hillsides in recent years to take advantage of the scenery and water sports. Bear Lake State Park offers a marina and campground on the west shore, a large camping area on the south shore at Rendezvous Beach, and undeveloped campgrounds on the east shore.

Bear Lake State Park: Marina
The 71,000 acres of Bear Lake give plenty of room to water-ski, sail, or fish. The marina, has boat slips protected by a breakwater, a boat ramp, swimming area, picnic tables, campground with showers, and ranger offices. Season is year-round; $3 day use, $9 camping ($10 Fri.-Sun.). On busy summer weekends it's a good idea to have reservations for the marina or Rendezvous Beach areas. The marina is one mile north of Garden City on US 89, Box 184, Garden City, UT 84028, tel. 946-3343 or (800) 322-3770 (reservations).

Bear Lake State Park: Rendezvous Beach

A wide sandy beach attracts visitors to the lake's southern shore. The park has a day-use area with a boat-rental concession and several campgrounds with showers. Ask at the entrance station for recommended places to camp; some sites have lake views, some offer hookups, and some are set up mainly for RVs. Open early May to late September; $3 day use, $9 camping ($10 Friday, Saturday, and holidays), $13 camping w/hookups ($15 Saturday, Sunday, and holidays). Located eight miles south of Garden City near Laketown Box 184, Garden City, UT 84028, tel. 946-3343 or (800) 322-3770 (reservations).

Bear Lake State Park: East Shore

Primitive campgrounds and day-use areas are located on the east side of Bear Lake. From south to north are First Point, Second Point (day-use only), South Eden, Cisco Beach, Rainbow Cove, and North Eden. Sites stay open all year; outhouses are provided but only South Eden had drinking water at press time; $3 day use, $5 camping. First Point and Rainbow Cove have boat ramps. Scuba divers like the steep underwater drop-offs near Cisco Beach. Turn north from Laketown.

Garden City And Vicinity

This small town (year-round pop. 300), on the east shore at the junction of US 89 and UT 30, comes to life in summer. You can learn about the area at a **tourist information cabin** at the highway junction; open daily 10 a.m.-6 p.m. from May to September. Classical and other forms of music fill the air the last two weeks in July during the **Great Music West Festival**, held at various locations. The town celebrates the harvest of its most famous crop during the **Raspberry Days Festival** on the first weekend in August with a parade, crowning of Miss Raspberry, Little Buckaroo Rodeo, crafts, and entertainment. **Bear Lake County Fair** has exhibits and entertainment in August at Montpelier, Idaho. The **Mountain Man Rendezvous** reenacts the big gatherings of fur trappers and Indians that took place at Bear Lake in the summers of 1826 and 1827; the modern event is held the third weekend of September at Rendezvous Beach, Bear Lake State Park, tel. 946-3343.

Bear Lake Motor Lodge, located just south of the highway junction at 50 S. Bear Lake Blvd. (UT 30), tel. 946-3271, is open all year and has a restaurant; rooms start at $43.60 s, $57.77 d. **Ideal Beach Resort,** tel. 946-3364 or (800) 634-1018 in Utah; located at 2144 S. Bear Lake Blvd., 3.3 miles south of Garden City, offers motel ($59.95 s or d) and condo accommodations (half week or longer) year-round; camping ($10 w/hookups) nearly a mile south of the resort gate. **The Landing** restaurant, tel. 946-3432, is open summer only daily for breakfast, lunch, and dinner; plus boat rentals, beach, swimming pools, tennis, and miniature golf. The nearby 9-hole **Bear Lake Golf Course,** tel. 946-8742, is open to the public. **Harbor Village,** 900 N. Bear Lake Blvd., tel. 946-3448 or (800) 324-6840, offers suites with full kitchens and fireplace ($108.91 s, $119.81 d) and use of tennis courts, pool, and hot tub and is open all year. **Fay's Trailer Park,** 285 N. Bear Lake Blvd., no phone, is open mid-April to late September, $7 tent or RV no hookups, $10 w/hookups; no showers. **Bear Lake KOA,** 0.8 mile north of Garden City on US 89, near the state park marina, tel. 946-3454, offers a swimming pool, miniature golf, tennis, store, showers, and laundry; open from May 1 to October 31; $15.81 tent or RV no hookups, $18 RV w/hookups, $24.52 cabins. **Bear Lake West** is four and one half miles north of Garden City, just across the Idaho border (three miles south of Fish Haven), tol. (208) 945-2222, and has a nine-hole golf course and a steak and seafood restaurant open in summer for Sunday brunch and Thurs.-Sat. for dinner. **Pickleville Playhouse,** 2.8 miles south of Garden City, tel. 946-2918 (Garden City) or 750-1044 (Logan), features family entertainment during summer evenings (call for days and times); a Western-style cookout precedes the show. A roadside picnic area is near the lake seven miles south of Garden City and one mile north of Rendezvous Beach.

Minnetonka Cave

Just after the turn of the century a grouse hunter retrieved a fallen bird after climbing a steep slope and noticed a cave entrance. Returning a few days later with friends and lights, the cave was found to be extensive and beautiful. Now you can visit this cave with a U.S. Forest Service ranger as your guide through its nine rooms. Wear comfortable shoes with good soles because the tour is 1,800 feet long with 484 stair steps (some are muddy and slick) and the route is repeated on the way out. Wear a light jacket and long pants because the temperature is 40° F and the humidity gives the cold a bite. Tours last one to one and one half hours (depending on group size); from the cave's sign at St. Charles, Idaho, go west 10 miles to the cave entrance parking lot. There are several USFS campgrounds along the route and a few designated free camping sites. Tours of the cave are given 10 a.m.-5:30 p.m. daily from mid-June until Labor Day; adults $4, children (6-15) $3; tel. (208) 945-2407.

Randolph

Rich County seat, Randolph (pop. 800) is a quiet rural town 19 miles south of Bear Lake. Farming and ranching have been the main activities ever since Randolph H. Stewart led the first settlers here from Idaho in 1870. **Rich County Round-Up Days,** held in August, has a rodeo, parade, and exhibits. No accommodations in town, just a drive-in.

elk (Cervus canadensis)

Pahvant Butte

WEST-CENTRAL UTAH

INTRODUCTION

Utah's Wild West remains nearly as wild as ever. Rugged mountain ranges and barren desert valleys have discouraged all but the most determined individuals. Explorers, pioneers in wagon trains, Pony Express riders, and telegraph linemen crossed the inhospitable land with only the desire to reach the other side. It took the promise of gold and silver to lure large numbers of people into the jagged hills. Fading ghost towns still show the industry of the early miners. Hardy ranchers also braved the isolation to grow hay and run their cattle and sheep. Shortage of water has always been the limiting factor to development. Travelers, however, can enjoy the solitude and the thrill of exploring a land little changed since white men first arrived. Roads provide surprisingly good access for such a remote region. Paved I-80, US 50/6, and UT 21 cross it, while dirt roads branch off in all directions. Driving along the Pony Express and Stage Route from Fairfield to Ibapah might be the most unique driving tour; you experience some of the same unfenced wilderness as did the tough young Pony Express riders. This and many other back roads can be negotiated by car in dry weather. For the adventurous, the wildly beautiful mountain ranges offer countless hiking possibilities—though you'll have to rough it. Hardly any developed trails exist.

THE LAND

Located in the Great Basin, west-central Utah has about equal amounts of valley and mountain terrain. Geologic forces have worked here on a grand scale. Great blocks of the earth's crust rising along faults formed the mountains, all of which run north-south. Volcanic activity has left well-preserved craters, cinder cones, and lava flows. The massive sandbars that once lined the southern shore of Lake Bonneville have blown northeastward to form impressive dunes at Little Sahara. Streambeds in west-central Utah actually drain into several different subbasins; the two largest are Great Salt Lake and Sevier Lake.

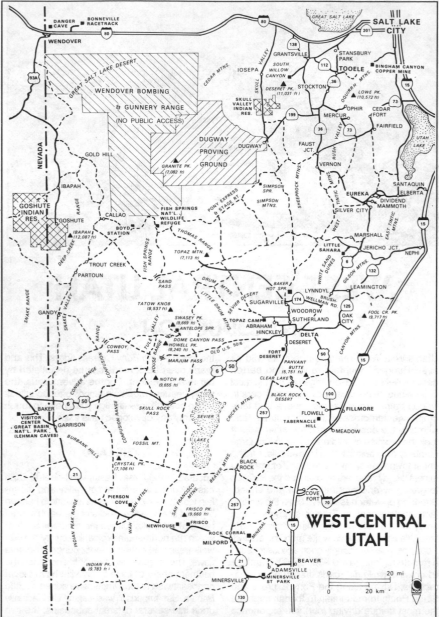

WEST-CENTRAL UTAH

© MOON PUBLICATIONS, INC.

Clouds moving in from the Pacific Ocean lose much of their moisture to the Sierra Nevada and other towering mountain ranges in California and Nevada. By the time the depleted clouds reach west-central Utah, only the Deep Creek, Stansbury, and southern Wah Wah mountains reach high enough to gather sufficient rain and snow to support permanent streams. Notable summits of the region include Ibapah (12,087 feet) and Haystack (12,020 feet) peaks of the Deep Creek Range, Deseret Peak (11,031 feet) of the Stansbury Mountains, Swasey (9,669 feet) and Notch (9,655 feet) peaks of the House Range, Frisco Peak (9,660 feet) of the San Francisco Mountains, and Crystal Peak (7,106 feet) of the Wah Wah Range.

Though west-central Utah is now one of the driest parts of the Great Basin, a far different scene existed 10,000 years ago. Freshwater Lake Bonneville then covered 20,000 square miles, one-fourth of Utah. Forests blanketed the mountains that poked above the lake waters. With time, the giant inland sea gradually shrank to much smaller remnants such as the Great Salt Lake, leaving behind the glistening salt flats of the Great Salt Lake Desert. Rainfall variations over time have caused Sevier Lake, southwest of Delta, to fluctuate between being a dry lakebed and the state's third-largest body of water.

Climate

Precipitation averages 8-10 inches annually over most of the region at the lower (4,000- to 6,000-feet) elevations. The rain and snow that do fall soon disappear because of the low humidity and abundant sunshine. Rainfall peaks in spring and again during the late summer-early autumn thunderstorm season. In this harsh semidesert, winter temperatures can drop into the subzeros, but the summer sun can send the thermometer climbing above 100 degrees. Visibility to 70 miles or more in the clean, dry air rewards mountain climbers with incredible views.

FLORA AND FAUNA

Vegetation in the valleys consists of sparse, low-growing plants such as saltbush, greasewood, black and bud sagebrush, shadscale,

beautiful thistle
(Cirsium pulchellum)

LOUISE FOOTE

little rabbitbrush, Mormon tea, and grasses. Big sagebrush, juniper, and piñon pine grow higher up. The highest peaks support mountain shrubs, aspen, and a variety of conifers, including the long-lived bristlecone pine.

Availability of water determines the quantity and variety of wildlife. Of the larger animals, mule deer and pronghorn are most widespread. Elk can be found in mountainous areas east of Delta. Rocky Mountain bighorn sheep have been reintroduced in the Deep Creek Range. Herds of wild horses roam the Confusion and House ranges. Other wildlife includes coyote, mountain lion, bobcat, kit fox, spotted and striped skunks, and black-tailed jackrabbit. Vast numbers of birds visit Fish Springs National Wildlife Refuge and other desert oases. Waterfowl and marsh birds stop over in greatest numbers during their early spring and late autumn migrations. Many smaller birds nest near water sources in late spring and early summer.

HISTORY

Indian Peoples

Paleo-Indians entered the region about 15,000 years ago to collect wild plants and to pursue the now-extinct mammoth and other big game. After 5,000 years or so, the drying climate and changing environment caused many of the large animals to disappear. Still nomadic, the Indian groups adapted by relying more on small game and wild plant foods. New technologies, including the bow and arrow, pottery, and small-scale agriculture, distinguished the Fremont people around A.D. 550. When the Fremont culture faded about 1300, perhaps because of drought and depletion of resources, the culturally distinct Shoshoni Indians moved in. These nomadic hunters and gatherers proved well suited to the dry environment. It's likely the modern Goshute (or Gosiutes) and Ute Indians descended from them.

Within the first decades of Utah's settlement by white men, all tribes suffered great losses of population and land. Even today the Indians struggle to adapt to modern ways. The Goshutes once occupied northwest Utah and adjacent Nevada; they now live in the Goshute and Skull Valley reservations. The Utes had the greatest range of all Utah's tribes, extending from west-central Utah into Colorado and New Mexico; they now have reservations in northeast Utah and southwest Colorado.

Explorers And Overland Trails

Imposing terrain and a scarcity of water discouraged early explorers from crossing the Great Basin region. In 1776, the Spanish became the first non-Indians to visit west-central Utah when members of the Dominguez-Escalante expedition left the Utah Lake area and headed southwest, passing near the present-day towns of Delta and Milford. Most American mountain men of the 1820s also kept to the Great Basin's edge, but not Jedediah Smith. With a party of 17 men, Smith set out in 1826 from northern Utah for Spanish California, searching for new fur-trapping areas. When Smith returned to Utah with two companions, the little group nearly perished from deep snows in the Sierra Nevada and from thirst in the desert.

Government explorer John C. Frémont named and made the first scientific studies of the Great Basin in 1845, putting to rest myths about the Great Salt Lake's monsters, whirlpools, and subterranean outlets to the Pacific.

In the following year, travelers began crossing the Great Basin as a shortcut to California. Horses and mules made the crossing safely, but the Donner-Reed wagon train met disaster. Mud of the Great Salt Lake Desert slowed the group so much that they ran out of water and lost some of their wagons and oxen. The exhausted

and demoralized group reached the Sierra Nevada late in the season, when snowstorms trapped and killed 40 of the 87 emigrants.

In 1859, Captain J.S. Simpson surveyed a military road to the south of the treacherous desert to connect Camp Floyd in central Utah with Carson Valley in western Nevada. Swift riders of the Pony Express used the road, known as the South-Central Overland Route, in 1860-61, before the telegraph ended this brief chapter of American history. The Lincoln Highway, America's first designated transcontinental motoring route, included part of this road from 1910 to 1927.

Gold!

Prospectors found placer gold deposits in the early 1860s, though significant production had to wait for arrival of the transcontinental railroad in 1869. Deposits of gold, silver, copper, lead, and zinc were found in quick succession. Major mining districts included Ophir, Mercur, and Tintic to the southwest of Salt Lake City; Gold Hill, Clifton, and Willow Springs in the far west of Utah; Detroit near Delta; and the San Francisco Mountains near Milford. Active gold mining continues in the Mercur, Tintic, and Detroit districts.

Bombs Away!

Much of the Great Salt Lake Desert is off-limits to visitors because of military activities. Jet aircraft and helicopters occasionally break the silence in flights above the Wendover Bombing and Gunnery Range. Scientists and engineers at Dugway Proving Grounds work on chemical and biological weapons. The base received some notoriety in 1968 after 6,500 sheep died on neighboring ranches. The military never admitted that it had released toxic warfare chemicals, but it did compensate the ranchers. Just south of Tooele you'll see the neat rows of buildings across the vast Tooele Army Depot, which functions as a storage, maintenance, repair, and training center.

WENDOVER AND VICINITY

Wendover began in 1907 as a watering station during construction of the Western Pacific Railroad. The highway went through in 1925, marking the community's beginnings as a travelers' stop. Wendover Air Force Base got its start in 1940 and soon grew to one of the world's largest military complexes. During WW II, crews of bombers and other aircraft learned their navigation, formation flying, gunnery, and bombing skills above the three and one half million acres of desert belonging to the base. Only after the war ended did the government reveal that one of the bomber groups had been training in preparation for dropping atomic bombs on Japan. Little remains of the base, once a city of nearly 20,000 people. Hill Air Force Base, near Ogden, continues to use the vast military reserve for training air crews.

Practicalities

This desert oasis has a split personality—half the town lies in Utah and half in Nevada. On both sides you'll find accommodations and restaurants where you can take a break from long drives on I-80. Five casino hotels, eight motels, and two campgrounds offer places to stay. Six casinos on the Nevada side provide a chance to lose your money in the usual gambling games. Most of the town's visitor facilities line Wendover Boulevard, also known as State Highway, which parallels the interstate. Stop in at the Nevada-Wendover Welcome Center, on the Nevada side at 937 Wendover Blvd. (Box 2460, Wendover, NV 89883), tel. (702) 664-3414 or toll-free (800) 426-6862, for information about the area. Open daily 8:30-11:30 a.m. and noon-5 p.m.; look for the WW II memorial supported by a B-29 model in front. Major annual events near Wendover include **Wendover Bor-** **dertown Bike Challenge,** three days in late April or early May for mountain bikes and road bikes. During the **Land Speed Opener** in July, attempts are made to set a new speed record. **Wendover Air Show** takes place in August or October, **Speed Week** in the third week of August, the smaller **World of Speed** in late September, and the **Bonneville World Finals** in mid-October at the Bonneville Salt Flats International Speedway.

Bonneville Salt Flats International Speedway

A brilliant white layer of salt left behind by prehistoric Lake Bonneville covers more than 44,000 acres of the Great Salt Lake Desert. For much of the year, a shallow layer of water sits atop the salt flats. Wave action planes the surface almost perfectly level—it's said that the curvature of the earth can be seen here. The hot sun usually dries out the salt flats enough for speed runs in summer and autumn. Cars began running across the salt in 1914 and continue to set faster and faster times each year. Rocket-powered vehicles have exceeded 600 mph. Expansive courses can be laid out; the main speedway is 10 miles long and 80 feet wide. A small tent city goes up near the course during the annual **Speed Week** on the third week of August; vehicles of an amazing variety of styles and ages take off individually to set new records for their class. The salt flats, just east of Wendover, are easy to access: Take I-80 Exit 4 and follow the paved road five miles north, then east. Signs and markers indicate if and where you

Jenkin's Mormon Meteor

can drive on the salt. Soft spots underlain by mud can trap vehicles venturing off the safe areas. Take care not to be on the track when racing events are being held!

Silver Island Mountains

These rugged mountains rise above the salt flats northeast of Wendover. You can visit them and their rocky canyons on a 54-mile loop drive. Take I-80 Exit 4, go north 1.2 miles, turn left 0.8 mile on a gravel road, then turn right at a sign for Silver Island Mountains. The road loops counter-clockwise around the mountains, crosses Lebby Pass, and returns to the junction near I-80. Another road goes north from Lebby Pass to Lucin in the extreme northwest corner of Utah. High-clearance vehicles do best on these roads, though cars can often negotiate them in dry weather. The Northern Utah map in the Utah Travel Council series shows approximate road alignments and terrain.

Danger Cave

Archaeologists from the University of Utah discovered thousands of prehistoric Indian artifacts in this cave. The five distinct layers of debris, the oldest dating back at least 10,000 years, have provided a wealth of new information on the region's early inhabitants. During field work in the 1950s, a huge piece of the cave's ceiling came crashing down. No one was hurt, but "Danger Cave" seemed an appropriate name. No exhibits or signs exist, so there's not much to see. If you'd like to visit the cave anyway, take I-80 Exit 4, turn north 0.4 mile, turn left (west) 1.4 miles on a paved road, and turn right (northwest) 1.8 miles on a gravel road (keep left past the gravel pits) to the cave. The road curves southwest along the face of the Silver Island Mountains. The cave entrance is easy to locate, about 200 feet from the road. Excavation work and the collapsed ceiling can be seen in the large room that once was home to ancient Indians. A bit farther down the road is another undeveloped cave that was used by off-duty military personnel for recreation. The cave floor was paved with concrete and a juke box was powered by a generator, creating a dance area that could be used even during blackouts. Juke Box Cave and Danger Cave are both part of an undeveloped Utah state park.

TOOELE

To sound like a native, pronounce the town's name "too-ILL-uh." Origin of the word is uncertain, but it may honor the Goshute Chief Tuilla. The attractive town (pop. 17,600) lies 34 miles southwest of Salt Lake City in the western foothills of the Oquirrh (OH-ker) Mountains. At its 4,900-foot elevation, Tooele offers fine views of the Great Salt Lake to the north and Tooele Valley and Stansbury Mountains to the west. Mormon pioneers settled here in 1849 to farm and raise livestock, but today the major industries are the nearby Tooele Army Depot, Dugway Proving Ground, and mining. Visitors wanting to know more about the region's history will enjoy the Tooele County Museum (exhibits on mining, smelting, and railroading), Benson Grist Mill (a pioneer mill and historic park), and DUP Museum (covers pioneer history) in Tooele and the Donner-Reed Pioneer Museum in nearby Grantsville. Other attractions in the area include a scenic drive and overlook in the Oquirrhs, Ophir ghost town, and hiking and camping in South Willow Canyon Recreation Area of the Stansbury Mountains.

SIGHTS

Tooele County Museum

A steam locomotive and a collection of old railroad cars surround Tooele's original (1909) train station. Step inside to see the restored station office and old photos showing railway workers, steam engines, and trestle construction. You might also meet and hear stories from retired railway men who volunteer as museum guides. Mining photos and artifacts illustrate life and work in the early days at Ophir, Mercur, Bauer, and other booming communities now faded to ghosts. Much of the old laboratory equipment and tools on display came from the Tooele Smelter, built by International Smelter & Refining Company in 1907-09. It processed copper, lead, and zinc until 1972. Ore came over the Oquirrh Mountains by aerial tramway from the Bingham Mine. More than 3,000 people worked here during the hectic WW II years. A highly detailed model shows the modern Carr Fork Mill, built near Tooele but used only 90 days before being dismantled and shipped to a more profitable site in Papua New Guinea. Two railroad cars, once part of an Air Force mobile ballistic missile train, contain medical equipment and antique furniture, Outside, kids can ride the scale railway (Saturday only), check out a caboose, or explore a replica of a mine. Tooele County Museum is open Tues.-Sat. 1-4 p.m. from Memorial Day to Labor Day weekends. Admission is by donation. Off-season visits can often be arranged by calling 882-8133. From downtown Tooele, go east a half mile on Vine St.; the museum is between Third East and Broadway, tel. 882-2836.

DUP Museum

Meet Tooele's pioneers in 128 framed pictures and see their clothing and other possessions at this museum, downtown at 39 E. Vine St., just a half block east of Main. The small stone

DUP Museum

building dates from 1867 and once served as a courthouse for Tooele County. The little log cabin next door, built in 1856, was one of the town's first residences. The DUP Museum is open some Saturdays in summer and for groups on request; call the numbers on the front.

Oquirrh Overlook

A look into the world's largest open-pit copper mine, panoramic views, and canyon scenery reward those who drive to this spot atop the Oquirrh Mountains. Views take in much of northern and western Utah: Great Salt Lake, Wasatch Range, Salt Lake City, Tooele Valley, and the Stansbury Mountains. Intricate patterns of the terraced **Bingham Canyon Copper Mine** lie directly below. To reach the overlook, 10.5 miles from town, head east on Vine Street and enter Middle Canyon. Forests of box elder and maple dominate the lower canyon, with firs and aspen farther up. After seven miles you'll see a picnic and parking area on the right. The pavement ends here: large RVs and vehicles with trailers should not go beyond it. The gravel road begins a steep one-mile climb with sharp curves to Butterfield Pass (elev. 8,400 feet). Turn left at the pass and continue 2.5 miles to the overlook (elev. 9,400 feet). Ice and snow close the road in winter.

Continue east at the pass and you'll descend on a gravel road through Butterfield Canyon into the Salt Lake Valley; ask about conditions as this road is sometimes closed. After seven miles, the road meets a bend in a paved highway (this junction may not be signed). Continue straight (east) 11 miles to I-15 (Exits 294 and 295) or turn left (north) five miles to UT 48 and the Bingham Canyon Copper Mine entrance.

Benson Grist Mill

Pioneers constructed this mill, one of the oldest buildings in western Utah, in 1854. Wooden pegs and rawhide strips hold the timbers together. E.T. Benson (the grandfather of LDS president Ezra Taft Benson) supervised its construction for the LDS church. The mill produced flour until 1938, then ground only animal feed until the 1940s. Local people began to restore the exterior in 1986. Much of the original machinery inside is still intact. Antique farm machinery, a granary, log cabin, blacksmith shop, and other buildings stand on the grounds to the east. Ruins of the Utah Wool Pullery, which once removed millions of tons of wool annually from pelts, stand to the west. The mill and historic park are usually open Tues.-Sat. 10 a.m.-4 p.m. from June 1 to September 1 and may be open on request. Benson Grist Mill is one block west of Mills Junction (UT 36 at UT 138), eight miles north of Tooele, four miles south of I-80 Exit 99, and 10 miles east of Grantsville, tel. 882-3302, 884-7137, or 884-7678.

PRACTICALITIES

Accommodations

All motels lie conveniently along Main Street (UT 36). From north to south are: **Villa Motel,** 475 N. Main, tel. 882-4551, $30 s or d, $40 kitchenette; **Best Western Tooele Inn,** 365 N. Main, tel. 882-5010 or 800-528-1234, has an indoor pool and spa, $48.49 s, $51.72 d; **Comfort Inn,** 491 S. Main, tel. 882-6100 or 800-228-5150, free breakfasts, pool, $52.37 s, $57.22 d; and **Valleyview Motel,** 585 Canyon Rd. at S. Main, tel. 882-3235, all kitchenettes, available by the week only at $115-135. No developed campgrounds are in town, but campers sometimes head east on Vine Street to Middle Canyon or southeast on Settlement Canyon Road (from south edge of town, 0.3 mile south of Valleyview Motel) into Settlement Canyon. Other possibilities are the BLM **Clover Creek Campground** 20 miles southwest (go 12 miles south on UT 36, then eight miles west on UT 199) and the forest service campgrounds in **South Willow Canyon Recreation Area,** and the **Grantsville Reservoir** 20 miles west of town (see "Stansbury Mountains" under "West of Tooele," below); none of the areas have water or a fee.

Food

For a variety of American food, including steaks, seafood, roast beef, veal, and sandwiches, try the **Glowing Embers Restaurant,** 494 S. Main (across from the Comfort Inn), tel. 882-0888, open daily for breakfast, lunch, and dinner. **Golden Corral Steakhouse,** 411 N. Main, tel. 882-6579, is an inexpensive family place open daily for lunch and dinner. Dine Chinese-Polynesian-American at the **Sun Lok Yuen,** 615 N. Main, tel. 882-3003, open Mon.-Sat. for lunch and dinner. Pick up pizza at **Pizza Hut,** 540 N.

Main, tel. 882-3924, open daily for lunch and dinner. **Tooele Pizza & Restaurant,** 21 E. Vine, tel. 882-8035, also has Greek foods; open Mon.-Sat. for lunch and dinner. For Mexican and American food it's **Casa del Cielo,** 100 N. Main, tel. 882-2000, open daily for breakfast, lunch, and dinner; or **Los Laureles,** 23 N. Main, tel. 882-2860, open Mon.-Sat. for lunch and dinner. **Subway Sandwiches,** 124 N. Main, tel. 882-8822, offers deli sandwiches; open daily for lunch and dinner.

Entertainment And Events
Catch movies at the **Ritz,** 111 N. Main, tel. 882-2273. Bowl at the **Sports Bowl,** near the corner of Main and Second North, tel. 882-8992. Annual events include the **High School Rodeo** the last weekend in March, the **Arts Festival** in June, the **Clover Stampede Rodeo** and a **Fourth of July parade** (fireworks rotate between here and Grantsville), **Tooele County Fair** in mid-August, **Tooele Gem & Mineral Show** in September, **Tooele Valley Cutters Race** in November, and the **Main Street Christmas Celebration** the first Saturday after Thanksgiving.

Services
In emergencies (police, fire, or paramedic), dial 911. The post office is downtown at 65 N. Main, tel. 882-1429. **Tooele Valley Regional**

Medical Center has 24-hour emergency services at 211 S. First East, tel. 882-1697.

The **city park** offers picnicking, playground, and an indoor swimming pool (open year-round) at the corner of Vine and Second West, tel. 882-3247. **Elton Park** at Second North and Broadway has tennis courts and ball fields. **Middle Canyon** has a picnic area seven miles from town (head east on Vine St.). **Settlement Canyon** contains a small reservoir (a local fishing and swimming spot) one-half mile up and **Legion Park,** a picnic area one and one half miles up. Play golf at the nine-hole **Oquirrh Hills Golf Course** at Seventh and Edgemont on the east side of town (tel. 882-4220) or at the 18-hole course in **Stansbury Park** eight miles north on UT 36, tel. 882-4162.

Information
The **Tooele Chamber of Commerce** can tell you about the sights and services here; its office is upstairs in the Key Bank at 202 N. Main (Tooele, UT 84074), tel. 882-0690. Open Mon.-Fri. about 9 a.m.-4 p.m. The **public library** is at 47 E. Vine St., tel. 882-2182, open Tues.-Saturday.

Transport
Utah Transit Authority (UTA) buses connect Tooele with Salt Lake City and other towns of the Wasatch Front Mon.-Saturday. The main bus stop is at Main and Fourth South, tel. 882-9031.

WEST OF TOOELE

GRANTSVILLE

Old buildings and tall Lombardy poplars reflect the pioneer heritage of this rural community, first settled in 1851 and named Willow Creek Fort. The museum in town offers a look at local history. Grantsville stretches along UT 138, nine miles northwest of Tooele. For hiking and camping in the Stansbury Mountains, crowned by 11,031-foot Deseret Peak, head south 10 miles to South Willow Canyon Recreation Area.

Donner-Reed Pioneer Museum
Early residents built this one-room adobe schoolhouse within the old fort walls in 1861.

Today it's a museum honoring the Donner-Reed wagon train of 1846. These pioneers crossed the Great Salt Lake Desert to the west with great difficulty, then became trapped by snow in the Sierra Nevada of California. Only 47 of the 87 who started the trip survived the winter. Museum displays include guns and relics abandoned on the salt flats by the desperate travelers; pottery, arrowheads, and other Indian artifacts; and more. Outside you can try out Grantsville's original iron jail and see an early log cabin, blacksmith shop, and old wagons. Another adobe building across the street served as a church and dates from 1866. The museum is open on request; free. To view the exhibits, visit or call the Grantsville Municipal Building (see

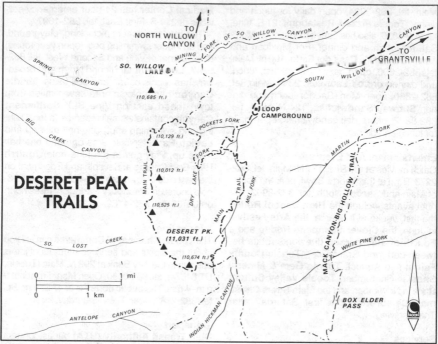

DESERET PEAK TRAILS

TO NORTH WILLOW CANYON

SPRING CANYON

SO. WILLOW LAKE

FORK OF SO WILLOW CANYON

MINING FORK

(10,685 ft.)

BIG CREEK CANYON

POCKETS FORK

(10,129 ft.)

FORK

MAIN TRAIL

(10,012 ft.)

DRY LAKE FORK

(10,525 ft.)

MAIN TRAIL

MILL FORK

LOOP CAMPGROUND

SOUTH WILLOW

TO GRANTSVILLE

CANYON

FORK

MARTIN

MACK CANYON-BIG HOLLOW TRAIL

DESERET PK. (11,031 ft.)

SO. LOST CREEK

(10,674 ft.)

WHITE PINE FORK

INDIAN HICKMAN CANYON

ANTELOPE CANYON

BOX ELDER PASS

0 ___ 1 mi
0 ___ 1 km

© MOON PUBLICATIONS, INC.

"Practicalities," below). From the municipal building, go two blocks west on Main to Cooley St., then one block north to the museum.

Bonneville Seabase
Scuba divers can enjoy ocean-type diving in the desert. A natural pool here was found to have salinity so close to that of the ocean that marine creatures could thrive in it. Several dozen species have been introduced including groupers, triggerfish, damsel fish, clown fish, and lobsters. The springs are geothermally heated, so winter cold is no problem. The original pool has been expanded and new pools created by dredging. User fees are $10 per person; full equipment can be rented whether scuba diving ($20) or snorkel diving ($10). The Seabase is five miles west of Grantsville on UT 138, tel. 884-8373 or 486-0513 (Salt Lake City).

Practicalities
The **city park** offers picnicking and a playground; turn south from Main on Quirk (220

East) Street. Local events include the **Old Folks Sociable** (entertainment, dinners, dances) in March, the **High School Rodeo** in late April, the **Fourth of July** parade and fireworks (the show alternates between here and Tooele each year), the **Tooele County Stock Show and Rodeo** in July, **Pioneer Day** (parade, dances, entertainment) on July 24, and a **Christmas Parade** the first week in December. Contact the Grantsville Municipal Building for details, open Mon.-Fri. 8:30 a.m.-5 p.m. at the corner of 7 Park and Main, tel. 884-3411.

STANSBURY MOUNTAINS

Not all western Utah is desert, as a visit to this section of Wasatch National Forest will show. Trails lead to Deseret Peak and other good day-hiking and overnight destinations. For more information about the area, contact the Salt Lake Ranger District of the Wasatch-Cache National Forest, 6944 S. 3000 East, Salt Lake City, UT

84121, tel. 524-5042. To reach South Willow Canyon from Salt Lake City, take I-80 to Exit 99, turn south four miles on UT 36, turn right (west) 10 miles on UT 138 to Grantsville, turn left (south) five miles on South Willow Rd., then right (southwest) five miles to the recreation area.

Campgrounds
South Willow Canyon Recreation Area, on the east slope of the range, has six small, free campgrounds along the South Fork of Willow Creek. They are open from early June to mid-September; no drinking water. Cottonwood, box elder, Douglas fir, and aspen thrive in the canyon. Elevations range from 6,080 feet at the first campground to 7,400 feet at the last one, at the end of the road. Sites can be crowded on summer weekends. **Grantsville Reservoir** has picnic tables, a ramada, parking, and trout fishing. Near the west end of town signs direct you south for the Willow Creek Recreation Areas. About four miles out of town you will see a paved road heading west. This road leads to the reservoir if you stay with the pavement. You can also continue on the dirt road at the first curve. After three miles you will find many sites for camping. The BLM recently opened the **Clover Creek Campground** south of the Stansbury Mountains; a spring in the campground feeds Clover Creek; no developed water or fee. It's located eight miles west on UT 199 from the junction with UT 36.

Deseret Peak
Hikers enjoy expansive views amidst alpine forests and glacial cirques in the Deseret Peak Wilderness Area, in the central portion of the Stansbury Mountains. The moderately difficult 3,600-foot climb to the summit is seven and one half miles roundtrip. Most of the way is easy to follow, though it's recommended that you carry the USGS topo maps Deseret Peak West and Deseret Peak East (7½-minute) or Deseret Peak (15-minute). The trail begins from Loop Campground at the end of the road up South Willow Canyon and connects to make a loop to the summit. After three-quarters of a mile the main summit trail turns left and follows Mill Fork (the trail forking right leads to an alternate summit trail and to North Willow Canyon). The main trail ascends two more miles through meadows, aspen, Douglas fir, limber pine, and a glacial cirque to a high ridge at 10,000 feet. Follow the ridge west three-quarters of a mile to Deseret Peak (elev. 11,031 feet). On a clear day atop the summit you can see much of the Wasatch Range on the eastern horizon, the Great Salt Lake to the north, Pilot Peak in Nevada to the northwest, Great Salt Lake Desert to the west, and countless desert ranges to the southwest. To make a loop, follow the trail along the north ridge about one and one half miles, contouring on the west side of three smaller peaks, then drop east a half mile into Pockets Fork. At the junction with the trail connecting North and South Willow canyons, turn right one and one half miles back to the trail junction in Mill Fork, three-quarters of a mile from the start.

For other trails and access roads in the Stansburys, see the topo and Wasatch-Cache National Forest maps. Only foot and horse travel are permitted in the wilderness area (west of

descending
Deseret Peak

Mack Canyon-Big Hollow Trail, north of Dry Canyon, and south of Pass Canyon).

SKULL VALLEY

Iosepa

Now a ghost town with little more than a cemetery, foundations, and a few houses, Iosepa once had a population of 226 Polynesian settlers. Devout Hawaiian Mormons who desired to live in the promised land of Utah began the settlement in 1889. All the good farmland around Salt Lake City had been taken, so the group wound up in this desolate valley west of the Stansbury Mountains. Undaunted by the harsh climate and scarcity of water, the Hawaiians laid out a townsite and named it Iosepa (Joseph) after the sixth president of the LDS church, Joseph F. Smith. Livestock were raised, crops and trees were planted, and roses bloomed in the new desert home. The islanders celebrated Pioneer Day on August 28, the date they arrived in Skull Valley, with feasts of poi and roast pig. Not all harvests produced a profit, however, and life here was hard. Leprosy appeared in 1896 and its several victims were forced to live in a separate building—Utah's only known leper colony. News in 1916 of a Mormon temple to be built in Hawaii brought a wave of homesickness, and within a year, the struggling settlement disbanded.

Today Iosepa is a large ranch along the road 15 miles south of I-80 Timpie Springs Exit 77. There's no sign at the ranch, but it's the largest in the area, with four houses along the road and several farm buildings. The two small frame houses belonged to the original Hawaiian settlement; two other surviving buildings are farther back. Residents don't mind people visiting the old townsite, but ask first. To see the cemetery, turn east past a group of mailboxes and the northernmost house, go through a gate,

then keep left at a fork. The cemetery, marked by six flagpoles, is three-quarters of a mile in; the road may be too rough for cars. Time and the elements have reduced the graves to mounds of gravel with just a few marble headstones. Their Hawaiian names seem out of place in this lonely desert valley.

Skull Valley Indian Reservation

From prehistoric times, Goshute Indians have ranged over this region to hunt and gather wild plant foods. And since the 1860s, they have been ranching and farming. If you've seen the hogans and sweat houses in the Four Corners area, this reservation will be something of a change: No culturally distinctive houses or outbuildings are found here.

SOUTH OF TOOELE

OQUIRRH MOUNTAINS GHOST TOWNS

Ophir

Picturesque old buildings and log cabins line the bottom of Ophir Canyon, which once boomed with saloons, dance halls, houses of ill repute, hotels, restaurants, and shops. In the 1860s, soldiers under General Patrick Connor heard stories of Indians mining silver and lead for ornaments and bullets. The soldier-prospectors tracked the Indian mines to this canyon and staked claims. By 1870 a town was born, named after the biblical land of Ophir where King Solomon's mines were located. Much of the ore went to General Connor's large smelter at nearby Stockton. Later the St. John & Ophir Railroad entered the canyon to haul away the rich ores of silver, lead, and zinc, and small amounts of gold and copper. Ophir's population peaked at 6,000, but unlike most other mining towns of the region, Ophir never quite died. People still live here and occasionally prospect in the hills. The city hall and some houses have been restored,

and the new **Ophir Gophir** sells groceries and refreshments (tel. 882-9903), but canyon vegetation has claimed the rest of the old structures.

Paved roads go all the way into town. From Tooele, head south 12 miles on UT 36 through Stockton, turn left five miles on UT 73, then left three and one half miles to Ophir. Tailings and foundations of a flotation mill built in 1930 are near the mouth of Ophir Canyon. The road to Ophir follows an old railroad grade; part of an abandoned passenger car still lies on the right just before the town. A gravel road continues up the canyon beyond Ophir, crossing Ophir Creek and weaving through forests of box elder and aspen before ending two and one half miles farther. You can camp here, but there are no facilities. Hikers can continue upstream and ascend Lowe Peak (elev. 10,572 feet) and other summits of the Oquirrh Mountains.

Mercur

General Connor's soldiers also discovered silver in the canyon southeast of Ophir during the late 1860s. After a slow start, prospectors made rich strikes and the rush was on. The mining

Golden Gate Mill at Mercur, ca. 1898

CHURCH OF JESUS CHRIST OF LATTER-DAY SAINTS

camp of Lewiston boomed in the mid-1870s, then busted by 1880 as the deposits worked out. Arie Pinedo, a prospector from Bavaria, began to poke around the dying camp and located the Mercur Lode of gold and mercury ore. He and other would-be miners were frustrated when all attempts to extract gold from the ore failed. Then in 1890, a new cyanide process proved effective, and a new boomtown with the Golden Gate Mill arose five years later. Though fire wiped out the business district in 1902, Mercur was rebuilt and had an estimated population of more than 8,000 by 1910. Only three years later the town closed up when ore bodies seemed depleted. Mining revived in the 1930s and again in the 1980s. Barrick Mercur Gold Mines now owns the ghost town site, of which little remains. Current technology allows profitable mining of both the massive old tailing piles (heaps of refuse pulled from the mines) and new deposits.

The company has an information center at the entrance gate with artifacts and photos of the early mining days; open daily in summer 10 a.m.-8 p.m.; tel. 268-4447. From the Ophir turnoff, continue southeast four miles on UT 73, then turn left three and one half miles on a paved road. A sign at the turnoff indicates if the center is open. If it's closed, there's no reason to drive in, as the mining and ghost town site can't be accessed without special permission. Tours of the operations can sometimes be arranged by calling in advance.

Other Ghost Towns
Stories of several other historic mining sites and the famous Ajax underground store make fascinating reading, but little remains at these sites. Good sources of information include *The Historical Guide to Utah Ghost Towns* by Stephen L. Carr and *Some Dreams Die: Utah's Ghost Towns and Lost Treasures* by George A. Thompson.

Stockton
The small town of Stockton is on the shore of Rush Lake, where sailboarding has gained great popularity in recent years. Soldier Canyon draws mountain bikers; go east three miles on Silver Street in Stockton.

PONY EXPRESS AND STAGE ROUTE

In 1860, Pony Express officials put together a chain of stations between St. Joseph, Missouri, and Sacramento, California. Relays of frontier-toughened men covered the 1,838-mile distance in 10 days. Riders stopped at stations spaced about 12 miles apart to change horses. Only after changing horses about six times did the rider complete his day's work. Despite the hazards of frontier travel, only one mail pouch was lost, and Indian wars held up service for only one month. Historians credit the daring enterprise with providing communications vital to keeping California aligned with the Union during the Civil War and proving that the West could be crossed in all kinds of weather—thus convincing skeptical politicians that a transcontinental railroad could be built. The Pony Express operated for only 18 months; completion of the transcontinental telegraph in October 1861 put the riders out of work. The company, which received no government assistance, failed to make a profit for its owners.

Relive some of the Old West by driving the Pony Express route across western Utah. The scenic route goes from spring to spring as it winds through several small mountain ranges and across open plains, skirting the worst of the Great Salt Lake Desert. Interpretive signs and monuments along the way describe how Pony Express riders rode swiftly on horseback to bring the country closer together. The 140 miles between Fairfield in the east and Ibapah near the Nevada border provide a sense of history and appreciation for the land lost to motorists speeding along I-80.

Allow at least a full day for the drive and bring food, water, and a full tank of gas. The Bureau of Land Management (BLM) has campgrounds at Simpson Springs and south of Callao. No motels or restaurants line the road, but Ibapah has two gas station/grocery stores. The well-graded gravel road can be traveled by car; just watch for the usual backcountry hazards of wildlife, rocks, and washouts. Adventurous travelers may want to make side trips for rockhounding, hiking, or visiting old mining sites. Always keep vehicles on existing roads—sand and mud flats can be treacherously deceptive!

You can begin your trip down the historic route from the Stagecoach Inn at Fairfield (from Salt Lake City or Provo, take I-15 to Lehi, then go 21 miles west on UT 73). You can also begin at Faust Junction (30 miles south of Tooele on UT 36) or Ibapah (51 miles south of Wendover off US 93A). The BLM has an information kiosk and small picnic area 1.8 miles west of Faust Junction. For the latest road conditions and travel information, contact the BLM Salt Lake District Office, 2370 S. 2300 West, Salt Lake City, UT 84119, tel. 977-4300. The following are points of interest along the route.

Stagecoach Inn At Fairfield
The inn was built for travelers in 1858 by John Carson, who had arrived as one of the first white settlers in the area around 1855. Now it's a state park. Inside the restored structure you can see where weary riders slept and sat around tables swapping stories. Stagecoach Inn is 36 miles northwest of Provo.

Simpson Springs
Indians had long used these excellent springs before the first white men came through. The name honors Capt. J.H. Simpson, who stopped here in 1859 while leading an Army survey across western Utah and Nevada. About the same time, George Chorpenning built a mail

station here that was later used by the Pony Express and Overland Express companies. A reconstructed stone cabin on the old site shows what the station looked like. Ruins of a nearby cabin built in 1893 contain stones from the first station. Foundations of a Civilian Conservation Corps camp lie across the road. In 1939, the young men of the CCC built historic markers, improved roads, and worked on conservation projects. The BLM campground higher up on the hillside has water (except in winter) and good views across the desert. A $2 per vehicle fee is charged; do not drink the water. Sparse juniper trees grow at the 5,100-foot elevation. Simpson Springs is 25 miles west of Faust Junction and 67 miles east of Callao.

Fish Springs National Wildlife Refuge
The Pony Express station once located here no longer exists, but you can visit the 10,000 acres of marsh and lake that attract abundant bird and animal life. Waterfowl and marsh birds stop over in greatest numbers during their early spring and late autumn migrations. Many smaller birds nest here in late spring and early summer, though they're difficult to see in the thick vegetation. Opportunistic hawks and other raptors circle overhead. A self-guided auto tour makes an 11.5-mile loop through the heart of the refuge. Most of the route follows dikes between the man-made lakes and offers good vantage points from which to see ducks, geese, egrets, herons, avocets, and other water birds.

Stagecoach Inn, built by John Carson in 1858

red-tailed hawk
(Buteo jamaicensis)

LOUISE FOOTE

The tour route and a picnic area near the entrance are open from sunrise to sunset; no camping is allowed in the refuge. Stop at the information booth near the entrance to pick up a brochure, to see photos of birds found at the refuge, and to read notes on the area's history. Fish Springs National Wildlife Refuge is 42 miles west of Simpson Springs and 25 miles east of Callao, tel. 831-5353.

Boyd Pony Express Station
Portions remain of the station's original rock wall, signs give the history of the station and the Pony Express. Find the station 13 miles west of Fish Springs and 12 miles east of Callao.

Callao
This cluster of ranches dates from 1859-60, when several families decided to take advantage of the desert grasslands and good springs here. The original name of Willow Springs had to be changed when residents applied for a post office—too many other Utah towns had the same name. Then someone suggested Callao (locally pronounced as "CAL-ee-o"), because the Peruvian town of that name has a similar setting of a valley backed by high mountains.

Residents raise cattle, sheep, and hay. Children go to Callao elementary school, one of the last one-room schoolhouses in Utah. Local people believe that the Willow Springs Pony Express station site was located off the main road at Bagley Ranch, but a BLM archaeologist contends that the foundation is on the east side of town. Callao is 67 miles west of Simpson Springs and 28 miles east of Ibapah (via Pony Express and Stage Route). A BLM campground, at the site of a former Civilian Conservation Corps camp, is four miles south beside Tom's Creek; no water or fee. The high Deep Creek Range rises to the west.

Canyon Station
(Follow signs for Sixmile Ranch, Overland Canyon, and Clifton Flat between Callao and Ibapah.) The original station used by Pony Express riders was in Overland Canyon, northwest of Canyon Station. Indians attacked in July 1863, burned the first station, and killed the Overland agent and four soldiers. The new station was built on a more defensible site. You can see its foundation and remnants of a fortification. A signed fork at Clifton Flat points the way to Gold Hill, a photogenic ghost town six miles distant; it's described below. Canyon Station is north of the Deep Creek Range, 13 miles northwest of Callao and 15 miles northeast of Ibapah.

Ibapah
Pronounce it "EYE-buh-paw" to avoid sounding like a tourist! Actually Ibapah is about the same size as Callao—little more than a group of some 20 ranches. Ibapah Trading Post (tel. 234-1166) and Pony Express Stop (tel. 234-1134) provide gas and groceries.

VICINITY OF IBAPAH

Continuing south a short way, the main road forks left to Goshute Indian Reservation, while the right fork crosses into Nevada to US 93 (58 miles) on the old Pony Express and Stage Route. From Ibapah you can also go north to Gold Hill ghost town (14 miles) and Wendover (58 miles) or south to US 50/6 near Great Basin National Park via Callao, Trout Creek, and Gandy (90 miles).

Goshute Indian Reservation

Goshute Indians mastered living in the harsh desert by knowing of every edible seed, root, insect, reptile, bird, and rodent, as well as larger game. Their meager diet and possessions appalled early white settlers, who referred disparagingly to the Indians as "diggers." Loss of land to ranchers and dependence on manufactured food put an end to the old nomadic lifestyle. In recent times the Goshute have gradually begun to regain independence by learning to farm and ranch. Several hundred members of the tribe live on the Goshute Indian Reservation, which straddles the Utah-Nevada border. Most of the reservation is off-limits to nonmembers without special permission.

Gold Hill

Miners had been working the area for three years when they founded Gold Hill in 1892. A whole treasure trove of minerals came out of the ground here—gold, silver, lead, copper, tungsten, arsenic, and bismuth. A smelter along a ridge just west of town processed the ore. But three years later Gold Hill's boom ended. Most people lived only in tents anyway, and soon everything but the smelter foundations and tailings was packed up. A rebirth occurred during WW I when the country desperately needed copper, tungsten, and arsenic. Gold Hill grew to a sizable town with 3,000 residents, a railroad line from Wendover, and many substantial buildings. Cheaper foreign sources of arsenic knocked the bottom out of local mining in 1924, and Gold Hill began to die again. Another frenzied burst of activity occurred in 1944-45 when the country called once more for tungsten and arsenic. The town again sprang to life, only to fade just as quickly after the war ended. Determined prospectors still roam the surrounding countryside awaiting another clamor for the underground riches. Decaying structures in town make a picturesque sight. (Several year-round residents live here; no scavenging allowed.) Visible nearby are the cemetery, mines, railroad bed, and smelter site. The smaller ghost town of **Clifton** lies over the hill to the south but little remains; No Trespassing signs make visitors unwelcome. Good roads (partly dirt) approach Gold Hill from Ibapah, Wendover, and Callao.

DEEP CREEK RANGE

The range soars spectacularly above the Great Salt Lake Desert. Few people know about the Deep Creeks despite their great heights, diverse wildlife, and pristine forests. Ibapah Peak ("EYE-buh-paw"; elev. 12,087 feet) and Haystack Peak to the north (elev. 12,020 feet) crown the range. Glacial cirques and other rugged features have been carved into the nearly white granite that makes up most of the summit ridge. Prospectors have found gold, silver, lead, zinc, copper, mercury, beryllium, molybdenum, tungsten, and uranium. You'll occasionally run across mines and old cabins in the range, especially in Goshute Canyon. Of the six perennial streams on the east side, Birch and Trout creeks still contain Lake Bonneville cutthroat trout that originated in the prehistoric lake; both creeks were closed to fishing at press time. Wildlife includes Rocky Mountain bighorn sheep (reintroduced), deer, pronghorn, mountain lion, coyote, bobcat, and many birds. Vegetation ranges from grass and sagebrush in the lower foothills to piñon pine and juniper, then to montane

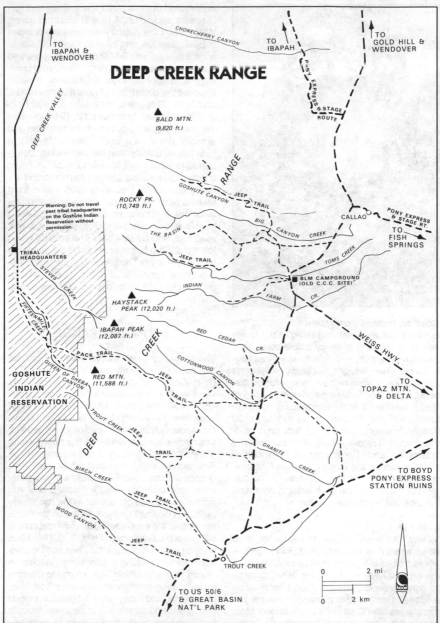

DEEP CREEK RANGE

TO IBAPAH & WENDOVER

CHOKECHERRY CANYON

TO IBAPAH

TO GOLD HILL & WENDOVER

DEEP CREEK VALLEY

BALD MTN. (9,820 ft.)

PONY EXPRESS & STAGE ROUTE

RANGE

GOSHUTE CANYON

JEEP TRAIL

ROCKY PK. (10,749 ft.)

Warning: Do not travel past tribal headquarters on the Goshute Indian Reservation without permission.

THE BASIN

BIG CANYON CREEK

CALLAO

PONY EXPRESS & STAGE RT.

TO FISH SPRINGS

TRIBAL HEADQUARTERS

STEVES CREEK

JEEP TRAIL

TOMS CREEK

BLM CAMPGROUND (OLD C.C.C. SITE)

INDIAN

FARM

CR.

FIFTEEN MILE CREEK

HAYSTACK PEAK (12,020 ft.)

IBAPAH PEAK (12,087 ft.)

RED CEDAR CR.

CREEK

WEISS HWY.

PACK TRAIL

QUEEN OF SHEBA CANYON

COTTONWOOD CANYON

TO TOPAZ MTN. & DELTA

GOSHUTE INDIAN RESERVATION

RED MTN. (11,588 ft.)

JEEP TRAIL

TROUT CREEK

JEEP TRAIL

DEEP

GRANITE CREEK

BIRCH CREEK

JEEP TRAIL

TO BOYD PONY EXPRESS STATION RUINS

WOOD CANYON

JEEP TRAIL

TROUT CREEK

0   2 mi

0   2 km

TO US 50/6 & GREAT BASIN NAT'L PARK

© MOON PUBLICATIONS, INC.

forests of aspen, Engelmann spruce, Douglas fir, white fir, subalpine fir, ponderosa pine, and limber pine. Bristlecone pine grows on some of the high ridges. Alpine tundra covers the highest peaks. The Deep Creek Range gets plenty of snow in winter, so the climbing season runs from about late June to late October. Aspen and some mountain shrubs put on colorful displays in September and early October. Streams in the range have good water (purify first), but the lower canyons are often polluted by the organisms that accompany cattle excrement. Carry water while hiking on the dry ridges.

Main Climbing Routes

Most of the canyons have roads into their lower reaches. Four-wheel-drive vehicles will be able to get farther up the steep grades than cars. Most hikers start up Granite or Indian Farm creeks and head for Ibapah or Haystack peaks. A trail along **Granite Creek** offers the easiest approach to Ibapah Peak, about 12.5 miles roundtrip and a 5,300-foot elevation gain from the beginning of the jeep trail. The road to Granite Creek turns west off Snake Valley Road 10 miles south of Callao (7.8 miles north of Trout Creek Ranch). Keep left at a junction about one mile in, then follow the most-used track. The road enters Granite Canyon after three miles. The first ford of Granite Creek, a half mile into the canyon, requires a high-clearance vehicle; the second ford, 0.8 mile farther, may require 4WD. The road deteriorates into a jeep track in another 0.6 mile at the border of Deep Crook Wilderness Study Area. Four-wheel-drive vehicles can climb the steep grade another two miles. Continue two miles on a pack trail to the beginning of a large meadow at the pass, then head cross-country one and one half miles to the small peak (11,385 feet) just before Ibapah; you should find a small trail on the east side of this peak that continues three-quarters of a mile to the summit of Ibapah. (This small trail probably once connected with the pack trail, but is little used today.)

Impressive panoramas take in the rugged canyons and ridges of the Deep Creek Range below and much of western Utah and eastern Nevada beyond. Remains of a heliograph station sit atop Ibapah. Early mapmakers measured the highest point in the range at 12,101 feet and named it "Haystack." A later survey determined the correct height to be 12,087 feet and renamed the peak "Ibapah"; the second highest peak was given the old Haystack name by default. Hikers can head cross-country two miles north from Ibapah to Haystack Peak (12,020 feet). The 7 1/2-minute Ibapah Peak topo map covers the entire hike to the summit of both peaks via Granite Creek.

Other Climbing Routes

Red Mountain (11,588 feet) can also be climbed from the pass above Granite Creek. The jeep trail to **Toms Creek** leads to a route to the head of the creek, from which Haystack Peak is about three miles south along the crest of the range; turnoff for Toms Canyon is 1.6 miles south of Callao and 8.4 miles north of the Granite Creek turnoff. A more direct route to Haystack Peak goes up through **Indian Farm Canyon.** Turnoff for this canyon is 4.3 miles south of Callao and 5.7 miles north of the Granite Creek turnoff. **Red Cedar Creek** in the heart of the Deep Creeks remains pristine —no trails, roads, or other developments. It's also very rugged; allow a day or two just to hike through one-way. Early ranchers mistook the Rocky Mountain juniper for red cedar. **Trout Creek** is another good hiking area. A trail goes most of the way up the valley.

Approaches to the peaks from the **Goshute Indian Reservation** have been less used because of travel restrictions. Also, this western slope is much drier. Probably the easiest way up from here is to drive though Goshute village to Fifteen Mile Creek and to hike the pack trail to the ridge between Ibapah Peak and Red Mountain, meeting the trail coming up from Granite Creek. To visit the west side you need to plan ahead and get permission from the Tribal Council, which meets once a month. Write to them at Box 6104, Ibapah, UT 84034, explaining the purpose of your trip and what you'll be doing, dates, roads and trails to be used, and the organization you're with, if any. Then on arrival, check in at the tribal offices. For more information call the executive secretary at 234-1136 or the law enforcement office at 234-1139.

Information

Hikers venturing into this remote range must be self-sufficient and experienced in wilderness travel. Topo maps you'll need are the 7 1/2-

minute Ibapah Peak and Indian Farm Creek for the central part of the range, the 7½-minute Goshute and Goshute Canyon for the northern part, and the 15-minute Trout Creek for the southern part. The metric 1:100,000 Fish Springs quad covers the whole area, but with less detail. For firsthand information, contact the BLM House Range Resource Area, 35 E. 500 North, Fillmore, UT 84631, tel. 743-6811. The Sierra Club book *Hiking the Great Basin* by John Hart has detailed trail descriptions.

All approaches to the Deep Creeks involve dirt road travel and generally sizable distances. Some of the ways in (to the Granite Creek road junction) are from Wendover via Gold Hill (92 miles), from Provo via the Pony Express and Stage Route (158 miles), from Delta via the Weiss Hwy. (93 miles), and from US 50/6 near the Utah-Nevada border via Gandy and Trout Creek (52 miles). Ibapah has the nearest gas and groceries (38 miles from Granite Creek turnoff).

EUREKA AND TINTIC MINING DISTRICT

The lucky prospectors who cried "Eureka! I've found it!" had stumbled onto a fabulously rich deposit of silver and other valuable metals. Eureka sprang up to be one of Utah's most important cities and the center of more than a dozen mining communities. Much can still be seen of the district's long history—mine headframes and buildings, shafts and glory holes, old styles of residential and commercial architecture, great piles of ore tailings, and forlorn cemeteries. Exhibits at the Tintic Mining Museum in Eureka show what life was like. Paved highways provide easy access: from I-15 Santaquin Exit 248 (south of Provo) go west 21 miles on US 6, from Delta go northeast 48 miles on US 6, or from Tooele go south 54 miles on UT 36.

History

Mormon stockherders began moving cattle here during the early 1850s to take advantage of the good grazing lands. Ute Indians under Chief Tintic, for whom the district was later named, opposed the newcomers but couldn't stop them.

Mineral deposits found in the hills remained a secret with the Mormons, as Church policy prohibited members from prospecting for precious metals. In 1869, though, George Rust, a gentile (non-Mormon) cowboy, noted the promising ores. Soon the rush was on—ores assaying up to 10,000 ounces of silver per ton began pouring out of the mines. Silver City, founded in 1870, became the first of many mining camps. New discoveries kept the Tintic District booming. Gold, copper, lead, and zinc added to the riches. By 1910 the district had a population of 8,000 with the end nowhere in sight. The hills shook from underground blasting and the noise of mills, smelters, and railroads. Valuable Tintic properties kept the Salt Lake Stock Exchange busy, while Salt Lake City office buildings and mansions rose with Tintic money. Mining began a slow decline in the 1930s but has continued, sporadically, to the present. Most of the old mining camps have dried up and blown away. Eureka and Mammoth drift on as sleepy towns— monuments to an earlier era. The ghosts of for-

Eureka mines, ca. 1900

mer camps can be worth a visit too, though most require considerable imagination to see them as they were. Do not go near decaying structures or mine shafts.

EUREKA

Mines and tailing dumps surround weather-beaten buildings. Eureka lacks the orderliness of Mormon towns; the main street snakes through the valley with side streets branching off in every direction. Few recent buildings have been added, so the town retains an authentic atmosphere from earlier in this century. Eureka now has a population of about 600, down from the 3,400 of its peak years.

Tintic Mining Museum

The varied exhibits of this small museum will give you an appreciation of the district and its mining pioneers. A mineral collection from the Tintic area has many fine specimens. You'll see early mining tools, assay equipment, a mine office, courtroom, blacksmith shop, a 1920s' kitchen, many historic photos, and displays that show social life in the early days. One display is dedicated to the influence of Jessie Knight, a Mormon financier and philanthropist. Knightsville, now a ghost town site near Eureka, gained fame as one of the few mining towns in Utah without a saloon or gambling hall. Knight also promoted mine safety and closed his mines for a day of rest on Sundays—both radical concepts at the time. Museum galleries are upstairs in the City Hall (built 1899) and next door in the former railroad depot (built 1925). The *Tintic Tour Guide* sold here describes a 35-mile loop to some of the nearby ghost towns and mines. The Tintic Mining Museum is usually open summer weekends and some weekdays, at other times on request. Admission is free, tel. 433-6842.

Bullion-Beck Mine

A large timber headframe on the west edge of town beside the highway marks one of the most productive mines in the district. John Beck arrived in 1871 and began sinking a shaft. At first people called him the "Crazy Dutchman," but the jeers ended when he hit a huge deposit of rich ore 200 feet down. The present 65-foot-high headframe dates from about 1890; originally a large wooden building enclosed it.

Practicalities

The small **Tintic Motel** is downtown on Main St., tel. 433-6311, $27.25 s, $30.52 d. **Gold Diggers Restaurant** (closed Monday) is also downtown. The **Pit Stop** serves fast food on the east edge of town. Eureka celebrates **Depot Days and Tintic Silver Festival** with a parade, a mountain men rendezvous, mine tours, arts and crafts exhibits, dances, and entertainment; it's held on the third weekend of August.

VICINITY OF EUREKA

Dividend

Emil Raddatz bought this property on the east slope of the Tintic Mountains in 1907, believing that the ore deposits mined on the west side of the Tintics also extended to here. Raddatz nearly went broke digging deeper and deeper, but the prized silver and lead ore 1,200 feet below proved him right. After his 1916 discovery, a modern company town grew up complete with hotel, movie theater, golf course, and ice plant. The miners, whose wages had been paid partly in stock certificates, chose the name Dividend because they had been so well rewarded. Mining continued until 1949, producing $19 million in dividends, but today only foundations, mine shafts, and large piles of tailings remain. A loop road east of Eureka will take you to this site and other mining areas. Walking or driving off the road is forbidden because of mine shafts and other hazards. Though the road is paved, some sections are badly pot-holed and need to be driven slowly. From downtown Eureka, go east one and one half miles on US 6 and turn right on the Dividend road (0.1 mile east of Milepost 141); the road climbs into hills and passes the Eureka Lily headframe and mine on the left after two and one half miles; continue 0.3 mile to Tintic Standard #1 shaft on right, then 0.3 mile more to the site of Dividend and the #2 shaft (signed); the road ends at a junction 0.9 mile farther; turn left 0.7 mile to US 6 (four miles east of Eureka). The Sunshine Mining Company currently operates the Burgin Mine about one mile east of Dividend.

Mammoth

Prospectors made a "mammoth" strike over the hill south of Eureka in 1870. The town of Mammoth, more mines, mills, and smelters followed. The eccentric mining engineer George Robinson built a second town, immodestly named after himself, one mile down the valley. Both towns prospered, growing together and eventually becoming just "Mammoth." Nearly 3,000 people lived here when activity peaked in 1900-10. Then came the inevitable decline as the high-grade ores worked out. By the 1930s, Mammoth was well on its way to becoming a ghost town. People still live here and have preserved some of the old buildings. The Mammoth glory hole and mine buildings overlook the town at the head of the valley. Ruins of smelters and mines cling to hillsides. From Eureka, go southwest two and one half miles on US 6, then turn left (east) one mile on a paved road. Upper and lower towns can now be distinguished.

Silver City

Optimistic prospectors named their little camp for the promising silver ore, but a city it was not to be. The cost of pumping water out of the mines cut too deeply into profit margins, then a 1902 fire nearly put an end to the town. At that point Mormon financier Jessie Knight stepped in to improve the mines and rebuild the town. He also built a smelter and later a mill. Silver City reached its peak about 1908 before declining to ghost town status in the 1930s. You can't miss the giant piles of tailings (light colored) and slag (dark colored) from the smelter and mill at the old townsite. Extensive concrete foundations show the complexity and size of the operations. Sagebrush has reclaimed the rest of the town, of which only debris and foundations survive. Mining and prospecting are still done in the area, though; a new mining operation is currently reprocessing the old smelter waste products. Silver City ghost town site lies 3.3 miles southwest of Eureka (0.8 mile past the Mammoth turnoff) just off US 6.

Other Tintic Ghost Towns

These towns exist mostly as memories. Diligent searching through the sagebrush may uncover foundations, tailings piles, broken glass, and neglected cemeteries. Yet behind many of the sites are dramatic stories of attempts to win riches from the earth. History buffs may want to look at the book *Faith, Hope and Prosperity: The Tintic Mining District* by Philip Notarianni, available at the Tintic Mining Museum. Also see *The Historical Guide to Utah Ghost Towns* by Stephen L. Carr and *Some Dreams Die* by George A. Thompson.

SHEEPROCK MOUNTAINS

Black Crook Peak (elev. 9,275 feet) tops this little-known range northwest of Eureka. Sheeprock Mountain Trail (Forest Trails #051 and #052) follows the crest of the mountains for most of their length. Several other trails connect from each side. See the Uinta National Forest map and the 7½-minute Erickson Knoll, Dutch Peak, Lookout Pass, and Vernon topo maps. Mining, which peaked in the early 1900s, still continues on a small scale for silver, lead, and zinc. Bald eagles winter here from about Dec.-March; their numbers appear to fluctuate with the rabbit population. Anglers can try for brook and brown trout in Vernon Reservoir and Vernon and Bennion creeks.

The small **Little Valley Campground** is open May-Nov.; no water or charge. Benmore Experimental Pastures, northeast of the mountains, dates from 1933 as a cooperative state and federal program to develop techniques of restoring and managing rangelands. Although the Sheeprock Mountains are in the Wasatch National Forest, the Spanish Fork Ranger Dis-

black-tailed jackrabbit (Lepus californicus)

LOUISE FOOTE

trict office of the Uinta National Forest manages this area, known as the Vernon Division, 44 W. 400 North, Spanish Fork, UT 84660, tel. 798-3571. Follow UT 36 northwest 17 miles from Eureka (or south 42 miles from Tooele) to a junction signed "Benmore," just east of Vernon, turn south five miles to Benmore Guard Station, then left two and one half miles for Vernon Reservoir. Little Valley Campground is off to the right in a side valley 2.3 miles past the reservoir. A road in via Lofgreen is a bit rough for cars. None of these roads are recommended in wet weather.

LITTLE SAHARA RECREATION AREA

Sand dunes have made a giant sandbox between Eureka and Delta. Managed by the BLM, the recreation area covers 60,000 acres of free-moving sand dunes, sagebrush flats, and juniper-covered ridges. Elevations range from about 5,000 to 5,700 feet. Varied terrain provides challenges for dune buggies, motorcycles, and 4WD vehicles. While offroad vehicles can range over most of the dunes, areas near White Sands and Jericho campgrounds have been set aside for children. The Rockwell Natural Area in the western part of the dunes protects 9,150 acres for nature study.

The dunes originated 150 miles away as sandbars along the southern shore of Lake Bonneville roughly 10,000 years ago. After the lake receded, prevailing winds pushed the exposed sands on a slow trek northeastward at a rate of about 18 inches per year. Sand Mountain, however, deflected the winds upward, and the sand grains piled up into large dunes downwind. Lizards and kangaroo rats scamper across the sands in search of food and, in turn, are eaten by hawks, bobcats, and coyotes. Pronghorn and mule deer live here all year. Juniper, sagebrush, greasewood, saltbush, and grasses are the most common plants. An unusual species of fourwing saltbush *(Atriplex canescens)* grows as high as 12 feet and is restricted to the dunes area.

A visitor center near the entrance is open irregular hours. Three developed campgrounds with water (White Sands, Oasis, and Jericho) and a primitive camping area (Sand Mountain) are open all year. In winter, water is available only at the visitor center on the way in. Visitors to Little Sahara pay a daily $5 fee per vehicle (a pickup truck or trailer carrying offroad vehicles counts as one vehicle), which includes use of campgrounds. In winter the campgrounds don't have water available. For more information or group camping permits, contact the BLM at 15 E. 500 North, Fillmore, UT 84631, tel. 743-6811. The entrance road is four and one half miles west of Jericho Junction; the distance from Nephi (I-15 Exits 222 and 228) is 31 miles via UT 132 and Juab County 148. From Eureka head south 17 miles on US 6, then west four and one half miles. From Delta go northeast 32 miles, then west four and one half miles. The distance from Salt Lake City is 115 miles.

DELTA AND VICINITY

The barren Pahvant Valley along the lower Sevier River had long been considered a wasteland. Then in 1905, some Fillmore businessmen purchased water rights from Sevier River Reservoir and 10,000 acres of land. The farm and town lots they sold became the center of one of Utah's most productive agricultural areas. Other hopeful homesteaders that settled farther from Delta weren't as fortunate. Thousands of families bought cheap land in the North Tract but found the going very difficult. Troubles with the irrigation system, poor crop yields, and low market prices forced most to leave by the late 1930s. A few decaying houses and farm buildings mark the sites of once-bustling communities. Farmers near Delta raise alfalfa seed and hay, wheat, corn, barley, mushrooms, and livestock. The giant coal-burning Intermountain Power Project (IPP) and the Brush Wellman beryllium mill have helped boost Delta's population to about 4,000. Miners have been digging into the Drum Mountains northwest of Delta since the 1870s for gold, silver, copper, manganese, and other minerals; some work still goes on there. The beryllium processed near Delta comes from large deposits of bertrandite mined in open pits in the Topaz and Spors mountains, farther to the northwest.

Great Basin Museum, 328 W. 100 North (turn north one block on 300 West from Main St.), tel. 864-5013, presents a varied collection of pioneer photos and artifacts, Indian arrowheads, a Topaz Camp exhibit, fossils, and minerals; antique farm machinery stands outside. Open Mon.-Fri. 10 a.m.-4 p.m. and Saturday 1-4 p.m.; free admission.

A pioneer log cabin (built 1907-08), now on Main Street in front of Delta's Municipal Building, was the second house and the first post office in Melville, which was later known as Burtner and finally as Delta in 1910. Historical markers near the cabin commemorate the Spanish Dominguez-Escalante expedition that passed to the south in 1776, and the Topaz Camp for Japanese-Americans interned during WW II. For travelers, Delta makes a handy base for visiting the surrounding historic sites, rockhounding, and exploring nearby mountain ranges.

Rockhounding

Beautiful rock, mineral, and fossil specimens await discovery in the desert surrounding Delta. Sought-after rocks and minerals include topaz, bixbyite, sunstones, geodes, obsidian, muscovite, garnet, pyrite, and agate. Some fossils to look for are trilobites, brachiopods, horn coral, and crinoids. The chamber of commerce in Delta is a good source of local information.

Gemstones from the area can be seen at West Desert Collectors and Tina's Jewelry & Minerals. Useful publications include *Guide to Rocks and Fossils* available at the chamber of commerce and *Collector's Guide to Mineral and Fossil Localities,* published by the Utah Geological and Mineral Survey (June 1977). A hat and plenty of water will add to comfort and safety when enjoying the outdoors. Always be watchful when hiking to avoid rattlesnakes and mine shafts. Both are occasionally found in caves, where the dim light makes them harder to see.

Accommodations

All of Delta's motels are on or close to Main Street. Rates listed are for summer; most drop a few dollars in winter. From west to east are **Starglo Motor Lodge,** 234 W. Main, tel. 864-2041, $21.80 s, $28.50 d; **Killpack Motor Lodge,** 201 W. Main, tel. 864-2734, $26.16 s, $28.34 d, also one kitchenette; **Rancher Motel,** 171 W. Main, tel. 864-2741, $27.25 s, $30.52 d; **Wilden Motel,** 127 W. Main, tel. 864-2906, $25 s, $28.35 d; **Deltan Inn Motel,** 347 E. Main, tel. 864-5318, $30.52 s, $33.79 d; **Budget Motel,** a half block south of Main on 350 East, tel. 864-4533, $27.44 s, $37 d; also kitchenettes; and **Best Western Plaza Motel,** just north on US 6 at the east edge of town, tel. 864-3882 or (800) 528-1234, $45.78 s, $49.05 d and up.

Campgrounds

B Kitten Klean Trailer Court, 181 E. Main, tel. 864-2614, has showers and is open all year; $6 tent, $12 RV w/hookups. **Antelope Valley RV Park,** 760 W. Main, tel. 864-4782, has showers and is open April 1 to early September; $10 tent, $12 RV no hookups, $18 RV w/hookups. **Oak Creek Campground** lies in a pretty wooded canyon in the Fishlake National Forest; sites have drinking water late May to early October, $5. Head east 14 miles on US 50 and UT 125 to Oak City, then turn right four miles on a paved road.

Food

Tops City Cafe, 313 W. Main, tel. 864-2148, serves standard American fare daily for breakfast, lunch, and dinner. The **Rancher Motel,** 171 W. Main, tel. 864-2741, has a cafe with American and Mexican food; a dining room upstairs serves steak and seafood. Open daily for breakfast, lunch, and dinner. **Chef's Palace,** 225 E. Main, tel. 864-2421, offers steak, seafood, chicken, and a salad bar; open Mon.-Sat. for dinner only. **Jade Garden,** at the Best Western Plaza Motel, just north on US 6 at the east edge of town, tel. 864-2947, has American and Chinese food; open daily for breakfast, lunch, and dinner. The **Pizza House,** 69 S. 300 East, tel. 864-2207, features pizza, pasta, barbecued ribs, a long list of sandwiches, and salad bar. Open Mon.-Sat. for lunch and dinner.

Several fast-food places and two supermarkets can be found in town. **Delta Valley Farms** has a family restaurant two miles northeast of Delta on US 6; open Mon.-Sat. for lunch. Call in advance if you'd like a tour of their cheese-making plant, tel. 864-3566.

Entertainment And Events

Catch movies at **T&T Twin Theatres** in Pendray Plaza (east end of town just north of US 6 and US 50 junction), tel. 864-4551. Annual events include **Fourth of July** fireworks and demolition derby, **Pioneer Day** (parade, rodeo, games) on July 24 in Hinckley, and **Millard County Fair** (parade, horse show, games, demolition derby, and street dance) at the fairgrounds on the east side of town in early August. In September enjoy the **Classy Chassy Car Show** and the **West Millard High School Rodeo** with hundreds of contestants.

Recreation, Shopping, And Services

The indoor **West Millard County Swimming Pool** is open year-round at the corner of 200 East and 300 North, tel. 864-3133. A **city park** with picnic facilities and tennis courts is at the corner of Main and 100 West; restrooms are in

the nearby municipal building. **Sunset View Golf Course** offers nine holes, three miles northeast of town on US 6, tel. 864-2508. **Gunnison Bend Park** west of town has picnicking, water-skiing, and fishing (catfish and largemouth bass); go west two and one half miles on US 50/6, then right two miles. **West Desert Collectors,** 298 W. Main, tel. 864-2175, has beautiful rocks, minerals, and fossils. **Tina's Jewelry & Minerals,** 320 E. Main, tel. 864-2444, offers beautiful gems.

The **post office** is at the corner of 300 East and 100 South, tel. 864-2811. **Delta Community Medical Center** provides emergency care at 126 S. White Sage Ave. (south off US 50 on east side of town), tel. 864-5591. In **emergencies** (police, fire, or medical) call 911.

Information

Delta Chamber of Commerce will tell you about services in town and sights in the surrounding area; the office is in the municipal building at Main and 200 West (80 N. 200 West, Delta, UT 84624), tel. 864-4316. Open Mon.-Fri. 10 a.m.-5 p.m. The **public library,** also in the municipal building, tel. 864-4945, is open Mon.-Fri. 2-8 p.m. and Saturday 1-5 p.m.

NORTH OF DELTA

Baker Hot Springs

Though Crater Springs Health Resort has closed, local people still come to soak in the hot springs. Water emerges from the ground at near boiling temperatures and flows into two surviving concrete tubs. The springs also feed shallow ponds that have colorful mineral deposits and strange-looking algae growths. Easiest way from Delta is to go northeast 11 miles on US 6, turn left (west) 19 miles on the paved Brush Wellman Road, then right (north) seven miles on a dirt road along a large black lava flow. Springs are on the right. Ruts may make this dry-weather-only road difficult for cars. (You can save about nine miles from Delta if you can navigate the maze of farm roads between the west edge of Delta and the Brush Wellman Road.) Adventurous motorists can also follow dirt roads from Baker Hot Springs north and east 35 miles to Little Sahara Recreation Area.

EAST OF DELTA

Canyon Mountains

Oak Creek Campground lies along the creek amid Gambel oak, cottonwood, maple, and juniper on the west side of the mountains. Canyon walls cut by Oak Creek reveal layers of twisted and upturned rock. This forest service campground (elev. 5,900 feet) has water from late May to early October ($5 for family sites). Groups can reserve a large area with amphitheater, sports area, and shelter. Oak Creek usually has good fishing for rainbow trout. Much of its flow comes from a spring at the upper end of the campground. From Delta go east 14 miles on US 50 and UT 125 to the small farming town of Oak City, then turn right four miles on a paved road. A gravel road continues upcanyon past the campground to other forest roads and hiking trails; see the Fishlake National Forest map. Unpaved roads also provide access to the steeper east side of the Canyon Mountains. Fool Creek Peak tops this small range at 9,717 feet. For more information, contact the Fillmore Ranger District office at 390 S. Main in Fillmore (Box 265, Fillmore, UT 84631), tel. 743-5721.

SOUTH OF DELTA

Fort Deseret

What remains of this fort represents a fading piece of pioneer history. Mormon settlers hastily built the adobe-walled fort in only 18 days in 1865 for protection against Indians during the Black Hawk War. The square fort had walls 550 feet long and 10 feet high with gates in the middle of each side. Bastions were located at the northeast and southwest corners. Indians never attacked the fort, though it came in handy to pen up cattle at night. Parts of the wall and stone foundation still stand. From Delta go west five miles on US 50/6, then turn left (south) four and one half miles on UT 257. The site is on the west side of the road near Milepost 65, about one and one half miles south of the town of Deseret.

Great Stone Face

A natural rock formation seven miles southwest of Deseret has a striking resemblance to the Mormon prophet Joseph Smith. To see the pro-file you have to view the rock from the west. From the town of Deseret, go south three miles on UT 257, then turn right (west) four miles (should be signed) on a dirt road. A short hike at road's end leads up a lava flow to the stone face.

Clear Lake State Waterfowl Management Area

Lakes and marsh country offer ducks, Canada geese, and other birds a refreshing break from the desert. Roads cross Clear Lake on a causeway and lead to smaller lakes and picnic areas to the north. Utah Division of Wildlife Resources manages the area. From the junction of US 50/6 and UT 257 west of Delta, go south 15.5 miles on UT 257, then turn left (east) seven miles on a good gravel road.

Pahvant Butte

Locally known as Sugar Loaf Mountain, this extinct volcano rises 1,000 feet above the desert floor. Waters of prehistoric Lake Bonneville leveled off the large terrace about halfway up. Remnants of a crater, now open to the southwest, are on this level. Another terrace line is at the bottom of the butte. Hikers can enjoy the volcanic geology, expansive panoramas, and a visit to the curious ruins of a windmill. Construction of the wind-powered electric power station began in 1923 but was never completed. A large underground room and two concentric rings of concrete pylons give an eerie Stonehenge-like atmosphere to the butte.

Easiest way up is an old road on the south side that goes to the windmill site. From Clear Lake (see above), continue east 3.3 miles to the second signed turn on the left for Pahvant Butte; there's a sign here "Pahvant Butte Road: 3 miles, Sugarloaf Well #1: 8 miles." Turn left three and one half miles at the sign, then turn left one-half mile on Pahvant Butte Road. Park before the road begins a steep climb. Daredevils in 4WDs have tried going straight up the slope from here, but the real road turns right and follows switchbacks 0.7 mile to the windmill site. This last 0.7 mile is closed to vehicles because of soft volcanic rock, but it's fine for walking; elevation gain is about 400 feet. Pahvant Butte's highest point is about a half mile to the north and 265 feet higher; you'll have to find your own way across if headed there. Dirt roads encircle Pahvant Butte and go northeast to US 50 and southeast to Tabernacle Hill and Fillmore. The Tabernacle Hill area provides good examples of volcanic features.

WEST OF DELTA

Topaz Camp

Topaz is easily Utah's most dispirited ghost town site. Other ghost towns had the promise of precious metals or good land to lure their populations, but those coming to Topaz had no choice—they had the bad fortune to be of the wrong ancestry during the height of WW II hysteria. About 9,000 Japanese, most of whom were American citizens, were brought from the West Coast to this desolate desert plain in 1942. Topaz sprang up in just a few months and included barracks, communal dining halls, post office, hospital, schools, churches, and recreational facilities. Most internees cooperated with authorities; the few who caused trouble were shipped off to a more secure camp. Barbed wire and watchtowers with armed guards surrounded the small city—Utah's fifth-largest for a time. All were released at war's end in 1945 and the camp came down almost as quickly as it had gone up. Salvagers bought and removed equipment, buildings, barbed wire, telephone poles, and even street paving and sewer pipes. An

on their way to Topaz

uneasy silence pervades the site today. Little more than the streets, foundations, and piles of rubble remain. You can still walk or drive along the streets of the vast camp, which had 42 neatly laid-out blocks. A concrete memorial stands at the northwest corner of the site.

One way to get here is to go west six miles from Delta on US 50/6 to the small town of Hinckley, turn right (north) four and one half miles on a paved road (some parts are gravel) to its end, turn left (west) two and one half miles on a paved road to its end in Abraham, turn right (north) one and one half miles on a gravel road to a stop sign, then turn left three miles on a gravel road; Topaz is on the left.

Drum Mountains

Strange subterranean noises can sometimes be heard in these desert mountains; some say the sounds are like thumps or rumblings of a drum. Prospectors began combing the parched hillsides in 1872 but did little mining development. Harry Joy and Charles Howard, mining engineers from Michigan, organized the Detroit Mining District here in 1879. They dug for gold, silver, and copper and built a smelter. Mining centered on the small town of **Joy.** Crumbling foundations are all that remain of the townsite, though dilapidated mine buildings can be found in nearby canyons. Western States Minerals has an active gold mine in the Drums. The mountains can be reached by continuing west from Topaz or from US 6 on the paved Brush Wellman Road.

HOUSE RANGE

This range about 45 miles west of Delta offers great vistas, scenic drives, wilderness hiking, and world-famous trilobite fossil beds. Swasey Peak (elev. 9,669 feet) is the highest point. From a distance, however, Notch Peak's spectacular 2,700-foot face stands out as the most prominent landmark in the region. What the 50-mile-long range lacks in great heights, it makes up for in massive sheer limestone cliffs and rugged canyons. Precipitous drops on the western side contrast with a gentler slope on the east. Hardy vegetation such as juniper, piñon pine, mountain mahogany, and sagebrush dominates the dry slopes. Bristlecone pines grow on high ridges of

Swasey and Notch peaks; the long-lived trees are identified by inward-curving bristles on the cones and by needles less than one and one half inches long in clusters of five. Some of the high country also harbors limber pine, ponderosa pine, white fir, Douglas fir, and aspen.

Wildlife includes mule deer, pronghorn, chukar partridge, bald and golden eagles, and peregrine falcon. Wild horses roam Sawmill Basin to the northeast of Swasey Peak. Permanent water supplies are found only at a few scattered springs in the range. Limestone caves attract spelunkers, especially Antelope Spring Cave near Dome Canyon Pass (ask directions at the BLM office in Fillmore or from the Speleological Society of Utah). Council Cave on Antelope Peak (between Notch and Swasey peaks) has an enormous opening, visible for more than 50 miles.

Mining in the range has a long history. Stories tell of finding old Spanish gold mines with iron tools in them that crumbled at a touch. More recent mining for tungsten and gold has occurred on the east side of Notch Peak. Outlaws found the range a convenient area to hide out; Tatow Knob (north of Swasey Peak), for example, was a favorite spot for horse thieves. Death Canyon got its name after a group of pioneers became trapped and froze to death; most maps now show it as Dome Canyon.

Driving In The House Range

The dirt roads here can be surprisingly good. Often you can zip along as if on pavement, but watch for loose gravel, large rocks, flash floods, and deep ruts that sometimes appear on these backcountry stretches. Roads easily passable by car connect to make a 43-mile loop through Marjum and Dome Canyon passes. You'll have good views of the peaks and go through scenic canyons on the west side of both passes. Drivers with high-clearance vehicles can branch off on old mining roads or drive past Antelope Spring to Sinbad Overlook for views and hiking near Swasey Peak. Shale beds near Antelope Spring have given up an amazing quantity and variety of trilobite fossils dating from about 500 million years ago. Professional collectors have leased a trilobite quarry, so you'll have to collect outside. Trilobites can also be found near Swasey Spring and near Marjum Pass. Flat-edged rock hammers work best to split open the shale layers. During WW I, a hermit took a liking to the House Range and built a one-room cabin in a small cave, where he lived until his death. He entertained visitors with a special home brew. Walk a quarter mile up a small side canyon from the road to see the cabin, which is on the right side of the road that comes down to the west from Marjum Pass.

Several roads connect US 50/6 with the loop through Marjum and Dome Canyon passes. Going west from Delta on US 50/6, you have the choice of the following turnoffs: after 10 miles, turn right 25 miles at the fork for the unpaved old US 50/6; or after 32 miles, turn right 10 miles on a road signed "Antelope Spring"; or after 42 miles, turn right 16 miles on a road also signed "Antelope Spring"; or after 63 miles (30 miles east of the Utah-Nevada border), turn right 14 miles on a road signed "Painter Spring."

Hiking In The House Range

Most hiking routes go cross-country through the wilderness. Springs are very far apart and can be polluted, so carry water for the whole trip. Bring topo maps and compass; help can be a long way off if you make a wrong turn. Because of the light precipitation, the hiking season at the high elevations can last from late April to late November. Most destinations, including Swasey and Notch peaks, can be visited on a day-hike. These peaks have fantastic views over nearly all of west-central Utah and into Nevada. For more information on the House Range, contact the BLM office at 35 E. 500 North in Fillmore (Box 778, Fillmore, UT 84631), tel. 743-6811.

Swasey Peak

A good half-day hike usually done as a loop. Total distance for the moderately difficult trip is about four and one half miles with a 1,700-foot elevation gain to the summit (elev. 9,669 feet). Drive to the Antelope Spring turnoff, two and one half miles east of Dome Canyon Pass, and follow the well-used Sinbad Overlook road 3.3 miles, passing the spring and trilobite area, up a steep grade to a large meadow below Swasey Peak. Cautiously driven cars might be able to get up this road, though it's safer to park low-clearance vehicles and walk the last one and one half miles. (Nonhikers with suitable vehicles will enjoy driving to Sinbad Overlook for views at the end of the road.) From the large meadow at the top of the grade, head northeast on foot up the ridge, avoiding cliffs to the left. After one and one quarter miles you'll reach a low summit; continue one-half mile along the ridgeline, curving west toward Swasey Peak. To complete the loop, descend one-half mile to the northwest along a ridge to bypass some cliffs, then head southwest three-quarters of a mile to the end of Sinbad Overlook road.

From here it's an easy one and one half miles by road back to the start; Sinbad Spring and a grove of ponderosa pines are about halfway. No signs or trails mark the route, but hikers experienced with maps shouldn't have any trouble. Topo maps for this hike are the 7½-minute Marjum Pass and Swasey Peak. Route-finding is easier when hiking the loop in the direction described. You'll get a close look at the mountain mahogany on Swasey Peak—some thickets of this stout shrub have to be crossed; wear long pants to protect your legs.

view north from Swasey Peak

Notch Peak

The 2,700-foot sheer rock wall on the western face of this prominent peak is only 300 feet less than El Capitan in Yosemite. Most hikers prefer the far easier summit route on the other side via Sawtooth Canyon. This moderately difficult canyon route is about nine miles roundtrip and has a 1,700-foot elevation gain. Bring water, as no springs are in the area. Like the Drum Mountains, Notch Peak has a reputation for strange underground noises. The 15-minute Notch Peak topo map is needed as much for navigating the roads to the trailhead as for the hiking. First take Antelope Spring Road to the signed turnoff for Miller Canyon, four and one half miles north of Milepost 46 on US 50/6 (42 miles west of Delta) and 11.5 miles south of old US 50/6 (35 miles west of Delta). Turn west 5.3 miles on Miller Canyon Road, then bear left to Sawtooth Canyon at a road fork. A stone cabin two and one half miles farther on the right marks the trailhead. The cabin is owned and used by people who mine in the area. Follow a rough road on foot into Sawtooth Canyon. After three-quarters of a mile the canyon widens where two tributaries meet; take the left fork in the direction of Notch Peak. A few spots in the dry creekbed require some rock-scrambling. Be on the lookout for flash floods if thunderstorms threaten. After about three miles the wash becomes less distinct; continue climbing to a saddle visible ahead. Then a short but steep quarter-mile scramble takes you to the top of 9,655-foot Notch Peak and its awesome drop-offs. Other ways up Notch Peak offer challenges for the adventurous. The other fork of Sawtooth Canyon can be used, for example, and a jeep road through Amasa Valley provides a northern approach.

CONFUSION RANGE

The Confusions lie in a long, jumbled mass west of the House Range. The sparse vegetation consists largely of piñon pine, juniper, sagebrush, shadscale, and cheatgrass. Some Douglas fir grow on the King Top Plateau, the highest area in the Confusion Range, where elevations reach 8,300 feet. Shortages of water and feed allow only small numbers of wild horses, pronghorn, deer, and smaller animals to eke out an existence.

1. Salt Lake Temple, Salt Lake City; **2.** Logan Temple, Logan; **3.** Box Elder Tabernacle, Brigham City; **4.** LDS Conference (Priesthood Session) in the Tabernacle, Salt Lake City; **5.** inside the Tabernacle Organ, Salt Lake City; **6.** Angel Moroni in Museum of Church History and Art, Salt Lake City (all photos by Bill Weir)

1. Maze wildflowers and meadows atop the Wasatch Plateau;
2. collared lizard *(Crotaphytus collaris)* of the Colorado Plateau (all photos by Bill Weir)

Fossil Mountain in the southeast part of the Confusions has an exceptional diversity of marine fossils, many very rare. Thirteen fossil groups of ancient sea creatures have been found in rocks of early Ordovician age (350-400 million years ago). Fossil Mountain stands 6,685 feet high on the west edge of Blind Valley. A signed road to Blind Valley turns south off US 50/6 between Mileposts 38 and 39 (54 miles west of Delta). Fossil Mountain is about 14 miles south of the highway.

GREAT BASIN NATIONAL PARK

Lehman Caves and Wheeler Peak lie just across the Nevada border in Nevada's only national park. Lehman Caves, a national monument since 1922, has long been known for its beautiful formations. Wheeler Peak (elev. 13,063 feet), with its glacial features, alpine lakes, forests, and great views, stands as one of the best examples of the Great Basin mountains. Legislation in 1986 joined the caves and peak to form Great Basin National Park. The 6,200-foot difference in elevation between the upper Sonoran Desert and the alpine tundra on Wheeler Peak encompasses the region's full spectrum of plant and wildlife habitats.

Lehman Caves

Long ago, underground heat turned layers of limestone on the east side of Wheeler Peak into marble. Much later, the caves formed as water containing carbon dioxide slowly worked into cracks and dissolved the rock. After the underground chambers had partly drained, stalactites, stalagmites, and other features typical of limestone caves began to grow. Indians knew about the caves in times past but didn't venture beyond the entrance room. A rancher named Absalom Lehman became the first to explore the wonders within. He had come to the area about 1869 to try his hand at ranching and raising fruit, knowing that nearby mining camps would provide a good market. (Some trees from his orchard still grow in front of the park's visitor center.) Word of the cave system spread quickly after its discovery in 1885 and hundreds of sightseers arrived in the first year. Lehman guided many of the visitors until his death in 1891.

Visitor Center

Cave entrance, exhibits, bookshop, cafe/gift shop, and park headquarters are in a piñon pine and juniper woodland on the east slope of Wheeler Peak. Views at the 6,825-foot elevation look over valleys and ranges of western Utah. A short film and exhibits introduce the geology of Lehman Caves and illustrate cave formations, flora, wildlife, and human history of the park. Books, topo maps, postcards, slides, and other interpretive materials can be purchased. **Rhodes Cabin,** just north of the visitor center, has additional historical and natural history exhibits. **Mountain View Nature Trail** begins a half-mile loop here; pick up a trail guide at the visitor center. You can plan your own nature hikes with materials in Family Adventure Packs, available at the visitor center information desk. In summer, rangers give evening programs nightly in two of the campgrounds and lead nature walks and hikes; check the posted schedule for locations and times. The visitor center is open daily 8 a.m.-5 p.m. (7:30 a.m.-6 p.m. Memorial Day to Labor Day weekends) except on New Year's Day, Thanksgiving, and Christmas. The only fees charged are for the cave tour and campsites. From Baker, Nevada (just west of the Utah-Nevada line and five miles south of US 50/6), head west five miles to the visitor center. The park is about 106 miles west of Delta, Utah. Contact the Great Basin National Park at Baker, NV 89311, tel. (702) 234-7331.

Cave Tours
Ranger-led tours begin daily (except on the holidays noted above) from the visitor center 8 a.m.-5 p.m. The schedule has frequent departures (hourly or half-hourly) in summer, decreasing to four tours a day in winter. In summer you can also take a daily candlelight tour of the cave and see it much as Ab Lehman did. The cave's cool interior (50° F) comes as a welcome relief from desert heat, and a jacket or sweater is recommended. Tours cover 0.6 mile with some stairs and inclines in a leisurely one and one half hours. Cost of this tour is $4 adult, $3 children 6-15, and $2 with Golden Age cards; no discount for Golden Eagle cards. Don't forget that Nevada is on Pacific time, one hour earlier than Utah.

Spelunking Tours
Tours lasting two and one half hours give participants an experience in the sport and science of cave exploring. These trips require considerable crawling and use of caving equipment. You'll visit parts of the cave system not normally seen by visitors. Contact the park in advance for information and required reservations. Trips take place on summer weekends; minimum age is 14 and fee is $6.

Wheeler Peak Scenic Drive
Cars can drive this 12-mile paved road from near the visitor center to Wheeler Peak Campground (elev. 9,880 feet) from about late May to October. It's not recommended for trailers or large RVs past Upper Lehman Creek Campground. You'll first pass Lower Lehman Creek Campground two miles in and Upper Lehman Creek Campground 0.6 mile farther. Once past the campgrounds, you'll enjoy great panoramas to the east and north, then, as the road swings around, of Wheeler Peak itself. Attractions include the Osceola gold mining ditch (reached by a one-third-mile trail), Mather Overlook, Wheeler Peak Overlook, and hiking trails.

Wildflowers bloom profusely beginning at lower elevations in spring and progressing to the high country by late summer.

Hiking Trails
Glaciers and streams have carved sheer cliffs and rugged canyons into lofty **Wheeler Peak** (elev. 13,063 feet). A ridge that extends north and south from the summit has many peaks exceeding 11,000 feet. Hikers can climb to Wheeler Peak's summit on the **Wheeler Peak Trail** from Summit Trailhead (elev. 10,161 feet), just before Wheeler Peak Campground. The strenuous trip takes six to eight hours for the 10 miles to the top and back. **Alpine Lakes Loop Trail** offers an easier hike of three miles past beautiful Stella and Teresa lakes. The trail, great for families, begins near the entrance to Wheeler Peak Campground; elevation gain is 400 feet.

Bristlecone Pine Trail branches off the Alpine Lakes Loop Trail between the trailhead and Teresa Lake, then winds around to a glacial moraine and a pine grove, four miles roundtrip from the trailhead with a 500-foot elevation gain. **Wheeler Peak Rock Glacier & Icefield Trail** continues about one mile past the bristlecone pine grove to a spectacular cirque below Wheeler Peak. A layer of broken rock covers the lower ice field—hence the term "rock glacier." A sign warns where hiking farther would be dangerous due to rock avalanches. The hike is six miles roundtrip from the trailhead with about a 1,000-foot elevation gain. Hikers on the easy, four-mile (one-way) **Lehman Creek Trail** cross four life zones, from spruce, fir, and aspen forests to cactus and sage 2,100 feet lower; most people arrange to be dropped off at the upper trailhead on the far side of Wheeler Peak Campground and picked up in Upper Lehman Creek Campground below. The **Baker and Snake creek drainages** in the park's central section have longer trails, good for day-hikes or backpacking trips.

Lexington Arch spans an opening 120 feet wide and 75 feet high in the southern section of the park; the arch has the unusual feature of being limestone, instead of the sandstone found in most other arches of the Southwest. Drive to Garrison, Utah, continue southeast on UT 21 to Milepost 6, and turn right 12 miles on a dirt road (high-clearance vehicles recommended) to the trailhead. The hike to Lexington Arch in

Arch Canyon is two miles roundtrip with a 1,000-foot elevation gain; trailhead elevation is 7,440 feet. Maps, trail descriptions, and backcountry permits are available at the visitor center; you can purchase the colorful book *Trails to Explore in Great Basin National Park* here with trail descriptions, topo maps, flora and fauna illustrations, and background information.

Baker Village Archaeology Site

Fremont Indians lived in the Snake Valley about 1,000 years ago, leaving what appears to be an exceptionally large village at this site seven miles east of Great Basin National Park. Full-scale excavations began in the summer of 1991 by the Brigham Young University Archaeological Field School in a cooperative effort with the Ely District of the BLM and White Pine Public Museum (Ely). Visitors have been able to tour the site and see archaeologists at work during past summers and they may be able to visit in the future too. Ask at the Great Basin National Park or the Ely District BLM office (tel. 702-289-4865).

Practicalities

Lehman Caves Gifts and Cafe at the visitor center is open for breakfast and lunch April-October. Picnic grounds are just a short distance away. **Campgrounds** in the park, with distances from the visitor center, are: Lower Lehman Creek (two miles; open all year; elev. 7,500 feet); Upper Lehman Creek (2.6 miles; open mid-May to mid-October; elev. 7,800 feet); Wheeler Peak (12 miles; open mid-June to mid-September; 9,880 feet), Baker Creek (3 miles; open mid-May to mid-September; elev. 8,000 feet), and Snake Creek (23 miles; open mid-May to late September; elev. 7,800 feet). All the campgrounds except Snake Creek have drinking water and charge a $5 fee.

The small town of **Baker** has the following accommodations and restaurants. **Silver Jack Motel,** tel. (702) 234-7323, is open April-Oct., $29 s, $33 d. **The Outlaw Cafe** serves lunch and dinner daily. **Whispering Elm Motel & RV Park,** tel. 234-7343, has rooms, $32.40 s, $37.80 d, and campsites, $16.20 for tent or RV w/hookups, from mid-May through mid-October, and a gas station/grocery store. The **"Y,"** on US 50/6 at the NV 487 turnoff for Baker, tel. (702) 234-7223, has a restaurant, open Mon.-Sat. for breakfast, lunch, and dinner, and RV

spaces, $5.40 no hookups, $10.80 w/hookups, year-round. The **Border Inn,** eight miles northeast of Baker, straddles the Utah-Nevada line on US 50/6, tel. (702) 234-7300, with motel rooms for $29.43-40.33 in Utah and a restaurant (serving breakfast, lunch, and dinner daily) and a gas station in Nevada.

WAH WAH MOUNTAINS

The Wah Wah Mountains extend south about 55 miles in a continuation of the Confusion Range. Elevation ranges from 6,000 to more than 9,000 feet. The name comes from a Paiute Indian term for salty or alkaline seeps. Sparse sagebrush, juniper, and piñon pine cover most of the land. Aspen, white fir, ponderosa pine, and bristlecone pine grow in the high country. Mule deer, pronghorn, and smaller animals roam the mountains. Carry water, maps, and compass into this wild country. Few people visit the Wah Wahs despite their pristine ecosystem. A 1986 BLM publication reported an estimated 155 visitor days per year for recreation in the Wah Wah Mountains Wilderness Study Area, which includes the northern and central parts of the range. That's an average of less than half a person per day!

Crystal Peak

This snow-white pinnacle in the north end of the Wah Wah Mountains stands out as a major landmark. The soft white rock of the peak is tuff, from an ancient volcano thought to predate the block-faulted Wah Wahs. The best way to climb the peak (elev. 7,106 feet) is to ascend the ridge just south of it from the east, then follow the ridge northeast up the peak. Be careful of soft crumbly rock. See the 15-minute Crystal Peak topo map for details.

Central Section

The heart of the Wah Wahs has some fine scenery and opportunities for nature study. Rugged cliffs mark the west edge of the range. A good hiking route begins at about 6,600 feet in elevation at the end of a dirt road going up Pierson Cove. Follow the dry wash upstream a short way to a split in the drainage, then take the left fork north through a canyon. After about two miles you'll come out of the canyon onto a high plateau. For the best views, turn northwest and continue climbing three-quarters of a mile to the summit of an 8,918-foot peak. See the 15-minute Wah Wah Summit topo map for back roads and hiking routes.

SAN FRANCISCO MOUNTAINS AND GHOST TOWNS

Frisco Peak (elev. 9,660 feet) crowns this small range northwest of Milford. The Wah Wah Valley and Mountains lie to the west. Silver strikes in the San Francisco Mountains in the 1870s led to the opening of many mines and the founding of the towns of Newhouse and Frisco. By 1920 the best ores had given out and both communities turned to ghosts. A jeep road goes to the summit of Frisco Peak.

Frisco
The Horn Silver Mine, developed in 1876 at the south end of the San Francisco Mountains, was the first of several prolific silver producers. Smelters, and charcoal ovens to fuel them, sprouted up to process the ore. A wild boom town developed as miners flocked to the new diggings. The railroad reached Frisco in 1880 and later extended to nearby Newhouse. Frisco's population of 6,000 included quite a few gamblers and other shady characters. Twenty-three saloons labored to serve the thirsty customers. Gunfights became almost a daily ritual for a while, keeping the cemetery growing. Yet all came to an end early in 1885 when rumblings echoed from deep within the Horn Silver Mine between shifts. The foreman luckily delayed sending the next crew down, and a few minutes later the whole mine collapsed with a deafening roar that broke windows in Milford 15 miles away. Out of work, most of the miners and business people moved on. More than $60 million in silver and other valuable ores had come out of the ground in the 10 frenzied years. Some mining has been done on and off since, but Frisco has died.

Today Frisco is one of Utah's best-preserved mining ghosts, with about a dozen stone or wood buildings surviving. A headframe and mine buildings, still intact, overlook the town from the hillside. Five beehive-shaped charcoal kilns stand on the east edge of Frisco. You can see the

kilns and the townsite if you look north from UT 21, 15 miles west of Milford, between Mileposts 62 and 63. Dirt roads wind their way in. A historical marker for Frisco is at the turnoff for the town; turnoff for the beehive kilns is 0.3 mile east. I liking off the roads can be very dangerous near the old mines and time-worn buildings.

Newhouse
Prospectors discovered silver deposits in 1870 on the southwest side of the San Francisco Mountains but lacked the funds to develop them. Mining didn't take off until 1900, when Samuel Newhouse financed operations. A sizable town grew here as ore worth $3.5 million came out of the Cactus Mine. Citizens maintained a degree of law and order not found in most mining towns: Even the saloon and the working girls had to operate outside the community. Deposits of rich ore ran out only 10 years later and the town's inhabitants departed. The railroad depot was moved to a nearby ranch and other buildings went to Milford. Today Newhouse is a ghostly site with about half a dozen concrete or stone buildings standing in ruin. Foundations of a smelter, mill, other structures, railroad grades, and lots of broken glass remain. A good dirt road turns north two miles to the site from UT 21 (between Mileposts 57 and 58), 20 miles west of Milford.

MILFORD

Miners on their way to Frisco and Newhouse crossed the Beaver River at a ford below a stamp mill, so Milford seemed the logical name for the town that grew up here. Most of Milford's businesses in the early days supplied the mining camps. Today the town serves as a center for the railroad, nearby farms, and a geothermal plant. Steam from wells at the Blundell Geothermal plant, 13 miles northeast of town, produces electricity for Utah Power and Light. Travelers heading west will find Milford their last stop for supplies before the Nevada border. Milford is at the junction of UT 21 and UT 257; Beaver is 32 miles east, Baker (NV) is 96 miles northwest, and Delta is 77 miles north.

Practicalities
The **Station Motel,** at the corner of 100 West and 500 South, tel. 387-2481, has rooms at

$26.16 s, $31.61 d in the old section and $32.70 s, $39.24 d in the new section. Its **Station Restaurant,** tel. 387-2804, is open daily for breakfast, lunch, and dinner. **Old Hickory Inn,** 485 W. Center, tel. 387-5042, also serves American food; open daily for lunch and dinner. **Hong Kong Cafe,** 433 S. Main, tel. 387-2251, prepares inexpensive Chinese and American food 24 hours daily.

The **city park** at 300 South and 200 West has a picnic area. An **outdoor pool** is behind the high school at 141 N. 200 West, tel. 387-2315. **Pavilion Park** has a free camping area just beyond the high school grounds on 300 West, open all year with water. Milford's five-hole **golf course,** on the west edge of town (about 1000 South and 700 West), tel. 387-2711 (city office), is open April 1 to October 31. The **post office** is at 458 S. Main. **Milford Valley Memorial Hospital** is at 451 N. Main, tel. 387-2411. **Milford City Office,** 302 S. Main (Box 69, Milford, UT 84751), tel. 387-2711, will answer questions about the area Mon.-Fri. 8 a.m.-3 p.m. During the summer you can obtain area information in the old caboose at 46 S. Main. The **public library,** 400 N. 100 West, tel. 387-5039, is open weekday afternoons.

Rock Corral Campground And Pass Road

The BLM has a campground and picnic area east of Milford in the Mineral Mountains, a popular area for rockhounding; no water or fee. From UT 21 on the southeast edge of Milford, turn east five and one half miles on Pass Road, then left (north) 5.2 miles. Returning to Pass Road, you can continue east 13.4 miles over the Mineral Mountains and loop back to UT 21 between Mileposts 102 and 103, 4.8 miles west of Beaver. Pass Road has a gravel surface with a dirt section near the pass.

MINERSVILLE STATE PARK

The 1,130-acre reservoir has good year-round fishing for rainbow trout and smallmouth bass (ice fishing in winter). Be sure to check with the rangers for information about fishing regulations for the park. Bait fishing is not allowed and there are special catch limits. Most people come here to fish, though some visitors go sailing or water-skiing. Park facilities include picnic tables, campsites (all with electric and water hookups), restrooms with showers, paved boat ramp, fish-cleaning station, and dump station. Fees are $3 day use, $11 for sites in the main campground with water and electric hookups ($12 on Friday, Saturday, and holidays), $9 for sites in the overflow area ($1 more camping on Friday, Saturday, and holidays). Reservations are a good idea on summer holidays. In winter the restrooms may be closed but water is available. For information about the park, write Box 1531, Beaver, UT 84713, tel. 438-5472 or (800) 322-3770 (reservations). Minersville Reservoir lies just off UT 21 in a sage- and juniper-covered valley, eight miles east of Minersville, 18 miles southeast of Milford, and 14 miles west of Beaver.

coyote
(Canis latrans)

LOUISE FOOTE

UTAH STATE HISTORICAL SOCIETY

Fort Utah (Provo); Timpanogos Peak rises in background

CENTRAL UTAH

In many ways, the geography and history of central Utah are extensions of the northern part of the state. The rugged Wasatch Range continues to act as an eastern boundary to the spread of the state's largest municipalities, which cluster at the base of the range. Here, smaller mountains and hills form a transitition to the basin and range terrain to the west. The mountains of the Wasatch Range are steeper and higher than those to the north, perhaps even more majestic, and are likely to be coated with snow. Just two years after the founding of Salt Lake City, Mormon pioneers began settling both this area and the Wasatch Plateau south of the range. Quiet Mormon villages occupy much of the lower country today.

PROVO

Utah's second-largest city (pop. 91,000) has a striking setting on the shore of Utah Lake, beneath the west face of the Wasatch Range. Provo is best known as the home of Brigham Young University, a large, dynamic school sponsored by the Mormon Church. Museums and cultural events on the BYU campus make it a popular destination.

Provo boasts one of the most majestic views of any of the Wasatch Front cities, possibly contributing to the city's consistently high marks in many publications' "liveability" ratings. It also offers a university town's full selection of cultural and sporting events; easy access to water sports, fishing, hiking, and skiing; and a relatively low crime rate.

History
In 1776, members of the Dominguez-Escalante expedition visited the Utah Valley, where Provo now is, and gave glowing reports of fertile soil, plentiful game, and beautiful countryside. The Spanish friars who led the group had hoped to return and establish missions for the local Indians, but political decisions prevented them from doing so. The expedition had friendly relations

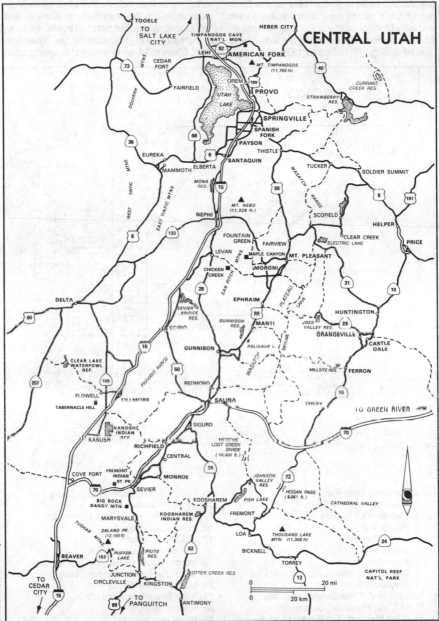

CENTRAL UTAH

with the Ute Indians (known here as the "Timpanogotzis"), as did most later mountain men and early Mormon settlers. Fur trappers included Etienne Provost, a French-Canadian who passed through in 1824 and 1825. His Anglicized name was adopted in 1849 when Mormons arrived in the Utah Valley to start their first settlement. Within the next two years, the communities of Lehi, Pleasant Grove, American Fork, Springville, and Payson also sprang up in

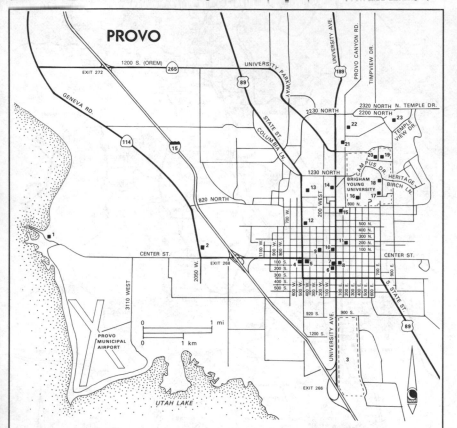

1. Utah Lake State Park
2. Fort Utah City Park
3. East Bay Golf Course
4. Pioneer Park
5. Provo City Library
6. post office
7. Provo Tabernacle
8. Utah County Travel Council (tourist info)
9. Greyhound Bus
10. Uinta Natl. Forest Supervisor's office
11. McCurdy Historical Doll Museum*
12. North Park and DUP Pioneer Museum
13. Utah Valley Regional Medical Center
14. Provo Recreation Center
15. Museum of Peoples and Cultures (BYU)
16. Visitor Center (BYU)
17. Wilkinson Center and BYU Bookstore (BYU)
18. Museum of Art (BYU)
19. Bean Life Science Museum (BYU)
20. Marriott Center (BYU)
21. Earth Science Museum (BYU)
22. Cougar Stadium
23. Provo Temple

the valley. Geneva Steel and other major industries established during the WW II years transformed the Provo area from an agrarian landscape to the major urban center it is today. The downtown business district, though, still features many distinctive buildings from the turn of the century and earlier.

BRIGHAM YOUNG UNIVERSITY

The university had a modest beginning in 1875 as the Brigham Young Academy, established under the direction of Mormon Church President Brigham Young. Like the rest of Provo, BYU's population and size have grown dramatically in recent decades. BYU is one of the largest church-affiliated schools in the world. Students aren't required to be Mormons, but about 95% of 28,000 do belong to the LDS church. High academic standards upheld by students and faculty have made the university a leader in many fields. Everyone attending the school must follow a strict dress and grooming code, something you'll notice immediately on a stroll across the modern campus.

Exhibits and concerts are held in the **Harris Fine Arts Center** (just north of the Wilkinson Center) and other locations on campus, tel. 378-7444 (music ticket office), 378-7447 (theater performances). BYU also goes all out to support its Cougars football and other athletic teams. Major sporting events take place in the 65,000-seat Cougar Stadium and the indoor 23,000-seat Marriott Center, tel. 378-2981 (ticket office).

You're welcome to visit the more than 600 acres of BYU's vast campus. The **Visitor Center** provides literature and advice about things to see, events, and facilities open to the public. It's open Mon.-Fri. 8 a.m.-5 p.m. on the brow of the hill near Maeser Building, south on Campus Drive, tel. 378-4678. Campus tours, either walking or in small open-air vehicles, introduce the university; student guides point out features of interest and tell about student life and research work. The free tours last about 45 minutes and depart Mon.-Fri. 9 a.m.-4 p.m. by reservation; tours also depart the same days at 11 a.m. and 2 p.m. on a walk-in basis (no reservation needed) from the Visitor Center. Free parking is available in front of the Visitor Center for those taking guided tours or needing information about the campus. Additional free visitor parking (signed) is near the north end of Campus Drive, near the Wilkinson Center (east across the street), and north of the Museum of Art.

Wilkinson Center serves as the social center for BYU. The main level has a choice of cafeterias and snack bars (open Mon.-Sat. for breakfast, lunch, and dinner), Varsity Theater (current movies), an art gallery, lounge areas, and an information desk. The **Skyroom Restaurant** on the sixth floor, tel. 378-2049, offers great views and fine dining (open Mon.-Fri. for lunch and Friday for dinner). The lower level has Out-

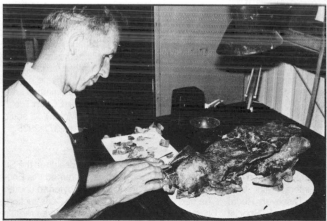

Head Preparator Dee Hall assembling skull of a female Uintatheruim, an Eocene herbivore; this prehistoric mammal had an exceptionally small brain in relation to its body size.

BYU EARTH SCIENCE MUSEUM

doors Unlimited (rentals of bicycles and equipment for sports, camping, boating, snowshoeing, cross-country skiing, and downhill skiing, tel. 378-2708) and a **post office**. Some of the other recreation facilities are open only to university students, faculty, and staff.

The **BYU Bookstore** occupies three levels on the west side of the Wilkinson Center with a good selection of general books, textbooks, LDS titles, art supplies, and BYU clothing and souvenirs. The **Harold B. Lee Library,** just west of the bookstore, has an impressive collection of books and maps on five levels; the genealogical library on the fourth floor ranks second in size only to the one in Salt Lake City, which is the largest in the world; main collections are open Mon.-Sat. 7 a.m.-midnight; tel. 378-2926.

BYU MUSEUMS

Small collections on campus include a series of salt- and freshwater aquariums in the basement of the Widtsoe Building, and Earth Science exhibits and a Foucault pendulum in the lobby and hallways of the Eyring Science Center. The Summerhays Planetarium in the Eyring Science Center presents programs to the public for a small charge; tel. 378-4361.

Museum of Art
In one of the largest art museums in the west you can see such famous works of art as Rembrandt's *Raising of Lazarus,* Gifford's *Lake Scene,* and Andy Warhol's *Marilyn.* These are just of few of the museum's 14,000 works ranging from Renaissance to modern, Asian to local. The building itself is a work of art, with a polished granite exterior, hardwood floors, and high-ceiling galleries bathed in natural light. Special exhibits have entrance fees, otherwise admission is free. Open Mon.-Sat., call for hours, tel. 378-8257 (office), 378-BYU1 (recording), or (800) 322-BYU1 (out of state).

Monte L. Bean Life Science Museum
Mounted animals and dioramas realistically depict wildlife of Utah and distant lands. The exhibits not only identify the many species on display but also show how they interact within their environments. The Children's Discovery Room has cages of insects and small animals. Special

presentations include movies, talks, workshops, and live-reptile, animal-adaptation, and other demonstrations; call for the schedule. The research library is open Mon.-Fri. 10 a.m.-5 p.m.; natural history items can be purchased in the gift shop. Museum exhibits are open Monday 10 a.m.-9 p.m. and Tues.-Sat. 10 a.m.-5 p.m.; admission is free. Located southeast of the Marriott Center on 1430 North, tel. 378-5051.

Earth Science Museum
This small museum features excellent exhibits of dinosaurs and early mammals. A popular dinosaur video program both entertains and educates. A viewing window lets you observe researchers cleaning and preparing bones. Open Mon.-Fri. 9 a.m.-5 p.m. (til 9 p.m. on Monday) and Saturday noon-4 p.m., free admission, 1683 N. Provo Canyon Rd. (across from Cougar Stadium), tel. 378-2232.

Museum Of Peoples And Cultures
The museum's purpose is to communicate knowledge about both modern and ancient peoples of the world. Exhibits reflect research in the Great Basin in Utah, the American Southwest, Mesoamerica, South America, the Near East, and Polynesia. Open Mon.-Fri. 9 a.m.-5 p.m., free admission, corner of 700 North and 100 East, tel. 378-6112.

OTHER PROVO SIGHTS

McCurdy Historical Doll Museum
Mrs. Laura McCurdy Clark, who started the collection, often used her dolls to teach history to students. The original collection has been expanded to about 4,000 dolls, representing U.S. presidents and their wives, other historical figures, and diverse nationalities. Private parties can be arranged here. The museum shop sells dolls, doll supplies, toys, and books. Open Tues.-Sat. noon-5 p.m (1-5 p.m. Jan.-March), $2 adult, $1 under 12; 246 N. 100 East, tel. 377-9935.

Provo Tabernacle
Architect William Folsom, who designed the St. George and Manti temples, patterned this English-style structure after a Presbyterian church he had visited in Salt Lake City. Construction, begun in 1883, required 15 years. Organ recitals

and other concerts take place here. Located at 100 S. University Avenue.

Provo Temple

The modern building of white cast stone incorporates floral elements and a central golden spire. It's particularly impressive at night lit up against the sky. Dedication took place in 1972 with 75,000 people in attendance. Church members carry out sacred work within the 283 rooms. Visitors can't go inside but are welcome to visit the landscaped grounds; 2200 N. Temple Dr. (turn east on 2230 North from University Ave. or drive north on 900 East).

Utah Lake State Park

The largest body of freshwater completely within the state, Utah Lake is 24 miles long (north to south) and 11 miles wide. Average depth is only 9.4 feet. Mountains form the skyline in all directions. Swans, geese, pelicans, ducks, and other migratory birds stop by. Best birdwatching is at the south end of the lake and near the Provo airport. The state park provides recreation facilities on the east shore, just a short drive from downtown Provo. Boaters come for water-skiing, sailboarding, and fishing; four paved boat ramps, docks, and slips are provided.

The swimming beach offers another way to cool off. Anglers catch white and black bass, channel catfish, walleyed pike, carp, and other warm-water fish during most of the year. The lake usually freezes over by late December and has good ice fishing; trout descend from the mountain rivers during this season. A visitor center has ice-skating in winter. The campground is open mid-March to October 31 with water and showers; $3 per vehicle day use, $7 or $9 per vehicle camping ($1 more for Friday, Saturday, and holiday camping). The park is open year-round at 4400 W. Center, Provo, UT 84601, tel. 375-0733 (recording), 375-0731 (office), or (800) 322-3770 (reservations). Head west four miles on Center from downtown Provo or take the I-15 exit for West Center and go west three miles.

Springville Museum Of Art

The museum started in the early 1900s as a collection of the Springville High School, but when it began to receive gifts of major works from artists Cyrus Dallin and John Hafen,

townspeople decided that a special building was needed. They built this fine Spanish-style structure during the Depression years with federal and LDS church assistance. The town is now also known as "Art City" for its patronship. The permanent collection contains 1,200 American works, including some of the best by early Utah pioneers and Native Americans, as well as the state's modern artists. Eleven galleries display visiting exhibits downstairs; a permanent collection is housed upstairs. The annual April Salon is a major show of Utah contemporary artists. The museum is open Sunday 2-5 p.m. and Tues.-Sat. 10 a.m.-5 p.m. (until 9 p.m. on Wednesday); closed Monday and state holidays (also closed for two weeks prior to the April Salon); free admission. The museum is at 126 E. 400 South in Springville, tel. 489-2727. From Provo, drive seven miles south on US 89 (South State Street) or take I-15 Exit 263 and go east.

Appeal to the Great Spirit; *Cyrus Dallin (1912)*

PROVO ACCOMMODATIONS
Add 10.75% tax to all prices; rates listed are for 1-2 persons

Best Value Western Inn; 40 W. 300 South; $25-00, tel. 373-0660 or (800) 500-5003; waterbeds, pool

Colony Inn Suites (National 9 Inn); 1380 S. University Ave.; $38-56; tel. 374-6800 or (800) 524-9999; suites, kitchens, sauna, pool

Columbian Motel (Best Western); 70 E. 300 South; $42-48; tel. 373-8973 or (800) 321-0055; pool

Comfort Inn (near BYU); 1555 N. Canyon Rd.; $62-65; tel. 374-6020 or (800) 221-2222; indoor pool, spa, Continental breakfast

Cottontree Inn (Best Western); 2230 N. University Parkway; $52-62; tel. 373-7044 or (800) 528-1234; pool, spa

Days Inn; 1675 N. 200 West; $53-58; tel. 375-8600 or (800) 325-2525; pool

East Bay Inn Provo; 1292 S. University Ave.; $42-44; tel. 374-2500 or (800) 326-0025; pool, hot tub, exercise room

Fairfield Inn by Marriott; 1500 S. University Ave.; $65-71, $95 suites; tel. 377-9500 or (800) 228-2800; pool, spa, Continental breakfast

Holiday Inn; 1460 S. University Ave.; $59-69; tel. 374-9750 or (800) HOLIDAY; pool

Horne's East Bay Inn; 1292 S. University Ave.; $42-44; tel. 374-2500 or (800) 326-0025; pool, hot tub, weight room

Hotel Roberts; 192 S. University Ave.; $18; tel. 373-3400; historic 1882 hotel

Motel 6; 1600 S. University Ave.; $30-36; tel. 375-5064; pool

Rome Inn (Best Western); 1200 S. University Ave.; $47-51; tel. 375-7500 or (800) 528-1234; kitchenettes, pool

Safari Motel; 250 S. University Ave.; $30-34; tel. 373-9672; kitchenettes, pool, spa

Provo Park Hotel; 101 W. 100 North; $75-335; tel. 377-4700 or (800) 777-7144; suites, pool, spa, weight room

Super 8 Motel; 1288 S. University Ave.; $37.88-42.88; tel. 375-8766 or (800) 800-8000

Travelodge; 124 S. University Ave.; $45-50; tel. 373-1974 or (800) 255-3050; pool

University Western Inn; 40 W. 300 South; $25-27; tel. 373-0660; kitchenettes, pool

Uptown Motel; 469 W. Center; $32-36; tel. 373-8248; kitchenettes, pool

PRACTICALITIES

Accommodations And Campgrounds
See the "Provo Accommodations" chart for motels, hotels, and bed & breakfasts. **Lakeside RV Campground** has sites for tents ($13.11) and RVs ($18.57 w/hookups) with showers, pool, laundry, store, and canoe rentals; open all year at 4000 W. Center (just before Utah Lake State Park), tel. 373-5267. **Provo KOA** has sites for tents ($14.11) and RVs ($14.65 no hookups, $19.25 w/hookups) with showers, pool, laundry, and store; open year-round at 320 N. 2050 West (a quarter mile west of I-15 on Center, then one block north), tel. 375-2994. **Silver Fox RV Resort,** 101 W. 1500 South (behind Motel 6 near I-15 Exit 266), tel. 377-0033, is open all year and offers sites for tents ($15) and RVs ($15 w/hookups) with showers, pool, and laundry.

Frazier Park lies along the Provo River, five miles up Provo Canyon, tel. 225-5346; $12.50 tent or RV w/hookups and showers; closed in winter. **Riverbend Trailer Park,** six miles up Provo Canyon on US 189, tel. 225-1863, has sites for RVs ($12 w/hookups; no tents) with showers and laundry; open April 15 to October 15. **Deer Creek Park** lies along the Provo River farther upstream near the dam for Deer Creek Reservoir, tel. 225-9783, $11.65 tent or RV no hookups, $13.75 RV with water, electricity, and showers. Open April 15 to October 15. You'll find **Forest Service campgrounds** near Provo along the Alpine Scenic Loop to the northeast, Squaw Peak Road to the east, and Hobble Creek-Diamond Fork Loop to the southeast.

Food
Good Earth Natural Foods, 384 W. Center, tel. 375-7444, has a cafe (open Mon.-Sat. for

lunch and dinner), bakery, and groceries. **Govinda's Buffet,** 260 N. University Ave., tel. 375-0404, features tasty vegetarian cuisine from around the world; open Mon.-Sat. for lunch and dinner. **Magleby's,** 1675 N. 200 West, tel. 374-6249, serves steak, seafood, and chicken in a European atmosphere; open Mon.-Fri. for lunch and Mon.-Sat. for dinner. The Excelsior Hotel offers fine dining in **Mingles,** 101 W. 100 North, tel. 377-4700, open daily for breakfast, lunch, and dinner. **The Underground,** downstairs at 65 N. University Ave., tel. 377-5044, features American and Mexican specialties and pizza in a Prohibition-era setting; open Mon.-Sat. for lunch and dinner. The **Sensuous Sandwich,** 163 W. Center, tel. 377-9244, has a great choice of ingredients for its hot and cold sandwiches, sold by the inch; open Mon.-Sat. for lunch and dinner. The **Sizzler,** 1385 S. University Ave., tel. 374-1516, serves steak and seafood with a big salad bar; open daily for lunch and dinner. **Chuck-A-Rama,** 1081 S. University Ave., tel. 375-0600, features buffet dining daily for lunch and dinner.

For Italian pasta, pizza, and baked goods, try **La Dolce Vita,** 61 N. 100 East, tel. 373-8482, open Mon.-Sat. for lunch and dinner, or the **Brick Oven,** 111 E. 800 North, tel. 374-8803, open Mon.-Sat. for lunch and dinner.

Four Winds Restaurant's varied menu includes Chinese, American, and Italian items at 250 W. Center, tel. 374-9323. Open Mon.-Sat. for lunch and dinner. **Taiwan Cafe,** 2250 N. University Parkway in the Plum Tree Shopping Center, tel. 373-0389, specializes in Mandarin cuisine and Mongolian barbecue Mon.-Sat. for lunch and daily for dinner. Other places for Chinese food include **Chinatown Restaurant,** 330 S. State, tel. 373-7699, open Mon.-Sat. for lunch and dinner; **China Chef Cao,** 1295 N. State (500 West), tel. 374-1007, open Mon.-Sat. for lunch and dinner; and **South China Restaurant,** 1700 N. State, tel. 374-9114, open daily for lunch and dinner. **Cafe Viet Hoa,** 278 W. Center, tel. 373-8373, presents a good variety of Vietnamese and some Chinese food; open Mon.-Sat. for lunch and dinner. **Osaka Japanese Restaurant** prepares tempura, sukiyaki, and other fare at 46 W. Center, tel. 373-1060; open Mon.-Sat. for lunch and dinner. **Tepanyaki Steak House,** 1240 N. 500 West, tel. 374-0633, prepares Japanese cuisine daily for dinner. **Many Lands,** 1145 N. 500 West, tel.

375-3789, is an Asian grocery store and Japanese fast-food place; open Mon.-Sat. for lunch and dinner.

Flavorful Mexican food is prepared at **Los Amigos,** 150 S. University Ave., tel. 377-3800, open daily for brunch, lunch, and dinner; **Los Hermanos,** 16 W. Center, tel. 375-5732, open Mon.-Sat. for lunch and dinner; **Joe Vera's,** 250 W. Center, tel. 375-6714, open Mon.-Sat. for lunch and dinner; and **Mi Rancherito,** 368 W. Center, tel. 373-1503, open Mon.-Sat. for lunch and dinner. **El Salvador Restaurant,** 232 W. Center, tel. 377-9411, is a small cafe with Salvadoran and Mexican items; open Mon.-Sat. for lunch and dinner.

Entertainment

Catch movies at the **Academy Theatre,** 56 N. University Ave., tel. 373-4470; **Mann 4 Central Square Theatre,** 175 W. 200 North, tel. 374-6061; **Movies 8,** Plum Tree Shopping Center at 2424 N. University Parkway, tel. 375-5667; or BYU's **Varsity Theatre,** Wilkinson Center, tel. 378-3311. **SCERA** offers family entertainment movies year-round inside the Show House at 745 S. State in Orem and summer plays and musicals in an outdoor shell at 699 S. State in Orem, tel. 225-2560 (recorded info) or 225-2569 (office). **Brigham Young University** has a busy calendar of cultural and sporting events; tel. 378-7444 (music ticket office), 378-7447 (theater performances), or 378-2981 (sporting events).

Events

For current happenings in Provo and nearby towns, check with the Utah County Travel Council at 51 S. University Ave., Suite 111, tel. 370-8393. Major annual events include:

May: The **Auto Expo and Pioneer Car Cruise** brings hundreds of antique and classic cars to Orem.

June: **Art City Days** takes place in Springville. **City of Orem Family Summerfest** presents a parade, talent show, 5K run, Dutch oven cook-off, and other entertainment. **Strawberry Days** is a community celebration with rodeos, softball tournament, games, and entertainment in Pleasant Grove. Sundance holds a **Bluegrass Festival.** Cowboys show their skills at the **Lehi Round-up and Rodeo.** Provo begins its **Freedom Festival** about mid-June; events reach their peak on July 4.

July: Provo celebrates the Fourth of July with a **Freedom Festival** grand parade, freedom run, sports events, concerts, arts festival, and fireworks. **Provo Arts Festival** has performing and visual arts and special programs for the kids. Springville presents groups of dancers from many countries in the **Springville World Folkfest. Steel Days** is a community celebration in American Fork. A **Pioneer Day** parade and entertainment take place on July 24 in Provo and other towns. **Fiesta Days** in Spanish Fork has a parade, rodeo, pioneer activities, 10K run, and entertainment for three days near July 24. Highland lets loose in its **Highland Fling** with a parade, 10K run, carnival, fireworks, entertainment, and children's games.

August: Alpine puts on the **Alpine Days Celebration** with a parade, 5K run, mountain bike race, games, and entertainment. **Utah County Fair** features a horse show, exhibits, and entertainment in Spanish Fork. The town of Payson puts on a **Scottish Festival.** Nationally recognized storytellers present traditional and new pieces in the **Timpanogos Storytelling Festival.**

September: Payson's **Golden Onion Days** celebrates with fireworks, a children's parade, carnival, runs, and entertainment.

Recreation

Provo Recreation Center next to Provo High School at 1155 N. University Ave., tel. 379-6610, has an indoor pool, racquetball/wallyball courts, and weight rooms. **North Park,** 500 W. 500 North, has Veterans' Memorial Pool & Waterslide Park, tel. 379-6614, picnic areas, playground, and a **DUP Pioneer Museum,** open Mon.-Fri. 2-5 p.m. in summer. **Fort Utah City Park** has picnic tables, playground, and a replica of the fort built by Provo's first settlers; from downtown, head west on Center past the I-15 interchange and turn north one block on UT 114 (2050 West). **Pioneer Park** has picnicking and a playground at Center and 500 West. The big **Seven Peaks Resort Water Park** contains two of the world's tallest slides, twisting tubes, and a variety of pools to cool off in; guests can also picnic or play games like volleyball, basketball, softball, and horseshoes. Other attractions include ice-skating in winter and an 18-hole executive golf course. Open about late May to early September; admission is $13 ($7.50 after

5 p.m.) age 12-59, $10 age 3-11, and free for toddlers (ages 2 and under) and seniors (60 and over); turn east on Center St. to its end and follow signs, tel. 373-8777. **Trafalga Family Fun Center,** 168 S. 1200 West in Orem (take I-15 Exit 274), tel. 224-7415, features a water-tube slide, mini golf, bumper boats, and arcade games. Play golf at the 27-hole **East Bay Golf Course** (turn east on East Bay Blvd. from South University Ave. near the I-15 interchange, tel. 379-6612) or the nine-hole **Cascade Fairways Public Golf Course,** 1313 E. 800 North in Orem, tel. 225-6677.

In winter, skiers hit the slopes at **Sundance Ski Area** 14 miles northeast of town, tel. 225-4100 (recording) or 225-4107 (office). Head out on horseback from **Big Springs Riding Stable** on one-hour, two-hour, half-day, and full-day rides; sleigh, overnight, three-day, and dropcamp trips are offered too. Drive up US 189 in Provo Canyon to the Chalet Cafe in Vivian Park (two miles past Bridal Veil Falls) and turn in three and one half miles on South Fork Road to the stables, tel. 225-8589. **Hansen Mountaineering,** 757 N. State, Orem, UT 84057, tel. 226-7498, leads trips and provides instruction and sales for rock-climbing, winter camping, and cross-country skiing.

Services

In **emergencies** (police, fire, medical), call 911. The **post office** is at 95 W. 100 South, tel. 374-2000. The **U.S. Forest Service** provides avalanche/mountain weather information during the snow season at 374-9770. **Utah Valley Regional Medical Center** is at 1034 N. 500 West, tel. 373-7850 (375-4673 for the 24-hour crisis line). **First Medical** clinic is at 745 N. 500 West, tel. 373-1633.

Information

Utah County Travel Council, Suite 111, 51 S. University Ave. in the old county courthouse (Box 912, Provo, UT 84601), tel. 370-8393 or (800) 222-UTAH out of state, offers advice on sights and services in Provo and the Utah Valley; open Memorial Day to Labor Day weekends Mon.-Fri. 8 a.m.-8 p.m. and Saturday and Sunday 10 a.m.-6 p.m., then Mon.-Fri. 8 a.m.-5 p.m. the rest of the year. The U.S. Forest Service has three offices in the area. The **Uinta National Forest Supervisor,** 88 W. 100 North, Provo, UT 84601, tel. 377-5780, has general information about all districts in the forest and some books and maps for sale; open Mon.-Fri. 8 a.m.-5 p.m. Contact the **Pleasant Grove Ranger District** office, 390 N. 100 East, Pleasant Grove, UT 84062, tel. 785-3563, for specific information about the Alpine Scenic Loop and other areas in the Uinta National Forest north of Provo; open Mon.-Fri. 8 a.m.-5 p.m. (plus 8 a.m.-5 p.m. Saturday in summer). The **Spanish Fork Ranger District** office, 44 W. 400 North, Spanish Fork, UT 84660, tel. 798-3571, covers the Uinta National Forest east and southeast of Provo and the Wasatch National Forest, Vernon Division, southwest of town; open Mon.-Fri. 8 a.m.-5 p.m. (daily 8 a.m.-4:30 p.m. in summer).

Provo City Library, 425 W. Center, tel. 379-6650, is open Mon.-Thurs. 9:30 a.m.-9 p.m., Fri.-Sat. 9:30 a.m.-6 p.m. BYU's **Harold B. Lee Library,** just west of the Wilkinson Center, tel. 378-2926, has an impressive collection of books and maps on five levels; open Mon.-Fri. 7 a.m.-

midnight and Saturday 8 a.m.-midnight, The **BYU Bookstore** at the Wilkinson Center, tel. 378-3584, has one of the best and largest selections in the state. **Valley Book Center** sells magazines and books downtown at 52 W. Center, tel. 374-6260. **Deseret Book** also has a good selection at the Kmart shopping center, 1201 S. University Ave., tel. 375-1009.

Transportation
Utah Transit Authority (UTA) provides local bus service in Provo and connects with Springville, Salt Lake City, Ogden, and other towns; buses don't run on Sunday and holidays except for a few services on Sunday in Salt Lake City and Ogden, tel. 375-4636. **Greyhound Bus,** 124 N. 300 West, tel. 373-4211, has at least two northbound and two southbound departures daily. **Amtrak** trains serve Provo, tel. (800) 872-7245. **Yellow Cab** provides taxi service, tel. 377-7070. Scheduled airline flights leave from the Salt Lake City airport.

NORTHWEST OF PROVO

Hutching's Museum Of Natural History
This amazingly diverse collection in the town of Lehi (LEE-high) began as a family museum. Highlights include pioneer rifles, Indian crafts, glittering minerals, ancient fossils, mounted birds of Utah, and colorful tropical shells. Open Mon.-Sat. 9:30 a.m.-5:30 p.m.; $2 adult, $1 children under 12. Located at 685 N. Center St. in Lehi (16 miles northwest of Provo on I-15), tel. 768-7180. The museum plans to relocate to 53 N. Center Street

Saratoga Resort
This family amusement park on the north shore of Utah Lake, tel. 768-8206/8205, features four swimming pools, a 350-foot-long "Kamikazi" water slide, arcade games, Kiddieland rides, miniature golf, boating on the lake, snack bar, picnicking, and camping. Mineral springs emerging from the ground at 111° F feed the pools, which are kept at about 95° (upper pool) and 85° (lower pool). The campground has showers with spaces for tents and RVs (w/electric hookups). Saratoga's season lasts from about Memorial Day to Labor Day weekends. Costs depend on facilities used; a small parking

fee is charged on weekends. From Lehi, drive west two miles on UT 73 and turn south 3.3 miles on 9550 West at the sign. The resort was closed for major renovation in 1994, so you should call for information about changes and campground rates.

Camp Floyd Stagecoach Inn State Park
A restored inn, an old U.S. Army building, and a military cemetery preserve a bit of pioneer history at Fairfield, a sleepy village on the other side of Utah Lake from Provo. John Carson, who had been one of the first settlers at the site in 1855, built a family residence and hotel three years later. About the same time, troops of the U.S. Army under Colonel Albert Johnston marched in and established Camp Floyd nearby. The soldiers had been sent by President Buchanan to put down a rumored Mormon rebellion. Upon finding that no "Utah War" existed, the colonel led his men to this site so as not to intimidate the major Mormon settlements. Fairfield jumped in size almost overnight to become Utah's third-largest city, with a population of about 7,000 including the 3,000 soldiers. Even for the times, it was rowdy—17 saloons served

the Army men. The camp (later named Fort Crittenden) served no real purpose, however, and was abandoned in 1861 so that troops could return east to fight in the Civil War. Carson's hotel, later known as the Stagecoach Inn, continued to serve travelers on the dusty main road across Utah. Pony Express riders, stagecoach passengers, miners, sheepherders, and every other kind of traveler stopped here for the night until the doors closed in 1947.

Now the inn is a state park, furnished as in the old days and full of exhibits showing frontier life. A shaded picnic area is beside it. The only surviving building of Camp Floyd has been moved across the street and has a diorama of the fort and some excavated artifacts. Camp Floyd's well-kept cemetery is a three-quarter-mile drive west and south of Fairfield. The Stagecoach Inn is open daily 11 a.m.-5 p.m. from about Easter weekend to the end of September. The season may be extended depending on visitation; it's a good idea to call ahead, especially if you are driving out just to see the exhibits, tel. 768-8932. Admission is $3/vehicle, $1/individual. From Provo or Salt Lake City, take I-15 to Lehi and turn west 21 miles on UT 73.

NORTH OF PROVO

TIMPANOGOS CAVE NATIONAL MONUMENT

Beautiful cave formations reward visitors who hike the trail to the cave entrance on the north side of Mt. Timpanogos. Branching helictites, icicle-like stalactites, rising stalagmites, and graceful flowstone formations appear snow white or in delicate hues of green, yellow, or red. Tunnels connect three separate limestone caves, each of which has a different character. The first was discovered by Martin Hansen in 1887 while tracking a mountain lion. Middle and Timpanogos caves weren't reported until 1921-22. Timpanogos Cave so impressed early explorers that a trail, lighting, and national monument protection came soon afterward.

Exhibits and a short slide show in the visitor center introduce the formation, history, and ecology of the caves. The staff provides information on special cave tours and on wildlife and plants of the area. A brochure available here identifies plants and trees along the trail to the caves and illustrates the geology and formation of the caves. Related books, hiking maps, posters, and slides are sold. Be sure to obtain tickets here for the cave tour before starting up the trail. Rangers schedule nature walks on the trail to the caves.

Allow about three hours for the complete trip, including 45-60 minutes for the cave tour. The three-mile roundtrip hike from the visitor center to the caves is moderately difficult; you'll climb 1,065 feet to an elevation of 6,730 feet. Points along the way have fine views up and down American Fork Canyon and out onto the Utah Valley. People with breathing, heart, or walking difficulties shouldn't attempt the trail; wheeled vehicles (including strollers) and pets aren't allowed. Rangers enforce safety rules that prohibit running, throwing rocks, or short-cutting; children under 16 must stay with their parents.

Ranger-led tours wind about one-third mile through the caves. Underground temperature is about 45° F all year, so bring a sweater or jacket. The caves close during winter because snow and ice make the trail too hazardous. The season lasts from about mid-May to mid-October; tickets are sold (in the visitor center only) 8 a.m.-3:30 p.m. (extended to 7 a.m.-5:30 p.m. in the peak summer season). On Saturday (all day), Sunday afternoons, holidays, and mid-summer weekdays, you may have a long wait at best. It's a good idea to call ahead to check hours and find out how busy the caves are. Tickets can also be purchased two to three weeks in advance by calling and paying with a credit card. Tours often sell out from mid-June to mid-August, when advance reservations are strongly recommended. Admission fees for the cave tours are $5 adult, $4 children 6-15, free for children under six; Golden Age card holders pay $2.50 but no discount is given with Golden Eagle cards.

A snack bar at the visitor center is open in summer. Picnickers can use tables across the road from the visitor center and at a site a quarter mile west. The U.S. Forest Service has several campgrounds nearby. Contact the monument at RR 3, Box 200, American Fork, UT 84003, tel. 756-5238. The visitor center is two miles up American Fork Canyon on the Alpine Scenic Loop (UT 92). You can take I-15 American Fork Exit 279 if you're coming north from Provo or the I-15 Alpine Exit 287 if coming south from Salt Lake City.

ALPINE SCENIC LOOP

The narrow paved highway twists and winds through some of the most beautiful alpine terrain in Utah. Mount Timpanogos rises to 11,750 feet in the center of the loop and presents sheer cliff faces and jagged ridges in every direction. More than a dozen campgrounds and several picnic areas line the way. Anglers can try for trout in swift clear streams. Timpanogos Cave National Monument on the north side of the loop, and the Bridal Veil Falls Skytram on the south side are major attractions. Autumn brings brilliant golds of aspen and scarlets of maples. Winter snows close the loop at its higher elevations and attract skiers to Sundance Resort. The most scenic sections of the loop lie along American Fork Canyon and its South Fork, Provo Canyon and its North Fork, and on the high pass between these drainages. A drive on US 89 or I-15 completes the approximately 40-mile loop. With a few stops, a full day can easily be spent on the drive. If you'd like to see Timpanogos Cave on the way, it's recommended to begin the loop there to avoid waiting in ticket lines, especially on weekend afternoons.

Most of the picnic areas and campgrounds lie along American Fork Canyon at elevations of 5,400 to 6,200 feet; their season begins in early May and lasts to late October. Higher recreation areas are **Granite Flat Campground** (elev. 6,800 feet), **Altamont Group Campground** (elev. 6,600 feet), **Timpooneke Campground** (elev. 7,400 feet), **Mt. Timpanogos Campground** (elev. 6,800 feet), and **Theatre in the Pines Picnic Area** (elev. 6,800 feet). The season runs from about Memorial Day weekend to the third week in September. Nearly all the recreation areas have water and a $12 fee (except Timpooneke and Mt. Timpanogos campgrounds, which are $10). Some areas can be reserved by calling (800) 280-CAMP. **Pleasant Grove Ranger District** office of the Uinta National Forest has information and maps for recreation areas along the Alpine Scenic Loop and for the Lone Peak and Mt. Timpanogos wildernesses; open Mon.-Fri. (daily in summer) 8 a.m.-5 p.m. at 390 N. 100 East, Pleasant Grove, UT 84062, tel. 785-3563. (You'll pass the office if taking US 89 and UT 146 between Provo/Orem and the mouth of American Fork Canyon.)

black-chinned hummingbird (Archilocus alexandri)

Lone Peak Wilderness

The summit of Lone Peak rises to 11,250 feet on the divide between Little Cottonwood and American Fork canyons. Despite its closeness to Provo and Salt Lake City, the wilderness (30,088 acres) offers good opportunities for solitude. Hikers sometimes spot mountain goats. A climb to the summit is a very strenuous dayhike; many people prefer taking two days. Some routes have dangerous drop-offs and require mountaineering skills. Lower elevations have fine scenery as well as easier hiking. Lake Hardy (southeast of the summit) is a popular destination. Four main trailheads provide access to the wilderness: Bells Canyon from lower Little Cottonwood Canyon to the north, Draper Ridge to the west, Alpine to the south, and Granite Flat Campground (off American Fork Canyon) to the southeast. Topo maps for the wilderness are the 7 1/2-minute Lehi, Draper, Dromedary Peak, and Timpanogos Cave. Trail descriptions are given in *Wasatch Trails, Volume Two* by Daniel Geery and *The Hiker's Guide to Utah* by Dave Hall. Contact the Salt Lake City Ranger District office for hiking information on the north slope, or the Pleasant Grove Ranger District office for the south side.

Mount Timpanogos Wilderness

Sheer cliffs of Mt. Timpanogos tower 7,000 feet above the Utah Valley and present one of the most dramatic sights of the Wasatch Range. Trails to the heights lead past waterfalls, flower-filled alpine meadows, lakes, and permanent snowfields. One trail continues to the 11,750-foot summit for superb vistas of central Utah. The climb is strenuous, especially the last three miles, but requires no special skills. You'll see whole families—from grandchildren to grandparents—on this popular mountain. Even short hikes can be very rewarding. Take care to bring storm gear in case the weather suddenly turns bad. A shelter at Emerald Lake provides a refuge from storms. Hike either the **Timpooneke Trail** from Timpooneke Campground or the **Aspen Grove Trail** from the Theatre in the Pines Picnic Area; both trailheads lie just off the Alpine Scenic Loop. One-way distances to the summit are 9.1 miles on the Timpooneke Trail (4,350-foot elev. gain) and 8.3 miles on the Aspen Grove Trail (4,900-foot elev. gain). A hike on both trails (highly recommended) can be done with a car shuttle. If a trip to the summit sounds too ambitious, you can stick to the 12 miles between the trailheads via Emerald Lake (elev. 10,300 feet).

The **Summit Trail** branches off west of Emerald Lake, climbs a steep slope to the jagged summit ridge, then follows the ridge southeast to the top. A large snowfield and the deep blue waters of Emerald Lake lie directly below. Chunks of ice break off the snowfield and float in the lake during even the hottest summer days. Local people often refer to the snowfield as a glacier, but technically it's just a snowfield. Some climbers continue southeast along the summit ridge and drop down onto the snowfield and slide or walk to Emerald Lake, but this can be a bit hazardous. Hiking season is from about mid-July to mid-October. In winter and spring, hikers must be equipped and experienced for snow travel. Topo maps are the 7¹/₂-minute Timpanogos Cave and Aspen Grove, though you're not likely to need them unless snow covers the trails. The Pleasant Grove Ranger District office can advise on hiking conditions.

on the Aspen Grove Trail

Cascade Springs

Crystal-clear water emerges amidst lush vegetation and flows down a long series of travertine terraces at this beautiful spot. The springs produce more than seven million gallons of water daily. Boardwalks (some handicapped accessible) and short trails with interpretive signs allow a close look at the stream and pools. Trout can be seen darting through the water (no fishing). Plantlife includes maple, oak, aspen, willow, water birch, box elder, cattails, watercress, and wildflowers. The drive to Cascade Springs is also very pretty, either from the Alpine Scenic Loop or from Heber Valley. A paved road (Forest Route 114) branches off the Alpine Scenic Loop near its summit (between Mileposts 18 and 19) and winds northeast seven miles to the springs. An unpaved road, passable by car if the road is dry, begins on the west edge of Heber Valley and climbs high above the valley with good views, then drops down to the springs; turn west seven miles on UT 220 from UT 113 (between Midway and Charleston) and follow signs.

Sundance Resort

Since actor/director Robert Redford purchased the land in 1969, he has worked toward obtaining an ideal blend of recreation, the arts, and natural beauty. Musicals and other entertainment of the **Sundance Summer Theatre** take place outdoors. Tickets can be purchased the day of the show or reserved by calling 225-4107; the information line recording is 225-4100. Redford founded the **Sundance Institute** in 1980 as a laboratory for independent filmmakers; its program is expanding and it may have screening rooms and other facilities open to the public.

Downhill skiing begins in mid-December and lasts into April. Two double chairlifts and two triple chairs take skiers high on the southeast slopes of Mt. Timpanogos. The 41 runs on 450 acres provide challenges for people of all abilities; total elevation drop is 2,150 feet. Ski instruction, rentals, accommodations, restaurants, and packages are available at the resort. Adult lift tickets cost $28 full day and $21 half day; children 12 and under ski for $17 full day and $14 half day. **Sundance Nordic Center** offers 15 km of nordic track, lessons, and rentals.

Accommodations in cottages cost $110-455 in summer, $170-600 in winter; mountain houses run $650 per night year-round. **Sundance Grill** serves breakfast, lunch, and dinner daily. The **Tree Room** prepares elegant dinners daily and a Sunday brunch. A barbecue is held prior to performances of the Sundance Summer Theatre. Reservations are recommended for all dining. Contact Sundance at RR 3, Box A-1, Sundance, UT 84604, tel. 225-4100 (recording of summer theater, events, and winter skiing) or 225-4107 or (800) 892-1600 (office). The resort can be easily reached by taking US 189 from Provo, Orem, or Heber City, then turning northwest two and one half miles on UT 92 (Alpine Scenic Loop).

Bridal Veil Falls Skytram

One of the world's steepest trams provides a thrilling ride with good views of Mt. Timpanogos, Provo Canyon, and Utah Valley. You'll also have a close look at the falls, which drop 607 feet in two cascades; they're a major tributary of the Provo River. The Swiss-made tramway rises 1,228 feet in a single 1,753-foot span; a pair of 14-ton counterweights provide tension for the track cables. At the top, you can turn right 200 feet to an overlook of the Utah Valley, or turn left one-third mile to see a smaller set of waterfalls not visible from the bottom. Short hiking trails also begin below at the Provo River and go to the base of the lower falls (an easy hike) and the base of the upper falls (more difficult). The Skytram runs daily 9 a.m.-9 p.m. from about mid-May to Labor Day, then 11 a.m.-8 p.m. until late October, weather permitting; $5.95 adult, $2.75 children 3-11, $4.95 seniors 65 and up; tel. 225-4461. The ticket office has a snack bar and gift shop. A dance hall on top jumps to music Friday and Saturday evenings from mid-June to late October. Trout swim in the clear pool at the base of the falls; they like to be fed, but you're not allowed to catch them. The falls and Skytram lie four miles up from the mouth of Provo Canyon on US 189.

Squaw Peak Road

This scenic drive follows the Wasatch Range east of Provo with many fine views over Utah Valley. The road turns south from US 189 in Lower Provo Canyon, then climbs high into the mountains. Pavement ends after five miles at the turnoff for **Hope Campground** (has water from late May to mid-October; $6; elev. 6,600 feet). The road continues south eight miles to

Rock Canyon Campground (a group area with water from late May to mid-October) and on to the Left Fork of Hobble Creek, east of Springville, for a total of 26 miles one-way. Squaw Peak Road has some rough spots in the middle section, but cars with good clearance can usually be driven through in dry weather. The Pleasant Grove Ranger District office can advise on camping, hiking, road conditions, and Rock Canyon group reservations.

HEBER CITY

Its setting in a lush agricultural valley surrounded by high mountains has earned Heber City the title "Switzerland of America." Many of its people work at farming, raising livestock, and dairying as their families have done since pioneer days. A massive snowslide blocked passage of the first settlers making their way up Provo Canyon in 1859, but they simply disassembled their wagons and portaged them to the other side. The town's name honors Heber C. Kimball, a counselor to Church President Brigham Young. Heber City (pop. 5,100) makes a handy stop for travelers exploring the nearby Wasatch and Uinta ranges or visiting the large Deer Creek and Strawberry reservoirs. Heber City offers reasonably priced accommodations a short drive from Park City.

Heber Valley Historic Railroad

Ride a turn-of-the-century train pulled by steam locomotive #618 past Deer Creek Lake into the scenic alpine Provo Canyon. You may choose a short round trip of two hours to the Deer Creek Dam or continue on to Vivian Park; adult fare $16, senior $14, and children $10. One-way rates are available and diesel locomotive rides cost $2 less. The depot is located at 450 South 600 West, tel. 654-5601 or (800) 982-3257.

Midway Fish Hatchery

Visitors are welcome at this state-run trout hatchery. It's open daily 8 a.m.-4:30 p.m.; located one mile south of Midway just off UT 113 (Charleston Road).

Accommodations

Places in town, from south to north, include **High Country Inn**, 1000 S. Main, tel. 654-0201,

$42-46 s, $46-50 d; the **Danish Viking Lodge,** 989 S. Main, tel. 654-2202 or (800) 544-4066, $37-40 s, $42-45 d; **Cottage Bed & Breakfast,** 830 S. Main, tel. 654-2236, $21.80 s, $27.25-38.15 d; **Mac's Motel,** 670 S. Main, tel. 654-0612, $35.97 s, $42.51 d; **Hylander Motel,** 425 S. Main, tel. 654-2150 or (800) 932-0355, $32 s, $42 d and up; **Swiss Alps Inn,** 167 S. Main, tel. 654-0722, $35.95 s, $41.95 d and up; and **Aloma Motel,** 90 N. Main, tel. 654-0231, $28-32 s, $32-38 d; also kitchenettes. In Midway, **Inn at the Creek Bed & Breakfast** offers rooms at 375 Rainbow Lane near Homestead Golf Course, tel. 654-0892, $103.55 d.

A hot-spring resort three miles west of town near Midway features mineral baths, swimming, and accommodations. "Hot pots" of natural hot springs dot the surrounding landscape. The spring water is believed to be good for the skin. Spacious grounds and stately buildings of **The Homestead** may remind you of an age long past, but the facilities are modern. A large volcanic-like cone beside the resort is actually composed of travertine deposited by the springs; water once flowed out of the top, but it's now piped to indoor and outdoor pools and hot tubs. (Pools and hot tubs are open only to hotel guests.) Golfers can play at the resort's 18-hole course. Stables offer horseback and hay rides (sleigh rides in winter) and bicycle rentals, tel. extension 440. Rooms cost $81.75-228.62 and should be reserved well in advance, especially for summer weekends. A restaurant serves breakfast, lunch, and dinner daily; reservations are requested for dinner. The Grill Room offers lighter fare in summer. Open all year at 700 N. Homestead Dr. (Midway, UT 84049), tel. 654-1102 or (800) 327-7220.

Food
High Country Inn's restaurant has a varied American menu at 1000 S. Main, tel. 654-2022, open daily for breakfast, lunch, and dinner. **Lakeside Cottage** offers home-style food at 3761 S. Charleston Road (UT 113 between Midway and Charleston), tel. 654-3456, open Wed.-Sat. for lunch and dinner. Other places for American food include **Hub Cafe,** 1165 S. Main, tel. 654-5463, open daily for breakfast, lunch, and dinner; **Chick's Cafe,** 154 S. Main, tel. 654-1771, open daily for breakfast, lunch, and dinner; and **Wagon Wheel Cafe,** 220 N.

Main, tel. 654-0251, open daily for breakfast, lunch, and dinner. **Blazing Saddles Restaurant** serves American and Mexican food at 605 W. 100 South, tel. 654-3300; open daily for lunch and dinner. **Das Burgermeister Haus Restaurant,** 79 E. Main St. in Midway, serves Swiss and American cuisine for lunch and dinner Mon.-Saturday. **Song's Chinese Restaurant,** 930 S. Main, tel. 654-3338, offers Cantonese, Mandarin, and American items; open Mon.-Sat. for lunch and daily for dinner. Pick up pizza at **Pizza Hut,** 750 S. Main, tel. 654-3636, open daily for lunch and dinner, or **The Pizza House,** 587 S. Main, tel. 654-1212, open Tues.-Sat. for lunch and Mon.-Sat. for dinner).

Events
Horse shows and rodeos take place through the summer in the Heber City area. A **Pow Wow** in June brings Indians for dances and craft sales. The **Utah High School Rodeo Finals** are also held in June. **Wasatch Fair Days** features a parade, rodeo, exhibits, livestock show, entertainment, and demolition derby in early August. **Swiss Days** are celebrated with a parade, entertainment, food, and flea market on the Friday and Saturday before Labor Day. The Experimental Aircraft Association sponsors the **E.A.A. Fly In** of experimental and vintage aircraft in September.

Services
The **city park** at Main and 300 South has picnic tables and a playground. **Wasatch Community Pool** has indoor swimming and racquetball at Wasatch Middle School, 200 E. 800 South (turn east from Main onto 600 South, then right on 200 East), tel. 654-3450. Wasatch County High School has **tennis courts** at 600 South and 200 East. **High Country Aviation** arranges sailplane rides at the airport, tel. 654-5831. The **post office** is at 125 E. 100 North, tel. 654-0881. **Wasatch County Hospital** is at 55 S. 500 East, tel. 654-2500. In **emergencies** (police, fire, paramedic), dial 911.

Information
The **Heber Valley Chamber of Commerce** has an Information Center at 475 N. Main (Box 427, Heber City, UT 84032), tel. 654-3666, open Mon.-Fri. 9 a.m.-5 p.m. (also on Saturdays and Sundays from June to September). **Heber**

Ranger District office, 2460 S. Hwy. 40 (Box 190, Heber City, UT 84032), tel. 654-0470, manages the Uinta National Forest lands east and southeast of Heber City. The staff provides literature and advice for camping, hiking, horseback riding, boating, fishing, cross-country skiing, snowmobiling, and back-road travel; open Mon.-Fri. 8 a.m.-5 p.m. (also some Saturday and Sunday June-Sept.). **Wasatch County Library,** 188 S. Main, tel. 654-1511, is open Mon.-Saturday.

VICINITY OF HEBER CITY

Wasatch Mountain State Park

Utah's largest state park encompasses 22,000 acres of valleys and mountains on the east side of the Wasatch Range. An excellent 27-hole golf course in the park has a pro shop and a cafe. Unpaved scenic drives lead north through Pine Creek Canyon to Guardsman Pass Road (turn right for Park City or left over the pass for Brighton), northwest through Snake Creek Canyon to Pole Line Pass and American Fork Canyon, and southwest over Decker Pass to Cascade Springs. Only a short nature trail has been developed, but you can set out on your own. Winter brings snow depths of three to six feet from about mid-December to mid-March. Separate cross-country ski and snowmobile trails begin near the golf course. **Homestead Cross-Country Ski Center,** tel. 654-1102, provides equipment for both sports.

The large **Pine Creek Campground** has showers and hookups from late April/early May to late October; located just north of the golf course at an elevation of 5,600 feet. A one and one half-mile **nature trail** begins near site #21 of the Oak Hollow Loop in Pine Creek Campground. The staff offers **campfire programs,** usually on Friday and Saturday evenings, at the campground's amphitheater. **Little Deer Creek Campground** is a smaller, more secluded area in an aspen forest; open with water from June to mid-September. It's also open earlier and later without water; check with the park office first because groups often reserve all the sites. You can get here by driving the seven-mile unpaved road to Cascade Springs, then turning north four miles on another unpaved road. The park visitor center, just before the golf course, has an information desk open all

year daily 8 a.m.-5 p.m.; Box 10, Midway, UT 84049, tel. 654-1791 or (800) 322-3770 (reservations). Make golf course reservations at tel. 654-0532 (local) or 266-0268 (Salt Lake City). Admission is $3 per vehicle day use, $11 camping w/electric hookups or $13 w/full hookups ($1 more for Friday, Saturday, and holiday camping plus $1 more for full hookups) at Pine Creek Campground; $7 per vehicle overnight at Little Deer Creek Campground. From Heber City, drive west three miles to Midway, then follow signs north two miles.

Deer Creek State Park

The seven-mile-long Deer Creek Reservoir lies in a very pretty setting below Mt. Timpanogos and other peaks of the Wasatch Range. A developed area near the lower end of the lake has a campground with showers, picnic area, paved boat ramp, dock, and fish-cleaning station; elevation is 5,400 feet. Island Beach Area, four and one half miles to the northeast, has a gravel swimming beach and a marina (open in summer with a store, snack bar, boat ramp, and rentals of fishing boats, ski boats, and Jet Skis); ice fishermen can park here in winter. Rainbow trout, perch, largemouth bass, and walleye swim in the lake. Good winds for sailing blow most afternoons. You'll often see a lineup of catamarans at the sailboat beach near the campground and crowds of sailboarders at the Island Beach Area. Deer Creek State Park is open mid-April to late October; Box 257, Midway, UT 84049, tel. 654-0171 or (800) 332-3770 for reservations (advised Memorial Day to Labor Day weekends). Admission fee is $3 per vehicle day use (includes Island Beach Area) or $9 ($10 Friday, Saturday, or holidays) per vehicle camping at the campground area. The campground is just off US 189, 11 miles southwest of Heber City and 17 miles northeast of Provo.

Deer Creek Island Resort, at the Island Beach area, tel. 654-4779, has boat rentals (fishing, ski, sport), and a snack bar in summer; a restaurant offers fine dining Friday and Saturday evenings year-round. **Snow's Marina,** on Wallsburg Bay 1.2 miles northeast of the state park campground, has a small store, snack bar, boat ramp ($3), RV park ($8 no hookups), and fishing-boat rentals (with or without motor). Open daily May to October.

sailboarding off Island Beach Area, Deer Creek State Park

Jordanelle State Park

This large reservoir upstream on the Provo River provides recreation for boaters and fishermen. It's located east off US 40, starting six miles north of Heber. There are two recreation areas. **Rock Cliff Recreation Site** is located at the upper end of the east arm of the reservoir and has walk-in camping sites with restrooms and hot showers, a nature center, boardwalks with interpretive displays, and pavilions for day use. Admission is $3 per carload, $1 per individual for day use; sites cost $7 tent or RV no hookups, $11 w/hookups, ($1 extra camping Friday, Saturday, and holidays). **Hailstone Recreation Site** was under construction at press time and will have 230 campsites with restrooms and showers, day-use shaded pavilions, a modern marina with 80 boat slips, a general store, a laundromat, and a small restaurant. Facilities will have wheelchair access with raised tent platforms. The season is April to mid-October; Box 309, Heber City, UT 84032, tel. 783-3030.

Heber Valley RV Park Resort offers camping sites, hot showers, a country store, and a laundromat just below the Jordanelle Reservoir dam, about six miles north of Heber City, tel. 654-4049, open all year, tent $11.94, RV no hookups $14.12, and RV w/hookups $17.39.

Historic Union Pacific Rail Trail State Park

Utah's new state park consists of a multi-use, nonmotorized trail built to accommodate hikers, bicyclists, horseback riders, and cross-country skiers. The trail runs 27 miles from Echo Reservoir to Park City with trailheads and information kiosks at Echo Reservoir, Coalville, Wanship, Star Pointe, and Park City. Other staging areas will be added as well as spurs connecting to the Mormon Pioneer Historic Trail, Rockport Lake State Park, and the Jordanelle State Park's proposed trail system. There are campgrounds near the trailheads and spurs but not on the trails. No fee is planned, but this could change; Box 309, Heber City, UT 84032, tel. 645-8036.

Strawberry Reservoir

This 17,000-acre reservoir lies on a high rolling plateau 23 miles southeast of Heber City. Creation of the original Strawberry Reservoir began in 1906 as a federal reclamation project to divert water from the Colorado Basin west to the Utah Valley. Soldier Creek Dam (constructed in 1973) greatly increased the reservoir's size. A section of lake called "The Narrows" separates Strawberry Arm on the west from the smaller Soldier Creek Arm on the east. The water at this 7,600-foot elevation is cold for water-skiing, but hardy souls in wet suits will often brave it. Fishing is good all year (through the ice in winter) for rainbow and cutthroat trout and some brook trout and kokanee salmon. Several winter parking areas along US 40 provide access for cross-country skiing, snowmobiling, and ice fishing. Check with the Heber Ranger District office for information on recreation at the reservoir and in the surrounding Uinta National Forest; tel. 654-0470.

The **Strawberry Visitor Center/Fish Hatchery** not only sells maps and books but also functions as a small museum with interactive displays explaining the history of the reservoir from its construction to its present-day fish-breeding programs. A 200-yard boardwalk with interpretive stations leads to the hatchery and an information kiosk. Open Mon -Thurs 9 a m - 5 p.m. and Fri.-Sun. 9 a.m.-6 p.m. from Memorial Day through the last weekend of October, tel. 548-2321.

The U.S. Forest Service maintains four campgrounds around the lake; all are open with water from late May to late October; $10 no hookups, $15 loop B w/hookups. **Strawberry Bay Recreation Complex,** on the west shore of Strawberry Bay, has a large campground, an overflow campground (group and individual family sites can be reserved), paved boat ramp, several fish-cleaning stations, and **Strawberry Bay Marina.** The marina has a cafe (open daily for breakfast, lunch, and dinner), store, gas pump, boat rentals (with and without motors), gas dock, and boat storage; open late April/early May through deer season (the cafe closes weekdays between Labor Day and deer season); tel. 548-2261. **Renegade Campground** sits on the south shore of Strawberry Reservoir. **Soldier Creek Recreation Complex** lies on the west shore of Soldier Creek Bay with a large campground, paved boat ramp, several fish-cleaning stations, and **Soldier Creek Marina.** The marina, tel. 548-2696, offers a store, gas pump, boat rentals (with and without motor), gas dock, and boat storage; open late April/early May through deer season. **Aspen Grove Campground** is a smaller area on the southeast side of Soldier Creek Bay; a paved boat ramp is nearby. **Aspen Grove Marina,** near the dam on Soldier Creek Bay, has supplies and boat rentals. **Picnickers** can stop at free day-use areas at Strawberry Bay, Chicken Creek, Haw's Point, and Soldier Creek. Haw's Point has handicapped fishing access.

Other Recreation Areas
In The Heber Ranger District
Whiskey Springs Picnic Area is near the mouth of Daniels Canyon, eight miles south-east of Heber City on US 40; water is available in summer. Elevation is 6,400 feet; signs along the short **Whiskey Springs Nature Trail** identify plants. **Lodgepole Campground** lies in upper Daniels Canyon, 16 miles southeast of Heber City on UC 40; open late May to late October with water; $10. Lodgepole pine and aspen grow at the 7,800-foot elevation.

Currant Creek Recreation Complex, on the southwest shore of **Currant Creek Reservoir** (elev. 8,000 feet), has a campground (with water from late May to late October and a $10 fee), paved boat ramp, fish-cleaning station, and handicapped fishing access. Anglers catch rainbow, cutthroat, and brook trout; ice fishing is good in winter. **Currant Creek Nature Trail** begins from loop D of the campground and climbs 400 feet in a one and a quarter mile loop; signs tell about the ecology. The best way to get here from Heber City is to drive southeast 42 miles on US 40 past Strawberry Reservoir, just before **Currant Creek Lodge** (motel and cafe, tel. 548-2226), turn northwest 19.5 miles along Currant Creek on Forest Route 083. High-clearance vehicles can take a slow, scenic route over Lake Creek Summit (elev. 9,900 feet); from Heber City, head east 31 miles on Center Street, which becomes Lake Creek/Currant Creek Road (Forest Route 083).

Mill Hollow Campground sits on the shore of small Mill Hollow Reservoir at an elevation of 8,800 feet in an Engelmann spruce forest, 37 miles from Heber City. It's open with water from mid-June to late October; $10; the reservoir has trout fishing. Take US 189 to Francis (northeast of Heber City), then UT 35 and Forest Route 054 (gravel).

Wolf Creek Campground is in an Engelmann spruce forest at 9,500 feet near Wolf Creek Pass, 38 miles from Heber City; open with water from early July to mid-October; $6; also group sites; from Heber City, drive north and east to Francis, then head southeast about 22 miles on UT 35 (part gravel); this scenic road continues on to Hanna and Duchesne in northeastern Utah.

SOUTH OF PROVO ALONG I-15

HOBBLE CREEK-DIAMOND FORK LOOP

Pleasant canyon and mountain views line this 34-mile scenic drive east of Springville. The road is open from about mid-May to late October and is normally fine for cars; all but about the middle eight miles are paved. Along the way you'll pass picnic spots, campgrounds, hiking trailheads, and fishing holes. Back roads branch off to Squaw Peak Road, Strawberry Reservoir, and other destinations. Hikers can choose from a trail network totaling about 100 miles. Contact the **Spanish Fork Ranger District** office for maps and recreation information at 44 W. 400 North, Spanish Fork, UT 84660, tel. 798-3571. Open Mon.-Fri. 8 a.m.-5 p.m. (plus Saturday 8 a.m.-4:30 p.m. in summer). Family and group sites at some campgrounds can be reserved by calling (800) 280-CAMP. To drive the loop from Main Street in Springville (take I-15 Exit 263), head east three miles on 400 South to the mouth of Hobble Creek Canyon and follow Forest Routes 058 and 029.

Stops, listed with mileages from the mouth of Hobble Creek Canyon are: **Hobble Creek Golf Course,** 2.7 miles, 18 holes, pro shop, and restaurant, tel. 489-6297; **Cherry Picnic Area and Campground,** 4.6 miles, open with

water from early May to mid-September, $2 day use, sites can be used for camping if they haven't been reserved, $10, elev. 5,200 feet; **Balsam Campground,** 10 miles, open mid-May to mid-September with water, $10, elev. 6,000 feet; **Road Summit** with scenic views at the pass between Hobble Creek and Diamond Fork drainages (13.8 miles); **Three Forks Trailhead,** 24 miles, elev. 5,600 feet; **Diamond Campground,** 28 miles, open early May to late September with water, $6, elev. 5,280 feet; **Palmyra Campground,** 29 miles, open early May to late September with water, $6, elev. 5,240 feet; and **end of drive** at US 6/89 (34 miles, turn right 12 miles to return to Springville).

NEBO SCENIC LOOP

This mountain drive loops off I-15 and winds into the heights of the southern Wasatch Range. You'll enjoy alpine forests, fine panoramas of the valleys below, and a close look at Mt. Nebo—highest peak in the range. The entire 13-mile length from Payson to Nephi is paved; it's open from about mid-June to late October. In winter and spring, cross-country skiers and snowmobilers come up to glide across the snow. You can begin the drive from Payson in the north (I-15 Exit 254) or Nephi in the south

Mount Nebo

(take I-15 Exits 222 or 228 and go east six miles on UT 132). A partly paved road from Santaquin (I-15 Exit 248) goes southeast 11 miles via Santaquin Canyon to connect with the main drive.

More than 100 miles of trails lead into the backcountry. Devil's Kitchen Geologic Area lies at the end of a quarter-mile trail, 28 miles south of Payson; eroded layers of red-tinted river gravel and silt form spires and sharp ridges. Mount Nebo Wilderness is west of the drive and can be reached by several trails. Strong hikers can climb the south summit (elev. 11,877 feet) by trail on a day or overnight trip. The higher north summit (elev. 11,928 feet) is two peaks farther north along a knife-edge ridge (no trail). The Hiker's Guide to Utah by Dave Hall has hiking descriptions for Mt. Nebo and Santaquin Peak.

The U.S. Forest Service provides recreation facilities, trailheads, and overlooks along the Nebo Scenic Loop. Contact the Spanish Fork Ranger District office for maps and information at 44 W. 400 North, Spanish Fork, UT 84660, tel. 798-3571, open Mon.-Fri. (daily in summer) 8 a.m.-5 p.m. If you're coming from the south, you can stop at the forest service's Nephi Ranger District office, 740 S. Main, tel. 623-2735, for info on the Nebo Scenic Loop; open Mon.-Fri. 8 a.m.-5 p.m. You can reserve sites at Payson, Blackhawk, Ponderosa, and Bear Canyon by calling (800) 280-CAMP.

Campgrounds and picnic areas, from north to south (with distances from Payson), are Maple Bench Campground, 7.6 miles, open with water from early May to mid-September, $6, elev. 5,800 feet, Maple Lake is one mile away; Payson Lakes Campground, 12 miles, open with water from late May to mid-September, $10, elev. 8,000 feet, several lakes are nearby; Blackhawk Campground, 16 miles, open with water from late May to mid-September, $10, elev. 8,000 feet, also has group reservation sites and horse facilities; Ponderosa Campground, 36 miles, open with water from mid-May to mid-September, $10, elev. 6,200 feet, along Salt Creek below Mt. Nebo; and Bear Canyon Picnic Area, 38 miles, open with water from mid-May to mid-September, $2 day use, $6 single family camping, elev. 6,800 feet, two miles upstream from Ponderosa Campground. Travelers taking the road from Santaquin can stop at Trumbolt Picnic Area, open

from mid-May to mid-September, free day use, elev. 6,200 feet; and Tinney Flat Campground, open with water from mid-May to mid-September, $10, elev. 7,000 feet. The private Nephi KOA campground is near the south end of the drive at the junction with UT 132 (six miles east of Nephi), tel. 623-0811, open mid-May to mid-October, sites cost $14.71 tent or RV no hookups, $17.44 RV w/hookups. At High Country RV Camp, 899 S. Main, tel. 623-2624, sites cost $6 tent, $8 RV no hookups, and $12 RV w/hookups.

NEPHI

This small town (pop. 3,850) serves as the commercial center for the region and as the seat of Juab County. The first settlers arrived in 1851 and named the place for a patriarch in the Book of Mormon. Pleasant scents fill the air at the Nephi Rose Garden, one block east of Main on 100 North.

About half a dozen motels and as many restaurants line Main between I-15 Exits 222 and 228. You can't miss the Whitmore Mansion Bed & Breakfast, an ornate Eastlake/Queen Anne-style structure built in 1898-1900 at 110 S. Main, tel. 623-2047, $54.50-70.85, lunches and dinners are served by reservation. Nephi's annual events are the Ute Stampede and Rodeo in July and the Juab County Fair in August. The city park has picnic tables, playground, and an outdoor pool at Main and 500 North. Canyon Hills Park Golf Course (nine holes) lies up a canyon at 1200 E. 100 North, tel. 623-9930. Central Valley Medical Center is at 549 N. 400 East, tel. 623-1242. The Nephi Ranger District office of the Uinta National Forest has information on the Nebo Scenic Loop at 740 S. Main (Nephi, UT 84648), tel. 623-2735, open Mon.-Fri. 8 a.m.-5 p.m. The public library is at 21 E. 100 North, tel. 623-0822.

YUBA STATE PARK

Sevier Bridge Reservoir, 26 miles south of Nephi, is 22 miles long and 11,000 acres when full; its elevation is 5,014 feet. Minerals give the lake a turquoise tint that varies with the lighting. There's plenty of space for both water-skiers and anglers. Sailboarders often find good wind conditions here and warmer water in springtime than at most other Utah lakes. Fishermen catch yellow perch, walleye, channel catfish, and northern pike; ice fishing, mostly for yellow perch, is done from January to early March. North Sandy Beach (on the main road to the campground) and East Beach (reached from UT 28) have the best swimming; there's also a beach at the campground. For many years the reservoir and state park were known as Yuba Lake, despite the fact that no such thing existed! The name "Yuba" refers to the dam, begun in 1902 and originally named "U.B." Farmers who helped to build the dam received water rights from the Deseret Irrigation Company in payment for their labor; if they stopped working they lost their stock, if they kept working they had to do additional work to pay for an assessment. An old song lamented that "U.B. damned if you do and U.B. damned if you don't."

The campground (has showers), picnic area, and a paved boat ramp lie on the west shore; take I-15 Exit 202 and follow signs 4.3 miles. North Beach is off to the left 2.2 miles in; a small store here is open on summer weekends. If driving to the campground from the south, you can save eight miles by taking the I-15 frontage road (west side) from Scipio. East Beach and Painted Rocks Pictograph Site, both on the east shore, can be reached by boat or from UT 28 (an unpaved road from North Beach provides a shortcut to UT 28). Boaters can also use a boat ramp near Painted Rocks Pictograph Site. The park and campground stay open all year, though the campground showers close Nov.-March. It's a good idea to reserve campsites for summer weekends. If the campground is full, ask a ranger about other areas around the lake. Admission fees are $3 per vehicle day use, $5 per vehicle camping at Painted Rocks (no water), $7 per vehicle in the overflow area, or $9 ($10 Friday, Saturday, and holidays) per vehicle camping at the main campground; group day-use and camp areas can also be reserved. Box 159, Levan, UT 84639, tel. 758-2611 (ranger) or (800) 322-3770 (reservations). Weather conditions for the park area are available from a recording, tel. 758-2683.

FILLMORE

In 1851, Brigham Young and the Utah Territorial Legislature designated Fillmore as the territorial capital, even before the town was established. They chose this site in the Pahvant Valley because it lay in the approximate geographic center of the territory. Their plans didn't work out, but Fillmore (pop. 2,430) has become the center of a large agricultural region and the Millard County seat. A state historical museum in the Territorial Statehouse contains a wealth of pioneer history.

Territorial Statehouse State Park
Completed in 1855, the statehouse is Utah's oldest government building. Architect Truman O. Angell designed the three-story sandstone structure, originally planned to have four wings capped by a large Moorish dome. Only the south wing was completed, though, because antagonism between the U.S. government and the Mormons blocked the appropriation of expected federal funds. Several legislatures met here, but only the fifth session in 1855 stayed for its full length; the sixth and eighth sessions opened here, then quickly adjourned to Salt Lake City's better-suited facilities.

Rooms are furnished to represent a typical pioneer bedroom, parlor, and kitchen. Other exhibits display clothing, tools, and Indian artifacts. Lawbreakers spent time in the jail, one of the building's many uses. Historic photos and paintings show pioneer families and leaders of the church and government in early Utah. Open daily 9 a.m.-5 p.m. (to 6 p.m. in summer season); $1.50 adult, $1 ages 3-15, or $6 per vehicle. Guided tours can be arranged with advance notice at no additional charge. You can visit a pair of 1880s log cabins on the grounds; one has pioneer furnishings, the other a wagon. Peek in the windows of the restored 1867 Little Rock School House nearby. Cabins and schoolhouse can be opened on request. Rose gardens surround the statehouse, located downtown at 50 W. Capitol Ave. (behind the Millard County Courthouse), tel. 743-5316.

Accommodations And Campgrounds
Six motels lie along or near the I-15 Business Loop through town; some have very low prices.

Wagons West RV Campground, 545 N. Main, tel. 743-6188, is open all year with showers, laundry, and store; $10.65 tent or RV no hookups, $15 w/hookups. **Fillmore KOA** one-half mile off the south end of the Business Route, near I-15 Exit 163, tel. 743-4420, has showers, laundry, and store $14.31 tent or RV no hookups, $17.17 w/hookups (may close in winter).

Food

The **Truck Stop Cafe** is open daily for breakfast, lunch, and dinner at 580 N. Main, tel. 743-6876. The **Garden of Eat'n Restaurant** at the Paradise Inn, 1035 North Main, tel. 743-5414, is open daily for breakfast, lunch, and dinner. **Cowboy Cafe** and **Deano's Pizza** are downtown.

Events

Quarterhorse racing is held in June. A parade, carnival, and fireworks celebrate **Fourth of July**.

Services

For **emergencies** (police, fire, paramedic), dial 911. The **city park** in front of the Territorial Statehouse has picnic tables and a playground. An indoor **swimming pool** is just west of the statehouse. **North Park** at 500 N. Main offers picnicking and a tourist information booth (open in summer). **Fillmore Community Medical Center** is at 690 S. Hwy. 99, tel. 743-5591.

Information And Transportation

An **information booth** is open in summer at North Park, 500 N. Main. **Millard County Tourism** has year-round information on the county and the Paiute ATV Trail; open variable hours at 195 N. Main (Box 1082, Fillmore, UT 84631), tel. 743-7803 or (800) 441-4ATV. The **Fillmore Ranger District** office of the Fishlake National Forest has information about camping, fishing, hiking, horseback riding, and back-road travel in the nearby Pahvant Range and Canyon Mountains; open Mon.-Fri. 8 a.m.-5 p.m. at 390 S. Main (Box 265, Fillmore, UT 84631), tel. 743-5721. Visit the office of the **BLM's Warm Springs and House Range** resource areas to learn about the valleys and rugged mountains of west-central Utah; open Mon.-Fri. 7:45 a.m.-4:30 p.m. at 35 E. 500 North (Box 778, Fillmore, UT 84631), tel. 743-6811. The **public**

library is at 25 S. 100 West, tel. 743-5314. The **Greyhound Bus** stops at the Truck Stop Cafe, 590 N. Main, tel. 743-6876.

VICINITY OF FILLMORE

Pahvant Range

These mountains east of Fillmore have seven summits over 10,000 feet; Mine Camp Peak (elev. 10,222 feet) is the highest. Elk, deer, and other wildlife live here. A network of trails and forest roads leads into the high country; contact the Fillmore Ranger District office for a Fishlake National Forest map, recreation information, and group campground reservations. Turn east six miles on 200 South from downtown Fillmore to reach four **picnic areas** along wooded Chalk Creek; they have water in summer; free; elevations are 5,700-6,100 feet. Anglers catch rainbow and German brown trout in the creek. **Adelaide Campground** lies along Corn Creek farther south near Kanosh; open with water from late May to early October; $5. Cottonwood, piñon pine, juniper, spruce, and maple grow at the 5,500-foot elevation. From the southernmost east-west street in Kanosh, turn east five miles on a gravel road (Forest Route 106). The road continues through pretty country and descends Mud Spring Hollow to I-70. Corn Creek has fishing for rainbow and German brown trout. Two recreation areas are in the northern part of the range: **Maple Hollow Picnic Area**, on the west side, has water from late May to early October (elev. 6,900 feet); take the I-15 South Holden Exit 174 and go east six miles; box elder, maple, oak, and fir trees grow in the hollow. **Maple Grove Campground** is open with water from late May to early October (elev. 6,400 feet); $5; turn west four miles on the signed paved road from US 50 (near Milepost 47 between Scipio and Salina); maple, water birch, oak, piñon pine, juniper, and aspen grow in the valley; Ivie Creek has fishing for rainbow trout.

Tabernacle Hill

Volcanic eruptions in the desert 15 miles southwest of Fillmore have covered the land with cinder cones, a tuff ring, a collapsed caldera, spatter cones, pit craters, pressure ridges, and squeeze-ups. When viewed from the north, the

Tabernacle Hill and surrounding lava beds

tuff ring resembles the Mormon Tabernacle in Salt Lake City. The first eruptions occurred 12,000-24,000 years ago when Lake Bonneville covered the region. Explosive cinder and ash eruptions built a circular ring of tuff 3,000 feet across and 200 feet or more high, rising above the lake waters. In a second period of eruptions 11,000-12,000 years ago, molten lava filled the tuff ring and spilled out to the north, forming a seven-square-mile island of black lava in the receding lake. About two-thirds of the tuff ring survives as Tabernacle Hill. The collapsed caldera inside is 1,000 feet across and 60 feet deep. Two spatter cones near the hill represent the last gasps of the final eruption. A lava-tube cave, most of which lies west of the caldera, can be traced (on the surface) for about a mile. Bats live in some of the cave sections. You can enter the cave where its roof has collapsed, though rock falls commonly block the passages. Watch for Great Basin rattlesnakes when exploring the caves and other features here.

You can visit Tabernacle Hill any time of the year, but in summer, try to visit early in the day. From Fillmore, go west six miles on 400 North (UT 100) to Flowell, turn left (south) one mile, turn right two miles (pavement ends), turn left (south) three and one half miles at the junction (the other road continues to cinder pits), continue on the main track toward Tabernacle Hill in the distance; at a major gravel road, turn west, then immediately turn south again on a narrow dirt road. Tabernacle Hill is two and one half miles farther. You may have to walk the last two miles, depending on road conditions. Tabernacle Hill can also be reached from Meadow, eight miles to the southeast. The BLM office in Fillmore has maps and information helpful in exploring this and other areas of Utah's Great Basin; tel. 743-6811.

Cove Fort

In 1867, during the Black Hawk War, Church President Brigham Young ordered construction of this fort to protect travelers on the overnight journey between Fillmore and Beaver. Walls of volcanic basalt 100 feet square and 13 feet high enclosed 12 rooms and a cistern. Gunports at the two entrances and along the upper walls discouraged Indians from ever attacking the fort. Now furnished and restored to its 1877 specifications, the fort is open daily 10 a.m.-dusk from about early April to mid-October; free admission. The south row of rooms has the telegraph, stagecoach, post offices, dining room, kitchen, and laundry. North rooms have the sleeping accommodations. Outbuildings that have been reconstructed or relocated to the site include a barn, blacksmith shop, pig pen, and cabin. An ice house will be constructed. A picnic area is across the street. Volunteers of the LDS church lead informal tours and relate the fort's history. Cove Fort stands near the junction of I-15 and I-70; take I-15 Exit 135 and go southeast two miles or take I-70 Exit 1 and go northwest one mile.

BEAVER

Mormon pioneers settled near the mouth of Beaver Canyon in 1856 to farm and raise livestock. Large flocks of sheep kept a woolen mill busy. The pastoral tranquility came to an end four years later when prospectors discovered silver and gold in the San Francisco Mountains to the west. The flood of rambunctious miners, distrust of the staid Mormon community, and fear of Indian attacks caused the community to call for federal troops. The Army arrived in 1872 and built a fort, later named Fort Cameron, and stayed until 1882. Today, Beaver (pop. 2,300) is a handy travelers' stop just east of I-15. Main Street (the I-15 business loop) has a good selection of motels and restaurants. Highway UT 21 (Center St.) goes west to Minersville State Park (fishing and boating) and the desert country of west-central Utah, a popular region for rockhounding. An entirely different world lies just to the east on UT 153 (200 North St.)—wooded canyons, alpine lakes, and a ski area in Utah's third-highest mountain range, the Tushars.

Historic Buildings

More than 200 historic houses of architectural interest lie scattered around town. You'll see many of them by driving along the side streets. A large stone building remaining from Fort Cameron still stands on the east edge of town across the highway from the golf course. The old **Beaver County Courthouse,** with an ornate clock tower, represents the architectural splendor of its period. Building started in 1877, and the courthouse served Beaver County from 1882 until 1975. It now houses a historical museum; drop by Tues.-Thurs. 12 a.m.-6 p.m. in

Beaver County's old courthouse

summer (Memorial Day to Labor Day weekends) to see pioneer portraits, historic documents, an 1892 wedding cake, other artifacts, and mineral specimens. Visit the courtroom on the top floor, then head down to the dungeonlike jail cells in the basement (check out the graffiti here). The adjacent Historical Park has a statue of Philo T. Farnsworth (1906-1971), the "Father of Television," born in a log cabin near Beaver. Located on Center one block east of Main.

Accommodations And Campgrounds

A dozen motels lie along the business route through town between I-15 Exits 109 and 112; some offer very low rates. **Beaver KOA** has showers, store, laundry, and pool at the north edge of town (take I-15 Exit 112, go south 0.6 mile on the business loop, then turn left on Manderfield Rd.), tel. 438-2924, sites cost $13.08 tent, $14.17 RV no hookups, $16.35 w/hookups, open February 1 to November 30. **De Lano Motel's RV Park** has showers at 480 N. Main, tel. 438-2418, $9.26 w/hookups (no tents), open all year. **Beaver Canyon Campground,** on the east side of town at 1419 E. Canyon Road (200 North), tel. 438-5654, has showers, laundry, and a Mexican restaurant (open daily for dinner); $8.72 tent or RV no hookups, $10.90 w/hookups; open May 1 to November 1. **United Beaver Camperland** offers showers, store, laundry, and pool at the south edge of town (near I-15 Exit 109), tel. 438-2808, sites cost $9.76 tents, $11.94 RV no hookups, $15.21 w/hookups; open all year. **Minersville State Park** has a campground 14 miles west on UT 21. The Tushar Mountains have good camping too (see below).

Food

You'll find American food at **Garden of Eat'n Restaurant,** at Paradise Inn on north edge of town; **El Bambi Cafe,** 935 N. Main; **Arshel's Cafe,** 711 N. Main; **The Cottage Inn,** 171 S. Main; and **Timberline Restaurant,** south I-15 Exit 109. **Mama Sarty's Italian Kitchen** has pizza, pasta, and subs at 1 N. Main, tel. 438-5868, open Mon.-Sat. for lunch and dinner. **Maria's Cocina** serves Mexican food at the Beaver Canyon Campground, 1419 E. Canyon Rd. (200 North), tel. 438-5654, open daily for dinner. **Kan Kun** offers Mexican food just off the south I-15 Exit 109, tel. 438-5908, open daily for lunch and dinner.

Entertainment And Events

Beaver City Birthday celebrates with historic programs on February 6. **Summer Theater** performances take place from mid June to late July in the Opera House Civic Center across from the old county courthouse. **Horse races** run through the summer. Beaver celebrates **Pioneer Day** on July 24 with a parade, fireworks, rodeo, horse racing, and games. The **Beaver County Fair** is held in August at the fairgrounds near Minersville to the west.

Recreation And Services

City parks offer picnic tables and playgrounds at Main and Center and at 400 East and 300 North. This second park also has the indoor **Municipal Swimming Pool,** tel. 438-5066. **Tennis** courts are at the rodeo grounds on the east edge of town. Play golf at the nine-hole **Canyon Breeze Golf Course** on the east edge of town, tel. 438-2601. There's good **rockhounding** in

the Mineral Mountains northwest of town and in other areas to the west; a brochure that describes collecting sites is available from many local businesses. The **post office** is at 20 S. Main, tel. 438-2321. **Beaver Valley Hospital** provides medical care at 85 N. 400 East, tel. 438-2531.

Information And Transportation

Foresters at the **Beaver Ranger District** office, 575 S. Main (Box E, Beaver, UT 84713), tel. 438-2436, can tell you about camping, fishing, hiking, and road conditions in the forest lands of the Tushar Mountains to the east; open Mon.-Fri. 8 a.m.-5 p.m. The **Beaver County Visitor Information Center,** Box 272, Beaver, UT 84713, tel. 438-2975, can tell you more about sights and services in the area. The **public library** is at 55 W. Center, tel. 438-5274. The **Greyhound Bus** stops at El Bambi Cafe, 935 N. Main, tel. 438-2229.

THE TUSHAR MOUNTAINS

Although higher than the Wasatch Range, the Tushars remain relatively unknown and un crowded. Travelers on surrounding highways get glimpses of their rocky summits, but people who hurry by rarely appreciate their size and height. Delano Peak (elev. 12,169 feet) crowns the Tushars and is the highest point in central Utah. Highway UT 153 (200 North St.) from Beaver winds into the alpine country of the Fishlake National Forest to a ski area, campgrounds, fishing spots, and hiking trails. (The first 19 miles are paved, followed by 21 miles of dirt.) The road takes you through meadows and forests before making a steep descent to the town of Junction on US 89. Forest Route 137 branches off UT 153 10 miles from Beaver to Kents Lake, Anderson Meadow, and other pretty areas, then returns to the highway to complete a scenic loop (54 miles roundtrip from Beaver). Drivers with high-clearance vehicles can journey amidst the summits on the Kimberly/Big John Road Backway between UT 153 and the Kimberly Scenic Drive; much of this trip goes above timberline with spectacular views of peaks above and canyons below. For recreation information and road conditions, visit the Beaver Ranger District office at the corner of 200 North and 100 East in Beaver, tel. 438-2436.

Camping And Picnicking

From Beaver, the first campground and picnic area reached is **Little Cottonwood,** six miles east on UT 153; sites are open with water from late May to early September; $6; elevation is 6,500 feet. **Ponderosa Picnic Area** is two and one half miles farther up Beaver Canyon on UT 153 in a grove of ponderosa pine; it has water in summer; its elevation is 7,000 feet. Little Cottonwood and Ponderosa lie along the rushing Beaver River, which has trout fishing. **Mahogany Cove Campground** overlooks Beaver Canyon 12 miles east of town on UT 153; open with water from late May to early October; $4. Its name comes from the abundant curlleaf mountain mahogany; other trees at the 7,500-foot elevation include ponderosa pine, Gambel oak, juniper, and cottonwood. **Puffer Lake,** 21 miles from town on UT 153, is set among forested hills of spruce, fir, and aspen at 9,700 feet. The lake, privately owned by **Puffer Lake Resort** on the other side of the highway, tel. 864-2751, has trout fishing, primitive camping, and a primitive boat ramp. The resort offers boat rentals, a small store, and cabins during the warmer months.

To reach additional campgrounds or to drive the scenic loop, turn southeast on Forest Route 137 at a junction 10 miles east of town (near Milepost 10 on UT 153). The first eight miles are on a good gravel road (to Anderson Meadow), then there are seven miles of dirt road to UT 153; the last half is passable when dry by cars with good clearance, but it can be too rough for RVs. **Little Reservoir Campground** is less than one mile in on Forest Route 137; sites are in a ponderosa pine forest at 7,350 feet; open with water and a $5 fee from late May to early October. The reservoir here covers only three acres but often has good trout fishing. **Kents Lake Campground** overlooks Kents Lake five miles in on Forest Route 137. Sites are in a forest of spruce, fir, and aspen at 8,800 feet; open with water and a $5 fee from mid-June to early October. The 100-acre lake offers trout fishing. **Tushar Lakeside Campground** is a county-managed group area below Kents Lake, tel. 438-2975. **Anderson Meadow Campground** lies in high forests and meadows overlooking Anderson Meadow Reservoir at 9,500 feet,

eight miles in on Forest Route 137. It's open with water and a $4 fee from mid-June to early October. The reservoir has trout fishing. **La Baron Reservoir** is another popular fishing spot four miles farther (12 miles in on Forest Route 137), but it has only primitive camping; its elevation is 9,900 feet. Three miles further you'll return to UT 153; turn right for City Creek Campground and the town of Junction or left for Puffer Lake, Elk Meadows Resort, and Beaver.

The gravel and dirt section of UT 153 from the town of Junction on US 89 makes a relentless five-mile climb from the valley to the mountains—you'll need to use low gears going up and have good brakes coming down. This drive isn't recommended for trailers or RVs. This east side of UT 153 is open from late June until sometime in October. **City Creek Campground** is located near the bottom of the grade; from the turnoff five miles northwest of Junction, follow a side road in for one mile. Sites lie along City Creek in a diverse forest of cottonwood, aspen, ponderosa pine, piñon pine, Gambel oak, and juniper at an elevation of 7,600 feet. Open with water from Memorial Day to Labor Day weekends; free.

Hiking

Relatively few hikers have discovered this area, but good trails for hiking and horseback riding lead into the high country. Contact the Beaver Ranger District office in Beaver for details. Three peaks of the Tushars rise above 12,000 feet and make good climbing destinations—Delano Peak (elev. 12,169 feet), Mt. Belknap (12,139 feet), and Mt. Baldy (12,082 feet). Each involves an ascent of about 2,000 feet and can be reached on a day-hike. (Strong hikers have climbed all three in one day!) Delano can be climbed by a route up its southwest slope, Mt. Belknap by a trail up its southeast side, and Mt. Baldy by a route from Blue Lake up its southeast side. All three trails are reached from the Big John Flat Road, which turns north from UT 153 between Mileposts 16 and 17. When dry, the dirt road is often okay for cars. Other climbing routes are possible too. Hikers can reach the top of Delano Peak in just an hour via the southwest route; follow the Big John Flat Road past Big John Flat and park at the pullout between Griffith and Poison Creeks, 5.6 miles north of UT 153. The hike begins at an old jeep track

1. Cedar Breaks National Monument; **2.** Weeping Rock, Zion National Park; **3.** North Fork of Virgin River from Gateway to Narrows Trail, Zion National Park (all photos by Bill Weir)

1. Maze District, Canyonlands National Park; **2.** confluence of Salt Creek and Colorado River in the Needles District, Canyonlands National Park (all photos by Bill Weir)

marked by a sign saying it's closed to vehicles; follow the jeep tracks, then just head up the grassy slope to the summit. You're likely to see deer, hawks, and summer wildflowers on any hike in the area. Topo maps for the peaks are the 15-minute Delano Peak or the 7¹/₂-minute Delano Peak, Mt. Brigham, Mt. Belknap, and Shelly Baldy Peak maps.

Elk Meadows Ski And Summer Resort

The resort offers skiing and year-round accommodations in the Tushars 18 miles east of Beaver. Ski season normally begins on Thanksgiving and lasts to mid-April. The ski area has a total of 40 runs, up to two and one half miles

long with a vertical drop of 1,200 feet; 14% of the runs are rated beginner, 62% intermediate, and 24% advanced. Two double chairs, one triple chair, a poma, and a T-bar serve the slopes. Lift tickets cost $25 adult (all day), $18 adult (morning or afternoon); a first-time beginner's special includes lesson, equipment, and beginner lift ticket for $25. Free shuttle buses connect the ski area. The resort offers a ski school, rentals, races, several restaurants, and condominium-style accommodations. Lodging costs run $60-285 depending on room, day of week, and season. Contact Elk Meadows Resort at Box 511, Beaver, UT 84713, tel. 438-5433 or (800) 248-SNOW.

SOUTH OF PROVO ALONG US 89

SKYLINE DRIVE

This scenic back road, nearly all of which is unpaved, follows the crest of the Wasatch Plateau for about 100 miles between US 6 in the north and I-70 in the south. Few people travel the entire length, however, preferring to do shorter sections reached from the many access roads. Much of the drive lies above 10,000 feet in vast meadows and alpine forests; above Ferron Reservoir, you'll reach the drive's summit at High Top, elev. 10,897 feet. Major attractions include sweeping vistas, fishing, hiking, horseback riding, and winter sports.

Probably the four most popular recreation areas on the plateau are **Scofield State Park, Huntington Canyon (UT 31), Joes Valley Reservoir,** and **Ferron Reservoir.** Cars can normally reach Skyline Drive from these places when the roads are dry. The easiest access to the drive is paved UT 31 between Fairview on the west and Huntington on the east; the road is kept clear in winter so that cross-country skiers, snowmobilers, and ice fishermen can reach the plateau. Other roads may be too rough for low-clearance vehicles or even occasionally closed to all traffic; it's best to check with the forest service offices when planning a trip. A snowbank on Skyline Drive near Jet Fox Reservoir (east of Manti) often blocks traffic until middle or late July. The rest of the drive can usually be traveled from about mid-June to middle or late

October. The drive may not be signed at either end; the north end is off US 6 at a highway rest area near Tucker (between Mileposts 203 and 204); the south end is reached from I-70 Ranch Exit 71. You'll need the Manti-La Sal forest map (Sanpete, Ferron, and Price ranger districts) and, for the southern end, the Fishlake forest map. Nearly all of the drive is in the Manti-La Sal National Forest. Get recreation information and road conditions from the supervisor's office at 599 W. Price River Dr., Price, UT 84502, tel. 637-2817. District offices are **Price Ranger District** (same address and phone as the supervisor's office) for the northeastern part of the Wasatch Plateau, **Ferron Ranger District,** Box 310, Ferron, UT 84523, tel. 384-2372, for the southeastern part of the plateau, and **Sanpete Ranger District,** 150 S. Main, Ephraim, UT 84027, tel. 283-4151, for the western half of the plateau. This office plans to relocate to 540 N. Main.

FAIRVIEW

Mormon farmers settled on the grasslands of the upper San Pitch (or Sanpete) River Valley in 1859, giving their community its original name of North Bend. Many pioneer buildings can still be seen in town. The unusual Fairview Museum of History and Art is worth a visit. Fairview (pop. 1,173) lies 42 miles south of Provo on US 89; turn east on UT 31 to reach the alpine lands of the Wasatch Plateau. Stay at the **Skyline Motel,** 236 N. State, tel. 427-3312; $27.25 s, $32.70 d. A couple of places to eat are in town, too.

Fairview Museum Of History And Art

Many of the varied exhibits show a sense of humor. You'll see stern-faced pioneer portraits, furniture, clothing, tools, telegraph and telephone equipment, mounted wildlife, Indian crafts, geology displays, and artwork. Noted Utah sculptor Dr. Avard Fairbanks donated much of the art, including *Love and Devotion,* depicting Peter and Celestia Peterson, Fairview residents who were married for 82 years. A large threshing machine and other antique farm equipment are outside. The museum is open from about mid-May to mid-October: Mon.-Sat. 10 a.m.-6 p.m. and Sunday 1-6 p.m.; free. Located in a former elementary school (built in 1900) at 85 N. 100 East; from US 89, turn east one block on 100 North, tel. 427-9216.

San Pitch Mountains

This small range rises northwest of Ephraim. **Maple Canyon Campground** (elev. 6,800 feet) on the east side has pretty scenery but no water or fee. You can hike from the campground up **Maple Canyon Trail** along the middle fork or up **Left Fork Maple Canyon Trail.** The trails can be done as a loop using a section of forest road. Maple Canyon is 3.75 miles west of Freedom. **Chicken Creek Campground** (elev. 6,200 feet) is on the west side of the range; open early May to early October with water and a $5 fee; head east four miles from Levan. A rougher forest road continues southeast past the campground and over to Wales, four miles south of Freedom. Although the San Pitch Mountains lie within the Uinta National Forest, they are administered by the Manti-La Sal National Forest; visit the Sanpete Ranger District office in Ephraim for information (see below). See the Fishlake National Forest map for ways to reach the campgrounds.

EPHRAIM

The first settlers arrived in 1854 and named this place after a tribe mentioned in the Book of Mormon. A fort guarded against Indian attacks during the first six years. Pioneer structures that date back more than a century can be seen on Ephraim's side streets. Turkey-raising is big business here and in nearby towns.

Snow College

One of the nation's leading junior colleges, Snow College began in 1888 as a Mormon academy. Today it's a state school with about 2,100 students and 75 faculty members. You're welcome to attend the plays, concerts, and lecture series on campus; call 283-4021, ext. 616 (public relations), for cultural events and general information. Many sports facilities at the Activity Center are open to the public too, including an indoor pool, track, basketball, racquetball, tennis, and fitness center; 300 East and Center, tel. 283-4021, ext. 381. The Badgers football team won the junior college national championships in 1985; call the Activity Center for schedules of their games and other sporting events. Union Building has a snack bar and bookstore at 100 East and Center. The library is at 250 E. Center, tel. 283-4021, ext. 364. For more information about Snow College, visit or write the Administration Building at 150 E. College Ave., Ephraim, UT 84627.

Practicalities

Stay at **Iron Horse Motel,** 670 N. Main, tel. 283-4223, $34.90 s, $39.25 d; or **Travel Inn Motel,** 330 N. Main, tel. 283-4071, $29.70 s, $41.80 d. **Ephraim Homestead Bed & Breakfast** has an 1860s log cabin year-round and an 1880s Victorian house in the summer at 135 W. 100 North, tel. 283-6367, $27.25-70.85 s, $38.15-81.75 d. Several cafes and fast-food places are also downtown. Turn east eight and one half miles on 4th South for **Lake Hill Campground** (open with water about mid-June to mid-September, $5, elev. 8,400 feet) and other areas of the Wasatch Plateau, the road continues to Skyline Drive. Ephraim celebrates the **Scandinavian Festival** in May (Memorial Day weekend) with historic town tours, pioneer demonstrations, craft sales, and a fun run. The **post office** is at 45 E. 100 North, tel. 283-4189. **Ephraim Medical Clinic** is at 9 E. 100 North, tel. 283-4076. **Sanpete Ranger District** office, 150 S. Main, Ephraim, UT 84627, tel. 283-4151, has recreation and road information for the western half of the Wasatch Plateau and for the San Pitch Mountains; open Mon.-Fri. 8 a.m.-noon and 12:30-4:30 p.m. The office is planning to relocate to 540 N. Main.

MANTI

The town dates from November 1849 and is one of the oldest in Utah. Brigham Young named it for a place mentioned in the Book of Mormon. An estimated 100 buildings built before 1880 can be seen on the side streets. Manti (pop. 2,200) is the Sanpete County seat.

Manti Temple

The temple, on a small hill, has a commanding position over the town. Brigham Young dedicated the site in April 1877, just three months before his death. Workers labored 11 years to complete construction, using locally quarried blocks of oolitic limestone. The temple architecture combines several 19th century styles in a rectangular plan similar to the first Mormon temples in the Midwest.

Practicalities

Manti House Inn, 401 N. Main, tel. 835-0161, provides bed and breakfast accommodations in an 1880 pioneer house; workers who built the temple stayed here in the 1880s, rates range from $53.95 to the $107.91 honeymoon suite. Other places to stay are the **Manti Motel and Outpost,** 445 N. Main, tel. 835-8533, $32.70 s or d, **RV** spaces cost $15.90 w/hookups; **Temple View Lodge,** 260 E. 400 North, tel. 835-6663, $29.40 s, $32.70 d; **Manti Country Village,** 145 N. Main, tel. 835-9300, $37.06 s, $39.24 d; **Brigham House Inn Bed & Breakfast,** 123 E. Union, tel. 835-8381, $43.60-70.85 d; **Yardley's Inn Bed & Breakfast,** 190 W. 200 South, tel. 835-1861, $44-104.50 d; and the **Grist Mill Inn,** 780 E. Canyon Rd., tel. 835-MILL, $49.05 s, $59.95 d. **Palisade Lodge,** four and one half miles south of Manti, tel. 835-5413, offers budget, deluxe, and group accommodations starting at $27.50 s, $33 d; recreation facilities include a pool, water slide, racquetball court, weight room, spas, and sauna.

Yogi Bear's Jellystone Park, tel. 835-CAMP, has children's activities, pool, store, showers, and laundry on the north edge of town; $16.35 tent, $18.53-20.71 RV w/hookups; may close in winter. **Manti Community Campground** is in the Manti-La Sal National Forest, seven miles east on 500 South/Manti Canyon Road (open with water from early June to early October; has a trout fishing

Manti Temple

pond; $5; elev. 7,400 feet); the road continues nine miles to Skyline Drive. Several cafes and a couple of fast-food places are in town.

The **Mormon Miracle Pageant** in July portrays the history of the Book of Mormon and of the pioneers and early church leaders. The very popular production takes place at night on Temple Hill; a large cast provides lots of action. **Sanpete County Fair** is held in August. A **city park** at 300 W. 200 North, tel. 835-4961, has picnic tables, playground, and an outdoor pool. The **post office** is at 140 N. Main, tel. 835-5081. **Manti Medical Clinic** is at 159 N. Main, tel. 835-3344. Manti's **public library** is downtown at 2 S. Main, tel. 835-2201.

VICINITY OF MANTI

Palisade State Park

People have been enjoying themselves at 70-acre Palisade Lake since 1873. A pleasure resort here once featured a dance hall and a steam excursion boat. Now a state park, the lake lies six miles south of Manti, then two miles east. Only nonmotorized craft may be used. Canoeing and sailboarding are popular here. Canoes can be rented at the park. Fishermen catch rainbow and cutthroat trout. The swimming beach and fishing conditions are best early in the season, before the water level drops. Cottonwoods shade the picnic area and campground. The campground is open with showers from early April to late October. Restrooms close in winter, but self-contained campers can still stay here. Admission fees are $3 per vehicle day use, $9 ($10 Saturday, Sunday, and holidays) per vehicle camping; Box H, Manti, UT 84642, tel. 835-7275 (ranger) or (800) 322-3770 (reservations). Campground reservations are a good idea on summer weekends.

The nine-hole **Palisade Golf Course,** just beyond the state park entrance, tel. 835-4653, has a clubhouse, pro shop, and driving range. **Cedar Crest Inn** is on the left about one mile before the state park, tel. 835-6352; it has bed and breakfast accommodations ($47.90-76.30 s, $53.35-82.75 d) and an elegant restaurant for guests only (closed Sundays).

Gunnison Reservoir, three miles west of the state park, has good water-skiing and fishing for bass and perch; there are no developed facilities here, though people use the shore to launch boats (west shore is best); ask directions in Manti. **Nine Mile Reservoir** has a fine reputation for rainbow and other trout; the small lake is west of US 89 and two miles south of Sterling.

Gunnison

The name honors Capt. John Gunnison, an Army surveyor killed by Indians in 1853 near Sevier Lake. Gunnison (pop. 1,300) is an agricultural center with two motels, a campground, and several places to eat. An information booth is open in summer in the park on North Main.

Salina

Salina (pronounced suh-LINE-uh by locals) is a Spanish word for "salt mine," one of which is found nearby. The first pioneers arrived in 1863, but Indian troubles forced them to evacuate the site from 1866 to 1872. Today, Salina is a handy travelers' stop, strategically located at the junction of US 89 and I-70. More than half a dozen motels and places to eat can be found down-

town and near the I-70 interchange. **Don's Texaco,** 215 W. Main, tel. 529-3531, has RV sites and showers ($7.63 no hookups, $10.90 w/hookups; no tents). **Butch Cassidy Campground,** 1100 S. State, between I-70 Exit 54 and downtown, tel. 529-7400, offers sites for tents ($6.56 s, $8.74 d) and RVs ($13.10 no hookups, $15.93-18.03 w/hookups) with showers, store, and laundry. **Salina Creek R.V. Camp,** behind the Texaco Station at 1385 S. State (near I-70 Exit 54), tel. 529-3711, costs $16.89 w/hookups; has showers, store, and laundry.

Fourth of July is the big annual event, celebrated with a rodeo, parades, contests, and fireworks. **Salina Medical Clinic** is at 310 W. Main, tel. 529-7411. The **public library,** at 90 W. Main, tel. 529-7753, is open Mon.-Fri. 1:30-6 p.m. and Saturday noon-2 p.m. The **city pool** is behind the library.

Vicinity Of Salina

The **Redmond Clay and Salt Company** operates an open-pit salt mine north of town (three miles north of Redmond); you're welcome to watch the operations from an overlook, open Mon.-Fri. 8 a.m.-4:30 p.m.; for more information, contact the office at 6005 N. 100 West at the mine, tel. 529-7402.

From I-70 east of Salina, you can turn north on back roads to Skyline Drive and the Wasatch Plateau or head south into the alpine country of the Fish Lake Mountains. The small **Gooseberry Campground** lies along Gooseberry Creek in an aspen forest of the Fish Lake Mountains; elevation is 7,800 feet. Open with water from late May to early November; free. Take I-70 Gooseberry Road Exit 61 and go south 10 miles (six miles of pavement, then four miles of gravel). Snowmobiling is popular in this area during winter. The road continues south, climbing steadily through forests and meadows to **Niotche-Lost Creek Divide** (elev. 10,320 feet) in another 10 miles; the road then winds down to Johnson Valley Reservoir, where pavement continues to Fish Lake.

RICHFIELD

The seat of Sevier County and center of a large agricultural region, Richfield (pop. 6,300) has a dozen motels, a good selection of restaurants, and other services for travelers; most are along the I-70 business route. See some local history in the museum exhibits inside the **Ralph Ramsey House** at 57 E. 200 North (behind the courthouse); hours vary, call 896-6439 (city offices) to schedule a visit. The stuccoed-adobe structure dates from 1873-74. Before settling in Richfield, Ralph Ramsey carved the original Eagle for the famous gate beside Brigham Young's residence in Salt Lake City.

Campgrounds
J.R. Munchies RV Park is open all year at 745 S. Main, tel. 896-9340, $9.90 RV no hookups, $15.40 w/hookups; has store, showers, and laundry. **Richfield KOA** is open all year with spaces for tents and RVs at 600 S. 600 West, tel. 896-6674, $16.39 no hookups, $20.67 w/hookups; has pool, store, showers, and laundry.

Events
Quarter Horse and Thoroughbred races take place during the summer, usually July 4 or soon after. **Sevier County Fair** in August presents entertainment, livestock shows, 4-H exhibits, and a demolition derby. September is a busy month with the **Rocky Mountain ATV Jamboree**, the **Fishlake Mountain Bike Festival**, the **Fall Festival of the Arts**, and the **Gathering of the Clans** with highland games and activities.

Services
The **city park** at Main and 300 North (where US 89 makes a bend) has covered picnic tables, playground, and an information booth (open in summer). An indoor/outdoor **swimming pool** is at 600 W. 500 North, tel. 896-8572. **K-C Waterslide**, 995 South 100 East, tel. 896-5334, offers another way to get wet in summer. **Cove View Municipal Golf Course** has nine holes on the southwest edge of town (take South Airport Rd. from South Main), tel. 896-9987. The **post office** is at 93 N. Main, tel. 896-6231. **Sevier Valley Hospital** is at 1100 N. Main, tel. 896-8271.

Information
For travel info, visit the **information booth** in an 1888 former hardware store moved to the city park at Main and 400 North (open Mon.-Sat. 10 a.m.-7 p.m. in summer) or contact the

Sevier County Travel Council at 220 N. 600 West (Richfield, UT 84701), tel. 896-8898 or (800) 662-8898; open year-round Mon.-Fri. 9 a.m.-5 p.m. The **Richfield Ranger District** office of the Fishlake National Forest has recreation and road information for the mountain country south and east of town; maps and books are sold; the **Supervisor's** office has general information for the entire forest; both offices are open Mon.-Fri. 8 a.m.-5 p.m. at 115 E. 900 North (Richfield, UT 84701), tel. 896-9233. The **BLM District Office** can give you information about recreation areas controlled by the BLM for much of this part of Utah; open Mon.-Fri. 7:45 a.m.-4:30 p.m.; across the street from the USFS offices at 150 East 900 North (Richfield, UT 84701). The **public library** is open Mon.-Sat. afternoons and evenings in a Carnegie building (built 1913-14) at 83 E. Center, tel. 896-5169.

VICINITY OF RICHFIELD

Paiute ATV (All-Terrain Vehicle) Trail
ATVers enjoy this 200-mile scenic loop trail and its many side trips in the scenic Pahvant Range, Tushar Mountains, and Monroe Mountain surrounding Richfield. Trail users travel among cool mountains, rugged canyons, and desert country. The trail is multi-use and can be enjoyed by mountain bikers, hikers, horseback riders, and even those with four-wheel drive automobiles. Not all the trail is suitable for each mode of travel; some parts are rough while other parts are narrow. Obtain up-to-date information before starting your route. Access points include Beaver, Richfield, Fillmore, Fremont Indian State Park, Kanosh, Piute State Park, Marysvale, and Circleville with more access points planned. Information and a brochure are available from the Fishlake National Forest office, see Richfield information above, and local tourist and state park offices. Information kiosks are also being built at the access points. Millard County Tourism also offers travel info for the entire trail; open Mon.-Fri. 9 a.m.-5 p.m. at 195 N. Main in Fillmore (Box 1082, Fillmore, UT 84631), tel. 743-7803 or (800) 441-4ATV.

Mystic Hot Springs
Steaming mineral water (168° F) from springs on a hillside above Monroe feeds a hot tub (102-

110° F) and heats a swimming pool at this resort. The hot tub stays open all year, but the pool is open only in summer. The campground has showers; $11 tent or RV no hookups, $16.50 w/hookups; may close in winter. Mystic Hot Springs is on the east edge of Monroe, about 10 miles south of Richfield on US 89 and UT 118 or five miles east of Joseph on UT 118; signs point the way; tel. 527-4014. From I-70, take Elsinore Exit 31 or Joseph Exit 24. The springs are under new ownership and changes are planned so call before visiting.

Monrovian Park

A paved road leads southeast from Monroe into this park in a pretty canyon. Cottonwood and Gambel oak trees shade picnic areas along gurgling Monroe Creek. Drinking water is available in summer. Four trails from the park area wind up onto the high Sevier Plateau above. Most spectacular is the trail that goes up Monroe Creek from the picnic areas, then follows Third Left Hand Fork to Scrub Flat Trail (six miles one-way); you'll have to do some wading. A narrow unpaved road with steep grades also climbs into the mountains. The Richfield Ranger District office in Richfield has detailed information about exploring this area. To reach the park, head south on Main St. in Monroe and follow signs four miles.

FREMONT INDIAN STATE PARK

The prehistoric Fremont people had lived over much of Utah, yet archaeologists weren't aware of this group's identity until 1931. Artifacts discovered along the Fremont River in central Utah indicated that the Fremont was a distinct culture. The largest excavated site was discovered in Clear Creek Canyon during construction of I-70 in 1983. The Five Finger Ridge Village site probably had more than 150 occupants at its peak around A.D. 1100; more people lived nearby in the canyon. The Fremont farmed in the canyon bottom and sought game and wild plant foods. They lived in pit houses and stored surplus food in carefully constructed granaries. More than 500 rock art panels in the canyon show their religious and hunting life in a cryptic form. Nothing remains at the village site, located across the canyon; workers constructing I-70

cut most of the ridge away to use as fill after the scientific excavations had been completed. Only an experienced eye can spot pit-house villages after nearly 1,000 years of weathering, so there was little to see at this village site anyway.

Visitor Center

The park's visitor center, dedicated in 1987, has excellent displays of artifacts found during excavations. Many aspects of Fremont life remain a mystery, but exhibits present ideas of how the Indians could have lived here. Children can use a Fremont mano and metate to grind corn. A 16-minute video program introduces the Fremont, their foods, events that may have caused their departure, and the excavation of Five Finger Ridge Village. The exhibit area also has short video programs on the Fremont. Models illustrate pit-house construction and how Five Finger Ridge Village may have looked. A full-size replica of a pit house includes audio explanations of the functions of the dwelling.

Three loop trails begin outside the visitor center. Pick up a pamphlet inside for the Show Me Rock Art and Discovery trails; keyed to numbered stops, the pamphlets provide more insight into Fremont life, partly by using Hopi Indian legends. **Show Me Rock Art Trail** (200 yards) leads past fine petroglyphs; the trail is level and graded and can be used by people with strollers or wheelchairs. **Discovery Trail** (200 yards) goes to more rock art and climbs a short way above the visitor center. **Canyon Overlook Trail** (1,000 feet) ascends about 500 feet above the visitor center for fine views of the canyon and surrounding mountains; this starts as a nature trail but continues another mile. Park staff can tell you of 10 other trails and rock art sites in the area too. New trails are currently under construction and all park trails allow mountain bike travel. Volunteers and rangers lead walks in summer.

You can purchase related books, maps, rock-art posters, petroglyph replicas, Indian crafts, T-shirts, and postcards. Video programs can be seen on request. Park staff will take groups to other sites in the canyon; call or write at least a week in advance; 15500 Clear Creek Canyon Rd., Sevier, UT 84766, tel. 527-4631. Open daily 9 a.m.-6 p.m. in summer and daily 9 a.m.-5 p.m. the rest of the year; closed on winter holidays;

$1.50 adult, $1 children 6-16, or $6 per vehicle (whichever is less). The park is near I-70 Exit 17 in Clear Creek Canyon, five miles west of US 89 and 16 miles east of I-15. Two picnic areas are on the frontage road east of the visitor center. You can camp at Castle Rock Campground; see below. A short scenic drive follows the old highway nine miles through Clear Creek Canyon between the visitor center and I-70 Ranch Exit 8.

VICINITY OF FREMONT INDIAN STATE PARK

Castle Rock Campground

Clear Creek cut its canyon through tuff, a soft rock formed of hot volcanic ash from eruptions in the Tushar Mountains area. Erosion has carved towering buttresses and narrow canyons at Castle Rock, just off the main canyon. Campsites lie in a cottonwood and oak forest beside Joe Lott Creek; open with drinking water during the warmer months; $7 ($8 Friday, Saturday, and holidays). Register at the state park visitor center. Take I-70 Fremont Indian State Park Exit 17, turn onto the south frontage road, and follow it 1.3 miles.

Kimberly Scenic Drive

This 16 mile unpaved road climbs to about 10,000 feet on the north slopes of the Tushar Mountains. You'll enjoy good views and cool forests of aspen and fir. Old Kimberly, a ghost-town site and once the center of the Gold Mountain Mining District, is reached about halfway. Miners started the town in 1888. Gold production peaked around the turn of the century, then dropped off after 1907; production has been only sporadic since. Little remains of the town, but you'll see mine shafts, tailings, mill ruins, and foundations. Prospectors haven't given up hope—more recent mining equipment can be seen along the road too. Cars with good clearance can usually negotiate the road if it's dry; ask locally or at the Beaver Ranger District office of the Fishlake National Forest, corner of 190 North and 100 East in Beaver, tel. 438-2436. Take I-70 Exit 17, turn west on the north frontage road, and follow it under I-70; the drive ends at Marysvale on US 89. Kimberly Scenic Drive connects with the Kimberly/Big John Road Backway (Forest Route 123) above Marysvale and winds through the alpine forests, rocky slopes, and meadows of the Tushar Mountains to UT 153 (high-clearance vehicle recommended). See the Fishlake National Forest map.

Big Rock Candy Mountain

This multicolored mountain, made famous in a song by Burl Ives, rises above the Sevier River. Cold mineral springs high on the mountainside are claimed to be very healthful and a cure for

company housing at
Upper Kimberly,
ca. 1900

UTAH STATE HISTORICAL SOCIETY

many ailments. The water, usually diluted before drinking, has a slight lemonade tang but no scent. You can walk behind the cafe for a closer look at the mountain and its small spring-fed stream. The resort, cafe, and rock shop were closed and up for sale at press time. Raft trips on the Sevier River cover four and one half miles on one and one half-hour trips; $18 adult, $9 children. Stop at the store across the road from the resort. The resort is on US 89, 24 miles south of Richfield and six miles north of Marysvale, tel. 326-4321.

JUNCTION

This tiny village (pop. 151), near the confluence of the south and east forks of the Sevier River, is the Piute County seat. The entire county has only 1,329 inhabitants. It's one of the smallest and most mountainous in the state, but local people say that if all the mountains were ironed out, the county would be one of Utah's largest! The outlaw Butch Cassidy grew up in this country and learned his first lawless ways here by altering cattle brands. The rustic cabin the Cassidys once called home still stands two and one half miles south of Circleville (between Mileposts 156 and 157 on US 89). The bright red county courthouse dates from 1902-03; drop in on weekdays for tourist information. **Junction Motel** is on the south edge of town, tel. 577-2629, open April 1 to late November $18 s or d, $22 kitchenettes s or d. **Fat's Country Cafe and RV Park** is one block west from the courthouse, tel. 577-2672, open daily, sites cost $3.27 tent, $5.45 RV no hookups, $10.90 RV w/hookups; no showers. **City Creek Campground** is five miles northwest on UT 153, then right one mile; sites lie along wooded City Creek at an elevation of 7,600 feet; open with water from Memorial Day to Labor Day weekends; free. The **"biggest little rodeo in the world"** is held in July in Marysvale. The **Piute County Fair** takes place in August. Vehicles with stout engines can follow UT 153 up a long grade into the Tushar Mountains to Puffer Lake (18 miles) and other scenic spots, then descend to Beaver (40 miles); pavement ends just outside Junction, then there's 25 miles of dirt road before pavement begins again. This road isn't recommended for trailers or RVs. See "The Tushar Mountains," above.

VICINITY OF JUNCTION

Piute State Park
The 3,300-acre Piute Reservoir is one of the largest in central Utah. It's relatively undeveloped, however, with just an outhouse or two and a place to launch boats plus some docks. Anglers catch rainbow trout. The lake also has plenty of room for water-skiers. The park has no drinking water, established sites, or fee. Contact Otter Creek State Park (see below) for more information. From the town of Junction, drive north six miles on US 89 and turn right 1.4 miles at the sign (near Milepost 172).

Otter Creek State Park
Otter Creek Reservoir has some of the best trout fishing in Utah; it's six and one half miles long and one-half to three-quarters of a mile wide (2,500 acres). Birdwatching is often good, especially in winter for raptors and swans, then in spring for waterfowl and songbirds. Shore fishing can be productive in spring and autumn, but in summer you really need a boat because of moss near the shore and because the fish move to deeper waters. The park stays open all year and offers ice fishing and ice-skating in winter. The campground area at the south end of the lake (elev. 6,400 feet) has showers, tables with windbreaks, boat ramp, dock, and a fish-cleaning station. Boats with motors can be rented just outside the park. You can make reservations for the developed sites, or you can nearly always find a slot in the adjacent overflow areas. People also camp and fish at Fisherman's Beach, Tamarisk Point, and South Point on the west shore; no water or charge (BLM land). Entrance fees at the state park are $3 per vehicle day use, $9 ($10 Friday, Saturday, and holidays) per vehicle camping, or $7 per vehicle camping at overflow areas ($1 more for camping Friday, Saturday, and holidays); Box 43, Antimony, UT 84712, tel. 624-3268 or (800) 322-3770 (reservations). From the town of Junction, go two miles south on US 89, then turn east 13 miles on UT 62. **Otter Creek RV Park Marina,** across the highway, tel. 624-3292 or (800) 441-3292, offers RV sites ($8.72 no hookups, $13.08 w/hookups), cafe (daily breakfast, lunch, and dinner), showers, boat rentals, and fishing supplies; open March 1 to October 31.

FISH LAKE AND VICINITY

The large lake and surrounding mountain country have great beauty. You'll see expansive vistas, pristine meadows, sparkling streams, and dense forests on drives through the area. Hikers can reach more remote spots, such as the 11,633-foot summit of the Fish Lake Hightop Plateau. Fish Lake formed when a block of the earth's crust dropped along faults. The water that filled the basin created one of Utah's largest natural lakes, six miles long and one mile wide. Fishermen angle for lake (mackinaw) and rainbow trout and splake (a hybrid of mackinaw and eastern brook trout). Swimming isn't recommended due to the cold (50° F) water temperatures. Summers are cool at this 8,800-foot elevation. Heavy winter snows provide recreation for snowmobilers and cross-country skiers. The lake and surrounding country lie in the Loa Ranger District of the Fishlake National Forest. The **Forest Information Center** in Fish Lake Lodge, tel. 638-1033, is open daily in summer; books, maps, and pamphlets are available. You can also contact the district office for the latest camping, fishing, hiking, and road conditions at 138 S. Main, Loa, UT 84747, tel. 836-2811; open all year Mon.-Fri. 8 a.m.-4:30 p.m. Paved UT 25 branches off UT 24 (31 miles southeast of Richfield, 14 miles northwest of Loa) and climbs seven miles over a pass to the lake; the road is usually kept open year-round.

FISH LAKE CAMPGROUNDS AND RESORTS

Most of the forest service campgrounds lie just off UT 25 along the lake's west shore. Dispersed camping isn't permitted near Fish Lake; you'll have to head farther into the backcountry if you'd like an undeveloped spot. The camping season runs from about late May to late October; all the campgrounds along the lake have water and a $8 fee. Picnic areas are free (groups can reserve for a charge). Half of the campsites, as well as group areas, can be reserved by calling (800) 280-CAMP. Recreation sites, with distances from the junction of UT 25 and UT 24, are: **Doctor Creek** (seven miles; in

an aspen grove on the southwest shore; group areas can be reserved; has a dump station); **Twin Creek Picnic Area** (8.8 miles; day use only; a ranger station is opposite the turnoff); **Mackinaw Campground** (nine miles; in an aspen grove overlooking the lake); **Bowery Creek Campground and Picnic Area** (10 miles; in an aspen grove overlooking the lake); **Joe Bush Fishermen Parking** (10.7 miles); **Pelican Promontory** (12 miles; turn left one mile for a panoramic view; not suitable for low-clearance vehicles); **Frying Pan Campground** (14.5 miles; on the edge of an aspen grove near Johnson Valley Reservoir); **Tasha Equestrian Campground** (14.7 miles, then one-half mile in; under construction; for people with horses); and **Piute Parking Area** (14.8 miles; access to the reservoir). At the junction just past the reservoir, you can turn north along Sevenmile Creek on Forest Route 640 to I-70 and Salina (36 miles) or south on Forest Route 036 to a boat ramp on Johnson Valley Reservoir (one mile), Fremont River (three miles), and Loa (20 miles). Both drives have exceptional scenery and go past many good spots for fishing and primitive camping; the roads are usually okay for cars.

Fish Lake Lodge and Lakeside Resort each offer accommodations, a store, and a marina on the lake's southwest shore. Fish Lake Resorts operates both areas. The marinas have rentals of fishing and pontoon boats, boat ramps, slips, bait, tackle, and boat gas. **Lakeside Resort** is 7.3 miles in on UT 25, where the highway first meets the lake, tel. 638-1000, cabins cost $27.25-136.25 ($31.61-163.50 weekends and holidays), some are open all year; RV sites with hookups are open May 15-Oct. 15 at $13.08 and $15.26. **Fish Lake Lodge**, 1.2 miles beyond Lakeside Resort, tel. 638-1000, is a huge rambling log structure built in 1932; it has a dining area, dance hall, and a small store open Memorial Day to Labor Day weekends. Rustic (old) cabins are open Memorial Day weekend to the end of hunting season for $30.52-41.42 ($34.88-45.78 weekends and holidays). New cabins are available all year and cost $49.05-261.60 ($65.40-299.75 weekends and holidays). The rustic dining room in the lodge has lake views and is open daily for breakfast and dinner. Showers are available to the public for a small fee. Accommodations for Lakeside Resort and Fish Lake Lodge can be reserved year-round by contacting Fish Lake Resorts, 10 E. Center, Hwy. 25, Richfield, UT 84701, tel. 638-1000.

Bowery Haven Resort lies near Fish Lake about 10 miles in on UT 25, Fish Lake, UT 84701, tel. 638-1040 (in season), 943-7885 (off-season). The resort's season lasts from late May to late October. Amenities include a marina (fishing boat rentals, ramp, slips, and supplies), cabins ($23.98 rustic, $56.68 modern), motel rooms ($57.77 s or d), RV park ($14.17 w/hookups; has showers and laundry; no tents), cafe (open daily for breakfast, lunch, and dinner), and a small store.

THOUSAND LAKE MOUNTAIN

This high plateau rises above the Fremont River to an elevation of 11,306 feet at Flat Top. Panoramas from the rim take in the wooded valleys surrounding Fish Lake to the west and the colorful rock formations and canyons of Cathedral Valley in Capitol Reef National Park to the east. Roads and trails provide access to viewpoints and fishing lakes on the plateau. Forest roads lead to the heights from UT 72 on the west and from the middle Desert and Cathedral Valley on the east. Actually Thousand Lake Mountain may have been misnamed because its lakes number far fewer than a thousand. Some people think that a mapmaker in the 1800s accidentally switched names between this and Boulder Mountain to the south, which has far more lakes. For more information, contact the Loa Ranger District office in Loa; maps are the 15-minute Torrey topo and the Fishlake National Forest.

Elkhorn Campground

The small campground makes a good base for hikes to lakes and the Flat Top summit. Open with water from about mid-June to late September; no charge. Meadows and a forest of aspen, fir, and spruce surround the sites; elevation is 9,300 feet. From the north edge of Loa, turn east and north 12 miles on UT 72 to Forest Route 206 and follow it eight miles to the campground. The winding mountain road is unpaved,

but passable by cars in dry weather. Desert View Overlook, three miles before the campground, has a fantastic view of Cathedral Valley and beyond. The road to Elkhorn Campground can also be approached from I-70 via UT 72; this paved road climbs over Hogan Pass (elev. 8,961 feet) past meadows, groves of aspen, and fine views of Cathedral Valley and surrounding country. Vehicles with high clearance (only) can drive up directly from Cathedral Valley via Forest Routes 020 and 022.

LOA

Pioneers settled here in the mid-1870s. A former Mormon missionary who had served in Hawaii suggested the town's unusual name. A commemorative marker (next to the 1897 Loa Tithing House, on Center Street one block west from Main) has a rock from Mauna Loa. The small town (pop. 364) is the Wayne County seat and a handy base for exploring the Fish Lake area to the north. **Wayne County Fair** on the third weekend in August has a parade, rodeo, exhibits, barbecue, and games.

Road Creek Inn, 90 S. Main, tel. 836-2485 or (800) 338-7688, is a bed and breakfast ($70.30-99.74); its restaurant features trout, steak, sandwiches, elk, buffalo, and Cornish game hen (open daily for dinner). **Wayne Wonderland Motel** is at 42 N. Main, tel. 836-9692, $38.15 s, $43.66 d. **Wood Motel** is at 23 N. Main, tel. 836-2777, $20 s or d. **Gina's Place Cafe** serves breakfast, lunch, and dinner daily at 289 N. Main, tel. 836-2873; motel rooms are available at $25-30 s or d; an RV park here costs $10 w/hookups (no tents); has showers and laundry. Loa's courthouse and post office are at the junction of Main and Center; step inside the courthouse to see a small rock and mineral collection in the lobby. The **Loa Ranger District** office has camping, fishing, hiking, and road condition information for the Fishlake National Forest lands north and east of town; there's also regional travel info; 138 S. Main, Loa, UT 84747, tel. 836-2811; open Mon.-Fri. 8 a.m.-4:30 p.m. You can visit the brook and rainbow trout at **Loa Fish Hatchery** 2.2 miles north of town; go north on Main and keep straight on the county road where UT 24 curves to the left; open daily 8 a.m.-4:30 p.m.; call before coming out, tel. 836-2858.

NORTHEASTERN UTAH
INTRODUCTION

Northeastern Utah has an extremely diverse landscape of barren desert, deep canyons, high plateaus, and the lofty Uinta Mountains. Thousands of well-preserved bones unearthed in the region tell of a time about 140 million years ago when dinosaurs roamed the land in a relatively moist subtropical climate amid tree ferns, evergreens, and ginkgo trees. You can meet the skeletons of these creatures in excellent museums in Vernal, Price, and Castle Dale and visit bone excavations at Dinosaur National Monument and Cleveland-Lloyd Dinosaur Quarry.

The high country of the Uinta Mountains has some of Utah's loveliest alpine scenery. Kings Peak tops the range at 13,528 feet—the highest point in the state. Fishermen seek trout and arctic grayling in the countless lakes and streams of the Uintas. Trails provide access for hiking and pack trips into the High Uintas Wilderness at the heart of the range. Other popular recreation areas include Flaming Gorge National Recreation Area, Dinosaur National Monument, Wasatch Plateau, and San Rafael Swell. Anglers and boaters have a choice of many large reservoirs, seven of which are state parks. River runners enjoy lively rides down the Green River through Red, Lodore, Whirlpool, Split Mountain, Desolation, and Gray canyons. You'll see two spellings in this region—Uinta and Uintah—both of which are pronounced "you-INT-ah." Geographical terms have no "h," as in Uinta Mountains and Uinta Basin. Political divisions usually have an "h," as in Uintah County and Uintah and Ouray Indian Reservation.

Climate
In summer, the valleys have average highs of about 90° F, which drop to the low 50s at night. Valley temperatures plummet in winter to about 30° during the day and 5° at night. The Wasatch Plateau and Uinta Mountains experience cool weather year-round. Above 10,000 feet, summer highs rarely exceed 70° in the day and drop to the 30s and 40s at night; freezing weather may occur at any time of year. Winter in the mountains brings highs in the 20s and lows well below zero. Annual precipitation changes dramatically with elevation, from about eight inches in the desert to 40 inches in the high country. Snowfall is widespread in winter and very heavy in the mountains.

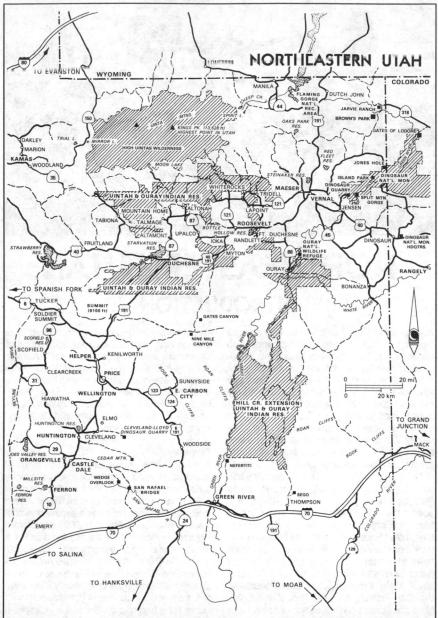

NORTHEASTERN UTAH

© MOON PUBLICATIONS, INC.

HISTORY

Prehistoric Indians

Paleo-Indians wandered across the land beginning at least 15,000 years ago. About A.D. 550, the Fremont culture emerged as a distinct group. The Fremont ranged widely in search of wild foods and places to grow their corn, beans, and squash. By 1300, however, the tribe had mysteriously disappeared, leaving behind village sites, artifacts, and intriguing rock art.

Ute Indians

Nomadic Ute Indians moved in at about the same time that the Fremont culture faded away, though the Utes seemed to have no knowledge of their more sophisticated predecessors. Utes guided the Spanish Dominguez-Escalante expedition through the Uinta Basin, south of the Uinta Mountains, in 1776, and they were the first Indian group encountered by the Mormons in Utah. Mountain men traded with the tribe during the 1820s and 1830s on beaver-trapping expeditions. Neither the Utes nor the mountain men, however, made permanent homes in the Uinta Basin. White men figured that this land, seemingly short of water and most other resources, was worthless. Pressures of settlements elsewhere in Utah and Colorado gradually forced more and more Utes from their traditional lands into the Uinta Basin. In 1861, President Lincoln issued an executive order making nearly the entire Uinta Basin into the Uintah Indian Reservation—about 2,287,000 acres. By 1864, the U.S. Army had moved nearly all the state's Utes onto the reservation. The Ouray Indian Reservation was established in 1881, then merged with the Uintah five years later. Whites started having second thoughts, though, when they discovered coal and oil and realized the agricultural potential that irrigation held for the area. Much Indian land was taken back. Heavily promoted homesteading programs beginning in 1905 brought in floods of settlers. The Utes recovered some cash awards for their lost lands during the 1950s and obtained the Hill Creek Extension south of the Uinta Basin. The reservation now covers approximately one million

acres in the Uinta Basin, in the foothills of the Uinta Range and Tavaputs Plateau, and in the remote East Tavaputs Plateau.

The Ute Indian tribe today consists of three bands, the Uintah (of Utah), the Whiteriver (moved from Colorado in 1880), and the Uncampahgre (moved from Colorado in 1882). About half of the current 2,830 Utes on the reservation and in nearby towns belong to the Uncampahgre band; the rest are equally divided between the Uintah and Whiteriver. Each band elects two members to the Ute tribal government. Tribal headquarters are east of Roosevelt at Fort Duchesne (pronounced "doo-SHAYN"), site of a U.S. Army base from 1886 to 1912. A tribal museum at nearby Bottle Hollow Resort displays Ute artifacts and historic exhibits; you can also ask at the resort about Native-American dances, pow wows, and rodeos. In summer you might be able to see the Sun Dance, an important religious and social ceremony passed down from the Wind River Shoshone. Other ceremonies are the Bear Dance (performed in the spring) and the Turkey Dance (held on many social occasions).

Early White Settlement

In the 1870s and early 1880s, the Mormon church sent out calls for members to colonize lands east of the Wasatch Plateau. Though at first the land looked harsh and barren, crops and orchards eventually prospered with irrigation. Nevertheless, it took some time for the first families to take a liking to this country. Mrs. Orange Seely of the Castle Dale area is credited with the quote, "The first time I ever swore was when we arrived in Emery County and I said 'Damn a man who would bring a woman to such a God-forsaken country!'" Individual families also came out on their own and started isolated farms and ranches in the Uinta Basin and along the eastern edge of the Wasatch Plateau to the south. Much of the land proved too dry or rugged for any use and remains in its natural state even today. Discoveries of coal in 1877 and oil in 1900 attracted waves of new people to the sleepy Mormon settlements east of the Wasatch Plateau. Immigrant miners fresh from Europe brought a new cultural diversity to the region.

UINTA MOUNTAINS

This outstanding wilderness area contains lofty peaks, lush grassy meadows, fragrant coniferous forests, crystal-clear streams, and thousands of tiny alpine lakes. The Uintas, unlike most other major ranges of the United States, run east-west. Underground forces pushed rock layers up into a massive dome 150 miles long and 35 miles wide. Ancient Precambrian rocks exposed in the center of the range consist largely of quartzite (metamorphosed sandstone). Outcrops of progressively younger rocks are found away from the center. Glaciers have carved steep ridges and broad basins and left great moraines. Barren rock lies exposed across much of the land, including the peaks and high ridges. Trees, from 10,000 feet to timberline at about 11,000 feet, include limber pine, Engelmann spruce, and subalpine fir. Lower slopes (7,000-10,000 feet) support dense unbroken forests of lodgepole pine (the most common tree in the Uintas), aspen, Douglas fir, white fir, blue spruce, and scattered stands of ponderosa pine. The remote setting of the Uinta Mountains has protected much of the forests from the ravages of logging industries. The central part received protection in 1931 as a primitive area and in 1984 as the High Uintas Wilderness. Four of Utah's major rivers have their source in these mountains: the Bear and Weber rivers on the north slope, and the Provo and Duchesne rivers on the south slope. Despite their great heights, the Uintas have a gentler terrain than the precipitous Wasatch Range. High plateaus and broad valleys among the peaks hold the abundant rain and snowfall in marshes and ponds, supporting large populations of wildlife and fish.

Elk, moose, mule deer, and Rocky Mountain goat (reintroduced) come here to graze in summer. Also foraging for food are black bear, mountain lion, coyote, bobcat, raccoon, porcupine, badger, pine marten, snowshoe hare, marmot, and pika. Fishermen seek out arctic grayling and native cutthroat, Eastern brook, rainbow, German brown, and golden trout. Aerial stocking keeps even the most remote lakes swimming with fish. Your luck at a lake or stream can range from lousy to fantastic, depending on when it was last stocked and how many other fishermen have discovered the spot.

Visiting The Uintas

Highway UT 150 winds over the western end of the range from the town of Kamas to the Wyoming border, with splendid panoramas and access to fishing lakes and hiking trails. On the east, US 191 and UT 44 provide access to the Uintas and Flaming Gorge Reservoir from Vernal. Unpaved roads also lead to trailheads on all sides of the range. Developed and primitive campgrounds can be found along these highways and at other locations, including many of the trailheads.

Most people prefer to visit the Uintas from mid-June to mid-September. Campers should be prepared for cold nights and freezing rain even in the warmest months. Afternoon showers are common in summer. Arm yourself with insect repellent to ward off the mosquitoes, especially in July. Snow stays on the ground until well into June and the meltwater can make trails muddy until early July. The lakes and campgrounds along UT 150 become crowded on summer weekends and holidays, though you can usually get off by yourself on a short hike into the backcountry.

An extensive trail system with about 20 trailheads goes deep into the wilderness and connects with many lakes. A great number of trips are possible, from easy day-hikes to rigorous treks lasting weeks. Climbers headed for the summits can take trails to a nearby pass, then rockscramble to the top. Kings Peak (elev. 13,528 feet) attracts the most attention because it's the highest point in Utah. The shortest approach is from Henrys Fork Trailhead on the north, requiring three days of hiking for the 32-mile roundtrip; elevation gain is about 4,100 feet. Southern approaches from Swift Creek or Uinta trailheads usually take an extra day. More than a dozen other peaks in the Uintas exceed 13,000 feet. No permits are needed for travel in the wilderness area, though it's recommended that you sign registers at the trailheads. Groups must not exceed 14 people. The High Uintas Wilderness, about 450,000 acres, is closed to

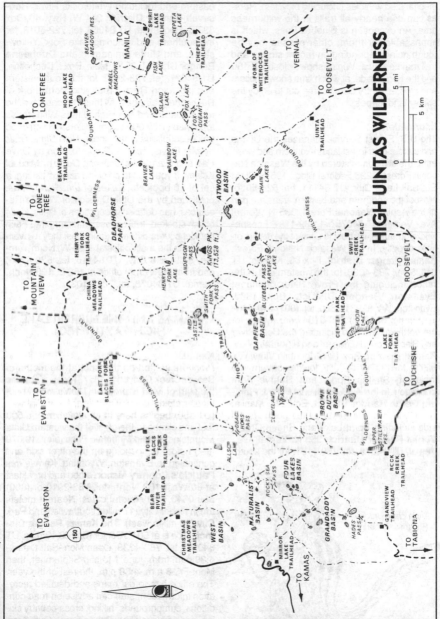

HIGH UINTAS WILDERNESS

mechanized vehicles (including bicycles). Horses can use nearly all trails in the wilderness area. An exception is Bluebell Pass, which is impassable for them; other passes may be rough going depending on recent storms and trail maintenance. Winter snows close UT 150 and the back roads, at which time snowmobilers and cross-country skiers come out to enjoy the snowy landscapes.

Information

The U.S. Forest Service manages the Uintas and surrounding forest lands. Northern and western parts are administered by the Wasatch National Forest, 8226 Federal Bldg., 125 S. State St., Salt Lake City, UT 84111, tel. 524-5030. Most of the southern and eastern areas are part of the Ashley National Forest, 355 N. Vernal Ave., Vernal, UT 84078, tel. 789-1181. For specific information, it's best to contact the district offices directly. In the Wasatch National Forest: **Kamas Ranger District,** Box 68, Kamas, UT 84036, tel. 783-4338, for the western end of the range including the Provo River drainage; **Evanston Ranger District,** Box 1880, Evanston, WY 82931-1880, tel. (801) 642-6662 in summer or (307) 789-3194 year-round, for the northwestern end including the Bear River and Blacks Fork drainages; and **Mountain View Ranger District,** Box 129, Mountain View, WY 82939, tel. (307) 782-6555, for the northern side including Smiths Forks and Henrys Fork drainages. In the Ashley National Forest: **Flaming Gorge Ranger District,** Box 278, Manila, UT 84046, tel. 784-3445, for the northeastern side including Spirit Lake and Sheep Creek; **Vernal Ranger District,** 355 N. Vernal Ave., Vernal, UT 84078, tel. 789-1181, for the south-

eastern end including Whiterocks River; **Roosevelt Ranger District,** 244 W. Hwy. 40, Box 333-6, Roosevelt, UT 84066, tel. 722-5018, for the southern end including Lake Fork, Yellowstone, and Uinta drainages; and **Duchesne Ranger District,** 85 W. Main, Box I, Duchesne, UT 84021, tel. 738-2482, for the southwestern end including Rock Creek and North Fork of Duchesne drainages. All these offices have the forest maps and the High Uintas Wilderness topo map (1:75,000 scale). Hikers will find good trail descriptions in the books *High Uinta Trails* by Mel Davis, *Hiker's Guide to Utah* by Dave Hall, and *Utah Mountaineering Guide* by Michael Kelsey. If you plan to do some serious fishing, a set of 10 booklets, *Lakes of the High Uintas,* published by the Utah Division of Wildlife Resources, has detailed descriptions of lakes, kinds of fish stocked, trail access, and camping. Each booklet covers different drainages; they're available from the main office at 1596 W. North Temple, Salt Lake City, UT 84116, tel. 538-4700; and from the Vernal office at 152 E. 100 North, Vernal, UT 84078, tel. 789-3103.

KAMAS AND THE MIRROR LAKE HIGHWAY (UT 150)

Kamas

Pioneers settled on this spot at the mouth of Beaver Creek Canyon in 1857. Today, Kamas is the start of what is probably Utah's most spectacular alpine drive. The Mirror Lake Highway (UT 150) begins here at an elevation of 6,500 feet and climbs to the crest of the western Uinta Mountains at Bald Mountain Pass (elev. 10,678 feet) before descending on the other side and continuing to Evanston, Wyoming. Kamas has **Patricia's Country Manor,** a bed and breakfast at 80 West 100 North, tel. 783-2910 or (800) 658-0643, and several cafes. Nearest motels are in Heber City (17 miles southwest) and Park City (19 miles west). The **Kamas Ranger District** office is at 50 E. Center (Box 68, Kamas, UT 84036), tel. 783-4338. Open Mon.-Sat. 8 a.m.-4:30 p.m. from June 1 to mid-September, then Mon.-Fri. 8 a.m.-4:30 p.m. the rest of the year. The office has forest maps and detailed recreation information; staff can advise on road conditions, campgrounds, hiking, cross-country skiing, and snowmobiling. **Paiute Creek Outfitters,**

*Uinta chipmunk
(Eutamias umbrinus)*

LOUISE FOOTE

just north of Kamas, 3000 N. 900 East, Kamas, UT 84036, tel. 783-4317 or (800) 225-0218 (outside Utah), organizes guided pack trips into the Uintas lasting from overnight to 10 days; hourly, half-day, and dinner rides are offered too.

Mirror Lake Highway

You can drive this scenic highway from about mid-June to mid-October. Campgrounds tend to fill on summer weekends, especially on holidays. Reservations can be made for some campsites by calling (800) 280-CAMP.

Snowplows keep the highway cleared in winter to Soapstone, 15.5 miles from Kamas, to provide access for cross-country skiing and snowmobiling. Five trails used by both skiers and snowmobilers begin along the highway and at Soapstone. Skiers using snowmobile trails will find the most solitude on weekdays. **Beaver Creek Cross-Country Trail** begins from Slate Creek (six miles east of Kamas) and parallels the highway to Pine Valley Campground, a distance of five and one half miles one-way with an elevation gain of 440 feet. This trail is easy; branching off from it are other ski trails rated intermediate and advanced. Obtain information and brochures for these and other skiing areas from the Kamas Ranger District office. Mileages given below correspond to mileposts along the highway:

Mile 0.0: Heading east on UT 150 from the junction with US 189 in Kamas.

Mile 0.1: Kamas Ranger District office on the right.

Mile 3.3: Kamas Fish Hatchery on the right; visitors welcome daily 8 a.m.-4 p.m.

Mile 3.7: Sign for "Beaver Creek Nudist Ranch" (someone's idea of a practical joke!).

Mile 6.1: Entering **Wasatch National Forest**; Slate Creek.

Mile 6.7: Yellow Pine Campground on the left. Sites are in a forest of ponderosa and lodgepole pines and juniper at an elevation of 7,200 feet; open late May to late October; no water, $5 fee. **Yellow Pine Creek Trail** begins just north of the campground and goes up the creek to Lower Yellow Pine Lake (elev. 9,600 feet; four miles one-way) and beyond; this is a good hike early in the season.

Mile 8.2: Beaver Creek Campground on the right. Sites line both sides of Beaver Creek amid lodgepole pine and willow at 7,300 feet;

pika (Ochotona princeps)

LOUISE FOOTE

open from early May to mid-October, no water, $5 fee.

Mile 8.9: Taylor Fork ATV Campground on the right; **Taylor Fork-Cedar Hollow ATV Trail** begins here. Sites are along Beaver Creek in lodgepole pine and aspen at 7,400 feet; water from early June to mid-September, $8 fee.

Mile 9.3: Shingle Creek Campground and Picnic Area on the right. Sites are in a mixed forest of pine, spruce, and fir at 7,400 feet; water from early June to mid-September, $9 fee (no charge for day use).

Mile 9.9: Shingle Creek Trail follows the creek upstream to East Shingle Lake (elev. 9,680 feet; five and one half miles one-way) and Upper Setting Trail; this is a good early-season hike. Past the trailhead, the highway climbs over a small pass to the Provo River and follows it upstream.

Mile 10.5: Lower Provo River Campground is one mile south on Pine Valley Road. Sites are along the Provo River in a pine and spruce forest at 7,600 feet; water from early June to mid-September, $8 fee. The nearby **Pine Valley Group Camping Area** is a group reservation area.

Mile 15.5: Soapstone Campground on the right. Sites are along the Provo River amid lodgepole pine at 8,200 feet; water from early June to mid-September, $10 fee.

Mile 17.0: Shady Dell Campground on the right. Sites lie along the Provo River at 8,200 feet; water from early June to mid-September, $10 fee.

Mile 17.7: West Portal of Duchesne Tunnel; a sign describes this six-mile conduit that brings water from the Duchesne River to the Provo River. **Duchesne Tunnel Camping Area** is a group reservation camping area with a $30 fee; call (800) 280-CAMP.

Mile 18.8: Cobblerest Campground on the right. Sites are near the Provo River in a pine and spruce forest at 8,500 feet; water from mid-June to mid-September, $9 fee.

Mile 22.3: Slate Gorge Overlook on the right.

Mile 23.1: Upper Provo Bridge Camping Area on the right at 9,200 feet; open early July to early September with tables and outhouses with no water and is available by group reservation only, $30 fee.

Mile 23.9: Provo River Falls Overlook on the left.

Mile 25.4: Trial Lake Campground is a quarter mile to the left on Spring Canyon Road. Sites are on the southeast shore of the lake in a pine and spruce forest at 9,500 feet; water from early July to early September, $10 fee. There's a fishermen's parking area near the dam. Spring Canyon Road continues past the dam to Washington and Crystal lakes and Crystal Lake Trailhead. **Notch Mountain Trail** begins at Crystal Lake Trailhead, goes north past Wall and Twin lakes, through The Notch to Ibantik and Meadow lakes, to the Weber River (elev. 9,000 feet; six and one half miles one-way), and to Bald Mountain Pass (elev. 10,678 feet; 10 miles one-way). The **Lakes Country Trail** starts at the Crystal Lake Trailhead and goes west past Long, Island, and other lakes before joining the Smith-Morehouse Trail after 3 miles.

Mile 26.4: Lilly Lake Campground to the left. Sites are in a spruce and fir forest at 9,800 feet; water from early July to early September, $9 fee. Lilly, Teapot, and Lost lakes lie within short walking distances.

Mile 26.7: Lost Creek Campground to the right. Sites are beside the creek in a spruce and pine forest at 9,800 feet; water from early July to early September, $9 fee. Lost Lake is a short walk to the southwest.

Mile 29.1: Bald Mountain Pass (elev. 10,678 feet). **Bald Mountain Picnic Area and Trailhead** are on the left. **Bald Mountain National Recreation Trail** climbs to the summit of Bald Mountain (elev. 11,947 feet) with great views all the way; the two-mile (one-way) trail climbs 1,269 feet, putting you in the midst of the Uinta

Range's alpine grandeur. Expect a strenuous trip because of the high elevation and steep grades; carry rain gear to fend off the cold wind (even in summer) and possible storms. From the top, weather permitting, you'll enjoy panoramas of the High Uintas Wilderness, the Lakes Roadless Area, and the Wasatch Range. **Notch Lake Trail** also begins near the picnic area and connects with Trial Lake.

Mile 30.5: Moosehorn Campground on the left. Sites are on the east and north shores of Moosehorn Lake in a spruce and fir forest at 10,400 feet; water from early July to early September, $8 fee. **Fehr Lake Trail** begins a quarter mile south and across the highway; it goes to Fehr Lake (one-half mile), Shepard Lake (one and one half miles), and Hoover Lake (one and one half miles).

Mile 31.2: Mirror Lake Campground and Picnic Area are a half mile to the right. This is the largest campground (91 sites) on the Mirror Lake Highway. Sites are near the lake in a forest of spruce, fir, and lodgepole pine at 10,200 feet; water from early July to early September, $10 fee. Parking for picnicking and fishing costs $2. Fishermen can park at the south end of the lake and at the Mirror Lake Trailhead. Boats can be hand launched; no motors at all are permitted on the lake. **Highline and North Fork Duchesne trails** lead from the trailhead to the High Uintas Wilderness.

Mile 32.1: Pass Lake Trailhead on the left, across the highway from Pass Lake. **Lofty Lake and Weber Canyon trails** begin here and connect with other trails. Weber Canyon Trail goes to Holiday Park Trailhead (elev. 8,000 feet; seven miles one-way), reached by road from Oakley.

Mile 33.9: Butterfly Lake Campground on the left. Sites are on the south shore of the lake in a spruce, fir, and lodgepole pine forest at 10,300 feet; water from early July to early September, $8 fee.

Mile 34.2: Hayden Pass (elev. 10,200 feet). **Highline Trailhead** is on the right. This is the closest point on the highway to the **High Uintas Wilderness.** The Highline Trail tends to be muddy, rocky, and heavily used. It winds east from here across the Uintas nearly 100 miles to East Park Reservoir north of Vernal. The highway makes a gradual descent from the pass along Hayden Fork of the Bear River. Contact the Evanston Ranger District offices for camping, hiking, and back-road travel in this area.

Mile 35.0: Ruth Lake Trailhead on the left; the lake is an easy three-quarter-mile hike west. There are only a few parking spots available.

Mile 38.9: Sulphur Campground on the right. Sites lie near the Hayden Fork of Bear River in a forest of lodgepole pine, fir, and spruce at 9,000 feet; water from early June to mid-September, $7 fee.

Mile 41.8: Beaver View Campground on the right. Sites overlook Hayden Fork of Bear River from a lodgepole pine and aspen forest at 8,900 feet; a beaver pond and lodge can be seen near the entrance station; water from early June to mid-September, $7 fee.

Mile 42.4: Hayden Fork Campground on the right. Sites lie along Hayden Fork of Bear River in a lodgepole pine and aspen forest at 8,900 feet; water from early June to mid-September, $7 fee.

Mile 45.6: Stillwater Campground on the right. Sites are in a lodgepole pine and aspen forest at 8,500 feet, near where Hayden Fork and Stillwater Fork meet the Bear River; water from early June to mid-September, $7 fee.

Mile 45.8: Christmas Meadow Road goes right four miles to **Christmas Meadow Campground** and **Stillwater Trailhead.** Sites overlook a large meadow from a forest of lodgepole pine at 9,200 feet; water from early June to mid-September, $7 fee. Stillwater Trailhead, near the campground, is the starting point for hikes to lakes in Amethyst, Middle, and West basins to the south. **Wolverine ATV Trailhead Campground** is one and one half miles in on Christmas Meadow Road, then one mile off; it offers sites for ATVers at 9,000 feet near a trailhead for a Lily Lake loop. Open mid-June to mid-September; no water or fee.

Mile 46.5: Bear River Ranger Station on the right. Stop here for recreation information in the northwestern part of the Uinta Range. The office is open Mon.-Thurs. 8 a.m.-4:30 p.m., Friday and Saturday 8 a.m.-6 p.m., and Sunday and holidays 8 a.m.-5 p.m.; the season is weekends only mid-May to late May, daily late May to mid-October, then weekends only to late October; tel. 642-6662. Off-season, you'll need to contact the Evanston, Wyoming, office, Box 1880, Evanston, WY 82931-1880, tel. (307) 789-3194, one mile south of I-80 at 1565 Hwy. 150, Suite A.

Mile 47.5: A road turns right two miles to **Lily Lake.** Most of the route is unmaintained dirt road.

Mile 48.2: Bear River Campground on the left. Sites are along the Bear River just upstream from the East Fork confluence in a lodgepole pine and aspen forest at 8,400 feet; water from early June to mid-September (handicap facilities will be added), $7 fee.

Mile 48.3: East Fork Bear River Campground on the left. Sites are along the Bear River just below the East Fork confluence in a lodgepole pine and aspen forest at 8,400 feet; water from early June to mid-September, $7 fee.

Mile 48.6: Forest Route 058 goes right about 17 miles to **Little Lyman Lake Campground.** Sites are near the east shore of the lake in a lodgepole pine forest at 9,200 feet; water from early June to mid-September, $7 fee. Lyman Lake is just a short walk away. **Meeks Cabin Reservoir and Campground** are two miles farther on Forest Route 058, then left about five miles on Forest Route 073. Sites here are along the southwest shore of the reservoir in a lodgepole pine forest at 8,800 feet; water from early June to mid-September, $7 fee.

Mile 48.7: Leaving **Wasatch National Forest.** This is approximately the end of the scenic drive. The valley opens up and supports sagebrush and scattered aspen groves.

Mile 48.9: Bear River Service, tel. 642-6290, offers gas, food, groceries, snowmobile rental, and lodging ($58.30 s or d). Since this facility is up for sale, call ahead to see what services are available under the new owner.

Mile 54.6: Wyoming border; highway becomes WY 150. Evanston is 23 miles ahead with several motels, two large groceries, two discount department stores, and a city recreation facility with hot showers (and athletic facilities) for $2.50.

VERNAL

One of the oldest and largest communities in northeastern Utah, Vernal makes a handy base for travels to the many sights of the region. The perennial waters of Ashley Creek, named for mountain man William H. Ashley who passed by in 1825, attracted the first settlers to the valley during the early 1870s. The small community went through a succession of names—Hatchtown, Ashley Center, and Ashley—before residents decided on Vernal in 1893. Rugged terrain and poor roads isolated the area from the rest of Utah for years. In 1916, when a local businessman wanted to order a shipment of bricks from Salt Lake City for the facade of a new bank, he solved the problem of expensive shipping costs by having the bricks sent by parcel post! Freight cost $2.50 per hundred pounds while the postal service charged only $1.05. Other Vernal residents caught on to the post office's bargain rates, and even started parcel-posting crops to market until the postal service changed its regulations. The Bank of Vernal, nicknamed the "Parcel Post Bank," still serves the town at the corner of Main and Vernal. Growth of the oil industry in recent decades has been a mixed blessing because of its boom-and-bust cycles. Vernal is the Uintah County seat and has a population of 7,500.

SIGHTS

Utah Field House Of Natural History

Come here to see the dinosaurs. More than a dozen full-size models stalk or fly in the Dinosaur Gardens outside. The natural setting makes the strange creatures seem almost alive. Inside, the Geology and Fossil Hall has displays of 45-million-year-old skulls of ancient mammals, crocodiles, and alligators that once roamed across Utah. Other exhibits have fossil specimens ranging in size from tiny insects to massive dinosaur bones. A geologic mural 36 feet across shows the structure of rock layers in northeastern Utah. Other exhibits trace Utah's Native Americans from the Desert Culture through Anasazi and Fremont groups to the modern Ute. The Natural History Hall offers a

close look at mounted wildlife of the state. The museum dates from 1948 and is now a state park. It's open daily 8 a.m.-9 p.m. from Memorial Day to Labor Day weekends, 9 a.m.-5 p.m. daily in winter. Admission is $1.50 adult, $1 ages 6-15. The gift shop sells dinosaur T-shirts, books, postcards, and other souvenirs. The Vernal Welcome Center in the museum building has area travel information. A city park behind the museum contains a playground and offers a shady spot for a picnic. The Utah Field House of Natural History is at 235 E. Main (Vernal, UT 84078), tel. 789-3799.

DUP Pioneer Museum

Get to know Vernal's pioneers here. The many historical photos and carefully labeled exhibits present a good idea of what life was like in the old days. The large collection includes a pioneer kitchen, spinning wheels, farm machinery, a buggy, old organs, clothing, guns, and a

portable drilling rig for oil wells, early 1920's

L.C. THORNE COLLECTION (VERNAL)

model of a Western town. You'll see Dr. Harvey Coe Hullinger's well-stocked medicine chest, last used in 1926 when he was 101 years old. One room of the museum is the stone tithing office, built in 1877. The Daughters of the Utah Pioneers operate the museum, open Mon.-Sat. 1-7 p.m. in summer and at other times by request (ask at the Vernal Welcome Center). Located across the street from the Uintah Stake Tabernacle at the corner of 200 South and 500 West.

Western Heritage Museum
See art and historic exhibits in this new museum in the Western Park Complex; the gun used by "Matt Dillon" in the TV series "Gunsmoke" is on display. Open in summer Mon.-Sat. 10 a.m.-6 p.m. (check off-season hours at the Welcome Center). Located at 300 East and 200 South, tel. 789-7399.

PRACTICALITIES

Accommodations
Motels, listed in order of increasing price, include: **Sage Motel,** 54 W. Main, tel. 789-1442, $29.43 s, $38.15 d; **Lazy K Motel,** east edge of town on Hwy. 40, tel. 789-3277, $32.70 s or d; **Econo Lodge,** 311 E. Main, tel. 789-2000 or (800) 424-4777, $39.20 s, $42.50 d; **Weston Lamplighter Inn,** 120 E. Main, tel. 789-0312, $39.24 s, $50.14 d, has kitchenettes and a pool; **Days Inn,** 260 W. Main, tel. 789-1011 or (800)

325-2525, $41.42 s, $56.68 d, has a pool; **Split Mountain Motel,** 1015 E. Hwy. 40, tel. 789-0020, $41.50 s, $45.88 d; **Weston Plaza Hotel,** 1684 W. Hwy. 40, tel. 789-9550, $52.32 s, $61.04 d, has an indoor pool and spa; **Antlers Best Western Motel,** 423 W. Main, tel. 789-1202 or (800) 528-1234, $59.95 s, $81.75 d, has a pool; and **Dinosaur Inn (Best Western),** 251 E. Main, tel. 789-2660 or (800) 528 1234, $68.67 s or d, has a pool. **Rodeway Inn** will open at 590 W. Main.

Campgrounds
Vernal KOA is on the west side of town (turn in beside the Weston Plaza Hotel), tel. 789-8935; facilities include a pool, store, showers, laundry, and playground; $14.17 tent or RV no hookups, $16.35 w/hookups. Open May 1 to September 30. **Campground Dina** is on the north side of town at 930 N. Vernal Ave., tel. 789-2148. It has showers, store, laundry, and miniature golf; $11.99 tent or RV no hookups, $17.99 w/hookups; open May 1 to September 30. **Fossil Valley RV Park,** 999 W. Hwy. 40, tel. 789-6450, has showers and laundry; $11.95 tent, $11.95-12.95 RV no hookups, $14.95 RV w/hookups. Open April to November. **Dinosaur Village Campground,** 11 miles east of town on the way to Dinosaur National Monument, tel. 789-5552, has showers; $5.30 tent or RV no hookups, $8.48-12.72 RV w/hookups; open mid-May to mid-September. Other campgrounds are north at Steinaker State Park (eight miles from Vernal), at Red Fleet Reservoir (11

miles), and in the Ashley National Forest (about 20 miles) and east in Dinosaur National Monument (23 miles).

Food

For American fare, try the **Crack'd Pot Restaurant,** 1089 E. Hwy. 40, tel. 781-0133, open 24 hours daily for breakfast, lunch, and dinner; **Sage Restaurant,** 56 W. Main, tel. 789-2277, open Mon.-Sat. for breakfast, lunch, and dinner; **Skillet Coffee Shop,** 251 E. Main in Dinosaur Inn, tel. 789-3641, open daily for breakfast, lunch, and dinner; **Seven-Eleven Ranch Restaurant,** 77 E. Main, tel. 789-1170, open daily except Sunday for breakfast, lunch, and dinner, plus a Saturday chuckwagon dinner; **Lamplighter Inn Restaurant,** 120 E. Main, tel. 789-0312, open daily for breakfast and lunch; **Great American Cafe,** 13 S. Vernal Ave., tel. 789-1115, open daily for breakfast, lunch, and dinner; and **JB's Big Boy,** 475 W. Main, tel. 789-4547, open daily for breakfast, lunch, and dinner. The **Golden Corral Family Steakhouse,** 1046 W. Hwy. 40, tel. 789-7268, offers steak and other items in an informal Western atmosphere, open daily for lunch and dinner.

H.R. Weston in the Weston Plaza Hotel, 1684 W. Hwy. 40, tel. 789-9550, offers a varied menu of Continental and American specialties. Open Mon.-Sat. for breakfast and dinner. **Jerry's Steak and Seafood,** 831 W. Main, tel. 789-9805, features fine dining with steak, seafood, and Mexican items. Open Mon.-Sat. for lunch and dinner. The **Pizza Barn,** part of Jerry's Steak and Seafood, same address, tel. 789-2030, serves pizza and pasta as well as Mexican food, open Mon.-Sat. for lunch and dinner. **Pizza Hut,** 1819 W. Hwy. 40, tel. 781-1048, is open daily for lunch and dinner. **Casa Rios,** 2015 W. Hwy. 40, tel. 789-0103, specializes in south-of-the-border cuisine, open Tues.-Sat. for lunch and dinner. **La Cabaña,** 2590 W. Hwy. 40, tel. 789-3151, also has good Mexican food, open Mon.-Sat. for lunch and dinner.

Entertainment

See movies at **Tri Cinema,** 1400 W. Hwy. 40; **Vernal Theatre,** 40 E. Main; or **Sunset Drive-In,** open in summer on W. Hwy. 40. Call the Movie Information Line to find out what's playing at the theaters, tel. 789-6139.

Events

May: The **Square Dance Festival** sets the town a-jumping. **Horse races** begin. **Governor's Invitational Fishing Derby** (Lucerne Valley) brings excitement to Flaming Gorge Reservoir. **Manila Fishing Derby** also takes place at Flaming Gorge Reservoir.

June: **Junior Livestock Show. Horse racing** continues. **Dinosaur Days** presents special programs at the Utah Field House and a variety of kids activities around town. The **Outlaw Trail Festival** brings in some wild characters for shooting events, a bank robbery, trail rides on old outlaw paths, musicals, western art competition, oil-painting workshop, and a song-writing contest; begins mid-June and lasts through July.

July: **Fireworks** on the Fourth. **Outlaw Trail Festival** continues. **Dinosaur Roundup Rodeo (PRCA)** pits man against beast and features a parade; country musicians show their stuff in the **True Value Country Showdown** a few days before the rodeo. A parade celebrates **Pioneer Day** on the 24th. **Dinosaur Triathlon.**

August: **Uintah County Fair.**

September: **Balloon races.** The Flaming Gorge Yacht Club organizes a **Parade of Lights** at Lucerne Bay on Labor Day weekend.

November: **Lighting of the Dinosaur Gardens** marks the beginning of the holiday season on the Friday after Thanksgiving.

Recreation

Aquanoodle has water-tube fun in summer at 1155 E. Hwy. 40, tel. 789-5281. **Naples Hydrosaurus Waterslides** provides another place to cool off at 1701 E. 1900 South, tel. 789-1010. An outdoor **swimming pool** is next to Independence Park at 170 S. 600 West, tel. 789-5775. Play **tennis** or **baseball** at the city park, corner of 400 North and 900 West. Golf at the 18-hole **Dinaland Municipal Golf Course,** 675 S. 2000 East, tel. 781-1428.

Services

In **emergencies** (police, medical, and fire), dial 911. The **post office** is near the corner of Main and 800 West, tel. 789-2393. **Ashley Valley Medical Center** provides hospital care at 151 W. 200 North, tel. 789-3342. Camping and fishing supplies are available at **Dez Murray's Sporting Goods,** 39 S. Vernal Ave., tel. 789-

5779; **Basin Sports,** 511 W. Main, tel. 789-2409; and **Gart Bros.,** 872 W. Main, tel. 789-0536. The **Plaza Shopping Center** has a Kmart and other stores at 1153 W. Hwy. 40.

Information

The staff at the **Vernal Welcome Center,** tel. 789-4002, knows about the many attractions of "Dinosaurland" and offers a short video program showing highlights of the region and other parts of Utah; a series of self-guided tour brochures has maps and mileages of suggested trips. The center is open daily 8 a.m.-9 p.m. in summer, then daily 9 a.m.-5 p.m. the rest of the year. You can also contact the **Dinosaurland Travel Board** for tourist info and events at tel. (800) 477-5558. Both offices are located in the Utah Field House of Natural History at 25 E. Main (Vernal, UT 84078). Foresters at the **Vernal Ranger District** office of the Ashley National Forest, 355 N. Vernal Ave. (Vernal, UT 84078), tel. 789-1181, can tell you about scenic drives, camping, hiking, cross-country skiing, and snowmobiling in the eastern Uinta Mountains. Books and forest maps are sold there; travel plans showing vehicle restrictions are free. Open Mon.-Fri. 8 a.m.-5 p.m. The **Ashley National Forest Supervisor's Office,** behind (same address and phone), has general information about the Flaming Gorge, Roosevelt, and Duchesne districts. The **Bureau of Land Management (BLM)** Vernal District office, 170 S. 500 East (Vernal, UT 84078), tel. 789-1362, knows about the John Jarvie Historic Ranch in the northeast corner of the state and areas south of Vernal such as Pelican Lake and the White River; land-use maps and a variety of brochures on recreation areas are available. Open Mon.-Fri. 7:45 a.m.-4:30 p.m.

For detailed fishing and hunting information, stop at the **Utah Division of Wildlife Resources** in the courthouse building, second floor, 152 E. 100 North (Vernal, UT 84078), tel. 789-3103. Books on fishing and wildlife are sold; open Mon.-Fri. 8 a.m.-5 p.m. The **U.S. Fish**

and Wildlife Service, 266 W. 100 North #2 (Vernal, UT 84078), tel. 789-0351, has information about the Ouray National Wildlife Refuge and the new Ouray National Fish Hatchery to the south and Jones Hole National Fish Hatchery to the northeast; open Mon.-Fri. 7 a.m.-4 p.m. The **Uintah County Library,** 155 E. Main, tel. 789-0091, has good reading; you can also see the **Ladies of the White House Doll Collection** here with dolls fashioned after each first lady, each wearing a handsewn dress. Open Mon.-Thurs. 10 a.m.-8 p.m., Friday and Saturday 10 a.m.-6 p.m. **Bitter Creek Books,** 672 W. Main, tel. 789-4742, offers a selection of regional and general titles and topo maps.

Tours

River trips down the Green or Yampa in Dinosaur National Monument provide the excitement of big rapids and the beauty of remote canyons. One-day and longer trips are offered by **Don Hatch River Expeditions,** Box 1150, Vernal, UT 84078, tel. 789-4316 or (800) 342-8243; **Adrift Adventures** summer address is Box 192, Jensen, UT 84035, tel. 789-3600, year-round address is 1816 Orchard Place, Ft. Collins, CO 80521, tel. (800) 824-0150; and **Dinosaur River Expeditions,** 540 E. Main, Vernal, UT 84078, tel. (800) 247-6197. Expect to pay about $50 for day-trips and about $100 per day for longer excursions, children usually got discounts. Both companies offer trips on other rivers of the West too. **Dinaland Aviation,** tel. 789-1612, and **Vernal Aviation,** tel. 789-8157, do scenic and charter flights.

Transportation

Greyhound buses, 38 E. Main, tel. 789-0404, travel at least once daily west to Salt Lake City and east to Denver. Rent cars from **Avis,** at the airport, tel. 789-7264, or **Showalter Ford,** 100 E. Main, tel. 789-3818. Catch a cab from **T-Rex Taxi,** tel. 790-7433. **Skywest Airlines,** tel. (800) 453-9417, has daily connections with Salt Lake City ($75 one-way) and other regional cities.

NORTH OF VERNAL

Drive Through The Ages

You cross 10 geologic formations going far back in time on the drive between Vernal and Flaming Gorge Reservoir. Uplift of rock layers during the creation of the Uinta Mountains and the erosion that followed have revealed an exceptionally thick geologic layer cake. The 30-mile drive begins four miles north of town on US 191; a tour map at a pullout shows the formations to be seen ahead. *Drive Through the Ages* brochures are available at the Vernal Welcome Center, U.S. Forest Service, and BLM offices. Signs on the drive identify and briefly describe each formation from the Mancos (80 million years old) to the Uinta Mountain Group (one billion years old).

Steinaker State Park

Water sports, camping, and picnicking at the park's 750-acre Steinaker Reservoir make this a popular place in summer. Fishermen catch largemouth bass, rainbow trout, and a few brown trout. Water-skiers have plenty of room on the lake's two-mile length. Warm weather brings bathers to a swimming beach near the picnic area. Scuba divers find the best conditions from midsummer to late autumn, when visibility is up to 30 feet. In winter, visitors come to ice fish or to cross-country ski. The campground (elev. 5,500 feet) is open with drinking water all year; no showers or hookups. Other facilities include two covered pavilion areas and a paved boat ramp. The park charges $3 per vehicle day use or $7 per vehicle camping ($8 Friday, Saturday, and holidays). From Vernal, go north six miles on US 191, then turn left two miles, tel. 789-4432 or (800) 322-3770 (reservations).

Red Fleet State Park

Colorful cliffs and rock formations, including three large outcrops of red sandstone, inspired the name of Red Fleet Reservoir. You can hike three-quarters of a mile or take a boat to see a dinosaur trackway. Anglers catch largemouth bass, rainbow trout, and some brown trout and bluegill. Like the larger Steinaker Reservoir, Red Fleet stores valuable water for irrigation and municipal use. A developed area offers covered picnic tables, water, restrooms, fish-cleaning station, and paved boat ramp; open all year. Charges are $3 per vehicle day use or $7 per vehicle camping ($8 Friday, Saturday, and holidays); call 789-6614 or contact Steinaker State Park for more information. From Vernal, go north 10 miles on US 191 to Milepost 211, then turn right two miles on a paved road to its end.

Jones Hole National Fish Hatchery

Canyon walls tower 2,000 feet above Jones Hole. Springs supply water for the young trout raised here that will later go to Flaming Gorge Reservoir and other areas. You may view the operation daily 7 a.m.-3:30 p.m. or see the outdoor raceways at any time during the day. The visitor center has exhibits on the trout and Jones Hole area. Tours can be arranged on weekdays with at least one day's notice. The fragile eggs usually aren't on display, but you can see the newly hatched fish swimming in tanks inside the buildings. Young trout spook easily, so they're kept indoors, where they eat better and grow faster. When the trout reach a length of three inches they go outside. At an age of 14 months, the trout are eight inches long and ready to be transplanted to the wild. The hatchery produces about three million rainbow, brown, brook, and cutthroat trout annually. Call 789-4481 for information. Jones Hole is 38 miles northeast of Vernal via paved roads; head east on 500 North and follow the signs over Diamond Mountain Plateau. Diamond Mountain is believed to be the site of a hoax played in the 1870s; two men salted the area with genuine diamonds, then sold out for a fortune; one culprit was caught, the other escaped. Unpaved roads connect Jones Hole Road with US 191 and Browns Park. Hatchery staff discourage visits from mid-November to mid-March because ice and drifting snow can make driving hazardous; it's best not to come then unless you call ahead, have 4WD, and are prepared for winter camping.

An easy hiking trail begins below the raceways and follows Jones Hole Creek four miles to the Green River in Dinosaur National Monu-

pictographs along the
Jones Hole Creek
hiking trail

ment. Hikers enjoy the spectacular canyon scenery, lush vegetation, a chance to see wildlife, and some Fremont Indian pictographs. The creek has good fishing; special regulations (posted) include use of artificial lures and flies only. You may camp midway on the trail near the confluence with Ely Creek by first obtaining a backcountry permit from Dinosaur National Monument. Ely Creek has good places to camp and explore. The trail begins at an elevation of 5,550 feet and descends 500 feet to the Green River in Whirlpool Canyon.

John Jarvie Ranch

Browns Park, along the Green River in Utah's northeast corner and adjacent to Colorado, has always been remote. The Wild Bunch and other outlaws often used the area as a hangout. John Jarvie settled here in 1880 and stayed until his death in 1909. He ran a store, post office, and ferry, while still having time to take care of the ranch and do some prospecting. A guided tour of the restored ranch takes in the original (1880s) corral, blacksmith shop and tools, farm implements, crude dugout, stone house, and other structures. Jarvie's store has been reconstructed and filled with shelves of canned goods, dried food, pots and pans, tools, harnesses, barbed wire, and other necessities of turn-of-the-century ranch life. Exhibits also show artifacts dug up from the original store site. The John Jarvie Ranch is open daily 8 a.m.-5 p.m. from May to October; free, tel. 885-3307 (or call

the BLM office in Vernal, tel. 789-1362). Winter visits are possible too; call first to find out road conditions. Boaters on the Green River can easily stop off to see the ranch; a sign marks where to pull in. You can camp at **Bridge Hollow Recreation Site** (water and $4 fee; one-quarter mile downstream of the ranch) and **Indian Crossing Recreation Site** (no water, $2 fee; one quarter mile upstream of the ranch); the ranch also has drinking water.

Trucks or cars with good clearance can drive to the ranch on an unpaved road through scenic Crouse Canyon; this route branches off Jones Hole Road 26 miles from Vernal, goes north past Crouse Reservoir and into the canyon, winds west through hills and parallels the Green River (the river is hard to see from the road), crosses a bridge over the swift-flowing Green, and turns left 0.3 mile; distance from Jones Hole Road is 28 miles. Another way in is to go north from Vernal on US 191 to 0.7 mile past the Wyoming border and turn right 22 miles on a gravel road; a steep 14% grade into Browns Park makes climbing back difficult for RVs and other underpowered vehicles. A third approach is from Maybell, Colorado, on CO 318 (paved until the Utah border); this is the best road, especially in winter. Highway CO 318 also provides access to Browns Park National Wildlife Refuge, a stopover point for migratory waterfowl in spring and autumn and a nesting habitat for ducks and Great Basin Canada geese. A gravel tour road goes through the refuge.

Ashley National Forest (Vernal District)

The southeastern part of the Uinta Mountains has very pleasant mountain country with scenic drives, fishing, hiking, camping, picnicking, and winter sports. Contact the U.S. Forest Service office in Vernal for road conditions and recreation information. Roads at the higher elevations open about the beginning of June and are often passable through October. Most roads to the campgrounds and reservoirs are okay for cars. Some areas may be closed to vehicle use because of wet conditions, wildlife habitat, sheep ranges, or erosion problems. **Lodgepole Campground** offers sites with water from late May to early September at an elevation of 8,100 feet; it's 30 miles north of Vernal on US 191 on the way to Flaming Gorge N.R.A.; $8; some sites can be reserved by calling (800) 280-CAMP. **East Park Campground,** at East Park Reservoir, has water and a $6 fee; go 20 miles north of Vernal on US 191, then 10 miles northwest on forest roads (all but the last mile is paved); elevation is 9,000 feet. **Iron Springs Campground and Picnic Area,** on the Red Cloud Loop Scenic Drive, is mainly a group area; individuals can also use the sites if there's room; a hand pump supplies water. Other campgrounds include **Red Springs** ($6 fee), **Oaks Park, Paradise Park, Kaler Hollow,** and **Whiterocks** ($6 fee).

Fishermen will find rainbow trout in most of the lakes and streams. Brown trout and native cutthroat trout live in some areas. Most hiking trails are rocky with some steep sections; topo maps should be carried. Trails lead into the High Uintas Wilderness from Chepeta Lake and West Fork of Whiterocks trailheads; road distances to the trailheads are relatively long, then there's a hike of about six to seven miles to the wilderness boundary. In winter, three cross-country ski trails lead west from US 191 into the Grizzly Ridge and Little Brush Creek areas; signed trailheads are about 25 miles north of Vernal. Most of these trails are rated intermediate to advanced, though some sections are good for beginners too. Snowmobilers have an extensive network of trails that mostly follow forest roads.

Red Cloud Loop Scenic Drive

This 74-mile loop winds through scenic canyons and mountains northwest of Vernal. Allow about half a day for just the drive. Side roads go to East Park and Oaks Park reservoirs, campgrounds, fishing streams, and hiking areas. Aspen trees put on a brilliant display in autumn. About half the drive follows unpaved forest roads, so it's a good idea to check road conditions first with the U.S. Forest Service office in Vernal. Cars with good clearance can usually make the trip if the roads are dry. Drive 20 miles north from Vernal on US 191 (or 15 miles south from the junction of US 191 and UT 44 in Flaming Gorge N.R.A.) and turn west on the paved East Park Reservoir Road at the sign that says "Red Cloud Loop." Signs then show the rest of the way. The Vernal Welcome Center's brochure *Red Cloud Loop* describes points of interest.

FLAMING GORGE NATIONAL RECREATION AREA

Flaming Gorge Reservoir winds through 91 miles of gentle valleys and fiery red canyons. The rugged land displays spectacular scenery where the Green River cuts into the Uinta Mountains—cliffs rising as high as 1,500 feet, twisted rock formations, and sweeping panoramas. Although much of the lake lies in Wyoming, most of the campgrounds and other visitor facilities, as well as the best scenery, are in Utah. Boating on the clear blue waters of the lake or the river below is one of the best ways to enjoy the sights. Water-skiers have plenty of room on the lake's 66 square miles. Swimming is popular too. Anglers regularly pull trophy trout and smallmouth bass from the lake and trout from the river. Rafting the lively Green River below the dam offers a thrilling ride that anyone with care and proper safety equipment can take—no special skills are needed. A permit system might be in place by summer 1995. Be sure you're properly equipped before setting out. The U.S. Forest Service and private concessions offer boating facilities and about two dozen campgrounds in the recreation area. Information centers at Flaming Gorge Dam and Red Canyon Overlook have exhibits, video programs, maps, and literature. Flaming Gorge N.R.A. can be easily reached by heading north 35 miles on US 191 from Vernal. In Wyoming, you can take WY 530 south from the town of Green River or US 191 south from near Rock Springs.

Look for groups of graceful pronghorn in the open country east of the lake at Antelope Flat (north of Dutch John) and in the Lucerne area on the west side. Other wildlife in the area includes deer, elk, moose, mountain lion, black bear, bighorn sheep, fox, bobcat, mink, and eagle.

Flaming Gorge Dam And Visitor Center

Nearly a million cubic yards of concrete went into the dam, completed in 1964. The structure rises 502 feet above bedrock and is 1,285 feet long at the crest. The dam is open for self-guided tours daily from about the first weekend in April to the last weekend in September and for guided tours daily about early May to late September; tours last 20-30 minutes and are free; check hours at the visitor center, on the west end of the dam. You'll descend inside for a look at the three giant generators in the power-plant room, then go one floor below where a shaft connects the turbine and generator of one of the units.

The visitor center has a large 3-D map of the area, exhibits, and video programs; books and maps are for sale and staff will answer your

Flaming Gorge; view uplake from Red Canyon Overlook

questions. Open Thurs.-Mon. 9 a.m.-5 p.m. year-round, and daily with extended hours in summer. The dam and visitor center are six and one half miles northeast on US 191 from the junction with UT 44, or 2.8 miles southwest of Dutch John.

Red Canyon Visitor Center

Sheer cliffs drop 1,360 feet to the lake below. The visitor center and nearby viewpoints have splendid panoramas up and down the canyon and to the lofty Uinta Mountains in the distance. A nature trail connects the overlooks and has signs about the ecology; the trail is wheelchair accessible. Exhibits inside describe local wildlife and flora, geology, Indian groups that once lived here, and early history and settlement of the area. Books and maps are for sale at an information desk; the staff answers visitor questions and offers video programs. Open daily 10 a.m.-5 p.m. from Memorial Day weekend to mid-September. Located three and one half miles west on UT 44 from the junction with US 191, then three miles in on a paved road.

Additional Information

Staff and volunteers at the Flaming Gorge Ranger District/Manila Headquarters office can answer your questions year-round; located at the junction of UT 44 and UT 43 in the center of Manila; open daily 8 a.m.-4:30 p.m. in summer and Mon.-Fri. 8 a.m.-4:30 p.m. the rest of the year (may also be open Saturday in autumn); forest and topo maps and some books are sold; Box 279, Manila, UT 84046, tel. 784-3445.

Off-Season Visits

Peace, quiet, and snow prevail in winter. Dedicated fishermen still cast their lines into the Green River or fish through the lake ice. Cross-country skiers and snowmobilers make their trails through the woods. Flaming Gorge Lodge, Grubbs Motel (Manila), Niki's Inn (Manila), and Steinaker's Motel (Manila) provide warm places to stay. Campgrounds are closed, though snow campers and hardy RVers can stop for the night in parking areas.

Sheep Creek Canyon Geological Area

Canyon walls on this scenic loop drive reveal rock layers deformed and turned on end by immense geological forces. The earth's crust broke along the Uinta North Fault and the south side rose 15,000 feet relative to the north. Fossils of trilobites, corals, sea urchins, gastropods, and other marine animals show that the ocean once covered this spot before the uplifting and faulting. Rock layers of yet another time preserve fossilized wood and tracks of crocodile-like reptiles. Nongeologists can appreciate and enjoy the drive too. The road through Sheep Creek Canyon is paved but has some narrow and rough places; it's closed in winter. The 13-mile loop branches off UT 44 south of Manila between Mileposts 14 and 15 and rejoins UT 44 at Milepost 22; the loop can be done in either direction. The *Wheels of Time* geology brochure, available at visitor centers and the Manila Headquarters, describes geologic formations at marked stops. Three picnic areas line the drive, two in the lower part of the canyon and one in Palisades Memorial Park upstream where the road climbs out of the canyon. Camping in the canyon has been restricted ever since a flash flood in 1965 killed a family of seven; Palisades Memorial Park marks the site. Only dispersed camping is allowed along the drive and only from October 1 to May 15. Two primitive campgrounds (outhouses but no water or established sites) lie just off UT 44 along lower Sheep Creek a short way from the entrance to the scenic loop.

Swett Ranch

Oscar Swett homesteaded near Flaming Gorge in 1909, when he was just 16 years old, then built up a large cattle ranch in this isolated region. With the nearest store days away, Oscar ran his own blacksmith shop and sawmill and did much of the ranch work; his wife Emma tended the garden, made the family's clothing, raised nine kids, and helped with the ranch chores. You can experience some of the early homestead life on a visit to the ranch by joining Forest Service tours, from Memorial Day to Labor Day, Thurs.-Mon. 9 a.m.-5 p.m. (check hours at the visitor centers). The house, cabins, spring house, root cellar, blacksmith shop, horse barn, cow shed, many other outbuildings, and farm machinery have been preserved. Drive north 0.3 mile on US 191 from the UT 44 junction (or south 1.6 miles from Flaming Gorge Lodge), then turn west and follow signs 1.3 miles on a gravel road.

Boating On Flaming Gorge Lake

Watch for strong winds on the lake which can whip up large waves without warning—even on a clear day. Rock reefs may appear and disappear as the lake level changes. Three marinas along the lake's length offer rentals, fuel docks, and supplies. Free paved boat ramps at these and several other locations are maintained by the U.S. Forest Service. **Cedar Springs Marina,** Box 337, Dutch John, UT 84023, tel. 889-3795, at the lower end of the lake, rents boats (fishing, ski, and pontoon) and fishing gear, and has a fuel dock, slips, store, scenic tours, and guided fishing trips; open April to October. Turnoff for the marina is 1.7 miles west of Flaming Gorge Dam on US 191. **Lucerne Valley Marina,** Box 356, Manila, UT 84046, tel. 784-3483, provides services on the broad central section of the lake near Manila; the marina has boat rentals (fishing, ski, pontoon, and houseboats), fishing gear rentals, a fuel dock, slips, store, and guided fishing trips; open mid-March to mid-November. The marina is eight miles east of Manila on paved roads. **Buckboard Marina** is on the west shore in Wyoming; services include boat rentals (fishing, ski, and pontoon), fishing gear rentals, a fuel dock, slips, store, scenic tours, and guided fishing trips; Star Route 1, Green River, WY 82935, tel. (307) 875-6927 or (800) 824-8155. It's 22.5 miles northeast of Manila on UT 43/WY 530, or 23.5 miles south of Green River on WY 530.

The Green River
Below Flaming Gorge Dam

The Green bounces back to life in Red Canyon below the dam and provides enjoyment for boaters, anglers, and hikers. Anyone in good shape with a raft, life jacket (must be worn), a paddle (and spare), bailing bucket, and common sense can put in at the launch area just below the dam and float downriver to Little Hole (two and one half hours for seven river miles) or to Indian Crossing just above the John Jarvie Historic Ranch (five to eight hours for 14.5 river miles). It's also possible to continue 11 miles beyond Indian Crossing to Swallow Canyon takeout or 35 miles to Gates of Lodore; these runs are mostly flat water and have troublesome sandbars at low water. Gates of Lodore marks the beginning of some big rapids in Dinosaur National Monument; you'll need permits

and whitewater experience here or you can make prior arrangements to join a commercial river trip.

People with canoes, kayaks, and dories can float all sections of the Green between the dam and Gates of Lodore, though river experience is needed for these craft. Permits may be required starting summer 1995. Have proper equipment before you get in and go. Raft rentals and shuttle services are provided by Flaming Gorge Lodge (tel. 889-3773), Flaming Gorge Recreation Services at the Dutch John Store (tel. 885-3191), and Flaming Gorge Flying Service at the Dutch John Airport (tel. 885-3338). Rentals typically cost $40 per day for a six-person raft or $60 per day for one holding eight, shuttles cost about $25 to Little Hole, $70 to Indian Crossing, and $85 to Swallow Canyon. Drivers can also drop their vehicles off at Little Hole and take an early morning shuttle back to the starting point.

Friday, Saturday, and holidays in summer often see large crowds on the river; you'll need reservations then for raft rentals and shuttles. For solitude, try to come Sunday to Wednesday. Guide services for boating and fishing trips can be contacted through the rental outfits. Life jackets (included with rentals) *must* be worn by all boaters—the water is too cold (57° F in summer, 40° in winter) to swim in for long. The 10 class-II rapids between the dam and Little Hole lend some excitement to the trip but aren't usually dangerous. Red Creek Rapid below Little Hole is a class-III rapid and can be difficult; scouting before running is recommended. Many groups portage this rapid. Camping is permitted

downstream of Little Hole at established primitive sites or dispersed sites. Bring drinking water or obtain some at Little Hole. No motors are allowed between the dam and Indian Crossing. Water flow varies according to power needs; allow more time if the flow is small. Call the Bureau of Reclamation for present conditions, tel. 885-3121.

Trips begin at the end of a 1.4-mile paved road (may not be signed) which turns off US 191 0.3 mile east of the dam. The parking area at the river is small, for unloading boats and passengers only. The main parking areas are 0.7 mile back up the road. Drivers can take either of two foot trails which descend from the parking lots to the river. The shuttle to Little Hole is only eight miles (paved) via Dutch John. The drive to Indian Crossing is much longer, 38 miles (25 unpaved); go north on US 191 to 0.7 mile beyond the Wyoming state line, then turn east on a gravel road to Browns Park and follow signs; one section of this road has a 14% grade.

Little Hole National Recreation Trail follows the north bank of the Green River through Red Canyon for seven miles between the main parking area below the dam and Little Hole. Many good fishing spots can be found along the way. No camping, horses, ground fires, or motorized vehicles are allowed. The Green River downstream of the dam has a reputation for some of western America's best river fishing. Trophy catches have included 22-pound rainbow, 18-pound brown, and 14-pound cutthroat trout. Modifications to the dam allow the ideal temperature mix of warmer water near the lake's surface and cold water from the depths. Special regulations apply here to maintain the high-quality fishing (check for current regulations). Trout between 13 and 20 inches (the most prolific breeders) must be returned to the water, there's a three-fish limit (two under 13 inches, one over 20 inches), and only artificial lures and flies may be used. Fishermen using waders should wear life jackets in case the river level rises unexpectedly; neoprene closed cell foam waders are recommended for their extra flotation and protection against hypothermia.

Hiking And Biking Trails
The **Canyon Rim Trail** is a popular 4.2 mile (one way) hike or mountain bike ride with trailheads at Red Canyon Visitor Center and at the Greendale Overlook, a short distance from the junction of US 191 and UT 44. **Browne Lake** is a popular starting point for hikes outside the recreation area: Trail #005 goes to the **Ute Mountain Fire Lookout Tower,** a national historic site (two miles one-way); Trail #016 goes to **Hacking Lake** (seven miles one-way); Trail #012 goes to **Tepee Lakes** (five miles one-way) and **Leidy Peak** (elev. 12,028 feet; eight miles one-way); and Trail #017 goes to **Spirit Lake** (15 miles one-way). Browne Lake is four and one half miles west on unpaved Forest Route 221 from the Sheep Creek loop drive, then one and one half miles southeast on the Browne Lake road; see the Ashley National Forest map. Visitor centers and forest service offices have maps of hiking and mountain bike trails and can suggest dirt roads suitable for either activity. The USGS topo maps are recommended too.

Campgrounds
The camping season begins with the opening of Lucerne Valley Campground (eight miles east of Manila), usually on Easter Sunday. By Memorial Day, everything should be open. Campgrounds begin closing after Labor Day, though at least one is left open through October for hunters. If you're here early or late in the season, stop by or call the Manila forest service office or Flaming Gorge Dam Visitor Center to find out what's available. Most campgrounds have water and a $5 base fee. Group sites and single family units in some areas can be reserved by calling (800) 280-CAMP. Two primitive campgrounds (outhouses but no water or

established sites) lie just off UT 44 along lower Sheep Creek. Some primitive campgrounds on the lake can be reached only by boat or trail; these include Kingfisher, Island, Gooseneck, Hideout, and Jarvies Canyon.

Accommodations
Flaming Gorge Lodge, seven miles southwest of Dutch John; Greendale, US 191, Dutch John, UT 84023, tel. 889-3773, offers motel rooms all year ($53.41 s, $59.95 d), condos ($90.47 s, $97.01 d) with reduced winter rates, and a restaurant serving breakfast, lunch, and dinner daily all year. The lodge also has a store, raft rentals, shuttles, and guided river fishing trips. **Red Canyon Resort,** Box 211145, Salt Lake City, UT 84121-8145, tel. 889-3759, sits beside the privately operated Green's Lake a short distance from the Red Canyon Visitor Center. The resort is open early April to late October and has rustic cabins for $30.52 or $45.78 s, $41.42 or $56.16 d, luxury duplex cabins for $97.20 per side, a restaurant open daily for breakfast, lunch, and dinner, a store with groceries and fishing supplies, and boat rentals for Green's Lake.

Other Services
Flaming Gorge Recreation/Dutch John Service, at the turnoff for Dutch John on US 191, tel. 885-3191, has a snack bar (open daily Memorial Day to Labor Day weekends), store (open early April to late October), raft rental and shuttle services, hot showers ($3), and a gas station (open all year). **Flaming Gorge Flying Service** at Dutch John Airport, tel. 885-3338, offers raft rentals, river trips, guided fishing trips, shuttle service, hot showers ($3), a laundromat, and airplane fuel. Dutch John has always been a government town. It sprang up in 1957-58 to house workers during construction of Flaming Gorge Dam and had a peak population of about 3,000. About 150 current residents work in various state and federal agencies.

The tiny town of Manila, just west of the recreation area, is the seat of Daggett County, the smallest and least populated in Utah. Year-round population of Manila totals only 284. The name commemorates Admiral Dewey's capture of Manila in the Philippines, which occurred in 1898 when surveyors were laying out the Utah townsite. Manila is a handy base for travel in the Flaming Gorge area. The town is 63 miles northwest of Vernal and 46 miles south of Green River (WY).

Stay at **Flaming Gorge Motel** in the center of town, tel. 784-3131, $30.52 s, $39.24 d; **Steinaker's Motel,** E. Hwy. 43, tel. 784-3363, $27 s, $30.52 d, check in at Chevron station; **Niki's Inn,** W. Hwy. 43, tel. 784-3117, $43.60 s, $47.96 d; or **Vacation Inn,** W. Hwy. 43, tel. 784-3259, all kitchenettes, $43.60 d and up, open April 1 to October 31. **Flaming Gorge KOA** on W. UT 43, tel. 784-3184, with showers, laundry, pool, and playground, is open from May 1 to October 31; tent or RV spaces cost $15.81 no hookups, $20.71 w/hookups. Dine at **Flaming Gorge Cafe,** in the center of town; open daily for breakfast, lunch, and dinner; or **Niki's Inn,** W. Hwy. 43, open daily for breakfast, lunch, and dinner. Both gas stations in the center of town have small stores and snack bars. The **3M Market** on E. Hwy. 43 has groceries and fishing supplies. **Cow Country Rodeo** in July is the big annual event. The **Flaming Gorge Ranger District** office is in the center of town (see "Additional Information," above).

Vicinity Of Flaming Gorge N.R.A.

Browne Lake has a small campground (elev. 8,200 feet; no water or fee) and fishing for native cutthroat trout. Several trails start nearby (see "Hiking and Biking Trails," above). Browne Lake

is four and one half miles west on unpaved Forest Route 221 from the Sheep Creek loop drive, then one and one half miles miles southeast on the Browne Lake road; see the Ashley National Forest map.

Ute Mountain Fire Lookout Tower (elev. 8,834 feet) has a good panorama of surrounding alpine lakes, Flaming Gorge Lake, and the Uintas. The tower has been restored as a historic site; ask at a visitor center for days and hours. Turn west one mile on Forest Route 221 from the Sheep Creek loop drive, then one and one half miles south on Forest Route 005.

Spirit Lake has a beautiful setting in high country of the Uintas. The lake (elev. 10,000 feet) offers fishing, boating, a campground, and a lodge. Hikers can take trails to nearby lakes (17 are within three miles!) and to the High Uintas Wilderness. **Spirit Lake Campground** is in a fir, spruce, and lodgepole pine forest; open early June to late October; $5; you may need to obtain water from the nearby Spirit Lake spring. **Spirit Lake Lodge,** 1360 Hallam Rd., Francis, UT 84036 (mailing address), tel. 783-2339 or (307) 780-8088 (mobile phone), offers cabins for $32.86 s or d, $37.10 for groups up to five, $40.28 for groups up to eight, $50.88 for groups up to 14. It also has a cafe, open daily for breakfast, lunch, and dinner and a small store, and offers guided pack trips, trail rides, and rowboat and canoe rentals; open early June to late Oc-

loading up for a pack trip at Spirit Lake Lodge

tober. Take unpaved Forest Route 221 west 10½ miles past the Ute Mountain Fire Lookout Tower and Browne Lake turnoffs to the junction with Forest Route 001, then follow 001 southwest six and one half miles to Spirit Lake;

this last section may have some rocky areas, but is usually passable for cars with good clearance. Spirit Lake is 69.5 miles from Vernal, 41 miles from Flaming Gorge Dam, and 31 miles from Lone Tree (WY).

EAST OF VERNAL

DINOSAUR NATIONAL MONUMENT

The monument owes its name and fame to one of the world's most productive sites for dinosaur bones. More than 1,600 bones of 11 different dinosaur species cover a rock face at the quarry. The spectacular canyons of the Green and Yampa rivers form another aspect of the monument. Harpers Corner Scenic Drive winds onto high ridges and canyon viewpoints in the heart of Dinosaur. River running allows a close look at the geology and wildlife within the depths and provides the bonus of thrilling rapids. Dinosaur National Monument straddles the Utah-Colorado border, but only the quarry, in the western end of the monument, has dinosaur bones.

The Land
From the original 80 acres reserved at the quarry in 1915, Dinosaur National Monument has grown to more than 200,000 acres of rivers, canyons, valleys, plateaus, and mountains. Elevations range from 4,750 feet at the Green River near the quarry to 9,006 feet atop Zenobia Peak of Douglas Mountain. The high country is part of the east flank of the Uinta Mountains, whose geology is graphically revealed in the deep canyons of the Green and Yampa rivers. Wildlife inhabiting this rugged terrain includes mule deer, elk, pronghorn, Rocky Mountain bighorn sheep, mountain lion, black bear, coyote, bobcat, red and gray fox, badger, striped and Western spotted skunks, ringtail cat, raccoon, beaver, bat, and many species of rats and mice. Streamside vegetation consists largely of cottonwood, box elder, willow, tamarisk, and some black birch. Desert plants such as sagebrush, greasewood, shadscale, saltbush, and rabbitbrush grow on the slopes at lower elevations. Middle elevations have piñon pine and juniper trees, serviceberry, buckbrush, and sagebrush. Douglas fir, aspen, ponderosa pine,

spruce, and mountain mahogany thrive on the mountains and in the protective shade of canyon walls. Annual precipitation averages about nine inches.

Dinosaurs
A fortunate combination of sand and water preserved the bones of dinosaurs, turtles, crocodiles, and clam shells at this spot about 145 million years ago. River floods washed the carcasses onto a sandbar where they were buried and preserved. Pressure from thousands of feet of additional sediments above gradually turned the sand to rock, and the bones within it were partially mineralized. Later, uplift of the Rockies and Uintas tilted the sandstone layer nearly on edge and exposed the overlying rocks to erosion.

In 1909, Earl Douglass, of the Carnegie Museum in Pittsburgh, PA, suspected that dinosaur bones might be found here because similar rock layers had yielded fine specimens in Colorado and Wyoming. He was right. A discovery of eight brontosaurus tail bones in their original position the following year became the first of many rewarding finds at the site. Douglass and other workers continued excavations until 1924, removing 350 tons of bones and attached rock that included 22 complete skeletons and parts of hundreds of other specimens. (Some of the best mounted skeletons can be seen at the Carnegie Museum.) After 1924, quarry work shifted emphasis from removing bones to exposing them in relief in their natural positions.

Dinosaur Quarry
A large enclosure protects the quarry face from the elements and houses laboratories and visitor exhibits. Near the entrance, you'll pass a realistic stegosaurus before climbing a spiral ramp to the quarry observation deck. Exhibits illustrate the sandbar and Morrison scene and place the quarry in context within the span of geologic

stegosaurus

time. The rock layer is 8-12 feet thick and dates from the Jurassic Period, about the middle of the Age of Dinosaurs. Workers have finished relieving the quarry bones and have left them in place as a permanent exhibit. Roughly three-quarters of the bones that you'll see come from sauropods—giant plant eaters with long necks and tails. All the bones appear in a jumble in the rock, just as they were deposited in the river sands long ago. One skeleton has a number marked on each bone; a diagram lets you figure out which piece is which. Models, artwork, and specimens on the lower level depict the variety of dinosaurs found here. Exhibits also show how workers remove bones from the rock and how they learn details about the dinosaurs' size, shape, diet, and muscle structure. Peek through windows of the paleontology lab to see bones under study and the instruments used. In winter, you may see researchers at work here.

Staff will answer questions about the quarry and other places to see in the monument. Handouts, available on request, include information on backcountry roads, hiking, river running, and Fremont rock art. A schedule posted during the main season lists times and places of ranger talks, nature walks, auto tours, children's programs, and campfire programs. A good selection of dinosaur and natural history books,

posters, postcards, slides, topo and geologic maps, bird and mammal lists, and film is sold. The Dinosaur Quarry is open daily 8 a.m.-4:30 p.m. (extended to about 7 p.m. Memorial Day to Labor Day weekends); closed Thanksgiving, Christmas, and New Year's Day. Mailing address is 4545 Hwy. 40, Dinosaur, CO 81610, tel. (303) 374-2216. From Vernal, drive east 13 miles on US 40 to Jensen, then turn north seven miles on UT 149. Admission to the quarry costs $5 per vehicle ($2 bicyclist or bus passenger); free for children under 16. Parking space is in short supply during the busy summer season, so a free shuttle operates every 15 minutes between the quarry and a separate parking area during most of the day. The rest of the year you can drive all the way in, as can handicapped people anytime. The privately owned **Dinosaur Quarry Gift Shop,** just outside the monument, has a snack bar; open summer only.

Quarry To Josie Morris Cabin Drive
Stop at the Dinosaur Quarry or a roadside pullout for the booklet *Tour of the Tilted Rocks,* which describes points of interest of an auto tour to the Cub Creek area. The drive goes 10 miles past the quarry turnoff to a historic ranch, passing sites of Fremont rock art and the Split Mountain and Green River campgrounds on the way. A small overhang known as the **"Swelter Shelter"** contains some petroglyphs; the pullout is one mile beyond the quarry turnoff; a trail leads 200 feet to the cave. **Sound of Silence Nature Trail** begins on the left 1.9 miles past the quarry turnoff; this unusual nature trail makes a three mile loop up Red Wash, enters an anfractuosity (a winding channel), crosses a bench and ridge with fine panoramas, then descends through some slickrock back to Red Wash and the trailhead; you'll need the trail guide (best purchased at the quarry or headquarters) for this hike. Red Wash is also good for short strolls—just avoid it if thunderstorms threaten! Continue on the drive to the Split Mountain Campground turnoff; the side road winds down one mile to the campground at the Green River. At press time, **Split Mountain Campground** was open only Nov.-March, when nearby Green Mountain Campground is closed; no water or fee. The Green River emerges from Split Mountain Canyon here after some of the roughest rapids on the whole river. **Desert Voices Nature Trail** begins at the

campground entrance and makes a two-mile loop; a trail brochure available at the quarry, headquarters, or near the start describes plants and geology seen along the way; allow one and one half to two hours.

Back on the main road, a Green River overlook is on the left 1.2 miles past the Split Mountain Campground turnoff. The road to Green River Campground is a short way farther on the left; **Green River Campground** is open only in summer and has water and an $8 fee. **Placer Point Picnic Area** is 1.1 miles beyond the junction, just before a bridge across the Green River. The main road continues past a private ranch, then pavement ends. A road fork on the right, 2.7 miles past the bridge, goes to Blue Mountain (high-clearance vehicles and good maps needed); keep left for the Josie Morris Cabin. A **petroglyph panel** is on the left beside the road 0.7 mile beyond the road fork. Continue past this panel 0.2 mile and park in a pullout on the right (may not be signed) for a look at no less than seven lizard petroglyphs on the cliffs above and to the left; a steep climb up the slope (no trail) allows a closer view of these and other figures. Large shade trees surround the **Josie Morris Cabin** at the end of the road, 0.9 mile farther. Josie grew up in Browns Park during the 1870s and 1880s and settled here about 1914. She spent much of the next 50 years alone at the ranch, tending the fields, garden, cows, pigs, and chickens. She was in her 90s when she died as a result of a hip broken in a riding accident. You can visit her cabin, outbuildings, orchards, and a nearby box canyon.

Monument Headquarters

A few exhibits and a 10-minute slide show (shown on request) introduce the monument's history, dinosaurs, and canyons. The staff offers handouts, books, and maps and will answer your questions. Open daily 8 a.m.-4:30 p.m. from Memorial Day to Labor Day weekends, then Mon.-Fri. 8 a.m.-4:30 p.m. the rest of the year; 4545 Hwy. 40, Dinosaur, CO 81610, tel. (303) 374-2216. The River Office here handles permits for groups running the Green or Yampa rivers within the monument. A self-guided scenic drive to Harpers Corner begins at the headquarters. Admission to the exhibits and scenic drive is free. You won't see any dinosaur exhibits in this part of the monument—the bones

are only at the quarry area. From Vernal, go 35 miles east on US 40 to the Colorado town of Dinosaur, then continue another two miles east to the monument headquarters. Dinosaur has a couple of small motels and places to eat.

Harpers Corner Road

This scenic drive begins at monument headquarters in Colorado and winds north past many scenic overlooks. The road opens in about early May and closes after the first big snowstorm in November. In winter, the road is kept clear to Plug Hat Butte overlook, 4.3 miles in. A booklet available at the quarry or headquarters has good background material on the area and describes the sights at numbered stops along the way. The paved road is 31 miles long (one-way); allow about two hours for the roundtrip or half a day if you also plan to hike the two nature trails. You'll pass three picnic areas along the way, but no water or campgrounds are available. The road climbs a series of ridges with fine views of much of the monument, including Island Park, Echo Park, and canyons of the Green and Yampa rivers. You'll see spectacular faulted and folded rock layers, and a complete range of vegetation, from the cottonwoods along the rivers far below to aspen and firs of the highlands.

Plug Hat Nature Trail is an easy half-mile loop in a piñon-juniper forest at a stop 4.3 miles from the beginning of the drive. At Island Park Overlook, about 26 miles along the drive, **Ruple Point Trail** heads west four miles (one-way) on an old jeep road to an overlook of the Green River in Split Mountain Canyon; carry water. The drive ends at Harpers Corner, a long and narrow peninsula. You can continue one mile on foot to the very tip by taking the **Harper's Corner Trail;** a brochure available at the start describes features visible from numbered stops. Cliffs on each side drop to a bend of the Green River at the beginning of Whirlpool Canyon, about 2,500 feet below. Echo Park, Steamboat Rock, and the sinuous curves of the Yampa River Canyon are visible too. Allow one and one half to two hours for the easy to moderately difficult walk. Binoculars come in handy for a better look at the geology and other features.

Echo Park

A rough dirt road branches off Harpers Corner Road 25 miles from monument headquarters and winds down more than 2,000 feet in 13 miles to Echo Park. The setting of Echo Park, near the confluence of the Green and Yampa rivers, is one of the prettiest in the monument. The massive sandstone fin of Steamboat Rock looms into the sky across the Green River. Echo Park offers a campground (water in summer; free), river access for boaters (permit needed), and a ranger station (open summer only). Cars with good clearance can often make this side trip, though it's better to have a truck. Like all dirt roads in Dinosaur National Monument, it shouldn't be attempted when wet with any vehicle. The clay surface becomes extremely slick after rains, yet it usually dries out in two to three hours. Hikers can follow an unmarked route from Echo Park along the banks of the Yampa River to the mouth of Sand Canyon; go up Sand Canyon until it opens out, cut across benchland to Echo Park Road in lower Pool Creek Canyon, and follow the road back to Echo Park. High water levels of the Yampa can block the route from about late May to late June; you'll need to do some rockscrambling in Sand Canyon. The loop is six to eight miles long, depending on the route taken.

Drivers with high-clearance trucks can also explore the backcountry on **Yampa Bench Road,** which turns off eight miles down the Echo Park Road. Yampa Bench Road has views of the Yampa River Canyon and Douglas Mountain to the north and Blue Mountain to the south; allow four to five hours to drive the 38 miles between Echo Park Road and US 40. It's always a good idea to get directions and the latest road conditions from a ranger before driving into the backcountry. Rains occasionally cut off travel, so it's recommended that you carry extra water, food, and camping gear.

Other Areas
Gates of Lodore, on the Green River, has a campground, a boat launching area for river runners, and a ranger station—all open year-round. **Gates of Lodore Campground** has water in summer and is free. **Gates of Lodore Trail** follows the river downstream to the dramatic canyon entrance, an easy one and one half mile roundtrip; get a trail leaflet at the ranger station or the trailhead. Gates of Lodore is 108 miles from monument headquarters via US 40, CO 318, and 10 miles of gravel road.

Deerlodge Park Campground at the east end of the monument sits just upstream from the Yampa River Canyon. Camping is primitive, with no designated sites, water, or fee; closed in winter. River trips on the Yampa usually begin here. The site is 53 miles from monument headquarters by paved roads.

Rainbow Park and **Ruple Ranch** are on the west shore of the Green River at opposite ends of Island Park. Both offer primitive campgrounds (no water or fee) and a place to launch or take out river boats. Easiest access is from the quarry area; distances are 26 miles to Rainbow Park and about another five miles to Ruple Ranch via the rough and unpaved Island Park Road. Cars with good clearance may be able to drive in, but the road is impassable during wet weather.

Hiking In The Monument
Any of the trails can easily be done on a day-trip. The two longest—Jones Hole and Ruple Point trails—are each about eight miles roundtrip and moderately difficult. The Echo Park-Sand Canyon route is also a similar distance. Easier, self-

Echo Park, from Harpers Corner Trail

Gates of Lodore

guided nature walks are Red Rock (two miles roundtrip), Plug Hat (half-mile roundtrip), Harpers Corner (two miles roundtrip), and Gates of Lodore (one and one half miles roundtrip). Each trail is described in the text above (see "North of Vernal," above, for visiting Jones Hole). Overnight trips are possible on the longer trails or on cross-country routes. Off-trail hikers must be able to navigate with map and compass and find (or carry) water, and they should have experience in desert travel over rugged terrain. One possibility is the three- to five-day hike from Echo Park to Gates of Lodore; before starting, though, you'll need to find river runners to take you across the Yampa. Obtain the required backcountry permit for overnight hikes from rangers at monument headquarters or at the Dinosaur Quarry.

River Running

Trips down the Green or Yampa rivers feature outstanding scenery and exciting rapids. All boaters in the monument must have permits or be with a licensed river-running company, even for day-trips. A one-day trip on the Green gives a feeling for the river at a modest cost; see "Tours" under "Practicalities" in the "Vernal" section earlier in this chapter. The most popular day run begins at Rainbow Park or Ruple Park; you bounce through the rapids of Split Mountain Canyon to takeouts at Split Mountain Campground. Longer trips usually begin on the Green at Gates of Lodore in the north end of the monument. Names of rapids like Upper and Lower Disaster Falls, Harp Rapids, Triplet Falls, and Hells Half Mile in Canyon of Lodore suggest that this isn't a place for inexperienced boaters.

In 1869, John Wesley Powell lost one of his four boats and many of the supplies at Disaster Falls on his first expedition. As a result, the rest of the trip was too hurried to make all the scientific studies he had planned. Powell's second trip in 1871 also had trouble when another boat was upset here.

Canyon depths reach 3,350 feet, the deepest in the monument. Echo Park marks the end of Canyon of Lodore 19 river miles later. The Yampa River joins the Green here and noticeably increases its size and power. Whirlpool Canyon begins downstream with modest rapids for the next 17 miles, followed by an interlude of slow water at Island Park. The river picks up speed again on entering the warped walls of Split Mountain Canyon and roars through Moonshine, S.O.B., Schoolboy, and Inglesby rapids on the eight miles to Split Mountain Campground. From here, the Green flows placidly the next 100 miles through open country.

The Yampa remains the last major undammed tributary of the Colorado River system. Snowmelt in the mountains of Colorado and Wyoming swells the Yampa to its highest and best levels from May to mid-July. Most boaters put in at Deerlodge Park at the east end of the monument. The next takeout point is 46 miles downriver at Echo Park. A series of rapids culminates in Warm Springs Rapids, the Yampa's wildest. Where the water is shallow, boaters may have difficulties with sandbars and rocks.

Guided river trips are often best for first-time visitors. Contact the monument for a list of river concessionaires. Private groups planning a trip on the Green or the Yampa should write far in advance to the River Unit at monument headquarters; the office will let you know about equipment regulations and how to obtain the required permits. One-day permits are the easiest to obtain. Contact the River Unit at Box 210, Dinosaur, CO 81610, tel. (303) 374-2468. The *Dinosaur River Guide* by Laura Evans and Buzz Belknap has maps and descriptions of both rivers in the monument.

VICINITY OF DINOSAUR NATIONAL MONUMENT

Stewart Lake State Waterfowl Management Area

Birders might want to make a short side trip south of Jensen to visit their feathered friends. Abundant vegetation in the water and on the shore of the shallow lake provides food and shelter for bird life. Take the small paved road south 1.4 miles from Jensen, then when the paved road curves right, keep going straight on the gravel road for 1.2 miles. The road is okay for cars, but is too narrow for large rigs or trailers.

SOUTH OF VERNAL

Ouray National Wildlife Refuge

This desert oasis along the Green River provides a lush habitat for migratory and nesting waterfowl. Other birds and animals also find food and shelter in the brush, grass, marsh, and trees. A list compiled at the refuge names 206 bird species. More than 4,000 ducks nest in summer. Migratory populations peak in April and again in October. Some mallards and Canada geese winter along the Green River.

A self-guided auto tour loops through a variety of habitats on the 11,480-acre refuge. The tour begins at an information booth, which has a brochure and other literature, then follows gravel roads for nine miles past 12 numbered stops. Open daily all year during daylight hours; free, tel. 545-2522 or 789-0351 (Vernal office). An observation tower gives a bird's-eye view of the marshlands. Hiking is permitted (take insect repellent). Some roads may close during spring flooding and autumn hunting; those in the east part of the refuge may require 4WD in wet weather. From Vernal, head southwest 14 miles on US 40, turn south 14 miles on UT 88, then turn into the refuge on a gravel road.

Ouray National Fish Hatchery

This facility is under construction inside Ouray National Wildlife Refuge with the goal of increasing the numbers of four endangered fish species: the Colorado squawfish, the humpback chub, the razorback sucker, and the longtail chub. For more information about these fish,

see the special topic "Endangered Fish of the Colorado River Basin." The fish hatchery will consist of 18 ponds and a number of buildings. Forces of nature cause the fish to be hatched in numbers much higher than the number that will survive. By collecting eggs and removing them from dangers in the stream, the hatchery insures that more of the fish will reach maturity and reproduce. Until an office is built, you can reach hatchery officials by calling Ouray National Wildlife Refuge.

Pelican Lake

Birds also stop in large numbers at this lake west of Ouray National Wildlife Refuge. The BLM has a campground (no water or fee) and a boat ramp on the south shore. From a junction northwest of the lake, go south on a narrow road (partly paved) that swings around the lake's west side to the campground and boat ramp. The lake has fishing for largemouth bass and bluegill. There's no swimming because of schistosomes (parasitic flatworms) in the water.

White River

The White has some of the best canoeing in Utah and is good for kayaking and rafting too. The river originates in Colorado's White Mountains and meanders west to meet the Green River near the town of Ouray, Utah. The scenic ride through White River Canyon has only a few rapids, and they're easy. Trips can be a day to a week long, depending on where you put in and take out. Boating provides good opportunities for viewing wildlife. Groves of cottonwoods make pleasant places to camp. The best time to go is during spring runoff, from mid-May to the end of June. No permits are needed—the BLM gives boaters the responsibility of proper boating safety and clean camping. Launch point is at the Bonanza Highway Bridge (40 miles south of Vernal) and takeout is at the Mountain Fuel Bridge, 40 river miles downstream. The shuttle between the two bridges is only 20 miles on graded dirt roads. The trip can be extended by putting in at Cowboy Canyon, nine miles upriver from Bonanza Highway Bridge on a very rough road, or by taking out at the confluence of the White and Green rivers, 22 miles downriver from the Mountain Fuel Bridge. Both the confluence and Mountain Fuel Bridge takeouts are on Ute Indian land; the tribe requires a permit to park or boat on Indian land (below Mountain Fuel Bridge); contact the Ute Indians at Box 190, Fort Duchesne, UT 84026,

tel. 722-5511. Bring life jackets, spare paddle, insect repellent, and drinking water. Obtain information and a brochure on this trip from the BLM Vernal District office at 170 S. 500 East, Vernal, UT 84078, tel. 789-1362.

Other Places
The remote desert country south of Vernal has many sites of geologic or historic interest for those who enjoy exploring back roads. The BLM office in Vernal can suggest places to go. Fantasy Canyon contains eroded sandstone formations, but a high-clearance vehicle is needed to get in; contact the BLM for a map. The old Uinta Railway grade from Mack (CO) to the ghost towns of Dragon, Watson, and Rainbow can be driven partway on a rough road. Gilsonite, a natural asphalt mined at these towns, provided the railway with most of its business. The narrow-gauge line operated 1904-39 and had some of the steepest slick track and sharpest curves in the world.

WEST OF VERNAL

UINTAH AND OURAY INDIAN RESERVATION

The reservation covers nearly one million acres scattered across the Uinta Basin and south on the East Tavaputs Plateau. Nonmembers must keep to the main roads on the reservation and purchase permits for most activities. Camping is allowed at the backcountry lakes open to fishing; you'll need either a fishing or a camping permit; boats need permits too. Some lakes have boat ramps. A brochure with map and regulations lists fishing areas and fees. Backcountry sites have outhouses and sometimes tables; bring your own water. Small-game hunting is permitted with a tribal license. You'll need special permission to explore outside the permitted areas. Obtain permits at the Ute Indian Tribe Fish & Game Department in Fort Duchesne, one and one half miles south of US 40, Box 190, Fort Duchesne, UT 84026, tel. 722-5511 or at sporting goods stores in Vernal, Price, Salt Lake City, and other towns.

Bottle Hollow Resort

The distinctive architecture of this resort uses tri-angular elements reminiscent of an Indian teepee. Bottle Hollow Resort includes a tribal museum, restaurant, gift shop, swimming pool, and facilities for boating and fishing. It's located 24 miles southwest of Vernal and six miles east of Roosevelt on the south side of US 40. The resort may close in winter.

The museum, on the west side of the motel complex, has exhibits of prehistoric artifacts, tribal history, ceremonies, early reservation life, and crafts. Ute crafts on display include moccasins, gloves, beadwork, ceremonial dress, and musical instruments. Open Mon.-Fri. 8:30 a.m.-4 p.m.; donation requested.

Motel rooms at the resort are available only by the month, tel. 722-3941, ext. 14. A restaurant serves American food and Indian tacos; open Mon.-Sat. for breakfast, lunch, and dinner. Check the gift shop for Indian art and craft items. The nearby 300-acre Bottle Hollow Reservoir has fishing for trout and channel catfish; be sure to have tribal fishing and boating permits. A boat ramp is located at the north end of the reservoir.

Events

The July Fourth **Northern Ute Indian Pow Wow and Rodeo** is the main annual event, with

Ute Indian Chief Sevara and family, ca. 1899

Indian tribes from all over the West participating. Dances, rodeo action, craft displays, and food booths entertain the crowds. Other pow wows, rodeos, and dances happen at different times of the year—ask at Bottle Hollow Resort.

ROOSEVELT

President Theodore Roosevelt opened the way for settlement of whites on the Uintah and Ouray Indian Reservation by a proclamation in 1902. Three years later, grateful homesteaders named two of their new towns in his honor—Theodore (later renamed Duchesne) and Roosevelt. Today Roosevelt (pop. 5,000) is the largest town in Duchesne County and a supply center for surrounding agricultural and oil businesses and for the Ute Indians. Roosevelt offers a good selection of places to stay and eat along the main highway (200 East and 200 North streets in downtown). The community is 30 miles west of Vernal and 146 miles east of Salt Lake City. Travelers can head north to Moon Lake and the High Uintas Wilderness. A scenic backcountry drive goes south to the many rock art sites in Nine Mile Canyon (see "Nine Mile Canyon Backcountry Byway" under "East of Price," below).

Accommodations

In order of increasing price are **Regal Motel,** 160 S. 200 East, tel. 722-4878, $21.80 s, $27.25 d; **Western Hills Motel,** 737 E. 200 North, tel. 722-5115, $29.40 s, $32.65 d; **Frontier Motel,** 75 S. 200 East, tel. 722-2201, $32.70 s, $36 d; and **Best Western Inn,** one mile east on US 40, tel. 722-4644 or (800) 528-1234, $43.60 s, $49 d.

Food

The **Frontier Grill,** 75 S. 200 East, next to the Frontier Motel, tel. 722-3669, is a family restaurant open daily for breakfast, lunch, and dinner. **Western Hills Cafe,** 737 E. 200 North, tel. 722-4562, offers American and Mexican favorites daily for breakfast, lunch, and dinner. **The Greenbriar,** just west of the Best Western Inn (one mile east of downtown), tel. 722-2236, is a family-style place open daily for breakfast, lunch, and dinner. The **Cow Palace,** just east of the Best Western Inn (one mile east of downtown), tel. 722-2717, offers steaks in an informal Western setting, open Mon.-Sat. for lunch and dinner. **Pizza Hut** serves pizza daily for lunch and dinner on the east edge of town, tel. 722-4586.

Events

Rough Rider Days, on the second weekend in June, focuses on hunting, fishing, and other outdoor sports. Festivities in the area on July 4 are the **Northern Ute Indian Pow Wow and Rodeo** at Fort Duchesne, **rodeos** in Neola and Tabiona, and a **Kid's Rodeo** in Altamont. **Altamont Longhorn Days & Rodeo** take place on July 24. The **U.B.I.C. (Uintah Basin In Celebration)** in early August is Roosevelt's biggest annual event with parades, craft shows, and entertainment. Anglers come to Starvation State Park in mid-August for the **Walleye Classic.**

Recreation And Services

The **city park** offers picnic tables, playground, and outdoor pool at 90 W. Lagoon, tel. 722-4851. **Roosevelt Golf Course** has nine holes about one and one half miles west of downtown, tel. 722-9644. Catch movies at **Roosevelt Twin Theatre** at 21 S. 200 East or **Uinta Theatre** at 41 N. 200 East, tel. 722-2095 for both places. The **post office** is at 81 S. 300 East. **Duchesne County Hospital** is at 250 W. 300 North, tel. 722-4691.

Information

The **Roosevelt Chamber of Commerce,** 48 S. 200 East (Box 1417, Roosevelt, UT 84066), tel. 722-4598, staff can tell you about points of interest in the area, events, and services. It's open Mon.-Fri. 8 a.m.-5 p.m. Foresters at the **Roosevelt Ranger District** office of the Ashley National Forest know about camping, fishing, hiking, and road conditions on the forest lands north of town, including the High Uintas Wilderness; forest maps, topo maps, and books are offered for sale; open Mon.-Fri. 8 a.m.-noon

WELCOME TO
ROOSEVELT
A "BULLY" GOOD TOWN!
ELEVATION 5280   POPULATION 5000

and 1-5 p.m. (8 a.m.-5 p.m. in summer). The office is on the west edge of town at 244 W. Hwy. 40 (Box 333-6, Roosevelt, UT 84066), tel. 722-5018. The **public library**, next to the city park at 70 W. Lagoon, tel. 722-4441, is open Mon.-Saturday

VICINITY OF ROOSEVELT

Ashley National Forest
Moon Lake is in the Uintas about 45 miles due north of Duchesne and 50 miles northwest of Roosevelt. Access roads are paved except for a seven-mile section crossing Indian lands. **Moon Lake Campground** (elev. 8,100 feet) is open from Memorial Day weekend to one week after Labor Day with water and an $8 fee. **Moon Lake Resort** offers cabins, boat rentals, store, mountain bike rides, horseback rides, and guided pack trips from June 1 to August 31 (the season will be extended in the future); write Mountain Home, UT 84051, tel. 454-3142 (in season). Major access points to the High Uintas Wilderness near Roosevelt are (from west to east): Lake Fork at Moon Lake (three trails), Center Park at the head of Hells Canyon, Swift Creek on the Yellowstone River (two trails), Uinta Canyon on the Uinta River, and West Fork of Whiterocks River. In winter, snowmobilers use trails in the Snake John area north of Whiterocks.

Five campgrounds are located along the Yellowstone River on Forest Routes 119 and 124 northwest of Roosevelt; elevations range from 7,700 feet at **Yellowstone Campground** to 8,100 foot at **Swift Creek Campground**; all have water and charge a $5 fee from late May to the week after Labor Day.

Uinta Canyon (no water, $5 fee Memorial Day weekend to week after Labor Day; also a group area) and **Wandin** (no water or fee) campgrounds and the **U-Bar Ranch** are along the Uinta River at an elevation of about 7,600 feet; take UT 121 and Forest Route 118 north of Roosevelt. The U-Bar Ranch, Box 680846, Park City, UT 84068, tel. 722-3560 or (800) 303-7256, offers cabins, horseback riding, and pack trips from May to October.

The **Pole Creek (Elkhorn) Scenic Loop** on Forest Route 117 winds through canyons and atop ridges east of the Uinta River; some sec-

tions may be rough, though the drive is usually passable by cars with good clearance. **Pole Creek Campground** (elev. 10,200 feet) is at the north end of the loop; no water or fee.

Big Sand Lake State Park
Good fishing attracts most of the visitors at this undeveloped park. The 390-acre reservoir has rainbow trout with some browns and cutthroats and lots of crayfish. People also come to water-ski and swim. Ice fishermen try their luck in winter. A boat ramp is on the southeast shore. No water or other services are available; admission is free. The park ranger is based at Starvation State Park near Duchesne, tel. 738-2326. From Roosevelt, go southwest five miles on US 40, turn west (then north) 10 miles to Upalco, continue straight (north) 0.7 mile where the main road curves left just past Upalco, then turn left 0.4 mile on a gravel road.

DUCHESNE

This small community, located at the confluence of the Duchesne and Strawberry rivers, is the seat of thinly settled Duchesne (doo-SHAYN) County. The name is said to honor a French Catholic nun or a French fur trapper or to be a corruption of the name of an Indian chief. Ranching, farming, and the oil industry provide most of the employment. Main attractions for visitors are the High Uintas Wilderness and other sections of the Ashley National Forest, Starvation Lake, and fishing on the Duchesne and Strawberry rivers.

Practicalities
Stay at the **Rio Damian**, 23 W. Main, tel. 738-2217, $38.50 s, $57.20 d, RV spaces cost $13 w/hookups; **Sportsmen Motel**, 145 E. Main, tel. 738-5733, $38.50 s, $57.20 d; or **Ell's Motel**, 220 E. Main, tel. 738-2215, $38.50 s, $57.20 d. **Country Kitchen Cafe** at 516 W. Main serves breakfast, lunch, and dinner daily except Sunday. **Cowan's Cafe** on East Main serves breakfast, lunch, and dinner daily. For steaks try **Well's Club**, 47 E. Main, tel. 738-9693.

The **city park** at Main and 100 West, tel. 738-2536, has picnic tables, playground, and an outdoor pool. **Footprints through Duchesne** on July 4 celebrates the area's homesteading with historic displays, fireworks, and entertainment. The **Duchesne County Fair,** usually on the third weekend of August, features a rodeo, parade, horse show, demolition derby, and other entertainment. People at the **Duchesne Ranger District** office of the Ashley National Forest have information on campgrounds, trailheads, and road conditions of the forest and the High Uintas Wilderness to the north and the Tavaputs Plateau to the south; forest maps, topo maps, and some books are sold; open Mon.-Fri. 8 a.m.-5 p.m. (and Sat. 8 a.m.-4:30 p.m. from Memorial Day to September 30). Offices are located at 85 W. Main (Box 981, Duchesne, UT 84021), tel. 738-2482.

VICINITY OF DUCHESNE

Uinta Mountains
Forest Route 144 turns north from Stockmore off UT 35, then follows the Duchesne River North Fork to **Aspen Grove Campground** (elev. 7,000 feet), **Hades Campground** (elev. 7,100 feet), and **Iron Mine Campground** (elev. 7,200 feet). All three campgrounds have water and a $5-8 fee from Memorial Day to one week after Labor Day; Iron Mine Campground also has a group reservation area ($25). **Defa's Ranch,** between Hades and Iron Mine campgrounds, Hanna, UT 84031, tel. 848-5590, offers cabins ($21.25-26.50), a cafe (breakfast, lunch, and dinner), RV park ($10.60), horseback riding, and pack trips; open May-October. Forest Route 315 turns east from Defa's Ranch to **Grandview Trailhead,** an access point for the southwestern part of the High Uintas Wilderness; the grade is steep and rough, though cars with good clearance can make it in dry weather.

The **Rock Creek** area and **Upper Stillwater Reservoir** are reached by going north from Duchesne on UT 87, turning north to Mountain Home, then west on Forest Route 134. The road is paved to the reservoir. **Miner's Gulch Campground** is a group campground at an elevation of 7,500 feet; no water, $25 charge, tel. 738-2482; **Fishermen's parking** is across the road. **Yellow Pine Campground** nearby (elev. 7,600 feet) has developed sites with water and a dump station from Memorial Day to one week after Labor Day; $10 (family), $16 (double), and $30 (group reservation sites). **Rock Creek**

Ranch has cabins ($39-53), restaurant (daily breakfast, lunch, and dinner), RV park ($13.08), pack trips, and trail rides; open May 1 to November 15; Box 510060, Mountain Home, UT 84051, tel. 454-3332. **Upper Stillwater Campground** (elev. 7,900 feet) lies just south of Upper Stillwater Reservoir; sites are open from mid-May to mid-October. Rates are $8 (family), $16 (double), and $30 (group sites). **Rock Creek Visitor Center,** near Upper Stillwater Campground has recreation and travel information in summer. **Rock Creek Trailhead** near the reservoir offers access into the High Uintas Wilderness.

Starvation State Park
The large Starvation Reservoir sits among rolling hills of high-desert country four miles west of Duchesne. Water-skiing is the biggest summer activity, followed by fishing, sailboarding, and sailing. Fishermen catch walleye (a state record was taken here), smallmouth bass, and some largemouth bass and German brown trout. The marina is open mid-April to Labor Day with boat rentals (fishing, Jet Skis, Wave Runners, and ski boats) and store. A developed campground with pull-through and tent sites with showers overlooks the water. This exposed location can be windy. Continue past the campground turnoff for a picnic area near a sand beach. A second developed campground is just past the picnic area. There are four primitive camping areas around the reservoir; other facilities include a paved boat ramp, a fish-cleaning station, and a dump station. The park is open all year. The main season, between Memorial Day and Labor Day weekends, is sometimes extended up to a month earlier and later; $3 day use, $5 primitive camping, or $9 developed camping ($10 Friday, Saturday, and holidays). The campground usually has vacancies except on major holiday weekends. Showers and restrooms close during the off-season, though outhouses are available. A paved four-mile road to the park turns off US 40 just west of Duchesne. Address is Box 584, Duchesne, UT 84021, tel. 738-2326 or (800) 322-3770 (reservations).

Over The Mountains To Price
From Duchesne, US 191 goes southwest 56 miles over the West Tavaputs Plateau to Price.

The route follows the Left Fork of Indian Canyon to a pass at an elevation of 9,100 feet, then descends through Willow Creek Canyon to the Price River. Snow may close the road in winter. **Avintaquin Campground** (elev. 8,800 feet) is reached by a short gravel road from just south of the pass; sites in a fir and aspen forest have water from Memorial Day to one week after Labor Day. Sites may have water and cost $5 (family), $8 (double), and $25 (group sites). The Bamberger Monument, between the pass and Price Canyon, commemorates construction of the highway by state prisoners in 1919; Governor Simon Bamberger gave the workers reduced sentences and other benefits for their efforts.

PRICE

In the beginning, Price was a typical Mormon community. Ranchers and farmers had settled on the fertile land surrounding the Price River in 1879. Four years later, everything changed when the railroad came through. A flood of immigrants from all over the world arrived to work in the coal mines and other rapidly growing enterprises. (An informal census taken in a pool hall at nearby Helper in the 1930s found 32 different nationalities in the room!) Coal mining has had its ups and downs in the last 100 years, but it continues to be the largest industry in the area. Price (pop. 8,712) is a modern city and a good base for exploring the surrounding mountains and desert. The highly recommended Prehistoric Museum and the Price Mural are in town; the Western Mining & Railroad Museum is in Helper to the north. Other places to visit lie tucked into the surrounding backcountry and include Nine Mile Canyon (rock art and historic sites), Cleveland-Lloyd Dinosaur Quarry, San Rafael Swell, and many ghost town sites. Roads wind up canyons to the cool forests and lakes on the Wasatch Plateau. Information and maps for Carbon and Emery counties can be obtained at the Castle Country Travel Office (see "Information" under "Practicalities," below). A walking tour leaflet available at the office describes historic buildings in Price.

saurus. See bones of the huge Huntington Canyon Mammoth recently discovered nearby. Mineralogy exhibits have colorful gemstones. The outstanding Indian collection has artifacts of teh prehistoric Fremont and the modern Ute Indians. The power and mystery of prehistoric rock art is conveyed in a replica of the Barrier Canyon mural. Modern art can be seen too, in rotating exhibits. Kids can explore the hands-on displays in the Children's Room. The College of Eastern Utah operates the museum, 155 E. Main, tel. 637-5060; open Mon.-Sat. (also Sunday in spring and summer) 10 a.m.-5 p.m.; sum-

SIGHTS

Prehistoric Museum

Excellent exhibits of the creatures and people that lived in prehistoric Utah fill the halls. Dramatic dinosaur displays include a fierce flesh-eating allosaurus, a plant-eating camptosaurus (not to be fooled with either), a camarasaurus, a chasmosaurus, a prosaurolophus, and a stego-

prehistoric petroglyph

LOUISE FOOTE

mer hours may be extended; donation. Regional and natural history books, fossils, T-shirts, and postcards are sold.

Price Mural
Artist Lynn Fausett captured the history of Price and Carbon County in a colorful mural four feet high and 200 feet long. It extends around all four walls in the foyer of the Price Municipal Building (enter from the east side). Look straight ahead for panels of the first settlers, Abram Powell and Caleb Rhodes. Follow the panels around to the right, past scenes of railroad workers, freight wagons, the first town hall in Price, religious leaders, the 1911 Fourth of July parade, and depictions of the coal-mining industry. A brochure available here gives details for each scene and identifies the self-portrait of the artist as a small boy. Fausett, a native of the area, used his own recollections and old photos for the project, which he worked on from 1938 to 1941. He also painted the Barrier Canyon mural replica in the Prehistoric Museum and *The Pioneer Trek* at This Is The Place Monument near Salt Lake City. Open Mon.-Fri. 8 a.m.-5 p.m.; free; located at the corner of Main and 200 East.

College Of Eastern Utah (CEU)
The two-year community college began as Carbon Junior College in 1938 and took its present name in 1965. CEU's current enrollment of about 2,300 students meets on a four-quarter system. Most of the facilities, cultural activities, and sporting events are open to the public. The Division of Continuing Education offers a varied program of evening classes. Gallery East hosts state and national art exhibits during the fall to spring quarters in the Main Building; exhibits change monthly. You'll find the bookstore, snack bar, cafeteria, and formal dining room in the Student Activities Center. A variety of concerts, plays, choirs, and ballets takes place on campus; call public relations at 637-2120, ext. 288, for the schedule. The library, located in the middle of campus, has a good collection that includes a set of topo maps covering Utah. Outdoor expeditions organized by the college are often open to the public and include backpacking trips into wilderness areas and river runs on the Green, Colorado, and San Juan

rivers. Each outing emphasizes ecological education; contact Wilderness Studies Director Sara or Eric Ewert at 637-2120, ext. 667 or ext. 609. Sporting events include women's volleyball and basketball and men's basketball and baseball; call 637-1300 for schedules. The Bunnell-Dimitrich Athletic Center (BDAC) has an exercise room, outdoor track, and facilities for aerobics, racquetball, handball, basketball, and volleyball, tel. 637-1300. The College of Eastern Utah is at 451 E. 400 North, Price, UT 84501.

PRACTICALITIES

Accommodations And RV Parks
In order of increasing cost are **Greenwell Inn,** 655 E. Main, tel. 637-3520, $26.15 s, $33.78 d and up; **El Rancho Siesta Motel and RV Park,** W. Main and 145 N. Carbonville Rd., tel. 637-2424, $29.40 s, $34.85 d, RVers pay $14.10 w/hookups, pool; **National 9,** 641 W. Price River Dr. in Creekview Shopping Center, tel. 637-7000, $31.61 s, $37.06 d; **Carriage House Inn,** 590 E. Main, tel. 637-5660 or 800-228-5732 in Utah, $32.70 s, $38.15 d, indoor pool and spa; **Days Inn,** 838 Westwood Blvd., tel. 637-8880 or (800) 325-2525, $53.41 s, $59.95 d and up, indoor pool, sauna, and spa.

Balance Rock Motel is an older place in a quiet canyon just north of Helper (seven miles north of Price), tel. 472-9942, $22 s, $24 d. **National 9** in the town of Wellington, seven miles to the southeast, tel. 637-7980 or (800) 221-2222, $31.61 s, $38.15 d, has an indoor pool; RVers stay for $13.73 w/hookups; a restaurant is open daily for breakfast, lunch, and dinner. **Rock Creek Ranch,** on the remote Tavaputs Plateau, Box 1736, Price, UT 84501, tel. 637-1236, offers packages with accommodations, meals, horseback riding, and jeep tours; guests can also ride with the seasonal cattle drives; open June 1 to September 30.

Food
Ricardo's Restaurant, at the Greenwell Inn, 655 E. Main, tel. 637-2020, serves American and Mexican food daily for breakfast, lunch, and dinner. **Golden Rock Cafe,** at the Days Inn just west of town, tel. 637-8880, offers varied fare including steak, prime rib, seafood, and pasta

daily for breakfast, lunch, and dinner. Some say that the **Matador Steak House**, 355 E. Main, tel. 637-9959, has the best steaks in town; open Mon.-Sat. for dinner. The **Crest Restaurant**, 601 E. Main, tel. 637-0843, is open Sun.-Fri. for breakfast and Mon.-Fri. for lunch. For American fare, try **Mallard's Restaurant**, on the third floor at 11 W. Main (follow the duck footprints from the entrance), tel. 637-7414 is open Mon.-Fri. for lunch and Mon.-Sat. for dinner. **Mecca Cafe**, 71 W. Main is open Mon.-Sat. for breakfast, lunch, and dinner; **Century Cafe**, 57 W. Main, is open Mon.-Sat. for breakfast, lunch, and dinner; and **Coffee Shop**, at Phillips 66, one block north on Carbonville Road from W. Main, is open daily for breakfast, lunch, and dinner.

The **Greek Streak**, 84 S. Carbon Ave., tel. 637-1930, specializes in Greek foods; open Mon.-Sat. for lunch and dinner. **Farlaino's Cafe**, 87 W. Main, tel. 637-9217, serves Italian and American cuisine; open Mon.-Sat. for breakfast and lunch and Wed.-Sat. for dinner. **China City Cafe**, 350 E. Main, tel. 637-8211, features a good selection of Chinese and American items; open daily for lunch and dinner. **El Salto**, 19 S. Carbon Ave., tel. 637-6545, brings south-of-the-border flavor to town; open Mon.-Sat. for lunch and dinner. **Luito's**, 86 E. 100 South, tel. 637-8224, prepares Mexican food Mon.-Fri. for lunch and Mon.-Sat. for dinner. Pick up pizza at **Pizza Hut** on the east edge of town, tel. 637-6410; open daily for lunch and dinner. **Castle Rock Café & Pizza Deli**, on the west edge of town in Creekview Shopping Center, tel. 637-8480, is open daily for breakfast, lunch, and dinner.

Entertainment And Events

Catch movies at the **King Coal Theaters 3**, 1171 E. Main; **Price Theatre**, 30 E. Main; or **Crown Theatre**, 30 W. Main, call 637-1705 for recorded information. The **State Quarter Horse Show** is held in May at the Carbon County Fairgrounds west of town. **Helper Outlaw Day** takes place in June at Helper with games, food, and a car show. **Black Diamond Stampede Rodeo** provides plenty of action in June. A **Demolition Derby** is also held in June. The **Greek Festival** in July features music, dancing, food, and tours of the Greek church. Wellington's **Pioneer Day** (July 24) festivities include a parade,

rodeo, games, and food. **International Days and Carbon County Fair** in August celebrate the area's ethnic diversity with a parade, rodeo, agricultural exhibits, entertainment, contests, and food.

Services

For **emergencies** (police, fire, paramedic), call 911. The **post office** is at the corner of Carbon Ave. and 100 South, tel. 637-1638. **Castleview Hospital** is at 300 N. Hospital Dr. on the west edge of town, tel. 637-4800. **Gart Bros. Sporting Goods** has camping and fishing gear in the Creekview Shopping Center on the west side of town, tel. 637-2077.

Recreation

Washington Park, 250 E. 500 North, tel. 637-7946, has picnic areas, playground, indoor swimming pool, outdoor Desert Wave Pool, tennis, volleyball, basketball, and horseshoe courts. Two historic log cabins dating from the 1880s and a fitness track are across to the north in **Pioneer Park**. **South Price Park** offers a picnic area and tennis courts at 400 South and 100 East. **Carbon Country Club Golf Course** has 18 holes, located four miles north of town on US 6/191, tel. 637-2388.

Information

Castle Country Travel Office offers literature and ideas for travel in Price and elsewhere in Carbon and Emery counties; open Mon.-Fri. 9 a.m.-5 p.m. in the Prehistoric Museum at 155 E. Main (Box 1037, Price, UT 84501), tel. 637-3009 or (800) 464-3790 in Utah. **Manti-La Sal National Forest** Supervisor's and Price District offices, across from the Creekview Shopping Center on the west edge of town (599 W. Price River Dr., Price, UT 84501), tel. 637-2817, have information about recreation in the beautiful alpine country of the Wasatch Plateau to the west; all the Utah forest maps and some regional books are sold; open Mon.-Fri. 8 a.m.-4:30 p.m. (till 5 p.m. in summer). The **Bureau of Land Management** has the Price River Resource Area and San Rafael Resource Area offices in Price, both offices have the same address and phone number: 600 Price River Drive (Price, UT 84501), tel. 637-4584. Staff can tell you about exploring the San Rafael Swell,

Cleveland-Lloyd Dinosaur Quarry, and Nine Mile Canyon, and about boating the Green River through Desolation, Gray, and Labyrinth canyons; land-use maps are sold; open Mon.-Fri. 7:45 a.m.-4:30 p.m. **Price City Library** is next to the Price Municipal Building at 160 E. Main, tel. 637-0744; open Mon.-Fri. in summer and Mon.-Sat. the rest of the year. Bookshops in town include **Walton Books,** 1187 E. Main in Castle Rock Square, tel. 637-8640, and the **Emerald**

Sun Book Store, new and used, 19 E. Main, tel. 637-5510.

Transportation
Greyhound buses travel west daily to Salt Lake City and east to Denver from the stop at Phillips 66, 277 N. Carbonville Rd., tel. 637-3457. **Amtrak** trains stop in nearby Helper on their runs between Denver and Salt Lake City, tel. (800) 872-7245.

NORTH OF PRICE

HELPER

In 1883, the Denver & Rio Grande Western Railroad began a depot, roundhouse, and other facilities here for its new line. Trains headed up the long grade to Soldier Summit needed extra locomotives or "helpers" based at the little railroad community, so the place became known as Helper. Miners later joined the railmen, and the two groups still make up most of the current population of 2,500. The fine examples of early 20th century commercial and residential buildings in downtown Helper have earned its designation as a national historic site. The local economy has suffered downturns from layoffs in the railroad and coal industries, and this is reflected in the many vacant structures awaiting new owners. The Western Mining & Railroad Museum offers a look into the past of Helper and surrounding mining towns. Helper is at the entrance to Price Canyon, seven miles north of Price.

Practicalities

The old hotels and motels downtown may or may not be open—Gone Fishing signs are common in these small municipalities. The Balance Rock Motel just north of town, tel. 472-9942 has rooms at $22 s, $24 d. Places to eat include Helper Newhouse Cafe, downstairs at 190 S. Main, and Jimbo's Steak House, 330 S. Main. The city park has shaded picnic tables, playground, outdoor pool (tel. 472-3329), tennis courts, and a ballpark east across the Price River. The post office is at 45 S. Main. The public library is open weekday afternoons at 19 S. Main. The Amtrak train station is downtown off Main.

Western Mining And Railroad Museum

A venerable red caboose and examples of coal-mining machinery sit outside next to the museum in downtown Helper at 296 S. Main, tel. 472-3009. Inside, you'll see two elaborate model railroad sets and photos of old steam locomotives in action. A mine room has models of coal mines (all are underground in this area) and equipment worn by the miners. Other exhibits illustrate Utah's two great mine disasters, the 1900 Scofield tragedy in which 200 men and boys died, and the 1924 Castle Gate explosion that killed 173. Other bits of history include ghost-town memorabilia, a Butch Cassidy exhibit, and a dentist's office. A company general store exhibit shows items that miners would buy with their company script. The new map room displays original maps showing hundreds of miles of tunnels. Video programs illustrate the area's mine and railroad history. The brick building housing the museum dates from about 1914 when it was the Hotel Helper; from 1942 to 1982 it served as a YMCA for railroad men. Open Tues.-Sat. 11 a.m.-4 p.m. from mid-May to the end of September; donation. It may also be possible to visit on other days; call the phone number posted on the front door.

Ghost Towns

Many coal-mining communities have bloomed and died in surrounding canyons and hillsides. Most have fared poorly since they were abandoned, yet their picturesque ruins can be worth seeking out. The mines and decaying buildings are dangerous and shouldn't be entered—security staff enforces no-trespassing rules. One former company town has survived intact. Kenilworth's residents bought their houses at low prices when the mines closed and have continued to live here; the large company store, however, now stands vacant; follow Helper's Main Street a short way south, then turn left (east) 3.8 miles on paved UT 157. A small Driving Tour Guide book describes coal mines and townsites in Carbon and Emery counties; it's sold at the museum in Helper. Also see the books Utah Ghost Towns by Stephen Carr and Some Dreams Die: Utah's Ghost Towns and Lost Treasures by George Thompson for histories and locations of the towns that have faded away.

Scenic Spring Canyon has some of the best and most easily visited ghost towns. The paved road begins as "Canyon Street" in east Helper (across US 6/191 from downtown Helper). You'll see railroad grades, mines, and ruins along much of the road's 6.7 miles. Sagebrush hides most of the Peerless ghost town site, 2.8 miles in. Only foundations and a few buildings survive from this community, which peaked in the 1920s and '30s with a population of about 300, then died in the '50s. A tramway brought coal down from the mine high on the hillside. Spring Canyon is a total ghost; only a loading platform remains of a community that had up to 1,000 people during the '20s, '30s, and '40s. The site is near a junction 3.8 miles in; keep straight at the junction (the road to the right is still used by mining companies and is gated).

A large concrete loading facility on the right greets you on arrival at Standardville, 4.9 miles in. The formerly attractive, well-planned community had a population of 550 during its best years and set a standard for other mining towns. Mines nearby operated from 1912 until 1950. A ghostly two-story stone building, once the Liberty Fuel Company offices, marks the site of Latuda, 5.9 miles in. Several hundred people lived here from about 1920 to 1950; Latuda died completely in the late 1960s. Extensive ruins of the mine can be seen on the slopes to the left. Only foundations remain from Rains, once a town of 500, located six and one half miles from Helper. A large stone ruin, once a store, stands at the site of Mutual, just beyond Rains. Most of the 250 or so residents lived to the north along a fork of Spring Canyon. You may have to park at the gate and walk a short distance on the road to Mutual.

Price Canyon Recreation Area
This pleasant spot in the woods makes a good stopping place for a picnic or a camp. From the turnoff 8.2 miles north of Helper, follow a narrow paved road three miles to the picnic area (free day use), a canyon overlook, and the campground (elev. 8,000 feet); open with water and a $5 fee from Memorial Day to late October. **Bristlecone Ridge Trail** begins at the far end of the campground loop and winds through a forest of Gambel oak, ponderosa pine, and mountain mahogany to a ridgetop. Grand views from the top take in surrounding mountains and Price and Crandall canyons below. The moderately difficult hike is about two miles roundtrip with an elevation gain of 700 feet. Bristlecone pines and lots of chipmunks live on the ridge.

Scofield State Park
The 3,000-acre reservoir lies in a broad mountain valley at an elevation of 7,600 feet. Anglers go after rainbow and cutthroat trout and crayfish.

victims of the mine disaster, Scofield, 1900

UTAH STATE HISTORICAL SOCIETY

Water-skiers and boaters have lots of room to roam. The main campground is on the east shore with a picnic area, showers, dump station, boat ramp, docks, and fish-cleaning station. Madsen Bay area at the north end, near the turnoff for Mountain View, has a campground, restrooms, fish-cleaning station, and dump station. The Mountain View area on the northwest side of the lake offers picnic and camping areas near a boat ramp and dock. The lake is accessible all year, though the park shuts down off-season; restrooms and showers are open from about early May to late October. In winter, Scofield Reservoir has excellent ice fishing. The State Division of Parks and Recreation grooms snowmobile trails nearby at Pond-Town Canyon (west side of the lake four miles north of the town of Scofield) and Left Fork of Whiteriver (near Soldier Summit). Cross-country skiing in the area is good too, though no facilities or trails have been developed. Entrance fees are $3 day use or $9 camping ($10 Friday, Saturday and holidays); Box 166, Price, UT 84501, tel. 448-9449 during the season, 637-8497 in winter. Call (800) 322-3770 for reservations. The park nearly always has room except during major summer holidays. From Price, drive 23 miles north on US 6, then turn left 13 miles on UT 96. Other approaches are from Provo (66 miles) via Soldier Summit or from UT 31 where it crosses the Wasatch Plateau to the south.

Scofield

Two coal mines operate near this tiny mining town south of Scofield Reservoir. Production began in 1879 and peaked about 1920, when the town had a population of nearly 2,000. Utah's worst mining disaster took place nearby on May 1, 1900, at the Winter Quarters Mine, where about 200 men and boys perished in an explosion of coal dust. Weathered tombstones in the cemetery on the hill east of town still give testimony to the tragedy. A paved road continues south and west from Scofield to UT 31 on the Wasatch Plateau. The **Lazy Anchor Campground,** with hot showers and a laundromat, is open from snowmelt to first winter snows at the edge of town on the road from the lake. Cost is $10 for tent or RV, tel. 448-9697. You can also stay at the **Winter Inn Bed and Breakfast** at the south edge of town, tel. 448-9253, $59.40-64.90 s or d.

Fish Creek

The forest lands surrounding Scofield have plenty of places for dispersed camping. The **Fish Creek Trailhead,** west of the lake, is suitable for primitive camping. This is also the start of the 10-mile **Fish Creek National Recreation Trail.** From Scofield, go northwest 3.7 miles on a partly paved road, then turn left one and one half miles at a fork up Fish Creek Valley. This last section of road is slippery when wet and may be too rough for cars at any time. The easy trail follows the creek through meadows and forests of aspen and evergreens. This is a good area to look for wildlife, including moose, elk, mule deer, black bear, mountain lion, bobcat, and beaver. Fishermen will find many places to cast a line; special fishing regulations (posted) apply in upper Fish Creek. The trail is good for both day and overnight hikes; Skyline Drive is 13 miles upstream.

EAST OF PRICE

Aside from a few ranches and coal mines, the rugged canyon country of the West Tavaputs Plateau remains largely a wilderness. Two especially good areas to visit here are Nine Mile Canyon (accessible by car) and Desolation and Gray canyons of the Green River (accessible by raft or kayak). Adventurous drivers with high-clearance vehicles can explore other places too; ask the BLM staff in Price about the back-country roads.

Nine Mile Canyon Backcountry Byway

A drive through this scenic canyon takes the visitor back in time to when Fremont Indians lived and farmed here, about 900 years ago. Although their pit-house dwellings can be difficult for a non-archaeologist to spot, the granaries and striking rock art stand out clearly. The canyon is especially noted for its abundant petroglyphs and smaller numbers of pictographs. You'll also see several ranches and the ghost town of Harper. Obtain a brochure for Nine Mile Canyon in Price from the Castle Country Tourist Office, Prehistoric Museum, or the BLM offices. The Roosevelt Chamber of Commerce has a less-detailed brochure. Nine Mile Canyon is actually more than 40 miles long; the origin of its misleading name is unclear. The drive is about 120 miles roundtrip from Price and takes most of a day. Another approach is from near Myton in the Uinta Basin via Wells Draw and Gate Canyon. When dry, all of these roads can be negotiated by cars with good clearance; Gate Canyon is the roughest section and may be impassable after storms. In the late 1800s and early 1900s, these roads through Nine Mile Canyon formed the main highway between Vernal and the rest of Utah. Today the distances and dusty roads may discourage the more casual traveler. This region is also fairly remote with no services; bring water, lunch, and a full tank of gas. From Price, drive 10 miles southeast (three miles past Wellington) on US 6/191 and turn north on 2200 East (Soldier Creek Road) at a sign for Nine Mile Canyon. The road passes Soldier Creek Coal Mine after 13 miles (pavement ends), continues climbing to an

aspen-forested pass, then drops into Nine Mile Canyon. Turnoff for the northern approach from US 40 is one and one half miles west of Myton.

Desolation And Gray Canyons
Of The Green River

The Green River leaves the Uinta Basin and slices deeply through the Tavaputs Plateau, emerging 95 miles downstream near the town of Green River. River runners enjoy the canyon scenery, hikes up side canyons, a chance to see wildlife, and visits to Fremont rock-art sites. John Wesley Powell named the canyons in 1869, designating the lower 36 miles as Gray Canyon. Boaters usually start at Sand Wash, the site of a ferry from the early 1920s to 1952;

Gunnison Butte overlooking lower Gray Canyon

a 42-mile road (36 miles are unpaved) south from Myton is the best way in. Another road turns east from Gate Canyon near Nine Mile Canyon. Some people save the long 200-mile car shuttle by flying from the town of Green River to an airstrip on a mesa top above Sand Wash. Swasey Rapids, north of the town of Green River, is the most common takeout point. The last part of Gray Canyon, between Neferti-ti and Swasey rapids, is a good day trip; see "Desolation and Gray Canyons of the Green River," below. Although not as difficult as

Cataract Canyon, Desolation and Gray canyons do have about 60 rapids and riffles, navigable by raft or kayak. Some are Class III and require river-running experience. Contact the BLM Price River Resource Area office in Price, 600 Price River Dr. (Price, UT 84501), tel. 637-4591 (river office), for information and the required permits. Open Mon.-Fri. 7:45 a.m.-4:30 p.m. Commercial trips through the canyons are available; the BLM can give you names of the companies. The *Desolation River Guide* by Laura Evans and Buzz Belknap has maps and descriptions.

SOUTH OF PRICE

CLEVELAND-LLOYD DINOSAUR QUARRY

You can learn more about dinosaurs and see their bones in an excavation here in the desert, 30 miles south of Price. Dinosaurs stalked this land about 147 million years ago, when it had a wetter and warmer climate. Mud in a lake bottom trapped some of the animals and preserved their bones. The mud layer, which later became rock of the Morrison Formation, has yielded more than 12,000 bones of at least 14 different dinosaur species at this site. Local ranchers discovered the bones, then interested the University of Utah, which started digs in 1928. Princeton University and Brigham Young Uni-

versity (which currently does excavations) also have participated in the quarry work.

Visitor Center

The BLM has built the visitor center, quarry exhibits, nature trail, and picnic sites here. Inside the visitor center, you'll see exhibits of the dinosaur family tree, techniques of excavating and assembling dinosaur skeletons, and local flora and fauna. A fierce allosaurus skeleton cast gazes down on you. Related books, postcards, and posters can be purchased. The enclosed dinosaur quarry, about 100 yards behind the visitor center, contains excavation tools and exposed allosaurus, stegosaurus, camptosaurus, and camarasaurus bones. **Rock Walk Nature Trail** begins outside; a brochure

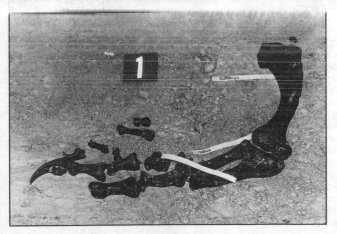

allosaurus arm,
Cleveland-Lloyd
Dinosaur Quarry

available at the start explains about geology, dinosaurs, uranium mining, and the ecology at numbered stops; allow 45 minutes. Usually the quarry can be visited from 10 a.m.-5 p.m. on weekends beginning at Easter, then daily from Memorial Day to Labor Day weekends. Admission is free; tel. 637-4584. The drive in is on graded dirt roads, though rains occasionally close them. From Price, drive south 13 miles on UT 10 and turn left 17 miles on UT 155 and follow the unpaved roads. From Huntington, go northeast two miles on UT 10 and turn right 20 miles on UT 155 and unpaved roads. Signs at the turnoffs from UT 10 indicate the days and hours the quarry is open. If it's closed, there's nothing to see. Visitors are not allowed to collect dinosaur bones at the quarry or on other public lands; bones are of greater scientific value when researchers can examine them in place.

Humbug Overlook Driving Tour
A brochure available at the visitor center describes the plants and animals living in this desert country. The drive begins at the quarry and goes southeast seven miles to the rim of Humbug Canyon. Cars with good clearance can negotiate the road in dry weather. The **Jump Trail** winds from the viewpoint down to the canyon floor, about a half mile one-way.

Look for hoodoos on the canyon walls. They are formed when water erodes rock material, stopping when a hard cap rock is reached. The resulting formation often resembles a mushroom or a human head on a thin neck.

Cedar Mountain Driving Tour
The overlook atop Cedar Mountain has a great panorama to the south across the gently curved dome of the San Rafael Swell and the many canyons cutting into it. Distant ranges include the Wasatch Plateau (west), Thousand Lake Mountains (southwest), Henry Mountains (south), and the Book Cliffs (east). A picnic area is at the second overlook at the end of the drive. **Fossil Ledge Nature Trail** makes a quarter-mile loop from the picnic area. Distances to the second overlook are 39 miles from Price, 27 miles from Huntington, or 25 miles from Cleveland-Lloyd Dinosaur Quarry. A graded dirt road climbs about 2,000 feet in elevation through woodlands of juniper, piñon pine, and pon-

derosa pine. Cars can easily drive the road in dry weather. A brochure describing points of interest along the way is available from the quarry visitor center or the BLM office in Price.

EXPLORING THE SAN RAFAEL SWELL (NORTHERN HALF)

About 65 million years ago, immense underground forces pushed rock layers into a dome about 80 miles long (north to south) and 30 miles wide. Erosion has exposed the colorful layers and cut deep canyons. I-70 divides the swell into roughly equal north and south halves. In the north, a 29-mile scenic drive, passable by cars in dry weather, branches off the road to Cedar Mountain and goes south past the Wedge Overlook, descends through Buckhorn Wash, crosses the San Rafael River, then winds across desert to I-70.

Much of the San Rafael Swell remains wild and remote. Seven sections of it are being considered for wilderness designation. The BLM

San Rafael River, just above the campground

San Rafael River from Wedge Overlook

San Rafael Resource Area office in Price has information about travel and wilderness status in this unique land; the office is at the corner of 900 North and 700 East (Price, UT 84501), tel. 637-4584. Good books for travel and historical background on this little-known region are *Canyoneering the San Rafael Swell* by Steve Allen, *Hiking Utah's San Rafael Swell* by Michael Kelsey, and *Utah's Scenic San Rafael* by Owen McClenahan. Allen's guide has by far the most detailed coverage of drives, hikes, and some rock climbs; Kelsey's book emphasizes history and hiking; while McClenahan's book mostly describes driving tours (about half of which can be done by car).

Wedge Overlook
An inspiring panorama takes in surrounding mountains and canyons and the 1,000-foot sheer drop into the "Little Grand Canyon." Rain and snowmelt on the Wasatch Plateau feed tributaries of the San Rafael River, which has cut this deep canyon through the San Rafael Swell. Downstream from the Little Grand Canyon, the river plunges through narrow canyons of the Black Boxes and flows across the San Rafael Desert to join the Green River. The signed turnoff for Wedge Overlook is on the way to the San Rafael Bridge and Campground; see the Utah Travel Council's Northeastern Utah map for the different approaches from Price (23 miles), Huntington (15 miles), and Castle Dale (13 miles). Drive in 6.6 miles from the turnoff, keeping left at a fork near the beginning, to the

first overlook, then continue to the left 0.9 mile for the best views at the end of the road. This area is fine for picnicking but be sure to drive only on designated roads and camp only in designated campgrounds. Walk along the rim for other views.

San Rafael Campground
Continue 12 miles past the Wedge Overlook turnoff to the bridge and campground at the San Rafael River. The road descends into the main canyon via pretty Buckhorn Wash and crosses the bridge to the camping area. The cottonwood trees at the campground mysteriously died, giving the area a bleak appearance. Tables and outhouses are provided but no water. From here the road continues south 20 miles to I-70 at Ranch Exit 129.

Floating The Little Grand Canyon
The 15-mile trip through this canyon provides one of the best ways to enjoy the scenery. The swift waters have a few riffles and small sand waves, but no rapids. Canoes, kayaks, and rafts can do the excursion in five to six hours with higher spring flows. An overnight trip will allow more time to explore side canyons. Best boating conditions occur during the spring runoff in May and June. Some people float through with inner tubes later in the summer. Life jackets should always be worn. No permits are needed for boating; the BLM in Price can advise on river flows and road conditions. Put-in is at Fuller's Bottom; the turnoff is near the Wedge Overlook

turnoff, then 5.4 miles to the river. Takeout is at the San Rafael Campground. Extremely dangerous rapids and waterfalls lie downstream of the campground in the Black Boxes; *don't* attempt these sections unless you really know what you're doing! Hikers can explore the canyons above and below the campground on day and overnight trips; autumn has the best temperatures and lowest water levels; wear shoes suitable for wading.

CASTLE VALLEY TOWNS

High cliffs of the Wasatch Plateau rise fortress-like to the west above the valley. Perennial streams flowing down the canyons enabled farmers to transform the desert into verdant orchards and fields of crops. Mormon pioneers didn't settle this side of the Wasatch Plateau until the 1870s, long after valleys on the other side of the plateau had been colonized. Water and good land began to run short by the time of the second generation of settlers, and many turned to jobs in nearby coal mines. Roads up the canyons lead to lakes and pretty alpine country.

HUNTINGTON

This small town at the mouth of Huntington Canyon dates from 1878 and has a population of 2,800. **Village Inn Motel** is at 310 S. Main, tel. 687-9888, rooms cost $29.98 s, $32.16 d. **Canyon Rim Cafe** offers fast food on the north edge of town. **Cozy Country Cafe** serves home-style cooking a half mile north of town, tel. 687-9080. It's open Mon.-Sat. for breakfast, lunch, and dinner. The community celebrates **Heritage Days** with a parade and fireworks on July 4. Travelers can turn west from town on paved UT 31 and soon be in the cool forests and meadows of the Wasatch Plateau or head east, to the Cleveland-Lloyd Dinosaur Quarry and the San Rafael Swell.

Huntington State Park
The 250-acre Huntington Reservoir is a popular destination for picnicking, camping, swimming, fishing, and water-skiing. Lots of grass and shade trees and a swimming beach make the park especially enjoyable in summer. Boaters can use the boat ramp and docks. Fishermen catch mostly largemouth bass and bluegill and some trout; crayfishing is good. The campground is open with showers from March to October. Reservations are a good idea for summer weekends. In winter, the park is open for ice-skating and ice fishing. Fees are $3 day use or $9 camping ($10 Friday, Saturday, and holidays). Located one mile north of town on UT 10, Box 1343, Huntington, UT 84528, tel. 687-2491 (ranger) or (800) 322-3770 (reservations).

Huntington Canyon
Highway UT 31 turns west up the canyon from the north edge of town. The giant Huntington power plant looks out of place in the agrarian landscape of the lower canyon. Beyond the power plant, **Bear Creek Campground** offers sites shaded by cottonwoods on the left near Milepost 39 (8.8 miles in from UT 10). It has water and a small charge in summer; elevation is 6,900 feet. The canyon narrows as the road climbs higher and enters groves of spruce, fir, and aspen. **Forks of Huntington Canyon Campground** sits in a side canyon among fir and spruce trees; it has water from early June to mid-September; fee is $5. The turnoff is on the left near Milepost 30 (18 miles in from UT 10); elevation is 7,600 feet. **Left Fork of Huntington Creek National Recreation Trail** begins at the end of the campground road and follows the creek up a pretty canyon. The trail offers easy walking and passes good trout-fishing spots; after four miles it comes to an open valley and connects with a jeep road.

Farther up the highway, **Old Folks Flat Campground** has sites in a spruce and aspen forest on the right; it has water and a $6 charge from mid-June to mid-September. Group sites are available; located between Mileposts 28 and 27 (20.5 miles in from UT 10); elevation is 7,800 feet; reservations can be made by calling (800) 280-CAMP. **Electric Lake** offers rainbow and cutthroat trout fishing; a boat ramp is at the upper (north) end. The turnoff is on the right near Milepost 14 (34 miles in from UT 10), then eight miles in. **Skyline Drive** lies near the top of the plateau amidst expansive meadows and groves of fir and aspen. The junction for Skyline Drive to the south is on the left between Mileposts 14 and 13; the turnoff for Skyline Drive to the north is five miles farther west along the highway. Roads branch off the northern section of Skyline Drive to Gooseberry Campground (one and one half miles), Flat Campground (four and one half miles), Electric Lake (six miles), and Scofield (17 miles). **Gooseberry Campground** is near Lower Gooseberry Reservoir; take the north Skyline Drive turnoff and follow signs one and one half miles; sites are open with water and a $5 fee from about mid-June to mid-September. Elevation is 8,400 feet. **Flat Canyon Campground** also provides a good base for fishing lakes of the high country; campsites are reached by a five and one half-mile paved road from the north Skyline Drive turnoff; open with water and a $6 fee from about mid-June to mid-September; elevation is 8,800 feet; reservations can be made by calling (800) 280-CAMP. From the campground, Boulger Reservoir is a quarter mile away, Electric Lake is two miles, and Beaver Dam Reservoir is two miles.

Other forest roads branch off the highway to more reservoirs and scenic spots; see the Manti La Sal Forest map available from the Sanpete, Ferron, and Price ranger districts. Highway UT 31 continues 10 miles down the other side of the plateau to Fairview on US 89. Snowplows keep UT 31 open in winter, though drivers must have snow tires or carry chains from November 1 to March 31. Snowmobilers can use groomed trails on the plateau.

CASTLE DALE

The story goes that after founding the community in 1877, citizens applied for a post office for their town of Castle Vale, but the name was recorded wrong. Because they couldn't agree on which side of Cottonwood Creek to settle, two towns grew up here—Castle Dale (current pop. 1,704) on the north side and Orangeville (current pop. 1,459) on the south. Castle Dale has a good historical museum and is the seat of Emery County. A memorial in front of the courthouse honors the 27 miners who died nearby in the Wilberg Coal Mine fire on December 19, 1984.

Emery County Pioneer Museum
Period rooms show life in the early days of Castle Valley settlements: a schoolroom, lawyer's office, country store, and kitchen. Pioneer rooms have farm and coal-mining tools and memorabilia of one-time outlaw Matt Warner. An art gallery exhibits local works. It's open Mon.-Sat. 10 a.m.-4 p.m. weekdays and 1-4 p.m Saturday all year; donations requested. It's located at 93 E. 100 North in the Castle Dale City Hall, one block north of the courthouse at 100 North and 100 East, tel. 381-5154.

Museum Of The San Rafael
This new facility is located at 64 N. 100 East, diagonally across the street from the courthouse. Exhibits include a paleontology room with life-size skeletons of dinosaurs including a 22-foot allosaurus. The dinosaurs displayed include only those species that have been found in Emery County. There are also exhibits of the prehistoric Fremont and Anasazi Indians including a rabbit-fur robe, pottery, baskets, tools, jewelry, and the famous Sitterud Bundle (bowmaker's kit). Admission is free, but donations are requested. Museum hours are 10 a.m.-4 p.m. weekdays and 1-4 p.m. Saturday, tel. 381-5252.

Practicalities
Village Inn Motel, 375 E. Main, tel. 381-2309 has rooms for $29.98 s, $32.16 d. **Big Moma's Pizza and Deli,** 340 E. Main, tel. 381-5080, offers pizza, spaghetti, and sandwiches Mon.-Sat. for lunch and dinner. The **K Bar K Cafe,** 41 W. Main, tel. 381-5474, serves American fare, open Mon.-Sat. for breakfast, lunch, and dinner.

Pioneer Day (July 24) is celebrated with a parade, rodeo, and games. **Castle Valley Pageant,** held in late July or early August, recounts the faith and trials of the pioneers who settled here; the pageant takes place on a hillside a short drive from town. The **Emery County Fair** is also in August; horse races are run in Ferron to the south, while the horse show, parade, and most exhibits are in Castle Dale.

The indoor **swimming pool** is open May to September; next to the city hall (one block north of the courthouse). The **city park,** between the courthouse and city hall, has covered picnic tables. Castle Dale's **library** is open Mon.-Fri. 11 a.m.-6 p.m., next door to the city hall.

Castle Valley Pageant

The High Country West Of Castle Dale

Head northwest from town toward Joes Valley Reservoir on the paved road along Cottonwood Creek. After about 10 miles you'll reach a fork; an unpaved road turns right (north) along Cottonwood Creek to Upper Joes Valley (10 miles). The main road (UT 29) enters Straight Canyon. Seely Creek below the dam in Straight Canyon has good fishing for German brown trout. Joes Valley Reservoir covers 1,170 acres in a large valley at the upper end of Straight Canyon, 16 miles from Castle Dale. A road turns off the highway at the north end of the lake and goes north to **Indian Creek Campground** (nine miles) and UT 31 (21 miles). Indian Creek Campground is open with water from late June to mid-September and a $5 fee; sites should be reserved at the Ferron Ranger District office; elevation is 9,000 feet. This campground is designed for groups but individuals are allowed to stay at unoccupied sites.

Joes Valley Campground has two sections on the west shore of the reservoir; they have water from mid-May to mid-September and a $6 fee. One loop stays open all year (no water or charge off-season); elevation is 7,100 feet.

Reservations can be made by calling (800) 280-CAMP. **Joes Valley Marina,** about 20 miles west of Castle Dale, tel. 381-2453, offers boat slips, rentals (fishing boats w/motors, rowboats, and paddle boats), a cafe (breakfast, lunch, and dinner daily), a campground, and a small store; open mid-May to early November. Anglers catch rainbow and cutthroat trout in the lake. Lowry Fork to the north has good trout fishing in the spring. Water-skiing is popular on the lake, but winds are too erratic for reliable sailing. Pavement ends after the turnoff for Joes Valley Campground. A forest road continues west and climbs 13 miles to Skyline Drive (elev. 10,200 feet) at the top of the Wasatch Plateau. The clay road surface is usually fine for cars in dry weather but treacherously slippery when wet for *any* vehicle. The road from Castle Dale to the reservoir is kept open in winter for ice fishing and snowmobile access.

North Dragon Road turns south between the two sections of Joes Valley Campground and goes about 15 miles to a spectacular overlook above Castle Dale; the San Rafael Swell and distant Henry, La Sal, and Abajo mountains can be seen on a clear day; the road is unpaved (high-clearance vehicles recommended).

FERRON

The town's name honors a surveyor who visited the valley in preparation for Mormon settlement. Millsite State Park and Ferron Reservoir are on a scenic road that connects Ferron with Skyline Drive. **Castle Country Motel** is on highway UT 10, tel. 384-2311, with rooms at $24.90 s, $27.40 d. The motel has a small cafe. Ferron (pop. 1,606) celebrates its pioneer heritage in September during **Peach Days** with horse races, a demolition derby, games, craft exhibits, a dance, and fireworks. The **Southeastern Utah Junior Livestock Show** takes place in July. The **Ferron Ranger District** office on the main highway, Box 310, Ferron, UT 84523, tel. 384-2372, can help you plan a trip to the Wasatch Plateau. Open Mon.-Fri. 8 a.m.-noon and 12:30-4:30 p.m.

Canyon Road To Skyline Drive

Turn west on Canyon Road beside the Ferron Ranger District office for a trip to Millsite State Park and the high county of the Wasatch Plateau. **Millsite State Park** is four miles from town at an elevation of 6,200 feet. The 450-acre Millsite Reservoir is about twice the size of Huntington Reservoir and has the area's best sailing conditions and the most space for water-skiing. Fishermen come to catch rainbow, cutthroat, and German brown trout. Ice fishing is done in winter. The park has picnic grounds, campground with showers (March-Oct.), boat ramp, and dock. Facilities, except for showers, stay open all year. Day use of the park costs $3, camping $9 ($10 Friday, Saturday, and holidays); tel. 384-2552 (ranger), 687-2491 (Huntington State Park) or (800) 322-3770 (reservations).

Millsite Golf Course, adjacent to the park, features nine challenging holes. Off-road vehicles are popular in the barren countryside near the reservoir; tel. 384-2887.

Pavement ends past the state park, but a fairly good gravel road, narrow and winding in places, continues high into the mountains. Stop at **Ferron Canyon Overlook** (14 miles from town) for a panorama of Millsite Reservoir, surrounding mountains and valleys, and the San Rafael Swell. Signs point out features and geology; elevation here is 8,200 feet. The road continues climbing to alpine country with pretty lakes and groves of fir and aspen.

Ferron Reservoir (28 miles from town) is the largest of the high-country lakes (57 acres). The forest service campground is open from mid-June to mid-September with water and a $5 fee; elevation is 9,400 feet. **Sky Haven Lodge** on the lake offers cabins, a small cafe (breakfast, lunch, and dinner daily), a small store, and boat rentals (with or without motors). Horseback rides and guided pack trips can be arranged. The road to Ferron Reservoir is open for vehicles

Wasatch Plateau from Skyline Drive, west of Ferron

only from about mid-June to late September, but the lodge plans to stay open in winter and organize snowmobile transportation. Skyline Drive is only two miles beyond Ferron Reservoir. Turn north on the drive to a fine view of the reservoir and canyon to the east and valleys near Manti to the west. The highest point on Skyline Drive, at 10,897 feet, is just 0.8 mile beyond the viewpoint. **Twelve Mile Flat Campground,** the only

one actually on Skyline Drive, is open with water from about mid-June to late September; $5. Elevation is 9,800 feet; it's about one and one half miles south of the Ferron road junction.

For additional information about outdoor activities in the area, and to buy books and maps, consult the U.S. Forest Service office at 115 West Canyon Road (Ferron, UT 84523), tel. 384-2372/2505.

Pink Cliffs of the Paunsaugunt Plateau

SOUTHWESTERN UTAH

INTRODUCTION

Visitors to Utah's "Dixie" enjoy marvelous scenery and a warm winter sun. The region's climate and varied terrain make it ideal for year round outdoor recreation. You can hike through serpentine canyons or flower-filled meadows, hit the slopes at the Brian Head ski area, glide on cross-country skis across a high plateau, explore the desert, or play a leisurely round of golf.

THE LAND

The Mohave Desert, Great Basin, and Colorado Plateau meet here to create a unique combination of climates and ecosystems. Plants and wildlife normally found only in Arizona and Southern California live in the arid plains and rocky ranges of the desert. The lofty cliffs of the Colorado Plateau rise east of the desert country with some of the most spectacular scenery on earth—the grandeur and colors have to be seen to be believed. Great faults break the Colorado Plateau into a staircase of lesser plateaus across southern Utah and into northern Arizona Angular features of cliffs and canyons dominate the landscape. Volcanic cones and lava flows have broken through the surface, some in geologically recent times. Elevations range from 2,350 feet at Beaver Dam Wash to 11,307 feet atop Brian Head Peak.

Climate

No matter what the season is, you can nearly always find pleasant temperatures in some part of the region. Ever since Brigham Young built a winter house at St. George to escape the cold and snow, people have been coming to take advantage of the mild climate. Midwinter temperatures at St. George (elev. 2,880 feet) may drop below freezing at night, but days are typically in the middle to upper 50s with bright sunshine. Spring and autumn bring ideal weather.

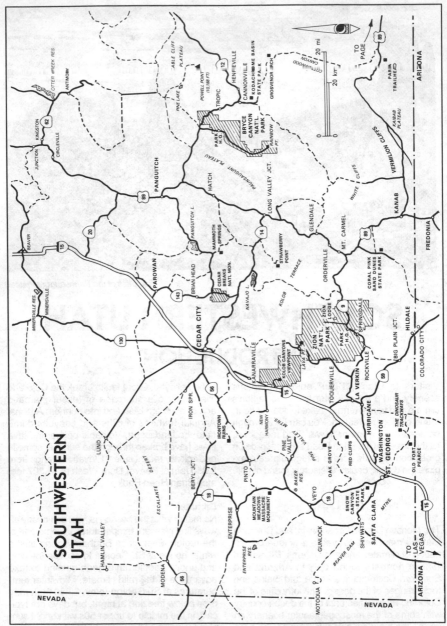

SOUTHWESTERN UTAH

© MOON PUBLICATIONS, INC.

Summer, when the highs often top 100° F, is the time to head for the mountains and high plateaus. The alpine meadows and cool forests of the Beaver Dam Mountains, Cedar Breaks National Monument, and Bryce Canyon National Park provide a welcome refuge from summer heat. Precipitation ranges widely from place to place and from year to year, though most falls in winter/early spring and in late summer. Annual precipitation averages 10.4 inches in St. George and more than 20 inches in the high country.

FLORA AND FAUNA

The land provides habitats for a great variety of plant and animal species. Sparse desert vegetation consists largely of big sagebrush, rabbitbrush, bitterbrush, blackbrush, yucca, cacti, and grasses. The distinctive Joshua tree, a member of the lily family, grows in the extreme southwestern corner of the state. Perennial streams support cottonwood, willow, velvet and singleleaf ash, tamarisk, rushes, and sedges. Creatures of the desert include the chuckwalla, Gila monster (a poisonous lizard), California king snake, and roadrunner. Above about 4,000 feet, woodlands of piñon pine and Utah juniper take over from the desert; you'll often find cliffrose, Utah serviceberry, live oak, and Gambel oak here too. At about 7,000-8,000 feet, ponderosa pine, Gambel oak, and Rocky Mountain juniper are common. Thriving in the cool mountain air above 8,000 feet are Douglas fir, subalpine fir, Engelmann spruce, aspen, and wildflowers. Larger wildlife, such as mule deer, elk, mountain lion, and coyote, migrate with the seasons between the high and low country. More than 200 bird species have been spotted in the region. Raptors include bald and golden eagles, redtailed and Cooper's hawks, peregrine and prairie falcons, and the American kestrel.

HISTORY

The Indians
Beginning about 15,000 years ago, groups of Paleo-Indians wandered across the region to hunt and gather wild plants. Only scant evidence remains of their long stay here. The more sophisticated Anasazi and Fremont cultures emerged about A.D. 500 with newly acquired agriculture. Their corn, beans, and squash enabled them to be less reliant on migration and to construct year-round village sites. Although both groups developed crafts such as basketry, pottery, and jewelry, only the Anasazi progressed to the construction of masonry buildings in their villages. The Fremont ranged across present-day central Utah, while the Anasazi stayed in what are now southern Utah and adjacent states. The Fremont and Anasazi mysteriously abandoned their Utah villages during the 1200s. Archaeologists have traced the Anasazi to modern pueblo tribes in Arizona and New Mexico but don't know what became of the Fremont.

Nomadic bands of Southern Paiutes, possible descendants of the Paleo-Indians, inhabited the region when the first white men came. The Paiutes befriended and guided the early explorers and settlers, but troubles soon began when the Indians saw their lands taken over by farmers and ranchers. Unable to maintain their old lifestyle or defeat the newcomers, the Indians settled near the white men's towns. They now have the Shivwits Reservation northwest of St. George and the Kaibab-Paiute Reservation in Arizona southwest of Kanab.

Explorers And Colonizers
In 1776, Spanish explorers of the Dominguez-Escalante expedition were the first white men to visit and describe the region. They had given up partway through a proposed journey from Santa Fe to California and returned to Santa Fe along a route passing through the sites of present-day Cedar City and Hurricane. In the first half of the 19th century, mountain men like Jedediah Smith and government surveyors such as John C. Fremont explored the land and learned about the Indians. In 1849-50, Mormon leaders in Salt Lake City took the first steps in colonizing the region when they sent an advance party led by Parley P. Pratt. Encouraging reports of rich iron ore west of Cedar Valley and of fertile land along the Virgin River convinced the Mormons to expand southward. Calls went out for members to establish missions and to mine the iron ore and supply iron products needed for the expanding Mormon empire. Parowan, now a sleepy community along I-15, became the first settlement and

Cedar City the second, both established in 1851. In 1855, a successful experiment in growing cotton along Santa Clara Creek, near present-day St. George, aroused considerable interest among the Mormons. New settlements soon arose in the Virgin River Valley. However, poor roads hindered development of the cotton and iron industries, most of which ended when cheaper products began arriving on the transcontinental railroad. Floods, droughts, disease, and hostile Indians discouraged some of Dixie's pioneers, but many of those who stayed prospered by raising food crops and livestock. The past 20 years have brought rapid growth to the region in the form of new industries, tourism, and retirement communities.

William Carter behind his plow at St. George, January 19, 1893. Carter plowed the first furrows at Salt Lake City on July 23, 1847.

CHURCH OF JESUS CHRIST OF LATTER-DAY SAINTS

ST. GEORGE

Southern Utah's largest town lies between lazy bends of the Virgin River on one side and rocky hills of red sandstone on the other. In 1861, more than 300 Mormon families in the Salt Lake City area answered the call to go south to start the Cotton Mission, of which St. George became the center. The settlers overcame great difficulties to farm and to build an attractive city in this remote desert. Brigham Young chose the city's name to honor George A. Smith, who had served as head of the Southern (Iron) Mission during the 1850s. (The title "Saint" means simply that he was a Mormon, a Latter-day Saint.) Visits to some of the historic sites will add to your appreciation of the city's past; ask for the brochure. Try the *St. George Historic Walking Tour,* at the chamber of commerce. The warm climate, dramatic setting, and many year-round recreation opportunities have helped make St. George (pop. 36,000) the fastest-growing city in the state. Local boosters claim that this is where Utah's summer sun spends the winter.

SIGHTS

St. George Temple
Visible for miles, the gleaming white temple rises from landscaped grounds in the center of St. George. In 1871, enthusiastic Mormons from all over the territory gathered to erect the temple. Dedicated on April 6, 1877, the structure was the church's first sacred house of worship in the West. The St. George Temple is the oldest active Mormon temple in the world. It's constructed of stuccoed stone in a castellated Gothic Revival style; a cupola with a weather vane caps the structure. Sacred ceremonies take place inside, so no tours are offered. But you're welcome to visit the grounds to admire the architecture. The temple is especially impressive at night when it's lit up against the black sky. A visitor center on the northeast corner of the grounds has short films and videos introducing the Mormon religion; it's open daily 9 a.m.-9 p.m. (8 a.m.-10 p.m. in summer). The visitor center and temple are at the corner of 400 East and 200 South, tel. 673-5181.

St. George Tabernacle
When Brigham Young visited the Cotton Mission after its first year, he found the community afflicted with difficulties and low morale. Soon after, he ordered construction of a tabernacle to help rally the members. The task, paid for with tithing revenues, took 13 years to complete. Builders used local red sandstone for the walls, and placed a slender white steeple on the roof, reminiscent of a New England church. Tour guides explain some of the tabernacle's history and construction details. The 20-minute film, *Windows of Heaven,* shown on request, dramatizes the revelation received here in 1899 by Church President Lorenzo Snow. Guides offer free tours daily about 9 a.m.-6 p.m.; occasional concerts (free) and other presentations take place too. The tabernacle is downtown at Main and Tabernacle streets, tel. 628-4072.

DUP Pioneer Museum
Drop in to see hundreds of pioneer portraits and the tools and clothing used by early settlers. The spinning wheels and looms on display served in the mission's cotton and silk industries. Open Mon.-Sat. 10 a.m.-5 p.m.; donation. The museum, staffed by the Daughters of the Utah Pioneers, is at 145 N. 100 East, behind the old county courthouse, tel. 628-7274.

Brigham Young Winter Home
Late in life, Brigham Young sought relief from rheumatism and other aches and pains by

Anasazi bowl found near St. George

BUREAU OF AMERICAN ETHNOLOGY

ST. GEORGE

1. Bluff Street Park
2. Bureau of Land Management offices
3. Brigham Young Winter Home
4. post office
5. St. George Chamber of Commerce; DUP Pioneer Museum
6. Pioneer Park
7. Greene Gate Village
8. St. George Tabernacle; Washington County Library
9. Vernon Worthen Park
10. St. George Temple
11. Dixie Regional Medical Center
12. swimming pool
13. Commercial Center
14. J.C. Snow Park
15. Pine Valley Ranger District office (USFS)
16. Dixie Center
17. Red Cliffs Mall

TO SNOW CANYON, VEYO, GUNLOCK RESERVOIR, AND PINE VALLEY MTNS.

DIXIE RED HILLS GOLF COURSE

SUNSET BLVD.

TO JACOB HAMBLIN HOME, SNOW CANYON, AND GUNLOCK RESERVOIR

600 NORTH
500 NORTH
400 NORTH
DIAGONAL ST.
400 WEST
300 WEST
200 WEST
200 NORTH
ST. GEORGE BLVD.
TABERNACLE ST.
100 SOUTH
200 SOUTH
300 SOUTH
400 SOUTH
100 WEST
MAIN ST.
100 EAST
200 EAST
700 SOUTH
300 EAST
400 EAST
900 SOUTH
800 EAST
900 EAST
1000 EAST

SKYLINE DR.

INDUSTRIAL RD.
HIGHLAND DR.
RED CLIFFS DR.

TWIN LAKES GOLF COURSE

EXIT 8

TO WASHINGTON, ZION N.P. AND CEDAR CITY

DIXIE COLLEGE

0   0.5 mi
0   0.5 km

AIRPORT DR.
AIRPORT
BLUFF ST.

INDIAN HILLS DR.
SANTA CLARA RIVER

HILTON DR.
EXIT 6

VIRGIN RIVER

RIVER RD.

TO DINOSAUR TRACKWAYS AND OLD FORT PEARCE

ST. GEORGE GOLF COURSE

TO VIRGIN RIVER GORGE AND LAS VEGAS

TONAQUINT DR.
SOUTHGATE GOLF COURSE

© MOON PUBLICATIONS, INC.

1. Greenshow of the Utah Shakespearean Festival, Cedar City; **2.** Greek Festival, Salt Lake City; **3.** Wayne County Fair exhibits, Loa; **4.** summer ski jump practice at the Utah Winter Sports Park (photo by Robert Blake); **5.** rodeo action at Utah State Fair, Salt Lake City; **6.** rafting through Red Canyon, Flaming Gorge National Recreation Area (all photos by Bill Weir except where noted)

MOUNT TIMPANOGOS
1. waterfall in Primrose Cirque; 2. summit view east to Deer Creek Reservoir and Heber City;
3. meadows and wildflowers above Primrose Cirque (all photos by Bill Weir)

mural detail on the
Fine Arts Building at
Dixie College

spending winters in Dixie's mild climate. This also gave him an opportunity to supervise more closely the affairs of the church here, especially construction of the temple. A telegraph line connected Young's house with Salt Lake City. He moved here late in 1873 and returned each winter until his death in 1877. The carefully restored adobe house contains furnishings of the era, including some that belonged to Young. Fruit and mulberry trees grow in the yard; mulberry leaves once fed the silkworms of a short-lived pioneer industry. Free tours begin at Young's office on the east side of the house. Open daily 9 a.m. (8 a.m. in summer) until about sunset; on 200 North between Main and 100 West, tel. 673-2517.

Jacob Hamblin Home
No one did more to extend the Mormons' southern settlements and keep peace with the Indians than Jacob Hamblin. He came west in 1850 with four children (his first wife refused to come) and settled in the Tooele area with wife number two. At Brigham Young's request, Hamblin moved to the south in 1856 and helped build the Santa Clara Fort. He built the present sandstone house after floods washed away the fort in 1862. Almost always on the move serving on missions, Hamblin had little time for home life. He moved to Kanab in 1870, then south to Arizona and New Mexico. Even so, he had four wives (never more than two at a time) and managed to father 24 children. The kitchen, work areas, and living rooms provide a good idea of what pioneer life was like. Free tours offer a

view of the house and tell of activities that once took place here. Open daily 9 a.m. until about sunset, tel. 673-2161. Located in the village of Santa Clara, four miles northwest of St. George.

Dixie College
A giant "D" on a hillside to the west watches over the "Home of the Rebels" and the surrounding town. The school began in 1911 as the St. George Stake Academy, founded by the Mormon Church. Later the name was changed to Dixie Normal School, then to Dixie Junior College, and finally to the present name in 1970. Dixie College is a two-year community college now run by the state. The approximately 3,100 students and 100 faculty meet on a four-quarter system. Visitors are welcome to attend cultural and sporting events and to use many of the facilities. The Fine Arts Building (700 East and 100 South) has exhibits inside, but you'll find the biggest work outside on the south wall. A mosaic more than 15 feet high and 127 feet long depicts the region's history from the days of the Fremont Indians to Mormon settlement. To find out what's going on at Dixie College, visit the Administration Building (700 East and 200 South) or call 628-3121 (student productions in the Fine Arts Theater); 673-4811, ext. 276 or 352 (Celebrity Concert Series Oct.-April), or 673-4811, ext. 383 (sporting events). The library is open during the main terms Mon.-Fri. 8 a.m.-10 p.m., Saturday 10 a.m.-5 p.m., and Sunday 1-8 p.m.; ext. 201. Recreation facilities open to the public include a swimming pool,

ST. GEORGE ACCOMMODATIONS
Add 9% tax to all prices; rates listed are for 1-2 persons

Ancestor Inn (Budget Motel); 60 W. St. George Blvd.; $34-42; tel. 673-4666 or (800) 864-6882; sauna, pool

Bluffs Motel; 1140 S. Bluff St.; $39-79; tel. 628-6699; kitchens, pool, spa

Desert Edge Inn; 525 E. St. George Blvd.; $29-35; tel. 673-6137; kitchens, pool

Budget 8 Motel; 1230 S. Bluff St.; $30-42; tel. 628-5234 or (800) 275-3494; kitchens, pool, spa

Budget Inn; 1221 S. Main; $40-45; tel. 673-6661 or (800) 929-0790; pool, spa, Continental breakfast

Chalet Motel; 664 E. St. George Blvd.; $30-40; tel. 628-6272; kitchens, pool

Claridge Inn; 1187 S. Bluff St.; $34-46; 673-7222 or (800) 367-3790; pool, spa

Comfort Inn; 999 E. Skyline Dr.; $38-52; tel. 628-4271 or (800) 221-2222; pool

Comfort Suites; 1239 S. Main; $64-69; tel. 673-7000 or (800) 245-8602; suites, pool, spa

Coral Hills (Best Western); 125 E. St. George Blvd.; $48-55; tel. 673-4844 or (800) 542-7733; pools, spas

Coronada Family Inn; 559 E. St. George Blvd.; $46-56; tel. 628-4436 or (800) 548-6007; kitchens, pool

Days Inn & Four Seasons Convention Center; 747 E. St. George Blvd.; $32-49; tel. 673-6111 or (800) 635-4441; suites, pool, spa, tennis, Continental breakfast

Days Inn South; 1165 S. Bluff St.; $35-49; tel. 628-4481 or (800) 231-4488; pool, spa, sauna

Desert Edge Inn; 525 E. St. George Blvd.; $30-35; tel. 673-6137; kitchens, pool

Diamond Valley Guest Ranch; 9 miles north on UT 18; $35-55; tel. 574-2281; horseback riding

Dixie Palms Motel; 185 E. St. George Blvd.; $23-26; tel. 673-3531; use of pool

Green Valley Resort (condominiums); 1515 W. Canyon View Dr.; $110-190; tel. 628-8060 or (800) 237-1068; pools, spa, tennis, racquetball; weight room

Greene Gate Village Bed & Breakfast Inn; 76 W. Tabernacle; $45-110; tel. 628-6999 or (800) 350-6999; pool, spa

Hilton Inn of St. George; 1450 S. Hilton Inn Dr.; $79-89; tel. 628-0463 or (800) 445-9667; pool, sauna, tennis

Holiday Inn; 850 S. Bluff St.; $67-75; tel. 628-4235 or (800) 457-9800; rec. area, pool, spa

Holiday Resort Realty; 141 Brigham Rd. #A; $67-160; tel. 673-6172; golf, tennis, pool, condos

Motel 6; 205 N. 1000 E. (Exit 8); $30-36; tel. 628-7979; pool

National 9 Inn (Regency Inn); 770 E. St. George Blvd.; $30-37; tel. 673-6119 or (800) 524-9999; pool, spa, sauna

Oasis Motel; 231 W. St. George Blvd.; $24-29; tel. 673-3551; kitchens, pool

Ramada Inn; 1440 E. St. George Blvd. (E of I-15 Exit 8); $59-135; tel. 628-2828 or (800) 228-2828; pool, spa, Continental breakfast

Ranch Inn; 1040 S. Main; $36-52; tel. 628-8000 or (800) 332-0400; kitchens, pool, spa

Red Cliffs Inn; I-15 Exit 10; $28-43; tel. 673-3537 or (800) 755-6755; pool

Red Mesa Motel; 247 E. St. George Blvd.; $26-28.50; tel. 673-3163; kitchens, pool

Regency Inn; 770 E. St. George Blvd.; $30-37; tel. 673-6119 or (800) 626-5810; kitchens, pool, spa, sauna

Sands Motel; 581 E. St. George Blvd.; $39-49; tel. 673-3501; pool

Seven Wives Inn Bed & Breakfast; 217 N. 100 West; $45-100; tel. 628-3737 or (800) 600-3737; pool

Singletree Inn; 260 E. St. George Blvd.; $44-54; tel. 673-6161 or (800) 528-8890; pool, spa

South Side Inn; 750 E. St. George Blvd.; $30-42; tel. 628-9000; pool, spa

Sullivan's Rococo Inn; 511 S. Airport Rd.; $35-45; tel. 628-3671; pool, jacuzzi

Sun Time Inn; 420 E. St. George Blvd.; $32-36; tel. 673-6181 or (800) 237-6253; kitchens, pool

Super 8 Motel; 915 S. Bluff St.; $38-43; tel. 628-4251 or (800) 800-8000; pool

Thunderbird Inn (Best Western); 150 N. 1000 East; $38-45; tel. 673-6123 or (800) 527-6543; pool, spa, sauna

ST. GEORGE ACCOMMODATIONS
(continued)

Travel Inn (Best Western); 316 E. St. George Blvd.; $42-45; tel. 673-3541 or (800) 528-1234; pool, spa

Travelodge East; 175 N. 1000 East; $41-44; tel. 673-4621 or (800) 255-3050; pool

Western Safari Motel; 310 W. St. George Blvd.; $21-24; tel. 673-5238; kitchens

Weston Inn; 460 E. St. George Blvd.; 30-35; tel. 673-4861; pool, spa

basketball court, and weight room at Dixie Center, and handball, tennis, and a jogging track at Hansen Stadium; both Dixie Center and Hansen Stadium are near the corner of 700 East and 400 South. The Student Union in the center of the campus has a cafeteria and snack bar; get your Dixie Rebels clothing and souvenirs at the bookstore. Visitors may park at the southeast corner of 700 East and 100 South (near the Fine Arts Building), along the west side of the gymnasium (700 East and 300 South), or on streets off campus. Mailing address is St. George, UT 84770.

PRACTICALITIES

St. George has a large number of places to stay and eat. Motel prices stay about the same year-round, though they may drop if business is slow in summer. Most are along the I-15 business route of St. George Blvd. (Exit 8) and Bluff St. (Exit 6). You'll find almost every fast-food place known to modern man just off the interstate on St. George Boulevard.

Campgrounds

Snow Canyon State Park has a campground with showers open all year in a pretty canyon setting; go 12 miles north on UT 18, then left two miles, tel. 628-2255 or (800) 322-3770 (reservations), $9 or $11 w/hookups ($1 more Friday, Saturday, or holidays), see "Vicinity of St. George," below. Closer to town are **St. George Campground & RV Park,** 2100 E. Middleton Dr., I-15 Washington Exit 10, tel. 673-2970, with

pool, laundry, and showers, $10.90 tent, $14.17 RV no hookups, $15.26 RV w/hookups; **Temple View RV Resort,** 975 S. Main, tel. 673-6400, with pool, laundry, and showers, $16.30 tent or RV no hookups, $19.57 RV w/hookups; **Redlands RV Park,** I-15 Washington Exit 10, tel. 673-9700, with pool, store, laundry, and showers, $15 tent, $19.35 RV w/hookups; **Settlers RV Park,** 1333 E. 100 South, near I-15 Exit 8, tel. 628-1624, with pool and showers, $14.17 RV no hookups, $18 RV w/hookups; **Hillside Palms RV Park,** 175 N. 600 East, tel. 673-2102/2809, $12 w/hookups, no showers, no tents; **The Palms RV Resorts,** 150 N. 3050 East, I-15 Washington Exit 10, tel. 628-2371, with pool, spa, sauna, and other recreational facilities, $16.75 RV w/hookups no tents; and **Valley View RV Park,** 2300 E. Middleton Dr., I-15 Washington Exit 10, tel. 673-3367, with showers, $10.90 RV no hookups, $16.35 RV w/hookups, no tents.

Food

For American and Continental food: **Basila's Greek Cafe** prepares Greek cuisine at 2 W. St. George Blvd. in Ancestor Square, tel. 673-7671, open Tues.-Sat. for lunch and dinner. **Dick's Cafe,** 114 E. St. George Blvd., tel. 673-3841, has been serving customers since 1935; open daily for breakfast, lunch, and dinner. **Andelin's Gable House,** 290 E. St. George Blvd., tel. 673-6796, presents elegant a la carte and three- and five-course dinners (reservations advised for multi-course dinners); open Mon.-Sat. for breakfast, lunch, and dinner. **Golden Corral Family Steak House,** 350 E. St. George Blvd., tel. 673-4213, is open daily for lunch and dinner. **Sizzler,** 405 E. St. George Blvd., tel. 628-1313, has an informal atmosphere for steak and seafood; open daily for lunch and dinner. **Rene's Restaurant,** at Weston Inn, 430 E. St. George Blvd., tel. 628-9300, serves American food and pasta dishes daily for breakfast, lunch, and dinner. The **McGuire's** varied menu includes Italian specialties at 531 N. Bluff St., tel. 628-4066, open Mon.-Sat. for dinner. The **San Franciscan Bakery Cafe,** 968 E. St. George Blvd., tel. 674-2800, serves pastry breakfasts and sandwich lunches Mon.-Saturday. The **Shed Restaurant** at the Four Seasons Inn, 747 E. St. George Blvd., tel. 673-7800, has steak, seafood, and other fine dining daily for dinner. **Shoney's**

Family Restaurant, 1410 E. St. George Blvd. (just east of I-15 Exit 8), tel. 628-8177, offers a breakfast bar and a salad bar with its American food; open daily for breakfast, lunch, and dinner. The Palms in the Holiday Inn, 850 S. Bluff St., tel. 628-4235, features steak, prime rib, and seafood dinners and a Sunday brunch; open daily for breakfast, lunch, and dinner. Tony Roma's Restaurant, 1450 Hilton Inn Dr. (off S. Bluff), tel. 628-0463, features prime rib and other fine dining in the Hilton Inn; open daily for breakfast, lunch, and dinner. Sullivan's Rococo Steak House offers prime rib, steak, seafood, and other specialties with memorable views atop a hill just west of town (take Airport Rd.), tel. 673-3305; open daily for dinner.

Dine Chinese at J.J. Hunan Chinese Restaurant, 2 W. St. George Blvd. in Ancestor Square, tel. 628-7219, open daily for lunch and dinner. Panda Garden Restaurant, 212 N. 900 East, tel. 674-1538, serves low sodium food cooked in low fat vegetable oil daily for lunch and dinner. Wok Express, a small cafe at 635 E. St. George Blvd., tel. 628-8452, is open daily for lunch and dinner. Authentic Mexican food is prepared at Los Hermanos, 46 W. St. George Blvd. in Ancestor Square, tel. 628-5989, open Mon.-Sat. for lunch and dinner; Paula's Cazuela, 745 W. Ridgeview Dr. on the northwest edge of town, tel. 673-6568, open Mon.-Sat. for lunch and dinner; El Torito, 929 W. Sunset Blvd. in Phoenix Plaza, tel. 674-2767, open Mon.-Sat. for lunch and dinner); and Pancho & Lefty's, 1050 S. Bluff St., tel. 628-4772, open daily for lunch and dinner. Pick up pizza at Pizza Factory, 2 W. St. George Blvd. in Ancestor Square, tel. 628-1234, and also at the corner of W. St. George Blvd. at Bluff St., tel. 634-1234, open Mon.-Sat. for lunch and dinner; Pizza Hut, 471 E. St. George Blvd., tel. 628-2641, and at 932 S. Bluff St., tel. 628-9290 both are open daily for lunch and dinner; and Little Caesar's Pizza, 700 E. 700 South, tel. 628-8100, and at 929 W. Sunset Blvd., tel. 628-8595, both are open daily for lunch and dinner.

Entertainment And Events

Staffs at the St. George Chamber of Commerce, tel. 628-1658, and the Washington County Travel & Convention Bureau, tel. (800) 869-6635 know about upcoming events, including concerts at Dixie Center and the Tabernacle and the many small sporting events that take place in St. George. Major annual events include:

February: Sunfest Trade Show of commercial exhibits especially for snow birds. Presidents Day Softball. Dixie Invitational Art Show hosts regional artists; it begins President's Day weekend at the Fine Arts Bldg. on Dixie College campus.

March: Daily Spectrum 10K Run. Color Country Barbershop Extravaganza. Antique Car Show in Hurricane on Easter weekend.

April: Dixie College D-Week (homecoming). St. George Arts Festival on Easter weekend.

May: Drag Racing at Dixie Raceway on Memorial Day.

July: Fourth of July Fireworks at the Sun Bowl, adjacent to Vernon Worthen Park. Gunlock Rodeo (amateur) on July 4. Enterprise Rodeo (amateur) on Thursday, Friday, and Saturday of July 24 weekend.

August: Veyo Rodeo on the first weekend. Washington County Fair in Hurricane. Corn Festival in Enterprise.

September: Southern Utah Folklife Festival. Lions Dixie Round-Up (PRCA) Rodeo.

October: St. George Marathon on the first Saturday. Invitational Art Show at Pioneer Courthouse for the first two weeks of the month. World Senior Games presents a wide variety of Olympic-type competitions for seniors; you'll be amazed at the enthusiasm and abilities.

November: Butch Cassidy 10K Walk/Run in Springdale. Celebrity Golf Tournament.

December: Jubilee of Trees (exhibition of decorated trees and handicrafts on the first Friday and Saturday). Dixie Rotary Bowl (football) and Band Competition on the first Saturday. Handel's Messiah takes place early in month.

Recreation

Vernon Worthen Park, 400 East and 200 South, offers shaded picnic tables, playground, and tennis courts. J.C. Snow Park, 400 East and 900 South, has picnic tables and playground (but little shade). Pioneer Park overlooks the city from the north; it's in desert country just off Skyline Drive (see map); the primitive park just has a few picnic tables. The outdoor public swimming pool, 250 E. 700 South, tel. 634-5867, features a hydro slide; open Memorial Day to Labor Day weekends. Tennis players may use the public courts at Dixie College and at Vernon Worthen Park. **Green Valley Resort,** 1515 W. Canyon View Dr., tel. 628-8060, has a tennis college and many courts for its guests (only). The city's **Leisure Services Department,** tel. 634-5850, offers a wide range of activities for adults and youth, including classes (art, music, sports), field trips, and lectures.

With seven golf courses, St. George has a reputation as Utah's winter golf capital. **Dixie Red Hills,** 1000 N. 700 West on the northwest edge of town, tel. 634-5852, is a nine-hole, par-34 municipal course. **Green Spring Golf Course,** 588 N. Green Spring Dr. just west of the I-15 Washington Exit 10, tel. 673-7888, has 18 holes, par 71. **Twin Lakes Golf Course,** 660 N. Twin Lakes Dr. on the northeast edge of town (take the I-15 west frontage road, Highland Dr.), tel. 673-4441, has nine holes, par 27. **Sunbrook Golf Course,** 2240 Sunbrook Dr. off Dixie Downs Rd., between Green Valley and Santa Clara, tel. 634-5866, has 18 holes, par 72. **St. George Golf Club** is an 18-hole, par-73 course south of town in Bloomington Hills, tel. 634-5854. **Southgate Golf Course,** 1975 S. Tonaquint Dr. on the southwest edge of town, tel. 628-0000, has 18 holes, par 70. **Bloomington Country Club,** southwest of town in Bloomington, tel. 673-2029, is private 18-hole, par-72 course; players need to be members, guests of members, or members of a club with a rooiprocal agreement.

Shopping
Red Cliffs Mall has the big Z.C.M.I., J.C. Penny, Wal-Mart, and other stores on Red Cliffs Drive, the east frontage road northeast of the I-15 St. George Blvd. Exit 8. **Zion Factory Stores** has many factory outlets nearby, just east of I-10 Exit 8. The **Commercial Center** is a shopping center with Kmart, Albertsons, and other stores at 700 S. Bluff. Outdoor supplies can be purchased at the **Outdoor Outlet,** 1062 E. Tabernacle, tel. 628-3611; **Hurst Sports Center,** 160 N. 500 West, tel. 673-6141; and **Wal-Mart,** Red Cliffs Mall, tel. 628-2802.

Services
The **post office** is at 180 N. Main, tel. 673-3312. **Dixie Regional Medical Center** provides hospital care at 544 S. 400 East, tel. 634-4000 (physician referral number is 628-6688). **Elder**

Hostel education and recreation programs (including activities as ambitious as raft trips and European tours) in St. George have been very popular with seniors, tel. 673-3704 or (800) 545-4653. Foreign currency can be exchanged at **First Security Bank,** 410 E. Tabernacle, tel. 628-2831.

Information
The **St. George Chamber of Commerce** can tell you about the sights, events, and services of southwestern Utah; it has brochures of accommodations, restaurants, a historic walking tour, and area ghost towns; open Mon.-Fri. 9 a.m.-5 p.m. and Saturday 9 a.m.-1 p.m. The office is in the old county courthouse (built 1866-76) at 97 E. St. George Blvd. (St. George, UT 84770), tel. 628-1658. See the **Pine Valley Ranger District** office, 289 E. Riverside Dr. (St. George, UT 84770), tel. 673-3431, for information on fishing, hiking, and camping in the Dixie National Forest north of town; maps of the forest and Pine Valley Wilderness are available; open Mon.-Fri. 8 a.m.-5 p.m. The **Bureau of Land Management** oversees vast lands in Utah's southwest corner and the Arizona Strip; open Mon.-Fri. 7:45 a.m.-4:30 p.m.; the offices for Dixie Resource Area, tel. 673-4654, and the Shivwits and Vermillion resource areas of the Arizona Strip, tel. 628-4491, are at 225 N. Bluff St. (St. George, UT 84770); the building is set back from the road behind a row of shops, look for it on the west side of Bluff St. between 200 and 300 North.

Washington County Library, just south of the Tabernacle at 50 S. Main, tel. 634-5737, has a good selection of books; a bulletin board lists community events and classes, open Mon.-Thurs. 9 a.m.-9 p.m., Friday and Saturday 9 a.m.-6 p.m. **Dixie College's library** sits in the center of campus, tel. 673-4811, ext. 201; open Mon.-Thurs. 7:30 a.m.-11 p.m., Friday 7:30 a.m.-5 p.m., Saturday 10 a.m.-5 p.m., and Sunday 1-8 p.m. during the main terms. **B. Dalton Bookseller,** in the Red Cliffs Mall, tel. 673-4224, offers a good assortment that includes regional and travel books. Other sources for Utah books include **R&K's Bookstore,** 116 E. City Center, tel. 673-5478, and **Deseret Book,** 801 S. Bluff St., tel. 628-4495. The **Book Peddler,** 25 N. Main, tel. 673-5827, specializes in used books.

Tours And Transportation

Scenic Airlines, tel. 628-0481, will show you spectacular scenery from the air on a variety of trips, including a half-hour flight over St. George and Snow Canyon ($40), one-hour trip across Zion National Park ($69), two-hour flight over Zion and Bryce ($119), two-hour tour of the Grand Canyon ($129), and a three and one half-hour loop to Zion, Grand Canyon, and Lake Powell ($339); prices are per person with a minimum of two. For a cab, call **Pete's Taxi,** tel. 673-5467, or **Bob's Taxi,** tel. 634-2343. See the telephone *Yellow Pages* for car rental agencies. **Dixie Stagecoach,** tel. 674-1250, offers a shuttle to the Virgin River and casinos in Mesquite, Nevada, at $5 each way. **St. George Shuttle** will take you to Las Vegas in a 15-passenger van for $20 from 850 S. Bluff St. (Holiday Inn), call for schedule, tel. 628-8320. **R & R Tours,** 135 N. 900 East, tel. 628-7710, has full day tours of Zion National Park at $59, Bryce Canyon National Park at $60, and shorter tours in the St. George area. **Greyhound** buses depart from McDonald's Restaurant at 1235 S. Bluff St. for Salt Lake City, Denver, Las Vegas, and other destinations; tel. 673-2933. **Skywest Airlines** flies to Salt Lake City (five times daily, $74-105 one-way), Page (one daily, $85 one-way), Las Vegas (two daily, $39-79 one-way), and other destinations; ask about weekend, roundtrip, and other special fares; tel. (800) 453-9417.

VICINITY OF ST. GEORGE

Some good scenic drives begin at St. George. Whether you're short on time or have all day, a good choice is the 24-mile loop through Snow Canyon State Park via UT 18, the park road (UT 300), and Santa Clara. The old highway to Littlefield (AZ) makes a 67-mile loop with I-15; this route follows former US 91 through the pioneer settlement of Santa Clara, the sparsely settled Shivwits Indian Reservation, and over a 4,600-foot pass in the Beaver Dam Mountains to Littlefield; the I-15 section goes through the spectacular Virgin River Gorge upstream from Littlefield. In summer, the cool forests of the Pine Valley Mountains 37 miles northwest of town are an especially attractive destination: you can make a 130-mile drive with many possible side trips by circling the mountains on UT 18, UT 56, and I-15. Zion National Park, with its grandeur and color, is about 40 miles northeast of St. George. Adventurous motorists may want to try some of the unpaved roads through the desert east and west of St. George; the back way to Hurricane via Fort Pearce can be driven by car in good weather.

SNOW CANYON STATE PARK

The park is a great place to explore and enjoy the desert scenery. Red-rock canyons, sand dunes, volcanoes, and lava flows have formed an incredible landscape. Walls of Navajo Sandstone 500-750 feet high enclose five-mile-long Snow Canyon. Hiking trails lead into the backcountry for a closer look at the geology, flora, and fauna. Common plants are barrel, cholla, and prickly pear cacti, yucca, Mormon tea, shrub live oak, cliffrose, and cottonwood. Delicate wildflowers bloom mostly in the spring and autumn, following the wet seasons, but cactus and the sacred datura can flower in the heat of summer. Wildlife includes sidewinder and Great Basin rattlesnakes, Gila monster, desert tortoise, kangaroo rat, squirrel, cottontail, kit fox, coyote, and mule deer. You may find some Indian rock art, arrowheads, bits of pottery, and ruins. Many of the place names in the park honor Mormon pioneers. Snow Canyon was named for Lorenzo and Erastus Snow—not for the rare snowfalls. Cooler months have the best weather; summers are too hot for comfortable hiking except in early morning. Highway UT 18 leads past an overlook on the rim of Snow Canyon and to the paved park road (UT 300) that drops into the canyon and follows it to its mouth and the small town of Ivins. Snow Canyon is about 12 miles northwest of St. George. It's reached either by UT 18, the faster way, or via Santa Clara and Ivins. The entrance fee is $3 per vehicle for day use, $9 for camping, or $11 for camping w/hookups ($1 more for Friday, Saturday, and holiday camping). Contact Snow Canyon State Park at Box 140, Santa Clara, UT 84765, tel. 628-2255 or (800) 322-3770 (reservations).

Practicalities

Set within the canyon, **Shivwits Campground** (elev. 2,600 feet) stays open all year with water, showers, and hookups. Camping reservations are recommended for spring and autumn weekends. Groups can also reserve picnic and overflow areas. **Snow Canyon Riding Stables**, tel. 628-6677, offers horseback riding, campfire breakfasts, and Western shows year-round; overnight pack trips in the Pine Mountains can be arranged in summer.

Hiking Trails

The park brochure has an aerial photo of the area on which trails and other features have been drawn in. **Hidden Piñon Trail**, also signed as "nature trail," begins across the road from the Shivwits Campground entrance, then weaves among sandstone hills and lava flows to Varnish Mountain Overlook above Snow Canyon. At the overlook, desert varnish on sandstone has turned the rock jet black. The easy trail is one and one half miles roundtrip and has a small elevation gain; some sections cross rough rocks and deep sand. It's an easy scramble from the overlook area to the canyon floor below. **West Canyon Trail** is the longest in the park; it begins near the stables (0.7 mile south of the campground) and goes northwest along an old road up Snow Canyon to West Canyon.

(You can also take cross-country hikes into other canyons passed on the way.) The trail is seven miles roundtrip with a small elevation gain. **Lava Tubes Trail** winds across a lava field to an area of lava caves; one mile roundtrip. The caves formed when molten lava broke out of the partly cooled flow and left rooms and tunnels behind. Artifacts indicate that Indians took shelter in the chambers. The trailhead is one and one half miles north of the campground. The steep and strenuous **Volcano Trail** ascends a cinder cone northeast of Snow Canyon. The 1,000-year-old volcano is on the east side of UT 18 one mile north of the turnoff for Snow Canyon.

TUACAHN AMPHITHEATER

Enjoy the spectacular musical drama *Utah* under the stars as a cast of 80 re-creates struggles of the early explorers and pioneers. Special effects include lightning bolts, waterfalls, floods, and Indian raids. Tuacahn has an outdoor amphitheater seating 1,900 set among 1,500-foot-high red rock cliffs. The Heritage Trails offer living history demonstrations of the lives of the Paiutes, Navajo, Hopi, Anasazi, and the early pioneers. A Dutch oven dinner is available before each production as well as free backstage tours. Admission is $14.50-24.50 ages 12 and over and $9-16 under 12. Tuacahn is located at the south entrance of Snow Canyon State Park. Call for reservations, tel. (800) 746-9882.

VEYO AND VICINITY

Veyo Resort
Warm-water springs feed a swimming pool in this pretty spot; the family resort here has picnic tables and a snack bar; open from about the last weekend in March to Labor Day; tel. 574-2744; take the Veyo Pool Resort Road from UT 18 southeast of town. The little village of Veyo lies along the Santa Clara River 19 miles northwest of St. George.

Gunlock State Park
The 266-acre reservoir is set among red and gray hills 10 miles southwest of Veyo. Parking area, docks, and paved boat ramp lie just off the road near the dam. The red-sand beach across the lake can be reached by boat or by a short walk across the dam. Largemouth bass, channel catfish, bluegill, and the odd trout swim in the waters. Open all year; no water or charge; check with Snow Canyon State Park for current info at Box 140, Santa Clara, UT 84765, tel. 628-2255. Gunlock Lake can be reached from St. George via Veyo or by the slightly shorter route through Santa Clara.

Baker Dam Recreation Site
This 50-acre reservoir on BLM land is on the Santa Clara River upstream from Veyo. Fishermen come for the rainbow and brown trout. An established campground is located just before the dam; drive across the dam to undeveloped camping areas and a boat ramp. Open all year; no water or charge. Go north four miles on UT 18 from Veyo, then turn right a half mile on a paved road (between Mileposts 24 and 25).

PINE VALLEY MOUNTAINS

A massive body of magma uncovered by erosion makes up the Pine Valley Mountains. Vegetation ranges from piñon pine and juniper woodlands on the lower slopes, to ponderosa pine and aspen at the middle elevations, to Douglas fir, subalpine fir, Engelmann spruce, and limber pine in the heights. Signal Peak (elev. 10,365 feet) tops the range, much of which has been designated the Pine Valley Mountain Wilderness Area.

Pine Valley
In 1856, pioneers arrived at Pine Valley (elev. 6,600 feet) to harvest the extensive forests and to raise livestock. Lumber from Pine Valley helped build many southern Utah settlements and even went into Salt Lake City's great tabernacle organ. The town's picturesque white chapel was built in 1868 by Ebenezer Bryce, who later homesteaded at what's now Bryce Canyon National Park; the chapel is open for tours daily 11 a.m.-5 p.m. from Memorial Day to Labor Day weekends. Most of today's residents come up just in summer for the cool mountain air. The Brandin' Iron Steakhouse serves dinners Friday and Saturday, tel. 574-2261. Pine Valley is 32 miles from St. George via Veyo.

Pine Valley Recreation Area

Continue three miles on the paved road past Pine Valley to the picnic areas, campgrounds, and trails in Dixie National Forest. At Pine Valley Reservoir, 2.3 miles up on the right, you can fish for rainbow and some brook trout. There's also fair fishing in the Santa Clara River upstream and downstream. **Ponderosa Picnic Area** is 0.4 mile farther on the right; free day use. Turn right just past the picnic area for **Pines Campground, Lower Pines Picnic Area,** and **Brown's Point Trailhead.** Continue straight for **Blue Springs** and **South and North Juniper campgrounds** and for **Whipple Trailhead.** Each campground has water and a $7 single-unit fee during the May 20 to October 31 season. Elevation is 6,800 feet. All campsites fill up most days in summer; try to arrive early or make reservations then. Reservations can be made by calling 800-280-CAMP for individual sites at Blue Springs Campground, the group campground at Upper Pines, and group picnic areas. The Pine Valley Ranger District office in

St. George can advise on camping and other recreation here, tel. 673-3431.

Pine Valley Wilderness

The 50,000-acre wilderness has the best scenery of the Pine Valley Mountains, but it can be seen only on foot or horseback. A network of trails from all directions leads into the wilderness. They're usually open from about mid-June into October. **Summit Trail** is the longest (35 miles one-way) and connects with many other trails. Several loops are possible, though most are too long for day-hikes. **Whipple National Recreation Trail** is one of the most popular for both day and overnight trips; it ascends 2,100 feet in six miles to Summit Trail. **Brown's Point Trail** also climbs to Summit Trail, but in four miles. Strong hikers can use the Brown's Point and Summit trails to reach the top of Signal Peak on a day-hike; the last part of the climb is a rockscramble. Generally, the trails from Pine Valley are signed and easy to follow; trails in other areas may be unmaintained. Take topo maps and a compass if you're going for more than a short stroll. The Pine Valley Ranger District office, 289 E. Riverside Drive (St. George, UT 84770), tel. 673-3431, in St. George has a recreation map that shows trails and trailheads. *The Hiker's Guide to Utah* by Dave Hall describes a 15-mile loop in the Pine Valley Mountains.

WEST OF PINE VALLEY MOUNTAINS

Mountain Meadows Massacre Historic Site
A short trip from UT 18 west of the Pine Valley Mountains leads to the site of one of the darkest chapters of Mormon history. The pleasant valley had been a popular rest stop for pioneers about to cross the hot desert country to the west. In 1857, a California-bound wagon train whose members had already experienced trouble with Mormons of the region was attacked by an alliance of Mormons and local Indians. About 120 people in the wagon train died in the massacre. Only some small children too young to tell the story were spared. The closely knit Mormon community tried to cover up the incident and hindered federal attempts to apprehend the killers. Only John D. Lee, who was in charge of Indian affairs in southern Utah at the time,

pools in a red rock canyon near St. George

was ever brought to justice. After nearly 20 years and two trials, authorities took him back to this spot to be executed by firing squad. Many details of the massacre remain unknown. The major causes seem to have been a Mormon fear of invasion, aggressive Indians, and poor communications between the Mormon leadership in Salt Lake City and southern Utah. A monument now marks the site of the tragedy; turn west one mile on a paved road from UT 18 between Mileposts 31 and 32.

Enterprise Reservoirs

Rainbow trout lurk in the lower and upper reservoirs. The larger Upper Enterprise Reservoir has a paved boat ramp and easier access. Nearby **Honeycomb Rocks Campground** (elev. 5,700 feet) has water and a $6 fee from about Memorial Day to October 31. Its name describes the outcrops of porous volcanic tuff. The open country here supports mostly grass, sage, and some ponderosa pine and Gambel oak. Drive to the town of Enterprise, 41 miles northwest of St. George and 47 miles west of Cedar City, then follow paved roads 11.5-miles west and south.

Pine Park Campground

This campground is located farther west from Enterprise in an isolated area of the Dixie National Forest near the Nevada border; open about Memorial Day to October 31; no water or fee. You may need 4WD, because the last part of the road is steep and rough. Sites are in a canyon eroded from volcanic tuff at an elevation of 6,200 feet.

NORTH OF PINE VALLEY MOUNTAINS

Irontown

This is one of Utah's best-preserved 19th-century iron smelter sites. The original Iron Mission near Cedar City had poor success during its brief life in the 1850s. In 1870, though, more extensive ore deposits farther west at this site encouraged another attempt at iron-making. Daily production rose to nearly five tons, and a town of several hundred workers grew up around the smelter. Profits began to decline in the 1880s when cheaper iron from the eastern states flooded in. The town soon died, though mining has since

continued on and off in the vicinity. A brick chimney and stone foundations of the smelter and a beehive-shaped charcoal kiln show the layout of the operation. Look around in the sagebrush for remnants of the townsite and for pieces of slag and iron. Drive 10 miles west from Cedar City or 30 miles east from Enterprise to the signed turnoff on UT 56 (just west of Milepost 41), then turn southwest 2.7 miles.

EAST OF PINE VALLEY MOUNTAINS

Leeds

This small community has two exits on I-15; southbound traffic on I-15 must use Exit 23 on the north side of town. Northbound traffic on I-15 must take Exit 22 south of town. **Leeds RV Park** has sites for $10.90 RV w/hookups and showers (no tents); turn east on Center at the sign, tel. 879-2450.

Silver Reef

This ghost town is probably Utah's most accessible. In about 1870, prospectors found rich silver deposits in the sandstone here, much to the surprise of mining experts who thought such a combination impossible. The town grew up several years later and boomed from 1878 to 1882. The population peaked at 1,500 and included a sizable Chinese community. Then a combination of lower silver prices, declining yields, and water in the mines forced the operations to close one by one, the last in 1891. Other attempts at mining have since been made from time to time, including some uranium production in the 1950s and '60s, but the town had died.

The **Wells Fargo building,** which once stood in the center of town, is now Silver Reef's main attraction. Built of stone in 1877, it looks as solid as ever. **Jerry Anderson Art Gallery** and the small **Silver Reef Museum** occupy the interior, open Mon.-Sat. 9 a.m.-5 p.m., tel. 879-2254. Encroaching modern houses detract a bit from the setting, but the ghosts are still here. Stone walls and foundations peek out of the sagebrush. A short walk on the road past the Wells Fargo building takes you to the ruins and tailings of the mills that once shook the town with their racket. Take I-15 Leeds Exit 22 or 23 and follow signs 1.3 miles on a paved road.

Wells Fargo building at Silver Reef ghost town

Oak Grove Campground

On the east side of the Pine Valley Mountains, Oak Grove (elev. 6,800 feet) is in a forest of Gambel and live shrub oak, ponderosa pine, and some spruce. The small campground has water from about Memorial Day to October 31; $5. Leeds Creek has trout fishing, but dense shrubbery along the banks can make access difficult. **Oak Grove Trail** winds three miles from the campground to Summit Trail in the Pine Valley Mountain Wilderness. Take I-15 Leeds Exit 22 or 23 and go northwest nine miles. The unpaved road may be rough, especially late in the season; it's usually passable by cars, but isn't recommended for trailers.

Red Cliffs Recreation Site

Weather-sculptured cliffs of reddish-orange sandstone rise above this pretty spot. The seasonal Quail Creek emerges from a canyon, flows through the middle of the campground, then goes on to Quail Creek Reservoir two miles away. The campground/picnic area (elev. 3,240 feet) is open all year with water; there's a $4 camping fee. **Desert Trail** starts on the left near the beginning of the campground loop and follows the creek a half mile into the canyon. Idyllic pools and graceful rock formations line the way. You'll need to do some wading to continue upstream past trail's end. A shorter but more rugged trail (one-quarter-mile roundtrip) begins near the end of the campground loop and crosses slickrock to Silver Reef Lookout Point. Here there's a good panorama of the area, though

you can't actually see Silver Reef ghost town. Take I-15 Leeds Exit 22 or 23, go south three miles on the frontage road, then turn west 1.7 miles on a paved road. Long trailers may drag on dips at stream crossings.

Quail Creek State Park

Barren rock hills surround the 590-acre reservoir. Most of the water comes from the Virgin River; Quail Creek also contributes its share. Curiously, the reservoir has two dams to hold back the waters. The state park on the west shore offers a campground (water but no showers or hookups), swimming beach, paved boat ramp, and docks. Fishermen come for the largemouth bass, rainbow trout, catfish, and bluegill. Other popular activities include water-skiing, Jet Skiing, and sailboarding. The park stays open all year; $3 per vehicle day use, $7 per vehicle camping ($8 Friday, Saturday, and holidays); Box 1943, St. George, UT 84770, tel. 879-2378 or (800) 322-3770 (reservations). If coming from the north, take I-15 Leeds Exit 23 and follow the frontage road south 3.4 miles, then turn left one and one half miles; from the south, take I-15 Hurricane Exit 16, go east 2.6 miles on UT 9, then north two miles on a paved road.

HURRICANE AND VICINITY

Legend has it that in the early 1860s a group of pioneers was descending the steep cliffs above the present townsite when a strong wind came up; Erastus Snow compared it with a hurricane and named the place Hurricane Hill. A canal to bring water from the Virgin River to Hurricane Bench took 11 years of hard work to build, beginning in 1893, but it allowed farming in the area for the first time. Settlers founded the town in 1906. Many retirees and winter visitors live here now. Hurricane is also a handy traveler's stop. The **Washington County Fair** is held in August.

Practicalities
Super 8, 65 S. 700 West, tel. 635-0808 or (800) 800-8000, offers a pool and sauna, $50 s, $54.37 d. **Weston's Lamplighter Inn (Best Western),** 280 W. State, tel. 635-4647 or (800) 528-1234, has a pool and spa, $52.32 s, $57.77 d. **Motel Park Villa,** 650 W. State, tel. 635-4010, has some kitchenettes, $32.70 s, $39.25 d and up. **Willow Park RV** is just west of town at 1150 W. 80 South, tel. 635-4154, $10.90 tent, $16.35 RV w/hookups, has showers. **Brentwood RV Park,** four and one half miles west of town, tel. 635-2320 or (800) 447-2239, is open year-round with a nine-hole golf course, indoor pool, tennis courts, recreation room, and showers, $13 tent, $17.44 RV w/hookups. A restaurant, bowling alley, water slide, and mini golf course are across the street, tel. 635-2320. **Quail Lake RV Park,** tel. 635-9960, is open year-round with pool, spa, store, and showers; six miles west of town, $13.08 w/hookups. **Quail Creek State Park** (see above) is six and one half miles west, then two miles north.

Cafes (all serving breakfast, lunch, and dinner) include **Grandma's Country Kitchen,** open Tues.-Sat.; **Chumley's,** 130 S. Main, has an international vegetarian menu, open Mon.-Sat. for breakfast, lunch, and dinner and a Sunday brunch; **El Chaparral Restaurant,** 270 W. State, open daily; **JB's Restaurant,** 640 W. State, open daily; and **Golden Circle Restaurant,** 1560 W. State.

Information
Enjoy the small but select collection of pioneer and Indian artifacts on display at the **Hurricane Valley Pioneer and Indian Museum** at 35 W. State Street; you can also obtain local and area information from well-informed personnel; open Mon.-Fri. 9:30 a.m.-5:30 p.m. and Saturday 10 a.m.-2 p.m. The new, well-stocked **public library** is at 36 S. 300 West, tel. 635-4621.

La Verkin
This small town, 2.7 miles north of Hurricane, has the **Gateway Trailer Park,** 511 N. State St., tel. 635-4533, open all year with showers and laundry, $9.81 tent or RV w/hookups; **Silver Springs RV Park,** 11 W. 500 North, tel. 635-7700, open all year at with showers, pool, and store, $10 tent, $16.36 RV w/hookups; and the **Virgin Territory RV Park,** 310 N. State, tel. 635-7618.

Pah Tempe Hot Springs
Hot mineral water gushes from springs along the Virgin River and fills three sandy bottom soaking pools (about 106° F) and a swimming pool (high 90s). The Dominguez-Escalante expedition passed by in 1776 and thought these hot springs characteristic of the entire river, which they named the Rio Sulfureo. A small resort at the springs maintains the pools, a bed and breakfast ($45 s, $55-75 d), and a campground ($25 s, $35 d). The resort is open daily 9 a.m.-10 p.m. Admission fees for the pools are $10 adult, $5 children 2-12, and free for younger children. The resort is on Enchanted Way, just off UT 9 one mile north of Hurricane, tel. 635-2879/2353.

With permission from the resort, you can take the old bridge across the river to see a group of undeveloped hot springs. Hikers can continue farther upstream to explore the canyon. Look for the Hurricane Canal in the cliffs high above the river.

The Dinosaur Trackways And Old Fort Pearce
Both of these sites illustrate periods of Utah's past. They're easily visited on a scenic backroad drive through the desert between Hurricane and St. George. Most of the road is unpaved and has some rough and sandy spots, but it should be okay for cautiously driven cars in dry weather. From Hurricane, drive south eight miles on 700 West, then turn west eight and one half miles to the dinosaur trackways turnoff and another two miles to the Fort Pearce turnoff. From St. George, head east on 700 South and follow the road as it turns south; turn left (east) 2.1 miles on a paved road immediately after crossing the Virgin River, turn left three and one half miles on another paved road after a curve, then turn left (east) 5.6 miles on an unpaved road to the Fort Pearce turnoff and another two

miles to the dinosaur trackways turnoff. Signs for Warner Valley and Fort Pearce point the way at many, but not all, of the intersections.

A group of dinosaur trackways documents the passage of at least two different species more than 200 million years ago. The well-preserved tracks, in the Moenave Formation, may have been made by a 20-foot-long herbivore weighing an estimated 8-10 tons and by a carnivore half as long. No remains of the dinosaurs themselves have been found here.

The name of Old Fort Pearce honors Capt. John Pearce, who led Mormon troops of the area during the Black Hawk War with Ute Indians from 1865 to 1869. In 1861, ranchers had arrived in Warner Valley to run cattle on the desert grasslands. Four years later, however, Indian troubles threatened to drive the settlers out. The Black Hawk War and periodic raids by Navajo Indians made life very precarious. Springs in Fort Pearce Wash, the only reliable water for many miles, proved the key to domination of the region. In December 1866, work began on a fort overlooking the springs. The stone walls stood about eight feet high and were more than 30 feet long. No roof was ever added. Much of the fort and the adjacent corral (built in 1869) have survived to the present. Local cattlemen still use the springs for their herds. Petroglyphs can be seen a quarter mile downstream from the fort along ledges on the north side of the wash.

ZION NATIONAL PARK

The sheer cliffs and great monoliths of Zion Canyon reach high into the heavens. Energetic streams and other forces of erosion created this land of finely sculptured rock. One can understand why the Mormon pioneers thought the name Zion appropriate here. The large park spreads across 147,000 acres and contains eight geologic formations and four major vegetation zones. Elevations range from 3,666 feet in lower Coalpits Wash to 8,726 feet atop Horse Ranch Mountain.

The highlight for most visitors is Zion Canyon, up to 2,400 feet deep. A scenic drive winds through it along the North Fork of the Virgin River past some of the most spectacular scenery in the park. Hiking trails branch off to lofty viewpoints and narrow side canyons. Adventurous souls can continue on foot past road's end into the eerie depths of the Virgin River Narrows in upper Zion Canyon. The spectacular Zion-Mt. Carmel Highway, with its switchbacks and tunnels, provides access to the canyons and high plateaus east of Zion Canyon. Two other roads enter the rugged Kolob section northwest of Zion Canyon. The Kolob, a Mormon name meaning "the brightest star, next to the seat of God," includes wilderness areas rarely visited by humans.

Zion's grandeur extends all through the year. Even rainy days can be memorable as countless waterfalls plunge from every crevice in the cliffs above. Spring and autumn are the choice seasons for the most pleasant temperatures and the best chances of seeing wildlife and wildflowers. From about mid-October to early November, cottonwoods and other trees and plants

Zion Canyon

blaze with color. Summer temperatures in the canyons can be uncomfortably hot with highs hovering above 100° F; this is also the busiest season. In winter, nighttime temperatures drop to near freezing; weather then tends to be unpredictable, with bright sunshine one day and freezing rain the next. Snow-covered slopes contrast with colorful rocks. Snow may block some of the high-country trails and the road to Lava Point, but the rest of the park is open and accessible year-round.

The Zion Canyon Visitor Center, at the mouth of Zion Canyon, is on UT 9 about midway between I-15 and US 89. It's 43 miles northeast of St. George, 60 miles south of Cedar City, 41 miles northwest of Kanab, and 86 miles southwest of Bryce Canyon National Park. Large RVs and bicycles must heed special regulations for the long tunnel on the Zion-Mt. Carmel Highway; see "East of Zion Canyon," below. Visitors short on time usually drop in at the visitor center, travel the Zion Canyon Scenic Drive, and take short walks on Weeping Rock or Riverside Walk trails. A stay of two days or longer is better to take in more of the grand scenery and to hike other inviting trails.

Kolob Canyons Road, in the extreme northwestern section of the park, begins just off I-15 Exit 40 and climbs to an overlook for great views of the Finger Canyons of the Kolob; the drive is 10 miles roundtrip. Motorists with more time may also want to drive the Kolob Terrace Road to Lava Point for another perspective of the park; this drive is about 44 miles roundtrip from Virgin (on UT 9) and has some unpaved sections. An entry fee of $5 ($2 bus passengers and bicyclists) is charged at the East and South entrance stations year-round; it's good for seven days. No charge is made for the Kolob Canyons or Lava Point drives.

Geology

The rock layers at Zion began as sediments of oceans, rivers, lakes, or sand dunes deposited 65-240 million years ago. Navajo Sandstone laid down in about the middle of this period forms most of the cliffs and great temples of the park. Look for the slanting lines of desert sand dunes turned to stone in this formation, which is more than 2,000 feet thick in some places. A gradual uplift of the Colorado Plateau, which continues today, has caused the former-

ly lazy rivers on its surface to pick up speed and knife through the rock layers. You can really appreciate these erosive powers during flash floods, when the North Fork of the Virgin River or other streams roar through their canyons. Erosion of some of the Virgin River's tributaries couldn't keep up with the main channel and were left as "hanging valleys" on the canyon walls. A good example is Hidden Canyon, reached by trail in Zion Canyon. Faulting has broken the Colorado Plateau into a series of smaller plateaus. At Zion you're on the Kolob Terrace of the Markagunt Plateau, whose rock layers are younger than those of the Kaibab Plateau at Grand Canyon National Park and older than those exposed on the Paunsaugunt Plateau at Bryce Canyon National Park.

Flora And Fauna

Many different plant and animal communities live in the rugged terrain of deep canyons and high plateaus. Because the park lies near the meeting place of the Colorado Plateau, Great Basin, and Mohave Desert, representatives of all three regions can be found here. Only desert plants can endure the long dry spells and high temperatures found at lower elevations away from permanent water; they include cacti (prickly pear, cholla, and hedgehog), blackbrush, creosote bush, honey mesquite, and purple sage. Pygmy forests of piñon pine, Utah juniper, live oak, mountain mahogany, and cliffrose grow between about 3,900 and 5,600 feet. High plateaus and the cooler canyons have ponderosa pine, Douglas fir, white fir, and aspen. Permanent springs and streams support a profusion of greenery such as cottonwood, box elder, willow, red birch, horsetail, and ferns. Watch out for poison ivy in moist, shady areas. Colorful wildflowers pop out of the ground at all elevations from spring through autumn.

You're likely to see mule deer, common throughout the park. Other wildlife includes elk, mountain lion, bobcat, black bear, bighorn sheep (reintroduced), coyote, gray fox, porcupine, ringtail cat, black-tailed jackrabbit, rock squirrel, cliff chipmunk, beaver, and many species of mice and bats. Birders have spotted more than 270 species in and near the park; common birds are red-tailed hawk, turkey vulture, quail, mallard, great horned owl, hairy woodpecker, raven, scrub jay, black-headed grosbeak, blue-gray gnatcatcher, canyon wren, Virginia's warbler, white-throated swift, and broad-tailed hummingbird. Hikers need to watch for western rattlesnakes, though these relatively rare snakes are unlikely to attack unless provoked.

History

As early as A.D. 285, the Kayenta-Virgin branch of the Anasazi built small villages of sunken pit houses in what's now the park. Their culture gradually developed over the centuries with improved agriculture and crafts until they left the region about 1200. Next came the Kaibab Band of Southern Paiutes, who spent part of the year here on seasonal migrations. The Paiutes relied heavily on wild seeds for food, supplemented by hunting and some agriculture. Anglo settlers and their livestock depleted the range and wildlife so much that the Paiutes had to abandon their old lifestyle.

Mormon pioneers pushed up the Virgin River Valley in 1859 and founded Grafton, the first of a series of towns south of the present-day park. In 1863, the Isaac Behunin family began farming in Zion Canyon and built a one-room cabin near where Zion Lodge now stands. Other families settled and farmed the canyon until the area's establishment as a national monument. The canyon's naming is credited to Isaac Behunin, who believed this spot to be a refuge from religious persecution. When Brigham Young later visited the canyon, however, he found tobacco and wine in use and declared the place "not Zion," which some dutiful followers then began calling it! A scientific expedition led by John Wesley Powell in 1872 helped make the wonders known to the outside world. Efforts by Stephen T. Mather, first director of the National Park Service, and others led to designation of Mukuntuweap ("Straight Canyon") National Monument in 1909 and establishment of Zion National Park in 1919.

ZION CANYON

You may want to begin your travels in the park with a stop at the Zion Canyon Visitor Center at the lower end of the canyon. Then drive 0.7 mile north to the turnoff for Zion Canyon Scenic Drive, a six-mile road that follows the North Fork of the Virgin River upstream. Monuments along the way include the Three Patriarchs, Mountain of the Sun, Lady Mountain, Great White Throne, Angels Landing, and Weeping Rock. Pullouts and hiking trails allow you to enjoy the many exhilarating views. Grotto Picnic Area offers shaded tables with water and restrooms. The road ends at Temple of Sinawava and the beginning of the Riverside Walk trail. In the busy summer months, vehicles over 21 feet have special parking restrictions in Zion Canyon; check at the entrance stations or visitor center.

Zion Canyon Visitor Center

A large exhibit room introduces the rock layers of Zion—how they formed and how they have changed. Photos and dioramas illustrate adaptation of plants and animals to the park's many habitats. Clay figurines, stone tools, and a clay jar containing 1,000-year-old corn belonged to the Anasazi, the first human culture to leave signs of habitation here. The Mormon pioneer exhibit commemorates the determined farmers who settled in the area. Staff will answer your questions about the park; they also have a variety of handouts and sales items on hiking, flora and fauna, history, and other aspects of the park. Many nature programs and hikes are offered from late March to November; check the posted schedule. Children's programs are held at Zion Nature Center near South Campground; ask at the visitor center for details. An excellent selection of books in the visitor center covers natural history, human history, and regional travel. Topo and geologic maps, posters, slides, postcards, and film are sold too. A Backcountry Shuttle Board allows hikers to coordinate transportation between trailheads. The Zion Canyon Visitor Center is open daily all year: 9 a.m.-5 p.m. in winter, extended to 8 a.m.-8 p.m. in summer. For more information, contact the park at Springdale, UT 84767, tel. 772-3256.

Zion Lodge

The rustic lodge sits in the heart of Zion Canyon, three miles up Zion Canyon Scenic Drive. Zion Lodge provides the only accommodations and dining places within the park. It's open year-round; reservations for rooms should be made as far in advance as possible. Costs run $72.88 s or d for the motel, $81.74 s or d for the western cabins, and $111.57 for motel suites. The moderately priced restaurant offers a varied American menu daily for breakfast, lunch, and dinner. Picnic lunches can be ordered in advance by calling 772-3213, ext. 160. A snack bar serves fast food (closes in winter). Zion Lodge organizes horseback rides along the Virgin River (one hour) and Sand Bench Trail (three hours). Tours in open-air vehicles provide narrated sightseeing trips in Zion Canyon; they run several times daily between Memorial Day and Labor Day weekends. The lodge also has evening programs, a post office counter (open Mon.-Sat.), and a gift shop. Make reservations for Zion Lodge through TW Services, Box 400, Cedar City, UT 84720, tel. 586-7686.

Zion Canyon Campgrounds
Campgrounds in the park often fill up on Easter and other major holidays and occasionally at other times. **South** and **Watchman campgrounds,** just inside from the South Entrance Station, have sites for $7 with water but no showers or hookups. Only group areas can be reserved. One of the campgrounds stays open in winter. Some of the pioneers' fruit trees in the campgrounds are still producing; you're free to pick what you'll be eating here. Additional campgrounds lie just outside the park in Springdale (see "Vicinity of Zion National Park," below).

ZION CANYON HIKES

The trails in Zion Canyon provide perspectives of the park not possible from the roads. Much of the hiking requires long ascents, but isn't too difficult at a leisurely pace. Water should be carried on most hikes. Descriptions of the following trails are given in order from the mouth of Zion Canyon to the Virgin River Narrows.

Experienced hikers can do countless off-trail routes in the canyons and plateaus surrounding Zion Canyon; rangers can suggest areas. Rappelling and other climbing skills may be needed to negotiate drops in some of the more remote canyons. Groups cannot exceed 12 hikers per trail or drainage. Overnight hikers must obtain free backcountry permits from either Zion Canyon or Kolob Canyons visitor centers. Some areas of the park, mainly those near roads and major trails, are closed to overnight use. Zion Lodge offers shuttle services for hikers or you

The rock squirrel (Citellus variegatus) *is a large ground squirrel that lives in rocky areas from high plateaus to the edge of the desert.*

can check the Backcountry Shuttle Board at the visitor center.

Rock climbers come to challenge the high cliffs, especially those of Navajo Sandstone. For route descriptions, see the climbing books available for reference at both visitor centers. Check to make sure your climbing area is open; some places are closed to protect wildlife. Climbing alone is discouraged.

Watchman Trail
From a trailhead north of Watchman Campground, the trail climbs 370 feet to a bench below Watchman Peak, the prominent mountain southeast of the visitor center. You'll enjoy views of lower Zion Canyon and the town of Springdale. The well-graded trail follows a side canyon past some springs, then ascends to the overlook; distance is 2.4 miles roundtrip and takes about two hours. A wide variety of trees and plants lines the way. In summer, it's best to get an early start. Rangers lead nature walks during the main season.

Court Of The Patriarchs Viewpoint
A short trail from the parking area leads to the viewpoint. The Patriarchs, a trio of peaks to the west, overlook Birch Creek; they are (from left to right) Abraham, Isaac, and Jacob. Mount Moroni, the reddish peak on the far right, partly blocks the view of Jacob. Better views can be obtained by hiking a half mile or so up Sand Bench Trail (see below).

Sand Bench Trail
This is an easy loop with good views of the Three Patriarchs, the Streaked Wall, and other

monuments of lower Zion Canyon. The trail is 1.7 miles long with a 500-foot elevation gain; allow about three hours. During the main season, Zion Lodge organizes three-hour horseback rides on the trail. The horses churn up dust and leave an uneven surface though, so hikers usually prefer to go elsewhere. You'll soon leave the riparian forest along Birch Creek as the trail climbs onto the dry benchland. Piñon pine, juniper, sand sage, yucca, prickly pear cactus, and other high-desert plants and animals live here. Hikers can park at Court of the Patriarchs Viewpoint, walk across the scenic drive, then follow a service road to the footbridge and trailhead. A 1.2-mile trail along the river connects the trailhead with Zion Lodge. Try to hike in early morning or late afternoon in the warmer months.

Emerald Pools Trails

Three spring-fed pools, small waterfalls, and views of Zion Canyon make the climb worthwhile. You have a choice of three trails. Easiest is the paved trail to the Lower Pool; cross the footbridge near Zion Lodge and turn right 0.6 mile. The Middle Pool above can be reached by continuing 0.2 mile on a smaller trail or by taking a different trail from the footbridge at Zion Lodge (after crossing the bridge, turn left, then right up the trail). Together these trails make a 1.8-mile roundtrip loop. The third trail begins from the Grotto Picnic Area, crosses a footbridge and turns left 0.7 mile; the trail forks left to the Lower Pool and right to the Middle Pool. A steep 0.4-mile trail leads from the Middle Pool to Upper Emerald Pool. This magical spot has a white-sand beach and towering cliffs rising above. Allow one to three hours to visit the pools. Photographers often get good pictures of rock reflections in the pools.

West Rim Trail

This strenuous trail leads to some of the best views of Zion Canyon. Backpackers can continue on the West Rim Trail to Lava Point and other destinations in the Kolob region. Start from Grotto Picnic Area (elev. 4,300 feet) and cross the footbridge, then turn right along the river. The trail climbs the slopes and enters the cool and shady depths of Refrigerator Canyon. Walter's Wiggles, a series of 21 closely spaced switchbacks, wind up to Scout Lookout and a trail junction, four miles roundtrip and a 1,050-foot elevation gain. Scout Lookout has fine views of Zion Canyon. The trail is paved and well graded to this point. Turn right a half mile at the junction to reach the summit of Angels Landing.

Angels Landing rises as a sheer-walled monolith 1,500 feet above the North Fork of the Virgin River. Though the trail to the summit is rough, chains provide security in the more exposed places. The climb is safe with care and good weather. Anyone steady on his feet should be able to make it out, but don't go if the trail is covered with snow or ice or if thunderstorms threaten. Once on top, you'll see why Angels Landing got its name—the panorama makes all the effort worthwhile. Average hiking time for the roundtrip between Grotto Picnic Area and Angels Landing is four hours.

Energetic hikers can continue 4.8 miles on the main trail from Scout Lookout to West Rim Viewpoint, which overlooks the Right Fork of North Creek. This strenuous 12.8-mile roundtrip from Grotto Picnic Area has a 3,070-foot elevation gain. West Rim Trail continues through Zion's backcountry to Lava Point (elev. 7,890 feet), where there's a primitive campground. A car shuttle and one or more days are needed for the 13.3 miles (one-way) from Grotto Picnic Area. You'll have an easier hike by starting at Lava Point and hiking down to Grotto Picnic Area; even so, be prepared for a *long* day-hike. The trail has little or no water in some seasons.

Weeping Rock Trail

A favorite with visitors, this easy trail winds past lush vegetation and wildflowers to a series of cliffside springs above an overhang. Thousands of water droplets glisten in the afternoon sun. The springs emerge where water seeping through more than 2,000 feet of Navajo Sandstone meets a layer of impervious shale. The paved trail is a half mile roundtrip with a 100-foot elevation gain. Signs along the way identify some of the trees and plants.

Observation Point Trail

The strenuous Observation Point Trail climbs 2,150 feet in 3.6 highly scenic miles to Observation Point (elev. 6,507 feet) on the edge of Zion Canyon. Allow about six hours for the roundtrip. Trails branch off along the way to Hidden Canyon, upper Echo Canyon, East Entrance, East Mesa, and other destinations. The first of many switchbacks begins a short way up from the trailhead at Weeping Rock parking area. You'll reach the junction for Hidden Canyon Trail (see "Hidden Canyon," below) after 0.8 mile. Several switchbacks later the trail enters sinuous Echo Canyon. This incredibly narrow chasm can be explored for short distances upstream and downstream to deep pools and pour-offs. **Echo Canyon Trail** branches to the right at about the halfway point; this rough trail continues farther up the canyon and connects with trails to Cable Mountain, Deertrap Mountain, and the East Entrance Station (on Zion-Mt. Carmel Highway). The East Rim Trail then climbs slickrock slopes above Echo Canyon with many fine views. Parts of the trail are cut right into the cliffs. You'll reach the rim at last after three miles of steady climbing. Then it's an easy 0.6 mile through a forest of piñon pine, juniper, Gambel oak, manzanita, sage, and some ponderosa pine to Observation Point. Impressive views take in Zion Canyon below and mountains and mesas all around. **East Mesa Trail** turns right about 0.3 mile before Observation Point and follows the plateau northeast to a dirt road outside the park.

Hidden Canyon

See if you can spot the entrance of Hidden Canyon from below! Inside the narrow canyon are small sandstone caves, a little natural arch, and diverse plantlife. The high walls, rarely more than 65 feet apart, block sunlight except for a short time at midday. Hiking distance on the moderately difficult trail is about three miles roundtrip between Weeping Rock parking area and the lower canyon; follow East Rim Trail 0.8 mile, then turn right 0.7 mile on Hidden Canyon Trail to the canyon entrance. Footing can be a bit difficult in places due to loose sand, but chains provide handholds on the more exposed sections. Steps chopped into the rock just inside Hidden Canyon help to bypass some deep pools. Allow three to four hours for the roundtrip; elevation change is about 1,000 feet. After heavy rains and spring runoff, the creek forms a small waterfall at the canyon entrance. The canyon is about one mile long and mostly easy walking, though the trail fades away. Look for the arch on the right about a half mile up the canyon.

Riverside Walk

This is one of the most popular hikes in the park. The nearly level paved trail begins at the end of Zion Canyon Scenic Drive and winds one mile upstream along the river to the Virgin River Narrows. Allow about two hours to take in the scenery. Countless springs and seeps on the canyon walls support luxuriant plant growth and swamps. Most of the springs occur at the contact between the Navajo Sandstone and the less permeable Kayenta Formation below. The water and vegetation attract abundant wildlife; keep an eye out for birds and animals and their tracks. At trail's end, the canyon is wide enough for only the river. Hikers continuing upstream must wade and sometimes even swim (see "The Narrows," below). Late morning is the best time for photography. In autumn, cottonwoods and maples display bright splashes of color.

The Narrows

Upper Zion Canyon is probably the most famous backcountry area in the park, yet it's one of the most strenuous. There's no trail and you'll be wading much of the time in the river, which is usually knee- to chest-deep. At places, the high fluted walls of upper North Fork of the Virgin River are only 20 feet apart, and very little sunlight penetrates the depths. Mysterious side canyons beckon exploration. Hikers should be well prepared and in good condition, as river hiking is more tiring than that over dry land. The major hazards are flash floods and hypothermia. Finding the right time to go through can be tricky: spring runoff is too high, summer thunderstorms bring hazardous flash floods, and winter is too cold. That leaves just part of early summer (mid-June to mid-July) and early autumn (mid-September to mid-October) as the best bets. You can get through the entire 16-mile (one-way) Narrows in about 12 hours, though two days is best to enjoy the beauty of the place. Children under 12 shouldn't attempt hiking the entire canyon. Talk with rangers at Zion Canyon Visitor Center before starting a trip; they also have a handout with useful information on planning a Narrows hike. You'll need a permit for hikes all the way through the Narrows even on a day-trip. No permit is needed if you're just going part way in and back in one day, though you must first check conditions and

*a short hike on the
Canyon Overlook Trail*

the weather forecast with rangers. The limited number of Narrows permits, for both day and overnight trips, become available after 5 p.m. on the day preceding the hike. A one-night limit applies. Overnight hikers must not leave vehicles at Riverside Walk trailhead; you can park at Zion Lodge or other designated roadside parking areas. No camping is permitted below Big Springs. Group size for hiking and camping is limited to 12 (of the same affiliation, family, etc.) on the *entire* route.

A hike downstream saves not only climbing but the work of fighting the river currents. In fact, the length of the Narrows should only be hiked downstream. The upper trailhead is near Chamberlain's Ranch, reached by an 18-mile dirt road that turns north from UT 9 east of the park. The lower trailhead is at the end of the Zion Canyon Scenic Drive. Elevation change is 1,280 feet. A good half-day trip begins at the end of Gateway to the Narrows Trail and follows the Narrows one and one half miles upstream to Orderville Canyon, then back the same way. Orderville Canyon makes a good destination in itself; you can hike quite a way up from Zion Canyon.

EAST OF ZION CANYON

The east section of the park is a land of sandstone slickrock, hoodoos, and narrow canyons. You can see much of the pretty scenery along the Zion-Mt. Carmel Highway (UT 9) between the East Entrance Station and Zion Canyon. Most of this region invites exploration on your own. Try hiking a canyon or heading up a slick rock slope (the pass between Crazy Quilt and Checkerboard mesas is one possibility). Highlights on the plateau include views of the White Cliffs and Checkerboard Mesa (both near the East Entrance Station) and a hike on the Canyon Overlook Trail (begins just east of the long tunnel). Checkerboard Mesa's distinctive pattern is due to a combination of vertical fractures and horizontal bedding planes, both accentuated by weathering. The highway's spectacular descent into Zion Canyon goes first through a 530-foot tunnel, then a 5,600-foot tunnel, followed by a series of six switchbacks to the canyon floor. Because of the narrow tunnel (completed in 1930) and the growing numbers of large vehicles visiting Zion, it's necessary for them to travel through in one-way traffic. Any vehicle over 7 feet 10 inches wide, 11 feet 4 inches high, or 40 feet long (50 feet with trailer) must go through in one-way traffic; a $10 fee is charged at the tunnel to do this. Bicycles must be carried through the long tunnel (it's too dangerous to ride). **Zican Indian Store**, just outside the East Entrance Station, is open all year with a cafe, groceries, gas station, and souvenirs. A campground is across the highway with hot showers, restrooms, tent sites ($10.90), and RV sites ($14.17 no hookups, $16.35 w/hookups); tel. 648-2154.

Canyon Overlook Trail

This popular hike features great views from the heights without the stiff climbs found on most other Zion trails. Allow about an hour for the one-mile roundtrip; elevation gain is 163 feet. A booklet available at the start or at the Zion Canyon Visitor Center describes the geology, plantlife, and clues to the presence of wildlife. The trail winds in and out along ledges of Pine Creek Canyon, which opens into a great valley. Panoramas at trail's end take in lower Zion Canyon in the distance. A sign at the viewpoint identifies Bridge Mountain, Streaked Wall, East Temple, and other features. The Great Arch of Zion, termed a "blind arch" because it's open on only one side, lies below; the arch is 580 feet high, 720 feet long, and 90 feet deep. Canyon Overlook Trail begins across from the parking area just east of the longer (west) tunnel on the Zion-Mt. Carmel Highway.

THE KOLOB

North and west of Zion Canyon lies the remote backcountry of the Kolob. This area became a second Zion National Monument in 1937, then was added to Zion National Park in 1956. You'll see all but one of the rock formations present in the park and evidence of past volcanic eruptions. Two roads lead into the Kolob. The paved five-mile Kolob Canyons Road begins at the Kolob Canyons Visitor Center just off I-15 and ends at an overlook and picnic area; it's open all year. Kolob Terrace Road is paved from the town of Virgin (15 miles west on UT 9 from the South Entrance Station) to the turnoff for Lava Point; snow usually blocks the way in winter.

Kolob Canyons Visitor Center

Though small with just a handful of exhibits, the visitor center is a good place to stop for information on exploring the Kolob region. Hikers can learn current trail conditions and obtain the permits required for overnight trips and Zion Narrows day-trips. Books, topo and geologic maps, posters, postcards, slides, and film are sold. Open daily 8 a.m.-4:30 p.m. (to 5 p.m. in summer); tel. 586-9548. The visitor center and the start of the Kolob Canyons Road lie just off I-15 Exit 40.

Campgrounds

The Kolob section of the park doesn't have a campground. The nearest one within the park is Lava Point Campground (see, "Lava Point," below). **Redledge Campground** in Kanarraville is the closest commercial campground to the Kolob Canyons area; go two miles north on I-15, take Exit 42, and continue four and one half miles into downtown Kanarraville, tel. 586-9150. The campground is open year-round with store, showers, and laundry; $13.08 tent or RV no hookups, $16.38 RV w/hookups. The tiny agricultural community was named after a local Paiute chief. A low ridge south of town marks the southern limit of prehistoric Lake Bonneville. Hikers can explore trails in Spring and Kanarra canyons of the **Spring Canyon Wilderness Study Area** just east of town.

Kolob Canyons Road

The five-mile scenic drive winds past the dramatic Finger Canyons of the Kolob to Kolob Canyons Viewpoint and a picnic area at the end of the road. The road is paved and has many pullouts where you can stop to admire the scenery. The first part of the drive follows the 200-mile-long Hurricane Fault that forms the west edge of the Markagunt Plateau. Look for the tilted rock layers deformed by friction as the plateau rose nearly one mile. **Taylor Creek Trail**, which begins two miles past the visitor center, provides a close look at the canyons (see "Taylor Creek Trail," below). Lee Pass, four miles beyond the visitor center, was named after John D. Lee of the infamous Mountain Meadows Massacre; he's believed to have lived nearby for a short time after the massacre. **La Verkin Creek Trail** begins at Lee Pass Trailhead for trips to Kolob Arch and beyond. Signs at the end of the road identify the points, buttes, mesa, and mountains. The salmon-colored Navajo Sandstone cliffs glow a deep red at sunset. **Timber Creek Overlook Trail** begins from the picnic area at road's end and climbs a half mile to the overlook (elev. 6,369 feet); views encompass the Pine Valley Mountains, Zion canyons, and distant Mt. Trumbull.

Taylor Creek Trail

An excellent day-hike from Kolob Canyons Road. The easy to moderate trail begins on the left two miles from Kolob Canyons Visitor

Center and heads upstream into the canyon of Middle Fork of Taylor Creek. Double Arch Alcove is 2.7 miles from the trailhead; a dry fall 0.2 mile farther blocks the way (water flows over it during spring runoff and after rains). A giant rock fall occurred here in June 1990. Other nearby canyons, such as North and South forks of Taylor Creek, can be explored too. **South Fork of Taylor Creek Trail** leaves the drive at a bend 3.1 miles from the visitor center, then goes in 1.2 miles.

Hiking To Kolob Arch

Kolob Arch vies with Landscape Arch in Arches National Park as the world's longest natural rock span. Differences in measurement techniques have resulted in a controversy as to which is longer: Kolob Arch's span has been measured variously at 292-310 feet, Landscape Arch's at 291-306 feet. Kolob probably takes the prize because its 310-foot measurement was done with an accurate electronic method. Kolob's height is 330 feet and its vertical thickness is 80 feet. The arch makes a

Taylor Creek, Zion National Park

fine destination for a backpack trip. Spring and autumn are the best seasons to go; summer temperatures rise into the 90s and winter snows make the trails hard to follow. You have a choice of two moderately difficult trails. **La Verkin Creek Trail** begins at Lee Pass (elev. 6,080 feet) on Kolob Canyons Scenic Drive, four miles beyond the visitor center. The trail drops into Timber Creek (intermittent flow), crosses over hills to La Verkin Creek (flows year-round; some springs too), then turns up side canyons to the arch. The 14-mile roundtrip can be done as a long day-trip, but you'll enjoy the best lighting for photos at the arch if you camp in the area and see it the following morning. Carry plenty of water for the return trip; the 800-foot climb to the trailhead can be hot and tiring.

You can also hike to Kolob Arch on the **Hop Valley Trail,** reached from Kolob Terrace Road. Hop Valley Trail is seven miles one-way to Kolob Arch with an elevation drop of 1,050 feet; water is available in Hop Valley and La Verkin Creek; you may have to do some wading in the creek. The trail crosses some private land (don't camp there).

Lava Point

The panorama from Lava Point (elev. 7,890 feet) takes in the Cedar Breaks area to the north, the Pink Cliffs to the northeast, Zion Canyon Narrows and tributaries to the east, the Sentinel and other monoliths of Zion Canyon to the southeast, and Mt. Trumbull on the Arizona Strip to the south. Signs help identify features. Lava Point, which sits atop a lava flow, is a good place to cool off in summer—temperatures are about 20° F cooler than in Zion Canyon. Aspen, ponderosa pine, Gambel oak, and white fir grow here. A small primitive **campground** near the point offers sites during the warmer months; no water or charge.

Two trails begin from West Rim Trailhead: either drive here or walk the one-mile **Barney's Trail** from Site 2 in the campground. **West Rim Trail** goes southeast to Zion Canyon, 13.3 miles one-way with an elevation drop of 3,600 feet (3,000 feet in the last six miles). Water can normally be found along the way at Sawmill, Potato Hollow (less reliable—was dry in summer 1990), and Cabin springs. **Wildcat Canyon Trail** heads southwest five miles to a trailhead on Kolob Terrace Road (16 miles north of Virgin); elevation drop is 450 feet. This trail lacks a reliable water source. You can continue east toward Kolob Arch by taking the four-mile **Connector Trail** to **Hop Valley Trail.** Snow blocks the road to Lava Point for much of the year; the usual season is May or June to early November. Check road conditions with Zion Canyon or Kolob Canyon visitor centers. From the South Entrance Station in Zion Canyon, drive west 15 miles on UT 9 to Virgin, turn north 21 miles on Kolob Terrace Road (signed "Kolob Reservoir"), then turn right 1.8 miles to Lava Point.

Kolob Reservoir

This high-country lake north of Lava Point has good fishing for rainbow trout. An unpaved boat ramp is at the south end near the dam. People sometimes camp along the shore, although there are no facilities. Most of the surrounding land is private. To reach the reservoir, continue north three and one half miles on Kolob Terrace Road from the Lava Point turnoff. The fair-weather road can also be followed past the reservoir to the Cedar City area. Blue Springs Reservoir, near the turnoff for Lava Point, is closed to the public.

VICINITY OF ZION NATIONAL PARK

SPRINGDALE

This small Mormon settlement (pop. 400) dates from 1862. Springdale lies just outside the park's south entrance and offers many services for travelers.

Zion Canyon Theatre

Meet Anasazi Indians, watch Spanish explorers seek golden treasure, witness the hardships of pioneer settlers, enter remote slot canyons, and join rock climbers hundreds of feet up vertical cliff faces in this I-Max facility with a screen six stories tall and 80 feet wide. The feature program is **Treasure of the Gods,** shot on large film for high-resolution viewing. Shows start on the half hour 8:30 a.m.-8:30 p.m. from April 1 to October 31 and from 10:30 a.m.-6:30 p.m. the rest of the year; $6.50 adults, $6 seniors, $4.50 children under 12.

Accommodations And Campgrounds

Places to stay and eat are listed in order of distance from the park entrance. All normally stay open year-round except as noted; rates may drop in winter. **Cliffrose Lodge,** 281 Zion Park Blvd., tel. 772-3234 or (800) 243-8824, offers luxury rooms, pool, and gardens; rooms run $74.80-85.80 s or d. suites are available too. **Flanigan's Inn,** 428 Zion Park Blvd., tel. 772-3244 or (800) 765-7787, has a restaurant and pool; rooms start at $53.90-86.96 s or d. **Zion Canyon Campground,** 479 Zion Park Blvd., tel. 772-3237, offers cabins ($33 s or d), tent sites ($15.95), and RV sites ($18.15 w/hookups), facilities include store, pizza parlor, game room, laundry, and showers. **Canyon Ranch Motel,** 668 Zion Park Blvd., tel. 772-3357, has some kitchenettes; rooms are $52.80 s or d and up. **Zion House Bed & Breakfast,** 801 Zion Park Blvd. (Box 323), tel. 772-3281, has rooms (nonsmoking only) for $52.80-74.80 s, $63.80-85.80 d. **Pioneer Lodge Motel,** 838 Zion Park Blvd., tel. 772-3233, has a restaurant, pool, and spa; rooms start at $59.40 s, $61.60 d. **Zion Park Motel,** 855 Zion Park Blvd., tel. 772-3251, has rooms for $57.20 s, $68.20 d. **Bumbleberry Inn,** 897 Zion Park Blvd., tel. 772-

3224, has a restaurant; $59.40 s, $64.90 d. **O'-Toole's Under the Eaves Guest House,** 980 Zion Park Blvd., tel. 772-3457, features homey bed and breakfast accommodations; $49.50-91.50 s, $61.50-104.50 d.

Morning Glory Bed & Breakfast, 26 Big Springs Rd., tel. 772-3301, has a guest pool table; $60.50-71.50. **Terrace Brook Lodge,** 990 Zion Park Blvd., tel. 772-3932, has a pool; $48.40 s, $53.90 d. **El Rio Lodge,** is at 995 Zion Park Blvd., tel. 772-3905, $44 s, $49.50 d and up. **Red Rock Inn Bed & Breakfast,** has opened at 998 Zion Park Blvd., tel. 772-3905, $71.50-77 s or d. **Driftwood Lodge (Best Western),** 1515 Zion Park Blvd., tel. 772-3262 or (800) 528-1234, has a restaurant, pool, and spa; $57.20-72.60 s or d and up. **The Blue House Bed & Breakfast Inn** sits in the small community of Rockville, five miles from the park entrance, tel. 772-3912, $49.50-60.50 s, $60.50-71.50 d. Also in Rockville is the **Handcart House Bed & Breakfast,** 244 W. Main, tel. 772-3867, $71.50 s or d.

Food

Oscar's Deli, 61 Zion Park Blvd., tel. 772-3232, offers food to eat in or take out with picnic meals or day pack fare prepared on order; open daily. **Electric Jim's,** 198 Zion Park Blvd., tel. 772-3838, offers fast food daily for lunch and dinner with breakfast available weekends. **Pizza To Go** serves pizza at Zion Canyon Campground, 479 Zion Park Blvd., tel. 772-3462; open daily for dinner. **Flanigan's Inn,** 428 Zion Park Blvd., tel. 772-3244, has varied Southwestern offerings; open daily for breakfast, lunch, and dinner. **Panda Garden Chinese Restaurant,** 805 Zion Park Blvd., tel. 772-3535, serves multi-region Chinese cuisine daily for lunch and dinner. The **Pioneer Restaurant,** 828 Zion Park Blvd., tel. 772-3009, serves American food daily for breakfast, lunch, and dinner. **Zion Pizza and Noodle,** 868 Zion Park Blvd., tel. 772-3815, dishes up pizza and pasta daily for breakfast, lunch, and dinner (may close winter). **Bumbleberry Inn's** menu of American food includes "bumbleberry" pies and pancakes at 897 Zion Park Blvd., tel. 772-3224; open

Mon.-Sat. for breakfast, lunch, and dinner. **Bit & Spur Restaurant,** 1212 Zion Park Blvd., tel. 772-3498, prepares flavorful chicken enchiladas, chiles rellenos, *toros colorado,* and other foods of the Southwest daily for dinner. **Driftwood Lodge,** 1515 Zion Park Blvd., tel. 772-3262, serves fine American food daily for breakfast, lunch, and dinner.

Other Practicalities
Tourist Information is available in summer at Town Center Old Church, 868 Zion Park Blvd., tel. 772-3072. The **Zion Canyon Field Institute,** tel. 772-3072, offers free nature walks from the Old Church as well as with other activities (children's stories, hikes, tours, and guided rock-climbing) at nominal charge. Old Church also houses **Zion Canyon Cycling Co.,** tel. 772-3929, where you may buy bicycling equipment, parts, maps, and books or rent bicycles. Also in Old Church is an art gallery, the **Zion Canyon Collection,** tel. 772-3620, where paintings, sculptures, and photographs by local artists are available. You may also want to check out the many art galleries, rock shops, and gift shops along Zion Park Boulevard. The **Grand Circle** multimedia show hosted by Dixie College portrays the splendor and history of Zion and other scenic areas in the Southwest; presented nightly from late May to early September at the O.C. Tanner Amphitheater in town (turnoff is opposite Zion Canyon Campground, then in 0.8 mile). Occasional concerts and dance performances are hosted as well; tel. 673-4811. A **Fourth of July Celebration** has a parade and fireworks. The **Southern Utah Folklife Festival** brings back the pioneer days with demonstrations, food, and entertainment in September. Roadside stands rent inner tubes in summer for tubing the Virgin River. Bicycles can also be rented in town. **Zion Canyon Medical Clinic** provides emergency services from about May to October; take the turnoff for the O.C. Tanner Amphitheater, tel. 772-3226. The **post office** is in the center of town on Zion Park Blvd., tel. 772-3950.

GRAFTON

Grafton is one of the best-preserved and most picturesque ghost towns in Utah. Photos of the deserted site grace the covers of no less than three books on the subject. Mormon families founded Grafton in 1859 near the Virgin River at a spot one mile downstream from the present site, but a big flood two years later convinced them to move here. Hostilities with the native Paiutes during the Black Hawk War forced residents to depart again for safer areas from 1866 to 1868. Floods and irrigation difficulties made life hard even in the best of times. Population declined in the early 1900s until only ghosts remained.

Moviemakers discovered Grafton and used the site for *Butch Cassidy and the Sundance Kid* and other films. You may notice a few fiberglass chimneys and other "improvements." A schoolhouse, store, houses, cabins, and a variety of outbuildings still stand. One story goes that the Mormon bishop lived in the large two-story house with wife number-one while wife number-two had to settle for the rough cabin across the road—probably not an amicable situation! Grafton's cemetery is worth a visit too; it's on the left at a turn 0.3 mile before the townsite. A monument commemorates three settlers killed by Indians in 1866. Many of Grafton's families now live in nearby Rockville; they tend the cemetery and look after the old buildings. From Springdale, follow UT 9 southwest two miles to Rockville and turn south three and one half miles on Bridge Road (200 East). The last 2.6 miles are unpaved but should be okay for cars in dry weather; keep right at a road junction 1.6 miles past Rockville.

THE VERMILION CLIFFS AND CANAAN MOUNTAIN

The rocky hills south of Springdale and Rockville offer fine scenery for back-road drives or hikes. The **Smithsonian Butte National Back Country Byway,** a 7.6-mile dirt road from the Grafton road, climbs into the scenic high country south of the Virgin River and continues to UT 59 (near Milepost 8) between Hurricane and Hildale on the other side; follow the directions to Grafton but turn left at the road junction 1.6 miles past Rockville. Panoramas take in Zion National Park, Smithsonian Butte, Canaan Mountain, and the rugged countryside all around. You can also find good places to hike or camp along the way. Cars with good clearance can usually make this trip if the road is dry.

Canaan Mountain (elev. 7,200 feet), a wilderness study area due south of Springdale, rises more than 2,000 feet above the surrounding land. The summit is a plateau of rolling slickrock, pinnacles, balanced rocks, and deep fractures similar to the plateaus of Zion National Park. High cliffs on three sides give you the feeling of being on an island in the sky. Eagle Crags Trailhead (elev. 4,400 feet) near Rockville provides access from the north past the Eagle Crags, a group of towering sandstone monoliths. Squirrel Canyon Trailhead (elev. 5,100 feet) near Hildale is the starting point for hikes from the south via Water or Squirrel canyons. See the USGS 7¹/2-minute topo maps Springdale West, Springdale East, Smithsonian Butte, and Hilldale. Contact the BLM office in St. George (tel. 673-4654) and use *The Hiker's Guide to Utah* by Dave Hall for hiking information.

VIRGIN

Mormon pioneers settled here in 1857 and named it for the nearby Virgin River. A few small eateries are in town. Kolob Terrace Road turns north to Lava Point in Zion National Park and continues on to Kolob Reservoir, high plateaus, and the Cedar City area. Virgin is on UT 9, 28 miles east of St. George and 15 miles west of the south entrance to Zion National Park.

CEDAR CITY

A cultural, tourist, and trade center, Cedar City is a popular stop for travelers. The excellent Utah Shakespearean Festival in summer presents several of the master's plays and a whole array of Elizabethan dances, concerts, sideshows, seminars, and backstage tours. Just east of town rise the high cliffs of the Markagunt Plateau—a land of panoramic views, colorful rock formations, desolate lava flows, extensive forests, and flower-filled meadows. The immense amphitheater of Cedar Breaks National Monument, eroded from the plateau, can be reached by a short but spectacular drive. Other areas to explore in the Cedar City area include Zion National Park to the south, Pine Valley Mountains to the southwest, and the remote desert country to the west and north. Cedar City is just east of I-15, 52 miles northeast of St. George and 253 miles southwest of Salt Lake City; take I-15 Exits 57, 59, or 62.

History

Cedar City began as a mission in 1851 to supply the Mormon settlements with much-needed iron products. Church leaders, upon hearing of promising iron ore and coal deposits, decided to launch the first major colonizing effort since the settlement of the Salt Lake City area. The first wagon loads of families and supplies left Provo in December 1850 for Parowan, 18 miles north-

east of present-day Cedar City. Other settlers arrived at Cedar City late the following year. All had to start from scratch. Farmers planted crops to feed the new communities while miners and engineers laid plans for iron-manufacturing industries. Hard winters, crop failures, floods, and shortages of skilled workmen nearly doomed the whole project. The final blow came when Johnston's Army and others brought cheaper iron from the East. Only a small amount of iron was produced, and operations ceased in 1858. Sizable quantities of iron ore did exist, though; large-scale mining west of Cedar City began in the 1920s, peaked in 1957, and has tapered off in recent years.

Paiute Indians have lived here since before pioneer days. Sponsorship by the Mormon community allowed them to remain when the federal government forced most other Indians in the state to move onto reservations. There's a Paiute village in the northeastern part of Cedar City. The tribe puts on the Paiute Restoration Gathering in mid-June.

SIGHTS

Utah Shakespearean Festival

The enthusiasm of the actors and the community make this summer festival come alive. The fes-

Cyrano (Randy Moore, left) and Valvert (Michael Stevenson) duel in Utah Shakespearean Festival's production of Edmond Rostand's romantic Cyrano de Bergerac, directed by John Neville-Andrews.

tival has such a high reputation and provides such a good learning experience that all participate eagerly. Their enthusiasm is contagious, and visitors soon find themselves caught up in the spirit. The festival presents three Shakespearean plays each season, choosing from both well-known and rarely performed works. The management's long-term goal is to produce every play from the Shakespeare canon! Most of the action centers on one of the most authentic Elizabethan stages in the world. The new indoor Randall Jones Theatre presents the "Best of the Rest"—works by other great playwrights such as Chekhov, Molière, and Arthur Miller.

Much work goes on backstage; for every actor, about seven people are involved with costumes, makeup, sets, and the many other aspects of staging plays. Production starts months ahead, then becomes frantic in the last weeks before the festival opens. Since it began at Southern Utah State College in 1962, the festival has continued to grow in quality and attendance.

Days at the festival are filled with entertaining and educational activities. Costumed actors stage the popular Greenshow each day before the performances with a variety of Elizabethan comedy skits, Punch and Judy shows, musicians, jugglers, food sellers, and pretty "wenches." Another activity, the Royal Feaste, presents dinner and entertainment of Tudor times. Backstage tours of the costume shop, makeup room, and stage show you how the festival works. At literary seminars each morning, actors and Shakespearean scholars discuss the previous night's play. The actors like to meet the audience, and you'll have plenty of opportunities to talk with them. Production seminars, held daily except Sunday, take a close look at acting, costumes, stage props, special effects, and other details of play production.

The season begins in late June and lasts to early September. The Greenshow and seminars are free; you'll have to pay for most other events. The main performances cost $10-24. Because the plays often sell out, it's best to purchase tickets well in advance. Both matinee and evening plays are scheduled, so you can plan a visit to see all six plays in just three days. Detailed brochures listing activities and dates of performances are available at many tourist offices in Utah or by mail from the Utah Shakespearean Festival, Cedar City, UT 84720, tel.

586-7878 (box office), 586-7880 (information desk), and 586-7790 (last-minute ticket sales).

The Adams Memorial Theatre on the Southern Utah University campus near the corner of Center and 300 West hosts the plays. Rain occasionally dampens the performances (Elizabethan theaters lacked a roof over the stage), and the plays move to a conventional theater next door, where the box office is located. The new, contemporary Randall Jones Theatre is across the street on 300 West.

Southern Utah University (SUU)

The towns of southern Utah eagerly sought a branch of the state's teacher training school after it had been authorized in 1897 by the Utah Legislature. A committee awarded the school to Cedar City, and classes began the same year in a borrowed church building. Some people say that Cedar City was chosen because it was the only one of the candidate towns without a saloon or pool hall! The school continued as a branch of the University of Utah and Utah State University until 1965, when it became independent as the four-year Southern Utah State College. In 1991 the college became a university. Major fields of study are education, arts and letters, science, and business. Graduate programs are offered in education and accounting. The attractively landscaped campus occupies 104 acres just west of downtown. SUU also operates a 1,000-acre farm in a valley west of town and a 3,700-acre ranch in Cedar Canyon to the east. **Braithwaite Fine Arts Gallery** presents changing exhibits in the Braithwaite Fine Arts Center; open during the Shakespearean Festival Mon.-Fri. 10 a.m.-7:30 p.m., Saturday and Sunday 1-5 p.m.; open the rest of the year Mon.-Thurs. and Saturday 10 a.m.-7:30 p.m., Friday 10 a.m.-5 p.m.; it's located about one block north of the intersection of 200 South and 400 West, tel. 586-5432. The Utah Shakespearean Festival is the main summer event on campus, but a variety of cultural and sports events takes place all through the year. Noted speakers can be heard at the Convocations Program in the Auditorium at Center and 300 West; programs are usually held Thursday at 11 a.m. Oct.-May. The scheduling office can tell you of upcoming convocations and other cultural happenings; tel. 586-7762. Sporting events on campus include football, basketball, baseball, softball,

CEDAR CITY ACCOMMODATIONS
Add 9% tax to all prices; rates listed are for 1-2 persons

Abbey Inn; 940 W. 200 North; $64-68; tel. 586-5500 or (800) 325-5411, pool, kitchenettes

Astro Budget Inn; 323 S. Main; $28-35; tel. 586-6557; kitchenettes, pool

Cedar Crest Motel; 583 S. Main; $42.50; tel. 586-6534; kitchenettes, pool

Comfort Inn; 250 N. 1100 West (I-15 Exit 59); $59-65; tel. 586-2082 or (800) 627-0374; kitchenettes, pool, spa, hot tub, Continental breakfast

Daystop Motel; 479 S. Main; $44-49; tel. 586-9471 or (800) 325-2525; Continental breakfast

Economy Motel; 433 S. Main; $21-25; tel. 586-4461

El Rey Inn (Best Western); 80 S. Main; $46; tel. 586-6518 or (800) 528-1234; suites, pool, sauna, spa

Holiday Inn; 1575 W. 200 North (I-15 Exit 59); $71; tel. 586-8888 or (800) HOLIDAY; pool, spa, sauna

Paxman House Bed & Breakfast; 170 N. 400 West; $60-69; tel. 586-3755

Quality Inn; 18 S. Main; $66-70; tel. 586-2433 or (800) 221-2222; pool

Raycap Motel; 2555 N. Main; $39-42; tel. 586-7435; pool, spa

Rodeway Inn; 281 S. Main; $53-55; tel. 586-9916 or (800) 424-4777; pool, sauna, spa

Super 7 Motel; 190 S. Main; $45-49; tel. 586-6566

Thrifty Motel; 344 S. Main; $38-44; tel. 586-9114; pool

Town & Country Inn (Best Western); 200 N. Main; $65-79; tel. 586-9911 or (800) 528-1234; suites, pools, spa

Village Inn Motel; 840 S. Main; $59-79; tel. 586-9926; kitchenettes, pool

Zion Inn; 222 S. Main; $45-55; tel. 586-9487; kitchenettes

gymnastics, and track; call 586-7872 for the schedule. Sports facilities open to the public include an indoor swimming pool, tennis and racquetball courts, and gym at the Physical Education Building, 600 W. 200 South, tel. 586-7815. The college can be contacted at the Information Services office, Southern Utah University, Cedar City, UT 84720, tel. 586-7752.

Iron Mission State Park
This large museum dedicates itself to the history of the cultures that have lived in and developed Iron County. Exhibits illustrate the Iron Mission's early hardships and the first iron production on September 30, 1852. Past members of the Iron Mission cast the old community bell on display. A diverse array of carriages is the museum's main attraction. You'll see everything from a bullet-scarred overland stagecoach to an elegant clarence carriage. All the sleighs, utility wagons, hearses, and many other forms of 19th-century transport have been meticulously restored. Also displayed are artifacts of prehistoric and modern Indian tribes. Pioneer memorabilia include clothing, furniture, saddles, and a

bathtub. A large collection of horse-drawn farm machinery sits out back. The museum is open daily 9 a.m.-7 p.m. from June 1 to Labor Day, then daily 9 a.m.-5 p.m. the rest of the year; closed Thanksgiving, Christmas, and New Year's Day; $1.50 adult, $1 ages 6-16. Located at 595 N. Main, tel. 586-9290.

Rock Church
Depression-era residents needed a new LDS church building but lacked the money to build one. Undaunted, they set to work using local materials and came up with this beautiful structure composed of many different types of rocks. Skilled craftspeople made the metal lamps, carpets, western red cedar pews, and most other furnishings. Open for tours Mon.-Sat. in summer; free admission; located at the corner of Center and 100 East.

PRACTICALITIES

With so much to see in the area and so many things going on in town, Cedar City is popular with visitors. A good selection of places to stay and eat line Main Street, the I-15 business route.

Campgrounds

Cedar City KOA, 1121 N. Main, tel. 586-9872, is open all year with showers, playground, and a pool; $16.35 tent or RV no hookups, $19.08 RV w/hookups. **Country Aire RV Park,** 1700 N. Main, tel. 586-2550, is open all year with showers and a pool; $14.17 tent or RV no hookups, $18.35 RV w/hookups and $20.16 for a cabin.

Food

The **Adriana's,** 164 S. 100 West, tel. 586-1234, has an English atmosphere for fine dining open in summer Mon.-Sat. for lunch and dinner; call for hours off-season. **Sullivan's Cafe,** 86 S. Main, tel. 586-6761, serves American food daily for breakfast, lunch, and dinner; its La Tajada Room features steak, seafood, and Italian dinners. The Western-style **Milt's Stage Stop,** five miles east of town on UT 14 in Cedar Canyon, tel. 586-9344, serves steak, prime rib, and seafood; open daily for dinner. An informal atmosphere for steak and seafood is offered by the **Sizzler,** 199 N. Main, tel. 586-0786, open daily for breakfast, lunch, and dinner; and **Golden Corral Family Steak House,** 755 S. Main, tel. 586-2396, open daily for lunch and dinner. **Sugar Loaf Restaurant,** 281 S. Main, tel. 586-6593, is an American cafe serving some Mexican favorites and Navajo tacos daily for breakfast, lunch, and dinner. **JB's Family Restaurant,** 127 S. Main, tel. 586-6911, has a breakfast bar and salad bar and variety of American entrees; open daily for breakfast, lunch, and dinner. **Shoney's Family Restaurant,** 980 W. 200 North (I-15 Exit 59), tel. 586-8012, has a breakfast bar and salad bar with its American food; open daily for breakfast, lunch, and dinner. The Holiday Inn's **Bristlecone Restaurant,** 1575 W. 200 North (I-15 Exit 59), tel. 586-8888, serves American food; open daily for breakfast, lunch, and dinner. **Dog & Duck Coffee House,** 50 W. Center, tel. 586-0355, has live entertainment summer evenings and serves coffee and sandwiches for breakfast, lunch, and dinner Mon.-Saturday.

Two Chinese cafes serve Cantonese-style food: **Hunan Restaurant,** 501 S. Main, tel. 586-8952, open daily for lunch and dinner; and **China Garden Restaurant,** 64 N. Main, tel. 586-6042, open daily for lunch and dinner. Good places for

Mexican and American food are **Pancho and Lefty's,** 2107 N. Main, tel. 586-7501, open daily for dinner; and **Escobar's,** 115 N. Main, tel. 865-0155, open Sun.-Fri. for late breakfast, lunch, and dinner. For pizza, try the **Pizza Factory,** 124 S. Main, tel. 586-3900, open Mon.-Sat. for lunch and dinner; or **Pizza Hut,** 579 S. Main, tel. 586-9896, open daily for lunch and dinner.

Events

April: Cowboys come to Parowan (18 miles north) for **Iron County Cowboy Days & Poetry Gathering.**

May: The **National Triple Crown Softball Tournament** brings many teams to town mid-month. **Horse Races** take place Memorial Day weekend at the Parowan Equestrian Park.

June: The local Indian community sponsors the **Paiute Restoration Gathering** with a parade, dances, traditional games, native food, and a beauty pageant on the second weekend in June. **Elks Annual Demolition Derby** cracks up on the second Saturday. Utah athletes compete in the **Utah Summer Games** during late June; events, patterned after the Olympic games, begin with a torch relay and include track and field, 10K and marathon runs, cycling, boxing, wrestling, basketball, tennis, soccer, karate, and swimming.

July: The **Fourth of July** is celebrated with a parade, fireworks, and games for the kids. **Hey Cedars Square Dance Jamboree** features lively dancing on the weekend following the fourth. Everyone dresses up in medieval style clothing for the **Utah Midsummer Renaissance Faire** of 16th-century entertainment, crafts, and food. **Pioneer Day** honors Utah's early settlers with a parade and games in town on July 24. Dances by the **American Folk Ballet** portray America's southern and western folk history (may take place in August).

August: Cowboys and cowgirls show their stuff in the amateur **Iron Rangers Rodeo** early in the month. Mountain men and Indians set up camp for black-powder shoots and games in the **Jedediah Smith High Mountain Rendezvous** in the mountains above Cedar City.

September: Iron County Fair presents a parade, rodeos, horse races, exhibits, and entertainment 18 miles north in Parowan during the Labor Day holiday.

November: Cedar City celebrates its birthday on the 11th with games and pioneer crafts in **Iron Mission Days**.

December: The holiday season arrives with a parade and festivities of Cedar City's **Winterfest and Christmas Light Parade** early in the month.

Recreation

The main **city park** has picnic tables, playground, and horseshoe courts at Main and 200 North; the Cedar City Chamber of Commerce office is here too. The **municipal swimming pools** at 400 Harding Ave. (400 W. 100 North), tel. 586-2869, have indoor and outdoor areas and a hydrotube. Look for **tennis courts** at Canyon Park (on UT 14, three blocks east of Main), the high school (703 W. 600 South), and the middle school (450 W. Center).

Shopping And Services

The **Renaissance Square** and **South Main Mall** shopping centers are on S. Main at the south edge of town. Camping and other outdoor supplies are sold at **Ron's Sporting Goods**, 138 S. Main, tel. 586-9901; **Gart Bros. Sporting Goods**, 606 S. Main, tel. 586-0687; **Wal-Mart**, 750 S. Main, tel. 586-0172; and **Kmart**, 889 S. Main, tel. 586-5208. **Valley View Medical Center**, 595 S. 75 East, tel. 586-6587, provides hospital care. The **post office** is at 10 N. Main, tel. 586-6701.

Information

Cedar City Chamber of Commerce has literature and advice on travel in the area; open Mon.-Fri. 8 a.m.-7 p.m., Saturday 9 a.m.-1 p.m. in summer, then Mon.-Fri. 8 a.m.-5 p.m. the rest of the year; located in the main city park at 286 N. Main (Box 220, Cedar City, UT 84721), tel. 586-4484. **Cedar City Ranger District** office of the Dixie National Forest has information on recreation and travel on the Markagunt Plateau; at 82 N. 100 East (Box 627, Cedar City, UT 84721-0627), tel. 865-3200. The Dixie National Forest **supervisor's office**, in the same building, provides general information for the entire forest; Box 580, Cedar City, UT 84721-0580, tel. 865-3700 (supervisor's office). The **BLM's Cedar City District** office can tell you about the BLM lands in southwestern Utah, including Beaver River, Dixie, Kanab, and Escalante resource areas; open Mon.-Fri. 7:45 a.m.-4:30 p.m.; located just off Main at 176 E. DL Sargeant

Dr. on the north edge of town (Cedar City, UT 84720), tel. 586-2401. For more specific info on the southern Wah Wah Mountains and other desert areas around town, visit the **BLM's Beaver River Resource Area** office; open Mon.-Fri. 7:45 a.m.-4:30 p.m.; at 366 E. Main, (Cedar City, UT 84720), tel. 586-2458. **Cedar City Public Library,** 136 W. Center, tel. 586-6661, has good reading material; open Mon.-Thurs. 9 a.m.-9 p.m., Friday and Saturday 9 a.m.-6 p.m. **Mountain West Bookstore,** 77 N. Main, tel. 586-3828, offers a selection of Utah history, travel, general reading, and LDS titles.

Transport

See the telephone *Yellow Pages* for car rental agencies. **Greyhound Bus,** 1355 S. Main (near the south I-15 interchange), tel. 586-1204, offers service at least twice daily to Salt Lake City, Denver, St. George, Las Vegas, and other destinations from the C-Mart. **Skywest Airlines** flies daily to and from Salt Lake City (three times daily, $89-117 one-way), St. George (once daily, $35 one-way), and other regional cities; call for weekend, roundtrip, and special fares, tel. (800) 453-9417.

PAROWAN

Although just a small town, Parowan (pop. 1,800) is southern Utah's oldest community and the seat of Iron County. Highway UT 143 turns south from downtown to the Brian Head Ski Area, Cedar Breaks National Monument, and other scenic areas on the Markagunt Plateau. To the west lies Utah's desert country. Accommodations in town offer a less expensive alternative to those in Brian Head. **Iron County Fair** presents a parade, rodeos, horse races, exhibits, and entertainment during the Labor Day holiday. The **Parowan City Office** will answer your questions about the area; open Mon.-Fri. 9 a.m.-4 p.m. at 5 S. Main (Box 576, Parowan, UT 84761), tel. 477-3331. Parowan is 18 miles northeast of Cedar City and 14 miles north of Brian Head; take I-15 Exits 75 or 78. The **public library** is across the street at 16 S. Main, tel. 477-3391.

Parowan Gap Petroglyphs

Indians have pecked many designs into the rocks at this pass 10.5 miles northwest of

Parowan. The gap was on the route of Indians and wildlife crossing the Red Hills, and it may have been an important site for hunting rituals. The meaning of this rock art hasn't been deciphered, but it probably represents the thoughts of many different Indian tribes over the past 1,000 or more years. Geometric designs, snakes, lizards, mountain sheep, bear claws, and human figures can be recognized. You can get here on a good gravel road from Parowan by going north on Main and turning left 10.5 miles on the last street (400 North). Or, from Cedar City, go north on Main (or take I-15 Exit 62), follow signs for UT 130 north 13.5 miles, then turn right two and one half miles on a good gravel road (near Milepost 19).

Practicalities

Jedediah's Inn and Restaurant, 625 W. 200 South (I-15 business route), tel. 477-3326, has rooms ($34.88 s, $41.42 d) and a restaurant (daily for breakfast, lunch, and dinner). **Swiss Village Motel (Best Western),** 580 N. Main, tel. 477-3391 or (800) 528-1234, offers rooms ($57.77 s, $67.58 d), a pool, spa, and restaurant (daily for breakfast and dinner). **Ace Motel,** 72 N. Main, tel. 477-3384, costs $24.50 s or d. **Grandma Bess' Cottage Bed & Breakfast,** 291 W. 200 South, tel. 477-8224, has rooms for $41.80 s or d. The **Pit Stop Restaurant** (fast food) has a campground with coin-operated showers at 492 N. Main, tel. 477-3714; $2 per person for tents, $6.54 RV no hookups, $11.99 RV w/hookups. **Parowan Cafe,** 33 N. Main, is open most days for breakfast, lunch, and dinner. **Pizza Barn,** 595 W. 200 South, tel. 477-8240, serves pizza and pasta daily for dinner.

Vermillion Castle Campground is in the Dixie National Forest at an elevation of 7,000 feet; open with water and a $5 fee from early May to mid-November; it may be open without water or fee the rest of the year; sites are among juniper and cottonwood trees along Bowery Creek; **Noah's Ark Trail** leads one steep mile to a high point with a great view of sunsets and picturesque rock layers including the Eocene Wasatch conglomerate; a group campground can be reserved by calling (800) 280-CAMP; go south four miles on UT 143, then left 1.4 miles on the road to Yankee Meadows Reservoir.

THE MARKAGUNT PLATEAU

Markagunt is an Indian name for "Highland of Trees." The large, high plateau consists mostly of gently rolling country, forests, and lakes. Black tongues of barren lava extend across some parts of the landscape. Cliffs at Cedar Breaks National Monument are the best-known feature of the plateau, but the land also drops away in the colorful Pink Cliffs farther southeast. Popular activities on the Markagunt include fishing, hiking, mountain bicycling, downhill and cross-country skiing, snowmobiling, and scenic drives. Highways UT 143 (across the northern part) and UT 14 (across the southern part) provide year-round access to the plateau. Contact the Cedar City Ranger District of the Dixie National Forest at 82 N. 100 East (Box 627, Cedar City, UT 84721-0627), tel. 865-3200, for a forest map and information on exploring the area. In summer, you can find volunteers or foresters at the visitor center on UT 14 opposite the Duck Creek Campground turnoff. Picnickers may stop at Duck Creek, Panguitch Lake, and Vermillion Castle campgrounds free of charge for up to two hours.

BRIAN HEAD

At an elevation of 9,850 feet, Brian Head is the highest municipality in Utah. Skiers like Brian Head for its abundant snow, challenging ski terrain, and good accommodations. Summer visitors come to enjoy the high country. The beautiful colors of Cedar Breaks National Monument lie just a few miles south. Panguitch Lake, to the east, receives high ratings for its excellent trout fishing. A winding paved highway provides year-round access to Brian Head's resort facilities; turn south 14 miles on UT 143 from Parowan (I-15 Exits 75 and 78). Other ways in are from Cedar City or Long Valley Junction via Cedar Breaks National Monument (road closed in winter) or from the town of Panguitch via Panguitch Lake (road usually open all year).

Brian Head Peak

The town takes its name from the flat-topped peak towering above to the east. Originally called Monument Peak, it got its present (misspelled) name in 1890 to honor the famed orator and politician, William Jennings Bryan. You can drive all the way to the 11,307-foot summit by car when the road is dry, usually from July to October. Panoramas from the top take in much of southwestern Utah and beyond into Nevada and Arizona. Sheep graze the grassy slopes below. From Brian Head, follow the highway about two miles south, then turn left (northeast) three miles on a gravel road to the summit. The stone shelter here was built by the Civilian Conservation Corps in the 1930s.

Brian Head Ski Resort

The town comes alive during the skiing season, from about mid-November to mid-April. Five triple and two double chairlifts carry skiers up both sides of the narrow valley to 48 runs. Forty percent of the terrain is rated beginner, 40% is intermediate, and 20% is advanced. The highest lift reaches an elevation of 10,920 feet on Brian Head Peak for a vertical drop of 1,161 feet. Lift tickets cost $32 adult full day, $24 adult half day; children 12 and under ski for $20 full day, $16 half day. Rentals, lessons, shops, and children's day care are available. Contact the resort and its reservation center at Box 190008, Brian Head, UT 84719, tel. 677-2035 or (800) 272-7426.

bobcat (Lynx rufus)

LOUISE FOOTE

Cross-Country Skiing

Brian Head Cross-Country Center (in the Brian Head Hotel) grooms about 22 km of trails in the area; ask for its map, tel. 677-2012. The short **North Rim Trail** goes to overlooks in Cedar Breaks National Monument. Experienced skiers with map and compass can head out on backcountry routes to the summit of Brian Head Peak and many other areas.

Accommodations

Brian Head Hotel is on the north (lower) side of town, tel. 677-3000 or (800) 468-4898; rooms go for $66 s, $71.50 d in summer; $93.50 s, $99 d winter weekdays; $104.50 s, $121 d winter weekends; and $132 s, $154 d winter holidays; condos and suites are available too. **The Lodge at Brian Head** up the street, tel. 677-3222 or (800) 386-5634, has rooms at $43.95-98.95 d in summer (call for winter rates). Nearly 20 **condominium** projects in town offer luxury accommodations with prices starting at about $65 d in summer; during the ski season expect to pay at least $75 ($125 holidays). You can either ask the chamber of commerce for a list of condominiums or contact one of the reservation offices: the **Accommodation Station,** Box 190128, Brian Head, UT 84719, tel. 677-3333 or (800) 572-9705; **Brian Head Condo Reservations,** Box 190217, Brian Head, UT 84719, tel. 677-2045 or (800) 722-4742; or **Brian Head Reservation Center,** Box 190055, Brian Head, UT 84719, tel. 677-2042 or (800) 845-9781. Many condominiums in town also offer ski packages.

Food

The Edge, tel. 677-3343, prepares sandwiches, steak, and seafood daily for lunch and dinner; closed part of spring and autumn. **Brian Head Hotel's** restaurant offers American cuisine daily for breakfast, lunch, and dinner; there's a deli, too; tel. 677-3000. The **Steakhouse at the Lodge,** in the Lodge at Brian Head, tel. 677-3222, serves steak, seafood, and pasta; open all year for breakfast, lunch, and dinner. **Pancho's & Lefty's,** 56 N. Hwy. 143, tel. 677-3322, serves Mexican dinners daily (in ski season). The **Black Diamond Cafe** serves breakfasts and sandwiches in the Brian Head Mall, tel. 677-3111; open daily for breakfast, lunch, and dinner (breakfast and lunch in summer). **Bump & Grind** serves gourmet coffee and pastries next

1. Deseret Peak (Great Salt Lake is visible in background); **2.** Raft River Mountains; **3.** Cedar Creek Canyon in the Deep Creek Mountains; **4.** Red Pine Lake (lower) in Little Cottonwood Canyon, Wasatch Range; **5.** Notch Peak at sunset, House Range; **6.** canyons of the Green River from Harpers Corner Trail, Dinosaur National Monument (all photos by Bill Weir)

1. Landscape Arch, Arches National Park; **2.** alcove along Harris Wash, Escalante River System; **3.** Green River sunset from Swasey Beach, near the mouth of Gray Canyon; **4.** Golden Throne (center) enveloped by mist, Capitol Reef National Park; **5.** Goosenecks of the San Juan River, Goosenecks State Park; **6.** foggy morning in Bryce Amphitheater, Bryce Canyon National Park (all photos by Bill Weir)

Cedar Breaks Amphitheater from Chocomon Ridge Overlook

door to the Black Diamond Cafe, tel. 677-2864. **Big O Pizza,** also in the Brian Head Mall, tel. 677 2300, dishes up pizza, spaghetti, and Italian sandwiches daily for lunch and dinner. **Brian Head Station** serves breakfast and lunch daily during the ski season next to Chairs 4 and 6, tel. 677-2035.

Services

The **post office** is in Brian Head Mall, near the center of town. Several shops have downhill ski rentals and supplies near the bases of the ski lifts. **Brian Head Cross-Country Center** specializes in cross-country skiing with rentals, instruction, guided tours, and sales; in summer the shop offers mountain bicycles (rentals, tours, maps, shuttle service, repairs, and sales), and hiking supplies; located in the Brian Head Hotel (Box 65, Brian Head, UT 84719), tel. 677-2012 or (800) 245-3754. **Crystal Mountain Recreation,** at the north edge of town, tel. 677-2386, offers guided snowmobile tours in winter.

Information

Brian Head Chamber of Commerce can be reached at Box 190068 (care of the City Offices), Brian Head, UT 84719, tel. 677-2013.

CEDAR BREAKS NATIONAL MONUMENT

Erosion on the west edge of the Markagunt Plateau has carved a giant amphitheater 2,500 feet deep and more than three miles across. A fairyland of forms and colors appears below the rim. Ridges and pinnacles extend like buttresses from the steep cliffs. Cottony patches of clouds often drift through the craggy landscape. Traces of iron, manganese, and other minerals have tinted the normally white limestone a rainbow of warm hues. The intense colors blaze during sunsets and glow even on a cloudy day. Rock layers look much like those at Bryce Canyon National Park and, in fact, are the same Claron Formation, but here they're 2,000 feet higher. Elevations range from 10,662 feet at the highest point on the rim to 8,100 feet at Ashdown Creek below. Cedar City and the valleys and ranges of the desert can be seen in the distance beyond the amphitheater. Dense forests broken by large alpine meadows cover the rolling plateau country away from the rim. More than 150 species of wildflowers brighten the meadows during summer; the colorful display peaks during the last two weeks in July.

A five-mile scenic drive leads past four spectacular overlooks, each with a different perspective. Avoid overlooks and other exposed areas during thunderstorms, which are common in summer afternoons. Heavy snows close the road most of the year. You can drive in only from about late May until the first big snowstorm of autumn, usually sometime in October. Winter visitors can come in on snowmobiles (unplowed roads only), skis, or snowshoes from Brian Head (two miles north of the monument) or from UT 14 (two and one half miles south). Cedar Breaks National Monument is 24 miles east of Cedar City, 17 miles south of Parowan, 30 miles southwest of Panguitch, and 27 miles northwest of Long Valley Junction. Nearest accommodations and restaurants are two miles north in Brian Head.

Visitor Center And Campground

A log cabin contains exhibits and an information desk. The exhibits provide a good introduction to the Markagunt Plateau and identify local rocks, wildflowers, trees, animals, and birds. Related books, topo and forest maps, posters, slides, and film are sold. Staff offer nature walks, geology talks, and campfire programs; see the schedule posted in the visitor center and at the campground. Open daily 8 a.m.-6 p.m. from about June 1 to mid-October. A $3 per vehicle entrance fee is collected near the visitor center; there's no charge if you're just driving through the monument without stopping. The small campground to the east has water and a $6 fee; camping is first come, first served. The campground is open from about June 1 to mid-September. There's a picnic area near the campground. Contact the monument at Box 749, Cedar City, UT 84720, tel. 586-9451.

Hiking Trails

Two easy trails near the rim give an added appreciation of the geology and forests here. Allow extra time while on foot—it's easy to get out of breath at these high elevations! Regulations prohibit pets on the trails. **Spectra Point/Wasatch Rampart Trail** begins at the visitor center, then follows the rim along the south edge of the amphitheater to an overlook. The hike is four miles roundtrip with some ups and downs. Weatherbeaten bristlecone pines grow at Spectra Point, about halfway down the trail.

Alpine Pond Trail forms a two-mile loop that drops below the rim into one of the few densely wooded areas of the amphitheater. The trail winds through enchanting forests of aspen, subalpine fir, and Engelmann spruce. Hiking distance can be cut in half with a car shuttle between the two trailheads or by taking a connector trail that joins the upper and lower parts of the loop near Alpine Pond. Begin from either Chessmen Ridge Overlook or the trailhead pullout 1.1 miles farther north. A trail guide is available at the start or at the visitor center.

ASHDOWN GORGE WILDERNESS

Experienced hikers can explore this wilderness on the Dixie National Forest and enter the Cedar Break National Monument's lower valleys. Although no trails within the monument itself wind from the rim down to the bottom, you can take **Rattlesnake Creek Trail** from a trailhead on the rim just outside the monument's north boundary. The rugged trail drops 3,400 feet in nine miles, following Rattlesnake and Ashdown creeks to the lower trailhead on UT 14 about seven miles east of Cedar City. Upon reaching Ashdown Creek, you have a choice of heading several miles upstream into the monument or entering the depths of Ashdown Gorge downstream. Check the weather forecast beforehand to avoid getting caught in a flash flood within the gorge. Hikers must be good at map reading and keeping an eye out for the next cairn or tree blaze. Rattlesnake and Ashdown creeks usually have water, though it can be silty or polluted by livestock. Some wading may have to be done in the gorge. Topo maps are the 7 1/2-minute Flanigan Arch or 15-minute Cedar Breaks. Check with staff at Cedar Breaks National Monument or Cedar City Ranger District for current trail conditions.

PANGUITCH LAKE AND VICINITY

This 1,250-acre reservoir sits in a volcanic basin surrounded by forests and barren lava flows. The cool waters have a reputation for outstanding trout fishing, especially for rainbow. Some German browns can also be caught in the lake and downstream in Panguitch Creek.

Recently, the lake has gained popularity for ice fishing. At least one resort has plans to open snowmobile trails and is considering having groomed cross-country ski tracks. The U.S. Forest Service has three campgrounds nearby; all are open with water from early June to mid-September. **Panguitch Lake North Campground,** on the southwest side of the lake, has developed sites in a ponderosa pine forest at an elevation of 8,400 feet; $7-14 fee. **Panguitch Lake South Campground,** across the highway, is more suited for small rigs; $5 fee. **White Bridge Campground** (elev. 7,900 feet) lies among cottonwoods and junipers along Panguitch Creek four miles northeast of the lake; $7 fee. Panguitch Lake lies along UT 143 about 16 miles southwest of Panguitch and 14 miles northeast of Cedar Breaks National Monument. The lake has public boat ramps on the south and north shores.

Panguitch Lake Resorts

Several fishing resorts encircle the lake. **Rustic Lodge** on the west shore, tel. 726-2627, has cabins ($136.25) and campsites ($9.81 tents and $16.35 RV w/hookups); open all year with lower winter cabin rates. **Deer Trail Lodge Resort,** northwest of the lake, tel. 676-2211, offers cabins ($49.05-136.25), campground ($8.18 tent or RV no hookups; $16.35 RV w/hookups; showers may be available), and restaurant (serving breakfast, lunch, and dinner daily); open year-round; take West or North Shore roads to Clear Creek Canyon Road, then turn west a half mile on it. **Beaver Dam Lodge** on the north shore, tel. 676-8339, has motel rooms ($65.40-81.75 summer, lower in winter), restaurant (open daily for breakfast, lunch, and dinner), small store, and boat rentals; open year-round; turn in three miles on West Shore Rd. from UT 143. **Panguitch Lake General Store and RV Park,** near the turnoff for West Shore Rd., tel. 676-2464, has an RV park ($15 w/hookups for self-contained RVs only), groceries, gas, gift shop and fishing supplies; the store is open all year.

Blue Springs Lodge is the area's newest resort, near the general store, tel. 676-2277. It has cabins that sleep six people ($81.75 summer, $54.50 winter) and plans to have an RV park. **Panguitch Lake Resort** on the south shore, tel. 676-2657 (in season) or 676-8326

(winter), has cabins ($59.95-65.40), RV park with showers ($16.90 w/hookups; no tents), restaurant (daily for breakfast, lunch, and dinner), small store, and boat rentals; open between about Memorial Day and Labor Day weekends. **Lake View Resort** is on the east shore, tel. 676-2650 (in season) or 628-2719 (winter), with cabins ($43.60-54.50), RV park ($16.35 w/hookups), small store, restaurant, post office, and boat rentals; open between about Memorial Day and Labor Day weekends.

Mammoth Springs

Moss and luxuriant streamside vegetation surround the crystal-clear spring waters at this beautiful spot. Mammoth Springs is about five and one half miles south of Panguitch Lake; the last two miles are on gravel Forest Route 068. See the Dixie National Forest map (Pine Valley and Cedar City ranger districts). A foot bridge leads across the stream to the springs.

Mammoth Cave

Step a few feet underground to explore the inside of a lava flow. When this mass of lava began to cool, the molten interior burst through the surface and drained out through a network of tunnels. A cave-in revealed this section of tunnel, which has two levels. One of the tunnels on the upper level can be followed through to another opening. The lower tunnel (with the large entrance) goes back about a quarter mile. To explore beyond that or to check out other sections, you'll have to stoop or crawl. Bring at least two reliable flashlights—the caves are very dark! Powerful flashlights work best. Mammoth Cave is about 14 miles south of Panguitch Lake; roads also lead in from Duck Creek on UT 14 and Hatch on US 89. You'll need the forest map to navigate the back roads, though there are some signs for Mammoth Cave.

RECREATION AREAS ALONG UT 14 (WEST TO EAST)

Cedar Canyon Campground

Sites lie along Crow Creek among aspen, fir, and spruce in a pretty canyon setting; elevation is 8,100 feet. Open with water from early June to mid-September; $5. Located 12 miles east of Cedar City on UT 14.

Zion Overlook

A sweeping panorama takes in the deep canyons and monuments of Zion National Park to the south. Located 16.5 miles east of Cedar City on the south side of the road.

Bristlecone Pine Trail

This easy half-mile loop, graded for wheelchair access, leads to the rim of the Markagunt Plateau and excellent views. A dense spruce-fir forest opens up near the rim, where storm-battered limber and bristlecone pines cling precariously near the edge. The bristlecone pines can be identified by their short-needled, "bottle-brush" branches. The trailhead is 17 miles east of Cedar City on the south side of UT 14.

Navajo Lake

Lava flows dammed this unusual three-and-one-half mile-long lake, which has no surface outlet. Instead, water drains through sinkholes in the limestone underneath and emerges as Cascade Falls (in the Pacific Ocean drainage) and Duck Creek (Great Basin drainage). From a pullout along the highway, 24 miles east of Cedar City, you can sometimes see three of the sinkholes at the east end; a dam prevents the lake from draining into them. Take the Navajo Lake turnoff, 25.5 miles east of Cedar City, for the campgrounds, marina, and lodge along the south shore. The U.S. Forest Service maintains **Spruces** and **Navajo campgrounds** along the lake and **Te-Ah Campground** one and one half miles west of the lake; all have water and a $7 fee from mid-June to mid-September; expect cool nights at the 9,200-foot elevation. Aspen, spruce, and fir grow along the lake. Boats can be rented and launched at **Behmer's Lodge and Landing**, between Spruces and Navajo campgrounds. **Navajo Lake Lodge,** at the west end of the lake, has cabins, a small cafe, store, boat rentals, and boat ramp; cabins cost $51.47 d, $109.92 for four persons, and up; open Memorial Day weekend to late October; tel. (702) 646-4197. Anglers catch rainbow trout and occasionally some eastern brook and brown trout; ice fishing is possible in winter. Small boats can be hand launched at Navajo Campground or from boat ramps at Navajo Lake Lodge and Behmer Lodge & Landing.

Virgin River Rim Trail

This new trail stretches about 38 miles along the rim between Deer Haven Group Campground and Strawberry Point. Beautiful panoramas of Zion National Park and the headwaters of the Virgin River reward trail users. You can also reach it at Te-Ah Campground, from Navajo Lake via short (one-half to three-quarter mile) spur trails, and at the start of the Cascade Falls National Recreation Trail. The entire length is open to hikers and mountain bikers. Off-highway vehicles can use the section from Deer Haven to Te-Ah campgrounds.

Cascade Falls National Recreation Trail

Splendid views and a waterfall make this an exciting trip. The easy trail is 1.1 miles roundtrip with some ups and downs. It begins at the south rim of the Markagunt Plateau, drops a short way down the Pink Cliffs, then winds along the cliffs to the falls. The falls gush from a cave and bounce their way down to the North Fork of the Virgin River and Zion Canyon. The flow peaks during spring runoff. Take the Navajo Lake turnoff from UT 14, go 0.3 mile, then turn left three miles on a gravel road to its end.

Duck Creek Campground

Turn north from UT 14 at Duck Lake, about 28 miles east of Cedar City. Sites (elev. 8,600 feet) are open early June to mid-September with water and a $7 fee. The adjacent creek and lake offer trout fishing. You'll see why Duck Lake got its name. A **visitor center**, staffed by the Dixie Interpretive Association, is open daily 10 a.m.-5 p.m. in summer across the highway from the campground turnoff. **Singing Pines Interpretive Trail,** just east of the visitor center, makes a half-mile loop; an amusing information sheet introduces the forest trees through songs. **Old Ranger Interpretive Trail** makes a one-third-mile loop from Duck Creek Campground; look for a large pullout on the left where the main campground road makes a curve to the right (near the amphitheater); the information sheet explains the forest through the eyes of an old-time forest ranger. Pick up information sheets for both trails from the visitor center. The **Lost Hunter Trail** makes a three-mile loop from the same trailhead in Duck Creek Campground to the top of Duck Creek Bench; elevation gain is about 600 feet with many fine views.

Ice Cave

Cool off inside this small cave, where the lava rock insulates ice throughout the summer. The road may be too rough for cars—ask conditions at the visitor center. Turn south on the dirt road beside the visitor center, keep left at the fork 0.2 mile in, keep right at another fork 0.8 mile farther, and continue 0.4 mile to the cave at the end of the road; signs mark the way.

Aspen Mirror Lake

Trout and scenic beauty attract visitors to this pretty reservoir. The turnoff is on the north side of UT 14 about midway between Duck Creek Campground and Duck Creek Village. Park, then walk the level trail about one-quarter mile.

Duck Creek Village

Hollywood has used this area since the 1940s to film such productions as *How the West Was Won*, *My Friend Flicka*, and the "Daniel Boone" TV series. The village lies at the edge of a large meadow (elev. 8,400 feet) about 30 miles east of Cedar City. The surrounding countryside is excellent for snowmobiling, a popular winter sport here. A big snowmobile race takes place on the weekend closest to Valentine's Day. Cross-country skiing is good too, on a variety of meadow, forest, and bowl terrain. The snow season lasts from about late November to late March. **Meadeau View Lodge** operates a bed and breakfast all year, tel. 682-2495; rates are $41.80-52.80 s, $55-66 d. **Falcon's Nest** offers cabins in the village, tel. 682-2556; $47.30-

66 year-round. **Thunder Inn Cafe** is open daily except Tuesday all year for breakfast, lunch, and dinner. **Loose Wheels,** tel. 682-2567, runs snowmobile tours and rentals, repairs snowmobiles, and rents cross-country skis; mountain bike rentals are offered in summer. For details on tours, offered jointly by Loose Wheels and Majestic Mountain Tours, call (800) 223-8264. A post office and stores are in town too.

To reach the rest of Duck Creek Village, drive one mile east, then a half mile south. **Pinewoods Inn,** tel. 682-2512, rents condominiums in the forest from May to October; $93.50 d. The **Pinewoods Restaurant,** tel. 682-2512, prepares prime rib, steak, seafood, and other fare all year; open daily for breakfast, lunch, and dinner. **Whispering Pines Lodge,** tel. 682-2378, has condominiums available all year; $82.50-126.50 for units sleeping from four to eight persons.

Strawberry Point

A magnificent panorama takes in countless ridges, canyons, and mountains south of the Markagunt Plateau. Zion National Park and even the Arizona Strip can be spotted from this lofty perch (elev. 9,016 feet). Erosion has cut delicate pinnacles and narrow canyons into the Pink Cliffs on either side below the viewpoint. Turn south from UT 14 between Mileposts 32 and 33 (32.5 miles east of Cedar City) onto a gravel road and go nine miles to its end. A 500-foot path continues to Strawberry Point. Take care near the edge—the rock is crumbly and there are no guardrails.

BRYCE CANYON NATIONAL PARK

A geologic fairyland of rock spires rises beneath the high cliffs of the Paunsaugunt Plateau. This intricate maze, eroded from a soft limestone, now glows with warm shades of reds, oranges, pinks, yellows, and creams. The rocks provide a continuous show of changing color through the day as the sun's rays and cloud shadows move across the landscape. Visitors perceive a multitude of wondrous forms. The natural rock sculptures can be Gothic castles, Egyptian temples, subterranean worlds inhabited by dragons, or vast armies of a lost empire. The Paiute Indian tale of the Legend People, relates how various animals and birds once lived in a beautiful city built for them by Coyote; when the Legend People began behaving badly toward Coyote, he transformed them all into stone. Bryce Canyon National Park contains some of the best scenery, though what's popularly called Bryce Canyon isn't a canyon at all, but the largest of a series of massive amphitheaters cut into the Pink Cliffs. You can gaze into the depths from viewpoints and trails on the plateau rim or descend moderate grades winding among the spires. More of the park can be seen along a 17-mile scenic drive south past Bryce Canyon to other overlooks and trailheads. The nearly 36,000 acres of Bryce Canyon National Park offers many opportunities to explore spectacular rock features, dense forests, and expansive meadows. Many wildlife and plant communities make their homes in the park.

Cool temperatures prevail most of the year at the park's 6,600- to 9,100-foot elevations. Expect pleasantly warm days in summer, frosty nights in spring and autumn, and snow in winter. The visitor center, scenic drive, and a campground stay open through the year. Allow a full day to see the visitor center exhibits, enjoy the viewpoints along the scenic drive, and to take a few short walks. Photographers usually obtain best results early and late in the day when shadows set off the brightly colored rocks. Memorable sunsets and sunrises reward visitors who stay overnight. Moonlit nights reveal yet another spectacle.

From Bryce Junction (on US 89, seven miles south of Panguitch), turn east 14 miles on UT 12, then south three miles on UT 63. Or, from Torrey (near Capitol Reef National Park), head west 103 miles on UT 12, then turn south three miles; winter snows occasionally close this section of UT 12. Both approaches have spectacular scenery. The park entrance fee of $5 per vehicle ($3 bicyclists) is good for seven days. A brochure available at the entrance station and visitor center has a map of major scenic features, drives, and trails.

The Hoodoos

The park's landscape originated about 60 million years ago as sediments in a large body of water, named Lake Flagstaff by geologists. Silt and calcium carbonate and other minerals settled on the lake bottom. These sediments consolidated and became the Claron Formation, a soft, silty limestone with some shale and sandstone. Lake Flagstaff had long since disappeared when the land began to rise as part of the Colorado

hoodoo at Agua Canyon Overlook

Plateau uplift about 16 million years ago. Uneven pressures beneath the plateau caused it to break along fault lines into a series of smaller plateaus at different levels known as the "Grand Staircase." Bryce Canyon National Park occupies part of one of these plateaus—the Paunsaugunt. The spectacular Pink Cliffs on the east edge contain the famous erosional features known as the "hoodoos," carved in the Claron Formation. Variations in hardness of the rock layers result in these strange features, which seem almost alive. Water flows through cracks, wearing away softer rock around hard, erosion-resistant caps. Finally, a cap becomes so undercut that the overhang allows water to drip down, leaving a "neck" of rock below the harder cap. Traces of iron and manganese provide the distinctive coloring. The hoodoos continue to change—new ones form and old ones fade away. Despite appearances, wind plays little role in creation of the landscape; it's the freezing and thawing, snowmelt, and rainwater that dissolve weak layers, pry open cracks, and carve out the forms. The plateau cliffs, meanwhile, recede at a rate of about one foot every 50-65 years; look for trees on the rim that now overhang the abyss. Listen, and you might hear the sounds of pebbles falling away and rolling down the steep slopes.

Flora And Fauna
Vegetation in the park changes considerably with elevation. Piñon pine, Utah juniper, and Gambel oak dominate the warmer and drier slopes below about 7,000 feet. Ponderosa pines rise majestically over greenleaf manzanita and other shrubs between elevations of 7,000 and 8,500 feet. Blue spruce, white fir, Douglas fir, limber pine, bristlecone pine, and aspen thrive in the cool moist conditions above 8,500 feet. Wildflowers put on a showy display from spring to early autumn. Springs and seeps below the rim support pockets of water birch, bigtooth maple, willows, and narrow-leaf cottonwood.

Larger wildlife visit the higher elevations in summer, then move down out of the park as winter snows arrive. You can often spot mule deer grazing in meadows, especially in morning and evening. Other residents include mountain lion, black bear, coyote, bobcat, gray fox, striped skunk, badger, porcupine, Utah prairie dog, yellow belly marmot, Uinta chipmunk, and golden-mantled ground squirrel. Beaver live near the

park on the East Fork of Sevier River. (Paunsaugunt is Paiute for "Home of the Beaver.") A few reptiles can be found despite the cool climate; look for the short horned lizard, skink, and Great Basin rattlesnake. Birds appear in greatest numbers from May to October. Violet-green swallows and white-throated swifts dive and careen among the hoodoos in hot pursuit of flying insects. Other summer visitors are the golden eagle, red-tailed hawk, western tanager, and mountain bluebird. Year-round residents include woodpeckers, owls, raven, Steller's jay, Clark's nutcracker, and blue grouse. Although some wild creatures may seem quite tame, they must not be fed or handled—rodents may have diseases, and young deer contaminated with human scent might be abandoned by their mothers. Also animals who become dependent on humans may die in winter when left to forage for themselves after the summer crowds have left.

History
Prehistoric Anasazi lived in the lower country surrounding Bryce and probably made frequent trips into what is now the park area to hunt game and gather piñon nuts and other wild foods. Nomadic groups of Paiute Indians later wandered into the area on seasonal migrations. Mormon pioneer Ebenezer Bryce homesteaded near the townsite of Tropic in 1875, but the work of scratching a living from the rugged land became too hard. He left five years later for more promising areas in Arizona. The name of the park commemorates his efforts. He is remembered as saying, "Well, it's a hell of a place to lose a cow."

A later settler, Ruben "Ruby" Syrett, recognized the tourist potential of the area and opened the first small lodge near Sunset Point in 1919, then Ruby's Inn in 1924. Enthusiasm for the scenic beauty led to creation of Bryce Canyon National Monument in 1923. The name changed to Utah National Park in the following year, then took its current name in 1928. Tours organized by the Union Pacific Railroad, beginning in the late 1920s, made Bryce well known and easily visited.

Visitor Center
From the turnoff on UT 12, follow signs past Ruby's Inn to the park entrance; the visitor center is a short distance farther on the right. A

brief slide show, screened on request, introduces the park. Geologic exhibits illustrate how the land was formed and how it has changed. Historic displays interpret the Paiute Indians, early explorers, and the first settlers. Trees, flowers, and wildlife are identified. Rangers present a variety of naturalist programs, including short hikes, from mid-May to early September; see the posted schedule. Staff sell travel and natural history books, maps of the park and adjacent Dixie National Forest, posters, postcards, slides, and film. Open daily all year (except Christmas) 8 a.m.-4:30 p.m., with extended hours during the warmer months. Contact the park at Bryce Canyon, UT 84717, tel. 834-5322.

Special hazards you should be aware of include crumbly ledges and lightning strikes. People who have wandered off trails or gotten too close to the drop-offs have had to be pulled out by rope. Avoid cliffs and other exposed areas during electrical storms, which are most common in late summer.

Winter Visits

Try a visit during the winter too. Snow on the rocks appears like frosting on a cake. The deep blue sky and crystal-clear air between storms make panoramas particularly inspiring. Roads and most viewpoints are plowed. Snowshoes (loaned free at the visitor center) or cross-country skis (rented at Ruby's Inn) allow excursions into the backcountry. **Paria Ski Trail** (five-mile loop) and **Fairyland Ski Trail** (two and one half-mile loop) are marked for snowshoers and cross-country skiers. A free backcountry permit is needed for overnight excursions.

SCENIC DRIVE

From elevations of about 8,000 feet near the visitor center, the scenic drive gradually winds 1,100 feet higher to Rainbow Point. About midway you'll notice a change in the trees from largely ponderosa pine to spruce, fir, and aspen. On a clear day, you can enjoy vistas of more than 100 miles from many of the viewpoints. Because of parking shortages on the drive, trailers must be left at the visitor center or campsite. The road beyond Inspiration Point will be closed to vehicular traffic during the summer of 1995 for road and parking lot improvements. Visitors

wishing to see the rest of the viewpoints may choose to walk on the Rim Trail.

Fairyland Point

To reach the turnoff (just inside the park boundary), go north 0.0 mile from the visitor center, then east one mile. Whimsical forms line Fairyland Canyon a short distance below. You can descend into the "fairyland" on the **Fairyland Loop Trail** or follow the **Rim Trail** for other panoramas.

Sunrise And Sunset Points

These overlooks are off to the left about one mile past the visitor center; they're connected by a half-mile paved section of the **Rim Trail.** Panoramas from each point take in large areas of Bryce Amphitheater and beyond. The lofty Aquarius and Table Cliff plateaus rise along the skyline to the northeast; you can recognize the same colorful Claron Formation in cliffs that faulting has raised about 2,000 feet higher. **Queen's Garden Trail** from Sunrise Point and **Navajo Trail** from Sunset Point provide different

a misty morning at Sunrise Point

experiences within the amphitheater. **Sunrise Nature Center,** near the parking area for Sunrise Point, has book sales, a few exhibits, and ranger information.

Inspiration Point

Walk south three-quarters of a mile along the **Rim Trail** from Sunset Point or drive a bit more than a mile to see a fantastic maze of hoodoos in the "Silent City." Weathering along vertical joints has cut many rows of narrow gullies, some more than 200 feet deep.

Bryce Point

This overlook at the south end of Bryce Amphitheater has memorable views to the north and east. It's also the start for the **Rim, Peekaboo Loop,** and **Under-the-Rim trails.** From the turnoff two miles south of the visitor center, follow signs 2.1 miles in.

Parla View

Cliffs drop precipitously into the headwaters of Yellow Creek, a tributary of the Paria River. You can see a section of Under-the-Rim Trail winding up a hillside near the mouth of the amphitheater below. Distant views take in the Paria River Canyon, White Cliffs (of Navajo Sandstone), and Navajo Mountain. The plateau rim in the park forms a drainage divide. Precipitation falling west of the rim flows gently into the East Fork of Sevier River and the Great Basin; precipitation landing east of the rim rushes through deep canyons in the Pink Cliffs to the Paria River and on to the Colorado River and Grand Canyon. Take the turnoff for Bryce Point, then keep right at the fork.

Farview Point

The sweeping panorama takes in a lot of geology. You can see levels of the Grand Staircase that include the Aquarius and Table Cliff plateaus to the northeast, Kaiparowits Plateau to the east, and White Cliffs to the southeast. Look beyond the White Cliffs to see a section of the Kaibab Plateau that forms the north rim of the Grand Canyon in Arizona. The overlook is on the left nine miles south of the visitor center.

Natural Bridge

This large feature lies just off the road on the left, 1.7 miles past Farview Point. The span is 54 feet wide and 95 feet high. Most likely it was formed by weathering from rain and freezing, rather than by stream erosion like a true natural bridge. Once the opening reached ground level, runoff began to enlarge the hole and to dig a gully through it.

Agua And Ponderosa Canyons

Sheer cliffs and hoodoos can be admired from Agua Canyon overlook on the left, 1.4 miles past Natural Bridge. With a little imagination, you might be able to pick out the Hunter and the Rabbit below. Ponderosa Canyon overlook, on the left 1.8 miles farther, offers a panorama similar to that at Farview Point.

Yovimpa Point And Rainbow Point

The land drops away in rugged canyons and fine views at the end of the scenic drive, 17 miles south of the visitor center. At an elevation of 9,105 feet, this is the highest area of the park. Yovimpa and Rainbow points lie only a short walk apart, yet they offer different vistas. **Bristlecone Loop Trail** is an easy one-mile loop from Rainbow Point to ancient bristlecone pines along the rim. **Riggs Spring Loop Trail** makes a good day hike; you can begin from either Yovimpa Point or Rainbow Point and descend into canyons in the southern area of the park. **Under-the-Rim Trail** starts from Rainbow Point and winds 22.5 miles to Bryce Point; dayhikers could make a seven and one half mile trip by using the Agua Canyon Connecting Trail and a car shuttle.

HIKING

Hikers enjoy close-up views of the wondrous erosional features. The approximately 61 miles of trails also add to an appreciation of the geology at Bryce. Most of the hiking is moderately difficult, with many ups and downs, but the paths are well graded and signed. Hikers not accustomed to the 7,000- to 9,000-foot elevations will find the going relatively strenuous and should allow extra time. A hat and sunscreen protect against sunburn, which can be a problem at these elevations. Don't forget rain gear because storms can come up suddenly. Always carry water for day-trips as only a few natural sources exist. Ask at the visitor center for hiking maps,

Bryce Canyon rock formations

current trail conditions, and water sources. Snow may block some trail sections in winter and early spring. Overnight hikers can obtain the required backcountry permits at the visitor center (camping is allowed only on the Under-the-Rim and Riggs Spring Loop trails). Backpack stoves must be used for cooking, because open fires and wood gathering damage the natural environment. Horses are permitted only on Peekaboo Loop. Pets must stay above the rim; they're allowed on the Rim Trail only between Sunset and Sunrise points. Don't expect much solitude during the summer on the popular Rim, Queen's Garden, Navajo, and Peekaboo Loop trails. Fairyland Loop Trail is less used and the backcountry trails are almost never crowded. September and October are the choice hiking months—the weather is best and the crowds smallest, though nighttime temperatures in late October can dip well below freezing.

Rim Trail
This easy trail follows the edge of Bryce Amphitheater for five and one half miles between

Fairyland Point and Bryce Point; elevation change is 540 feet. Most people walk just sections in leisurely strolls or use the trail to connect with five others. The half-mile section near the lodge between Sunrise and Sunset points is paved and nearly level; other parts are gently rolling.

Fairyland Loop Trail
The trail winds in and out of colorful rock spires in the northern part of Bryce Amphitheater. Though it's well graded, remember the 900-foot climb you'll make when you exit. You can take a loop hike of eight miles from either Fairyland Point or Sunrise Point by using a section of the **Rim Trail;** a car shuttle saves three hiking miles. The whole loop is too long for many visitors, who enjoy short trips down and back to see this "fairyland."

Queen's Garden Trail
A favorite of many people, this trail drops from Sunrise Point through impressive features in the middle of Bryce Amphitheater to a hoodoo resembling a portly Queen Victoria. The hike is one and one half miles roundtrip and has an elevation change of 320 feet, which you'll have to climb on the way back. This is the easiest excursion below the rim and takes about one and one half hours. Queen's Garden Trail also makes a good loop hike with **Navajo** and **Rim trails;** most people who do the loop prefer to descend the steeper Navajo and climb out on Queen's Garden Trail for a three and one half mile hike. Trails also connect with the **Peekaboo Loop Trail** and go to the town of Tropic.

Navajo Loop Trail
From Sunset Point, you'll drop 520 feet in three-quarters of a mile through a narrow canyon. At the bottom, the loop leads into the deep, dark **Wall Street**—an even narrower canyon a half mile long, then returns to the rim; total distance is about one and one half miles. Other destinations from the bottom of Navajo Trail are **Twin Bridges, Queen's Garden Trail, Peekaboo Loop Trail,** and the town of Tropic. The one and one half mile trail to Tropic isn't as scenic as the other trails, but it does provide another way to enter or leave the park; ask at the visitor center or in Tropic for directions to the trailhead.

Peekaboo Loop Trail

An enchanting walk full of surprises at every turn—and there are lots of turns! The trail is in the southern part of Bryce Amphitheater, which has some of the most striking rock features. You can start from Bryce Point (six and one half miles roundtrip), from Sunset Point (five and one half miles roundtrip via Navajo Trail), or from Sunrise Point (seven miles roundtrip via Queen's Garden Trail). The loop itself is three and one half miles long with many ups and downs and a few tunnels. Elevation change is 500-800 feet, depending on the trailhead you choose.

Under-The-Rim Trail

The longest trail in the park winds 22.5 miles below the Pink Cliffs between Bryce Point in the north to Rainbow Point in the south. Allow at least two days to hike the entire trail; elevation change is about 1,500 feet with many ups and downs. Four connecting trails from the scenic drive allow you to travel Under-the-Rim Trail as a series of day-hikes too. Another option is to combine Under-the-Rim and **Riggs Spring Loop** trails for a total of 31.5 miles.

The **Hat Shop** of delicate spires capped by erosion-resistant rock makes a good day-hiking destination; begin at Bryce Point and follow Under-the-Rim Trail for about two miles. Most of this section is downhill (elevation change of 900 feet), which you'll have to climb on the way out.

Bristlecone Loop Trail

The easy one-mile loop begins from either Rainbow or Yovimpa points and goes to viewpoints and ancient bristlecone pines along the rim. These hardy trees survive fierce storms and extremes of hot and cold that no other tree can. Some of the bristlecone pines here are 1,700 years old.

Riggs Spring Loop

One of the park's more challenging day-hikes or a leisurely overnighter, this trail begins from either Yovimpa Point or Rainbow Point and descends into canyons in the southern area of the park. The loop is about nine miles with an elevation change of 1,625 feet. A shortcut bypassing Riggs Spring saves three-quarters of a mile.

Mossy Cave Trail

This easy trail near the east edge of the park goes up Water Canyon to a cool alcove of dripping water and moss. Sheets of ice and icicles add beauty to the scene in winter. The hike is only one mile roundtrip with a small elevation gain. A side trail, just before the cave, branches right a short distance to a little waterfall; look for several small arches in the colorful canyon walls above. Although the park lacks perennial natural streams, the stream in Water Canyon flows even during dry spells. Mormon pioneers labored three years to channel water from the East Fork of the Sevier River through a canal and down this wash to the town of Tropic. Without this irrigation, the town might not even exist. From the visitor center, return to UT 12 and turn east 3.7 miles toward Escalante; the parking area is on the right just after a bridge (between Mileposts 17 and 18). Rangers schedule guided walks to the cave and waterfall during the main season.

PRACTICALITIES IN THE PARK

Accommodations and campsites can be hard to find from April to October in both the park and nearby areas. Advance reservations at lodges and motels are a good idea then; otherwise, plan to arrive by late morning. **Bryce Canyon Information Line,** an area reservation service, can be reached at tel. (800) 444-6689. Park campgrounds operate on a first-come, first-served basis; arrive by noon in the main season to be assured of a spot.

Bryce Canyon Lodge

Set among ponderosa pines a short walk from the rim, Bryce Canyon Lodge has by far the best location. It's open from about mid-April to late October. You have a choice of motel rooms ($67.50-73.74 s or d), western cabins ($78.50-85.73 s or d), or a lodge suite ($109.16). The lodge dining room offers a varied menu with moderate prices; open daily in season for breakfast, lunch, and dinner (reservations advised for dinner). Box lunches can be ordered 12 hours in advance. The lodge organizes horseback rides, park tours, evening entertainment, and ranger talks; a gift shop sells souvenirs. Try to make reservations for accommodations as far in advance as possible (eight is months advised) with TW Services, Box 400, Cedar City, UT 84720, tel. 586-7686 (reservations service in Cedar City) or 834-5361 (Bryce Canyon Lodge).

North And Sunset Campgrounds

The two campgrounds have water, some pull-through spaces, and a ¢7 fee. North Campground is on the left just past the visitor center. Sunset Campground is about two and one half miles farther on the right, across the road from Sunset Point; both campgrounds have a loop for tenters. Sunset has handicapped-accessible spaces. Groceries, camping supplies, and coin-operated showers and laundry are available from mid-May to late September at the **General Store,** between North Campground and Sunrise Point. During the rest of the year, you can go outside the park to Ruby's Inn for these services. Try to arrive early for a space during the busy summer season; both campgrounds usually fill by 1 or 2 p.m. then. Only group areas may be reserved.

PRACTICALITIES OUTSIDE THE PARK

Ruby's Inn

The large motel, part of the Best Western chain, offers many year-round services on UT 63 just north of the park boundary (Bryce, UT 84764), tel. 834-5341 or (800) 528-1234. Rooms start at $87.20 s or d in summer and $45.18 s or d in winter; kitchenettes and family rooms cost extra. An indoor heated pool is open except in winter. The restaurant serves breakfast, lunch, and dinner daily; no reservations needed. A snack bar is open for lunch and dinner April-October. The **campground,** tel. 834-5341, is open from early April to late October with spaces for tents ($12.54) and RVs ($19.62 w/hookups); showers and laundry are open all year. The **general store** has a large stock of groceries, camping and fishing supplies, film and processing, Indian crafts, books, and other souvenirs. The **Bryce post office** is at the store too. Horseback rides, helicopter tours, and airplane rides are arranged in the lobby. In winter, cross-country skiers can rent gear and use trails located near the inn as well as in the park. Snowmobile trails are available (snowmobiles may not be used within the park). Western-fronted shops across from Ruby's Inn offer trail rides, chuckwagon dinners, mountain bicycle rentals, souvenirs, and a petting farm. **Rodeos** take place in the nearby arena nightly Mon.-Sat. in season. Rooms should be reserved as far in advance as possible for the April-Oct. season.

Bryce Village Inn

This motel is on UT 12 at the turnoff for the park, tel. 834-5303. Motel rooms cost $74.94 s, $79.74 d from about April 1 to October 31; cabins go for $43.60 and $74.94 during the same season; prices may drop in winter. Its restaurant features steak and barbecue; open daily for breakfast, lunch, and dinner; closed in winter. **Foster's Family Steak House,** about two miles west on UT 12, tel. 834-5227, serves breakfast, lunch, and dinner daily (dinner only in winter) and has a **motel** ($54.45 s or d in season, less in winter), supermarket, bakery, and AAA car service.

Bryce Canyon Pines

The motel is six miles west on UT 12 from the park turnoff, tel. 834-5441. Rooms cost $60 s, $70.80 d from March 15 to November 15; rates drop off-season. A covered pool is open during the warmer months. The restaurant is open daily for breakfast, lunch, and dinner from early April to late October. **Red Canyon Trail Rides** has horseback riding from May to October. The **Bryce Canyon Country Store** a quarter mile west of the motel, tel. 834-5441, has a campground for tents ($9.81 s, $10.81 d) and RVs ($15.26 w/hookups) with showers, laundry, store, and pool; open about April-November.

Dixie National Forest Campgrounds

All three campgrounds have a scenic setting in the woods. Often they'll have room when campgrounds in the park have filled. Group sites can be reserved but the rest are available on a first-come, first-served basis. The campgrounds may also be open before and after the main season without water or charge. **Kings Creek Campground** is in a ponderosa pine forest at 8,000 feet on the west shore of Tropic Reservoir; open with water and a $6 fee from late May to late September; drive west 2.8 miles on UT 12 from the park turnoff, then turn south seven miles on the gravel East Fork Sevier River Road. Tropic Reservoir has a boat ramp and fair trout fishing. **Red Canyon Campground** lies in a ponderosa pine forest at 7,400 feet below brilliantly colored cliffs; open with water and a $7 fee from late May to late September; drive west 10 miles on UT 12 from the park turnoff (or four miles east on UT 12 from US 89). **Red Canyon Campground Trail** begins at Site #23 in the campground and climbs 450 feet in 0.8 mile for fine views of erosional forms and Red Canyon. **Pine Lake Campground** is just east of Pine Lake in a forest of ponderosa pine, spruce, and juniper at 7,700 feet; open with water and a $6 fee from mid-June to mid-September; from the highway junction north of the park, head northeast 11 miles on UT 63 (gravel), then turn southeast six miles. Contact the Powell Ranger District office

in Panguitch (tel. 676-8815) for more information on Kings and Red Canyon campgrounds, and the Escalante Ranger District office in Escalante (tel. 826-4221) for Pine Lake.

Red Canyon Indian Store And RV Park
The campground has showers and sites for tents ($8.72) and RVs ($12 w/hookups) from late March to late October; cabins cost $18.53 s, $23.98 d; tel. 676-2690. The adjacent Indian Store has Indian crafts, souvenirs, and a rock shop; closed in winter. **Harold's Place Cafe** is nearby across the highway, 0.9 mile east of US 89 on UT 12.

black bear (Ursus americanus)

LOUISE FOOTE

VICINITY OF BRYCE CANYON NATIONAL PARK

Red Canyon

The drive on UT 12 between US 89 and the turnoff for Bryce Canyon National Park passes through this well-named canyon. You may think that it should have been included in the national park, as the brightly colored rocks belong to the same Claron Formation that's exposed at Bryce. Staff at **Red Canyon Visitor Center** can tell you of scenic backcountry roads, horseback trails, and hiking routes that wind through the area; books and maps are sold; open daily about 8 a.m.-6 p.m. during the warmer months; located between Mileposts 3 and 4 on UT 12, a quarter mile west of Red Canyon Campground. You can contact the Powell Ranger District office in Panguitch for information year-round, tel. 676-8815. For details about **Red Canyon Campground,** see "Practicalities Outside the Park," above.

The U.S. Forest Service has many scenic hiking trails that wind back from the highway to give you a closer look at the geology. **Pink Ledges Trail,** the easiest and most popular, loops a half mile past intriguing erosional features from Red Canyon Visitor Center. Signs identify some of the trees and plants; elevation gain is 100 feet. **Birdseye Trail** winds through formations and connects the visitor center with a parking area on UT 12 just inside the forest boundary, 0.8 mile away. **Buckhorn Trail** begins from Site #23 in Red Canyon Campground and climbs one mile for views of erosional forms and Red Canyon; the campground is on the south side of UT 12 between Mileposts 3 and 4. **Tunnels Trail** ascends 300 feet in 0.7 mile for fine views of the canyon. The trail begins from a pullout on the south side of UT 12 just west of a pair of tunnels, crosses the streambed, then climbs a ridge to viewpoints on the top. Other good trails in the area can be explored too; ask at the visitor center.

Powell Point

Even in a state with many superb viewpoints, Powell Point (elev. 10,188 feet) is outstanding. Yet surprisingly few people know about this lofty perch at the southern tip of the Table Cliff Plateau, a southwestern extension of the Aquarius Plateau. Its light-colored cliffs stand about 15 air miles northeast of Sunset Point in Bryce Canyon National Park. Getting to Powell Point involves a bit of adventure. Cars with good clearance can be driven within 4.3 miles of the point; high-clearance vehicles can go to within 0.6 mile of the point. From the highway junction north of the national park, drive northeast 11 miles on UT 63 (gravel), turn southeast six miles to Pine Lake, continue east six miles on Forest Route 132 up onto the plateau, then look for the one-lane dirt road on the right to Powell Point; high-clearance vehicles can turn in 3.7 miles to the Powell Point trailhead. If you're not equipped for driving this rough road, you'll still find it good for hiking or mountain bicycling. The road ends where the ridge becomes too narrow for it; a clearing here is fine for camping (no facilities).

A foot trail continues 0.6 mile to the very end of Powell Point. On the way you'll pass through an extremely weather-beaten and picturesque forest of bristlecone and limber pine. Panoramic views begin well before trail's end; at the point itself you'll feel as though you're at the end of the world. Much of southern Utah and northern Arizona stretches out below to the far horizon. The colorful cliffs of the Claron Formation lie directly underfoot; take care near the crumbly cliff edges. Avoid Powell Point if thunderstorms threaten. (Note the many lightning scars on trees here!) The Escalante Ranger District office may have current road conditions to Powell Point, tel. 826-4221.

Tropic

Mormon pioneers settled six villages near the upper Paria River between 1876 and 1891. The towns of Tropic, Cannonville, and Henrieville still survive. Tropic lies just east of Bryce Canyon National Park and can be seen from many of the park's viewpoints. A log cabin built by Ebenezer Bryce has been moved to a site beside the Bryce Pioneer Village Motel; ask to see the cabin's small collection of pioneer and Indian artifacts. **Bryce Pioneer Village Motel,** tel. 679-8546, has rooms at $49.05-76.30 s or d regular, $59.95 d kitchenette and family; the RV park (closed in winter) has showers and costs $12.72 w/hookups. **Bryce Valley Inn,** tel. 679-8811 or (800) 442-1890, has rooms ($67.58 s or d), restaurant with American and some Mexican items (breakfast, lunch, and dinner daily), and a gift shop. **Under the Rim Inn,** tel. 679-8502, has rooms at $60 s or d. **Doug's Place,** tel. 679-8633, has motel rooms ($54.45 s or d), a restaurant (breakfast, lunch, and dinner daily), and a store; open all year. **Bryce Point Bed & Breakfast,** tel. 679-8629, and **Charley Francisco's Bed & Breakfast,** tel. 679-8721, also offer accommodations. A **tourist booth** in the center of town is open daily about 11 a.m.-7 p.m. from early May to late October.

KODACHROME BASIN STATE PARK

Visitors come to this basin southeast of Bryce Canyon National Park to see not only colorful cliffs but also strange-looking rock pillars that occur nowhere else in the world. Sixty-seven rock pillars (here called "sand pipes") found in and near the park range in height from six to nearly 170 feet. One theory of their origin is that earthquakes caused sediments deep underground to be churned up by water under high pressure. The particles of calcite, quartz, feldspar, and clay in the sand pipes came from underlying rock formations, and the pipes appeared when the surrounding rock eroded away. Most of the other rocks visible in the park are Entrada Sandstone: the lower orange layer is the Gunsight Butte Member and the white layer with orange bands is the Cannonville Member. Signs name some of the rock features. "Big Stoney," the phallus-shaped sand pipe overlooking the campground, is so explicit that it doesn't need a sign! An article, "Motoring into Escalante Land," by Jack Breed in the September 1949 issue of *National Geographic* brought attention to the scenery and renamed the area "Kodachrome Flat." The state park makes a worthwhile stop, both as a day-trip to see the geology and as a pleasant spot to camp. Entrance costs $3 per vehicle day use or $9 per vehicle camping ($10 Saturday, Sunday,

and holidays); Box 238, Cannonville, UT 84718, tel. 679-8562 or (800) 322-3770 (reservations).

To reach the park, drive to Cannonville (on UT 12, 12 miles southeast of the Bryce Canyon National Park turnoff and 36 miles southwest of Escalante) and follow signs south and east for nine miles on paved roads. Adventurous drivers can also approach the park from US 89 to the south via the Cottonwood Canyon road (39 miles) or the Skutumpah road through Bull Valley Gorge and Johnson Canyon (48 miles). These routes may be impassable in wet weather but may be okay for cars with good clearance in dry weather; ask about current conditions at Kanab, Paria Ranger Station (on US 89 near Milepost 21), or the visitor center at Glen Canyon Dam.

Campground
The state park's campground sits in a natural amphitheater at an elevation of 5,800 feet. It's open all year and has restrooms, showers, and dump station. Restrooms and showers may close in winter but pit toilets will be available. The campground usually has room except on summer holidays, though reservations can be made.

Hiking Trails
The short **Nature Trail** introduces the park's ecology. **Panorama Trail** loops through a highly scenic valley with sand pipes and colorful rocks; the easy trail is three miles roundtrip and takes about two hours. **Angel's Palace Trail** begins just east of the group campground and makes a three-quarter-mile loop with fine views; elevation gain is about 300 feet. **Grand Parade Trail** makes a one-and-one-half-mile loop with good views of rock pinnacles; begin from the concession or group campground. **Eagles View Trail,** a historic cattle trail, climbs nearly 1,000 feet up steep cliffs above the campground, then drops into Henrieville, two miles away; the highest overlook is a steep half-mile ascent from the campground. **Arch Trail** is a half-mile roundtrip hike to a natural arch; the trail can be reached by a signed dirt road or on a two-mile (roundtrip) trail; a brochure and numbered stops identify local plants.

Horseback Riding
Scenic Safaris operates guided horseback and horse-drawn coach rides in the park. You can

arrange rides at **Trailhead Station,** a small store in the park that sells groceries and camping supplies from about early April to late October, or contact Box 278, Cannonville, UT 84718, tel. 679-8536/8787.

SOUTH OF KODACHROME BASIN STATE PARK

Several highly scenic canyon systems cut deep into the plateaus south of Kodachrome Basin. The book *Hiking and Exploring the Paria River* by Michael Kelsey outlines some of the hiking possibilities in the region. The BLM staff at the Paria Ranger Station (on US 89 near Milepost 21) or at the office in Kanab (tel. 644-2672) knows about current road and hiking conditions. Hikers may encounter cattle and off-road vehicles in some areas, but most of the land remains a wilderness. Spring and autumn are the best hiking seasons, when you'll avoid the desert extremes found in winter and summer. Gnats and biting flies can be troublesome from

a sand pipe

late May into July; bring repellent and long pants.

Cottonwood Canyon And Grosvenor Arch
The road from Cannonville continues past the turnoff to Kodachrome Basin State Park and drops into the upper reaches of Cottonwood Creek (a tributary of the Paria River) and follows it for about 15 miles. Total distance on this scenic drive between Cannonville and US 89 is 46 miles one-way, nearly all of which is dirt. If coming from the south, look for the turnoff on US 89 between Mileposts 17 and 18. Cars with good clearance can do the trip anytime of year if the road is dry. Be especially cautious if any of the washes have water—cars sometimes get stuck in them. When wet, the road is slippery and hazardous even with 4WD vehicles. Check current conditions at Kodachrome Basin State Park, Paria Ranger Station (on US 89 near Milepost 21), Kanab, or the visitor center at Glen Canyon Dam. A one-mile side road leads to the magnificent Grosvenor Arch; the largest of the two openings is 99 feet across. The 1949 National Geographic Society expedition named the double arch in honor of the society's president. The turnoff is 10 miles from the state park turnoff and 29 miles from US 89.

Hackberry Canyon
Hikers can travel the 18-mile length of this scenic canyon in two to three days. The headwaters lie just south of the Cottonwood Canyon road between Kodachrome Basin State Park and Grosvenor Arch at an elevation of about 6,000 feet. The lower canyon meets Cottonwood Canyon at an elevation of 4,700 feet. Cottonwood Canyon road provides access to both ends. A small spring-fed stream flows down the lower half of Hackberry. Many side canyons invite exploration. One of them, Sam Pollock Canyon, is on the west about four and one half miles upstream from the junction of Hackberry and Cottonwood canyons; follow it one and three quarters miles up to **Sam Pollock Arch** (60 feet high and 70 feet wide). Available topo maps include the metric 1:100,000 Smoky Mountain or the 7¹/₂-minute Slickrock Bench and Calico Peak. Kelsey's book contains trail and trailhead information and a history of the Watson homestead, located a short way below Sam Pollock Canyon.

Upper Paria River Canyon
Although not as well known as the lower canyon, the upper section has some beautiful scenery and offers many side canyons to explore too. The Paria lies west of both Hackberry and Cottonwood canyons. Access to the upper end is from the Skutumpah or Cottonwood Canyon roads near Kodachrome Basin State Park (elev. about 5,900 feet). The usual lower entry is from near Pahreah ghost town (elev. 4,720 feet); turn north six miles from US 89 between Mileposts 30 and 31 and continue past the Pahreah movie set to road's end. (The clay road surface is very slippery when wet but is okay for cars when dry.) The upper canyon is about 25 miles long, and the hike takes three to four days (allowing some time to explore side canyons). Water can be found at springs along the main canyon and in many side canyons (purify first); try not to use water from the river itself as it may contain chemical pollution. Topo maps are the metric 1:100,000 Kanab and Smoky Mountain or the 7 1/2-minute Cannonville, Bull Valley Gorge, Deer Range Point, and Calico Peak. Again, Kelsey's book is a good source of history and hiking information for this area.

ALONG US 89: PANGUITCH TO KANAB

PANGUITCH

Pioneers arrived in 1864, but hostile Ute Indians forced evacuation just two years later. A second attempt by settlers in 1871 succeeded, and Panguitch (Indian for "Big Fish") is now the largest town in the area. The early 20th century commercial buildings downtown have some of their original facades. On side streets you can see sturdy brick houses built by the early settlers. Stop by the **DUP Museum** in the old bishop's storehouse at 100 East and Center to see historic exhibits of Panguitch; open Mon.-Sat. about 4-8 p.m. in summer and by appointment the rest of the year; phone numbers are on the door.

Practicalities
About 11 motels and six cafes line US 89 (Main and Center) in town. **Hitch-N-Post Campground,** 420 N. Main, tel. 676-2436 or (800) 282-9633, offers year-round spaces for tents ($8.75) and RVs ($13 w/hookups); has showers and laundry. **Big Fish KOA Campground,** 555 S. Main, tel. 676 2225, on the road to Panguitch Lake is open April 1 to October 31 with a pool, recreation room, laundry, and showers; $15.26 tent or RV no hookups, $17.44 RV w/hookups, $27.25 kamping kabins. **Sportsman's Paradise RV Park** is two miles north on US 89, tel. 676-8348; open May-Oct. for tents or RVs no hookups ($8.72) and RVs ($13.08 w/hookups); has a store, showers, pool, and laundry.
Major annual **events** include **Fourth of July** celebrations (parade, fireworks, and FFA junior rodeo in town; also fireworks at Panguitch Lake), **Pioneer Day** on July 24 (parade and rodeo), and **Garfield County Livestock Show and Fair** in mid-August. The **city park** on the north edge of town has picnic tables, a playground, tennis courts, and a tourist information cabin.

wooden Indian in front of a Panguitch store

A **swimming pool** is at 250 E. Center by the high school, tel. 676-8806. The **post office** is at 65 N. 100 West, tel. 676-8853. **Garfield Memorial Hospital** provides medical services at 224 N. 400 East, tel. 676-8811 (hospital), 676-8842 (clinic). The **Information Center** in the city park, tel. 676-8131 or (800) 444-6689 (Bryce Canyon Information Line), offers brochures and suggestions for services in Panguitch and travel to Bryce Canyon National Park and other scenic destinations nearby; open daily 9 a.m.-5 p.m. from early May to late October; closed in winter. **Garfield County Travel Council** can be contacted year-round at Box 200, Panguitch, UT 84759, tel. 676-2311. The **Powell Ranger District** of the U.S. Forest Service has information on campgrounds, hiking trails, fishing, and scenic drives in the forest and canyons surrounding Bryce Canyon National Park; open Mon.-Fri. 8 a.m.-4:30 p.m. at 225 E. Center (US 89) or write Box 80, Panguitch, UT 84759, tel. 676-8815. The **public library** is at 75 S. 400 East (across the street from the Forest Service), tel. 676-2431.

HATCH

The Hatch family started a ranch in the upper Sevier River Valley during the early 1870s. Colorful cliffs of the Paunsaugunt Plateau contrast with the blue sky to the east. Stop in at the **DUP Museum** to learn about the pioneers and see their artifacts; it's usually open summer afternoons (except Sunday), or you can call the telephone numbers posted on the front; turn west one block at the sign in the center of town. **Mountain Ridge Motel,** tel. 735-4258, is open about April-Oct.; rooms cost $36-40 s or d; an RV park with showers has spaces for tents ($8) and RVs ($12 w/hookups). **New Bryce Motel,** tel. 735-4265, has a cafe (open daily for breakfast, lunch, and dinner) and rooms ($45.78 s, $49.05 d and up); open about mid-March to late October. **Galaxy Motel,** tel. 735-4327, also has a cafe (open daily for breakfast, lunch, and dinner) and basic rooms ($27.25 s, $37.06 d); open late March to September. **Riverside Motel and Campground** is just north of town, tel. 735-4223, with rooms ($30.52 s, $38.15 d) and sites for tents ($10.72) and RVs ($12.75) year-round; it also offers trout fishing in the Sevier River, store, laundry, and showers. **Garfield Infor-**

mation Center, just south of town, is open daily 9 a.m.-5 or 6 p.m. from early May to late October with literature and advice for travel in Garfield County.

Mammoth Creek Hatchery
This is one of about 11 state hatcheries producing trout and other game fish. You're welcome to visit during daylight hours. Indoor areas house the eggs and fry; larger fish swim in the outdoor raceways. Go one mile south of Hatch on US 89 and turn west two miles on a paved road at the sign. An unpaved road continues to Mammoth Cave and other attractions on the Markagunt Plateau.

LONG VALLEY

Highway US 89 follows the East Fork of the Virgin River past a series of small Mormon towns north of Kanab. Nearly all travelers visiting the national parks of the region will pass through this forested valley. Most of the towns in Long Valley offer a handful of motels, campgrounds, and restaurants.

Long Valley Junction
The junction (elev. 7,200 feet) marks the divide between the East Fork of the Virgin River to the south and the Sevier River to the north. Turn west on UT 14 to visit Cedar Breaks National Monument and the alpine country of the Markagunt Plateau. Continue south 13 miles for Glendale or north 13 miles on US 89 for Hatch.

Glendale
The original settlers named their community Berryville in 1864. A small fort helped protect against Navajo raids, but continued Indian troubles forced all the valley's inhabitants to leave by 1866. A new group arrived in 1871 and renamed the site Glendale after the town in Scotland. **Smith Hotel** (1927), on the north side of town, tel. 648-2156, has been restored as a bed and breakfast; all rooms have bath, $38.50 s, $44-55 d. **The Homeplace Bed & Breakfast** will reopen at the south end of town with a new telephone number; call information. **Bauer's Canyon Ranch RV Camp,** one block east of the highway on Center St., tel. 648-2564, offers hot

showers and a laundromat; open early March to early November; $9.78 tent or RV no hookups, $13.70 w/hookups. **Bryce-Zion KOA Kampground,** five miles north of Glendale, tel. 648-2490, has a pool, store, horseback rides, laundry, and showers; open May 1 to October 15; $16.50 tent or RV no hookups, $18.70-20.35 w/hookups, $27.50 kamping kabins.

Orderville

Residents began a communal life in 1875 as part of the Mormon United Order. Everyone worked on cooperative farms and industries, divided income according to need, shared meals at a common table, and met twice daily for worship. The experiment succeeded admirably for about 10 years, longer than in any other Mormon town. A combination of internal disagreements and external pressures eventually convinced community leaders to end the United Order and to return its property to private ownership. The **Orderville DUP Museum** contains pioneer artifacts; open on request (call telephone numbers posted on door). Inexpensive accommodations are offered by the **Orderville Motel,** tel. 648-2380, **Parkway Motel,** tel. 648-2380, and **Starlight Motel,** tel. 648-2060. **Hummingird Bed & Breakfast,** at the south end of town, has rooms at $35-50 s or d, tel. 648-2415. Orderville also has a few cafes. **Tortoise and the Hare Campground,** one mile north of town,

tel. 648-2312, has sites for tents ($9) and RVs ($11 w/hookups) with showers and laundry; open early April to late October.

Mt. Carmel

This agricultural community, a few miles north of Mt. Carmel Junction, was first settled in 1865 as Winsor. Threats by Navajo and Paiute Indians forced its abandonment a year later and it wasn't reestablished until 1871, when it was named Mt. Carmel for a mountain in Israel. The Elkhart Cliffs of white Navajo Sandstone rise to the east. **Mt. Carmel Motel and RV Park** is a small place on the south edge of town, tel. 648-2323; closed in winter; rooms are $22-24.20 s or d; the RV park is $6.75 for tents or RVs no hookups, $9.90 w/hookups.

Mt. Carmel Junction

Highway UT 9 turns west here from US 89 to Zion National Park. **Thunderbird Motel (Best Western),** tel. 648-2203 or (800) 528-1234, features a restaurant, nine-hole golf course, and a pool; $70.40 s or d in summer. **Thunderbird Restaurant** serves breakfast, lunch, and dinner daily. **Golden Hills Motel,** tel. 648-2268, costs $40.30 s, $44 d in summer; **Golden Hills Restaurant** serves breakfast, lunch, and dinner daily. **East Zion Trailer Park,** next to the Shell station, tel. 648-2326, has RV sites year-round for $13 w/hookups (no tents).

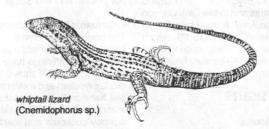

*whiptail lizard
(Cnemidophorus sp.)*

LOUISE FOOTE

Kanab, beneath the Vermilion Cliffs, late 1800s

KANAB AND VICINITY

Striking scenery surrounds this small town in Utah's far south. The Vermilion Cliffs to the west and east glow with a fiery intensity at sunrise and sunset. Streams have cut splendid canyons into surrounding plateaus. The Paiute Indians knew the spot as Kanab, meaning "Place of the Willows," which still grow along Kanab Creek. Mormon pioneers arrived in the mid-1860s and tried to farm along the unpredictable creek. Irrigation difficulties culminated in the massive floods of 1883, which in just two days gouged a section of creekbed 40 feet below its previous level. Ranching proved better suited to this rugged and arid land. Hollywood discovered the dramatic scenery in the 1920s and has filmed more than 150 movies and TV series here since. Several western sets near Kanab have been constructed by film crews, but most lie on private land and are difficult to visit. The Pahreah set east of town, however, is on BLM land and open to the public.

Travelers find Kanab (pop. 3,500) a handy stopover on trips to Bryce, Zion, and Grand Canyon national parks and to the Glen Canyon National Recreation Area. A good selection of motels and restaurants lines US 89, which zigzags through town. Short detours on many of the side streets reveal 19th-century houses of Kanab's pioneer days.

SIGHTS

Kanab Heritage House
This 1895 Queen Anne-style Victorian house reflects the prosperity of two of Kanab's early Mormon residents. Henry Bowman built it, but he lived here only two years before going on a mission. He sold the property to Thomas Chamberlain, who led a busy life serving as a leader in the Mormon's United Order and caring for his six wives and 55 children. (There's a family photo in the sitting room.) A guide will show you around the house and explain its architectural details. Photos, furnishings, and artifacts give an idea of what life was like in early Kanab. The town had no stores when the house was built, so each family grew its own vegetables and fruit. The grape arbor, berry bushes, and trees here represent those grown during pioneer times; fruit is free for the picking to visitors. The house is usually open for tours in summer Mon.-Fri. 9:30 a.m.-noon and 1:30-5 p.m.; free admission. You might be able to visit at other times by appointment; call the number posted on the front of the house. Located one block off US 89 at the corner of Main and 100 South.

Lopeman's Frontier Movie Town
The owners assembled this movie-set replica in Kanab to show tourists a bit of the "Old West." Some of the buildings have seen actual use in past movies and TV shows. Many small exhibits display western and movie memorabilia. Shops sell handicrafts and snacks. Local tour information is available too. Groups can arrange cowboy cookouts and western shows. Movie Town entry costs $2 ages 12 and up; it's open

April 1 to October 31 about 10 a.m.-9 p.m. Turn in off W. Center between Brandon Motel and Gift City, tel. 644-5337.

Squaw Trail

This well-graded trail provides a close look at the geology, plantlife, and animals of the Vermilion Cliffs just north of town. Allow about an hour on the moderately difficult trail to reach the first overlook (two miles roundtrip with a 400-foot elevation gain) or one and one half hours to go all the way up (three miles roundtrip with an 800-foot elevation gain). Views to the south take in Kanab, Fredonia, Kanab Canyon, and the vast Kaibab Plateau. At the top, look north to see the White, Gray, and Pink cliffs of the Grand Staircase. Some maps show the trail continuing across the mesa to Hog Canyon, but the BLM has not completed that part of the tail. The trailhead is at the north end of 100 East near the city park. Pick up a trail guide at the Information Center (brochures may also be available at the trailhead or BLM office). Bring water. Try to get a very early start in summer.

Moqui Cave

A tourist attraction with a large collection of Indian artifacts. Most of the arrowheads, pottery, sandals, and burials were excavated locally. A diorama re-creates an Anasazi ruin located five miles away in Cottonwood Wash. Fossils, rocks, and minerals are exhibited too, including what's claimed to be one of the largest fluorescent mineral displays in the country. The collections and a gift shop lie within a spacious cave that stays pleasantly cool even in the hottest weather. Open daily except Sunday from early March to mid-November; summer hours are 8:30 a.m.-7:30 p.m., with shorter hours in spring and autumn; $3.50 adult, $3 senior, $2.50 children 13-17, and $1.50 ages 6-12. The cave is five miles north of Kanab on US 89, tel. 644-2987.

PRACTICALITIES

Canyonlands International Youth Hostel

This is a great place to meet other travelers, many from foreign countries. Guests stay in simple dorm-style accommodations. Facilities include kitchen, laundry, TV room, patio, lawn, locked storage, and a reference library of regional maps and books. Open year-round; check in is 9 a.m.-11 p.m.; $9 (no hostel card required). Centrally located a half block off US 89 at 143 E. 100 South, tel. 644-5554.

Motels

Reservations are a good idea during the busy summer months. Motels are listed in order of increasing price. (Summer rates shown; they may drop in winter.) All of the motels and campgrounds lie along US 89, which follows 300 West, Center, 100 East, and 300 South through town.

Premium Motel has basic accommodations at the corner of US 89 and 100 South (99 S. 100 East), tel. 644-2449, $24.20 s, $28.60 d. **Coral Sands Motel** is at 60 S. 100 East, tel. 644-2616 or (800) 654-0805, $35.20 s, $39.60 d and up. **Treasure Trail Motel** is at 150 W. Center with a pool, tel. 644-2687, $38.50 s or d. **Aiken's Lodge** (National 9) is at 79 W. Center with a pool, tel. 644-2625, $36.30 s, $38.50 d and up. **Sun-N-Sand Motel** at 347 S. 100 East has a pool, spa, and kitchenettes, tel. 644-5050, $41.80 s, $46.20 d and up. **K-Motel** is at 330 S. 100 East, tel. 644-2611, $39.60 s, $46.20 d and up. **Parry Lodge** is a large white colonial building at 89 E. Center with a pool, tel. 644-2601 or (800) 748-4101, $47.30-56.10 s, $50.60-69.30 d. (Parry Lodge has hosted many famous movie stars; ask for the room where your favorite star has stayed. Ronald Reagan once had number 125.) **Brandon Motel** is at 223 W. Center with a pool, tel. 644-2631, $44 s, $50.60 d and up. **Quail Park Lodge** at 125 N. 300 West has a pool, tel. 644-2639, $48.40 s or d and up. **Shilo Inn** features a pool, spa, free Continental breakfast, and mini-suites at 296 W. 100 North, tel. 644-2562 or (800) 222-2244, $73.70-96.80 s or d. **Four Seasons Motel** at 36 N. 300 West has a pool, tel. 644-2635, $81.40 s, $85.80 d, $101.20 suite. **Red Hills Motel (Best Western)** at 124 W. Center has a pool, tel. 644-2675 or (800) 528-1234, $65.40-68.67 s or d. **Super 8** is one of the newest Kanab motels at 70 S. 200 West, tel. 644-5500 or (800) 995-5532, $65.88, $70.28 d. **Holiday Inn Express** is a mile east of downtown at 815 E. Hwy. 89 and offers a nine-hole golf course, free breakfast bar, pool, and hot tub, tel. 644-8888 or (800) HOLI-DAY, $74.80 s or d.

Campgrounds

Kanab RV Corral has sites with hot showers, pool, and laundromat open all year at 483 South 100 East, tel. 644-5330, $14.85 tent, $17.60 RV w/hookups. **Hitch'n Post RV Park** has sites with showers open all year at 190 E. 300 South, tel. 644-2681, $9 tent, $10.50 RV no hookups, $13 w/hookups. **Coleman's Exxon RV Park,** 355 E. 300 South, tel. 644-2922, offers sites with showers for RVs, open all year, $12.50 w/hookups. **Crazy Horse Campark,** 625 E. 300 South, tel. 644-2782, has sites with pool, store, game room, and showers, open mid-April to late October, $10.45 tent or RV no hookups, $16.50 RV w/hookups.

Food

Parry's Lodge features steak and seafood at 89 E. Center, tel. 644-2601; open daily for breakfast, lunch, and dinner (closed 2-6 p.m.). Photos of former movie-star guests decorate the walls. The **Moon Shadow Steak House,** 625 E. 300 South, tel. 644-5744, has steak and seafood in a Western atmosphere; open Sunday for brunch, Mon.-Fri. for lunch, and daily for dinner. Other good places for American food are **1950's Style Restaurant,** 22 N. 300 West, tel. 644-2635, open daily for breakfast, lunch, and dinner; **Chef's Palace Restaurant,** 176 W. Center, tel. 644-5052, open daily for breakfast, lunch, and dinner, offers steak, prime rib, and seafood; and **Paula's Gold Dust Cafe,** 176 S. 100 East, tel. 644-5938, open Tues.-Sat. for breakfast and lunch. For a choice of Mexican and American cuisine, try **Nedra's Too,** 310 S. 100 East in Heritage Center, tel. 644-2030, open daily for breakfast, lunch, and dinner with a homey atmosphere; or **Houston's Trail's End Restaurant,** 32 E. Center, tel. 644-2488, open daily for breakfast, lunch, and dinner. **Pizza Hut,** 421 S. 100 East, tel. 644-2513, serves up pizza daily for lunch and dinner. The **Wok Inn,** 86 S. 200 West, tel. 644-5400, has Hunan and Szechuan cuisine; open weekdays for lunch and dinner and weekends for dinner only; closed in winter.

Entertainment And Events

Kanab Theatre has movies at 29 W. Center, tel. 644-2334. **Kanab 10K** run is in May. **Zane Grey Horse Show** takes place the fourth weekend in June. **Fourth of July** is celebrated with a parade, cookout, and fireworks. Another parade and a cookout commemorate **Pioneer Day** on July 24. **Kane County Fair,** on the third weekend in August, presents rodeo action, livestock shows, and arts and crafts at Orderville (22 miles north). **Kanab West Fest** features a rodeo, western art, and festivities in October.

Services And Shopping

The **city park** has picnic tables, playground, tennis courts, and a ball field at the north end of 100 West; the trailhead for Squaw Trail starts here (see "Squaw Trail" under "Sights," above). An outdoor **swimming pool** is open in summer at 44 N. 100 West (behind the State Bank), tel. 644-5870. **Coral Cliffs Golf Course** has nine holes and a driving range on the east edge of town, tel. 644-5005. **Trail rides** (hourly, three-, five-, and 10-day) and stagecoach rides can be arranged through Lopeman's Frontier Movie Town, tel. 644-5337. The **post office** is at 34 S. Main, tel. 644-2760. **Kane County Hospital** provides emergency care at 221 W. 300 North, tel. 644-5811.

Gift City, 288 W. Center across from Four Seasons Motel, specializes in "Kanab Wonderstone" slabs; this natural sandstone, found nearby, has curious patterns (possibly caused by deposits from mineral springs) that resemble scenic landscapes; prices range from a few dollars for a pocket-sized piece to $1,000 for a five-foot by two-and-one-half-foot work. Several other shops sell Indian crafts and assorted souvenirs. **Alderman & Son Photo,** 19 W. Center, tel. 644-5981, supplies film and camera needs (including repairs) beyond what you would expect in a town this size. The also shop almost qualifies as an antique camera museum.

Information

Staff at the **Information Center** offers literature and advice for services in Kanab and travel in Kane County, they're in the center of town at 70 S. 100 East (Kanab, UT 84741), tel. 644-5033; open Mon.-Sat. 8 a.m.-8 p.m. all year. Visit the **BLM** office to learn about hiking and back roads in the Kanab area at 318 N. 100 East (Kanab, UT 84741), tel. 644-2672; open Mon.-Fri. 7:45 a.m.-4:30 p.m. The **public library** is at 13 S. 100 East, tel. 644-2394.

Tours

Cowboy Aviation will take you on a 40-minute flight over the scenic Kaibab Plateau at $79 per person (minimum two people, $70 each for three or more passengers) and on an 85-minute flight over the Grand Canyon for $125 per person (minimum two people, $100 each for three or more passengers); flights leave from the airport three miles south of town on US 89A, toward Fredonia, tel. 644-2299. **Angel Canyon Tours** runs scenic jeep trips to Anasazi sites and movie locations in this privately owned canyon; self-guided, sunset, photography, and hiking tours are offered too; tel. 644-2001. You can travel like pioneers in covered wagons, ride horseback, or participate in cattle drives across southern Utah and northern Arizona with the **Honeymoon Trail Company,** Moccasin, AZ 86022, tel. (602) 643-7292.

CORAL PINK SAND DUNES STATE PARK

Churning air currents funneled by surrounding mountains have deposited huge sand dunes in this valley west of Kanab. The ever-changing dunes reach heights of several hundred feet and cover about 2,000 of the park's 3,700 acres.

Moviemakers have used the location for filming. Tiny particles of quartz make up the sand; the "coral pink" refers only to the color. Average summer temperatures at the 6,000-foot elevation range from about 55° F at night to 95° during the day; winter days have highs of about 55°, falling to below freezing at night. Most wildlife is difficult to spot, though you may see tracks in the sand. Coyotes are often heard at night. Wildflowers put on a fine show in June and July. Different areas in the park have been set aside for hiking, off-road vehicles, and a campground with hot showers. If you see what looks like a family reunion, it might be just a man and his wives from the nearby polygamist settlements of Colorado City or Hildale!

From Kanab, the shortest drive is to go north eight miles on US 89 (to between Mileposts 72 and 73), turn left 9.3 miles on the paved Hancock Road to its end, then turn left (south) one mile on a paved road into the park. From the north, you can follow US 89 three and one half miles south of Mt. Carmel Junction, then turn right (south) 11 miles on a paved road. The back road from Cane Beds in Arizona has about 16 miles of gravel and dirt with some sandy spots; ask a park ranger for current conditions. Entrance fees are $3 per vehicle for day use or $9 per vehicle ($10 Friday, Saturday, and holidays) for camping. The park can be contacted at Box 95, Kanab, UT 84741, tel. 874-2408 or (800) 322-3770 (reservations).

Day-Use Area
On the left just past the contact station, a short boardwalk leads into a protected section of the dunes; signs explain the geology and illustrate some animals and plants that live in this semiarid desert. Photographers and families can explore on foot and use the sheltered picnic area.

Riding The Dunes
Drivers of off-road vehicles can head for the sands from a trailhead between the day-use area and campground. The thrills of traveling across the Sahara-like landscape attract motorcyclists, ATVers, and dune buggy enthusiasts. Paddle-type tires work best on the soft sand. Park regulations ask drivers to attach an eight-foot whip with a flag to their vehicle, to observe quiet hours from 10 p.m.-9 a.m., and to avoid riding across vegetation. All vehicles must be registered for

off- or on-highway use. It's a good idea to ride where you can be seen by other drivers. Rangers have a complete list of regulations.

Campground
The pleasant campground site in a piñon pine, juniper, and oak woodland. Facilities include restrooms with showers, paved pull-through sites, and a dump station. Ice, firewood, and off-road vehicle whips may be sold by park staff. Open all year, but the water is shut off from late October until Easter; winter campers need to bring their own. Reservations are recommended for the busy Memorial Day to Labor Day season.

Other Areas
The canyon country surrounding the park has good opportunities for hiking and off-road vehicle travel; the BLM office in Kanab can supply maps and information. The BLM maintains **Ponderosa Grove Campground** on the north edge of the dunes; no water or fee (but improvements and fees are planned); it's on the paved Hancock Road that turns off one mile north of the park or eight miles north of Kanab from US 89 (between Mileposts 72 and 73). The campground is two miles in from the road to the park and 7.3 miles in from US 89. Drivers with 4WD vehicles can turn south on Sand Springs Road (one and one half miles east of Ponderosa Grove Campground) and go one mile to Sand Springs and another four miles to South Fork Indian Canyon Pictograph Site in a pretty canyon. Visitors may not enter the Kaibab-Paiute Indian Reservation, which is south across the Arizona state line, from this side.

horned lark
(Eremophila alpestris)

LOUISE FOOTE

THE ARIZONA STRIP

Lonely and vast, the "Strip" lies north and west of the Colorado River and south of Utah. Phoenix and the rest of Arizona seem a world away. The Arizona Strip's history and geography actually tie it more closely to Utah. Some beautiful desert and mountain country await the adventurous traveler. In addition to Grand Canyon National Park, nine designated wilderness areas totaling nearly 400,000 acres protect the most scenic and unique sections. See the *Arizona Handbook* for places to visit in the backcountry. Several tiny communities in the Arizona Strip offer food and accommodations for travelers. More extensive facilities lie just outside the region: Kanab and St. George across the Utah border to the north and Page across the river to the east.

PIPE SPRING NATIONAL MONUMENT

Step back to the days when cowboys and pioneers first settled this land. Excellent exhibits in Winsor Castle, an early Mormon ranch south west of Kanab, provide a look into frontier life. Abundant spring water attracted prehistoric Indians, who settled nearby more than 1,000 years ago, then departed. Nomadic Paiute Indians came more recently and now live on the surrounding Kaibab-Paiute Indian Reservation. Mormons discovered the springs in 1858 and began ranching five years later, but swift Navajo raiding parties stole some stock and killed two men who pursued the Indians. A treaty signed in 1870 between the Mormons and Navajo ended the raids and opened the land to development.

Brigham Young, the Mormon president, then decided to locate the church's southern Utah tithing herd at Pipe Spring. A pair of two-story stone houses went up, with walls connecting the ends to form a protected courtyard. Workmen added gun ports "just in case," but the settlement was never attacked. The structure became known as Winsor Castle because the ranch's superintendent, Anson P. Winsor, possessed a regal bearing and was thought to be related to the English royal family. Winsor built

up a sizable herd of cattle and horses and oversaw dairying and farming at the ranch. A telegraph office (Arizona's first) opened in 1871, bringing Utah closer to the rest of the world. So many newlyweds passed through the area, after having been married in the St. George Temple, that their route became known as the Honeymoon Trail. In the 1880s, the Mormon Church entered a period of turmoil and feared that the federal government would seize church property in the dispute over polygamous marriages. Winsor Castle, whose importance to the church had been declining, was sold to a non-Mormon.

President Harding proclaimed Pipe Spring a national monument in 1923 "as a memorial of Western pioneer life." National Park Service staff keeps the frontier spirit alive by maintaining the ranch as it was in the 1870s. Activities such as cattle branding, gardening, weaving, spinning, quilt-making, and baking still take place on a small scale. You can take a short tour of Winsor Castle or explore the restored rooms and outbuildings on your own. A half-mile loop trail climbs the small ridge behind the ranch to a viewpoint; signs tell of local history and geology.

Visitor Center
Historic exhibits are open daily 8 a.m.-4:30 p.m. year-round; $2 per person admission; tel. 643-7105. A short video introduces the monument. Demonstrations of blacksmithing, branding, and other cowboy skills sometimes take place in the summer months. Produce from the garden and goodies from the kitchen may be sold or given away. A shop offers regional books and Southwestern Indian arts and crafts. The snack bar's menu includes such items as cowboy beans and beef, similar to those eaten here 100 years ago. The Paiute tribe operates **Heart Canyon Campground** a half mile northeast of the monument; sites have showers and stay open all year: $5, or $10 w/hookups. Nearest grocery stores, restaurants, and motels are in Fredonia. Pipe Spring National Monument is just off AZ 389, 21 miles southwest of Kanab.

PARIA CANYON

The wild and twisting canyons of the Paria River and its tributaries offer a memorable experience for experienced hikers. Silt-laden waters have sculptured the colorful canyon walls, revealing 200 million years of geologic history. Paria means "Muddy Water" in the Paiute language. You enter the 2,000-foot-deep gorge of the Paria in southern Utah, then hike 37 miles downstream to Lees Ferry in Arizona, where the Paria empties into the Colorado River.

Ancient petroglyphs and campsites show that Pueblo Indians traveled the Paria more than 700 years ago. They hunted mule deer and bighorn sheep while using the broad, lower end of the canyon to grow corn, beans, and squash. The Dominguez-Escalante expedition stopped at the mouth of the Paria in 1776 and were the first white men to see the river. John D. Lee and three companions traveled through the canyon in 1871 to bring a herd of cattle from the Pahreah settlement to Lees Ferry. After Lee began a Colorado River ferry service in 1872, he

the Paria Narrows

and others farmed the lower Paria Canyon. Prospectors came here to search for gold, uranium, and other minerals, but much of the canyon remained unexplored. In the late 1960s, the Bureau of Land Management organized a small expedition whose research led to protection of the canyon as a primitive area. The Arizona Wilderness Act of 1984 designated Paria Canyon a wilderness, along with parts of the Paria Plateau and Vermilion Cliffs.

Allow four to six days to hike Paria Canyon because of the many river crossings and because you'll want to make side trips up some of the tributary canyons. The hike is considered moderately difficult. Hikers should have enough backpacking experience to be self-sufficient, as help may be days away. Flash floods can race through the canyon, especially July to September. Rangers close the Paria if they think a danger exists. Because the upper end has the narrowest passages (between Miles 4.2 and 9.0), rangers require that all hikers start here in order to have up-to-date weather information. You must register at a trailhead or the visitor center, or the Kanab Area Office at 318 N. 100 East in Kanab, Utah, 84741, tel. 644-2672 (open Mon.-Fri. 7:45 a.m.-4:30 p.m. year-round). The visitor center and the office both provide weather forecasts and brochures with map and hiking information. The visitor center always has the weather forecast posted at an outdoor information kiosk. Current BLM plans are to have the new visitor center manned with a volunteer who will give area information.

All visitors need to take special care to minimize impact on this beautiful canyon. Check the BLM "Visitor Use Regulations" for the Paria before you go. They include no campfires in the Paria and its tributaries, a pack-in/pack-out policy, and that latrines be made at least 100 feet away from river and campsite locations. Also, remember to take some plastic bags to carry out toilet paper; the stuff lasts years and years in this desert climate. You don't want to haunt future hikers with TP flowers!

The Paria ranger recommends a group size of six maximum; regulations specify a 10-person limit. The best times to travel along the Paria are from about mid-March to June and October to November. May, especially Memorial Day weekend, tends to be crowded. Winter hikers often complain of painfully cold feet. Wear shoes suitable for frequent wading; canvas shoes are better than heavy leather hiking boots. You can get good drinking water from springs along the way (see the BLM hiking brochure for locations); it's best not to use the river water because of possible chemical pollution from farms and ranches upstream. Normally the river is only ankle deep, but it can be waist deep in a few spots in the spring or after rainy spells. During thunderstorms, it can be over 20 feet deep in the Paria Narrows, so heed weather warnings! Quicksand, most prevalent after flooding, is more of a nuisance than a danger—usually it's just knee deep. Many hikers carry a walking stick to probe the opaque waters for good crossing places.

Wrather Canyon Arch

One of Arizona's largest natural arches lies about one mile up this side canyon. The massive structure has a 200-foot span. Turn right (southwest) at Mile 20.6 on the Paria hike. (The mouth of Wrather Canyon and other points along the Paria are unsigned; you need to follow your map.)

Trailheads

The BLM Paria Canyon Ranger Station is in Utah, 43 miles east of Kanab on US 89 near Milepost 21. It's on the south side of the highway, just east of the Paria River. The actual trailhead is two miles south on a dirt road near an old homestead site called White House Ruins. Exit trailhead is in Arizona at Lonely Dell Ranch of Lees Ferry, 44 miles southwest of Page via US 89 and 89A (or 98 miles southeast of Kanab on US 89A).

Shuttle Services

You'll need to do a 150-mile-roundtrip car shuttle for this hike or make arrangements for someone else to do it for you, using either your car (about $55) or theirs ($125-150). Contact: Marble Canyon Lodge, tel. (602) 655-2225; Ken Berlin, (602) 655-2286; Richard Clark, (602) 655-2281; Rona Levein, (602) 655-2262; Sharon Rodgers, (602) 655-2254; or Steve Knisely, (602) 655-2295; all can be reached at Marble Canyon, AZ 86036. In Fredonia, there's Dick Walker, (602) 643-7494/7333. In Page, try Harley Stomberg, (602) 645-9471. The (602) area code will change to (520) sometime in 1995.

Buckskin Gulch

This amazing tributary of the Paria has convoluted walls hundreds of feet high, yet it narrows to as little as four feet in width. In places the walls block out so much light that it's like walking in a cave. Be *very* careful to avoid times of flash-flood danger. Hiking can be strenuous with rough terrain, deep pools of water, and log and rock jams that may require the use of ropes. Conditions vary considerably from one year to the next. You can descend into Buckskin from two trailheads, Buckskin and Wire Pass, both reached by a dirt road, not always passable by cars. The hike from Buckskin Trailhead to the Paria River is 16.3 miles long (one-way) and takes 12 or more hours. From Wire Pass Trailhead it's 1.7 miles to Buckskin Gulch, then 11.8 miles to the Paria. You can climb out on a route to a safe camping place about halfway down Buckskin Gulch. Carry water to last until the mouth of Buckskin Gulch.

Lees Ferry

The deeply entrenched Colorado River cuts one gorge after another as it crosses the high plateaus of southern Utah and northern Arizona. Settlers and travelers found the river a dangerous and difficult barrier until well into this century. A break in the cliffs above Marble Canyon provided one of the few places to build a road to the water's edge. Until 1929, when Navajo Bridge spanned the canyon, vehicles and passengers had to cross by ferry. Zane Grey expressed his thoughts about Lees Ferry, in *The Last of the Plainsmen* (1900). "I saw the constricted rapids, where the Colorado took its plunge into the box-like head of the Grand Canyon of Arizona; and the deep, reverberating boom of the river, at flood height, was a fearful thing to hear. I could not repress a shudder at the thought of crossing above that rapid."

The Dominguez-Escalante expedition tried to cross at what's now known as Lees Ferry in 1776, but without success. The river proved too cold and wide to swim safely, and winds frustrated the attempts to raft across. The Spaniards had to go 40 miles upstream into present-day Utah before finding a safe ford. About 100 years later, Mormon leaders began eyeing the Lees Ferry crossing as the most convenient route for expanding Mormon settlements from Utah into Arizona. After Jacob Hamblin led a failed at-

Jacob Hamblin

John Doyle Lee

tempt at rafting the river in 1860, he returned four years later and made it across safely. Mormons built a guard post in 1869 to prevent others from taking over the strategic spot. Although Hamblin was the first to recognize the value of this crossing, it now bears the name of John D. Lee. This colorful character gained notoriety in the 1857 Mountain Meadows Massacre. To get Lee out of sight, the Mormon Church leaders asked him to start a regular ferry service on the Colorado River, which he began in 1872. One of Lee's wives remarked on seeing the isolated spot, "Oh, what a lonely dell!" which became the name of their place. Lee managed to establish the ferry service despite boat accidents and sometimes hostile Navajo, but his past

caught up with him. In 1877, authorities took Lee back to Mountain Meadows where a firing squad and casket awaited.

Miners and farmers came to try their luck along the Colorado River and its tributaries. The ferry service continued too, though it suffered fatal accidents from time to time. The last run took place in June 1928 while the bridge was being constructed six miles downstream. The ferry operator on that trip lost control in strong currents and the boat capsized; all three persons aboard and a Model-T Ford were lost. Fifty-five years of ferryboating had come to an end. Navajo Bridge opened in January 1929, an event hailed by the Flagstaff *Coconino Sun* as the "Biggest News in Southwest History."

SOUTHEASTERN UTAH

INTRODUCTION

The Colorado River and its tributaries have carved extraordinary landscapes in southeastern Utah. Intricate mazes of canyons, delicate arches, and massive rock monoliths make this a region like no other. First-time visitors often need a while to appreciate this strange land before they're won over by the infinite colors and beauties of the sculptured rock. The thousands of canyons invite exploration—they offer solitude, ruins of prehistoric villages, wildlife, and dramatic records of geologic history.

THE LAND

About 300 million years ago, this land was at times a great Sahara-like desert and at others covered by water. Thick layers of sediment built up one on top of the other. During the last 50 million years, powerful forces within the earth

slowly pushed the entire region a mile upward. The ancestral Colorado River and other streams appeared and began to carve the deep gorges seen today. Some of the younger rock layers of the uplifted Colorado Plateau have been eroded, yet the deposits that remain represent more than 150 million years. Ancient dunes, turned to stone, make up many of the sheer canyon cliffs, arches, and spires of the region. Delicate crossbedded lines of the former dunes add grace to these features. Forces within the restless plateau have also buckled and folded rock layers into great reefs as long as 100 miles. Weathering then carved them into rainbow-hued rock monuments. Volcanic pressures deep in the earth also shaped the land. Thick sediments above, however, prevented most of the molten rock from reaching the surface. Massive intrusions of magma bowed up overlying rock layers before cooling and solidifying. Erosion has since

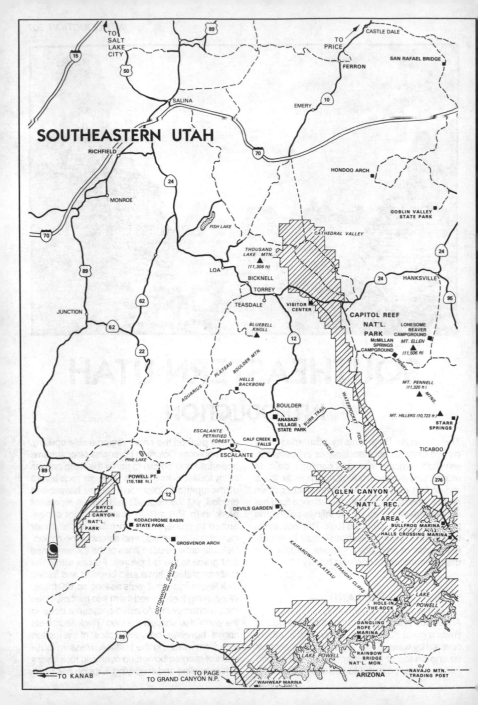

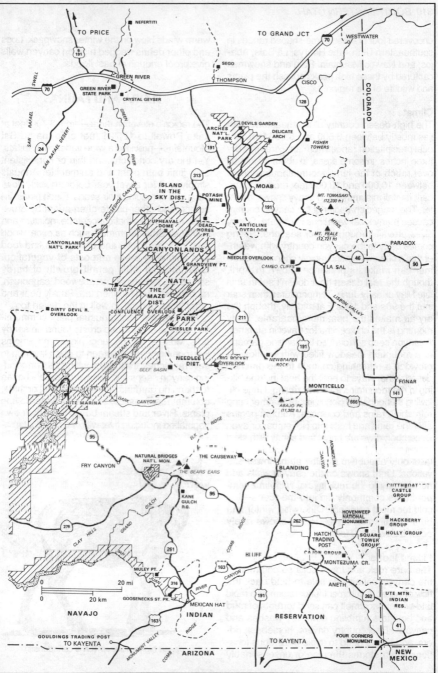

TO PRICE

NEFERTITI

TO GRAND JCT

WESTWATER

70

GREEN RIVER

6
191

70

SAN RAFAEL SWELL

GREEN RIVER
STATE PARK

CRYSTAL GEYSER

SEGO

THOMPSON

CISCO

128

SAN RAFAEL DESERT

24

GREEN RIVER

HORSESHOE CANYON

ARCHES
NAT'L
PARK

DEVILS GARDEN

DELICATE
ARCH

FISHER
TOWERS

191

ISLAND
IN THE
SKY DIST.

313

MOAB

POTASH
MINE

191

MT. TOMASAKI
(12,230 ft.)

UPHEAVAL
DOME

DEAD
HORSE
PT.

ANTICLINE
OVERLOOK

LA SAL
MTNS.

MT. PEALE
(12,721 ft.)

PARADOX

CANYONLANDS
NAT'L PARK

CANYONLANDS

NAT'L

GRANDVIEW PT.

NEEDLES OVERLOOK

CAMEO CLIFFS

LA SAL

46

90

HANS FLAT

THE
MAZE
DIST.

PARK

211

LISPON VALLEY

DIRTY DEVIL R.
OVERLOOK

CONFLUENCE OVERLOOK

CHESLER PARK

NEWSPAPER
ROCK

191

FGNAR

141

CATARACT CANYON

DARK CANYON

NEEDLES
DIST.

BEEF BASIN

BIG POCKET
OVERLOOK

MONTICELLO

666

HITE MARINA

95

ELK RIDGE

ABAJO PK.
(11,302 ft.)

MONTEZUMA CANYON

FRY CANYON

NATURAL BRIDGES
NAT'L MON.

THE CAUSEWAY

THE BEARS EARS

BLANDING

CUTTHROAT
CASTLE
GROUP

GULCH

276

CLAY HILLS

KANE
GULCH
R.S.

95

COMB RIDGE

GRAND

262

HOVENWEEP
NATIONAL
MONUMENT

HATCH
TRADING
POST

SQUARE
TOWER
GROUP

HACKBERRY
GROUP

HOLLY GROUP

261

HI LIFE

CAJON GROUP

MONTEZUMA CR.

MULEY PT.

316

SAN JUAN

163

RIVER

CANYON

191

ANETH

262

UTE MTN.
INDIAN
RES.

0   20 mi

0   20 km

GOOSENECKS ST. PK.

MEXICAN HAT

RESERVATION

41

NAVAJO

INDIAN

FOUR CORNERS
MONUMENT

NEW
MEXICO

GOULDINGS TRADING POST
TO KAYENTA

163

COMB RIDGE

MONUMENT VALLEY

TO KAYENTA

ARIZONA

© MOON PUBLICATIONS, INC.

uncovered four of these dome-shaped ranges in southeastern Utah—the Henrys, La Sals, Abajos, and Navajo Mountain. Rain and snowmelt captured by these high peaks nourish the plants and wildlife of the region.

Climate

The high-desert country of southeastern Utah lies mostly between 3,500 and 6,500 feet. Annual precipitation ranges from an extremely dry three inches, in some areas, to about 10 inches over much of the land. Mountainous regions between 10,000 and 13,000 feet receive abundant rainfall in summer and heavy snows in winter. The rugged character of the canyon country causes many local variations in climate. Sunny skies prevail through all four seasons. Spring comes early to the canyon country with weather that's often windy and rapidly changing. Summer can make its presence known in April, though the real desert heat doesn't set in until late May or early June. Temperatures then soar into the 90s and 100s F at midday, though the dry air makes the heat more bearable. Early morning is the choice time for travel in summer. A canyon seep surrounded by hanging gardens or a mountain meadow filled with wildflowers provides a refreshing contrast to the parched desert; other ways to beat the heat include hiking in the mountains and river rafting. Huge billowing thunderstorm clouds in late summer bring refreshing rains and coolness. Autumn begins after the rains and lasts into November or even December; days are bright and sunny with ideal temperatures, but nights become cold. Winter lasts only about two months at the lower elevations. Light snows on the canyon walls add new beauty to the rock layers. Nighttime temperatures commonly dip into the teens—too cold for most campers. Otherwise winter can be a fine time for travel. Heavy snows rarely occur below 8,000 feet.

Flash Floods

The bare rock and loose soils so common in the canyon country do little to hold back the flow of water. A summer thunderstorm or a rapid late-winter snowmelt can send torrents of mud and boulders rumbling down dry washes and canyons. Backcountry drivers, horseback riders, and hikers need to avoid hazardous locations when storms threaten or unseasonably warm winds blow on the winter snowpack. Logs and other debris wedged high on canyon walls give proof enough of past floods.

FLORA AND FAUNA

The region's elevation range—from 3,700 feet at Lake Powell to 12,721 feet atop the La Sal Mountains—provides a wide variety of habitats. Yet the dry conditions and thin or nonexistent soils limit both plant and animal life. Annuals simply wait for a wet year before quickly flowering and spreading their seeds. Piñon pines, junipers, and other plants often adapt by growing in rock cracks that concentrate moisture and nutrients. Small mammals such as mice, wood rats, rock squirrels, and chipmunks find food and shelter in these outposts of vegetation. Even meager soils permit growth of hardy shrubs like blackbrush, greasewood, sagebrush, rabbitbrush, and Mormon tea. Prickly pear and other types of cacti do well in the desert too.

Perhaps the most unusual plant communities are the cryptobiotic crusts found on sandy soils. Mosses, lichens, fungi, algae, and diatoms live together in a gray-green to black layer up to several inches thick. Microclimates surrounding canyon seeps and springs provide a haven for hanging gardens of grasses, ferns, orchids, columbines, mosses, and other water-loving plants. River and stream banks have their own vegetation including river willows, cattails, tama-

desert bighorn sheep (Ovis canadensis)

LOUISE FOOTE

Navajo medicine man with his ceremonial sand painting

risks, and cottonwoods. Wildlife you might see in the semiarid desert are mule deer, desert bighorn sheep, pronghorns, coyotes, bobcats, foxes, skunks, porcupines, and many species of rodents. Ravens, eagles, hawks, owls, falcons, magpies, and smaller birds fly overhead. Watch out for the poisonous rattlesnakes and scorpions, though these shy creatures won't attack unless provoked.

At elevations between 7,000 and 8,500 feet, the desert gives way to forests of aspen, Gambel oak, ponderosa pine, and mountain mahogany. Conifers dominate up to the treeline, at about 12,000 feet. Alpine flowering plants, grasses, sedges, and mosses cling to the windy summits of the La Sal Mountains. Wildlife of the forests includes many of the desert dwellers, as well as elk, bear, mountain lion, marmot, and pika. A herd of bison roam freely in the Henry Mountains; the surrounding desert keeps them from going elsewhere.

HISTORY

Prehistoric Indians
Nomadic bands of hunter-gatherers roamed the canyon country for at least 5,000 years. The climate was probably cooler and wetter when the first Indians arrived; food plants and game animals would have been more abundant than

today. Agriculture introduced from the south about 2,000 years ago brought about a slow transition to a settled village life. The Fremont culture emerged in the northern part of the region and the Anasazi in the southern part. Thousands of stone dwellings, ceremonial kivas, and towers built by the Anasazi still stand. Both groups also left behind intriguing rock art, either pecked in (petroglyphs) or painted (pictographs). The Anasazi and Fremont departed from this region about 800 years ago, perhaps because of drought, warfare, or disease. Some of the Anasazi moved south and joined the Pueblo tribes of present-day Arizona and New Mexico. The fate of the Fremont Indians remains a mystery.

After the mid-1200s and until white men arrived to settle in the late 1800s, small bands of nomadic Ute and Paiute moved through southeastern Utah. The Navajo began to enter Utah in the early 1800s. None of the three Indian groups established firm control of the region north of the San Juan River. A remnant of the Ute and Paiute Indian tribes now lives on the small White Mesa Reservation south of Blanding.

The Navajo
Relatives of the Athapascans of western Canada, the seminomadic Navajo wandered into New Mexico and Arizona between A.D. 1300 and 1500. This adaptable tribe learned agricul-

ture, weaving, pottery, and other skills from their pueblo neighbors, and they became expert horsemen and sheepherders with livestock obtained from the Spanish. Later, though, the old Navajo habits of raiding neighboring tribes and white settlements almost brought their down fall. In 1863-64 the U.S. Army rounded up all the Navajo they could find and forced the survivors on "The Long Walk" from Fort Defiance in northeastern Arizona to a bleak camp in eastern New Mexico. This internment was a dismal failure, and the Navajo were released four years later.

In 1868 the federal government "awarded" land to the Navajo that has since grown to a giant reservation spreading from northeastern Arizona into adjacent Utah and New Mexico. The Navajo Nation, with 172,000 members, now ranks as the largest Indian tribe in the country. Their Utah land lies mostly south of Lake Powell and the San Juan River in the extreme southeastern corner of the state but includes some acreage north of the San Juan near Montezuma Creek. Oil, gas, and ranching are important sources of income. The Navajo own the spectacular Monument Valley Tribal Park on the Utah-Arizona border.

Religion is a vital part of Navajo culture. Most ceremonies involve healing and often take place late at night. If someone is sick, his or her family calls in a medicine man who uses sandpaintings, chants, and dancing to affect a cure. The Navajo make beautiful silver jewelry and woven rugs. You'll see these in trading posts on and off the reservation. Colorful velveteen blouses and long flowing skirts like those worn by Navajo women are sometimes available for purchase; the style was adopted during the tribe's New Mexico internment in the 1860s. It was what the U.S. Army wives were then wearing!

Exploration And Settlement

The Spanish Dominguez-Escalante expedition skirted the east edge of the region in 1776 in an unsuccessful attempt to find a route west to California. Retreating back to New Mexico, the explorers encountered great difficulties in the canyons of southern Utah before finding a safe ford across the Colorado River. This spot, known as the "Crossing of the Fathers," now lies under Lake Powell. Later explorers established the Old Spanish Trail through Utah to connect New Mexico with California. The route crossed the Colorado River near present-day Moab and was used from 1829 to 1848, when the United States acquired the western territories. Fur trappers also traveled the canyons in search of beaver and other animals during the early 1800s; inscriptions carved into the sandstone record their passage. The U.S. Army's Macomb Expedition visited southeastern Utah in 1859 and made the first documented description of what's now Canyonlands National Park. Major John Wesley Powell's pioneering river expeditions down the Green and Colorado in 1869 and 1871-72 filled in many blank areas on the maps.

Hostile Indians discouraged early attempts by the Mormons to start settlements in southeastern Utah. The Elk Ridge Mission, founded in 1855 near present-day Moab, lasted only a few months before Ute Indians killed three Mormons and sent the rest fleeing for their lives. Church members had better success during the 1870s in the Escalante area (1876) and Moab (1877).

For sheer effort and endurance, no group of pioneers is cited as much as the Hole-in-the-Rock Expedition of 1879-80. Sixty families with 83 wagons and more than 1,000 head of livestock crossed some of the West's most rugged canyon country in an attempt to settle at Montezuma Creek on the San Juan River. They almost didn't make it: A journey expected to take six weeks turned into a six-*month* ordeal. The exhausted company arrived on the banks of the San Juan River on April 5, 1880. Too tired to continue just 20 easy miles to Montezuma Creek, they stayed and founded the town of Bluff. The Mormons established other towns in southeastern Utah too, relying on ranching, farming, and mining for their livelihoods. None of the communities in the region ever reached a large size; Moab is the biggest with a population of 4,600. More and more people have come to realize that the scenery and wilderness qualities of this unique land are its most valuable resources.

ESCALANTE

The outstanding scenery of the countryside surrounding the town of Escalante has just begun to be discovered. Highlights of a visit include seeing the Escalante River system's magnificent canyons, driving the historic Hole-in-the-Rock Road across a landscape little changed from pioneer days, fishing the trout lakes on the high Aquarius Plateau, and enjoying the area's splendid panoramas. Motorists traveling between Capitol Reef and Bryce Canyon national parks can take a shortcut through the town of Escalante, thanks to recent completion of UT 12. The drive provides a good introduction to the region's wonders.

History

Anasazi and Fremont Indians lived here from about A.D. 1050 to 1200. You can spot their petroglyphs, pictographs, artifacts, storage rooms, and village sites while you're hiking in the canyons of the Escalante River and its tributaries. High alcoves in canyon walls protect small stone granaries; check the floors of sandstone caves for things left behind—pieces of pottery, arrowheads, mats, sandals, and corncobs. (Federal laws prohibit removal of artifacts; please leave everything for the next person to enjoy.) You can visit an excavated Anasazi village, along with a modern replica of the original, 27 miles east in Boulder.

Southern Paiute arrived in the 1500s and stayed until white settlers took over. The nomadic Paiute had few possessions and left little behind despite their long stay. Mormon colonists didn't learn about the Escalante region until 1866, when Captain James Andrus led his cavalry east from Kanab in pursuit of Paiute Indians. Reports of the expedition described the upper Escalante, which was named Potato Valley after the wild tubers growing there.

Major John Wesley Powell's expedition down the Green and Colorado rivers in 1869 had failed to recognize the mouth of the Escalante River; it seemed too shallow and narrow for a major tributary. In 1872, a detachment of Powell's second expedition led by Almon H. Thompson and Frederick S. Dellenbaugh stumbled across the Escalante on an overland journey.

After some confusion they realized that an entire new river had been found, and they named it for Spanish explorer and priest Silvestre Valez de Escalante. The elusive river was the last to be discovered in the contiguous United States. Mormon ranchers and farmers arrived in the upper valleys of the Escalante in 1876 from Panguitch and other towns to the west, not as part of a church-directed mission but simply in search of new and better lands.

At first glance Escalante looks like a town that time has passed by. Only 800 people live here, in addition to the resident cows, horses, and chickens that you'll meet just a block off Main Street. Yet this little community is the biggest place for more than 60 miles around and a center for ranchers and travelers. Escalante (elev. 5,813 feet) has the neatly laid-out streets and trim little houses typical of Mormon settlements. The former LDS Tithing Office (behind the Griffin grocery store) dates from 1884. Pioneers had little cash then and paid their tithes in potatoes, fruit, and other produce. The building now has historic exhibits of the Daughters of the Utah Pioneers; open by appointment (phone numbers are listed on the door).

ESCALANTE PETRIFIED FOREST STATE PARK

This pleasant park just northwest of town offers camping, boating, fishing, picnicking, hiking, a visitor center with displays of petrified wood and dinosaur bones, and a chance to see petrified wood along trails. Rivers of 140 million years ago carried trees to the site of present-day Escalante and buried them in sand and gravel. Burial prevented decay as crystals of silicon dioxide gradually replaced the wood cells. Mineral impurities added a rainbow of colors to the trees as they turned to stone. Weathering has exposed this petrified wood, water-worn pebbles, and sand of the Morrison Formation. For a look at some colorful petrified wood, follow the **Petrified Forest Trail** from the campground up a hillside wooded with piñon pine and juniper. At the top of the 240-foot-high ridge, continue on a loop trail to the petrified wood; allow 45-60 minutes for the one-mile round trip. **Rainbow Loop Trail** (three-quarters of a mile) branches off the Petrified Forest Trail to more areas of petrified wood.

The campground stays open all year, offering drinking water and showers but no hookups. The adjacent 139-acre Wide Hollow Reservoir offers fishing, boating, and birdwatching. The park is one and one half miles west of town on UT 12, then 0.7 mile north on a gravel road; $3 per vehicle day use, $9 per vehicle to camp ($10 Friday Saturday, and holidays). Box 350, Escalante, UT 84726, tel. 826-4466 (ranger) or (800) 322-3770 (reservations).

PRACTICALITIES

Accommodations

Prospector Inn, 380 W. Main, tel. 826-GOLD, is Escalante's newest motel with rooms available in summer only ($49.05-$70.85). **Moqui Motel,** 480 W. Main, tel. 826-4210, has rooms and some kitchenettes ($27.25 s, $32.70-54.50 d) and an RV park ($12.72 w/hookups; no tents). **Circle D Motel,** 475 W. Main, tel. 826-4297, has rooms ($38.15-43.60 s, $43.60-49.05 d). **Quiet Falls Motel,** at the corner of W. Main and 100 West, tel. 826-4250, has rooms ($27.25 s, $37.06 d and up). The **Padre Motel,** 20 E. Main, tel. 826-4276, offers rooms ($32.70 s, $43.60 d and up). Bunkhouse style cabins are available at **Escalante Outfitters,** 310 W. Main, tel. 826-4266, ($27.25 s or d).

Campgrounds

Besides the state park described above, you can stay at **Triple-S RV Park,** which has cabins (starting at $18), sites for tents ($9.50) and RVs ($12 w/hookups), plus showers and a laundromat; closed in winter. 495 W. Main; tel. 826-4959.

Calf Creek Recreation Area lies in a pretty canyon 15.5 miles east of Escalante on UT 12; sites are open early April to late October ($6); group sites can be reserved through the BLM office. **Calf Creek Falls Trail** (five and one half miles roundtrip) begins at the campground and follows the creek upstream to the 126-foot-high falls.

Campgrounds at **Posey Lake** (16 miles north) and **Blue Spruce** (19 miles north) sit atop the

Aquarius Plateau in Dixie National Forest. Sites are open from around Memorial Day weekend to mid-September ($5). Take the dirt Hell's Backbone Road from the east edge of town.

Food

Cowboy Blues Diner and Bakery, 530 W. Main, tel. 826-4251, serves Western-style food and bakery goods. The **Circle D Restaurant,** 475 W. Main, tel. 826-4282, serves American and Mexican food. **Golden Loop Cafe,** 39 W. Main, tel. 826-4433, has standard American fare. All three are open daily for breakfast, lunch, and dinner. The **Frosty Shop,** open daily, serves carry-out fast food across from the Padre Motel. Buy groceries at either of the two stores on Main Street.

Services

Kazan-Ivan Memorial Clinic, on Center St. behind Bob Munson's Grocery, tel. 826-4374, offers medical care Monday and Thursday. The **Municipal Park** on the west edge of town has covered picnic tables, restrooms with water (except in winter), grills, and a small playground. **Escalante Outfitters,** 310 W. Main, tel. 826-4266, probably has that camping item you forgot as well as topo maps and books.

Information

Obtain travel advice and literature from the **information booth,** open daily about 10 a.m.-6 p.m. from mid-May to mid-September, near the Padre Motel. The new Escalante Interagency Office at 755 W. Main on the west edge of town has an **Information Center** for visitors to Forest Service, Bureau of Land Management, and National Park Service areas around Escalante; open Mon.-Fri. (daily from early March to late October), 8 a.m.-5 p.m. Write Box 246, Escalante, UT 84726; tel. 826-5499. Staff offers hiking and travel information, maps, books, and brochures for the high lake and forest country north of Escalante, Hole-in-the-Rock Road, Escalante River and its tributaries, and other beautiful areas nearby. Normally it's best to contact the Information Center first, but you can also communicate directly with the **Dixie National Forest** office, Box 246, Escalante, UT 84726, tel. 826-5400; the **Bureau of Land Management (BLM)** office, Box 225, Escalante, UT 84726, tel. 826-4291; or the **National Park Service**

(NPS) office, Box 511, Escalante, UT 84726, tel. 826-4315. Hikers headed for overnight trips on the Escalante River system can obtain permits at the Information Center or at trailheads. Techni-

cally the BLM administers the upper Escalante River while the NPS takes care of the lower section within Glen Canyon N.R.A., but only a single permit is needed for an overnight hiking trip.

VICINITY OF ESCALANTE

Hell's Backbone Road
This scenic 38-mile drive climbs high into the forests north of Escalante with excellent views of Death Hollow and Sand Creek canyons and the distant Navajo, Fiftymile, and Henry mountains. **Posey Lake Campground** (elev. 8,700 feet) offers sites amid aspen and ponderosa pines; open with drinking water from Memorial Day weekend to mid-September ($5). Rainbow and brook trout swim in the adjacent lake. A hiking trail (two miles roundtrip) begins near space number 14 and climbs 400 feet to an old fire lookout tower with good views of the lake and surrounding country. Posey Lake is 14 miles north of Escalante, then two miles west on a side road.

Blue Spruce Campground (elev. 7,860 feet) is another pretty spot but has only six sites. Fishermen can try for pan-sized trout in a nearby stream. The campground, surrounded by blue spruce, aspen, and ponderosa pine, has drinking water from Memorial Day weekend to mid-September ($5); go north 19 miles from town, then turn left and drive a half mile. Hell's Backbone Road reaches an elevation of 9,200 feet on the slopes of Roger Peak before descending to Hell's Backbone, 25 miles from town. Mule teams used this narrow ridge, with precipitous canyons on either side, as a route to Boulder until the 1930s. At that time a bridge built by the Civilian Conservation Corps allowed the first vehicles to make the trip. You can still see the old mule path below the bridge. After 38 miles the road ends at UT 12; turn right 24 miles to return to Escalante or turn left three miles to Boulder. Cars can usually manage the gravel and dirt Hell's Backbone Road when it's dry. Snows and snowmelt, however, block the way until about late May. Check with the U.S. Forest Service office in Escalante for current conditions. Trails and rough dirt roads lead deeper into the backcountry to more vistas and fishing lakes.

Calf Creek Recreation Area
Calf Creek Campground lies in a pretty canyon

15.5 miles east of Escalante on UT 12; sites are open with drinking water from early April to late October ($6). Group sites can be reserved through the BLM office. The hike to Calf Creek Falls offers a good introduction to the pleasures of hiking in the Escalante River system. Walking between high cliffs of Navajo Sandstone streaked with desert varnish, you'll see beaver ponds, Indian ruins and pictographs, and the misty 126-foot-high Lower Calf Creek Falls. A brochure available at the trailhead next to the campground identifies many of the desert and riparian plant species along the way. Roundtrip is five and one half miles with only a slight gain in elevation; bring water and perhaps a lunch. Summer temperatures can soar but the falls and the crystal-clear pool beneath stay cool. Sheer cliffs block travel farther upstream.

HOLE-IN-THE-ROCK ROAD

The building of this road by determined Mormons was one of the great epics in the colonization of the West. Church leaders organized the Hole-in-the-Rock expedition to settle the wild lands around the San Juan River of southeastern Utah, feeling a Mormon presence would aid in ministering to the Indians there and prevent non-Mormons from moving in. In 1878, the Parowan Stake issued the first call for a colonizing mission to the San Juan, even before a site had been selected. Preparations and surveys took place the following year as the 236 men, women, and children received their calls. Food, seed, farming and building tools, 200 horses, and more than 1,000 head of cattle would be taken along. Planners ruled out lengthy routes through northern Arizona or eastern Utah in favor of a straight shot via Escalante that would cut the distance in half. The expedition set off in the autumn of 1879, convinced that they were part of a divine mission. Yet hints of trouble to come filtered back from the advance group as they discov-

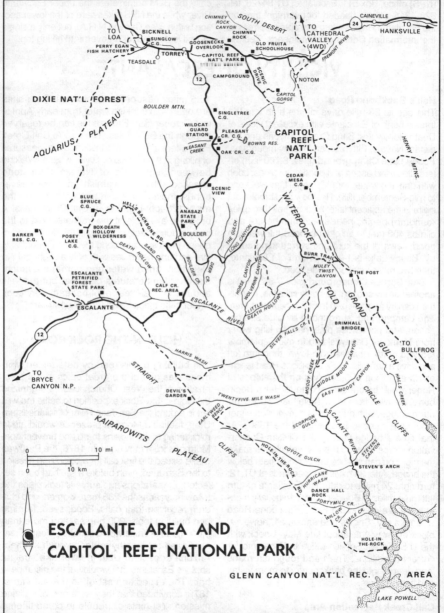

ESCALANTE AREA AND
CAPITOL REEF NATIONAL PARK

GLENN CANYON NAT'L. REC.   AREA

© MOON PUBLICATIONS, INC.

ered the Colorado River crossing to be far more difficult than first believed. Lack of springs along the way added to their worries. From their start at Escalante, road builders progressed rapidly for the first 50 miles, then slowly over rugged slickrock for the final six miles to Hole-in-the-Rock. A 45-foot sheer drop below this narrow notch was followed by three-quarters of a mile of extremely steep slickrock to the Colorado River. The route looked impossible, but three crews of workers armed with picks and blasting powder worked simultaneously to widen the notch and to construct a precarious wagon road down to the river and up cliffs on the other side. The job took six weeks. Miraculously, all the people, animals, and wagons made it down and were ferried across the Colorado River without a serious accident. Canyons and other obstacles continued to block the way as the weary group pressed on. Only after six months of exhausting travel did they stop at the present-day site of Bluff on the San Juan River.

Today, on a journey from Escalante, you can experience a bit of the same adventure the pioneers knew. Except for scattered signs of ranching, the land remains unchanged. If the road's dry, vehicles with good clearance can drive to within a short distance of Hole-in-the-Rock. The rough conditions encountered past Dance Hall Rock require more clearance than most cars. Bring sufficient gas, food, and water for the on tire 126-mile roundtrip from Escalante. The turnoff from UT 12 is five miles east of town. In addition to rewarding you with scenic views, Hole-in-the-Rock Road passes many side drainages of the Escalante River to the east and some very remote country of the Kaiparowits Plateau high above to the west. Staff at the Information Center just west of Escalante can give current road conditions and suggest hikes.

Metate Arch and other rock sculptures decorate **Devil's Garden**, 12.5 miles down Hole-in-the-Rock Road. Turn west 0.3 mile at the sign to the parking area, as you can't really see the "garden" from the road. Red- and cream-colored sandstone formations sit atop pedestals or tilt at crazy angles. Delicate bedding lines run through the rocks. There are no trails or markers—just wander about at your whim. The BLM has provided picnic tables, grills, and outhouses for day use. No overnight camping is permitted at Devil's Garden.

Dance Hall Rock (38 miles down Hole-in-the-Rock Road) jumped to fiddle music and lively steps of the expedition members in 1879. Its natural amphitheater has a relatively smooth floor and made a perfect gathering spot when the Hole-in-the-Rock group had to wait three weeks at nearby Fortymile Spring for road work to be completed ahead. Dance Hall Rock is an enjoyable place to explore and only a short walk from the parking area. Solution holes, left from water dissolving in the rock, pockmark the Entrada Sandstone structure.

At road's end (57 miles from UT 12) continue on foot across slickrock to the notch and views of the blue waters of Lake Powell below. Rockslides have made the descent impossible for vehicles, but hikers can scramble down to the lake and back in about an hour. Elevation change is 600 feet. The half-mile roundtrip is strenuous. After a steep descent over boulders, look for steps of Uncle Ben's Dugway at the base of the notch. Below here the grade is gentler. Drill holes in the rock once held oak stakes against which logs, brush, and earth supported the outer wagon wheels. The inner wheels followed a narrow rut four to six inches deep. About two-thirds of the route down is now under water, though the most impressive road work can still be seen.

Elizabeth Morris Decker described the descent in a letter to her parents on February 22, 1880: "If you ever come this way it will scare you to death to look down it. It is about a mile from the top down to the river and it is almost strait down, the cliffs on each side are five hundred feet high and there is just room enough for a wagon to go down. It nearly scared me to death. The first wagon I saw go down they put the brake on and rough locked the hind wheels and had a big rope fastened to the wagon and about ten men holding back on it and then they went down like they would smash everything. I'll never forget that day. When we was walking down Willie looked back and cried and asked me how we would get back home."

HIKING THE ESCALANTE RIVER AND ITS TRIBUTARIES

The maze of canyons presents exceptional hiking opportunities. You'll find everything from easy day-hikes to challenging backpacking treks. The Escalante's canyon begins just downstream from the town of Escalante and ends at Lake Powell about 85 miles beyond. In all this distance only one road (UT 12) bridges the river. Many side canyons provide additional access to the Escalante and most are as beautiful as the main gorge. The river system covers such a large area that you can find solitude even in spring, the busiest hiking season. The many eastern canyons remain virtually untouched. The Escalante canyons preserve some of the quiet beauty once found in Glen Canyon, now lost under the waters of Lake Powell. Prehistoric Anasazi and Fremont Indians have left ruins, petroglyphs, pictographs, and artifacts in many locations. These archaeological resources are protected by federal law. Please don't collect or disturb them.

Practicalities
Visit the people at the Information Center on the west edge of Escalante for the required permit and the latest trail and road conditions before setting out (see Escalante "Information" under "Practicalities" in the "Escalante" section earlier in this chapter). You can also obtain topo maps and literature that show trailheads, mileages, and other info useful in planning trips. A useful book, *Hiking the Escalante* by Rudi Lambrechtse, introduces the region and describes 43 trips with comments on the geology, flora and fauna, and history. Best times for a visit are early March to early June and mid-September to early November. Summertime trips are possible too—just be prepared for higher temperatures and greater flash-flood danger in narrow canyons. Travel along the Escalante River involves frequent crossings, and there's always water in the main canyon, usually ankle-to knee-deep. Pools in the "Narrows" section between Scorpion Gulch and Stevens Canyon can be up to chest deep in spots (which you can bypass), but that's the exception. All this wading can destroy leather boots, so it's best to wear canvas shoes or boots. High-topped "Vietnam boots," available at surplus stores, work well and prevent gravel from getting inside. Occasional springs, some tributaries, and the river itself provide drinking water. Always purify it first; the NPS and BLM warn of the unpleasant disease giardiasis, caused by an invisible protozoan. Don't forget insect repellent—mosquitos

and deer flies seek out hikers in late spring and summer. Long-sleeved shirts and long pants also discourage biting insects and protect against the brush.

Walking Softly
Only great care and awareness can preserve the pristine canyons. You can help if you pack out all trash, avoid trampling on the fragile cryptobiotic soils (dark areas of symbiotic algae and fungus on the sand), travel in groups of 12 or fewer, don't disturb Indian artifacts, and leave your dogs at home to protect wildlife. (Dogs must be leashed within Glen Canyon N.R.A.) Most important—bury human waste well away from water sources, trails, and camping areas; unless there's a fire hazard, burn toilet paper to aid decomposition. Some parts of the canyons have abundant firewood; try to use only existing fire rings or build your fire without rings below the floodline. The NPS is considering a ban on

Tony Rose on the Escalante River (near Silver Falls Creek)

campfires in the Escalante subdistrict to better preserve the land. The use of backpacker stoves is recommended by the NPS and the BLM. Visitors are encouraged to maximize efforts to leave no trace of their passage in the area.

Floating The Escalante

For most of the year, shallow water and rocks make boat travel impossible, but river levels may rise high enough for two to three weeks during spring runoff, which peaks between early April and late May. (In some years there may not be enough water in any season.) Keep in touch with the Information Center in Escalante to hit the river at its highest. Shallow draft and maneuverability are essential, so inflatable canoes or kayaks work best. Also, they are easier to carry out at trip's end or if water levels drop too low for floating. Not recommended are rafts (they're too wide and bulky) and hard-shelled kayaks and canoes (they get banged up on the many rocks). The usual launch is the UT 12 bridge; Coyote Gulch (a 13-mile hike) is a good spot to get out, as are Crack in Wall route (a two-and-three-quarter-mile hike on steep sand from the junction of Coyote and Escalante canyons to Forty-Mile Ridge Trailhead; 4WD needed; a rope is required to negotiate the vessel over the canyon rim), and Hole-in-the-Rock (a 600-foot ascent over boulders; rope suggested). You could also arrange for a friend to pick you up by boat from the Halls Crossing or Bullfrog marinas. River boaters need a backcountry permit from either the BLM or NPS.

Trailheads

The many approaches to the area allow all sorts of trips. Besides the road access at Escalante and the UT 12 bridge, hikers can reach the Escalante River through western side canyons from Hole-in-the-Rock Road or eastern side canyons from Burr Trail Road. The western-canyon trailheads on Hole-in-the-Rock Road can be more easily reached by car, thus facilitating vehicle shuttles. To reach eastern-canyon trailheads, with the exceptions of Deer Creek and The Gulch on Burr Trail Road, you'll need lots of time and, if the road is wet, a 4WD vehicle. You'll also need to carry water for these more remote canyons. With the exception of Deer Creek, they're usually dry.

Town Of Escalante To UT 12 Bridge
(15 miles)

This first section of canyon offers easy walking and stunning canyon scenery. Tributaries and sandstone caves invite exploration. You'll find good camping areas all along. Usually the river here is only ankle deep. Either enter Escalante River at the bridge next to the sawmill, or go one mile east of town on UT 12 and turn north past the cemetery (visible from highway) and town dump. Almost immediately the river knifes its way through the massive cliffs of the Escalante Monocline, leaving the broad valley of the upper river behind.

Death Hollow, far prettier than the name suggests, comes in from the north after seven and one half miles. Several good swimming holes

Phipps Arch near Escalante

carved in rock lie a short hike upstream from the Escalante; watch for poison ivy among the greenery. Continue farther up Death Hollow to see more pools, little waterfalls, and outstanding canyon scenery. Some pools can be bypassed, others have to be swum (bring a little inflatable boat, air mattress, or waterproof bag to ferry packs). Hikers looking for a real challenge can start from a trailhead 24 miles north of town on Hell's Backbone Road, then scramble and swim their way to the Escalante River (22.5 extremely strenuous miles one-way), then walk the Escalante seven and one half miles to town or the UT 12 bridge. The first 11 miles of this route are dry, then you're swimming! Allow four or five days. The average hiker would most enjoy exploring Death Hollow up from its confluence with the Escalante River.

Sand Creek, on the Escalante's north side four and one half miles downstream from Death Hollow, is also worth exploring; deep pools begin a short way up from the mouth. After another half mile down the Escalante, a natural arch appears high on the canyon wall. Then the Escalante Natural Bridge comes into view about a half mile farther, just two miles from the UT 12 bridge. In fact, Escalante Natural Bridge makes a good day-hike destination from the highway.

UT 12 Bridge To Harris Wash
(26.5 miles)
In this section, the Escalante Canyon offers a varied show: In places the walls close in to make constricted narrows, at other places they step back to form great valleys. Side canyons filled with lush greenery and sparkling streams contrast with dry washes of desert, yet all can be fun to explore. A good hike of four to six days begins at the highway bridge, goes down the Escalante to Harris Wash, then up Harris to a trailhead off Hole-in-the-Rock Road (37 miles total).

From the UT 12 parking area, a trail leads to the river. Canyon access goes through private property; cross the river at the posted signs to avoid barking dogs at the ranch just downstream. **Phipps Wash** comes in from the south (right side) after one and one half miles and several more river crossings. Turn up its wide mouth a half mile to see Maverick Bridge in a drainage to the right. To reach Phipps Arch, continue another three-quarters of a mile up the main wash, turn left into a box canyon, and

scramble up the left side (see 7 1/2-minute Calf Creek topo map).

Bowington (Boynton) Arch is an attraction of a north side canyon known locally as Deer Creek. Look for this small canyon on the left one mile beyond Phipps Wash; turn up it one mile past three deep pools and then turn left a short way into a tributary canyon. In 1878, gunfire resolved a quarrel between local ranchers John Boynton and Washington Phipps. Phipps was killed, but both their names live on.

Waters of **Boulder Creek** come rushing into the Escalante from the north in the next major side canyon, five and three quarters miles below the UT 12 bridge. The creek, along with its Dry Hollow and Deer Creek tributaries, provides good canyon walking; deep areas may require swimming or climbing up on the plateau. (You could also start down Deer Creek from the Burr Trail Road where they meet, six and one half miles southeast of Boulder at a primitive BLM campground; starting at the campground, follow Deer Creek seven and one half miles to Boulder Creek, then three and one half miles down Boulder to the Escalante.) Deer and Boulder creeks have water year-round.

High sheer walls of Navajo Sandstone constrict the Escalante River in a narrow channel below Boulder Creek, but the canyon widens again above **The Gulch** tributary, 14 miles below the highway bridge. Hikers can head up The Gulch on a day-hike or start from Burr Trail Road (the trailhead is 10.8 miles southeast of Boulder). The hike from the road down to the Escalante is 12.5 miles, but there's one difficult spot: A 12-foot waterfall in a section of narrows about halfway down has to be bypassed. When Rudi Lambrechtse, author of *Hiking the Escalante,* tried friction climbing around the falls and the pool at their base, he fell 12 feet and broke his foot. That meant a painful three-day hobble out. Instead of taking the risk, Rudi recommends backtracking about 300 feet from the falls and friction climbing out from a small alcove in the west wall (look for a cairn on the ledge above). Climb up Brigham Tea Bench, walk south, then look for cairns leading back east to the narrows, and descend to the stream bed (a rope helps to lower packs in a small chimney section).

Most springs along the Escalante are difficult to spot. One that's easy to find is in the first south bend after The Gulch; water comes straight out of the rock a few feet above the river. The Escalante Canyon becomes wider as the river lazily meanders along. Hikers can cut off some of the bends by walking in the open desert between canyon walls and riverside willow thickets. A bend cut off by the river itself loops to the north just before Horse Canyon, three miles below The Gulch. Along with its tributaries **Death Hollow** and **Wolverine Creek, Horse Canyon** drains the Circle Cliffs to the northeast. Floods in these mostly dry streambeds wash down pieces of black petrified wood. (Vehicles with good clearance can reach the upper sections of all three canyons from a loop road off Burr Trail Road.) Horse and Wolverine Creek canyons offer good easy-to-moderate hiking, but if you really want a challenge, try Death Hollow (sometimes called "Little Death Hollow" to distinguish it from the larger one near Hell's Backbone Road). Starting from the Escalante River, go about two miles up Horse Canyon and turn right into Death Hollow; rugged scrambling over boulders takes you back into a long section of twisting narrows. Carry water for upper Horse Canyon and its tributaries; Lower Horse Canyon usually has water.

About three and one half miles down the Escalante from Horse Canyon, you'll enter Glen Canyon N.R.A. and come to Sheffield Bend, a large grassy field on the right. Only a chimney remains from Sam Sheffield's old homestead. Two grand amphitheaters lie beyond the clearing and up a stiff climb in loose sand. Over the next five and one half river miles to Silver Falls Creek you'll pass long bends, dry side canyons, and a huge slope of sand on the right canyon wall. Don't look for any silver waterfalls in **Silver Falls Creek**—the name comes from streaks of shiny desert varnish on the cliffs. Upper Silver Falls Creek can be approached by a rough road from Burr Trail Road, but a car shuttle between here and any of the trailheads on the west side of the Escalante River would take all day. Most hikers visit this drainage on a day-hike from the river. Carry water.

When the Hole-in-the-Rock route proved so difficult, pioneers figured there had to be a better way to the San Juan Mission. Their new wagon road descended Harris Wash to the Escalante River, climbed part of Silver Falls Creek, crossed the Circle Cliffs, descended Muley Twist

Canyon in the Waterpocket Fold, then followed Hall's Creek to Hall's Crossing on the Colorado River. Charles Hall operated a ferry there from 1881 to 1884. Old maps show a jeep road through Harris Wash and Silver Falls Creek canyons, used before the National Park Service closed off the Glen Canyon N.R.A. section. Harris Wash lies just a half mile downstream and across the Escalante from Silver Falls Creek.

Harris Wash
(10.25 miles one-way from trailhead to river)
Clear shallow water glides down this gem of a canyon. High cliffs streaked with desert varnish are deeply undercut and support lush hanging gardens. Harris Wash provides a beautiful route to the Escalante River, but it can also be a destination in itself; tributaries and caves invite exploration along the way. The sand and gravel streambed makes for easy walking. Reach the trailhead from UT 12 by turning south 10.8 miles on Hole-in-the-Rock Road, then left 6.3 miles on a dirt road (keep left at the fork near the end). Don't be dismayed by the drab appearance of upper Harris Wash. The canyon and creek appear a few miles downstream.

Harris Wash To Lake Powell
(42.75 miles)
The Escalante continues its spectacular show of wide and narrow reaches, side canyons to explore, and intriguing rock formations. A trip all the way from Harris Wash Trailhead to the Escalante, down the Escalante to near Lake Powell, then out to the Hurricane Wash Trailhead is 66.25 miles, taking 8-10 days. Many shorter hikes using other side canyons are possible too.

Still in a broad canyon, the Escalante flows past **Fence Canyon** (on the west) five and one half miles from Harris Wash. Fence Canyon has water and is a strenuous three-and-one-half-mile cross-country route out to the end of Egypt Road. Get trail directions from a ranger and bring a topo map. (Adventurous hikers could do a three-day, 20-mile loop via Fence Canyon, the Escalante River, and the northern arm of Twentyfive Mile Wash.) To reach the trailheads, take Hole-in-the-Rock Road 17.2 miles south of UT 12, then turn left (east) 3.7 miles on the Egypt Road for Twentyfive Mile Wash Trailhead or 9.1 miles for Egypt Trailhead.

Twentyfive Mile Wash, on the west side 11.5 miles below Harris Wash, is a good route for entering or leaving the Escalante River. The moderately difficult hike is 13 miles one-way from trailhead to river. Scenery transforms from that of an uninteresting dry wash in the upper part to a beautiful canyon with water and greenery in the lower reaches. To get to the trailhead, take Hole-in-the-Rock Road 17.2 miles south of UT 12, then turn left 3.7 miles on Egypt Road.

Moody Creek enters the Escalante six meandering river miles below Twentyfive Mile Wash (or just two and one quarter miles as the crow flies). A rough road off Burr Trail Road gives access to Moody Creek, Purple Hills, and other eroded features. Distance from trailhead to river is seven miles one-way (moderately strenuous), though most hikers find it more convenient to hike up from the Escalante. **Middle Moody Creek** enters Moody Creek three miles above the Escalante. Moody and Middle Moody canyons feature colorful rock layers, petrified wood, a narrows, and solitude. Carry water, as springs and waterpockets cannot be counted on. Canyons on the east side of the Escalante tend to be much drier than those on the west side.

East Moody Canyon enters the Escalante one and one half miles downstream from Moody Canyon, and it too makes a good side trip. There's often water about one-half mile upstream. Continuing down the Escalante, look on the left for a rincon, a meander cut off by the river. **Scorpion Gulch** enters through a narrow opening on the right, six and one half miles below Moody Canyon. A strenuous eight-mile climb up Scorpion Gulch over rockfalls and around deep pools brings you to a trailhead on Early Weed Bench Road. Experience, directions from a ranger, and a topo map are needed. A challenging four-day, 30-mile loop hike uses Fox Canyon, Twentyfive Mile Wash, the Escalante River, and Scorpion Gulch. Water is found only in lower Twentyfive Mile Wash, the river, and lower Scorpion Gulch. Early Weed Bench turnoff is 24.2 miles south on Hole-in-the-Rock Road from UT 12; head in 5.8 miles to Scorpion Gulch Trailhead.

In the next 12 miles below Scorpion Gulch, Escalante Canyon is alternately wide and narrow. Then the river plunges into the **Narrows,** a five-mile-long section choked with boulders; plan on spending a day picking a route through.

Watch out for chest-deep water here! Remote and little visited, **Stevens Canyon** enters from the east near the end of the Narrows. Stevens Arch stands guard 580 feet above the confluence; the opening measures 225 feet wide and 100 feet high. The upper and lower parts of Stevens Canyon usually have some water.

Coyote Gulch, on the right one and one half miles below Stevens Canyon, marks the end of the Escalante for most hikers. In some seasons Lake Powell comes within one mile of Coyote Gulch and occasionally floods the canyon mouth. Coyote can stay flooded for several weeks, depending on the release flow of Glen Canyon Dam and water volume coming in. The river and lake don't have a pretty meeting place—quicksand and dead trees are found here. Log jams make it difficult to travel in from the lake by boat.

Coyote Gulch has received more publicity than other areas of the Escalante, and you're more likely to meet other hikers here. Two arches, a natural bridge, graceful sculpturing of the stream bed and canyon walls, deep undercuts, and a cascading creek make a visit well worthwhile. The best route in starts where Hole-in-the-Rock Road crosses Hurricane Wash, 34.7 miles south of UT 12. It's 12.5 miles one-way from the trailhead to the river and the hike is moderately strenuous. For the first mile you follow the dry, sandy wash without even a hint of being in a canyon. Water doesn't appear for three more miles. You'll reach Coyote Gulch, which has water, at five and one quarter miles from the trailhead. Another way into Coyote Gulch begins at the Red Well Trailhead; it's 31.5 miles south on Hole-in-the-Rock Road, then one and one half miles east (keep left at the fork). A start from Red Well adds three-quarters of a mile more to the hike than the Hurricane Wash route but is less crowded.

Other Adventures

Dry Fork of Coyote Gulch contains three enchanting canyons named Peek-a-boo, Spooky, and Brimstone. Enjoy the narrows, natural bridges, and deep pools. See *Hiking the Escalante,* by Rudi Lambrechtse, for directions.

Three canyons near the end of Hole-in-the-Rock Road lead down to Lake Powell: Fortymile Gulch (strenuous, 12 miles roundtrip), Willow Gulch (moderately difficult, six miles roundtrip), and Fiftymile Creek (easy to moderately difficult, eight miles roundtrip). As none are signed, you'll need a topo map or directions from a ranger or *Hiking the Escalante* to find them.

BOULDER

About 150 people live in this farming community at the base of Boulder Mountain. Ranchers began drifting in during the late 1870s, though not with the idea of forming a town. By the mid-1890s Boulder had established itself as a ranching and dairy center. Remote and hemmed in by canyons and mountains, Boulder remained one of the last communities in the country to rely on pack trains for transportation. Motor vehicles couldn't drive in until the 1930s. Today Boulder is worth a visit to see an excavated Anasazi village and the spectacular scenery along the way. Take paved UT 12 either through the canyon and slickrock country from Escalante or over the Aquarius Plateau from Torrey (near Capitol Reef National Park). Burr Trail Road connects Boulder with Capitol Reef National Park's southern district via Waterpocket Fold and Circle Cliffs. A fourth way in is from Escalante on the dirt Hell's Backbone Road, which comes out three miles west of Boulder at UT 12.

Anasazi State Park

Museum exhibits, an excavated village site, and a pueblo replica provide a look into the life of these ancient people. The Anasazi stayed here for 50-75 years sometime between A.D. 1050 and 1200. They grew corn, beans, and squash in fields nearby. Village population peaked at about 200, with an estimated 40-50 dwellings. Why the Anasazi left or where they went aren't known for sure, but a fire swept through much of the village before it was abandoned. Perhaps they burned the village on purpose, knowing they would move on. University of Utah students and faculty excavated the village, known as the Coombs Site, in 1958 and 1959. Pottery, ax heads, arrow points, and other tools found at the site can be seen in the museum, as can more perishable items like sandals and basketry that came from more protected sites elsewhere. A diorama shows how the village might have appeared in its heyday. Video programs on the Anasazi and modern tribes can be seen on request.

The self-guided tour of the ruins begins behind the museum. You'll see a whole range of Anasazi building styles—a pit house, masonry walls, jacal walls (mud reinforced by sticks), and combinations of masonry and jacal. Replicas of habitation and storage rooms behind the museum show complete construction details. The park is open daily 8 a.m.-6 p.m. from mid-May to mid-September, then 9 a.m.-5 p.m. the rest of the year. Admission is $1.50 adult, $1 children 6-15, or $6 per vehicle (whichever is the least). Books, videos, T-shirts, and postcards are sold. Located on UT 12, 28 miles northeast of Escalante and 38 miles south of Torrey, tel. 335-7308.

Information And Services

Circle Cliffs Motel has just three units on UT 12, tel. 355-7329. **Hall's Store,** next to Anasazi State Park, tel. 335-7304, runs a small RV park ($8.72; self-contained, no tents). **Poole's Place** (closed in winter), across the road from the state park, tel. 335-7422, has a motel ($38.15 s, $45.78 d), cafe, and gift shop. **Burr Trail Cafe** (open Memorial Day weekend until autumn) is at the intersection of UT 12 and Burr Trail Road. Look for a **visitor information** booth in town, open daily May-Oct. about 9 a.m.-6 p.m.; usually it's in front of Burr Trail Cafe. The two gas stations in Boulder sell groceries and snack food.

BOULDER MOUNTAIN SCENIC DRIVE

Utah 12 climbs high into forests of ponderosa pine, aspen, and fir on Boulder Mountain between the towns of Boulder and Torrey. The modern highway replaces what used to be a rough dirt road. Travel in winter is usually possible now, though heavy snows can close the road. Viewpoints along the drive offer sweeping panoramas of the Escalante canyon country, Circle Cliffs, Waterpocket Fold, and the Henry Mountains. Hikers and anglers can explore the alpine country of Boulder Mountain and seek out the 90 or so trout-filled lakes. The Dixie National Forest map (Escalante and Teasdale ranger districts) shows the back roads, trails, and lakes. The U.S. Forest Service has three developed campgrounds about midway along

Chriss Lake, one of many pretty spots on Boulder Mountain

this scenic drive: **Oak Creek** (18 miles from Boulder, elev. 8,800 feet), **Pleasant Creek** (19 miles from Boulder, elev. 8,700 feet), and **Singletree** (24 miles from Boulder, elev. 8,600 feet). Season with water lasts from about late May to mid-September; sites cost $6. Campgrounds may also be open in spring and autumn without water at $3. **Lower Bowns Reservoir** (elev. 7,400 feet) has primitive camping (no water or fee) and fishing for rainbow and some cutthroat trout; turn east five miles on a rough dirt road (not recommended for cars) just south of Pleasant Creek Campground. Contact the **Teasdale Ranger District office,** near Torrey, tel. 425-3702, for recreation information in the northern and eastern parts of Boulder Mountain; contact the **Escalante Ranger District office,** Escalante, tel. 826-5499/5400, for the southern and western areas. **Wildcat Information Center,** near Pleasant Creek Campground, has forest information; open in the summer with irregular hours.

TORREY AND VICINITY

This little town is only 11 miles west of the Capitol Reef National Park visitor center. **Sky Ridge Bed and Breakfast** is one mile east of downtown, tel. 425-3222, with rooms ($70.85-103.55 s or d). **Wonderland Inn,** just east of town near the UT 12 turnoff for Boulder, tel. 425-3775, has rooms for $47.96 s, $58.86 d and a restaurant serving breakfast, lunch, and dinner daily.

Chuck Wagon Motel, tel. 425-3288, open mid-April to mid-November, offers motel rooms ($30.52-51.94 s, $35.52-56.94 d), campground with showers ($6 tent or RV no hookups, $11.32 RV w/hookups), and a grocery store with bakery. **Capitol Reef Inn and Cafe,** tel. 425-3271, (closed in winter) has rooms ($39.24 s, $43.60 d), a small cafe serving breakfast and dinner, and a gift shop. **Boulder View Inn** is opening at 385 W. Main, tel. 425-3800, with rooms available all year ($50 s, $54 d). **Thousand Lakes RV Park,** one mile west of town on UT 24, tel. 425-3500, has sites with showers, laundry, and store from April 1 to October 31; $9.81 tent or RV no hookups, $13.08 RV w/hookups. **Boulder Mountain Homestead RV Park** offers sites four miles south on UT 12 from the junction with UT 24, tel. 425-3586; it may close in winter, $13 w/hookups (no tents or showers). **La Buena Vida Mexican Food,** on the west edge of town in a little white house with red trim, tel. 425-3759, prepares excellent south-of-the-border meals for lunch and dinner; open Thurs.-Sun. from June to October, irregular hours in spring and autumn, then closed in winter.

Teasdale Ranger Station of the Dixie National Forest has info about hiking, horseback riding, and road conditions in the northern and eastern parts of Boulder Mountain and the Aquarius Plateau; books and forest maps are available. The office is two miles west of Torrey on UT 24, then one and one half miles south to Main and 138 East (Box 99, Teasdale, UT 84773), tel. 425-3702; open Mon.-Fri. 8 a.m.-

4:30 p.m. **Hondoo Rivers & Trails,** Box 98, Torrey, UT 84775, tel. 425-3519, leads horse-back, rafting, and driving tours of one to eight days in the scenic backcountry of southern Utah.

East Of Torrey
Two motels offer lodging, restaurants, and fine views three miles east of town toward Capitol Reef National Park. **Best Western Capitol Reef Resort,** tel. 425-3761 or (800) 528-1234, fea-tures luxury accommodations and a pool ($82.84 s or d) and an attractive restaurant (open daily for breakfast, lunch, and dinner). **Rim Rock Rustic Inn,** tel. 425-3843 or (800) 243-0786, has basic rooms and a pool ($49.05 s or d and up), a campground open all year with showers ($8.48 tent or RV no hookups, $10.60 RV w/hookups), restaurant (open daily for breakfast, lunch, and dinner), horseback riding, indoor pool, and spa.

Bicknell
This small town is eight miles west of Torrey on UT 24. The **Sunglow Motel,** tel. 425-3821, has rooms ($27.25 s, $37.06 d) and a cafe (open daily for breakfast, lunch, and dinner). The

Aquarius Motel, tel. 425-3835, offers rooms ($27.14 s, $32.59 d), kitchenettes ($38.31 d), and a cafe (open daily for breakfast, lunch, and dinner). The Aquarius Motel also has an **RV park** four blocks away for self-contained units; $7.50 w/hookups. **Sunglow Campground** (U.S. Forest Service) is just east of Bicknell; sites are open mid-May to late October with water and a $5 charge; elevation is 7,200 feet; the sur-rounding red cliffs really light up at sunset. **Pleasant Creek Trail Rides,** tel. 425-3315, has half-day, full-day, and pack trips in the area.

The **J. Perry Egan Fish Hatchery** produces 25-30 million trout eggs a year. It's the largest in Utah and supplies eggs for most of the state's other hatcheries. Visitors are welcome to see the operation, open during daylight hours. The raceways have fish divided according to species, strain, and age. Trout spawn when three years old and are kept to produce here for another three years, after which they're released into high-pressure fishing areas. You'll see cutthroat, German brown, brook, and four to six strains of rainbow trout (including albinos). Turn south two and one half miles on a paved road off UT 24 between Mileposts 63 and 64 (southeast of Bicknell).

CAPITOL REEF NATIONAL PARK

Wonderfully sculptured rock layers in a rainbow of colors put on a fine show here. Though you'll find these same rocks through much of the Four Corners region, their artistic variety has no equal outside Capitol Reef National Park. About 70 million years ago, gigantic forces within the earth began to uplift, squeeze, and fold more than a dozen rock formations into the central feature of the park today—Waterpocket Fold, so named for the many small pools of water trapped by the tilted strata. Erosion has since carved spires, graceful curves, canyons, and arches. Water-pocket Fold extends 1100 miles between Thou-sand Lake Mountain in the north and Lake Pow-ell in the south. The most spectacular cliffs and rock formations of Waterpocket Fold form Capi-tol Reef, located north of Pleasant Creek and curving northwest across the Fremont River to-ward Thousand Lake Mountain. The reef was named by explorers who found Waterpocket Fold a barrier to travel and likened it to a reef blocking

passage on the ocean. The rounded sandstone hills reminded them of the Capitol dome in Wash-ington, D.C.—hence the name Capitol Reef.

Roads and hiking trails in the park provide access to the colorful rock layers and to the plants and wildlife that live here. You'll see rem-nants of the area's long human history too—petroglyphs and storage bins of the prehistoric Fremont Indians, a schoolhouse and other struc-tures built by Mormon pioneers, and several small uranium mines of the 20th century. Leg-ends tell of Butch Cassidy and other outlaw members of the "Wild Bunch" who hid out in these remote canyons in the 1890s.

NATURAL HISTORY

The Geologic Story
Exposed rocks reveal windswept deserts, rivers, mud flats, and inland seas of long ago. Nearly all

the layers date from the Mesozoic Era (65-230 million years ago), when dinosaurs ruled the earth. Later uplift and twisting of the land—which continues to this day—built up the Colorado Plateau of southern Utah and the Rocky Mountains to the east. Immense forces squeezed the rocks until they bent up and over from east to west in the massive crease of Waterpocket Fold.

Climate

Expect hot summer days (highs in the upper 80s and low 90s) and cool nights. Winter brings cool days (highs in the 40s) and night temperatures dropping into the low 20s and teens. Snow accents the colored rocks while rarely hindering traffic on the main highway. Winter travel on the back roads and trails may be halted by snow, but it soon melts when the sun comes out. Annual precipitation averages only seven inches, peaking in the late summer thunderstorm season.

Flora And Fauna

Ponderosa pine and other cool-climate vegetation grow on the flanks of Thousand Lake Mountain (7,000-9,000 feet high) in the northwest corner of the park. Most of Waterpocket Fold, however, is at 5,000-7,000 feet, covered

plain titmouse (Parus inoratus), *a common year-round resident in the park*

LOUISE FOOTE

with sparse juniper and piñon pine that cling precariously in cracks and thin soils of the slickrock. The soil from each rock type generally determines what will grow. Mancos Shale forms a poor clay soil supporting only saltbush, shadscale, and galleta grass. On Dakota Sandstone you'll see mostly sage and rabbitbrush. Clays of the Morrison Formation repel nearly all plants, while its sandstones nurture mostly juniper, piñon pine, and cliffrose; uranium prospectors discovered that *astragalus* and prince's plume commonly grow near ore deposits. Sands of the Summerville Formation nourish grasses and four-wing saltbush. The Fremont River and several creeks provide a lush habitat of cottonwood, tamarisk, willow, and other water-loving plants.

Streamside residents include beaver, muskrat, mink, tree lizard, Great Basin spadefoot toad, Rocky Mountain toad, and leopard frog. Spadefoot toads, fairy shrimp, and insects have adapted to the temporary water pockets by completing the aquatic phase of their short life cycles in a hurry. Near water or out in the drier country, you might see mule deer, coyote, gray fox, porcupine, spotted and striped skunks, badger, black-tailed jackrabbit, desert cottontail, yellow belly marmot, rock squirrel, Colorado chipmunk, Ord's kangaroo rat, canyon mouse, and five known species of bats. With luck, you may sight a relatively rare mountain lion or black bear. While you can't miss seeing the many small lizards along the trails, snakes tend to be more secretive; those in the park include the striped whipsnake, Great Basin gopher snake, wandering garter snake, and the rarely seen desert faded pygmy rattlesnake. Some common birds are the sharp-shinned hawk, American kestrel, chukar, mourning dove, white-throated swift, black-chinned and broad-tailed hummingbirds, violet-green swallow, common raven, piñon and scrub jays, canyon and rock wrens, and rufous-sided towhee. Most wildlife, except birds, wait until evening to come out, and they disappear again the following morning.

HUMAN HISTORY

Prehistoric Man

By A.D. 700, Fremont Indians had found good

farming land in some of the valleys. They grew corn, beans, and other crops to supplement hunting and the gathering of wild plants. They protected food from rodents and insects by carefully constructing stone or wooden storage rooms. Many of these have survived in sheltered cliff overhangs, but the pit house dwellings have nearly vanished. Intriguing pictographs and petroglyphs portray the Fremont adorned with headdresses, shields, sashes, and jewelry. Figures of desert bighorn sheep are seen too. Was this artwork casual doodlings? Or did it have religious importance? The meaning of this art hasn't been deciphered. Archaeologists first described and named the Fremont culture from sites along the Fremont River at Capitol Reef in 1929. Droughts and possible conflict with other tribes may have been factors in the disappearance of the Fremont from the area about 1250. Until the white man came, small groups of Ute and Paiute spent winters hunting here, then moved to the high country in summer.

Mormon Settlement

You can see why early explorers detoured around this natural barrier, though some trappers may have entered its canyons. Capitol Reef remained one of the last places in the West to be discovered. First reports came in 1866 from a detachment of Mormon militia pursuing renegade Indians. In 1872, Professor Almon H. Thompson of the Powell expedition led the first scientific exploration in the fold country and named several park features along the group's Pleasant Creek route. Mormons, expanding their network of settlements, arrived in the upper Fremont Valley in the late 1870s and spread downriver to Hanksville. Junction (renamed Fruita in 1902) and nearby Pleasant Creek (Sleeping Rainbow/Floral Ranch) were settled about 1880. Floods, isolation, and transport difficulties forced many families to move on, especially downstream from Capitol Reef. Irrigation and hard work paid off in Fruita with prosperous fruit orchards and the sobriquet "the Eden of Wayne County." Fruita averaged about 10 families who grew alfalfa, sorghum (for syrup), vegetables, and a wide variety of fruit. Getting the produce to market required long and difficult journeys by wagon. The region remained one of the most isolated in Utah until after WW II.

Creation Of The Park

In the 1920s local residents began to extol the wonders of Capitol Reef to the outside world. Impressed visitors lobbied for a national monument, which President Franklin D. Roosevelt granted in 1937. The original 37,060-acre Capitol Reef National Monument included the highly scenic areas around the Fremont River canyon and Capitol Gorge. Expansions to the north and south in 1969, followed by more additions and national park status in 1971, brought the park to its current 241,904 acres. Fruita residents moved out in the 1960s as the National Park Service purchased the old homesteads. The schoolhouse, Behunin cabin, Merin Smith's blacksmith shop, and other buildings survive to commemorate Fruita's pioneer settlers. And the orchards still produce fruit that visitors may pick.

VISITING THE PARK

The visitor center and main highway (UT 24) through Capitol Reef stay open all year. Even travelers short on time will enjoy a quick look at visitor center exhibits and a drive on UT 24 through an impressive cross section of Capitol Reef cut by the Fremont River. More of the park can be seen on the Scenic Drive, a narrow paved road that heads south from the visitor center. The drive passes beneath spectacular cliffs of the reef and enters scenic Grand Wash and Capitol Gorge canyons; allow at least one and one half hours for the 21-mile roundtrip (plus side trips). The fair-weather Notom/Dullfrog Road (paved as far as Notom at press time) heads south along the other side of the reef for almost 00 miles with fine views of Waterpocket Fold. Burr Trail Road (dirt inside the park) in the south actually climbs over the fold in a steep set of switchbacks, connecting Notom Road with Boulder. Only drivers with high-clearance vehicles can explore Cathedral Valley in the park's northern district. All these roads provide access to viewpoints and hiking trails. A $4 per vehicle park entrance fee is collected on the Scenic Drive.

Visitor Center

Start with a 10-minute slide show, shown on request, introducing Capitol Reef's natural wonders and history. A giant relief map gives you a bird's-eye view of the entire park. Rock samples and diagrams illustrate seven of the geologic formations you'll be seeing. Photos identify plants and birds found here. Prehistoric Fremont Indian artifacts on display include petroglyph replicas, sheepskin moccasins, pottery, basketry, stone knives, spear and arrow points, and bone jewelry. Other historic exhibits outline exploration and early Mormon settlement. Visitors headed for the back roads should ask at the desk about conditions and the weather forecast. Hikers planning overnight trips can get the required backcountry permit free. Besides answering questions, rangers will give out or sell info sheets for special interests. Hikers can pick up a map of trails that are near the visitor center and of longer routes in the southern park areas; naturalists will want the checklists of plants, birds, mammals, and other wildlife; and history buffs can learn more about the area's settlement and founding of the park. You can also choose from a good selection of pamphlets and books about the park, natural history, archaeology, pioneer history, and regional travel. Topo maps, posters, postcards, film, petroglyph and pottery replicas, and other souvenirs can be purchased too. Rangers offer nature walks, campfire programs, and other special events from Easter to mid October; the bulletin board outside the visitor center lists what's on. Hours at the visitor center are daily 8 a.m.-7 p.m. June-Sept., and daily 8 a.m.-4:30 p.m. the rest of the year. The visitor center is on UT 24 at the turnoff for Fruita Campground and the Scenic Drive. For more information, contact Capitol Reef National Park, Torrey, UT 84775, tel. 425-3791.

Hiking And Rock Climbing

Fifteen day-hiking trails begin within a short drive of the visitor center. Of these, only Grand Wash, Capitol Gorge, Sunset Point, and Goosenecks are easy. The others involve moderately strenuous climbs and travel over irregular slickrock. Signs and rock cairns mark the way, but it's all too easy to wander off if you don't pay attention to the route. Rewards of hiking in the park include superb views, a chance to see wildlife and flora, and a deeper appreciation of the area's geologic history. Innumerable canyon and cross-country possibilities exist all over the park; talk to the rangers for ideas. To avoid intimidating the wildlife, pets may not be taken on trails or into the backcountry. Be cautious on slickrock: Although it's not really slippery unless wet, hikers have gotten into trouble by attempting too steep a slope. You'll need a canteen on most hikes because few of the canyons and natural waterpockets are reliable water sources. Spring and autumn offer the most comfortable temperatures and less chance of bothersome insects (worst from mid-May to late June). Though most trails can easily be done in a day, backpackers might want to try longer trips in Chimney Rock/Spring Canyons in the north or Muley Twist Canyon and Halls Creek in the south. Obtain the required backcountry permit (free) from a ranger and camp at least a half mile from the nearest maintained road or trail. (Cairned routes like Chimney Rock Canyon, Muley Twist Canyon, and Halls Creek don't count as trails but are backcountry routes.) Bring a stove for cooking, as backcountry users may not build fires. Avoid camping or parking in washes at any time—torrents of mud and boulders can carry away everything! Technical rock climbers should check with rangers to learn about restricted areas; registration is voluntary. Climbers must use "clean" techniques (no pitons or bolts) and keep at least 25 feet from rock-art panels.

Fruit Picking

Though Fruita's citizens have departed, the National Park Service still maintains the old orchards. Visitors are welcome to pick and carry away the cherries, apricots, peaches, pears, and apples during the harvest seasons. Harvest times begin in late June or early July and end in October. You'll be charged about the same as in commercial pick-your-own orchards. You may also wander through any orchard and eat all you want on the spot before and during the designated picking season (no charge).

PRACTICALITIES

In The Park

Fruita Campground stays open all year and has drinking water but no showers or hookups ($6); Nov.-April you have to get water from the visitor center. The surrounding orchards and lush grass make this an attractive spot, one mile from the visitor center on the Scenic Drive.

Sites often fill by early afternoon in the busy May-Oct. season. One group campground (by reservation only) and a picnic area are nearby. If you're just looking for a place to park for the night, check out the public land east of the park boundary off UT 24. Areas on both sides of the highway (about nine miles east of the visitor center) may be used for primitive camping; no facilities or charge. The five-site **Cedar Mesa Campground** is in the park's southern district just off Notom-Bullfrog Road (dirt); campers here enjoy fine views of Waterpocket Fold and the Henry Mountains. Open all year, no water or charge; from the visitor center, go east 9.2 miles on UT 24, then turn right 22 miles on Notom-Bullfrog Road (avoid if wet). **Cathedral Valley Campground** serves the park's northern district; it has five sites (no water or charge) near the Hartnet Junction, about 30 miles north of UT 24; take either the Caineville Wash or Hartnet (has a river ford) roads; both are dirt and should be avoided if wet.

Other Areas

Accommodations, campgrounds, and restaurants are at Capitol Reef Resort and Rim Rock Ranch (eight miles west of the visitor center), Torrey (11 miles west of the visitor center), and Bicknell (19 miles west of the visitor center); see "Torrey and Vicinity" under "Vicinity of Escalante" earlier in this chapter. Caineville has a campground 15 miles east of the visitor center and a restaurant 21.5 miles east of the visitor center. The U.S. Forest Service has three developed campgrounds (open with water from late May to mid-September) on UT 12 between Torrey and Boulder. With distances from the park and elevations, they are: **Singletree** (22 miles, 8,200 feet); **Pleasant Creek** (27 miles, 8,600 feet); and **Oak Creek** (28 miles, 8,800 feet). **Lower Bowns Reservoir** has primitive camping (no water or fee) and fishing for rainbow trout and some cutthroat (elev. 7,400 feet); turn east five miles on a dirt road just south of Pleasant Creek Campground. **Hondoo Rivers & Trails** offers 4WD and horseback tours of the park and nearby areas; Box 98, Torrey, UT 84775, tel. 425-3591. Horseback trips are also offered by **Pleasant Creek Trail Rides** at Rim Rock Rustic Inn and Bicknell, tel. 425-3315 and by **Bestwestern Capitol Reef Resort** three miles east of Torrey, tel. 425-3761.

SIGHTS AND DAY-HIKES ALONG UTAH 24 (LISTED WEST TO EAST)

Chimney Rock Trail

The trailhead is three miles west of the visitor center on the north side of the highway. Towering 660 feet above the highway, Chimney Rock is a fluted spire of dark-red rock (Moenkopi Formation) capped by a block of hard sandstone (Shinarump Member of the Chinle Formation). A three-and-one-half-mile loop trail ascends 540 feet from the parking lot (elev. 6,100 feet) to a ridge overlooking Chimney Rock; allow two and one half hours. Panoramic views take in the face of Capitol Reef. Petrified wood along the trail has been eroded from the Chinle Formation (the same rock layer found in Petrified Forest National Park in Arizona). It is not legal to take any of the petrified wood.

Spring Canyon Route

This moderately difficult hike begins at the top of the Chimney Rock trail. The wonderfully eroded forms of Navajo Sandstone present a continually changing exhibition. The riverbed is normally dry; allow about six hours for the 10-mile (one-way) trip from Chimney Rock parking area to the Fremont River and UT 24. (Some maps show all or part of this as "Chimney Rock Canyon.") Check with rangers for the weather forecast before setting off—flash floods can be dangerous, and the Fremont River (which you must wade across) can be high. Normally the river is easily crossed (less than knee deep) to UT 24 (3.7 miles east of the visitor center). With luck

leopard frog (Rana pipiens)

LOUISE FOOTE

you'll have a car waiting for you. Summer hikers can beat the heat with a crack-of-dawn departure. Carry water, as this section of canyon lacks a reliable source. From the Chimney Rock parking area, hike Chimney Rock Trail to the top of the ridge and follow signs for Chimney Rock Canyon. Enter the unnamed lead-in canyon and follow it downstream. A sign marks Chimney Rock Canyon, which is two and one half miles from the start. Turn right six and one half miles (downstream) to reach the Fremont River. A section of narrows requires some rock-scrambling (bring a cord to lower backpacks), or the area can be bypassed on a narrow trail to the left above the narrows. Farther down, a natural arch high on the left marks the halfway point.

Upper Chimney Rock Canyon could be explored on an overnight trip. A spring (purify before drinking) is located in an alcove on the right side about one mile up Chimney Rock Canyon from the lead-in canyon. Wildlife use this water source, so camp at least a quarter mile away. Chimney Rock Canyon, the longest in the park, begins high on the slopes of Thousand Lake Mountain and descends nearly 15 miles southeast to join the Fremont River.

Sulphur Creek Route

This moderately difficult hike begins by following a wash across the highway from the Chimney Rock parking area, descending to Sulphur Creek, then it heads down the narrow canyon to the visitor center. The trip is about five miles long (one-way) and takes three to five hours. Park rangers sometimes schedule guided hikes on this route. Warm weather is the best time because you'll be wading in the normally shallow creek. Three small waterfalls can be bypassed fairly easily; two falls are just below the goosenecks and the third is about a half mile before coming out at the visitor center. Carry water. The creek's name may be a mistake as there's no sulphur along it; perhaps outcrops of yellow limonite caused the confusion. You can make an all-day eight-mile hike in Sulphur Creek by starting where it crosses the highway between Mileposts 72 and 73, five miles west of the visitor center.

Panorama Point,
The Goosenecks, And Sunset Point

The turnoff is two and one half miles west of the visitor center on the south side of the high-

way. Follow signs south for 0.15 mile to Panorama Point and views of Capitol Reef to the east and Boulder Mountain to the west. A sign explains how glacial meltwaters carried basalt boulders from Boulder Mountain to the reef 8,000-200,000 years ago. Goosenecks of Sulphur Creek are 0.9 mile farther on a gravel road. A short trail leads to the Goosenecks Overlook on the rim (elev. 6,400 feet) for dizzying views to the creek below. Canyon walls display shades of yellow, green, brown, and red. Another easy trail leads a third mile to Sunset Point and panoramic views of the Capitol Reef cliffs and the distant Henry Mountains.

Fruita Schoolhouse

Located 0.8 mile east of the visitor center on the north side of the highway. Early settlers completed the one-room log structure in 1896. Teachers struggled at times with rowdy students, but the kids learned their three R's in grades one through eight. Mormon church meetings, dances, town meetings, elections, and other community gatherings took place here. Lack of students caused the school's closing in 1941. Rangers are on duty some days in summer (ask at the visitor center). At other times you can peer inside the windows and listen to a recording of a former teacher recalling what school life was like.

Petroglyphs

Located 1.2 miles east of the visitor center on the north side of the highway, Fremont petroglyphs of several human figures with headdresses and mountain sheep decorate the cliff. More petroglyphs can be seen by walking to the left and right along the cliff face. Stay on the trail and do not climb the talus slope.

Hickman Natural Bridge,
Rim Overlook, And Navajo Knobs Trails

The trailhead is two miles east of the visitor center on the north side of the highway. The graceful Hickman Natural Bridge spans 133 feet across a small streambed. Numbered stops along the self-guiding trail correspond to descriptions in a pamphlet available at the trailhead or visitor center. Starting from the parking area (elev. 5,320 feet), the trail follows the Fremont River's green banks a short distance before gaining 380 feet in the climb to the bridge. The last section of trail follows a dry wash shaded by cottonwood, juniper, and

Indian artifacts illustrate a talk at the petroglyphs.

piñon pine trees. You'll pass under the bridge (eroded from the Kayenta Formation) at trail's end. Capitol Dome and other sculptured features of the Navajo Sandstone surround the site. The two-mile roundtrip hike takes about one and one half hours. Joseph Hickman served as principal of Wayne County High School and later in the state legislature during the 1920s; he and another local man, Ephraim Pectol, led efforts to promote Capitol Reef.

A splendid overlook 1,000 feet above Fruita beckons hikers up the Rim Overlook Trail. Take the Hickman Natural Bridge Trail a quarter mile from the parking area, then turn right two miles at the signed fork. Allow three and one half hours from the fork for this hike. Panoramic views take in the Fremont River valley below, the great cliffs of Capitol Reef above, the Henry Mountains to the southeast, and Boulder Mountain to the southwest.

Continue another 2.2 miles and more than 500 feet higher from the Rim Overlook to reach Navajo Knobs. Rock cairns lead the way over slickrock along the rim of Waterpocket Fold. A magnificent panorama at trail's end takes in much of southeastern Utah.

Cohab Canyon And Frying Pan Trails

Park at Hickman Natural Bridge trailhead, then walk across the highway bridge. This trail climbs Capitol Reef for fine views in all directions and a close look at the swirling lines in the Navajo

Sandstone. After three-quarters of a mile and a 400-foot climb, you'll reach a trail fork: keep right one mile to stay on Cohab Canyon Trail and descend to Fruita Campground or turn left onto Frying Pan Trail to Cassidy Arch (three and one half miles away) and Grand Wash (four miles away). The trail from Cassidy Arch to Grand Wash is very steep. All these interconnecting trails offer many hiking possibilities, especially if a car shuttle can be arranged. For example, you could start up Cohab Canyon Trail from UT 24, cross over the reef on Frying Pan Trail, make a side trip to Cassidy Arch, descend Cassidy Arch Trail to Grand Wash, walk down Grand Wash to UT 24, then walk (or car shuttle) 2.7 miles along the highway back to the start (10.5 miles total).

Cohab is a pretty little canyon in the Wingate Sandstone overlooking the campground. Mormon polygamists supposedly used the canyon to escape federal marshals during the 1880s. Hiking the Frying Pan Trail involves an additional 600 feet of climbing from either Cohab Canyon or Cassidy Arch trails. Once atop Capitol Reef, the trail follows the gently rolling slickrock terrain.

Grand Wash

The trailhead is 4.7 miles east of the visitor center on the south side of the highway. One of only five canyons cutting completely through the reef, Grand Wash offers easy hiking and great scenery. There's no trail—just follow the dry gravel riverbed. Flash floods can occur during storms. Canyon walls of Navajo Sandstone rise 800 feet above the floor and close in to as little as 20 feet in width. Cassidy Arch trailhead (see "Grand Wash Road," below) is two miles away, and parking for Grand Wash from the Scenic Drive is a quarter mile farther.

Behunin Cabin

Located 6.2 miles east of the visitor center on the south side of the highway. Elijah Cutlar Behunin used blocks of sandstone to build this cabin about 1882. He moved on, though, when floods made life too difficult. Small openings allow a look inside the dirt-floored structure, but no furnishings remain.

Small Waterfall In The Fremont River

Parking is 6.9 miles east of the visitor center on the north side of the highway. The river twists through a narrow man-made crack in the rock

The "Castle" stands near the visitor center.

before making its final plunge into a pool below. A sign warns of hazardous footing above the falls, which are dangerous for children. Instead, take the sandy path from the parking area to below the falls where they can be safely viewed. Use extreme caution if you intend to cool off in the pool at the base of the waterfall, as there is a very strong and dangerous undertow.

SIGHTS AND DAY-HIKES ALONG THE SCENIC DRIVE

Turn south from UT 24 at the visitor center to experience some of the reef's best scenery and to learn more about its geology. An illustrated pamphlet, available on the drive or in the visitor center, has keyed references to numbered stops along the 25-mile (roundtrip) drive. Descriptions identify rock layers and explain how they were formed. Just a quick tour takes one and one half hours, but several hiking trails may tempt you to extend your stay. The Scenic Drive is paved, though side roads have gravel surfaces. You'll first pass orchards and several of Fruita's buildings. A **blacksmith shop** (0.7 miles from the visitor center on the right) displays tools, harnesses, farm machinery, and Fruita's first tractor. The tractor didn't arrive until 1940—long after the rest of the country had modernized. In a recording, a rancher tells about living and working in Fruita.

Fremont Gorge Overlook Trail
From the start at the blacksmith shop, the trail crosses Johnson Mesa and climbs steeply to the overlook about 1,000 feet above the Fremont River; roundtrip distance is four and one half miles.

Picnic Area
Located 0.8 mile from the visitor center on the left, fruit trees and grass make this a pretty spot for lunch. A short trail crosses orchards and the Fremont River to the Fruita Schoolhouse.

Cohab Canyon Trail
The trailhead is across the road from Fruita Campground, 1.3 miles from the visitor center. The trail follows steep switchbacks during the first quarter mile, then more gentle grades to the top, 400 feet higher and one mile from the campground. You can take a short trail to viewpoints or continue three-quarters of a mile down the other side of the ridge to UT 24. See description under "Sights and Day-Hikes Along Utah 24" above. Another option is to turn right at the top on Frying Pan Trail to Cassidy Arch (three and one half miles one-way) and Grand Wash (four miles one-way).

Fremont River Trail
From the trailhead near the amphitheater at Fruita Campground, 1.3 miles from the visitor center, the trail passes orchards along the Fremont River (elev. 5,350 feet), then begins the climb up sloping rock strata to a viewpoint on Miner's Mountain. Sweeping views take in Fruita, Boulder Mountain, and the reef. The round-

trip distance of two and one half miles takes about one and one half hours; elevation gain is 770 feet.

Grand Wash Road

Turn left off the Scenic Drive 3.6 miles from the visitor center. This side trip follows the twisting Grand Wash for one mile. At road's end you can continue on foot two and one quarter miles (one-way) through the canyon to its end at the Fremont River (see "Grand Wash" under "Sights and Day-Hikes Along Utah 24," above).

Cassidy Arch Trail begins near the end of Grand Wash Road. Energetic hikers will enjoy good views of Grand Wash, the great domes of Navajo Sandstone, and the arch itself. The three and one mile roundtrip trail ascends the north wall of Grand Wash (Wingate and Kayenta formations), then winds across slickrock of the Kayenta Formation to a vantage point close to the arch, also of Kayenta. Allow about three hours, as the elevation gain is nearly 1,000 feet. The notorious outlaw Butch Cassidy may have traveled through Capitol Reef and seen this arch. Frying Pan Trail branches off Cassidy Arch Trail at the one-mile mark, then wends its way across three miles of slickrock to Cohab Canyon; see "Cohab Canyon and Frying Pan Trails" under "Sights and Day-Hikes Along Utah 24," above.

Old Wagon Trail

Wagon drivers once used this route as a short-cut between Grover and Capitol Gorge. Look for the trailhead 0.7 mile south of Slickrock Divide, between Grand Wash and Capitol Gorge. The old trail crosses a wash to the west, then ascends steadily through piñon and juniper woodland on Miners Mountain. After one and one half miles, the trail leaves the wagon road and goes north a half mile to a high knoll for the best views of the Capitol Reef area. The four-mile, roundtrip hike climbs 1,000 feet.

Pleasant Creek Road

Turn right 8.3 miles from the visitor center where the Scenic Drive curves east toward Capitol Gorge. Pleasant Creek Road turns south and continues below the face of the reef. After three miles the sometimes rough, dirt road passes Sleeping Rainbow/Floral Ranch (closed to pub-

lic) and ends at Pleasant Creek. A rugged 4WD road continues on the other side but is much too rough for cars. Floral Ranch dates back to Capitol Reef's early years of settlement. In 1939 it became the Sleeping Rainbow Guest Ranch, from the Indian name for Waterpocket Fold. Now the ranch belongs to the park, but the former owners still live here. Pleasant Creek's perennial waters begin high on Boulder Mountain to the west and cut a scenic canyon completely through Capitol Reef. Hikers can head downstream through the three-mile-long canyon and return, or continue another three miles cross-country to Notom Road.

Capitol Gorge

This is the end of the Scenic Drive, 10.7 miles from the visitor center. Capitol Gorge is a dry canyon through Capitol Reef much like Grand Wash, though with a somewhat different character. Believe it or not, the narrow, twisting Capitol Gorge was the route of the main state highway through south-central Utah for 80 years! Mormon pioneers laboriously cleared a path so wagons could go through, a task repeated every time flash floods rolled in a new set of boulders. Cars bounced their way down the canyon until 1962, when the present UT 24 opened, but few traces of old road remain today. Walking is easy along the gravel riverbed, but don't enter if storms threaten. The first mile downstream is the most scenic: Fremont Indian petroglyphs (in poor condition) appear on the left after 0.1 mile; narrows of Capitol Gorge close in at 0.3 mile; a "pioneer register" on the left at one-half mile consists of names and dates of early travelers and ranchers scratched in the canyon wall; natural water tanks on the left at three-quarters of a mile are typical of those in Waterpocket Fold. Hikers can continue another three miles downstream to Notom Road.

Golden Throne Trail also begins at the end of the Scenic Drive. Instead of heading down Capitol Gorge from the parking area, turn left up this trail for dramatic views of the reef and surrounding area. Golden Throne is a massive monolith of yellow-hued Navajo Sandstone capped by a thin layer of red Carmel Formation. The four-mile roundtrip trail climbs 1,100 feet in a steady grade to a viewpoint near the base of Golden Throne; allow four hours.

THE NORTH DISTRICT

Only the most adventurous travelers get into the remote canyons and desert country of the north. The few roads cannot be negotiated by ordinary cars. In good weather, high-clearance vehicles can enter the region from the east, north, and west. The roads lead through stately sandstone monoliths of Cathedral Valley, volcanic remnants, badlands country, many low mesas, and vast sand flats. Foot travel allows closer inspection of these features or lengthy excursions into the canyons of Polk, Deep, and Spring creeks, which cut deeply into the flanks of Thousand Lake Mountain. Much of the north district is good for horseback riding too. **Cathedral Valley Campground's** five sites provide a place to stop for the night; rangers won't permit car camping elsewhere in the district. The **Upper Cathedral Valley Trail,** just below the campground, is an enjoyable one-mile walk offering excellent views of the Cathedrals. Hikers with a backcountry permit must camp at least a half mile from the nearest road. A small guide to this area can be purchased at the visitor center.

THE SOUTH DISTRICT

Notom-Bullfrog Road

Capitol Reef is only a small part of Waterpocket Fold. By taking the Notom-Bullfrog Road, you'll see nearly 80 miles of the fold's eastern side. This route crosses some of the younger geologic layers, such as those of the Morrison Formation that form colorful hills. In other places, eroded layers of the Waterpocket Fold jut up at 70-degree angles. The Henry Mountains to the east and the many canyons on both sides of the road add to the memorable panoramas. The road has been paved as far as Notom (more will be paved in the future) but it is still dirt and gravel to Bullfrog. Keep an eye on the weather before setting out—the dirt and gravel surface is usually okay for cars when dry but can be too slippery and gooey for *any* vehicle when wet. Sandy spots and washouts may present a problem for low-clearance vehicles; contact the visitor center to check current conditions. Have a full gas tank and carry extra water and food because no services are available between UT

24 and Bullfrog Marina. A small guide to this area can be purchased at the visitor center. Features and mileage along the drive from north to south include:

Mile 0.0: The turnoff from UT 24 is 9.2 miles east of the visitor center and 30.2 miles west of Hanksville (another turnoff from UT 24 is three miles east).

Mile 2.2: Pleasant Creek; the mouth of the canyon is five to six miles upstream, though it's only about three miles by heading cross-country from south of Notom. Hikers can follow the canyon three miles upstream through Capitol Reef to Pleasant Creek Road (off the Scenic Drive).

Mile 4.1: Notom Ranch is to the west; once a small town, Notom is now a private ranch.

Mile 8.1: Burrow Wash; hikers can explore the narrow canyon upstream.

Mile 9.3: Cottonwood Wash; another canyon hike just upstream.

Mile 10.4: Five Mile Wash; yet another canyon hike.

Mile 13.3: Sheets Gulch; a scenic canyon lies upstream here too.

Mile 14.1: Sandy Ranch junction; high-clearance vehicles can turn east 16 miles to the Henry Mountains.

Mile 14.2: Oak Creek Access Road to the west; turn here for Oak Creek. The creek cuts a two-mile-long canyon through Capitol Reef that's a good day-hike. Backpackers sometimes start upstream at Lower Bowns Reservoir (off UT 12) and hike the 15 miles to Oak Creek Access Road. The clear waters of Oak Creek flow all year but must be treated for drinking.

Mile 14.4: Oak Creek crossing.

Mile 20.0: Entering Capitol Reef National Park; a small box has info sheets.

Mile 22.3: Cedar Mesa Campground to the west; the small five-site campground is surrounded by junipers and has fine views of Waterpocket Fold and the Henry Mountains. Sites have tables and grills; there's an outhouse but no drinking water; free. **Red Canyon Trail** begins here and heads west into a huge box canyon in Waterpocket Fold; four miles roundtrip.

Mile 26.0: Bitter Creek Divide; streams to the north flow to the Fremont River; Halls Creek on the south side runs through Strike Valley to Lake Powell, 40 miles away.

Mile 34.1: Burr Trail Road junction; turn west up the steep switchbacks to ascend Waterpocket Fold and continue to Boulder and UT 12 (36 miles). Burr Trail is the only road that actually crosses the top of the fold and it's one of the most scenic in the park. Driving conditions are similar to the Notom-Bullfrog Road—okay for cars when dry. Pavement begins at the park boundary and continues to Boulder. Although paved, the Burr Trail still needs to be driven slowly because of its curves and potholes. The section of road through Long Canyon has especially pretty scenery.

Mile 36.0: Surprise Canyon trailhead; a hike into this narrow, usually shaded canyon takes one to two hours.

Mile 36.6: The Post; a small trading post here once served sheepherders and some cattle men, but today this spot is just a reference point. Park here to hike to Headquarters Canyon. A trailhead for Lower Muley Twist Canyon via Halls Creek lies at the end of a half-mile-long road to the south.

Mile 37.5: Leaving Capitol Reef National Park; a small box has info sheets. Much of the road between here and Glen Canyon National Recreation Area has been paved.

Mile 45.5: Road junction; turn right (south) to continue to Bullfrog Marina (25 miles) or go straight (east) for Starr Springs Campground (23 miles) in the Henry Mountains.

Mile 46.4: The road to the right (west) goes to Halls Creek Overlook. This turnoff is poorly signed and easy to miss; look for it 0.9 mile south of the previous junction. Turn in and follow the road three miles, then turn right at a fork 0.4 mile to the viewpoint. The last 0.3 mile may be too rough for low-clearance cars. A picnic table is the only "facility" here. Far below in Grand Gulch, Halls Creek flows south to Lake Powell. Look across the valley for the double Brimhall Bridge in the red sandstone of Waterpocket Fold. A steep trail descends to Halls Creek (1.2 miles one-way) and it's possible to continue another 1.1 miles up Brimhall Canyon to the bridge. A register box at the overlook has info sheets on this route. Note, however, that the last part of the hike to the bridge requires difficult rockscrambling and wading or swimming through pools! Hikers looking for another adventure might want to follow Halls Creek 10 miles downstream to the narrows. Here, convoluted walls as high as 700 feet narrow to little more than arms' length apart. This beautiful

area of water-sculpted rock sometimes has deep pools that require swimming.

Mile 49.0: Colorful clay hills of deep reds, creams, and grays rise beside the road. This clay turns to goo when wet, providing all the traction of axle grease.

Mile 54.0: Beautiful panorama of countless mesas, mountains, and canyons. Lake Powell and Navajo Mountain can be seen to the south.

Mile 65.3: Junction with paved UT 276; turn left (north) for Hanksville (59 miles) or right (south) to Bullfrog Marina (5.2 miles).

Mile 70.5: Bullfrog Marina (see the "Glen Canyon National Recreation Area," later in this chapter).

Lower Muley Twist Canyon

"So winding that it would twist a mule pulling a wagon," said an early visitor. This canyon has some of the best hiking in the southern district of the park. In the 1880s, Mormon pioneers used the canyon as part of a wagon route between Escalante in the west and new settlements in southeastern Utah, replacing the even more difficult Hole-in-the-Rock route. Unlike most canyons of Waterpocket Fold, Muley Twist runs lengthwise along the crest for about 18 miles before finally turning east and leaving the fold. Hikers starting from Burr Trail Road can easily follow the twisting bends down to Halls Creek, 12 miles away. Two trailheads and the Halls Creek route allow a variety of trips. You could start from Burr Trail Road near the top of the switchbacks (2.2 miles west of Notom-Bullfrog Road) and hike down the dry gravel stream bed. After four miles you have the options of returning the same way, taking the Cut Off route east two and one half miles to the Post trailhead (off Notom-Bullfrog Road), or continuing eight miles down Lower Muley Twist Canyon to its end at Halls Creek. Upon reaching Halls Creek, turn left (north) five miles up the creekbed or the old jeep road beside it to the Post. This section of creek lies in a open dry valley. With a car shuttle, the Post would be the end of a good two-day, 17-mile hike, or you could loop back to Lower Muley Twist Canyon via the Cut Off route and hike back to Burr Trail Road for a 23.5-mile trip. It's a good idea to check the weather beforehand and avoid the canyon if storms threaten.

Cream-colored cliffs of Navajo Sandstone lie atop the red Kayenta and Wingate formations.

Impressively deep undercuts have been carved in the lower canyon. Spring and autumn offer the best conditions (summer temperatures can exceed 100° F). Elevations range from 5,640 feet at Burr Trail Road to 4,540 feet at the confluence with Halls Creek to 4,894 feet at the Post. An info sheet available at the visitor center and trailheads has a small map and route details. Topo maps off Wagon Box Mesa, Mt. Pennell, and Hall Mesa or the 1:100,000-scale Escalante and Hite Crossing are sold at the visitor center. You'll also find this hike described in Dave Hall's *Hiker's Guide to Utah* and in Michael Kelsey's *Canyon Hiking Guide to the Colorado Plateau* and *Utah Mountaineering Guide*. Carry all water for the trip, as natural sources are often dry or polluted.

Upper Muley Twist Canyon

This part of the canyon has plenty of scenery. Large and small natural arches along the way add to its beauty. Upper Muley Twist Road turns north off Burr Trail Road about one mile west from the top of a set of switchbacks. Cars can usually go in a half mile to a trailhead parking area, while high-clearance 4WD vehicles can head another two and one half miles up a wash to the end of the primitive road. Look for natural arches on the left along this last section. **Strike Valley Overlook Trail** (three-quarters of a mile

roundtrip) begins at the end of the road and leads to a magnificent panorama of Waterpocket Fold and beyond. Return to the canyon, where you can hike as far as six and one half miles (one-way) to the head of Upper Muley Twist Canyon.

Two large arches lie a short hike upstream; Saddle Arch, the second one on the left, is one and three quarters miles away. The **Rim Route** begins across from Saddle Arch, climbs the canyon wall, follows the rim (good views of Strike Valley and the Henry Mountains), and descends back into the canyon at a point just above the narrows, four and three quarters miles from the end of the road. (The Rim Route is most easily followed in this direction.) Proceed upcanyon to see several more arches. A very narrow section of canyon beginning about four miles from the end of the road must be bypassed to continue; look for rock cairns showing the way around to the right. Continuing up the canyon past the Rim route sign will take you to several small drainages marking the upper end of Muley Twist Canyon. Climb a high tree-covered point on the west rim for great views; experienced hikers with a map can follow the rim back to Upper Muley Road (no trail or markers on this route). Bring all the water you'll need, as there are no reliable sources in Upper Muley Twist Canyon.

EAST OF CAPITOL REEF NATIONAL PARK

HANKSVILLE

Ebenezer Hanks and other Mormon settlers founded this out-of-the-way community in 1882 along the Fremont River, then known as the Dirty Devil River. The isolation attracted polygamists like Hanks and other fugitives from the law. Butch Cassidy and his gang found refuge in the rugged canyon country of "Robbers' Roost" east of town. Hanksville hasn't grown much. The population is only about 400, but it has outlasted several other farm communities upstream. Today most people work at ranching, farming (hay, corn feed, and watermelons), mining, or tourism. The old stone church (on Center one block south of the highway) and several houses survive from the 19th century. Travelers exploring this scenic region find Hanksville a handy stopover; Capitol Reef National Park lies to the west, Lake Powell and the Henry Mountains to the south, the remote Maze District of Canyonlands National Park to the east, and Goblin Valley State Park to the north. The book *Hiking and Exploring Utah's Henry Mountains and Robbers Roost* by Michael Kelsey has a wealth of history and travel information about the Hanksville area.

Wolverton Mill

E.T. Wolverton built this ingenious mill during the 1920s at his gold-mining claims in the Henry Mountains. A 20-foot waterwheel, still perfectly balanced, powered ore-crushing machinery and a sawmill. Owners of claims at the mill's original site didn't like a steady stream of tourists coming through to see the mill, so it was moved to the BLM office at Hanksville. Drive south a half mile on 100 West to see the mill and some of its original interior mechanism.

Practicalities

Desert Inn Motel, just west on UT 24, tel. 542-3241, offers rooms for $32.70 s, $43.60 d. **Fern's Place,** one quarter mile west on UT 24, tel. 542-3251, has several kitchenettes at $32.70–48.15 s or d. **Whispering Sands Motel,** next to Stan's Burger Shack on the south side of town, tel.

542-3238, costs $42.80 s, $49.39 d. **Redrock Campground,** in the center of town, tel. 542-3235 or (800) 894-3242 for reservations, offers sites for tents and RVs, $8.48 tent, $10.60 van, $12.72 RV w/hookups; has showers and laundry; open March 15 to October 31. The **Redrock Restaurant** (adjacent to the campground) serves American food daily for breakfast, lunch, and dinner; closed in winter. **Blondie's Eatery** and **Stan's Burger Shack** on the south edge of town are open daily with fast food. The **post office** is at 118 E. 100 North, tel. 542-3422. The **Bureau of Land Management** staff has regional travel literature and can tell you about road conditions, hiking, camping, and the buffalo herd in the Henry Mountains. A recreation map and USGS topo maps are available; open Mon.-Fri. 7:45 a.m.-noon and 12:45-4:30 p.m.; turn south a half mile on 100 West from UT 24 or write Box 99, Hanksville, UT 84734, tel. 542-3461.

Caineville

Mormons founded this village on the Fremont River midway between the present-day Capitol Reef Visitor Center and Hanksville. **Sleepy Hollow Campground,** at Milepost 95 on UT 24, tel. 456-9130, has a store, showers, and sites for tents and RVs; $10 no hookups, $13 w/electric. Facilities are shut down in winter but primitive camping is permitted with reduced fees. **Luna Mesa Cantina,** between Mileposts 101 and 102, tel. 456-9141, serves Mexican/American lunches and dinners daily and offers motels rooms ($28-32 s or d), teepee accommodations ($25 s or d), and RV campsites w/hookups ($13). Closed winters.

HENRY MOUNTAINS AND VICINITY

Great domes of intrusive igneous rock pushed into and deformed surrounding sedimentary layers about 70 million years ago. Erosion later uncovered the domes, revealing mountains towering 5,000 feet above the surrounding plateau. Mount Ellen's North Summit Ridge (elev. 11,522 feet) and Mt. Pennell (elev. 11,320 feet) top the

Mt. Ellen in the
Henry Mountains,
from Burr Trail Road

range. Scenic views and striking geologic features abound in and around the Henrys. Rock layers tilt dramatically in Waterpocket Fold to the west and in the Pink Cliffs on the south side of Mt. Hillers. Sheer cliffs of The Horn, between Mt. Ellen and Mt. Pennell, attract rock climbers.

The arid land and rugged canyons surrounding the Henry Mountains so discouraged early explorers and potential settlers that the range wasn't even named or described until 1869, when members of the Powell river expedition sighted it. Powell later named the range in honor of one of his supporters, Professor Joseph Henry of the Smithsonian Institution. Indian tales of a lost Spanish gold mine have long enticed prospectors, yet only modest amounts of the yellow metal have been found. Bromide Basin has been the major site for gold and silver mines of the past and present. A brief gold boom here in the early 1890s gave rise to Eagle City mining camp along Crescent Creek. The rich vein soon worked out and the town faded away. Other minerals occur in the area too; a uranium mine is just south of the Henrys in Shootaring Canyon, near Ticaboo.

Vegetation ranges from sparse desert plants such as galleta grass and blackbrush on the lower slopes to piñon pine and juniper woodlands higher up, then to forests of ponderosa pine, aspen, Douglas fir, spruce, and bristlecone pine. Alpine plants and grasslands cover the highest summits. Buffalo, brought to the Henrys from Yellowstone National Park in 1941,

form one of the few free-roaming herds in the United States. They winter in the southwestern part of the mountains, then move higher as the snow melts. Mule deer keep mostly to the higher elevations, while pronghorn stay in the desert country to the east. Most of the bighorn sheep are found in the Little Rockies, a southeastern extension of the Henry Mountains. Mountain lions live near the Henrys too, but they're more likely to see you than you are to see them!

Exploring The Henry Mountains
Roads with panoramic views cross the range between the high peaks at Bull Creek, Pennellen, and Stanton passes. Most driving routes are best suited for high-clearance vehicles. The road through Bull Creek Pass (elev. 10,485 feet) is snow-free only from about early July to late October. Rains, which peak in August, occasionally make travel difficult in late summer. Roads tend to be at their best after grading in autumn, just before the deer-hunting season. Travel at the lower elevations is possible all year, though spring and autumn have the most pleasant temperatures. Check in first with the BLM office in Hanksville before exploring the backcountry. Staff members can advise you about water sources, road and trail conditions and, in case of trouble, they will have an idea of where to look for you. Take precautions for desert travel, and have water, food, and extra clothing with you. The Henry Mountains remain a remote and little-traveled region.

Campgrounds

Starr Springs Campground sits in an oak forest at the base of Mt. Hillers. Sites (elev. 6,300 feet) stay open all year and usually have water for a $4 fee from early May to early October. **Panorama Knoll Trail** begins from the campground and makes a half-mile loop to an overlook. A good gravel road to Starr Springs Campground turns off UT 276 near Milepost 17 (23 miles north of Bullfrog and 43 miles south of Hanksville) and goes in four miles. **Lonesome Beaver Campground** lies in a very pretty spot surrounded by ponderosa pine and Douglas fir; its five sites usually have water and a $4 fee; season runs May-Oct. (elev. 8,000 feet). To get here from Hanksville, turn south 27 miles on 100 East (next to the post office) or follow the road along Crescent Creek from UT 95 to the east; both unpaved roads are marginal for cars (check first with the Hanksville BLM office). **Dandelion Flat Picnic Area** usually has water in season; it's just one-half mile before Lonesome Beaver on the road from Hanksville. **Horseshoe Trail** begins at the picnic area and climbs to Log Flat (one mile) and East Saddle (four miles). **McMillan Springs Campground** is in a ponderosa pine forest at an elevation of 8,400 feet with a great view of Waterpocket Fold, especially at sunrise; open April-Nov., usually with water, located on a steep and rough road (not recommended for cars) between Notom Road and Bull Creek Pass.

Hiking

Countless mountain and canyon hiking possibilities exist in the range; Kelsey's book on the Henry Mountains has trip suggestions and practical advice. Most routes go cross country or follow old mining roads. The **Mt. Ellen summit route** is a good day-hike and probably attracts the greatest number of hikers. Easiest way is to follow the North Summit Ridge north from the road at Bull Creek Pass; there's an unsigned trail the first mile and on the final climb up Mt. Ellen; elevation gain is 1,030 feet. Nearly all of this route lies above timberline with spectacular panoramas. Another popular approach begins from Dandelion Flat Picnic Area; a trail follows an old road that climbs the slopes part of the way, then it's cross-country; elevation gain is 3,400 feet. Either route is about four miles roundtrip and takes half a day. Interestingly, Mt.

Ellen Peak shown on the maps isn't the true high point: the North Summit Ridge of Mt. Ellen, just to the south, is 16 feet higher at 11,522 feet. You can also hike the South Summit Ridge south of Bull Creek Pass. See the 7 1/2-minute Mount Ellen and Dry Lakes Peak or the 15-minute Mt. Ellen topo maps.

Little Egypt

Eerie rock formations similar to those in Goblin Valley, but covering a smaller area, lie east of the Henrys. Kids will enjoy exploring the area and it's a fine place for a picnic. Turn southwest one and one half miles from UT 95 between Mileposts 20 and 21; the gravel road is usually okay for cars when dry. No facilities or even a sign mark the site, so note mileage from UT 95.

Dirty Devil Canyon Overlook

The muddy waters of the Dirty Devil River have carved a deep canyon southeast of Hanksville. Views from the overlook at Burr Point take in some impressive scenery. Desperadoes around the turn of the century hid out in the rugged

Dirty Devil River

canyonlands of "Robbers' Roost" across the river. In 1869, when one of Powell's expedition members was asked if the waters had trout, he replied with disgust that the smelly and muddy river was "a dirty devil." An unpaved road winds east for 11 miles from UT 95 (between Mileposts 15 and 16). Cars with good clearance should be okay in dry weather. Park near where the road makes a sharp right just before the edge, or follow the road south for other views. Walking along the rim also affords different perspectives.

GOBLIN VALLEY STATE PARK

Thousands of spooky rock formations inhabit this valley. Little eyelike holes in the "goblins" make you wonder who's watching whom. All of the goblins have weathered out of the Entrada Formation, here a soft red sandstone and even softer siltstone. **Carmel Canyon Trail** (one and one half mile loop) begins at the northeast side of the parking lot at road's end, then leads into a strange landscape of goblins, spires, and balanced rocks. Just wander about at your whim; this is a great place for the imagination! **Curtis Bench Trail** begins on the road between the parking lot and the campground and goes south to a viewpoint of the Henry Mountains; cairns mark the one and one half mile (one-way) route. The state park provides a campground with showers on the drive in and a covered picnic area and an overlook at the end of the road. The park stays open all year; $3 per vehicle

day use or $9 per vehicle camping ($10 Friday, Saturday, and holidays). Box 637, Green River, UT 84525, tel. 564-8110 or (800) 322-3770 (reservations). The turnoff from UT 24 is at Milepost 137, 21 miles north of Hanksville and 24 miles south of I-70; follow signs west five miles on a paved road, then south seven miles on a gravel road.

The park is also a good base for exploring the **San Rafael Swell** area to the northwest. Deep canyons, otherworldly landscapes of rock and sand, old uranium mines, and Hondoo Arch await discovery here. Popular hikes near the state park include the Little Wild Horse and Bell canyons loop, Chute and Crack canyons loop, and Wild Horse Canyon. **Temple Mountain Bike Trail** traverses old mining roads, ridges, and wash bottoms about 12 miles north of the state park. Rangers at the park can tell you about the San Rafael Swell area; for detailed info contact the BLM San Rafael Resource Area, 900 North and 700 East, Price, UT 84501, tel. 637-4584.

GREEN RIVER

The small town began in 1878 as a mail station on the long run between Salina in central Utah and the Colorado border. Today Green River is still the only sizable settlement (nearly 1,000 people) on this route, now I-70. Travelers can stop for a rest or meal here, or use it as a base for exploring the scenic San Rafael Swell country nearby.

*rock formations
at Goblin Valley
State Park*

The Green River flows placidly below Gray Canyon.

River Running

Boaters enjoy trips on the Green River. Desolation and Gray canyons lie upstream of the town of Green River, while Labyrinth and Stillwater canyons are downstream. Several river companies organize day and multi-day trips through these areas. **Adventure River Expeditions,** 185 S. Broadway, tel. 564-3648 or (800) 564-3648. **Colorado River and Trail Expeditions,** 1000 North, off Long St., tel. 564-8170. **Holiday River and Bike Expeditions** (no local office), tel. 564-3273 (summer only) or (800) 624-6323. **Moki-Mac River Expeditions,** 100 Silliman Lane, tel. 564-3001. These businesses can provide shuttle services as well. The Green River Information Center can also supply names of individuals willing to supply shuttle services. You can also drive or do your own boat trip through the lower section of Gray Canyon; see "Green River Scenic Drive" under "Vicinity of Green River," below. Most river running on the Green is done with rafts, though regular power boats can also follow the river below town to the confluence with the Colorado River and head up the Colorado to Moab, two to three days and 186 river miles away. The town of Green River sponsors an annual **Friendship Cruise** on this route on Memorial Day weekend. A popular four-day canoe or raft trip goes to Mineral Bottom, 68 miles south near Canyonlands National Park; **Tex's Riverways,** Box 67, Moab, UT 84532, tel. 259-5101, provides canoes and shuttle services. Most boaters use the launch area at Green River State Park, 150 S. Green River Boulevard.

John Wesley Powell River History Museum

Stop by this fine museum to learn about Powell's daring expeditions down the Green and Colorado rivers in 1869 and 1871-72. An excellent multimedia presentation about the Green and Colorado rivers uses narratives from Powell's trips; 21 minutes; free. Historic river boats on display include a replica of Powell's *Emma Dean*. Other exhibits show places to visit in the area. The Grand County Travel Council in the museum has local travel information. A gift shop sells books, maps, Indian crafts, T-shirts, and other souvenirs. The Powell Museum, on the east bank of the Green River, is at 885 E. Main (the I-70 business route through town), tel. 564-3427/3428. Open daily 9 a.m.-8 p.m. in summer and daily 9 a.m.-5 p.m. the rest of the year.

Practicalities

Travelers have a selection of more than a dozen motels and a similar number of restaurants and fast-food places. You'll find these along the business route (Main Street) between I-70 Exits 158 and 162. To really get away, **Tavaputs Plateau Ranch** offers guest accommodations and activities in the high country north of Green River, reached by a long drive or short charter flight; Box 418, Green River, UT 84525, tel. 564-3463.

Four campgrounds, all with showers, have sites for tents and RVs: **Shady Acres RV Park,** 360 E. Main, tel. 564-8290, costs $14.24 no hookups, $17.55 w/hookups; open all year with store, showers, and laundry. **United Campground,** 910 E. Main, tel. 564-8195, is $12 no hookups, $16.20 w/hookups; open April 1 to October 15 with a pool, store, showers, and laundry. **Green River State Park,** 150 S. Green River Blvd., tel. 564-3633 or (800) 322-3770 (reservations), offers pleasant sites shaded by large cottonwoods and a boat ramp for $3 day use, $9 camping ($10 Friday, Saturday, and holidays); open all year. **Green River KOA,** 550 S. Green River Blvd., tel. 564-3651, runs $14.24 tent, $14.24 RV no hookups, $16.98 w/hookups, $26.29 kamping kabins. Open April 1 to October 15 with a pool, store, and laundry.

The community is known for its excellent melons, available in season at fruit stands along Main Street. **Melon Days** celebrates the harvest on the third weekend of September with a parade, city fair, music, canoe race, games, and free melons. A pleasant **city park** offers shaded tables, playground, and tennis courts at the corner of Main and 100 East. **Grand County Travel Council,** 885 E. Main in the John Wesley Powell Museum (Box 335, Green River, UT 84525), tel. 564-3526, has information about services in town and places to see in the area; open daily 8 a.m.-8 p.m. in summer (may be extended to 9 a.m. to 9 p.m.), then reduced hours the rest of the year. The **post office** is on E. Main. **Green River Medical Center,** 250 E. Main, tel. 564-3434, offers services Mon.-Fri. 9 a.m.-5 p.m. The emergency number is 911. See some of southeastern Utah's incredible landscapes with **Redtail Aviation,** Box 515, Moab, UT 84532, tel. 259-7421 (Moab) or 564-3412 (Green River) or (800) 842-9251; flights normally leave from the airport 18 miles north of Moab, but the pilot will pick you up at Green River for $10 extra per person. You can fly over Canyonlands National Park (Needles, Island in the Sky, and the Maze), Dead Horse Point, and other spectacular landscapes. Flights operate all year. Green River's airport is south of town.

VICINITY OF GREEN RIVER

Green River Scenic Drive

Splendid cliffs of Gray Canyon enclose the Green River 10 miles north of town. An unpaved road winding eight and one half miles into the canyon allows drivers easy access to the scenery. Cars with good clearance can travel through the clay road in dry weather. (When wet, the clay road surface shouldn't be attempted by any vehicle.) From downtown Green River, head east on Main Street and turn north on Hastings Road (1200 East); it's the first paved road to the north past the bridge. After two miles the road follows the banks of the Green River a short way with views north to the castle-like cliffs of the Beckwith Plateau, through which the Green River has carved Gray Canyon. At 6.3 miles after turning off Main, make a right turn onto an unpaved road just before the paved road enters a ranch. The turn may have a small sign for "Nefertiti." Follow the unpaved road 3.8 miles across a wash, then along the river to Swasey Beach and Rapids near the mouth of Gray Canyon. A primitive camping area under the cottonwoods is an inviting place to spend the night. The camping area has an outhouse; no drinking water or charge. A large sandy beach stretches along the shore just below the rapids. The road becomes a bit rougher and narrows to a single lane in spots past Swasey Beach for the eight and one half spectacular miles to road's end at Nefertiti. You'll see Price River Canyon entering Gray Canyon on the other side of the river two miles before Nefertiti. Look for petroglyphs near the end of the road. Hikers can explore many rugged side canyons or follow cattle trails a long distance upstream. Cowboys on horseback still work the range on the plateaus to the north much as they've always done. Cattle are driven on these trails to the high country in spring and brought back down in autumn. Kelsey's book *Canyon Hiking Guide to the Colorado Plateau* details hiking possibilities through Gray and Desolation canyons and their side canyons. Commercial raft trips provide a more relaxed way of enjoying this extremely remote part of Utah; see "Desolation and Gray Canyons of the Green River" under "East of Price" in the Northeastern Utah chapter.

River runners enjoy half a dozen lively rapids on the section of river from the boat launch just above Nefertiti Rapid to the take-out at Swasey Beach. This makes a good day-trip with rafts or kayaks; canoeists will find the whitewater very challenging. All boaters must wear life jackets and carry proper equipment (spare oar or paddle, extra life jacket, and bail bucket or pump). You will also need a portable toilet and, if a campfire is desired, a firepan to contain the ashes. You won't need a permit, though the BLM has a register at the put-in.

San Rafael Swell

This massive fold and uplift of the earth's crust is crossed by I-70 about 19 miles west of Green River. The east face and "flat irons" of the Swell, known as the San Rafael Reef, rise dramatically 2,100 feet above the desert. View areas allow stopping for a look at the colorful rock layers. San Rafael Swell is 80 miles long (north to south) and 30 miles wide. The geology, sheer cliffs, and narrow canyons attract adventurous travelers to the back roads and hiking routes. This little-known region also has a rich history of outlaws, ranchers, and miners. Boaters with canoes or rafts can float a section of the San Rafael River beneath 1,000-foot-high canyon walls upstream of the San Rafael Recreational Site camping area; see "Floating the Little Grand Canyon" in the Northeastern Utah chapter. Good books for background and travel are *Canyoneering the San Rafael Swell* by Steve Allen, *Hiking Utah's San Rafael Swell* by Michael Kelsey, and *Utah's Scenic San Rafael* by Owen McClenahan. Allen's book has the most detailed and up-to-date hiking information and some climbing notes; Kelsey's book emphasizes history and hiking, while McClenahan's book mostly describes driving tours (about half of which can be done by car). The BLM is studying six areas within the San Rafael for wilderness designation. The San Rafael Resource Area office administers this region: 900 North and 700 East, Price, UT 84501, tel. 637-4584.

Black Dragon Canyon

Don't worry about the dragon; he doesn't bite. This narrow canyon in the San Rafael Swell is just off I-70, 15 miles east of Green River. A quarter-mile walk up the streambed leads to a pair of pictograph panels of the dragon (he's actually red), human figures, a dog, and geometric designs. Continue farther upcanyon for more good scenery. To reach the trailhead, turn north on a dirt road from the I-70 westbound lane just past Milepost 145; this isn't a regular exit and is not signed. If coming from the west,

you'll have to turn around at the Hanksville Exit 147 and backtrack two miles. The dirt road crosses a wash (best to walk from here if it's filled with water), goes through a second gate, and crosses the streambed from Black Dragon Wash, 1.1 miles from I-70. Turn left 0.4 mile up the streambed (normally dry) to the canyon entrance. High-clearance vehicles can drive a short way up the canyon.

Hondoo Arch Loop

Dirt roads south of I-70 provide a scenic drive into some of the San Rafael's prettiest country. Either turn south and west 15 miles from I-70 Ranch Exit 129 or take the Goblin Valley State Park turnoff from UT 24 and head west 20 miles to the beginning of the loop. The 29-mile loop drops into Reds Canyon with fine panoramas on the descent. Look for Hondoo Arch high in the cliffs across the Muddy River. Side roads off the loop go to Muddy River (beside Tomsich Butte), Hidden Splendor Mine, and other old mining areas. The Tomsich Butte area has old cabins and uranium mines (dangerous to enter). Hikers can do many adventurous trips along the Muddy River, washes, and canyons of the area; *Canyoneering the San Rafael Swell* by Steve Allen has hiking details. The San Rafael Desert 1:100,000 topo map covers the loop area. Roads can become impassable after rain or snow; drivers with cars need to be especially careful in this remote area.

Crystal Geyser

With some luck, you'll catch the spectacle of this cold-water geyser on the bank of the Green River. The gusher shoots as high as 60 feet but only three or four times daily, so you may have to spend a half day here in order to see it. Camping is possible nearby (no facilities), so you might be able to see the geyser by moonlight. Staff at the Grand County Travel Council often know the latest eruption schedule. An eruption typically lasts seven minutes and discharges 4,350 cubic feet of salt water. Carbon dioxide and other gases power the gushing water. A 2,267-foot-deep petroleum test well drilled in 1935-36 concentrated the geyser flow, but thick layers of old travertine deposits attest that mineral-laden springs have long been active at this site. Colorful newer travertine forms delicate terraces around the opening and down to the river. The orange and dark red of the minerals and algae make this a pretty spot, even if the geyser is only quietly gurgling.

Crystal Geyser is 10 miles south of town by road (boaters should look for the geyser deposits on the left about four and one half miles downstream from Green River). From downtown, drive east one mile on Main, turn left three miles on signed Frontage Road (near Milepost 4), then turn right six miles on a narrow paved road just after going under a railroad overpass. The road goes under I-70, then is unpaved for the last four and one half miles; keep right at a fork near some power lines. Some washes have to be crossed, so the drive isn't recommended after rains. Other times it's okay for cars. Buildings and antennas passed on the way belong to the Utah Launch Complex of White Sands Missile Range. From 1963 to 1979 several hundred Pershing and Athena rockets blasted off for targets at White Sands, New Mexico, 400 miles away.

Woodside Geyser

This geyser is a smaller version of Crystal. Woodside goes up more often than Crystal and sometimes puts on a good show. Colorful travertine terraces surround the opening. When railroad workers drilled for water here in 1910 they got a 75-foot spout of useless mineral water! The geyser sits just west of US 191/6, 23 miles northwest of Green River and 37 miles southeast of Price. The site was once a developed tourist attraction and may be again. However, at press time the owners had posted the property so you may wish to check with the Grand County Travel Council before planning a visit.

SEGO CANYON AND GHOST TOWN

Prehistoric rock art and ruins of a coal-mining town lie within scenic canyons of the Book Cliffs just a short drive north from Thompson and I-

70. In the early 1900s, a local rancher discovered thick seams of high-quality coal here. A mining camp, served by the Ballard and Thompson Railroad, sprang to life at the site. Residents named their little town after Utah's state flower, the sego lily, which grew profusely in the canyons. Population peaked at about 500; families lived in fine houses or in rustic dugouts, while the bachelors stayed in a two-story boardinghouse. Production continued through water shortages, fires, and management troubles until the early 1950s, when the railroads switched to diesel locomotives and no longer needed Sego's coal. The town folded and was sold for salvage. Plenty of good coal remains; if steam locomotives ever come back into style, perhaps Sego will too!

Stone walls of the company store, the frame boardinghouse, dugout houses, railroad grades, and foundations of coal-handling structures can still be seen. The road in can be traveled by cars with good clearance if the weather is dry; don't enter the canyons after recent rains or if storms threaten. Take I-70 Thompson Exit 185 (25 miles east of Green River or five miles east of the US 191 turnoff to Moab) and drive one mile north to Thompson. The small railroad community has a cafe and convenience store near I-70. Continue north across the tracks on a paved road, which becomes dirt after half a mile, into Thompson Canyon. At the first creek ford, three and one half miles from town, look for petroglyphs and pictographs on cliffs to the left. Recently, a pit toilet and picnic tables have been added. More rock art, though in poorer condition, can be seen to the right at the second ford, just past the first. Look for a road fork on the right leading through a notch into Sego Canyon 0.3 mile after the second ford. This turnoff is easily missed. The ghost town lies one mile up Sego Canyon. Both the Sego and Thompson canyon roads lead deeper into the rugged Book Cliffs. Drivers with 4WD and hikers can explore more of this land, seldom visited except in deer season.

MOAB

By far the largest town in southeastern Utah, Moab (pop. 5,500) makes an excellent base for exploring the surrounding canyon country. The area offers Arches and Canyonlands national parks, scenic drives, jeep touring, river running, mountain bicycling, and hiking. Moab lies near the Colorado River in a green valley enclosed by high sandstone cliffs. The original Moab was a biblical kingdom at the edge of Zion. Early settlers must have felt themselves at the edge of their world too, being so isolated from Salt Lake City, the Mormon city of Zion. Moab's existence on the fringe of Mormon culture and the sizable gentile population have given the town a unique character. Yet the incredible canyons, mesas, and mountains around Moab remain its biggest draw. Movie and advertising photographers come from all over the world to work in these dramatic settings.

The landscape invites exploration. Adventurous drivers with 4WD vehicles have many places to go; a set of booklets and maps of off-road vehicle and mountain bicycle trails by F.A. Barnes (see the "Booklist" at the end of this book) will get you started. Mountain bicyclists enjoy the challenges of the back roads too and delight in riding the Moab Slickrock Bike Trail. The Trails Illustrated "Bike Map" #501 of the Moab area has mountain bicycle routes color coded according to difficulty. Hikers can visit even more places; talk to the National Park Service, BLM, and U.S. Forest Service people. The books *Canyon Country Hiking* by Barnes and *Canyon Hiking Guide to the Colorado Plateau* by Kelsey describe hiking areas near Moab. In summer when high daytime temperatures prevail at the low 4,000-foot elevation, it's worth getting an early start in the cool of the morning.

History

Prehistoric Fremont and Anasazi Indians once lived and farmed in the bottoms of the canyons. Their rock art, granaries, and dwellings can still be seen. Nomadic Ute Indians had replaced the earlier groups by the time the first white men arrived. The Old Spanish Trail, opened in 1829 between New Mexico and California, passed through Spanish Valley and crossed the Colorado near present-day Moab. Mormon missionaries tried to establish the Elk Mountain Mission here in 1855. They managed to plant some fields, build a stone fort, and convert some of the Utes before a series of attacks killed three missionaries and sent the others fleeing back to civilization. The valley reverted to the Indians and small numbers of explorers, outlaws, ranchers, and trappers for the next 20 years. Settlers with better success founded Moab in the 1870s. Indian troubles ceased after 1881 and the community became a quiet farming and ranching center. Oil exploration in the 1920s caused some excitement, but nothing like that of the uranium boom that began in 1952. Moab's population tripled in just three years as eager prospectors swarmed into the canyons. One of these hopefuls, Charlie Steen, did hit it big. Experts had laughed at Charlie's efforts until he discovered the Mi Vida uranium bonanza about 30 miles south of town. An instant multimillionaire, he built a large mansion overlooking Moab and hosted lavish parties attended by Hollywood celebrities. Charlie Steen and most of the prospectors have moved on, but Moab has never been the same since.

Moab (Dan O'Laurie) Museum

Step inside to learn about Moab's and Grand County's past. Prehistoric Indian artifacts include pottery, baskets, sandals, and tools. More recent crafts represent the Ute Indians, who no longer live near Moab. An exhibit of early explorers commemorates work of daring Spanish and American expeditions. Photos and tools show pioneer Moab life, much of which centered around ranching or mining. See colorful rocks and minerals, as well as bones of huge dinosaurs that once tracked across this land. Visiting shows can be seen too. Step upstairs to view rotating art exhibits. Ask for a *Moab Area Historic Walking Tour* leaflet to learn about historic buildings in town. Open in summer Mon.-Sat. 1-5 p.m. and 7-9 p.m., then the rest of the year Mon.-Thurs. 3-5 p.m. and 7-9 p.m., Fri.-Sat. 1-5 p.m. and 7-9 p.m; free admission. Located at 118 E. Center, tel. 259-7985.

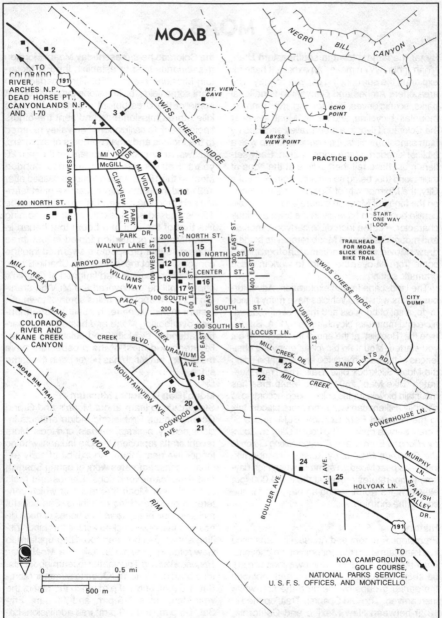

MOAB

MOAB

1. Slickrock Country Campground, Sundowner Restaurant, and Western River Expeditions
2. Grand Old Ranch House
3. Mi Vida Restaurant (Steen Mansion)
4. Chamber of Commerce
5. Allen Memorial Hospital
6. Holiday Haven RV Park
7. City Park and swimming pool
8. Moab Rock Shop (Lin Ottinger's Tours)
9. North American River Expeditions and Canyonlands Tours
10. Tag-A-Long Tours
11. Rim Cyclery and Rim Tours
12. Honest Ozzie's Cafe
13. Grand Emporium
14. post office
15. Hollywood Stuntmen's Hall of Fame
16. Moab (Dan O'Laurie) Museum and Grand County Public Library
17. Moab Information Center
18. Canyonlands Campark
19. Slickrock Cinemas
20. Miller's Shopping Center
21. BLM District Office
22. Bar M Chuckwagon Supper
23. Moab Rotary Park
24. Moab Lanes
25. Lazy Lizard Hostel

Hollywood Stuntmen's Hall Of Fame And Museum

Here action photos show the amazing stunts done in movies and television, from the early days to the present. You'll also see many costumes, weapons, and stunt equipment used in film. This Hall of Fame and Museum—the only one of its kind—is dedicated to preserving the history of the stunt profession in movies and TV. The Dave Sharpe Action Theatre presents a variety of old and new films. The curator/artist is a professional stuntman who located the museum in Moab because he had heard so much about the area from fellow film professionals. A gift shop sells stunt and movie memorabilia. Open in spring and summer daily Mon.-Fri. 10 a.m.-9 p.m., Saturday noon-9 p.m., and Sunday noon-6 p.m.; call for hours off-season. Entry is $3 adult, $2 ages 12-18 and seniors, and $1 ages 3-11. Located one

block north of the Dan O'Laurie Museum at 111 E. 100 North, tel. 259-6100.

Hole 'N The Rock

Albert Christensen worked 12 years to excavate his dream home within a sandstone monolith south of town. When he died in 1957, his wife Gladys worked another eight years to complete the project. The interior has notable touches like a 65-foot chimney drilled through the rock ceiling, paintings, taxidermy exhibits, and a lapidary room. The 14-room home is open for tours daily 9 a.m.-6 p.m. in summer and daily 9 a.m.-5 p.m. the rest of the year; $2.25 adult, $1.25 ages 6-12; it also has a gift shop, tel. 686-2250. A picnic area and snack bar are outside. Located 15 miles south of Moab on US 191.

PRACTICALITIES

Accommodations

See the chart "Moab Accommodations" for most of the motels, guesthouses, and bed-and-breakfasts. **Moab Central Reservations,** tel. 259-5125 or (800) 748-4386, can make bookings for all of the bed-and-breakfasts and many of the motels, condos, and cabins in the area.

Youth Hostel

The **Lazy Lizard** hostel costs just $7.63 a night for simple dorm-style accommodations, no hostel card needed; includes hot tub, kitchen, and coin-op laundry. Camping ($4 per person), showers for nonguests ($2), single rooms ($21.80), and doubles ($21.80) are offered too. Located one mile south of downtown in the red-and-white house behind A-1 Storage; the turnoff is about 200 yards south of Moab Lanes, tel. 259-6057.

Campgrounds

Old Spanish Trail RV Park, 2980 S. Hwy. 191, tel. 259-2411, is open Mar. 1-late November. Sites cost $15.53 tent, $16.35 RV no hookups, and $19.89 w/hookups. **Canyonlands Campark,** 555 S. Main, tel. 259-6848, is open all year; it has showers, laundry, store, and pool; $15.50 tent, and $21 w/hookups. **Holiday Haven RV Park,** 400 North and 500 West, tel. 259-5834, is open March 1 to October 31; has laundry and pool. $15.54 RV no hookups, $20 w/hookups.

MOAB ACCOMMODATIONS

Add 11% tax to all prices; summer rates shown for 1-2 persons; those in winter typically drop $5

Apache Motel; 166 S. 400 East; $63-100; tel. 259-5727; kitchenettes, pool

Bowen Motel; 169 N. Main; $53-61; tel. 259-7132 or (800) 874-5439; kitchenettes, pool

Canyon Country Bed & Breakfast; 590 N. 500 West; $45-66; tel. 259-5262 or (800) 635-1792; mountain bike rentals and tours

Canyonlands Inn (Best Western); 16 S. Main; $83-140; tel. 259-2300 or (800) 528-1234; suites, pool, fitness room, spa

Castle Valley Inn Bed & Breakfast; in Castle Valley 2.3 mi. in from UT 128; $75-125; tel. 259-6012; dinners, wilderness setting, hot tub

Cedar Breaks Condos; Center and 400 East; $70; tel. 259-7830; kitchenettes

Colorado River Lodge; 512 N. Main; $40-48; tel. 259-6122

Comfort Suites; 800 S. Main; $80-90; tel. 259-525 or (800) 221-2222; suites, indoor pool, spa, exercise room

Cottonwood Condos; 338 E. 100 South; $40-55; tel. 259-8897 or (800) 447-4106; kitchens

Greenwell Motel (Best Western); 105 S. Main; $89; tel. 259-6151 or (800) 528-1234; pool

Hotel Off Center; 96 E. Center; $35-45 or $10 dorm; tel. 259-4244 or (800) 237-4685; old-style hotel (bath down hall)

Inca Inn Motel; 570 N. Main; $35-38; tel. 259-7261; pool

Kokopelli Lodge; 72 S. 100 East; $49; tel. 259-7615

Landmark Motel; 168 N. Main; $66-86; tel. 259-6147 or (800) 441-6147; pool

Luxury Inn; 426 N. Main; $55-58; tel. 259-4468 or (800) 325-2525; pool

Moab Travelodge; 550 S. Main; $64-76; tel. 259-6171 or (800) 325-6171; pool

Moab Valley Inn; 711 S. Main; $67-125; tel. 259-4419 or (800) 831-6622; pool, spa

Nichols Lane Accommodations; 543 Nichols Lane; $45; tel. 259-5047; kitchens

Pack Creek Ranch; La Sal Mountains. foothills; $110 per person; tel. 259-5505; cabins, meals, kitchens, riding, sauna

Prospector Lodge; 186 N. 100 West; $30-50; tel. 259-5145

Ramada Inn; 182 S. Main; $89; tel. 259-7141 or (800) 228-2828; pool, spa

Red Rock Lodge; 51 N. 100 West; $38-59; tel. 259-5431; hot tub

Red Stone Inn; 535 S. Main; $50-60; tel. 259-3500 or (800) 772-1972; sauna

Ron Tez; 450 E. 200 South; $60; tel. 259-7273; kitchens

Rustic Inn Motel; 120 E. 100 South; $55-75; tel. 259-6177 or (800) 231-8184; kitchenettes, pool

Sandi's Bed & Breakfast; 450 Walker St.; $40-50; tel. 259-6359

Silver Sage Inn; 840 S. Main; $39-42; tel. 259-4420

Sunflower Hill Bed & Breakfast; 185 N. 300 East; $64-78; tel. 259-2974

Sunset Motel; 41 W. 100 North; $59-109; tel. 259-5191; kitchenettes, pool

Super 8 Motel; 889 N. Main; $73.88; tel. 259-8868 or (800) 800-8000; pool, hot tub

The Virginian Motel; 70 E. 200 South; $37-55; tel. 259-5951; kitchenettes

Westwood Guest House; 81 E. 100 South; $45-59; tel. 259-7283 or (800) 526-5690; kitchenettes

Slickrock Campground, one mile north on US 191, tel. 259-7660, is open March 1 to November 1; it has showers, store, outdoor cafe, and pool; $14.72 tent or RV no hookups, $21 w/hookups, and $29.43 for cabins. **Moab Valley RV & Campark,** two miles north on US 191 (opposite turnoff for UT 128), tel. 259-4469, is open March 1 to October 31; it has showers; $14.17 tent or RV no hookups, $18.53 w/hookups. **Moab KOA,** four miles south on US 191, tel. 259-6682, is open February 15 to November 15; it has showers, laundry, store, mini golf, and pool; $16.35 tent or RV no hookups, $19.25 w/hookups; kamping kabins go for $29-36. **Up the Creek Campground,** 210 East 300 South, tel. 259-2213, is open April 1 to October 31 with walk-in tent camping, showers, and restrooms at $7 per person.

The Bureau of Land Management now requires that all camping along the Colorado River (accessible by road above and below Moab), Kane Creek, and near the Moab Slickrock Bike Trail *must* be in **developed designated sites** (restrooms nearby; small fee) or **undeveloped designated sites** (your own porta-potty required; no restrooms or fee). The following four camping areas are being improved and will have water; they are along UT 128 with the distance given from the US 191/UT 128 junction: JayCee Park (4.2 miles), Hal Canyon (6.6 miles), Oak Grove (6.9 miles), and Big Bend Recreation Site (7.4 miles). Contact the Moab Information Center for locations of additional campgrounds. You'll also find campgrounds farther out at Arches and Canyonlands national parks, Dead Horse Point State Park, La Sal Mountains, and Canyon Rims Recreation Area.

Food

The Grand Old Ranch House serves elegant meals in an 1896 pioneer house on the north edge of town, tel. 259-5753; specialties include German cuisine, steak, prime rib, veal, seafood, and trout. Open daily for dinner (reservations recommended). **Mi Vida Restaurant** in Charlie Steen's mansion has a sweeping view of the valley; take the signed drive on the north edge of town, tel. 259-7146. Chefs offer steak, seafood, and other fare Saturday and Sunday for brunch, Mon.-Fri. for lunch, and daily for dinner. **Sundowner Restaurant,** on the north edge of town (next to Slickrock Country Campground), tel. 259-5201, prepares German and Southwestern cuisines; open daily for dinner. **Center Cafe,** downtown at 92 E. Center, tel. 259-4295, features fine dining and a varied menu; open Mon.-Sat. for dinner. **Honest Ozzie's Cafe,** 60 N. 100 West, tel. 259-8442, features tasty breakfasts, deli lunches, and dinners made with natural ingredients; it also has the best selection of vegetarian food in town; open daily. The **Rio Colorado Restaurant** can fill the bill for most any appetite—sandwiches,

Mexican food, steak, seafood, chicken, pasta, and salads; open Saturday and Sunday for breakfast and daily for lunch and dinner. Turn west one block on Center from Main, tel. 259-6666. **Bar M Chuckwagon Supper,** on the banks of Mill Creek at 541 S. 400 E. Mulberry Lane (see Moab map), tel. 259-2276, serves up tasty cowboy food, followed by a variety of live western entertainment; open for dinner (call to check on time) Mon.-Sat. April to October. **Cattleman's Restaurant,** two miles south of town on US 191, tel. 259-6585, rustles up American food including steak and seafood; open 24 hours daily for breakfast (served anytime), lunch, and dinner. The adjacent lounge has dancing with live country/Western or rock bands on Friday and Saturday nights. **Westerner Grill,** 331 N. Main, tel. 259-9918, is a favorite with locals; open daily for breakfast (anytime), lunch, and dinner. The **Ramada Inn,** 182 S. Main, tel. 259-7141, offers varied American fare in the Arches and Pancake Haus dining rooms, including sirloin, prime rib, and trout; open daily for breakfast, lunch, and dinner. **Golden Stake Restaurant,** 550 S. Main, tel. 259-7000, has the American favorites including steak and seafood. Open daily for breakfast, lunch, and dinner. **Cafe Ruisseau,** next to the Greenwell Motel at 105 S. Main, tel. 259-2599, also has a menu with a choice of standard American items. Open daily for breakfast, lunch, dinner, and takeout. **Fat City Smoke House,** 36 S. 100 West, tel. 259-4302, specializes in Texas-style pit barbecue for lunch and dinner; open Mon.-Saturday. **JH's Cafe,** 1075 S. US 191 (south edge of town), tel. 259-8352, features Western-style breakfasts; open daily for breakfast and lunch. **Pack Creek Ranch** offers fine dining in a remote mountain setting, 16 miles southeast of Moab off the LaSal Mountain Loop Road, tel. 259-5505, open daily for dinner (reservations recommended).

La Hacienda, 574 N. Main, tel. 259-6319, offers Mexican and gringo food; open daily for lunch and dinner. **Dos Amigos,** 56 E. 300 South, tel. 259-7903, presents a long list of Mexican specialties. You can dine indoors or out on the patio; open daily for breakfast, lunch, and dinner. **Catarina's,** 51 N. Main, tel. 259-6070, serves Italian cuisine with choices of vegetarian, meat, and seafood entrees (pizza too) in both indoor and outdoor settings; open daily except Monday for dinner; closed in winter. **Pasta Jay's,** 16 S. Main, tel. 259-2900, offers Italian sandwiches, pasta dishes, and pizza with informal indoor and outdoor seating; open daily for lunch and dinner. The **Slickrock Cafe** is opening at 5 W. Center for family dining. **Eddie McStiff's,** 57 S. Main in Western Plaza, tel. 259-BEER, has a dining room for their pasta, pizza, steaks, chicken, and Mexican food and a pub (they make their own beer). Open daily for dinner. **Poplar Place Pub & Eatery,** Main and 100 North, tel. 259-6018, serves pizza and has a pub; open daily for lunch and dinner. **Subway,** 74 S. Main, tel. 259-SUBS, serves breakfast, lunch, and dinner, daily, with sandwiches made to order. **Pizza Hut,** 265 S. Main, tel. 259-6345, specializes in pizza; open daily for lunch and dinner. **Grand Ice Cream Parlor,** at the corner of Main and 200 South, tel. 259-5853, is a popular spot for fast food and ice cream; open daily for breakfast, lunch, and dinner. You'll find an old-fashioned **soda fountain** in the T-Shirt Shop, 38 N. Main. **Moab Community Co-op,** 111 N. 100 West, tel. 259-5712, is a grocery store offering health food and a variety of books

Entertainment And Events

The Canyon's Edge, a multimedia presentation on the wonders of the Colorado Plateau, is given at the Moab Information Center, tel. 259-7750, from June to September at 7 and 8 p.m. (consult the Information Center for additional showtimes for the rest of the year). Cost is $4 adult, $3 seniors, and $2 children 12 and under. Tag-A-Long Expeditions, tel. 259-8946 or (800) 453-3292, presents **Canyon Classics,** performances of classical music, ballet, and opera in a wilderness setting, accessible by jetboat or raft tours on the Colorado River.

To find out about local happenings, contact the Moab Information Center, tel. 259-8825. Softball, golf, and other sport competitions take place through the warmer months. Major annual events include:

March: Moab Half Marathon (third Saturday) and **Jeep Safari** (Easter weekend).

April: Canondale Cup Bicycle Race.

May: Green River to Moab Friendship Cruise (Memorial Day weekend).

June: P.R.C.A. Rodeo (first weekend). **Canyonlands Rodeo** (with rodeo parade,

dance, horse racing, and 4-H gymkhana; third or fourth weekend).

July-August: Celebration on **Fourth of July, Little Buckaroo Rodeo, Grand County Fair** (agricultural, crafts, and arts judging in August).

September: Moab Music Festival (jazz, bluegrass, and other groups), **Moab Movie Jubilee** (Moab Film Commission shows films made in the area; early September), **Desert Duster Ladies Golf Tournament** (mid-September), **Red Rock 4-Wheeler Labor Day Campout** (overnight; on Labor Day weekend).

October: Arts Festival of the Canyonlands (art sales, music, Greek theater; early October), **Gem and Mineral Show** (second weekend), **Fat Tire Festival** (mountain bicycle guided tours, hill climb, workshops, and entertainment; week before Halloween day).

November-December: Christmas Parade and Crafts Fair (late November or early December), **Winter Sun Run** (first or second weekend in December).

Shopping And Services

Rockhounds and anyone wanting to learn more about geology will enjoy a stop at **Lin Ottinger's Moab Rock Shop,** 600 N. Main, tel. 259-7312. From mid-April to mid-October, Lin Ottinger leads tours of the area. He presents free slide shows of the backcountry in the evening May to September. The **Grand Emporium** at Main and West Center has art galleries and Indian art and craft shops; **Hogan Trading Co. Gallery** at 100 S. Main offers an upscale selection of Indian art; other shops lie scattered around town. **Global Expeditions,** 711 N. 500 West, tel. 259-6604, rents camping and mountaineering gear and offers instruction in climbing and cross-country ski touring. **Rim Cyclery,** 94 W. 100 North, tel. 259-5333, sells outdoor gear for bicycling, backpacking, climbing, river running, and skiing. Rentals include mountain bicycles and cross-country skis; mountain bicycle tours are offered too. Mountain bike rentals and tours are also at **Kaibab Mountain/Desert Bike Tours,** 391 S. Main, tel. 259-7423; **Poison Spider Bicycles,** 497 N. Main, tel. 259-7882; and **Western Spirit Cycling,** 38 S. 100 West, tel. 259-8732. **Canyon Climber ATVs,** one and one half miles south of town on US 191, tel. 259-6274/5301, rents all-terrain vehicles (four-wheelers) and has a recreational track and guided tours.

The **post office** is downtown at 50 E. 100 North, tel. 259-7427. **Allen Memorial Hospital** provides medical care at 719 W. 400 North, tel. 259-7191. For **emergencies** (ambulance, sheriff, police, or fire), dial 911.

Recreation

For a selection of movies head for **Slickrock Cinemas** at 580 Kane Creek Blvd., tel. 259-4441. The **City Park,** 181 W. 400 North, tel. 259-8226, has shaded picnic tables, a playground, and an outdoor swimming pool. The **Lions Park** offers picnicking along the Colorado River two miles north of town. **Tennis courts** are beside the Grand County Middle School, 217 E. Center. **Moab Lanes** has bowling action at 1145 S. Hwy. 191, tel. 259-5188. **Moab Golf Club** features an 18-hole course, driving range, and pro shop; at 2705 S. East Bench Road (go south five miles on US 191, turn left two miles on Spanish Trails Road, then right a quarter mile on Murphy Lane), tel. 259-6488. **Sunset Trail Rides,** nine miles south of Moab, tel. 259-4362, does day and evening horseback rides ($10 an hour for day rides; $30 for an evening ride with a Dutch oven cookoff). **Pack Creek Ranch,** tel. 259-5505, offers two hour horseback rides in Arches National Park and the La Sal Mountains. Pack trips tour the La Sals and canyon country.

Information

The **Moab Information Center,** Main and Center, tel. 259-8825, is the place to start for nearly all local and area information. The National Park Service, the Bureau of Land Management, the U. S. Forest Service, the Grand County Travel Council, and the Canyonlands Natural History Association all are represented in this multi-agency facility. Visitors needing help from any of these agencies should start at the Information Center rather than at the agency offices. A lot of free literature is available and a large selection of books and maps are sold. The office is open from 8 a.m.-9 p.m. in summer (reduced hours the rest of the year). The **Moab Chamber of Commerce** is on the north edge of town at 805 N. Main (Box 550, Moab, UT 84532), tel. 259-7531 or (800) 635-6622. The staff knows about services in town and can suggest many places to go in the area; free literature is available. Hours are 9 a.m.-5 p.m. daily.

The **National Park Service** office in Moab, 2282 Southwest Resource Blvd., Moab, UT 84532 (three miles south of downtown), tel. 259-7164/7164, is headquarters for Canyonlands and Arches national parks and Natural Bridges National Monument. Open Mon.-Fri. 8 a.m.-4:30 p.m. **Manti-La Sal National Forest** offices are also at 2282 Southwest Resource Blvd., tel. 259-7155; open Mon.-Fri. 8 a.m.-noon and 12:30-4:30 p.m. The **Bureau of Land Management** has an office in Moab. The **BLM District** office is at 82 E. Dogwood on the south side of town behind Comfort Suites, (Box 970, Moab, UT 84532), tel. 259-6111 or 259-819 (general info) and 259-4421 (river info from 8 a.m.-noon) and is open Mon.-Fri. 7:45 a.m.-4:30 p.m. Some land-use maps are sold. River runners need to visit the Moab Information Center for Colorado River info and Westwater Canyon permits. Most river runners obtain their permits by applying in January and February for a March drawing; the Moab Information Center BLM ranger can advise on this process and on cancellations available.

The **Grand County Public Library,** 25 S. 100 East (next to the Dan O'Laurie Museum), tel. 259-5421, is a good place for local history and general reading; open Mon.-Thurs. 1-9 p.m., Friday 1-5 p.m., and Saturday 10 a.m.-2 p.m. **Back of Beyond Books,** 83 N. Main, tel. 259-5154, features an excellent selection of regional books and maps. **B. Osborn's Books & Magazines,** 50 S. Main, tel. 259-2665, has a good selection of regional books, paperbacks, magazines, and maps. A good selection of books and maps is sold at **Times Independent Maps** at 5 E. Center St., tel. 259-7525.

River Tours

Rafts and other watercraft can take you through beautiful canyons near Moab. Western River Expeditions, Downstream River Works, and Tag-A-Long Tours rent rafts and inflatable kayaks for those who would rather organize their own boat trips. The most popular run near Moab starts upstream on the Colorado River near Fisher Towers and bounces through several moderate rapids on the way back to town. The Green and Colorado rivers also offer relatively gentle travel above their confluence; see "River District" under "Canyonlands National Park, below" The longer river trips provide more of a wilderness experience (thrilling rapids too in Westwater, Cataract, and Desolation canyons). Most one-day raft excursions cost about $35-50 per person. Expect to pay at least $100-150 per person per day for overnight trips. The rafting season runs April to September; jetboat tours are February to November. Contact the Moab Information Center and the National Park Service office for lists or brochures of tour operators.

Canyonlands by Night tours leave at sunset in an open boat and go several miles upstream on the Colorado River; a guide points out canyon features. The sound and light show begins on the way back; music and historic narration accompany the play of lights on canyon walls. Cost is $18 adult, $9 ages 6-17; boats run May to mid-October. **Canyonlands by Day** trips go downriver into the Colorado River canyon near Dead Horse Point; $52 adult, $25 ages 6-17, $5 under 6; tour operates March-October. Trips depart from the Spanish mission-style office just across the Colorado River and from Moab, tel. 259-5261.

Navtec Expeditions, 321 N. Main (Box 1267, Moab, UT 84532), tel. 259-7983 or (800) 833-1278, organizes Colorado River raft trips (oar) above Moab (full day: $38 adult, $29 children 17 and under; half day or sunset: $30-32 adult, $24-26 children 17 and under; overnight: $150 adult, $120 children 17 and under); sportboat trips above Moab (half day: $58 adult, $39 children 12 and under); sportboat excursions downriver to Dead Horse Point ($52 adult, $29 children 17 and under); sportboat rides through

Cataract Canyon (one day: $250 per person; also two- or three-day sportboat and four- or five-day raft trips); oar-powered raft trips through Westwater Canyon (one day, $100; also overnight); and winter sportboat trips that explore the Sea of Cortez off Baja. Navtec uses sportboats because of their speed across calm water (20 mph) and maneuverability.

Sheri Griffith Expeditions, Box 1324, Moab, UT 84532 (office is three miles south of downtown on US 191), tel. 259-8229 or (800) 332-2439, leads trips through Westwater Canyon (two to three days by oar; two-day trips cost $294 and three-day trips run $433 with a minimum age of 10), Cataract Canyon (five days by oar, three to four days by motorboat), Desolation and Gray canyons of the Green River (four to five days by paddleboat), and Dolores River (three and five days by oar); paddleboats can be substituted for oar boats on all the canyons.

Adrift Adventures, 378 N. Main (Box 577, Moab, UT 84532), tel. 259-8594 or (800) 874-4483, leads one-day raft (oar or paddle) and inflatable kayak trips on the Colorado River upstream from Moab ($38 adult, $26 children 7-17); half-day and sunset trips are available too; half-day jetboat trips cost $42-45, or you can take the full-day combination jeep tour/jetboat trip for $69; longer trips are in Cataract Canyon on the Colorado (three to four days by motor, five days by oar) and in Desolation and Gray canyons of the Green River (four to five days by oar or paddle).

a peaceful morning on the Colorado River, below Moab

rafting the Colorado above Moab

Wildwater: The Moab Rafting Co., tel. 259-7238 or (800) RIO-MOAB, does raft trips (oar) on the Colorado River above Moab (full day: $34 adult, $24 children; half day: $25 adult, $20 children) and the San Juan River (two to five days by oar).

Western River Expeditions, guides one-day trips (oar) upstream on the Colorado ($40 adult, $25 children 17 and under) and overnight trips ($105-175 per person); rafts and inflatable kayaks can be rented from their Moab office, 1371 N. Main, Moab, UT 84532, tel. 259-7019. Western River Expeditions also runs longer raft trips through Westwater Canyon (three days by oar), Cataract Canyon (four days by oar/motorcraft), Desolation and Gray canyons of the Green River (four to five days oar or paddle), and Grand Canyon (three to six days by motorboat, 12 days by oar); for these longer trips contact their main office at 7258 Racquet Club Dr., Salt Lake City, UT 84121, tel. 942-6669 or (800) 453-7450 out of state.

Tag-A-Long Tours, 452 N. Main, Moab, UT 84532, tel. 259-8946 or (800) 453-3292, offers raft trips (oar) on the Colorado River above Moab (half day: $32 adult, $28 children under 17; full day: $40 adult, $30 children under 17) and full-day jetboat/jeep excursions ($89 adult, $82 children under 17); longer raft trips go through Westwater Canyon (two days by oar), Cataract Canyon (three to four days by oar/motorboat), and Green River canyons (four to five days by oar in rafts or inflatable kayaks, four days in canoes). You can rent canoes and inflatable kayaks; a shuttle service from the Green-Colorado confluence is provided too.

North American River Expeditions & Canyonlands Tours, 543 N. Main, Moab, UT 84532, tel. 259-5865 or (800) 342-5938 out of state, operates raft (oar) trips on the Colorado above Moab (full day: $38 adult, $28 children 7-17; half day or sunset: $32 adult, $26 children 7-17), paddle rafts and inflatable kayaks (full day: $44 adult, $32 children 7-17; half day or sunset: $32 adult, $26 children 7-17); half-day jetboat trips ($57 adult, $31 children under 17), full-day jetboat and jeep tour combinations ($78 adult, $57 children under 17), and one- to five-day raft trips (motorized) through Cataract Canyon.

Canyon Voyages, 352 N. Main St., Moab, UT 84532, tel. 259-6007 or (800) 488-5884, runs trips on the Colorado upstream from Moab (full day: $41 adult, $31 children 17 and under; half day or evening: $31-33 adult, $24-26 children 17 and under; overnight: $155 adult, $120 children 17 and under).

World Wide River Expeditions, 625 N. River Sands Rd., Moab, UT 84532, tel. 259-7515 (Moab, May to August), 566-2662 (Salt Lake City, year-round), or (800) 231-2769, runs rafts on the Colorado above Moab (full day: $35 adult, $28 children 17 and under, Westwater Canyon; two and one half days by oar), Cataract Canyon (three to four days motor, five days oar) and Desolation and Gray canyons of the Green River (four or five days by motor/oar).

Tex's Riverways, a quarter mile off Main at 691 N. 500 West (Box 67, Moab, UT 84532), tel. 259-5101, will put you in a canoe for one-day ($40 for two people) and half-day ($30 for two people) unguided trips below Moab (costs are lower if you have your own canoe); other packages include canoes and jetboat shuttle services on the Colorado River to the Green-Colorado confluence (one to three days) and down the Green River to the confluence (4-10 days). Hikers can arrange to be dropped off and picked up in remote areas of Canyonlands National Park on jetboat trips down the Colorado. **River Runner Sports,** 401 N. Main (Box 336, Moab, UT 01500), tel. 259-4121 or (800) 258-4121, rents rafts inflatable kayaks, and equipment for river trip outfitting. **Red River Canoe Rentals,** 38 S. 100 West, tel. 259-7722, also offers canoe rentals and shuttles for the Colorado and Green rivers.

Road Tours
Moab Rock Shop/Lin Ottinger's Tours, 600 N. Main, Moab, UT 84532, tel. 259-7312, offers backcountry driving trips from mid-April to mid-October. Lin has been poking around the canyons of this area since the uranium boom of the 1950s, and he knows the best places; frequent stops allow plenty of time to walk around for a look at Indian art and scenic and geologic features. $45-50 all day.

Tag-A-Long Tours, 452 N. Main, Moab, UT 84532, tel. 259-8946 or (800) 453-3292, has a variety of one-day ($55-89) and multi-day ($395 for three days) jeep tours April-October.

North American River Expeditions & Canyonlands Tours, 543 N. Main, Moab, UT 84532, tel. 259-5865 or (800) 342-5938, explore the backcountry of the Island in the Sky ($72 adult, $62 children under 17) and Needles ($110 adult, $89 children under 17) districts of Canyonlands National Park year-round.

Adrift Adventures, 378 N. Main (Box 577, Moab, UT 84532), tel. 259-8594 or (800) 874-4483, has a half-day jeep tour to Dead Horse Point and Island in the Sky at $47 or you can take a full-day combination jeep tour/raft trip for $65 or a jeep tour/jetboat trip for $85.

Canyonlands Field Institute, 1320 S. Hwy. 191 (Box 68, Moab, UT 84532), tel. 259-7750, offers many educational programs—hiking, driving, rafting, and canoeing tours, naturalist walks, photography workshops, seminars, and youth programs.

Mountain Bicycle Tours
Rim Tours, 94 W. 100 North, Moab, UT 84532, tel. 259-5223 or (800) 626-7335, leads half-day ($25), day ($45), and multi-day ($330-990) trips on mountain bicycles through the canyon country; some tours combine a river excursion too.

Bicycles can be rented or you can bring your own. **Kaibab Desert and Mountain Bike Tours,** 391 S. Main, Moab, UT 84532, tel. 259-7423 or (800) 451-1133, explore Canyonlands National Park and other scenic areas March-Oct.; Daily trips in spring and autumn visit the Canyonlands' Island in the Sky ($60); multi-day trips operate mostly in spring and autumn to Maze District of Canyonlands (two days bicycling, one day hiking, and two days rafting through Cataract Canyon; $895), White Rim of Canyonlands (four days; $520), the Maze (four days; $590), and Grand Canyon North Rim. Rentals, supplies, and shuttle services are offered too.

Nichols Expeditions, 497 N. Main, tel. 259-7882 or (800) 635-1792, goes to all three districts of Canyonlands National Park—the Needles (five days, $575), Island in the Sky (five days; $575), and the Maze (six days; $600); other bike trips go to Grand Canyon North Rim and Idaho. Utah rides go in spring or autumn.

Western Spirit Cycling, Box 411, Moab, UT 84532, tel. 259-8732 or (800) 845-BIKE, specializes in multi-day tours of the Moab area during spring and autumn and the high country of Colorado, Idaho, and Montana in summer. Utah trips include the White Rim (four to five days, $495) and Abajos (five days, $595). Custom trips can be arranged to places such as Lockhart Basin and Kokopelli's Trail; day-trips (on request with a four-person minimum), rentals, and instructional clinics are offered too.

Air Tours
You'll have a bird's-eye view of southeastern Utah's incredible landscape from Moab or Green River airports with **Redtail Aviation,** Box 515, Moab, UT 84532, tel. 259-7421 (Moab), 564-3412 (Green River) or (800) 842-9251. Flights feature Canyonlands National Park (Needles, Island in the Sky, and the Maze districts; one hour, $60). Longer tours are available too. Rates are based on two or more persons; add $10 per person for tours out of Green River. Flights operate all year. **Slickrock Air Guides,** 2231 S. Hwy. 191, Moab, Utah, 84532, tel. 259-6216 or (800) 332-2439, offers three air tours at per person rates of $75 (75 minutes over the Canyonlands area), $192 (three hours over Canyonlands, Natural Bridges, and the Lake Powell area

with a visit to Gouldings Trading Post), and $494 (two days/one night with an overnight stay in the Bryce Canyon area). **Mountain Flying Service** offers three tours priced at $60 (one hour), $129 (two hours), and $198 (four hours); reservations can be made at NAVTEC Expeditions Office, 321 N. Main, tel. 259-8050. The airport is 18 miles north of Moab on US 191.

Helicopter tours are also available with a minimum of three passengers and a lower rate with four. **Arches Helicopters,** 1515 N. Hwy. 191, tel. 259-4637, has 15 minute flights at $35-45 per person and 30 minutes at $70-90. **Two Jays,** three miles south of Moab on Hwy. 191, tel. 259-8900, has the same rates plus a one hour flight at $135-180.

The Wild West Balloon Adventure, tel. 259-9000, will take you up over the Moab area April to October. Flights of one to two hours cost $139 per person with a minimum of two people.

Transportation
Rent jeeps and other 4WD vehicles at **Great Jeep'n Guides,** 550 N. Main, tel. 259-4567, drive-yourself tours are also available; **Farabee**

4X4 Adventures, 234 N. Main, tel. 259-7494; **Slick Rock 4X4 Rental,** 284 N. Main, tel. 259-5678; **Certified Ford,** 500 S. Main, tel. 529-6107; and **Thrifty,** 400 N. Main, tel. 259-7317. **Taxi** service includes shuttles for bicyclists and river runners, tel. 259-TAXI. **Alpine Air,** tel. (800) 748-4899 or 373-1508 (Provo) for reservations, flies daily roundtrip to Salt Lake City and Grand Junction, CO.

Wine Tasting
Arches Vineyards (Utah's only producer of premium wines) offers free wine tasting Mon.-Thurs. 11 a.m.-7 p.m. and Fri.-Sat. 11 a.m.-9 p.m. (except holidays) at 2182 S. Hwy. 191. Call for winter hours; tel. 259-5397.

Fishing
Portal Fishery (privately owned), just north of downtown at 1261 N. Hwy. 191, tel. 259-6108, offers trout fishing from 8 a.m. until dark. Catch-and-release fly fishing is $10 per hour. You can keep your catch at 25 cents per inch up to 12 inches and $3.50 per pound over 12 inches. No license, tackle, or bait required.

long-tailed weasel (Mustela frenata)

LOUISE FOOTE

EXPLORING THE CANYON COUNTRY NEAR MOAB

Except for the La Sals and the national parks, most of the canyon country surrounding Moab is administered by the Bureau of Land Management (BLM). Staff can offer advice on exploring this area at the two BLM offices in Moab (see "Information" under "Practicalities" in the "Moab" section earlier in this chapter). The offices also have literature, books, and maps. BLM people can also give locations of the developed and undeveloped designated campsites near the Moab Slickrock Bike Trail, Kane Creek, and along the Colorado River; you must use the designated sites in these areas.

MOAB SLICKROCK BIKE TRAIL

Undulating slickrock just east of Moab challenges even the best mountain-bicycle riders. This is not an area to learn mountain-bike skills. Originally motorcyclists laid out this route, though now about 99% of riders rely on leg and lung power. The practice loop near the beginning allows first-time visitors a chance to get a feel for the slickrock. The "trail" consists only of painted white lines. Riders following it have less

chance of getting lost or finding themselves in hazardous areas. Plan on about five hours to do the 9.6-mile main loop and expect to do some walking. Side trails lead to viewpoints overlooking Moab, the Colorado River, and arms of Negro Bill Canyon. Panoramas of surrounding canyon country and the La Sals add to the pleasure of biking. Take care if venturing off the trail—it's a long way down some of the sheer cliff faces! The trail's steep slopes and sharp turns can be tricky—a helmet is a must. Knee pads and riding gloves also protect from scrapes and bruises. Fat bald tires work best on the rock; partially deflated knobby tires do almost as well. Carry plenty of water—one gallon in summer, half a gallon in cooler months. Tiny plant associations, which live in fragile cryptobiotic soil, don't want you tearing through their homes; stay on the rock and avoid sand areas. Shops in Moab offer rentals, supplies, books, and tours. Obtain a trail map there or from the Moab Information Center. To reach the trailhead from Main St. in Moab, turn east 0.4 mile on 300 South, turn right 0.1 mile on 400 East, turn left (east) a half mile on Mill Creek Dr., then left two and one half miles on Sand Flats Road.

On the Moab Slickrock Bike Trail; La Sals stand in the distance.

The practice loop also makes an enjoyable two and one half mile hike. Precipitous drop-offs into tributaries of Negro Bill Canyon have breathtaking views. It's best to walk off to the side of the white lines marking the route. You'll reach the practice loop a quarter mile from the trailhead.

Kokopelli's Trail

Mountain bicyclists have linked together a series of back roads through the magical canyons of eastern Utah and western Colorado. You can start on Sand Flats Road in Moab and ride east to Castle Valley (21.1 miles), Fisher Valley (44.9 miles), Dewey Bridge (62.9 miles), Cisco Boat Landing (83.5 miles), Rabbit Valley (108 miles), and Loma (140 miles). Lots of optional routes and access points allow for many possibilities. Campsites along the trail have tables, grills, and outhouses. See the small book *The Utah-Colorado Mountain Bike Trail System, Route 1—Moab to Loma* by Peggy Utesch for detailed descriptions. An excellent brochure, *Kokopelli's Trail Map,* is available free at the Moab Information Center.

KANE CREEK SCENIC DRIVE AND TRAILS

This road heads downstream along the Colorado River on the same side as Moab. The four miles through the Colorado River's canyon are paved, followed by six miles of good dirt road through Kane Springs Canyon. People with high-clearance vehicles or mountain bicycles can continue across a ford of Kane Springs Creek to Hurrah Pass and an extensive network of 4WD trails. The book and separate map *Canyon Country Off-Road Vehicle Trails: Canyon Rims & Needles Areas* by F.A. Barnes has detailed back-road information.

Moab Rim Trail

The high cliffs just southwest of town provide fine views of the Moab Valley, highlands of Arches National Park, and the La Sal Mountains. The trail turns off Kane Creek Blvd. one and one half miles downriver from Moab. (Total driving distance from the junction of Main St. and Kane Creek Blvd. is 2.6 miles; look for the trailhead on the left 0.1 mile after a cattle guard.)

The sky can be seen through Little Arch across the river from the trailhead. Four-wheel-drive vehicles can also ascend the Moab Rim Trail, though the rough terrain is considered difficult for them; the first 200 yards will give drivers a feel for the difficulty. The trail climbs northeast one and one half miles along tilted rock strata of the Kayenta Formation to the top of the plateau. This is a moderately difficult hike with good views nearly all the way. Elevation gain is 940 feet. Once on top, hikers can follow jeep roads southeast to Hidden Valley Trail and descend on a hiking trail to US 191 south of Moab, a five-and-one-half-mile trip (total one-way). Experienced hikers can also head south from the rim to **Behind the Rocks,** a fantastic maze of sandstone fins.

To reach the Hidden Valley Trail, continue on the jeep road, which turns south and drops into a slickrock area flanked by two large domes of Navajo Sandstone. The road follows a wash at the bottom, then climbs a large sand hill (there are several ways up). About a half mile farther, two side roads turn left to viewpoints; the main road continues south into a wash, curves to the east up a slope, and ends near the upper end of Hidden Valley Trail. From here it's a one-third-mile hike to a low divide and another two miles to the lower trailhead near US 191. You'll need a car shuttle for a one-way hike.

Hidden Valley Trail

You'll see not only a "hidden valley" but also panoramas of the Moab area and Behind the Rocks. The moderately difficult trail ascends 500 feet in a series of switchbacks to a broad shelf below the Moab Rim, then follows the shelf ("hidden valley") to the northwest. It then crosses a low pass and follows a second shelf in the same direction. Near the end of the second shelf, the trail turns left to a divide, where you can see a portion of the remarkable fins of Behind the Rocks. This divide is one mile from the start (one-way) and 680 feet higher in elevation. The trail continues a third of a mile from the divide down to the end of the Moab Rim Trail, a jeep road and hiking trail. Or, instead of turning left to the divide, you can make a short side trip (no trail) to the right for views of Moab. To reach the Hidden Valley Trailhead, drive south three miles on US 191 from Moab, turn right 0.4 mile on Angel Rock Road to its end (the turnoff is just south of Milepost 122), then right 0.3 mile on Rimrock Lane.

Behind The Rocks

A look at the topo map will show that something strange is going on here. Massive fins of Navajo Sandstone 100-500 feet high, 50-200 feet thick, and up to a half mile long cover a large area. Narrow vertical cracks, sometimes only a few feet wide, separate the fins. Archaeological sites and several arches are in the area. No maintained trails exist here, and some routes require technical climbing skills. The maze offers endless exploration routes. If you get lost (very easy to do), remember that the fins are oriented east-west; the rim of the Colorado River canyon is reached by going west, and Spanish Valley is reached by going east. Bring plenty of water, a topo map (Moab 7 1/2-minute), and a compass. Access routes are Moab Rim and Hidden Valley trails (from the north and east) and Pritchett Canyon (from the west and south). Though only a couple of miles from Moab, Behind the Rocks seems a world away. The BLM is studying a possible wilderness designation to protect the solitude and character of this strange country.

Pritchett Canyon

A very difficult jeep road, also popular with mountain bicyclists, winds up this canyon to Pritchett Arch (four and one half miles one-way) and several other arches. Canyon scenery and good views of Behind the Rocks are other attractions. Turnoff is on the left 4.8 miles down Kane Creek Blvd., just before the road turns up Kane Creek Canyon; look for a small canyon with a fence across it. According to the BLM, a private landowner is charging a toll across his land; $2 per vehicle, $1 per hiker or biker.

Hunters Canyon

Hikers enjoy seeing the arch and other rock formations in the canyon walls and the lush vegetation along the creek. Off-road vehicles have made tracks a short way up, then you'll be walking, mostly along the creekbed. Short sections of trail lead around thickets of tamarisk and other water-loving plants. Look for Hunters Arch on the right about a half mile up. Most of the water in Hunters Canyon comes from a deep pool surrounded by hanging gardens of maidenhair

fern. This pretty spot is three miles (one-way) and 240 feet higher than the start. A dry fall and a small natural bridge lie above the pool. After the three-mile point the hike becomes very brushy. To reach the trailhead from Moab, drive eight miles on Kane Creek Blvd. along the Colorado River and up Kane Creek Canyon. The road is asphalted where it fords Hunter Creek but the asphalt is usually covered with dirt washed over it by the creek.

A longer hike can be made by going up Hunters Canyon and descending on Pritchett Canyon Road. The road crosses the normally dry creekbed just upstream of the deep pool. To bypass the dry fall above the pool, backtrack 300 feet down the canyon and rockscramble up a short, steep slope (on the right heading upstream). At a junction just east of there, a jeep road along the north rim of Hunters Canyon meets Pritchett Canyon Road. Walk northeast a half mile on Pritchett Canyon Road to a spur trail on the left leading to Pritchett Arch. Then continue four and one half miles on Pritchett Canyon Road to Kane Creek Boulevard. This country is more open and desertlike than Hunters Canyon. A 3.2-mile car shuttle or hike is needed to return to Hunters Canyon Trailhead.

UTAH SCENIC BYWAY 279 AND TRAILS

Utah Highway 279 goes downstream through the Colorado River canyon on the other side of the river from Moab. Pavement extends 16 miles past fine views, prehistoric rock art, arches, and hiking trails. A potash plant marks the end of the highway, where a rough dirt road continues to Canyonlands National Park. From Moab, head north three and one half miles on US 191, then turn left on UT 279. Soon you'll see Moab's radioactive lake on the left atop a huge pile of uranium tailings. Charlie Steen built the mill in the mid-1950s to process ore from his Mi Vida Mine. The water helps keep the hazardous dust down. Needless to say, no swimming or trespassing is allowed! The highway enters the canyon at the "Portal," 2.7 miles from the turnoff. Towering cliffs of sandstone rise on the right and the Colorado River is just below on the left.

Indian Ruins Viewpoint

Stop at a signed pullout on the left to see a small prehistoric Indian ruin tucked under a ledge across the river. The stone structure was probably used for food storage. The viewpoint is 0.6 mile past the canyon entrance.

Portal Overlook Trail

A trail switchbacks up a slope, then follows a sloping sandstone ledge of the Kayenta Formation to an overlook. A panorama takes in the Colorado River, Moab Valley, Arches National Park, and the La Sals. The hike is one and one half miles (one-way) with an elevation gain of 980 feet. This trail is a twin of the Moab Rim Trail across the river. Begin from the Jaycee Park Campground on the right, 3.8 miles from the turnoff at US 191; mulberry trees shade the attractive spot. Expect to share this trail with many mountain bikers.

Petroglyphs

Groups of petroglyphs cover cliffs along the highway 5.2 miles from US 191. These may not be signed, but they are 0.7 mile beyond Milepost 11. Look across the river to see The Fickle Finger of Fate among the sandstone fins of Behind the Rocks. A petroglyph of a bear is 0.2 mile farther down the highway. Archaeologists think that Fremont and the later Ute Indians did most of the artwork in this area.

Dinosaur Tracks

Tracks and petroglyphs are visible on rocks above to the right. Sighting tubes help locate the features. It's possible to hike up the steep hillside for a closer look. The signed pullout is on the right, 6.2 miles from US 191.

bear petroglyph

LOUISE FOOTE

Corona Arch And Bowtie Arch

A one and one half mile (one-way) hike across slickrock country leads to these impressive arches. You can't see them from the road, though a third arch—Pinto—is visible. Signed trailhead is on the right 10 miles from US 191 (midway between Mileposts 5 and 6); you'll see railroad tracks just beyond the trailhead. The trail climbs up from the parking area, crosses the tracks, and follows a bit of a jeep road and a small wash to an ancient gravel bar. Pinto (or Gold Bar) Arch can be seen to the left, though there's no trail to it. Follow cairns to Corona and Bowtie. Handrails and a ladder help in the few steep spots. Despite being only a few hundred yards apart, each arch has a completely different character and history. Bowtie formed when a pothole in the cliffs above met a cave underneath. It used to be called "Paul Bunyan's Potty" before the name was appropriated for an arch in Canyonlands National Park. The hole is about 30 feet in diameter. Corona Arch, reminiscent of the larger Rainbow Bridge, eroded out of a sandstone fin. The graceful span is 140 feet long and 105 feet high. Both arches are composed of Navajo Sandstone. If you have time for only one hike in the Moab area, this one is especially recommended.

Jug Handle Arch

This aptly named formation is close to the road on the right, 13.6 miles from US 191. The opening is 46 feet high and three feet wide. Ahead the canyon opens up. Underground pressures of salt and potash have folded the rock layers into an anticline.

Moab Salt Plant

The mine injects water underground to dissolve the potash and other chemicals, then pumps the solution to evaporation ponds. The ponds are dyed blue to hasten evaporation, which takes about a year. These colorful solutions can be seen from Dead Horse Point and Anticline Overlook on the canyon rims. High-clearance vehicles can continue on the unpaved road beyond the plant. The road passes through varied canyon country with views overlooking the Colorado River. At a road junction in Canyonlands National Park (Island in the Sky District), you have a choice of turning left for the 100-mile White Rim Trail (4WD only past Musselman

Arch) or continuing up the steep switchbacks of the Shafer Trail Road (4WD recommended) to the paved park road or returning the way you came.

UTAH SCENIC BYWAY 128 AND TRAILS

Utah Highway 128 turns northeast from US 191 just south of the Colorado River bridge, two miles north of Moab. This exceptionally scenic canyon route follows the Colorado for 30 miles upstream before crossing at Dewey Bridge and turning north to I-70. The entire highway is paved. In 1986, a new bridge replaced the narrow Dewey suspension bridge that once caused white knuckles on drivers of large vehicles. Lions Park picnic area at the turnoff from US 191 is a pleasant stopping place. Big Bend Recreation Site is another good spot seven and one half miles up UT 128. A popular one-day raft trip with mild rapids begins from the Hittle Bottom Recreation Site, 23.5 miles up UT 128 near Fisher Towers, and ends 14 river miles downstream at Take-out Beach, 10.3 miles up UT 128 from US 191. Rafts and life jackets (required) can be rented in Moab. No permit is needed on this section of river. A network of highly scenic jeep roads branches off Castle Valley and Onion Creek roads into side canyons and the La Sal Mountains. These are described in the book and separate map *Canyon Country Off-Road Vehicle Trails: Arches & La Sals Areas* by F.A. Barnes.

Negro Bill Canyon

The route follows a lively stream surrounded by abundant greenery and sheer canyon cliffs. Beaver and other wildlife live here. Morning Glory Natural Bridge, in a side canyon, is the sixth longest natural rock span in the country at 243 feet. The trailhead is on the right just after crossing a concrete bridge three miles from US 191. A trail leads upcanyon, at some places along the creek, at others high on the banks. Small beaver ponds provide a place to cool off on a hot day. To see Morning Glory Natural Bridge, head two miles up the main canyon to the second side canyon on the right, then follow a good side trail a half mile up it to the long slender bridge. The spring and small pool un-

derneath keep the air cool even in summer; ferns, columbines, and poison ivy grow here. Elevation gain is 330 feet. William ("Nigger Bill") Granstaff was a mulatto who lived in the area from about 1877 to 1881. Modern sensibilities have changed his nickname to "Negro Bill."

Experienced hikers can continue up the main canyon about eight miles and rockscramble (no trail) up the right side, then drop into Rill Creek that leads to the North Fork of Mill Creek and into Moab. Total distance is about 16 miles one-way; you'll have to find your own way between canyons. The upper Negro Bill and Rill canyons can also be reached from Sand Flats Road. The Moab and Castle Valley 15-minute and Moab 1:100,000 topo maps cover the route. This would be a good overnight trip, though fast hikers have done it in a day. Expect to do some wading and rockscrambling. Water from the creeks and springs is available in both canyon systems; purify first.

A car shuttle is necessary between the Negro Bill and Mill Creek trailheads. Mill Creek is reached from the end of Powerhouse Lane on the east edge of Moab (see the Moab map), but DON'T PARK HERE. Vehicle break-ins are a serious problem. Either have someone meet or drop you off here or park closer to town near houses. A hike up the North Fork offers very pretty scenery. A deep pool and waterfall lie three-quarters of a mile upstream; follow Mill Creek upstream and take the left (north) fork. Negro Bill and Mill Creek canyons are BLM wilderness study areas.

La Sal Mountains Loop Road

This paved scenic road goes through Castle Valley, climbs high into the La Sals, then loops back to Moab. Allow at least three hours to drive the 62-mile loop. Turnoff from UT 128 is 15.5 miles up from US 191. See "La Sal Mountains" later in this chapter.

Onion Creek Road

A graded county road turns southeast off the highway 20 miles from US 191 and heads up Onion Creek, crossing it many times. Avoid this route if storms threaten. The unpleasant-smelling creek contains poisonous arsenic and selenium. Colorful rock formations of dark-red sandstone line the creek, and you'll cross an upthrusted block of crystalline gypsum. After about eight miles the road climbs steeply out of Onion Creek to upper Fisher Valley and a junction with Kokopelli's Trail, which follows a jeep road over this part of its route.

Fisher Towers

Gothic spires of dark-red sandstone soar as high as 900 feet above Professor Valley. The BLM has a picnic area nearby and a hiking trail that skirts the base of the three main towers; Titan, the highest, is the third one. Titan is one mile from the picnic area, and a viewpoint overlooking Onion Creek is 1.1 miles farther. Carry water for this moderately difficult hike. In 1962, three climbers from Colorado made the first ascent of Titan Tower. The almost vertical rock faces, overhanging bulges, and sections of rotten rock made for an exhausting three and one half days of climbing (the party descended to the base for two of the nights). Their final descent from the summit took only six hours. See the November 1962 issue of *National Geographic* magazine for the story and photos. Supposedly, the name "Fisher" is not that of a pioneer, but a corruption of the geologic term "fissure" (a narrow crack). An unpaved road turns southeast off UT 128 near Milepost 21 (21 miles from US 191) and continues in two miles to the picnic area.

Dewey Bridge

A modern two-lane concrete bridge has replaced the picturesque wood and steel suspension bridge built in 1916. Here, the BLM has built the Dewey Bridge Recreation Site with a picnic area, trailhead, boat launch, and a small campground. Bicyclists and hikers can still use the old bridge; an interpretive sign explains its history. Drivers can continue on the highway to I-70 through rolling hills nearly devoid of vegetation.

Westwater Canyon

Wild rapids lie upstream of Dewey Bridge. The Colorado River cut this narrow gorge into dark metamorphic rock. A river trip by raft or kayak can be done in one day or in a more leisurely two days. Camping is limited to a single night. Unlike most desert rivers, this section of the Colorado also offers good river running at low water levels in late summer and autumn. Westwater Canyon's inner gorge, where boaters face their greatest challenge, is only about three and one

half miles long. Scenic sandstone canyons, however, are enjoyed upstream and downstream. Boaters can put in at the BLM's Westwater Ranger Station in Utah or at Loma boat launch in Colorado. A start at Loma adds a day or two to the trip and the sights of Horsethief and Ruby canyons. Normal take out is at Cisco, though it's possible to continue 16 miles on slow-moving water through open country to Dewey Bridge. The **Dolores River,** also enjoyed by river runners, joins the Colorado about two miles upstream from Dewey Bridge. The season lasts mid-May to mid-June—none at all in dry years. Boaters need a permit and experience for both rivers; kayakers should have their rolls down well. The BLM office in Moab handles permits and provides information for these rivers.

Top-Of-The-World Road

This bumpy 4WD road climbs to an overlook with outstanding views of Fisher Towers, Fisher Valley, Onion Creek, and beyond. I turn right (east) on the Entrada Bluffs Road (just before crossing Dewey Bridge). After five and one half miles, keep straight on a dirt road when the main road curves left, then immediately turn right (south) and go uphill 100 yards through a gate (gateposts are railroad ties) and continue about four and one half miles on the Top-of-the-World Road to the rim. Elevation here is 6,800 feet, nearly 3,000 feet higher than the Colorado River.

NORTH OF MOAB

Mill Creek Dinosaur Trail

A short trail with numbered stops identifies the bones of dinosaurs who lived here 150 million years ago. You'll see fossilized wood too. Pick up the brochure from the Moab Information Center or at the trailhead. From Moab, go 14 miles north on US 191 (or four miles north of the Dead Horse Point turnoff) and turn left two miles on a dirt road, keeping right at a fork 1.1 miles in. Many other points of interest can be seen nearby. A copper mill and tailings dating from the late 1800s lies across the canyon. Halfway Stage Station ruins, where travelers once stopped on the Thompson to Moab run, are a short distance down the other road fork. Jeepers and mountain bikers can do a 13- to 14-mile loop to Monitor and Merrimac buttes (an information sign just in from US 191 has a map and details).

Other Areas
Many areas just outside Canyonlands and Arches national parks have beautiful canyon country. You'll find a 4WD, high-clearance vehicle necessary here for most of the roads. Mountain bikers and hikers can find good places to explore too. Near Canyonlands National Park, the author especially enjoyed the Gemini Bridges Road; mountain bicyclists like the trip and often arrange a shuttle to pick them up at the bottom. Farther north, the author did a three-day drive on jeep roads to Spring Canyon Point (overlooking Green River), Rainbow Rocks (colorful sand-stone hills), Tenmile Point (overlook of Green River), Tenmile Wash (desert oasis), Red Wash (red-rock desert), White Wash (slickrock, huge sand dunes), and Crystal Geyser (cold-water geyser near town of Green River). Klondike Bluffs, just west of Arches National Park, has very scenic slickrock and fins. You'll find detailed travel information on these and other places in the books and separate maps by F.A. Barnes *Canyon Country Off-Road Vehicle Trails: Island Area* (north of Canyonlands National Park) and *Canyon Country Off-Road Vehicle Trails: Arches & La Sals Areas* (around Arches National Park). The BLM takes care of nearly all this land; staff in the Moab offices may know current road and trail conditions.

porcupine (Erethizon dorsatum)

LOUISE FOOTE

LA SAL MOUNTAINS

The forests and lakes in Utah's second-highest mountain range provide a dramatic contrast to the barren slickrock and sands of the surrounding desert. Mount Peale (elev. 12,721 feet) crowns the range at a height nearly 9,000 feet above the Colorado River. Volcanic intrusions formed the La Sals about 30 million years ago, twisting and upturning surrounding rock layers at the same time. Streams and glaciers later carved knife-like ridges in the peaks and deep canyons in the foothills. The range comprises three distinct mountain groups in an area about 15 miles long from north to south and six miles wide. Major peaks in the northern part are Mt. Waas (12,331 feet), Manns Peak (12,273 feet), and Mt. Tomasaki (12,230 feet). The middle group contains Mt. Mellenthin (12,646 feet), Mt. Peale (12,721 feet), and Mt. Tukuhnikivatz (12,483 feet). The Indian name of this last mountain is reputed to mean "Land Where the Sun Shines Longest." South Mountain (11,798 feet) dominates the southern group.

Wildlife you might see includes black bear (one of the state's largest populations lives here), Rocky Mountain elk, mule deer, mountain lion, badger, ringtail cat, porcupine, pika, Merriam's turkey, and golden eagle. Native cutthroat and some brook and brown trout swim in streams at the middle to higher elevations. Deer and Mill Creek contain rainbow trout. Early Spanish explorers, seeing the range when it was covered with snow, named it La Sal ("Salt"). Other names include "Salt Mountains" and "Elk Mountains." Gold fever peaked near the turn of the century with activity concentrated in Miners and Gold basins. Old mines and ruins of former mining camps can still be found in these areas.

Hiking In The La Sals
Miners traveling through the mountains during the boom years built many of the trails in use today. The current network of about 18 trails totals about 65 miles. Trails cross the range from north to south and branch off to scenic lakes, basins, and canyons. Hiking conditions range from easy to difficult. Horseback riders can use the trails too. Signs mark most trailheads and

junctions, but backcountry users should still have topo maps and a compass. Nearly all the canyons and valleys have springs or streams (purify first). Climbers can choose from half a dozen peaks exceeding 12,000 feet. All summit routes require rockscrambling and route-finding skills. Hazards include loose rock, lightning, and altitude sickness. Mount Peale can be climbed from the south off La Sal Pass Road from about three-quarters of a mile east of La Sal Pass; a jeep track here can be followed up a valley to either Mt. Peale or Mt. Tukuhnikivatz. Look for the most gradual slope; the best footing is found near the trees where roots have stabilized the dirt and rocks. The pass itself also makes a good starting point for Mt. Tukuhnikivatz. See the 7½-minute topo maps or the 1:100,000 La Sal map. Road conditions may be good enough for cars on the east side via UT 46, but the west side from Pack Creek has much steeper and rougher conditions—don't try this road without a high-clearance vehicle! The Moab Information Center is the place to start your search for trail and climbing information.

Winter Sports
Cross-country skiers often head to Miners Basin, Beaver Basin, Geyser Pass, Gold Basin, La Sal Pass, and Dark Canyon. The La Sal Mountains Loop Road (southern section) and four and one half miles of the Geyser Pass Road are plowed. Snowmobilers may also use the roads and trails in the mountains. Travelers here need proper experience, equipment, and knowledge of avalanche hazards and means of rescue. Always go with a companion. The Moab Information Center has information on groomed trails and marked routes for skiers and snowmobilers; you can also call 250-SNOW for information.

LA SAL MOUNTAINS LOOP ROAD

This paved road on the west side of the range provides a good introduction to the high country. Side roads and trails lead to lakes, alpine meadows, and old mining areas. Viewpoints overlook Castle Valley, Arches and Canyonlands national parks, Moab Rim, and other scenic features. Vegetation along the drive runs the whole range from cottonwoods, sage, and rabbitbrush of the desert to forests of aspen, fir, and spruce. The 62-mile loop road can easily take a full day with stops for scenic overlooks, a picnic, and a bit of hiking or fishing. Because of the high elevations, the loop's season usually lasts May through October. The following road log lists the major points of interest along the way (the loop is equally good driven in the other direction too). Stock up on supplies in Moab, as there aren't any stores or gas stations after leaving town. It's a good idea to check current backroad conditions with the U.S. Forest Service office in Moab before venturing off the Loop Road.

Mile 0.0: Downtown Moab; head south on US 191 (Main St.).

Mile 8.0: Turn left (east) on the La Sal Mountains Loop Road near Milepost 118.

Mile 10.1: Ken's Lake, an undeveloped fishing and swimming area, is reached by a gravel road to the left. Fishermen angle for rainbow trout and bass. A 645-foot tunnel brings water from Mill Creek.

Mile 13.4: Pack Creek Picnic Area is three miles to the right on a paved road; elevation is 6,800 feet. The nearby Pack Creek Ranch offers accommodations, meals, and guided pack trips (tel. 259-5505). The La Sal Pass Road (high-clearance vehicles required because of rough and steep grades) continues past the picnic area to the 10,100-foot pass south of Mt. Tukuhnikivatz and Mt. Peale. The pass usually doesn't open until late June.

Mile 20.1: Geyser Pass Road (dirt) on the right climbs to Gold Basin (seven and one half miles), 10,600-foot Geyser Pass (eight miles), and other areas in the La Sals. Cars can usually be driven to the pass and lower edge of Gold Basin; elsewhere high-clearance vehicles may be needed. Geyser Pass doesn't open until late June in most years.

Mile 21.5: Mill Creek bridge; Oowah Lake is three miles to the right on an unpaved road (usually okay for cars when dry); road is open from about early June to late October. Steep forested slopes enclose this pretty reservoir at an elevation of 8,800 feet. A small **campground** near the lake is free; no drinking water. Trails go to Warner Lake (one and one half miles), Clark

Lake (one and one half miles), Boren Mesa (a half mile), Geyser Pass Road (three miles), and other destinations.

Mile 22.8: Warner Lake is five and one half miles to the right on a gravel road, which follows a ridge with good views of the peaks to the east and canyon country to the west. **Warner Campground** at the end of the road has drinking water from early June to early October ($5); elevation is 9,200 feet. A short walk across a meadow leads to Warner Lake. Trail destinations from the road's end include Oowah Lake (one and one half miles), Burro Pass (three and one half miles), and Dry Fork (one and one half miles).

Mile 25.3: Sand Flats Road to Moab (20 miles) turns left through very scenic canyon country; a high-clearance vehicle is recommended.

Mile 27.7: An overlook on the left side of the road with a great panorama of Castle Valley and Arches National Park.

Mile 29.2: Miners Basin is three miles right and Pinhook Battleground Monument is two miles left; a high-clearance vehicle may be needed for either road. The lure of gold still brings prospectors to Miners Basin; some claims may be closed to visitors. The last Indian conflict in the region took place in 1881 in Pinhook Valley. A headstone marks the grave of eight whites killed in the engagement.

Mile 33.8: Gateway Road to right. This road crosses the northern slopes of the La Sals to the old mining town of Gateway, Colorado. Back roads branch south into the La Sals and north into canyon country. Castleton townsite is near the Gateway Road turnoff. Castleton was founded in about 1890 as a supply center for miners and ranchers. Its population quickly exceeded that of Moab, but it faded away in the early 1900s and little remains today.

Mile 37.5: Round Mountain, an old volcanic neck, rises from the center of Castle Valley.

Mile 39.5: The prominent rock spires of Castle Rock and of the Priest and Nuns tower above the north side of the valley.

Mile 44.5: Junction with UT 128 along the Colorado River. Turn left 17.5 miles for Moab to complete the loop or right for Fisher Towers and Dewey Bridge. See "Utah Scenic Byway 128 and Trails" under "Exploring the Canyon Country near Moab," above.

ARCHES NATIONAL PARK

A concentration of arches of marvelous variety has formed within the maze of sandstone fins at the park. Balanced rocks and tall spires add to the splendor. Paved roads and short hiking trails provide easy access to some of the more than 1,500 arches in the park. If you're short on time, a drive to the Windows Section (23.5 miles roundtrip) allows a look at some of the largest and most spectacular arches. To visit all the stops and to hike a few short trails would take all day. The entrance fee of $4 per vehicle ($2 bicyclists) is good for seven days at Arches only. The park brochure available at the entrance station and visitor center has a map of major scenic features, drives, trails, and back roads.

How The Arches Got Here

An unusual combination of geologic forces created the arches. About 300 million years ago, evaporation of inland seas left behind a salt layer more than 3,000 feet thick in the Paradox Basin of this region. Sediments, including those that later became the arches, then covered the salt. Unequal pressures caused the salt to gradually flow upward in places, bending the overlying sediments as well. Those upfolds, or anticlines, later collapsed when ground water dissolved the underlying salt. The faults and joints caused by the uplift and collapse opened the way for erosion to carve hundreds of free-standing fins. Alternate freezing and thawing action and exfoliation (flaking caused by expansion when water or frost penetrates the rock) continued to peel away more rock until holes formed in some of the fins. Rockfalls within the holes helped to enlarge the arches. Nearly all arches in the park eroded out of Entrada Sandstone.

Eventually all the present arches will collapse, but we should have plenty of new ones by the time that happens! The fins' uniform strength and hard upper surfaces have proved ideal for arch formation. Not every hole in the rock is an arch. The opening must be at least three feet in one direction and light must be able to pass through. Although the term "windows" often refers to openings in large walls of rock, windows and arches are really the same. Water seeping through the sandstone from above has created a second type of arch—the pothole arch. You may also come across a few natural bridges, cut from the rock by perennial water runoff.

Desert Life

Elevation at the park ranges from 3,960 feet along the Colorado River to 5,653 feet in the Windows area. Annual precipitation averages only 10-11 inches. Even so, plants and wildlife have found niches in this rugged high desert country. Shrubs and grasslands cover most of the land not occupied by barren rock. Cottonwood trees grow along some of the washes while piñon pine and juniper form pygmy forests at the higher elevations. Specially adapted plant communities can be found in the dark cryptobiotic crusts on the soil. Hanging gardens surround springs and seeps. Tracks across the sands show the presence of shy or nocturnal wildlife. Animals include mule deer, coyote, gray fox, porcupine, bobcat, ringtail cat, kangaroo rat, antelope ground squirrel, collared lizard, and midget faded rattlesnake.

History

Prehistoric Anasazi and Fremont Indians hunted in the area and collected wild plant foods. The modern Utes hunted here too. Chert, a hard rock from Salt Valley, provided material for toolmaking. Rock art and artifacts mark the former presence of these tribes. Most of the early settlers and cowboys of the region paid little attention to the scenery. However, in 1923 a prospector by the name of Alexander Ringhoffer interested officials of the Rio Grande Railroad in the scenic attractions at what he called "Devils Garden" (now known as Klondike Bluffs). The railroad men liked the area and contacted Stephen Mather, first director of the National Park Service. Mather started the political process that led to designation of two small areas as a national monument in 1929, but Ringhoffer's Devils Garden wasn't included until later. Early visitors had to endure travel over nonexistent or barely passable roads; see the August 1947 issue of *National Geographic* magazine for a well-written account of the monument as it once was. It grew in size over the years and became Arches National Park in 1971. The park now has 73,379 acres—it's small enough to be appreciated in one day, yet large enough to warrant extensive exploration.

Visitor Center

Located just past the entrance booth, the visitor center provides a good introduction of what to expect ahead. Exhibits identify the rock layers, describe the geologic and human history, and illustrate some of the wildlife and plants of the park. Staff will present a short slide program upon request and answer your questions. Details of special activities are posted. Rangers host campfire programs and lead a wide variety of guided walks during the main season (April through September). Checklists, pamphlets, books, maps, posters, postcards, and film can be purchased. Hikers may obtain advice and the required free backcountry permit (for overnight trips) from a ranger. The easy 0.2-mile **Desert Nature Trail** begins in front of the visitor center and identifies some of the native plants. Picnic areas are located outside the visitor center and at Balanced Rock and Devils Garden. The park is open all year; visitor center hours are daily 8 a.m.-4:30 p.m. (may be extended in summer). Arches National Park is five miles north of downtown Moab on US 191, Box 907, Moab, UT 84532, tel. 259-8161.

Devils Garden Campground

The park's campground is located near the end of the 18-mile scenic drive. It's open all year with water; $8. Try to arrive early during the busy Easter to October season; only groups

can reserve spaces. Elevation here is 5,355 feet. During summer evenings, rangers at the Campfire Circle tell about the park's geology, history, wildlife, flora, and environment.

Hiking, Biking, And Climbing

Established trails lead to many fine arches and overlooks that can't be seen from the road. You're free to wander cross-country too, but please stay on rock or in washes to avoid damaging the fragile cryptobiotic soils. Wear good walking shoes with rubber soles for travel across slickrock. The summer sun can be especially harsh on the unprepared hiker—don't forget water, hat, and sunscreen. The desert rule is to carry at least one gallon of water per person for an all-day hike. Take a map and compass for off-trail hiking. Be cautious on the slickrock; the soft rock can crumble easily. Also, remember that it's easier to go up a steep slickrock slope than to come back down! Almost any spot in the park can be reached on a day-hike, though there are some good overnight possibilities. Areas for longer trips include Courthouse Wash in the southern part of the park and Salt Wash in the eastern part. All backpacking is done off trail. A backcountry permit must be obtained from a ranger before camping in the backcountry. Hiking regulations include no fires, no pets, camping out of sight of any road (at least one mile away) or trail (at least a half mile away), and camping at least 300 feet from a recognizable archaeological site or nonflowing water source. Bicycles *must* stick to established roads in the park; cyclists have to contend with heavy traffic on the narrow paved roads and dusty, washboarded surfaces on the dirt roads. Beware of the deep sand on the 4WD roads. Nearby BLM and Canyonlands National Park areas offer much better mountain biking. Rock climbers don't need a permit, though they should first discuss their plans with a ranger. Most features named on USGS maps are *closed* to climbing.

ringtail cat
(Bassariscus astutus)

LOUISE FOOTE

SIGHTS AND HIKES ALONG THE PARK ROAD

A road guide to Arches National Park, available at the visitor center, has detailed descriptions that correspond to place names along the main road. Be sure to stop only in parking lots and designated pullouts. Watch out for others who are sightseeing in this popular park. The following are major points of interest.

Moab Fault

The park road begins a long but well-graded climb from the visitor center up the cliffs to the northeast. A pullout on the right after 1.1 miles gives a good view of Moab Canyon and its geology. The rock layers on this side of the canyon have slipped down more than 2,600 feet in relation to the other side. Movement took place about 6 million years ago along the Moab Fault, which follows the canyon floor. Rock layers at the top of the far cliffs are nearly the same age as those at the *bottom* on this side! If you could stack the rocks of this side on top of rocks on the other side, you'd have a complete stratigraphic column of the Moab area—more than 150 million years' worth.

Park Avenue

South Park Avenue Overlook and Trailhead are on the left 2.1 miles from the visitor center. Great sandstone slabs form a "skyline" on each side of this dry wash. A trail goes north one mile down the wash to North Park Avenue Trailhead (1.3 miles ahead by road). Arrange to be picked up there or backtrack to your starting point. The large rock monoliths of Courthouse Towers rise north of Park Avenue. Only a few small arches exist now, though major arches may have formed in the past.

Balanced Rock

This gravity-defying formation is on the right eight and one half miles from the visitor center. A boulder more than 55 feet high rests precariously atop a 73-foot pedestal. Chip Off the Old Block, a much smaller version of Balanced Rock, stood nearby until it collapsed in the winter of 1975-76. For a closer look at Balanced Rock, take the 0.3-mile trail encircling it. There's a picnic area across the road. Author Edward Abbey lived in a trailer near Balanced Rock during a season as a park ranger in the 1950s; his journal became the basis for the classic *Desert Solitaire.*

Windows Section

Turn right two and one half miles on a paved road past Balanced Rock. Short trails one-quarter to one mile long (one-way) lead from the road's end to some massive arches. Windows Trailhead is the start for North Window (an opening 51 feet high and 93 feet wide), South Window (66 feet high and 105 feet wide), and Turret Arch (64 feet high and 39 feet wide). Double Arch, a short walk from a second trailhead, is an unusual pair of arches; the larger opening measures 105 feet high and 163 feet wide—best appreciated by walking inside. The smaller opening is 61 feet high and 60 feet wide. Together, the two arches frame a large opening overhead, but this isn't considered a true arch.

Garden of Eden Viewpoint, on the way back to the main road, has a good panorama of Salt Valley to the north. Under the valley, the massive body of salt and gypsum that's responsible for the arches comes close to the surface. Tiny Delicate Arch (described below) can be seen across the valley on a sandstone ridge. Early visitors to the Garden of Eden saw rock formations resembling Adam (with an apple) and Eve. Two other viewpoints of the Salt Valley area lie farther north on the main road.

Delicate Arch

Drive north two and one half miles on the main road from the Windows junction and turn right 1.8 miles to the Wolfe Ranch, where a bit of pioneer history survives. John Wesley Wolfe came to this spot in 1888, hoping the desert climate would provide relief for health problems related to a Civil War injury. He found a good spring high in the rocks, grass for cattle, and water in Salt Wash to irrigate a garden. The ranch that he built provided a home for him and some of his family for more than 20 years, and cattlemen later used it as a line ranch. Then sheepherders brought in their animals, which so overgrazed the range that the grass has yet to recover. A trail guide available at the entrance tells about the Wolfe family and features of their ranch. The weather-beaten cabin built in 1906 still survives. A short trail leads to petroglyphs above Wolfe Ranch; figures of horses indicate that Ute Indians did the artwork. Park staff can give directions for other rock-art sites; great care should be taken not to touch the fragile artwork.

Delicate Arch stands in a magnificent setting atop gracefully curving slickrock. Distant canyons and the La Sal Mountains lie beyond. The span is 45 feet high and 33 feet wide. A moder-

Delicate Arch

ately strenuous hike to the arch begins at Wolfe Ranch and crosses the swinging bridge, climbs a slickrock slope, follows a gully, then contours across steep slickrock to the main overlook. Roundtrip distance is three miles with an elevation gain of 500 feet; carry water. This is one of the most scenic hikes in the park. Just before the end of the trail, walk up to a small arch for a framed view of the final destination. The classic photo of Delicate Arch is taken late in the afternoon when the sandstone glows with golden hues.

Another perspective of Delicate Arch can be obtained by driving 1.2 miles beyond Wolfe Ranch. Look for the small arch high above. A steep trail (a half mile roundtrip) climbs a hill for the best panorama.

Fiery Furnace

Return to the main road and continue three miles to the Fiery Furnace Viewpoint and Trailhead on the right. Closely packed sandstone fins form a maze of deep slots, with many arches and at least one natural bridge inside. The Fiery Furnace can be fun to explore (with the required free permit, obtainable at the Visitor Center), though route-finding is tricky. What look like obvious paths often lead to dead ends. Drop-offs and ridges make straight-line travel

impossible. It's easy to get lost! Ranger-led hikes of about one and one half hours during the summer season provide the best way to see the wonders within. You'll need a reservation for this trip, obtainable in person only from the visitor center up to 48 hours in advance. The Fiery Furnace gets its name from sandstone fins that turn flaming red on occasions when thin cloud cover at the horizon reflects the warm light of sunrise or sunset. Actually, the shady recesses provide a cool respite from the hot summer sun.

Broken Arches

Trailhead is on the right 2.4 miles past the Fiery Furnace turnoff. A short trail leads to small Sand Dune Arch (opening is eight feet high and 30 feet wide) tucked within fins. A longer trail (one mile roundtrip) crosses a field to Broken Arch, which you can also see from the road. The opening is 43 feet high and 59 feet wide. Up close, you'll see that the arch isn't really broken. These arches can also be reached by trail from near comfort station #3 of Devils Garden Campground. Low-growing Canyonlands biscuitroot, found only in areas of Entrada Sandstone, colonize sand dunes. Hikers can protect the habitat of the biscuitroot and other fragile plants by keeping to washes or rock surfaces.

Skyline Arch

Located on the right one mile past Sand Dune/Broken Arch Trailhead. In desert climates, erosion may proceed imperceptibly for centuries until a cataclysmic event happens. In 1940, a giant boulder fell from the opening of Skyline Arch, doubling the size of the arch in just seconds. The hole is now 45 feet high and 69 feet wide. A short trail leads to the base of the arch.

Devils Garden Trail

The trailhead, Devils Garden Picnic Area, and the campground all lie near the end of the main park road. Devils Garden offers fine scenery and more arches than any other section of the park. The trail leads past large sandstone fins to Landscape and six other named arches. Carry water if the weather is hot or if you might want to continue past the one-mile point at Landscape Arch. Adventurous hikers could spend days exploring the maze of canyons among the fins.

deep within the Fiery Furnace, on a ranger-led hike

The first two arches lie off a short side trail to the right. Tunnel Arch has a relatively symmetrical opening 22 feet high and 27 feet wide. The nearby Pine Tree Arch is named for a piñon pine that once grew inside; the arch has an opening 48 feet high and 46 feet wide. Continue on the main trail to Landscape Arch, which has an incredible 306-foot span (six feet longer than a football field!). This is one of the longest unsupported rock spans in the world. The thin arch looks ready to collapse at any moment. A rockfall from the arch on September 1, 1991, worries some people who fear the end may be near. Height is 106 feet. Distance from the trailhead is two miles roundtrip, an easy one-hour walk.

The trail narrows past Landscape Arch and continues a quarter mile to Wall Arch, in a long wall-like fin. The opening is 41 feet high and 68 feet wide. A short side trail branches off to the left beyond Wall to Partition Arch (26 feet high and 28 feet wide) and Navajo Arch (13 feet high and 41 feet wide). Partition was so named because a piece of rock divides the main opening from a smaller hole eight feet high and eight and one half feet wide. Navajo Arch is a rockshelter type; perhaps prehistoric Indians camped here. The main trail continues northwest and ends at Double O Arch (four miles roundtrip from the trailhead). Double O has a large oval-shaped opening (45 feet high and 71 feet wide) and a smaller hole (nine feet high and 21 feet wide) underneath. Dark Angel is a distinctive rock pinnacle a quarter mile northwest; cairns mark the way. Another primitive trail loops back to Landscape Arch via Fin Canyon. This route goes through a different area of Devils Garden but adds about one mile to your trip (three miles back to the trailhead instead of two). Pay careful attention to the trail markers to keep on the correct route.

Klondike Bluffs And Tower Arch

Relatively few visitors come to the spires, high bluffs, and fine arch in this northwestern section of the park. A fair-weather dirt road turns off the main drive 1.3 miles before Devils Garden Trailhead, winds down into Salt Valley, and heads northwest. After seven and one half miles, turn left one mile on the road signed "Klondike Bluffs" to the Tower Arch Trailhead. These roads may be washboarded but are usually okay in dry weather for cars; don't drive on them if storms threaten. The trail to Tower Arch winds past the Marching Men and other rock formations; the distance is three miles roundtrip. Alexander Ringhoffer, who discovered the arch in 1922, carved an inscription on the south column. The area can also be fun to explore off trail (map and compass needed). Those with 4WD vehicles can drive close to the arch on a separate jeep road. Tower Arch has an opening 34 feet high by 92 feet wide. A tall monolith nearby gave the arch its name.

Four-Wheel-Drive Road
A rough road near Tower Arch in the Klondike Bluffs turns southeast past **Eye of the Whale Arch** in Herdina Park to Balanced Rock on the main park road, 10.8 miles away. The road isn't particularly difficult for 4WD enthusiasts, though normal backcountry precautions should be taken. A steep sand hill north of Eye of the Whale Arch is very difficult to climb for vehicles coming from Balanced Rock; it's better to drive from the Tower Arch area instead.

Colorado Gooseneck and canyon country from Dead Horse Point

DEAD HORSE POINT STATE PARK

The land drops away in sheer cliffs from this lofty perch west of Moab. Nearly 5,000 square miles of rugged canyon country lie in the distance. Two thousand feet below, the Colorado River twists through a gooseneck on its long journey to the sea. The river and its tributaries have carved canyons that reveal a geologic layer cake of colorful rock formations. Even in a region of impressive views around nearly every corner, Dead Horse Point stands out for its exceptionally breathtaking panorama. You'll also see below you, along the Colorado River, the result of powerful underground forces: salt, under pressure, has pushed up overlying rock layers into an anticline. This formation, the Shafer Dome, contains potash that is being processed by the Moab Salt Plant. You can see the mine buildings, processing plant, and evaporation ponds (tinted blue to hasten evaporation).

A narrow neck of land only 30 yards wide connects the point with the rest of the plateau. Cowboys once herded wild horses onto the point, then placed a fence across the neck to make a 10-acre corral. They chose the desirable animals from the herd and let the rest go. According to one tale, a group of horses left behind after such a roundup became confused by the geography of the point. They couldn't find their way off and circled repeatedly until they died of thirst within sight of the river below. You may hear other stories of how the point got its name.

Besides the awe inspiring views, the park also offers a visitor center (with displays), campground, picnic area, group area, nature trail, and hiking trails. The point has become popular with hang gliders. If you are lucky in timing your visit, you may see one or more crafts gliding back and forth above or below the viewpoint. Dead Horse Point is easily reached by paved road, either as a destination itself or as a side trip on the way to Island in the Sky District of Canyonlands National Park. From Moab, head northwest 10 miles on US 191, then turn left 22 miles on UT 313. The drive along UT 313 climbs through a scenic canyon and tops out on a ridge with panoramas of distant mesas, buttes, mountains, and canyons. Several rest areas are along the road.

Visitor Center And Campground

Stop here for registration ($3 per vehicle for day use or $7 per vehicle camping Sun.-Thurs., $8 Friday, Saturday, and holidays) and exhibits about the park. Staff will answer questions and provide checklists of local flora and fauna. A short slide presentation is given on request. In summer, rangers give talks at the amphitheater behind the visitor center. Books, maps, posters, postcards, film, T-shirts, charcoal, ice, and soft drinks can be purchased. Open daily 8 a.m.-6 p.m. in summer (May 16 to September 15) and 9 a.m.-5 p.m. the rest of the year. Contact the park at Box 609, Moab, UT 84532, tel. 259-2614 or (800) 322-3770 (reservations). A short nature trail that begins outside introduces the high-desert country and its plants. Continue one and one half miles on the main road to viewpoints and picnic areas on the point itself. Primitive trails connect the point with several other overlooks, the visitor center, and the campground. Ask for a map at the visitor center.

Kayenta Campground, just past the visitor center, offers sites with electric hookups but no showers; open with water from about mid-March to late October. The campground nearly always fills up during the main season. Either make reservations or try to arrive by early afternoon to ensure a space. Winter visitors may camp on the point; no hookups are available but the restrooms have water.

CANYONLANDS NATIONAL PARK

The canyon country of southeastern Utah puts on its supreme performance in this vast park, which spreads across 527 square miles. The deeply entrenched Colorado and Green rivers meet in its heart, then continue south as the mighty Colorado through tumultuous Cataract Canyon Rapids. These two rivers form the **River District** and divide Canyonlands National Park into three other districts. **Island in the Sky** lies north between the rivers, the **Maze** is to the west, and **Needles** is to the east. Each has its own distinct character. No bridges connect the three land districts, so most visitors have to leave the park to go from one region to another. The huge park can be seen in many ways and on many levels. Paved roads reach a few areas, 4WD roads go to more places, and hiking trails reach still more, yet much of the land shows no trace of man's passage. To get the big picture, fly over this incredible complex of canyons (see "Air Tours" under "Practicalities" in the "Moab" section earlier in this chapter). However, only a river trip or a hike lets you experience the solitude and detail of the land. The park can be visited in any season of the year, with spring and autumn the best choices. Summer temperatures can get into the 100s F; carrying (and drinking) water becomes critical then; carry at least one gallon per person per day. Arm yourself with insect repellent from late spring to mid-summer. Winter days tend to be bright and sunny, though nighttime temperatures can dip into the teens or subzeros. Visitors coming in winter should inquire about travel conditions, as snow and ice occasionally close roads and trails at the higher elevations.

Visiting The Park

Come to any of the districts for great views, spectacular geology, a chance to see wildlife, and endless opportunities to explore. You won't find crowds or elaborate park facilities—most of Canyonlands remains a primitive backcountry park.

Island in the Sky District has paved roads on its top to impressive overlooks and to Upheaval Dome, a strange geologic feature. If you're short on time or don't want to make a rigorous back-

country trip, you'll find this district the best choice. The "Island," actually a large mesa, is much like Dead Horse Point on a giant scale. A narrow neck of land connects the north side of the Island with the "mainland." Hikers and those with suitable vehicles can drop off the Island in the Sky and descend about 1,300 feet to the White Rim 4WD Road, which follows cliffs of the White Rim around most of the Island.

Few visitors make it over to the **Maze District,** some of the wildest country in the United States. Only the rivers and a handful of 4WD roads and hiking trails provide access. Experienced hikers can explore the "maze" of canyons on unmarked routes. **Horseshoe Canyon Unit,** a detached section of Canyonlands National Park northwest of the Maze District, protects the Great Gallery, a group of pictographs left by prehistoric Indians.

Colorful rock spires prompted the name of the **Needles District.** Splendid canyons contain many arches, strange rock formations, and archaeological sites. Hikers enjoy day-hikes and backpack treks on the network of trails and routes within the district. Drivers with 4WD vehicles have their own challenging roads through canyons and other highly scenic areas. Overlooks and short nature trails can be enjoyed from the paved scenic drive in the park. State Highway 211 branches off US 191 south of Moab providing easy access to the Needles District.

The **River District** includes long stretches of the Green and Colorado. River running provides one of the best ways to experience the inner depths of the park. Boaters can obtain helpful literature and advice from park rangers. Groups planning their own trip through Cataract Canyon need a river-running permit. Flat water permits are also required and payment of a fee may be necessary.

Geology

Deep canyons of the Green and Colorado have sliced through rocks representing 150 million years of deposition. The Paradox Formation, exposed in Cataract Canyon, contains salt and other minerals responsible for some of the folded and faulted rock layers in the region. Under immense pressure of overlying rocks, the Paradox flows like plastic, forming domes where the rock layers are thinnest and causing cracks or faults as pressures rise and fall. Each of the overlying formations has a different color and texture; they're the products of ancient deserts, rivers, and seas that once covered this land. Views from any of the overlooks reveal that an immense quantity of rock has already been washed downriver toward California. Not so evident, however, is the 10,000 vertical feet of rock that geologists say once lay across the high mesas. The dry climate and sparse vegetation allow clear views of the remaining rock layers and the effects of erosion and deformation. You can read the geologic story at Canyonlands National Park in the 3,500 feet of strata that remain, from the bottom of Cataract Canyon to the upper reaches of Salt Creek in the Needles District.

Desert Life
Extremes of flash flood and drought, hot summers and cold winters, discourage all but the most hardy and adaptable life. Desert grasses, small flowering plants, cacti, and shrubs like blackbrush and saltbush survive on the mostly thin soils and meager eight to nine inches of annual precipitation. Trees either grow in cracks that concentrate rainfall and nutrients or rely on springs or canyon streams for moisture. Piñon pine and juniper prefer the higher elevations of the park, while cottonwoods live in the canyon bottoms that have permanent subsurface water. Tamarisk, an exotic streamside plant, and willows often form dense thickets on sandbars along the Green and Colorado rivers. The hanging gardens of lush vegetation that surround cliffside springs or seeps seem oblivious to the surrounding desert. Fragile desert ecology can easily be upset. Cattle, especially in the Needles District, once overgrazed the grasslands and trampled cryptobiotic crusts and other vegetation. Increased erosion and growth of undesirable exotic plants like cheatgrass have been the result. Scars left by roads and mines during the uranium frenzy of the 1950s can still be seen, most commonly in the Island in the Sky District.
Fewer than 10 species of fish evolved in the canyons of the Colorado and the Green. These fish developed streamlined bodies and strange features, such as humped backs, to cope with the muddy and varying river waters. Species include the Colorado squawfish, humpback chub, bonytail chub, and humpback sucker; most of these live nowhere else. All have suffered greatly reduced populations and restricted ranges due to recent dam building.
Of the approximately 65 mammal species living in the park, about one-third are rodents and another third are bats. You're most likely to see chipmunk, antelope ground squirrel, and rock squirrel, which are often active during the day. Most other animals wait until evening to come out and feed; in the morning look for tracks of mule deer, bighorn sheep, coyote, gray fox, badger, porcupine, spotted skunk, beaver, black-tailed jackrabbit, wood rat, kangaroo rat, and many species of mice.

History
Prehistoric Anasazi Indians once settled throughout this area, while the Fremont lived mostly west of the Green and Colorado rivers. Both groups departed from the region in the middle to late 1200s. They left behind hundreds of archaeological sites with rock art, granaries, dwellings, and stone tools. Nomadic Ute Indians later roamed through the canyons and drew rock art of their own. The Navajo may have made trips into the park area from the south during the 1800s.
At least one mountain man, Denis Julien, visited the Colorado and Green canyons in 1836, leaving his signatures but little else to tell of his travels. Julien may have been the first person to raft the rivers here. In 1859, Capt. John Macomb and his party noted the beautiful rock sculptures in Needles on an overland trip, but they judged the country worthless. Major John Wesley Powell led the first scientific expedition by boat through the Green and lower Colorado river canyons in 1869, then repeated this part of the journey in 1871-72. Cowboys brought in cattle during the 1870s. Some of their camps, corrals, and inscriptions still survive, though grazing no longer takes place in the park. The Powell expedition and the later cowboys named many of the park's features. Uranium prospectors swarmed through the area with Geiger counters during the 1950s, staking thousands of

ENDANGERED FISH OF THE COLORADO RIVER BASIN

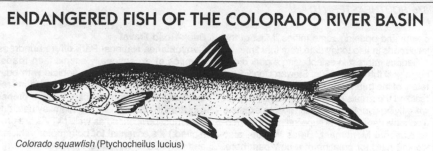

Colorado squawfish (Ptychocheilus lucius)
Native only to the Colorado and its major tributaries, this species is the largest minnow in North America. It has been reported as weighing up to 100 pounds and measuring six feet long. Loss of habitat due to dam construction has greatly cur- *tailed its size and range. Fishermen often confuse the smaller and more common roundtail chub (Gila robusta) with the Colorado squawfish; the chub is distinguished by a smaller mouth extending back only to the front of the eye.*

humpback chub (Gila cypha)
Scientists first described this fish only in 1940 and know little about its life. The small fish usually weighs in under two pounds and under 13 inches. Today the humpback chub hangs on the verge of extinction; it has retreated to a few small *areas of the Colorado River where the water still runs warm, muddy, and swift. The bonytail chub (Gila robusta elegans) has a similar size and shape, but without a hump; its numbers are also rapidly declining.*

humpback or razorback sucker
(Xyrauchen texanus)
This large sucker grows to weights of 10-16 pounds and lengths of about three feet. Its numbers have been slowly decreasing, especially above the Grand Canyon. They require warm, fast-flowing water to reproduce. Mating is done *as a bizarre ritual in the spring. When the female has selected a suitable spawning site, two male fish press against the sides of her body. The female begins to vibrate her body until the eggs and spermatozoa are expelled simultaneously. One female can spawn three times, but she uses a different pair of males each time.*

claims and opening some mines. Most of the jeep roads in use today date from that time.

Serious interest in establishing a park didn't begin until the early 1960s. Stewart Udall, Secretary of the Interior under President Kennedy, realized the area's potential as a national park while flying over the Colorado River to examine a possible dam site. The superintendent of Arches National Monument, Bates Wilson, also worked hard for creation of a new park here. Canyonlands National Park became a reality in 1964 and enlarged to its present size in 1971.

Visitor Centers And Information

Each of the three land districts has a visitor center near the park entrance, but you may find it convenient to stop at the Moab Information Center, corner of Main and Center, tel. 259-8825. The headquarters address for Canyonlands National Park is 2282 S.W. Resouce Blvd., Moab, UT 84532, tel. 259-7164 or 259-3911 (information). Any of the offices has brochures, maps, and books, as well as someone to answer your questions.

Vehicle camping is allowed only in established campgrounds and designated backcountry campsites. Except for the main campgrounds at Willow Flat (Island in the Sky) and Squaw Flat (Needles), you'll need a backcountry permit for overnight stays. There is a $10 fee for a backpacking permit and a $25 fee for a vehicle site permit. Each of the three districts has a different policy for backcountry vehicle camping—so it's a good idea to make sure that you understand the details. Backcountry permits will also be needed for any technical climbing and trips with stock; check with a ranger for details. Pets aren't allowed on trails and must always be leashed. No firewood collecting is permitted in the park; backpackers need stoves for cooking. Vehicle and boat campers can bring in firewood but must use grills or fire pans. The best maps for the park are a series of expensive topos printed on waterproof paper by Trails Illustrated; these have the latest trail and road information. A giant USGS topo map, Canyonlands National Park and Vicinity, has the same 1:62,500 scale at a lower cost, but without the updated information and fancy paper. Handouts from the ranger offices describe natural history, travel, and other aspects of the park.

Back-Road Travel

Canyonlands National Park offers hundreds of miles of exceptionally scenic jeep roads. Normally you must have a vehicle with both 4WD *and* high clearance. Park regulations require ALL motorized vehicles to have proper registration and licensing for highway use; drivers must be licensed as well. (ATV's are prohibited.) It's essential for both motor vehicles and bicycles to stay on existing roads to prevent damage to the delicate desert vegetation. Carry tools, extra fuel, water, and food in case of breakdown in a remote area. Mountain bicyclists enjoy travel on many of the backcountry roads too. Before making a trip, drivers and cyclists should talk with a ranger to register and to learn of current road conditions, which can change drastically from one day to the next. Also, the rangers will be more knowledgeable about where to seek help in case you become stuck. Primitive campgrounds are provided on most of the roads, but you'll need a backcountry permit from a ranger. Local author F.A. Barnes has written three sets of guidebooks and maps covering parts of Canyonlands National Park: *Canyon Country Off-Road Vehicle Trails: Island Area, Canyon Country Off-Road Vehicle Trails: Canyon Rims & Needles Areas,* and *Canyon Country Off-Road Vehicle Trails: Maze Area.* (Jack Bikers wrote the Maze book.)

the heart of Cataract Canyon

Cataract Canyon
(Colorado River)
by Navtec sportboat

RIVER DISTRICT

River Running Above The Confluence
Both the Green and Colorado rivers flow smoothly through their canyons above the confluence. Almost any shallow-draft boat can navigate these waters. Canoes, kayaks, rafts, and power boats are commonly used. Any travel requires advance planning because of the remoteness of the canyons and the scarcity of river access points. No campgrounds, supplies, or other facilities exist past Moab on the Colorado River or the town of Green River on the Green. All river runners must follow park regulations, which include the carrying of life jackets, use of a fire pan for fires, and packing out all garbage and solid human waste. The river flow on both the Colorado and the Green averages a gentle two to four mph (7-10 mph at high water). Boaters typically do 20 miles per day in canoes and 15 miles per day in rafts.

The Colorado has one modest rapid called the Slide, one and one half miles above the confluence, where rocks constrict the river to one-third of its normal width; the rapid is roughest during high water levels in May and June. This is the only difficulty on the 64 river miles from Moab. Inexperienced canoeists and rafters may wish to portage around it. The most popular launch points on the Colorado are the Moab Dock (just upstream from the US 191 bridge near town) and the Potash Dock (17 miles downriver on the Potash Road, UT 279).

On the Green, boaters at low water need to watch for rocky areas at the mouth of Millard Canyon (33.5 miles above the confluence, where a rock bar extends across the river) and at the mouth of Horse Canyon (14.5 miles above the confluence, where a rock and gravel bar on the right leaves only a narrow channel on the left side). The trip from the town of Green River through Labyrinth and Stillwater canyons is 120 miles. Launch places include Green River State Park (Green River) and Mineral Canyon (52 miles above the confluence, reached on a fair-weather road from UT 313).

No roads go to the confluence. Easiest return to civilization for nonmotorized craft is a pick-up by jetboat from Moab by Tex's Riverways or Tag-A-Long Tours (see "River Tours" under "Practicalties" in the "Moab" section earlier in this chapter). A far more difficult way out is hiking either of two trails just above the Cataract Canyon rapids to 4WD roads on the rim. Park rangers require that boaters above the confluence obtain a backcountry permit either in person from the Moab office or by mail (two weeks in advance). River notes on boating the Green and Colorado are available on request from the Moab office, tel. 259-3911. Belknap's *Canyonlands River Guide* has river logs and maps pointing out items of interest for the Green River below the town of Green River (UT) and all of the Colorado from the upper end of Westwater Canyon to Lake Powell. Don Baar's *A River Runner's Guide to Cataract Canyon* also has good coverage.

River Running
Through Cataract Canyon

The Colorado River enters Cataract Canyon at the confluence and picks up speed. The rapids begin four miles downstream and extend for the next 14 miles to Lake Powell. Especially in spring, the 26 or more rapids give a wild ride equal to the best in the Grand Canyon. The current zips along (up to 16 mph) and forms waves more than seven feet high! When the excitement dies down, boaters have a 34-mile trip across Lake Powell to Hite Marina; most people either carry a motor or arrange for a power boat to pick them up. Because of the real hazards of running the rapids, the National Park Service requires boaters to have proper equipment and a permit. Many people go on a commercial trip in which everything has been taken care of (write the park for a list of boat companies). Private groups need to contact the Canyonlands River Unit far in advance for permit details at 2282 W. Resource Blvd., Moab, UT 84532, tel. 259-3911.

ISLAND IN THE SKY DISTRICT

Panoramic views from the "Island" can be enjoyed from any point along the rim. You'll see much of the park and southeastern Utah. Short hiking trails lead to overlooks, Mesa Arch, Aztec Butte, Whale Rock, Upheaval Dome, and other features. Longer trails make steep, strenuous descents from the Island to the White Rim 4WD Road below. Elevations on the Island average about 6,000 feet. *Bring water for all hiking, camping, and travel on Island in the Sky.* No services are available, except at the visitor center in emergencies (bottled water is sold).

Visitor Center

Stop here for information about Island in the Sky and to see some exhibits; books and maps can be purchased. A $4 per vehicle charge is made unless you have a receipt issued within the last seven days from the Needles District of Canyonlands. Obtain a backcountry permit ($10 for backpack camping and $25 for a vehicle campsite) if making an overnight hike or planning to stay at campgrounds along the White Rim 4WD Road (reservations by mail, phone, or in person are required for sites; $25 reservation fee). Open daily 8 a.m.-4:30 p.m.

with reservations made from 12:30-4:30 pm. Mon.-Sat. (may close noon-1 p.m. in winter), tel. 259-4351. A bulletin board outside has park information. The visitor center is located just before crossing "The Neck" to Island in the Sky. From Moab, go northwest 10 miles on US 101, turn left 15 miles on UT 313 to the junction for Dead Horse Point State Park, then continue straight seven miles.

Shafer Canyon Overlook

Continue a half mile past the visitor center to this overlook on the left (just before crossing The Neck). Shafer Trail Viewpoint, across The Neck, provides another perspective a half mile farther. The Neck is a narrow land bridge just wide enough for the road, and it's the only vehicle access to the 40-square-mile Island in the Sky. The overlooks have good views east down the canyon and the incredibly twisting **Shafer Trail Road.** Cattlemen Frank and John Schafer built the trail in the early 1900s to move stock to additional pastures (the "c" in their name was later dropped by mapmakers). Uranium prospectors upgraded the trail to a 4WD road during the 1950s so that they could reach their claims at the base of the cliffs. Today the Shafer Trail Road connects the mesa top with the White Rim 4WD Road and the Potash Road 1,200 feet and four miles below. High-clearance vehicles should be used on the Shafer, preferably with 4WD if you plan to climb up. Road conditions can vary considerably, so it's a good idea to first contact a ranger.

Neck Spring Trail

The trail begins near the Shafer Canyon Overlook. A brochure should be available at the trailhead. This moderately difficult hike follows a five-mile loop down Taylor Canyon to Neck and Cabin springs, formerly used by ranchers, then climbs back to the Island in the Sky road at a second trailhead, a half mile south of the start. Elevation change is 300 feet. Water at the springs supports maidenhair fern and other water-loving plants. Also watch for birds and wildlife attracted to this spot. Bring water with you, as the springs aren't suitable for drinking.

Lathrop Trail

This is the only marked hiking route going all the way from Island in the Sky to the Colorado

River. The trailhead is on the left, 1.3 miles past The Neck. The first two and one half miles cross Gray's Pasture to the rim, then the trail descends steeply, dropping 1,600 feet over the next two and one half miles to the White Rim 4WD Road. Part of this section follows an old mining road past several abandoned mines, all relics of the uranium boom; don't enter the shafts as they're in danger of collapse and may contain poisonous gases. From the mining area, the route descends through a wash to the White Rim 4WD Road, follows the road a short distance south, then goes down Lathrop Canyon Road to the Colorado River, another four miles with a descent of 500 feet. Total distance for the strenuous hike is nine miles one-way with an elevation change of 2,100 feet. The trail has little shade and can be very hot.

Mesa Arch Trail
This easy trail leads to an arch on the rim. The trailhead is on the left five and one half miles from The Neck. On the way, the road crosses the grasslands and scattered juniper trees of Gray's Pasture. A trail brochure available at the start describes the ecology of the mesa. Hiking distance is only a half mile roundtrip with an 80-foot elevation change. The arch, eroded from Navajo Sandstone, frames views of rock formations below and the La Sal Mountains in the distance.

Murphy Point And Grand View Point
Go straight at the road junction just past the Mesa Arch Trailhead for these and other spectacular viewpoints. After two and one half miles, a rough dirt road turns right 1.7 miles to Murphy Point. Hikers can take **Murphy Trail,** which begins off the road to the point, to the White Rim 4WD Road. This strenuous route forks partway down; one branch follows Murphy Hogback (a ridge) to Murphy Campground on the 4WD road, and the other branch follows a wash to the road one mile south of the campground. A loop hike along both branches is nine miles roundtrip with an elevation change of 1,100 feet.

Continue two and one half miles on the main road past the Murphy Point turnoff to **Grand View Picnic Area,** a handy lunch stop. Two trails start here. **White Rim Overlook Trail** is an easy one-and-one-half-mile hike (roundtrip) east along a peninsula to an overlook of Monument

Basin and beyond. **Gooseberry Trail** drops off the mesa and descends some extremely steep grades to the White Rim 4WD Road just north of Gooseberry Campground; the strenuous trip is two and one half miles one-way with an elevation change of 1,400 feet.

Continue one mile on the main road past the picnic area to **Grand View Point,** perhaps the most spectacular panorama from Island in the Sky. Monument Basin lies directly below, and countless canyons, the Colorado River, the Needles, and mountain ranges are in the distance. **Grand View Trail** continues past the end of the road for other vistas from the point, which is the southernmost tip of Island in the Sky. The easy hike is one and one half miles roundtrip.

Green River Overlook And Willow Flat Campground
Return to the road junction, turn west a quarter mile, then turn south one and one half miles on an unpaved road to the overlook. Soda Springs Basin and a section of the Green River (deeply entrenched in Stillwater Canyon) can be seen below. Small Willow Flat campground is passed on the way to the overlook; it's open all year (no water or charge). Rangers present campfire programs here spring through autumn. Sites often fill except in winter; a sign near the visitor center indicates when they're full.

Aztec Butte Trail
The trailhead is on the right, one mile northwest of the road junction. Aztec Butte is one of the few areas at Island in the Sky with Indian ruins; shortage of water prevented permanent settlement. An easy trail climbs 200 feet in half a mile to the top of the butte for a good panorama of the Island.

Whale Rock
The trailhead is on the right, 4.4 miles northwest of the road junction. An easy trail climbs this sandstone hump near the outer rim of Upheaval Dome. Distance is a half mile roundtrip with an ascent of 100 feet.

Upheaval Dome
Continue to the end of the road, 5.3 miles northwest of the road junction, for a look at this geological curiosity. There's also a small **picnic area** here. The easy **Crater View Trail** leads

contorted rock layers inside Upheaval Dome

to overlooks on the rim of Upheaval Dome; the first viewpoint is a half mile roundtrip, and the second is one mile roundtrip. A fantastically deformed pile of rock lies below within a crater about three miles across and 1,200 feet deep. For many years, Upheaval Dome has kept geologists busy trying to figure out its origin. They once assumed that salt of the Paradox Formation pushed the rock layers upward to form the dome. Now, however, there is strong evidence that a meteorite impact caused the structure. The surrounding ring depression (caused by collapse) and the convergence of rock layers upward toward the center correspond precisely to known impact structures. Shatter cones and microscopic analysis also indicate an impact origin. When the meteorite struck, sometime in the last 150 million years, it formed a crater up to five miles across. Erosion removed some of the overlying rock, perhaps as much as a vertical mile. The underlying salt may have played a role in uplifting the central section.

Energetic hikers can reach Upheaval Dome from the parking area at the overlook or from White Rim 4WD Road below. **Syncline Loop**

Trail makes a strenuous eight-mile circuit completely around Upheaval Dome; elevation change is 1,200 feet. The trail crosses Upheaval Dome Canyon about halfway around from the overlook; walk east one and one half miles up the canyon to enter the crater itself. This is the only nontechnical route into the center of the dome. A hike around Upheaval Dome with a side trip to the crater totals 11 miles, best done as an overnight trip. Carry plenty of water for the entire trip; this dry country can be very hot in summer. The Green River is the only reliable source of water. From near Upheaval Campsite on White Rim 4WD Road, you can hike four miles on **Upheaval Trail** through Upheaval Canyon to a junction with the Syncline Loop Trail, then another 1 1/2 miles into the crater; elevation gain is about 600 feet.

Alcove Spring Trail
Another hiking possibility in the area, the Alcove Spring Trail leaves the road one and one half miles before the Upheaval Dome parking area and connects with the White Rim 4WD Road in Taylor Canyon. Total distance is 10 miles one-way (five miles on the trail in Trail Canyon and five miles on a jeep road in Taylor Canyon); elevation change is about 1,500 feet. Carry plenty of water—the strenuous trail is hot and dry.

White Rim Four-Wheel Drive Road
This driving adventure follows the White Rim below the sheer cliffs of Island in the Sky. Travel along the winding road presents a constantly changing panorama of rock, canyons, river, and sky. Keep an eye out for desert bighorn sheep. You'll see all three levels of Island in the Sky District, from the high plateaus to the White Rim to the rivers. Only 4WD vehicles with high clearance can make the trip. With the proper vehicle, driving is mostly easy but slow and winding; a few steep or rough sections have to be negotiated. The 100-mile trip takes two or three days. Allow an extra day to travel all the road spurs. Mountain bikers find this a great trip too; most cyclists arrange an accompanying vehicle to carry water and camping gear. Primitive campgrounds along the way provide convenient stopping places. You'll need to obtain reservations and a backcountry permit for the White Rim campsites from the Island in the Sky Visitor

Center; this can be done in person, by mail, or by phone, tel. 259-4351 Mon.-Sat. 12:30-4:30 p.m. Demand exceeds supply during the popular spring and autumn seasons, when you should make reservations as far in advance as possible. A $25 fee per reservation applies for White Rim trips. No services or developed water sources exist anywhere on the drive, so be sure to have plenty of fuel and water with some to spare. Access points are Shafer Trail Road (from near Island in the Sky) and Potash Road (UT 279 from Moab) on the east and Mineral Bottom Road on the west. White Rim Sandstone forms the distinctive plateau crossed on the drive. A close look at the rock reveals ripple marks and cross-beds laid down near an ancient coastline. The plateau's east side is about 800 feet above the Colorado River. On the west side, the plateau meets the bank of the Green River.

MAZE DISTRICT

Only adventurous and experienced travelers will want to visit this rugged land west of the Green and Colorado rivers. Vehicle access wasn't even possible until 1957, when mineral-exploration roads first entered what later became Canyonlands National Park. Today, you'll need a high-clearance 4WD vehicle, a horse, or your own two feet to get around. The National Park Service plans to keep this district in its remote and primitive condition. An airplane flight, recommended if you can't come overland, provides the only easy way to see the scenic features here. However, the National Park Service is currently studying the future of such flights and they may be curtailed or discontinued. The names of erosional forms describe the landscape—Orange Cliffs, Golden Stairs, the Fins, Land of Standing Rocks, Lizard Rock, the Doll House, Chocolate Bars, the Maze, and Jasper Canyon. The many-fingered canyons of the Maze gave the district its name. Although not a true maze, these canyons give that impression.

Ranger Station And Information

Glen Canyon National Recreation Area borders the Maze District on the west with scenic canyons, cliffs, rock monuments, and overlooks of its own. The Hans Flat Ranger Station for the Maze District lies inside Glen Canyon N.R.A.;

the station is open daily 8 a.m.-4:30 p.m., tel. 259-2652. (In winter the station may close, but a ranger is usually available.) *There are no developed sources of water in the Maze District.* Hikers can obtain water from springs in some canyons (check with a ranger to find which are flowing) or from the rivers; purify all water before drinking. The Maze District has nine camping areas (two at Maze Overlook, seven at Land of Standing Rocks) with a 15-person, three-vehicle limit. A backcountry permit is needed for these or for backpacking. Note that a backcountry permit in this district is *not* a reservation—you may have to share a site with someone else, especially in the popular spring months. Also, as in the rest of the park, only designated sites can be used for vehicle camping. You don't need a permit to camp in the Glen Canyon N.R.A. or on BLM land. The Trails Illustrated topo map of the Maze District describes and shows the few roads and trails here; some routes and springs are marked on it too. Agile hikers experienced in desert and canyon travel may want to take off on cross-country routes, which are either unmarked or lightly cairned. Extra care must be taken for preparation and travel in both Glen Canyon N.R.A. and the Maze. Always talk with the rangers beforehand to find out current conditions. Be sure to leave an itinerary with someone reliable who can contact the rangers if you're overdue. Unless the rangers know where to look for you in case of breakdown or accident, a rescue could take weeks!

Dirt roads to the Hans Flat Ranger Station and Maze District branch off from UT 24 (a half mile south of the Goblin Valley State Park turnoff), and UT 95 (take Hite/Orange Cliffs Road between the Dirty Devil and Hite bridges at Lake Powell). Easiest way in is the graded 46-mile road from UT 24; it's fast, though sometimes badly corrugated. The Hite Road (also called Orange Cliffs Road) is longer, bumpier, and, for some drivers, tedious; it's 54 miles from the turnoff at UT 95 to the Hans Flat Ranger Station via the Flint Trail. In winter or other times when the Flint Trail is closed, drivers must take the Hite Road to reach the Maze Overlook, Land of Standing Rocks, and the Doll House areas. All roads to the Maze District cross Glen Canyon National Recreation Area. From UT 24, 2WD vehicles with good clearance can travel to Hans

Flat Ranger Station and other areas near, but not actually in, the Maze District. (All the mileages given here come from the author's vehicle—they're not always the same as signs.)

North Point
Hans Flat Ranger Station, and this peninsula that reaches out to the east and north, lie at an elevation of about 6,400 feet. Panoramas from North Point take in the vastness of Canyonlands, including all three districts. From **Millard Canyon Overlook,** just 0.9 mile past the ranger station, you can see arches, Cleopatra's Chair, and features as distant as the La Sals and Book Cliffs. For the best views, drive out to Panorama Point, about 10.5 miles one-way from the ranger station. A spur road goes left two miles to Cleopatra's Chair, a massive sandstone monolith and area landmark. The trailhead for **North Trail Canyon** begins just down the North Point Road (or 2.4 miles from the ranger station). Two-wheel-drive vehicles can usually reach this spot, where hikers can follow the trail down seven miles (1,000-foot elev. change) through the Orange Cliffs, follow 4WD roads six miles to the Maze Overlook Trail, then one more mile into a canyon of the Maze. Because North Point belongs to the Glen Canyon N.R.A., you can camp on it without a permit.

Flint Trail
This narrow, rough, 4WD road connects the Hans Flat area with the Maze Overlook, Doll House, and other areas below. The road, driver, and vehicle should all be in good condition before driving it! Winter snow and mud close the road from late December into March, as can rainstorms anytime. Check conditions first with a ranger. If you're starting from the top, stop at the signed overlook just before the descent to scout for vehicles headed up (the Flint Trail has very few places to pass). The top of the Flint Trail is 14 miles south of Hans Flat Ranger Station; at the bottom, 2.8 nervous miles later, you can turn left two miles to the Golden Stairs Trailhead or 12.7 miles to the Maze Overlook; keep straight 28 miles to the Doll House or 39 miles to UT 95.

The Golden Stairs
Hikers can descend this steep two-mile (one-way) foot trail to the Land of Standing Rocks Road in a fraction of the time it takes for drivers to follow roads! The trail offers good views of Ernies Country and the Fins, but lacks shade or water. The upper trailhead is east two miles from the road junction at the bottom of the Flint Trail.

Maze Overlook
Now you're actually in Canyonlands National Park and at the edge of the sinuous canyons of the Maze. You can stay at primitive camping areas (backcountry permit needed) and enjoy the views. **Maze Overlook Trail** drops one mile into the South Fork of Horse Canyon; a rope helps to lower packs in a difficult section. Once in the canyon you can walk around to the Harvest Scene, a group of prehistoric pictographs, or do a variety of day-hikes or backpacks. These canyons have water in some places; check with the ranger when getting your permits. At least four routes connect with the 4WD road in Land of Standing Rocks; see the Trails Illustrated map. Hikers can also climb Petes Mesa from the canyons or head downstream to explore Horse Canyon (a dry fall blocks access to the Green River, however).

Land Of Standing Rocks
Here, in the heart of the Maze District, strange-shaped rock spires stand guard over myriad canyons. Six camping areas offer scenic places to stay (permit needed). Hikers have a choice of many ridge and canyon routes from the 4WD road, a trail to a confluence overlook, and a trail that descends to the Colorado River near Cataract Canyon. The well-named Chocolate Bars can be reached by a hiking route from The Wall near the beginning of the Land of Standing Rocks. A good day-hike makes a loop from Chimney Rock to the Harvest Scene pictographs; take the ridge route (toward Pete's Mesa) in one direction and the canyon fork northwest of Chimney Rock on the other. Follow your topo map through the canyons and cairns between the canyons and ridge. Other routes from Chimney Rock lead to lower Jasper Canyon (no river access) or into Shot and Water canyons and on to the Green River. Tall, rounded rock spires near the end of the road reminded early visitors of dolls, hence the name Doll House. The Doll House makes a delightful place to explore in itself, or you can head out on routes and trails. **Spanish Bottom Trail** begins here, then drops steeply to Spanish Bottom beside

the Colorado River in 1.2 miles (one-way); a thin trail leads downstream into Cataract Canyon and the first of a long series of rapids. **Surprise Valley Overlook Trail** branches right off the Spanish Bottom Trail after about 300 feet and winds south past some dolls to a T-junction; turn right for views of Surprise Valley, Cataract Canyon, and beyond. The trail ends at some well-preserved granaries; one and one half miles one-way. The **Colorado/Green River Overlook Trail** heads north five miles (one-way) from the Doll House to a viewpoint of the confluence. See the area's *Trails Illustrated* map for routes, trails, and roads.

Getting to the Land of Standing Rocks takes some careful driving, especially on a three-mile stretch above Teapot Canyon. The many washes and small canyon crossings here make for slow going. Short-wheelbase vehicles have the easiest time, as usual. The turnoff for Land of Standing Rocks Road is 6.6 miles from the junction at the bottom of the Flint Trail via a wash shortcut (add about three miles if driving via the four-way intersection). The lower end of The Golden Stairs foot trail is 7.8 miles in, western end of Ernies Country route trailhead is 8.6 miles in, The Wall is 12.7 miles in, Chimney Rock is 15.7 miles in, and the Doll House is 19 miles in at the end of the road. If you drive from the south on the Hite/Orange Cliffs Road, stop at the self-registration stand at the four-way intersection, about 31 miles in from UT 95; you can write your own permit for overnights in the park here. This may change, however, so check with a ranger for current information.

HORSESHOE CANYON UNIT

This canyon contains exceptional prehistoric rock art in a separate section of Canyonlands National Park. Ghostly life-size pictographs in the "Great Gallery" provide an intriguing look into the past. Archaeologists think that the images had religious importance, although the meaning of the figures remains unknown. The Barrier Canyon style of these drawings has been credited to an Archaic Indian Culture beginning at least 8,000 years ago and lasting until about A.D. 450. Horseshoe Canyon also contains rock art left by the subsequent Fremont and Anasazi. The relation between the earlier and later prehistoric groups hasn't been determined.

Great Gallery

Horseshoe Canyon lies northwest of the Maze District. Two moderately difficult trails and a very rough jeep road lead down the canyon walls. In dry weather, cars with good clearance can be driven to a trailhead on the west rim. To reach this trailhead from UT 24, drive to a junction a half mile south of Goblin Valley State Park turnoff, then turn east 30 miles on a dirt road (keep left at the Hans Flat Ranger Station/Horseshoe Canyon turnoff 25 miles in). From the rim, the trail descends 800 feet in one mile on an old jeep road, now closed to vehicles. At the canyon bottom, turn right two miles upstream to the Great Gallery. The sandy canyon floor is mostly level; trees provide shade in some areas.

mysterious figures from the past . . . Great Gallery detail

A 4WD road goes north 21 miles from Hans Flat Ranger Station and drops steeply into the canyon from the east side. The descent on this road is so rough that most people prefer to park on the rim and hike the last mile of road. A vehicle barricade prevents driving right up to the rock art panel, but the one-and-one-half mile walk is easy. A branch off the jeep road goes to the start of **Deadman's Trail** (one and one half miles one-way), which is less used and more difficult.

Look for other rock art along the canyon walls on the way to the Great Gallery. Take care not to touch any of the drawings; they're very fragile as well as irreplaceable. (The oil from your hands will remove the paints.) Horseshoe Canyon also offers pleasant scenery and spring wildflowers. Carry plenty of water. Neither camping nor pets are allowed in the canyon, but you can stay on the rim. Contact the Hans Flat Ranger Station or the Moab office for road and trail conditions.

NEEDLES DISTRICT

The Needles District showcases some of the finest rock sculptures in Canyonlands National Park. Spires, arches, or monoliths appear in almost any direction you look. Prehistoric ruins and rock art exist in greater variety and quantity than elsewhere in the park. Year-round springs and streams bring greenery to the desert. A paved road, several 4WD roads, and many hiking trails offer a variety of ways to explore the Needles.

Needles Outpost

A general store just outside the park boundary offers a campground ($10 tent or RV no hookups, $12.72 RV with water and sewer), groceries, ice, gas, propane, snack bar, showers, jeep rentals and tours, and scenic flights. Call or write ahead, if possible, to arrange for jeep tours and scenic flights: Box 1107, Monticello, UT 84535, tel. 259-2032 (mobile phone) or 259-8545. The season at Needles Outpost is mid-March to late October. Turnoff from UT 211 is one mile before the Needles Visitor Center. The store is up for sale and new ownership may change everything, so call ahead before making plans.

Visitor Center

Stop here to find out about hiking, back roads, and other aspects of travel in the Needles. The staff has backcountry permits (required for all overnight stays in the backcountry), maps, brochures, and books. Open daily 8 a.m.-5 p.m., tel. 259-4711. A $4 per vehicle charge is made unless you have a receipt issued within the last seven days from Island in the Sky of Canyonlands. Outside of office hours, get information at the bulletin board. To reach the Needles District, go 40 miles south from Moab (or 14 miles north of Monticello), turn west on UT 211, and continue 38 miles.

Scenic Drive

The main road continues six and one half miles past the visitor center to Big Spring Canyon Overlook. On the way, you can stop at several nature trails, turn off on 4WD roads, or take short spur roads to trailheads and Squaw Flat Campground.

Roadside Ruin is on the left 0.4 mile past the visitor center. A one-third-mile loop trail goes near a well-preserved granary left by Anasazi Indians. A trail guide available at the start tells about the Anasazi and the local plants.

Cave Spring Trail introduces the geology and ecology of the park and goes to an old cowboy line camp. Turn left 0.7 mile past the visitor center and follow signs about one mile to the trailhead. Pick up the brochure at the beginning. The 0.6-mile loop goes clockwise, crossing some slickrock; two ladders assist on the steep sections. Cowboys used the cave as a line camp from the late 1800s until establishment of the park in 1964; the line camp is just 50 yards in from the trailhead.

A road to **Squaw Flat Campground** and **Elephant Hill** turns left 2.7 miles past the ranger station. The campground, about a half mile in from the main road, has water and a $6 fee from mid-March to September; it's open the rest of the year with no water or charge (water can be obtained year-round at the visitor center). Rangers present evening programs at the Campfire Circle on Loop A from spring through autumn. A **picnic area** is at the base of Elephant Hill, three miles past the campground turnoff and on the scenic drive. Hiking trails lead into wonderful rock forms and canyons from both the campground and picnic areas. Only experienced drivers in 4WD vehicles should continue past the picnic area up Elephant Hill.

Pothole Point Nature Trail is on the left of the main road, 5.0 miles past the visitor center. Highlights of this 0.6-mile loop hike are the many potholes dissolved in the Cedar Mesa Sandstone. A brochure illustrates the fairy shrimp, tadpole shrimp, horsehair worm, snail, and other adaptable creatures that spring to life when rains fill the potholes. You'll also enjoy fine views of distant buttes from the trail.

Slickrock Trail begins on the right 6.2 miles past the visitor center. The trail makes a loop of 2.4 miles roundtrip and takes you north to an overlook of the confluence of Big Spring and Little Spring canyons. Hiking is easy and offers good panoramas.

Big Spring Canyon Overlook, six and one half miles past the visitor center, marks the end of the scenic drive but not of the scenery. The **Confluence Overlook Trail** begins here and winds west to an overlook of the Green and Colorado rivers (see "Confluence Overlook Trail," below).

Hiking

The Needles District has about 55 miles of backcountry trails. Many interconnect to provide all sorts of day and overnight trips. Cairns mark the trails; signs point the way at junctions. You can normally find water in upper Elephant Canyon and canyons to the east in spring and early summer, though the remaining water often becomes stagnant by midsummer. Always ask the rangers about water sources. Don't depend on it being there. Treat water from all sources, including springs, before drinking. Chesler Park and other areas west of Elephant Canyon are very dry; you'll need to bring all water. Mosquitoes, gnats, and deer flies can be very pesky from late spring to midsummer, especially in the wetter places—bring insect repellent. To plan your trip, obtain the small hiking map available from the visitor center, Trails Illustrated's Needles District map, or USGS topo maps.

Confluence Overlook Trail

This trail goes west five and one half miles from Big Spring Canyon Overlook (at the end of the scenic drive) to a fine viewpoint overlooking the Green and Colorado rivers 1,000 feet below. You might see rafts in the water or bighorn sheep on the cliffs. The trail crosses Big Spring and Elephant canyons and follows a jeep road for a short distance. Higher points have good views of the Needles to the south. Except for a few short steep sections, this trail is level and fairly easy. A very early start is recommended in summer, as there's little shade. Carry water even if you don't plan to go all the way. This enchanting country has lured many a hiker beyond his original goal!

Hiking Trails From Squaw Flat Trailhead

The main trailhead sits a short distance south of the campground and is reached by a separate signed road. You can also begin from a trailhead in the campground itself.

Peekaboo Trail winds southeast five miles (one-way) over rugged terrain, including some steep sections of slickrock (best avoided when wet, icy, or covered in snow). There's little shade; carry water. The trail follows Squaw Canyon, climbs over a pass to Lost Canyon, then crosses more slickrock before descending to Peekaboo Campground on Salt Creek 4WD Road. Look for Anasazi ruins on the way and rock art at the campground. A rock slide took out Pookaboo Spring, shown on some maps. Options on this trail include a turnoff south through Squaw Canyon or Lost Canyon to make a loop of 8.75 miles or more.

Squaw Canyon Trail follows the canyon south for 3.75 miles one-way. Intermittent water can often be found until late spring. You can take a connecting trail (Peekaboo, Lost Canyon, and Big Spring Canyon) or cross a slickrock pass to Elephant Canyon.

Lost Canyon Trail, 3.25 miles long one-way, is reached via Peekaboo or Squaw Canyon trails and makes a loop with them. Water supports abundant vegetation; you may need to wade. Most of the way is in the wash bottom, except for a section of slickrock to Squaw Canyon.

Big Spring Canyon Trail crosses an outcrop of slickrock from the trailhead, then follows the canyon bottom to the head of the canyon, 3.75 miles one-way. You can usually find intermittent water along the way except in summer. At canyon's end, a climb up steep slickrock (hazardous if covered by snow or ice) takes you to Squaw Canyon Trail and back to the trailhead for a good seven-and-one-half-mile loop. Another possibility is to turn southwest to the head of

Squaw Canyon, then hike over a slickrock saddle to Elephant Canyon for a 10.5-mile loop.

Hiking Trails From Elephant Hill Trailhead
Drive west three miles past the campground turnoff to the picnic area and trailhead at the base of Elephant Hill. Sounds of racing engines and burning rubber can often be heard from above as vehicles attempt the difficult 4WD road that begins just past the picnic area. All of the following destinations can also be reached by trails from the Squaw Flat Trailhead, though distances will be slightly greater.

Chesler Park is a favorite hiking destination. A lovely desert meadow contrasts with the red and white spires that gave the Needles District its name. An old cowboy line camp is on the west side of the rock island in the center of the park. Distance on **Chesler Park Trail** is about six miles roundtrip. The trail winds through sand and slickrock before ascending a small pass through the Needles to Chesler Park. Once inside, you can take **Chesler Park Loop Trail** (five miles) completely around the park. The loop includes the unusual half-mile **Joint Trail** that follows the bottom of a very narrow crack. Camping in Chesler Park is restricted to certain areas; check with a ranger.

Druid Arch reminds many people of the massive stone slabs at Stonehenge, popularly associated with the Druids, in southern England. The arch is an 11-mile roundtrip (15 miles if you start at Squaw Flat Trailhead). Follow the Chesler Park Trail two miles to Elephant Canyon, turn up the canyon three and one half miles, then make a quarter-mile climb to the arch. Upper Elephant Canyon has seasonal water but the narrow canyon is closed to camping.

Lower Red Lake Canyon Trail provides access to Cataract Canyon of the Colorado River. This is a long, strenuous trip best suited for experienced hikers and completed in two days. Distance from the Elephant Hill Trailhead is 19 miles roundtrip; you'll be walking on 4WD roads and trails. If you can drive Elephant Hill 4WD Road to the trail junction in Cyclone Canyon, the hike is only eight miles roundtrip. The most difficult trail section is a steep talus slope that drops 700 feet in a half mile into the lower canyon. Total elevation change is 1,000 feet. The canyon has little shade and lacks any water source above the river. Summer heat can make the trip grueling; temperatures tend to be 5-10° hotter than on other Needles trails. The river level drops between midsummer and autumn, allowing hikers to go along the shore both downstream to see the rapids and upstream to the confluence. Undertows and strong currents make the river dangerous to cross.

Upper Salt Creek Trail
Several impressive arches and many inviting side canyons attract adventurous hikers to the extreme southeast corner of the park. The trail begins at the end of the 13.5-mile 4WD road up Salt Creek, then goes south 12 miles up-

Chesler Park from its southern edge (near the Joint Trail)

Salt Creek's twisting canyon

canyon to Cottonwood Canyon/Beef Basin Road near Cathedral Butte, just outside the park boundary. The trail is nearly level except for a steep climb at the end. Water can usually be found. Some wading and bushwhacking may be necessary. The famous All-American Man pictograph, shown on some topo maps (or ask a ranger), is in a cave a short way off to the east at about the mid-point of the trail; follow your map and unsigned paths to the cave but don't climb in—dangerous to both you and the ruins and pictograph inside. Many more archaeological sites can be discovered near the trail; they're all fragile and need great care when visited.

Four-Wheel-Drive Roads

A backroad tour allows you to see beautiful canyon scenery, arches, and Indian rock-art sites in the Needles District. Check with a ranger about special hazards before setting out. Also obtain a backcountry permit ($25 per vehicle) if you plan to use one of the campgrounds available along Salt Creek or in the area past Ele-

phant Hill. Mountain bicyclists enjoy the challenge of going up Elephant Hill Road and the roads beyond. Colorado Overlook 4WD Road is good riding too, but Salt Creek and the other eastern canyons have too much loose sand.

Salt Creek Canyon 4WD Road begins near Cave Spring Trail, crosses sage flats for the next two and one half miles, then heads deep into this spectacular canyon. Roundtrip distance, including a side trip to 150-foot-high Angel Arch, is 26 miles. Agile hikers can follow a steep slickrock route into the window of Angel Arch. You can also explore side canyons of Salt Creek or take the Upper Salt Creek Trail (the All American Man pictograph makes a good day-hike destination of 12 miles roundtrip). **Horse Canyon 4WD Road** turns off to the left shortly before the mouth of Salt Canyon. Roundtrip distance, including a side trip to Tower Ruin, is about 13 miles; other attractions include Paul Bunyan's Potty, Castle Arch, Fortress Arch, and side-canyon hiking. Salt and Horse canyons can easily be driven with 4WD vehicles. Usually Salt Canyon is closed due to quicksand after flash floods in summer or shelf ice in winter.

Four-wheel-drive roads enter **Davis Canyon** and **Lavender Canyon** from UT 211, east of the park boundary. Both canyons are accessed through Davis Canyon Road off UT 211 and contain great scenery, arches, and Indian sites, and both are easily visited. Davis is about 20 miles roundtrip and Lavender is about 26 miles roundtrip. Try to allow plenty of time in either canyon as there is much to see and many inviting side canyons to hike. You can camp on BLM land just outside the park boundaries but not in the park itself.

Colorado Overlook 4WD Road begins beside the visitor center and follows Salt Creek to Lower Jump Overlook. Then it bounces across slickrock to a view of the Colorado River (upstream from the confluence). Driving is easy to moderate, though very rough the last one and one half miles. Roundtrip distance is 14 miles.

Elephant Hill 4WD Loop Road begins three miles past the Squaw Flat Campground turnoff. Only experienced drivers with stout vehicles should attempt the extremely rough and steep climb up Elephant Hill (coming up the back side of Elephant Hill is even rougher!). The loop is about 10 miles roundtrip. Connecting roads go to the Confluence Overlook Trailhead (viewpoint is one mile roundtrip on foot), the Joint Trailhead (Chesler Park is two miles roundtrip on foot), and several canyons. Some road sections on the loop are one-way. The parallel canyons in this area are grabens caused by faulting where a layer of salt has shifted deep underground. In addition to Elephant Hill, a few other difficult spots must be negotiated. This area can also be reached by a long route south of the park using Cottonwood Canyon/Beef Basin Road from UT 211, about 60 miles one-way. You'll enjoy spectacular vistas from the Abajo highlands. Two *very* steep descents from Pappys Pasture into Bobbys Hole effectively make this section one-way; travel from Elephant Hill up Bobbys Hole is possible but much more difficult than going the other way, and may require hours of roadbuilding. The Bobbys Hole route may be impassable at times—ask about conditions at the BLM office in Monticello or at the Needles Visitor Center.

Newspaper Rock detail

UTAH'S SOUTHEASTERN CORNER

NEWSPAPER ROCK
STATE HISTORICAL MONUMENT

At Newspaper Rock a profusion of petroglyphs depicts human figures, animals, birds, and abstract designs. These represent 2,000 years of human history during which archaic tribes and Anasazi, Fremont, Paiute, Navajo, and Anglo travelers have passed through Indian Creek Canyon. The patterns on the smooth sandstone rock face stand out clearly, thanks to a coating of dark desert varnish. Newspaper Rock lies just 150 feet off UT 211 on the way to the Needles District of Canyonlands National Park. A quarter-mile nature trail introduces you to the area's desert and riparian vegetation. Picnic areas, which can also be used for camping, lie along Indian Creek across the highway. The park is relatively undeveloped; no drinking water or charge. From US 191 between Moab and Monticello, turn west 12 miles on UT 211. In the future, Newspaper Rock will revert to the BLM and the campground will be closed.

CANYON RIMS RECREATION AREA

Viewpoints atop the high mesa east of Canyonlands National Park offer magnificent panoramas of the surrounding area. The BLM has provided two fenced overlooks, two campgrounds, and good access roads. Other overlooks and scenic spots can be reached on jeep roads or by hiking. The 20-mile-long mesa, shown on maps as Hatch Point, features rock monoliths, canyons, slickrock, and rolling hills. You have a good chance of seeing the graceful antelope-like pronghorn that thrive in this high-desert country. The turnoff for Hatch Point of Canyon Rims is at Milepost 93 on US 191, located 32 miles south of Moab and seven miles north of the UT 211 junction for the Needles District. Canyon Rims Recreation Area has been greatly expanded recently to include surrounding BLM lands and the Beef Basin and Dark Canyon areas. Author and BLM volunteer Fran Barnes has written and published the large book *Canyon Country's Canyon Rims Recreation Area* about exploring the new areas. The book includes a 235-mile long "Canyon Rims Recreation Area Mountain Bike Challenge Route." For back-road travel in this area, you'll find Fran Barnes's book and separate map *Canyon Country Off-Road Vehicle Trails: Canyon Rims Recreation Area* very helpful. Cyclists will also find good info in Peggy & Bob Utesch's *Mountain Biking in Canyon Rims Recreation Area.*

Needles Overlook

Follow the paved road 22 miles west to its end (turn left at the junction 15 miles in). The BLM has a picnic area and interpretive exhibits here. A fence protects visitors from the sheer cliffs that drop off more than 1,000 feet. You can see much of Canyonlands National Park and southeastern Utah. Look south for Six-Shooter Peaks and the high country of the Abajo Mountains; southwest for the Needles (thousands of spires reaching for the heavens); west for the confluence area of the Green and Colorado rivers, the Maze District, the Orange Cliffs, and the Henry Mountains; northwest for the lazy bends of the Colorado River's canyon and the sheer-walled mesas of Island in the Sky and Dead Horse Point; north for the Book Cliffs; and northeast for the La Sal Mountains. The changing shadows and colors of the canyon country make for a continuous show throughout the day.

Anticline Overlook

Head west 15 miles on the paved road, then go straight (north) 17 miles on a good gravel road to the fenced overlook at road's end. Here you're standing 1,600 feet above the Colorado River. The sweeping panorama over the canyons, the river, and the twisted rocks of the Kane Creek Anticline is nearly as spectacular as that from Dead Horse Point, only five and one half miles west as the crow flies. Salt and other minerals of the Paradox Formation pushed up overlying rocks into the dome visible below. Downcutting by the Colorado River has revealed the twisted rock layers. The Moab Salt mine across the river to the north uses a solution technique to bring up potash from the Paradox Formation several thousand feet underground. Pumps then transfer the solution to the blue-tinted evaporation ponds. Look carefully on the northeast horizon to see an arch in the Windows Section of Arches National Park, 16 miles away.

You can reach **Pyramid Butte Overlook** by a gravel road that turns west off the main drive two miles before Anticline Overlook; the road goes around a rock monolith to viewpoints on the other side (1.3 miles roundtrip). Vehicles with 4WD can go west out to **Canyonlands Overlook** (17 miles roundtrip) on rough unmarked roads. The turnoff, which may not be signed, is about 0.3 mile south of the Hatch Point Campground turnoff.

Campgrounds

Each camping area has water (mid-April to mid-October), tables, grills, outhouses, and a $6 fee. **Windwhistle Campground,** backed by cliffs to the south, has fine views to the north and a nature trail: follow the main road from US 191 for six miles and turn left. At **Hatch Point Campground,** in a piñon-juniper woodland, you can enjoy views to the north; water available April to mid-October, $6. Go 24 miles in on the paved and gravel roads toward Anticline Overlook, then turn right one mile.

Trough Springs Trail

Hikers can follow this old livestock trail on the east side of Hatch Point. To reach the trailhead, turn east 0.6 mile on a dirt road five miles north of the Hatch Point Campground turnoff (or four miles south of Anticline Overlook). The trail begins from an abandoned well pad and follows the canyon to its mouth at Kane Creek Road. The first one-third mile follows a jeep road, then cairns mark the way. Carry water. The moder-

descent into Bobby's Hole, Canyon Rims Recreation Area

the incredible vastness of Canyonlands National Park; Needles District from Big Pocket Overlook

ately difficult hike is five miles roundtrip and has an elevation change of 1,200 feet.

Beef Basin

The rugged canyon country south of Canyonlands National Park's Needle District contains beautiful scenery, knock-out panoramas, and Anasazi pueblo ruins. You'll need a 4WD, high-clearance vehicle, maps, camping gear, and emergency supplies to explore this remote region. Drive in either from the east via Cottonwood Canyon Road (turn off UT 211 near the Dugout Ranch) or from the south over the Abajo highlands of the Manti-La Sal National Forest. Although these approach roads are graded, high-clearance vehicles are still recommended. Snow and mud close the roads in winter and spring, especially from the Abajo highlands. The Beef Basin Road drops from the forests into a series of grassy parks. Spur roads branch out to other canyons and parks and make a loop in Beef Basin.

Many Anasazi pueblos stand out in the open in Middle and Ruin parks; others lie tucked into canyon alcoves. One road (badly eroded in 1992) runs northwest past Ruin Park, makes two *very* steep and rough descents into Bobbys Hole, then continues to Elephant Hill in Canyonlands National Park. Only hard-core jeepers should consider this route into Canyonlands National Park! The road may be impassable in the reverse (uphill) direction or totally impassable altogether; ask at the BLM office in Monticello or the Needles Visitor Center in the park.

Big Pocket Overlook

A rough jeep road branches north two and one half miles from the Cottonwood Canyon/Beef Basin Road to spectacular panoramas of upper Salt and Lavender canyons. Binoculars help to pick out natural arches and other details. The road, also good for hiking or mountain biking, makes a loop along the east side of this narrow peninsula. Although on BLM land, you'll be surrounded by some of the best views in the Needles District of Canyonlands National Park. A hiking trail into upper Salt Creek Canyon begins about one mile west of the Big Pocket Overlook turnoff.

Cameo Cliffs

Canyons, arches, and panoramas attract visitors to this little-known area east of US 191. Author Fran Barnes called it "Cameo Cliffs" because the pink cliffs reminded him of an old-fashioned pink-and-white cameo locket. You're not likely to see this unofficial name on maps, however. Barnes describes the area, divided by UT 46 into Cameo Cliffs North and South, in a small guidebook and separate map *Cameo Cliffs: Biking-Hiking-Four-Wheeling.*

MONTICELLO

The Mormon settlers who arrived in 1888 found the cool climate more suited to raising sheep and cattle than crops. Monticello (pronounced "mon-ti-SELL-o") lies at an elevation of 7,050 feet just east of the Abajo ("uh-BAH-hoe") Mountains. The small town is the seat of San Juan County (Utah's largest, at five million acres) and serves as a base for travelers to visit surrounding mountains and canyons, including the Needles District of Canyonlands National Park. Monticello is 54 miles south of Moab and 21 miles north of Blanding. US Highway 666 (Central) goes east from downtown to the Colorado border (17 miles) and Mesa Verde National Park (89 miles).

The **Monticello Museum**, in the library building at the city park, 80 N. Main, has exhibits of Anasazi artifacts, pioneer memorabilia, historic documents, and mineral specimens; open Mon.-Thurs. 2-9 p.m., Friday 2-6 p.m., and Saturday 10 a.m.-2 p.m. from June 1 to August 31.

Accommodations

(Summer rates shown; they drop at most places in winter.) **Canyonlands Motor Inn,** 197 N. Main, tel. 587-2266, $36.30 s, $40.70 d and up, has a spa and sauna. **National 9 Inn** (Navajo Trail Motel) is at 248 N. Main, tel. 587-2251 or (800) 524-9999, $42.71 s or d. **Days Inn** is at 549 N. Main, tel. 587-2458 or (800) 325-2525, $54.75 s, $61.32 d; has indoor pool and spa. **Triangle H Motel,** 164 E. Central, tel. 587-2274 or (800) 657-6622; starts at $46 s or d. **Wayside Motor Inn (Best Western),** 195 E. Central, tel. 587-2261 or (800) 633-9700, $64.60-$69 s or d, has a pool. **The Grist Mill Inn,** 64 S. 300 East, tel. 587-2597 or (800) 645-3762, offers unique bed and breakfast accommodations in a restored flour mill, $47.75 s, $61.34 d.

Campgrounds

Mountain View RV Park, 632 N. Main, tel. 587-2974, is open May 1 to October 31 (maybe in winter without piped water), $8.76 tent, $15.26 RV w/hookups; has showers and laundry. **Montclair RV Park,** 340 S. Main, tel. 587-2503, costs $12 RV no hookups, $15 w/hookups and has showers. **Westerner Trailer Park,** 516 S. Main, near the golf course, tel. 587-2762 costs $11 tent or RV no hookups, $14 w/hookups; it has showers and may close in winter. **Monticello/Canyonlands KOA,** tel. 587-2884, is on a ranch with buffalo, cows, horses, and other farm animals; go east five miles on Central/US 666, then north a half mile; open May 1 to September 30, $15.26 tent or RV no hookups, $19.62 w/hookups, $26 kamping kabins; has showers, store, pool.

The U.S. Forest Service has two campgrounds located nearby on paved roads in the Abajos. **Dalton Springs** (elev. 8,400 feet) has water early June to early October; $5. Go west 5.3 miles on 200 South. **Buckboard** (elev. 8,700 feet) has water mid-June to early October; $5. Go west six and one half miles on 200 South. Campgrounds may also be open off-season without water or fee.

Food

Houston's of Monticello, 296 N. Main, tel. 587-2531, serves homemade American and ethnic food daily (except Tuesday) for breakfast, lunch, and dinner. **Wagon Wheel Pizza,** 164A S. Main, tel. 587-2766, spins out pizza, sandwiches, and salads daily for lunch and dinner. **MD Ranch Cookhouse,** 380 S. Main, tel. 587-3299, dishes up cowboy food including steaks and buffalo in a western atmosphere with genuine ranching artifacts; open daily for breakfast, lunch, and dinner (closed December to Febrary). **Slider's Cafe,** 65 S. Main, tel. 587-2591, serves fast food and Mexican cuisine daily for lunch and dinner. **Juniper Tree Restaurant,** 133 E. Central, tel. 587-2870, features steak, prime rib, roast beef, and other items daily for dinner. **Lamplight Restaurant,** 655 E. Central, tel. 587-2170, offers similar fine dining Mon.-Sat. for dinner. **Hoagies Restaurant,** 216 E. Central, tel. 587-2550, serves American food and pizza daily for breakfast, lunch, and dinner. **La Casita,** 280 E. Central, tel. 587-2959, has Mexican and American food Mon.-Sat. for lunch and dinner.

Entertainment And Events

Watch movies at **The Movies,** 696 E. Central, tel. 587-2535. **Annual events** include **Monticello/Canyonlands Triathlon** in mid-March, **Pioneer Day** (parade, softball, games, and food) on July 24, **San Juan Amateur Golf Tourney and Mountain Cookout** in early August, and **San Juan County Fair** (rodeo, exhibits, and dance) on the third weekend in August.

Services And Recreation

The **post office** is at 197 S. Main, tel. 587-2294. **San Juan Hospital** provides medical care at 364 W. 100 North, tel. 587-2116. The **city park** has picnic areas and a playground at Main and Central. A covered swimming pool (open in summer, tel. 587-2907), tennis courts, and ball fields are three blocks west of Main on Central. **Blue Mountain Meadows Public Golf Course,** 549 S. Main (south edge of town), tel. 587-2468, has nine holes, pro shop, and snack bar. **Four Corners School of Outdoor Education** offers programs on the wildlife, geology, and archaeology of the Southwest. Write for a brochure at Box 1029, Monticello, UT 84535, tel. 587-2859.

Guest Ranch

Live the life of a cowboy on a working ranch operated by third and fourth generation cowboys on their original site. Operations cover 200,000 acres near Monticello. Depending on the season, you will be involved in trailing, moving pastures, and gathering and working cattle. **Dalton Gang Adventures** provides the horse, cattle, and range at $125 per person per day. Contact the ranch for a brochure that gives the activities of the different seasons: Box 8, Monticello, UT 84534, tel. 587-2416.

Information

Visit the **Monticello Multi-Agency Visitor Center,** on the side of the county courthouse at 117 S. Main (Box 490, Monticello, UT 84535), tel. 587-3235 or (800) 574-4386, for info about San Juan County towns and backcountry; staff and literature represent San Juan County Travel Council, Natl. Park Service, U.S. Forest Service, Bureau of Land Management, Canyonlands Natural History Association, and Utah Travel Council; regional books and maps are sold too. Open April 1 to October 31 Mon.-Fri. 8 a.m.-5 p.m. and Saturday and Sunday 10 a.m.-5 p.m., then Mon.-Fri. 9 a.m.-5 p.m. the rest of the year. The **Bureau of Land Management** (San Juan Resource Area), 435 N. Main (Box 7, Monticello, UT 84535), tel. 587-2141, knows about Grand Gulch, Fish and Owl canyons, Dark Canyon, Arch Canyon, and many other fine hiking areas; they can also advise on back-road travel in San Juan County. Open Mon.-Fri. 7:45 a.m.-4:30 p.m. The **Manti-La Sal National Forest** office, 496 E. Central (Box 820, Monticello, UT 84535), tel. 587-2041, has information about roads, camping, and hiking in the Abajos and surrounding high country; its Monticello district includes the upper reaches of Dark Canyon. Open Mon.-Fri. 8 a.m.-noon and 12:30-4:30 p.m. The

public library at 80 N. Main in the city park, tel. 587-2281, has general reading and an extensive collection of southeastern Utah history; open Mon.-Thurs. 2-9 p.m., Friday 2-6 p.m., and Saturday 10 a.m.-2 p.m.

Tours

Midway Aviation, tel. 587-2774, flies over spectacular Canyonlands National Park on 45-minute tours ($45 per person) and does an all-day trip to Canyonlands, Lake Powell, and Monument Valley with a jeep tour and lunch at Monument Valley ($180 per person); a two-person minimum applies. The airport is four miles north of Monticello.

VICINITY OF MONTICELLO

Abajo Peak

The rounded Abajos, or "Blues" as they're sometimes called, actually rise higher than they seem to. Early Spanish explorers climbed the La Sals to the northeast and named these mountains Abajo ("Below"). Intrusive volcanic rocks created the range in much the same way as they formed the Henry and La Sal mountains. Abajo Peak tops the range at 11,362 feet. You can easily reach the summit by road (high-clearance vehicles work best); head west 0.9 mile on 200 South from US 191, then turn left 13 miles on South Creek Rd. (pavement ends one mile in at Loyd's Lake). You'll likely see deer and raptors, as well as summer wildflowers, on the drive up. Panoramas on a clear day at the top take in the Four Corners Region including mountain ranges in Colorado, Shiprock in New Mexico, Chuska Mountains in Arizona, Monument Valley, Cedar Mesa, Henry Mountains, Needles District of Canyonlands National Park, the La Sal Mountains, and the forests and meadows of the Abajos. Other peaks and canyons of the Abajos have good hiking trails; see the foresters in Monticello and the Manti-La Sal forest map and the more detailed Trails Illustrated topo map for the back roads and trails of the area. The metric 1:100,000 Blanding topo map covers nearly all the range.

You can enjoy several scenic drives in the Abajos. Cars with good clearance can often do these trips in dry weather; ask at the U.S. Forest Service office in Monticello. The range can be crossed to Blanding by heading west on 200 South, turning southwest on Forest Route 079 up North Canyon, then descending along Johnson Creek (about 37 miles total one-way). A longer drive continues west from Forest Route 079 and 095 junction to Elk Ridge and through the Bears Ears to UT 95 near Natural Bridges National Monument. The drive has great views of rugged canyons and forested hills. You'll cross a knife-edge ridge on the Causeway at about the middle of Forest Route 095. At the west end of Forest Route 095, turn south around the upper drainages of Dark Canyon to the Bears Ears on Forest Route 088 or turn north to Beef Basin and Big Pocket Overlook roads (see "Canyon Rims Recreation Area," above). Winter visitors come to the mountains for cross-country skiing and snowmobiling, though no trails or ski areas exist (Blue Mountain Ski Area has closed). The road from Monticello to Dalton Springs is plowed for winter access. A good scenic loop saves about 16 miles from the highway route between Monticello and Canyonlands National Park; take Forest Route 105 about nine miles to Forest Route 174, perhaps stopping to enjoy a beautiful scenic overlook of Canyonlands from a high point before descending to Route 174. After turning on Rt. 174, another six miles will bring you to UT 211 near Newspaper Rock.

BLANDING

The largest town in San Juan County, Blanding (pop. 4,000) is also a handy travelers' stop. The state park on the northwest edge of town provides an excellent introduction to the Anasazi Indians, who left behind many ruins in the Four Corners area. Pioneers began work on an irrigation system in 1897 to bring water from the Abajo Mountains to the rich soil of White Mesa. The first families arrived at the townsite, then known as Sidon, in 1905. Many of the Mormon farmers who followed had been driven from Mexico by political and religious intolerance or had lost their farms to floods at nearby Bluff. Residents apparently liked to change the name of their community. Originally known as Sidon, the town became Grayson, then Blanding. The story goes that in 1915 townsfolk jumped at the offer of a free library by Thomas W. Bicknell on

the condition that they name their town after him. The town of Thurber in central Utah also wanted the library, so it was divided between the two communities; Thurber became Bicknell and Grayson became Blanding, the maiden name of Mrs. Bicknell.

Edge Of The Cedars State Park

Prehistoric Anasazi built at least six groups of pueblo structures between A.D. 700 and 1220 just outside present-day Blanding. The state museum features an excellent array of pottery, baskets, sandals, jewelry, and stone tools. The pottery collection on the second floor stands out for its rich variety of styles and decorative designs. Other displays illustrate Anasazi life and how archaeologists have learned about these ancient peoples through studies of stratigraphy, dendrochronology, and village layouts. The Special Exhibits room has changing shows related to the region and inhabitants. An observation tower in the museum provides panoramic views of the ruins outside and of mountains in four states; signs identify the features.

A short trail behind the museum leads past six clusters of ruins, each of which contains both rectangular rooms on the surface and circular depressions of underground kivas and pit houses. Only Complex 4 has been excavated and partly restored to give an idea of the village's appearance when the Anasazi lived here. You may enter the kiva by descending a ladder through the restored roof; the walls and interior features are original. The other five ruin groups haven't been restored and require some imagination. A large pit near Complex 4 is all that re-

Anasazi cup

mains of a great kiva, a structure rarely seen this far north. Edge of the Cedars likely served as an important community center in its day.

The museum also has exhibits and artifacts of the people who followed the Anasazi—the Ute and Navajo Indians and the early Anglo pioneers. You may enter a Navajo hogan outside. Videos and slide presentations, shown on request in the auditorium, illustrate Anasazi, Navajo, and pioneer cultures. There's often an art or photo exhibition in the auditorium, as well as in the art gallery. **Archaeology Week,** held in spring, has demonstrations and talks. A gift shop sells books on the region's Indians and pioneer history. Picnic tables outside provide a spot for having lunch. Edge of the Cedars is open daily 9 a.m.-6 p.m. from May 16 to September 15, then daily 9 a.m.-5 p.m. the rest of the year; closed Thanksgiving Day, Christmas Day, New Year's Day, Civil Rights Day and Presidents' Day; $1.50 adult, $1 ages 6-16, tel. 678-2238. Head north on Main from downtown and follow signs one mile.

Nations Of The Four Corners Cultural Center

This interesting park is dedicated to the four cultures that built in this area. Trails lead to an Anasazi style tower that gives a fine view of the surrounding area and to a pioneer cabin, a small Spanish hacienda, and Ute and Navajo villages. Tours are offered from May 15 through September 30th with gates opening at 4:30 p.m.; tours leave every 30 minutes starting at 5 p.m. For $30 you can enjoy a western style dinner starting at 6:30 p.m. followed by entertainment in an amphitheater built in slickrock. The park is sponsored by the College of Eastern Utah and proceeds, after operating expenses, are used for student scholarships. To reach the facility, turn west off Main Street at 500 South and go seven blocks, tel. 678-2323.

BLANDING PRACTICALITIES

Accommodations

The **Gateway Motel (Best Western),** 88 E. Center. tel. 678-2278 or (800) 528-1234, $44.69 s, $51.23 d and up, has a pool. **Cliff Palace Motel** is at 132 S. Main, tel. 678-2264 or (800) 553-8093, $33 s, $37 d. **Prospector Motor**

Lodge is at 591 S. Hwy. 191 (south edge of town), tel. 678-3231, $40 s, $45 d and up. **Comfort Inn** is at 711 S. Hwy. 191, tel. 678-3271, $55.59 s, $69.76 d. The **Sunset Inn** is at 88 W. Center, tel. 678-3323, starting at $24. The **Four Corners Inn,** 131 E. Center, tel. 678-3257, $43.60 s, $53.32 d, is the newest motel in town. **The Old Hotel Bed & Breakfast** features rooms in a Victorian house at 118 E. 300 South (turn east one block at Cedar Mesa Pottery), tel. 678-2388, $44 s, $56 d, closed in winter.

Campgrounds

KamPark has a store and showers on S. Hwy. 191 (south edge of town), tel. 678-2770, $10 tent, $11 RV no hookups, $14 w/hookups. **Devil's Canyon Campground** (elev. 7,100 feet) in the Manti-La Sal National Forest has sites with water from early May to late October; $6, no water or fee off-season. A quarter-mile nature trail begins at the far end of the campground loop. Go north eight miles on US 191, then west 1.3 miles on a paved road (turnoff is between Mileposts 60 and 61). **Nizhoni Campground** (elev. 7,760 feet), also in the Manti-La Sal National Forest, has sites with water from early June to late September; $6. Turn north 14 miles on 100 East in Blanding (last part is a gravel road). You can also reach Nizhoni on backways from Monticello via the Abajo Peaks or from Natural Bridges National Monument via the Bears Ears, Elk Ridge, and the Causeway.

Food

Elk Ridge Restaurant, 120 E. Center, tel. 678-3390, offers a varied American menu with a few Mexican items; open daily (except Sunday) for breakfast, lunch, and dinner. **Kenny's Restaurant,** N. Hwy. 191, tel. 678-9986, is an American cafe offering some Mexican dishes. Open daily for breakfast, lunch, and dinner. **Patio Drive-In, Mr. Bee's,** and **Cedar Pony** have fast food on N. Hwy. 191. **Food Town** on the south edge of town is a supermarket with a deli and bakery.

Events And Services

A three-day **Fourth of July Celebration** has fireworks, parade, horse events, "meller-dramas," and a mudbog competition. Navajo and Ute Indians produce handpainted ceramics at **Cedar Mesa Pottery,** Main and 300 South, tel.

678-2241. You can step in the adjacent factory on weekdays to watch the craftspeople at work. **Blue Mountain Trading Post,** one mile south of town, has a large selection of high-quality Indian art and crafts; the adaptable Navajo produce much of the work—even the kachina dolls (borrowed from Hopi traditions). **White Mesa Institute,** 639 W. 100 South (50-1), Blanding, UT 84511, sponsored by the College of Eastern Utah, offers educational programs for youth and adults on the archaeology, modern Indian tribes, pioneer history, wildlife, and geology of the Southwest. The **post office** is at the corner of Main and 100 North, tel. 678-2627. **Blanding Clinic** provides medical services at 930 N. 400 West, tel. 678-2254. Contact the county hospital in Monticello at 678-2830.

Recreation

Blanding Pool and a tennis court are at 50 West and 200 South, tel. 678-2157. **Reservoir Park** (picnic area and playground) and the nine-hole **Blanding Golf Course** are north three miles on 300 West; the small reservoir has trout fishing. **Recapture Reservoir** offers boating and trout fishing three miles northeast of town; head northeast 1.3 miles on US 191, turn left (north) on a paved road between Mileposts 53 and 54 (just before the highway enters a road cut), then go 1.7 miles to the lake's southern shore; this road is the old highway and makes a good boat ramp where submerged. For access to the north and west sides of the reservoir, follow US 191 across the dam, continue a half mile, then turn west onto a gravel road. Fishermen can also turn in at either end of the dam to fish from the shore. No facilities are at the reservoir, though people sometimes camp (west end is best).

Information And Tours

The staff at the state park knows about Blanding and can tell you of other Anasazi ruins in the area. The **public library** is at Main and 300 South. Open Mon.-Sat., tel. 678-2335.

Flights by **Scenic Aviation** go over spectacular country. Some destinations with costs per person (based on two or more) include: Comb Ridge and nearby canyons (half hour; $23), Canyonlands National Park (one hour; $45), Canyonlands and Lake Powell (one and three quarters hours; $80), Monument Valley (one and one quarter hours; $55), and Monument Valley, Rainbow Bridge, and San Juan River (one and one quarter hours; $80), tel. 678-3222. The airport is three miles south of town.

HOVENWEEP NATIONAL MONUMENT

The Anasazi Indians built many impressive masonry buildings during the early to mid-1200s, near the end of their 1,300-year stay in the area. A drought beginning in A.D. 1274 and lasting 25 years probably hastened their migration from this area. Several centuries of intensive farming, hunting, and woodcutting had already taken their toll on the land. Archaeologists believe the inhabitants retreated south in the late 1200s to sites in northwestern New Mexico and northeastern Arizona. The Ute Indian word Hovenweep means "Deserted Valley," an appropriate name for the lonely high-desert country left behind. The Anasazi at Hovenweep had much in common with the Mesa Verde culture, though the Dakota Sandstone here doesn't form large alcoves suitable for cliff-dweller villages. Ruins at Hovenweep remain essentially unexcavated, awaiting some future archaeologist's trowel.

The Anasazi farmers had a keen interest in the seasons because of their need to know the best time for planting crops. Astronomical stations (alignments of walls, doorways, and tiny openings) allowed the sun priests to determine the equinoxes and solstices with an accuracy of one or two days. This precision also may have been necessary for a complex ceremonial calendar. Astronomical stations at Hovenweep have been discovered at Hovenweep Castle and Unit-Type House of Square Tower Ruins and at Cajon Ruins.

Visitor Center And Campground

Hovenweep National Monument protects six groups of villages left behind by the Anasazi. The sites lie near the Colorado border southeast of Blanding. Square Tower Ruins Unit, where the visitor center is located, has the greatest number of ruins and the most varied architecture. In fact, you can find all of the Hovenweep architectural styles here. The visitor center has a few exhibits on the Anasazi and photos of local wildlife. A ranger will answer your questions, provide brochures and handouts about various aspects of the monument, and give directions for visiting the other ruin groups. Related books can be purchased. Hours at the visitor center are 8 a.m.-5 p.m. year-round; the ruins stay open all the time. Mesa Verde National Park administers Hovenweep at Mesa Verde National Park, CO 81330, tel. (303) 529-4465. The campground, one mile from the visitor center, is open all year; April-Oct. it has water, restrooms, and a $6 fee. The closest accommodations are at Blanding and Bluff in Utah and Cortez in Colorado. Nearest places for groceries and fuel are Aneth (20 miles south in Utah; has a telephone), Hatch Trading Post (groceries only; 16 miles west in Utah) and Ismay Trading Post (14 miles southeast in Colorado). Gnats can be very pesky in May and June; be sure to bring insect repellent.

One approach from US 191 between Blanding and Bluff is to head east nine miles on UT 262, continue straight six miles on a small paved road to Hatch Trading Post, then follow signs 16 miles. A good way in from Bluff is to go west 21 miles on the paved road to Montezuma Creek and Aneth, then follow signs north 20 miles. A scenic 58-mile route through Montezuma Canyon begins five miles south of Monticello and follows unpaved roads to Hatch and on to Hovenweep; you can stop at the BLM's Three Turkey Ruin on the way. From Colorado, take a partly paved road west and north 41 miles from US 666 (the turnoff is four miles south of Cortez).

Tower at Cajon Ruins; archaeologists recently removed the small ring of stones at upper left (reconstructed earlier this century) because the ring wasn't authentic.

ern rattlesnake), which is active at night in summer and during the day in spring and autumn. Please stay on the trail—don't climb ruin walls or walk on rubble mounds.

Square Tower Ruins

This extensive group of Anasazi towers and dwellings lines the rim and slopes of Little Ruin Canyon, a short walk from the visitor center. Obtain a trail guide booklet from the ranger station; the booklet's map shows the several loop trails. You can take easy walks of less than a half mile on the rim or combine all the trails for a loop of about two miles with only one up and down section in the canyon. The booklet has good descriptions of Anasazi life and architecture and of the plants growing along the trail. You'll see towers (D-shaped, square, oval, and round), cliff dwellings, surface dwellings, storehouses, kivas, and rock art. Take care not to disturb the fragile ruins. Keep an eye out for the prairie rattlesnake (a subspecies of the west-

Other Ruins

These are good to visit if you'd like to spend more time in the area. You'll need a map and directions from a ranger to find them, as they aren't signed. One group, the Goodman Point near Cortez (CO), has relatively little to see except unexcavated mounds.

Holly Ruins group is noted for its Great House, Holly Tower, and Tilted Tower. Most of Tilted Tower fell away after the boulder on which it sat shifted. Great piles of rubble mark the sites of structures built on loose ground. Look for remnants of farming terraces in the canyon below the Great House. A hiking trail connects the campground at Square Tower Ruins with Holly Ruin; the route follows canyon bottoms and is about eight miles roundtrip. Ask a ranger for a map and directions. Hikers could also continue to Horseshoe Ruins (one mile farther) and Hackberry Ruins (one-third mile beyond Horseshoe). All of these lie just across the Colorado border and about six miles (one-way) by road from the visitor center.

Horseshoe and **Hackberry** ruins are best reached by an easy trail (one mile roundtrip) off the road to Holly Ruins. Horseshoe House, built in a horseshoe shape similar to Sun Temple at Mesa Verde, has exceptionally good masonry work. Archaeologists haven't determined the purpose of the structure. An alcove in the canyon below contains a spring and small shelter. A round tower nearby on the rim has a strategic view. Hackberry House has only one room still intact. Rubble piles and wall remnants abound in the area. The spring under an alcove here still has a good flow and supports lush growths of hackberry and cottonwood trees along with smaller plants.

Cutthroat Castle Ruins were remote even in Anasazi times. The ruins lie along an intermittent stream rather than at the head of a canyon like most other Hovenweep sites. Cutthroat Castle is a large multistory structure with both straight and curved walls. Three round towers stand nearby. Look for wall fragments and the circular depressions of kivas. High-clearance vehicles can go close to the ruins, about 11.5 miles (one-way) from the visitor center. Visitors with cars can drive to a trailhead and then walk to the ruins (1.5 miles roundtrip on foot).

Cajon Ruins are at the head of a little canyon on Cajon Mesa in the Navajo Reservation in Utah, about nine miles southwest of the visitor center. The site has a commanding view across the San Juan Valley as far as Monument Valley. Buildings include a large multiroom structure, a round tower, and a tall square tower. An alcove just below has a spring and some rooms. Look for pictographs, petroglyphs, and grooves in rock (used for tool grinding). Farming terraces were located on the canyon's south side.

BLUFF

The 1880 Hole-in-the-Rock expedition arrived here after an epic journey by wagon train from Escalante. Too tired to go any farther, they chose this section of the San Juan River canyon in which to plant their fields and build new homes. They hoped that their presence here would secure the region for Mormon settlement and lead to conversion of the Indians. The settlers tried repeatedly to farm the fertile canyon soils, only to have the river wash their fields away. Most residents gave up and moved to more promising areas, but many of those who stayed prospered with large cattle herds. Today Bluff is a sleepy community of about 250 inhabitants. Take the signed "Bluff City Historic Loop" to see pioneer houses along the back streets. Many visitors also drive to the cemetery atop a small hill to read inscriptions and enjoy views of the valley (turn in beside Turquoise RV Park, turn left just past the Decker house, and follow the paved road to the top). Indians from the Navajo Reservation across the river occasionally have dance performances, horse races, rodeos, and other get-togethers in Bluff.

Accommodations

Recapture Lodge, Box 309, Bluff, UT 84512, tel. 672-2281, offers rooms and kitchenettes ($30.52 s, $32.70 d and up), swimming pool, hot tub, laundromat, tours, and llama pack trips. Groups can reserve rooms in the 1898 Decker pioneer house. The owners know of Indian ruins and scenic places in the backcountry. They offer free slide shows in the evenings during the season and can suggest places to go. Or you can take one of their organized naturalist tours to Monument Valley, Comb Ridge, Recapture Pocket, and other locations; $70 full day (minimum of four persons). Guided camping trips can also be arranged in the canyon country of southeastern Utah. They also can provide a shuttle service for rafting trips. **Kokopelli Inn Motel,** tel. 672-2322 or (800) 541-8854, to the south has rooms at $41.42 s, $45.78 d. **Mokee Motel** on the south edge of town, tel. 672-2217, has rooms for $28 s, $36 d. **Bluff Bed & Breakfast,** tel. 672-2220, lies in a secluded canyon spot on the northeast edge of town; $59.40 s, $64.80 d.

Campgrounds

Kokopelli Inn Motel, tel. 672-2322, has sites for RVs ($8.72 no hookups, $13.08 w/hookups); no showers. **Turquoise RV Park,** tel. 672-2219, offers sites for self-contained RVs, $8.48

w/hookups (no tents). **Sand Island Recreation Area** is a primitive camping area along the San Juan River, three miles south of town; large cottonwood trees shade this pretty spot. No drinking water or charge; tenters need to watch for thorns in the grass. River runners often put in at the campground. You can see a panel of pictographs along the cliff one-third mile downstream of the camping area along a gravel road.

Food, Shopping, And Information

The **Thai House Restaurant**, 1st North and 2nd West, tel. 672-2355, serves authentic Thai cuisine; a delicious and varied menu offers spicy and mild selections served in the historic Jens Nielson house one block off the highway. **Cow Canyon Cafe**, tel. 672-2208, serves homemade dinners in an old trading post on the northeast edge of town; open Thurs.-Mon. April to October. The trading post is open all year with Indian crafts. The **Sunbonnet Cafe** on the Bluff City Historic Loop has American and Indian foods, including Navajo tacos; open Mon.-Sat. for breakfast, lunch, and dinner. **Turquoise Restaurant** is a small cafe offering steaks, chops, Navajo tacos, sandwiches, and other items; open daily for breakfast, lunch, and dinner on the main highway. The **Dairy Cafe** has fast food. **Twin Rocks Trading Post** offers a good selection of high-quality Indian crafts, much of it produced locally by Navajo Indians; on the Bluff City Historic Loop. The **post office** is on the main highway. A small **library/travel information center**, open irregular hours, sits on the Historic Loop behind the post office.

River Trips

Wild Rivers Expeditions offers a variety of oar-powered raft and dory trips on the San Juan River. Day excursions to Mexican Hat cost $75 (motors may be used if water level is low). Other trips go from Bluff to Mexican Hat in two to three days ($300-435, with a minimum of four fares) and all the way to Lake Powell in five to six days ($720-830, with a minimum of six fares). Mexican Hat to Lake Powell takes three to four days ($435-580, with a minimum of six fares). The Montezuma Creek to Mexican Hat trip lasts four days and specializes in archaeological sites along the river ($690, with a minimum of six). A 16-day dory trip in May takes in the San Juan

from Shiprock, New Mexico, to Lake Powell. Boating through Cataract Canyon takes five to eight days by oar-powered raft or dory ($790-1195, with a minimum of six). The office is on the main highway through town, or write Box 118, Bluff, UT 84512, tel. 672-2244 or (800) 422-7654 out of state. See "Mexican Hat," below, for other river tours and "River Running on the San Juan" under "Vicinity of Mexican Hat" for a description of the river.

VICINITY OF BLUFF

The canyon country of Cedar Mesa, Comb Ridge, and other nearby areas has beautiful scenery, Anasazi ruins, and abundant wildlife. Recapture Pocket has unusual rock formations (it's *west* of Recapture Creek, not east as some maps show). Local information should be obtained for backcountry trips.

St. Christopher's Episcopal Mission

Father Harold Lieber came to the Bluff area in 1943 and established this mission for the Navajo Indians. Relying on donations and volunteer help, he built a school, chapel, and other buildings. The current priest, Father Steven Plummer, is Navajo. Visitors are welcome to the pleasant tree-shaded grounds; go east two miles on the paved road from the northeast edge of Bluff.

San Juan Footbridge And 14-Window Ruin

An easy walk of about two miles roundtrip crosses a suspension bridge over the San Juan River and follows roads to this Anasazi cliff dwelling. From Bluff, drive east two miles on the paved road to St. Christopher's Episcopal Mission, continue straight 1.3 miles, and turn right a half mile on a dirt road (it may not be signed; keep right at a fork 0.1 mile in) to the footbridge. Walk across the bridge, follow dirt roads winding southeast about a half mile to a road running beneath the cliffs, turn right (west) a half mile, and look for the ruins in an alcove on the left. You can scramble up for a closer look—but don't enter the rooms as the ruins can easily be damaged. The walk passes farm lands on the Navajo Reservation; please resist the temptation to take shortcuts across the fields.

WEST OF BLANDING TO NATURAL BRIDGES NATIONAL MONUMENT

Highway UT 95 turns west from US 191 four miles south of Blanding and crosses Comb Ridge, Cedar Mesa, and many canyons. Follow UT 95 to Natural Bridges National Monument or continue on to Hite Marina at Lake Powell. UT 261 turns south along Cedar Mesa before twisting down the hairpin curves of the Moki Dugway north of Mexican Hat. UT 276 turns off for Halls Crossing Marina and the ferry across Lake Powell to Bullfrog Marina. Fill up with gas before venturing out on UT 95; you won't find any gas stations on the highway until Hanksville, 122 miles away. Hite and the other Lake Powell marinas do have gas and supplies, however.

Cedar Mesa and its canyons have an exceptionally large number of prehistoric Anasazi Indian sites. Several groups of ruins lie just off the highway. Hikers will discover many more. If you would like to explore the Cedar Mesa area, be sure to drop in at the **Kane Gulch Ranger Station,** located four miles south on UT 261 from UT 95. Bureau of Land Management (BLM) staff issues the permits required to explore the Cedar Mesa backcountry at $5 per person for overnight stays in Grand Gulch, Fish Creek Canyon, and Owl Creek Canyon. The number of people permitted to camp at a given time is limited, so you may wish to call ahead: tel. 587-2141. BLM people will also tell you about archaeological sites and their values, current hiking conditions, and locations of water.

Butler Wash Ruins
Well-preserved pueblo ruins left by the Anasazi lie tucked under an overhang across the wash, 11 miles west on UT 95 (between Mileposts 111 and 112) from US 191. At the trailhead on the north side of the highway, follow cairns a half mile through juniper and piñon pine woodlands and across slickrock to the overlook.

Comb Ridge
Geologic forces have squeezed up the earth's crust in a long ridge running 80 miles south from the Abajo Peaks into Arizona. Sheer cliff faces plunge 800 feet into Comb Wash on the west side. Engineering the highway down these cliffs took considerable effort. A parking area near the top of the grade offers expansive panoramas across Comb Wash. The overlook is between Mileposts 108 and 109, two and one half miles west of Butler Wash ruins. Scenic **jeep roads** between UT 95 and US 163 follow the west side of Comb Ridge through Comb Wash and the east side of Comb Ridge through Butler Wash. Another jeep road traces the route of the 1880 Mormon Hole-in-the-Rock expedition between UT 261 on Cedar Mesa and Comb Wash (high-clearance vehicle is needed to go down, 4WD to go up).

In 1923, the West's last shoot-out between Indians and settlers took place in the Comb Ridge area. Conflicts between Ute Indians and ranchers had simmered for 57 years, with the white men taking the Indian's land and the Utes taking the white men's livestock. A group of renegade Utes under Chief Posey fled to this rugged area, knowing that the Blanding posse would have great difficulty in finding the few trails that existed then. The posse, however, caught up with the Indians, killing one of them. The disheartened Utes then surrendered. Old Chief Posey, who had been shot earlier in Blanding, evaded capture only to die of his wounds about a week later, alone in a cave. The event drew national attention to the plight of the tribe, which was later given the White Mesa Indian Reservation 12 miles south of Blanding.

Arch Canyon
This tributary canyon of Comb Wash has spectacular scenery and many Indian ruins. Much of the canyon can be seen on a day-hike, but two or three days are needed to explore the upper reaches. The main stream beds usually have water (purify before drinking). To reach the trailhead, turn north two and one half miles on a dirt road in Comb Wash (between Mileposts 107 and 108 of UT 95), go past a house and water tank, then park in a grove of cottonwood trees before a stream ford. This is also a good place to camp. The mouth of Arch Canyon lies just to the northwest (it's easy to miss!). Sign in at the register here. Look for an Indian ruin just up Arch Canyon on the right. More ruins lie tucked under alcoves farther upcanyon. From the trailhead (elev. 5,200 feet), the canyon extends about 13 miles upstream into Elk Ridge and has several tributary canyons worth exploring. The first one is two and one half miles

up on the right; it goes in one and one half miles to a ruin and spring. A second canyon on the right six miles up the main canyon also has a ruin and springs one and one half miles up. You'll reach Texas Canyon on the left seven and one half miles up (elev. 5,600 feet) in a grove of ponderosa pines; look across Arch Canyon from this junction to see a large arch. Texas Canyon goes back about five miles and has one fork. Continuing up Arch Canyon, you'll see a second arch on the right, then Butts Canyon on the right, nine miles from the trailhead. From this point, Arch and Butts canyons each extend about four miles to their heads (elev. 7,500 feet). Spring and autumn are the best times for hiking, though the upper reaches can be fine in summer too. In late spring and early summer, arm yourself with long pants and insect repellent against the deer flies. Most of the route follows the canyon bottoms; sometimes off-road vehicles travel the lower few miles. See the 7 1/2-minute topos, the 1:100,000 Blanding map, or Trails Illustrated's Grand Gulch Plateau map. The BLM offices at Kane Gulch or Monticello can advise on hiking.

Arch Canyon Overlook

A road and short trail to the rim of Arch Canyon provide a beautiful view into the depths. Turn north four miles on Texas Flat Road (County 263) from UT 95 between Mileposts 102 and 103, park just before the road begins a steep climb, and walk east on an old jeep road about a quarter mile to the rim. This is a fine place for a picnic, although it has no facilities or guardrails. Texas Flat Road is dirt but okay when dry for cars with good clearance. Trucks can continue up the steep hill to other viewpoints of Arch and Texas canyons.

Mule Canyon Ruin

Archaeologists have excavated and stabilized this Anasazi village on the gentle slope of Mule Canyon's South Fork. A stone kiva, circular tower, and 12-room structure can be seen, all originally connected by tunnels. Cave Towers (see above), two miles to the southeast, would have been visible from the top of the tower here. Signs describe the ruin and periods of Anasazi development. Turn north 0.3 mile on a paved road from UT 95 between Mileposts 101 and 102. Hikers can explore other Indian ruins in

North and South forks of Mule Canyon; check with the Kane Gulch Ranger Station for advice and directions. You might see pieces of pottery and other artifacts in this area. Please leave *every* piece in place so that future visitors can enjoy the discovery too. Federal laws also prohibit removal of artifacts.

NATURAL BRIDGES NATIONAL MONUMENT

Streams in White Canyon and its tributaries cut deep canyons, then formed three impressive bridges. Silt-laden floodwaters sculpted the bridges by gouging tunnels between closely spaced loops in the meandering canyons. You can distinguish a natural bridge from an arch because the bridge spans a stream bed and was initially carved out of the rock by flowing water. In the monument, these bridges illustrate three different stages of development, from the massive, newly formed Kachina Bridge, to the middle-aged Sipapu Bridge, to the delicate and fragile span of Owachomo. All three natural bridges will continue to widen and eventually collapse under their own weight. A nine-mile scenic drive has overlooks of the picturesque bridges, Anasazi ruins, and the twisting canyons. You can follow short trails down from the rim to the base of each bridge or hike through all three bridges on an 8.6-mile trail loop. Paved highways allow easy access to the monument: from Blanding, drive 42 miles west on UT 95; from Hite Marina, drive 50 miles southeast on UT 95; from Halls Crossing Marina, drive 59 miles northeast on UT 276; or from Mexican Hat, drive 44 miles north via UT 261 (there's a three-mile section of steep unpaved switchbacks). The National Park Service has a visitor center and a small campground.

History

Ruins, artifacts, and rock art indicate a long Indian occupation by tribes ranging from archaic groups to the Anasazi. Many fine cliff dwellings built by the Anasazi still stand. In 1883, prospector Cass Hite passed on tales of the huge stone bridges that he had discovered on a trip up White Canyon. Adventurous travelers, including a 1904 *National Geographic* magazine expedition, visited this isolated region to marvel at the bridges. The public's desire for their protection led President Theodore Roosevelt to proclaim the area a national monument in 1908. Federal administrators then changed the original bridge names of "Edwin," "Augusta," and "Caroline" to the Hopi names used today. Although the Hopi never lived here, the Anasazi of White Canyon very likely have descendants in the modern Hopi villages in Arizona.

Visitor Center

From the signed junction on UT 95, drive in four and one half miles on UT 275 to the visitor center (elev. 6,505 feet). Monument Valley Overlook, two miles in, has a panorama south across a vast expanse of piñon pine and juniper trees to Monument Valley and distant mountains. A slide show in the visitor center illustrates how geologic forces and erosion created the canyons and natural bridges. Exhibits introduce the Indians who once lived here, as well as the geology, wildlife, and plants. Outside in front, labels identify common plants of the monument. Rangers will answer your questions about the monument and surrounding area. If asked, staff will provide details on locations of ruins and rock-art sites. You can purchase regional books, topo and geologic maps, postcards, slides, and film. Checklists of birds, other wildlife, and plants are available too. Hours at the visitor center are daily 8 a.m.-5 p.m. Mar. 1-May 1 and Oct. 1-Oct. 31, 8 a.m.- 6 p.m. May 1-Oct. 1, and 9 a.m.-4:30 p.m. the rest of the year (extended to 6 p.m. in summer); closed holidays Oct.-April. Admission is $4 per vehicle ($2 bicyclist). The Bridge View Drive is always open during daylight hours except after heavy snowstorms. A winter visit can be very enjoyable; ice or mud often close the steep Sipapu and Kachina trails, but the short trail to Owachomo Bridge usually stays open. Pets aren't allowed on the trails or in the backcountry at any time. Address is Box 1, Natural Bridges, Lake Powell, UT 84533, tel. 259-5174. The nearest accommodations and cafe are at Fry Canyon, 26 miles northwest of the visitor center on UT 95; the closest gas is 40 miles east near Blanding or 50 west miles at Hite.

Photovoltaic Array

A large solar electric-power station sits across the road from the visitor center. This demonstration system, the largest in the world when constructed in 1980, has a quarter-million solar cells spread over nearly an acre and produces up to 100 kilowatts. Batteries, located elsewhere, store a two-day supply of power. The monument lies far from the nearest power lines, so the solar cells provide an alternative to continuous running of diesel-powered generators.

Campground

Drive 0.3 mile past the visitor center and turn right into the campground, set in a forest of piñon pine and juniper. Sites stay open all year; $5. Obtain water from a faucet in front of the visitor center. Rangers give talks several evenings each week during the summer season. The campground is often full, but there is a designated overflow area near the intersection of Highways 95 and 261. RVs or trailers more than 21 feet long will also have to use this parking area.

Bridge View Drive

The nine-mile drive begins its one-way loop just past the campground. You can stop for lunch at a picnic area. Allow about one and one half hours for a quick trip around. To make all the stops and do a bit of leisurely hiking will take most of a day. The crossbedded sandstone of the bridges and canyons is the 265-million-year-old Cedar Mesa Formation.

Sipapu Bridge viewpoint is two miles from the visitor center. The Hopi name refers to the gateway from which their ancestors entered this world from another world below. Sipapu Bridge has reached its mature or middle-aged stage of development. The bridge is the largest in the monument and has a span of 268 feet and a height of 220 feet. Many people think Sipapu the most magnificent of the bridges. Another view and a trail to the base of Sipapu are 0.8 mile farther. The viewpoint is about halfway down on an easy trail; allow a half hour. A steeper and rougher trail branches off the viewpoint trail and winds down to the bottom of White Canyon, probably the best place to fully appreciate the bridge's size. Total roundtrip distance is 1.2 miles with an elevation change of 600 feet.

Horse Collar Ruin, built by the Anasazi, looks as though it has been abandoned only a few decades, not 800 years. At 3.1 miles from the visitor center, a short trail leads to an overlook. The name comes from the shape of the doorway openings in two storage rooms. Hikers walking in the canyon between Sipapu and Kachina bridges can scramble up a steep rock slope to the site. Like all ancient ruins, these are very fragile and must not be touched or entered. Only with such care will future generations of visitors be able to admire the well-preserved structures. Other groups of Anasazi dwellings can be seen in or near the monument too; ask a ranger for directions.

Kachina Bridge viewpoint and trailhead are 5.1 miles from the visitor center. The massive bridge has a span of 204 feet and a height of 210 feet. A trail, one and one half miles roundtrip, leads to the canyon bottom next to the bridge; elevation change is 650 feet. Look for pictographs near the base of the trail. Some of the figures resemble Hopi kachinas (spirits) and prompted the bridge's name. Armstrong Canyon joins White Canyon just downstream from the bridge; floods in each canyon abraded opposite sides of the rock fin that later became Kachina Bridge.

Owachomo Bridge viewpoint and trailhead are 7.1 miles from the visitor center. An easy

Owachomo Bridge (from Armstrong Canyon)

walk leads to Owachomo's base, a half mile roundtrip with an elevation change of 180 feet. Graceful Owachomo spans 180 feet and is 106 feet high. Erosive forces have worn the venerable bridge to a thickness of only nine feet. Unlike the other two bridges, Owachomo spans a smaller tributary stream instead of a major canyon. Two streams played a role in the bridge's formation. Floods coming down the larger Armstrong Canyon surged against a sandstone fin on one side while floods in a small side canyon wore away the rock on the other side. Eventually a hole formed, and waters flowing down the side canyon took the shorter route through the bridge. The name Owachomo means "flat-rock mound" in the Hopi language; a large rock outcrop nearby inspired the name. Before construction of the present road, a trail winding down the opposite side of Armstrong Canyon provided the only access for monument visitors. The trail, little used now, connects with UT 95.

Hiking
A canyon hike through all three bridges can be the highlight of a visit to the monument. Unmaintained trails make an 8.6-mile loop in White and Armstrong canyons and cross a wooded plateau. The trip is easier if you start from Sipapu and come out the relatively gentle grades at Owachomo. Most people take five to six hours for this moderately difficult hike. You can save two and one half miles by arranging a car shuttle between Sipapu and Owachomo trailheads. Another option is to go in or out on the Kachina Bridge Trail midway, cutting the hiking distance in about half. On nearing Owachomo Bridge from below, a small sign points out the trail which bypasses a deep pool. The canyons remain in their wild state; you'll need some hiking experience, water, proper footwear, compass, and map (the handout available at the visitor center is adequate). USGS 7 1/2-minute topo maps also cover this area. When hiking in the canyons, keep an eye out for natural arches and Indian writings. Please don't step on midget faded rattlesnakes or other living entities (such as the fragile cryptobiotic soil). Be aware of flash-flood dangers, especially if you see big clouds billowing in the sky in an upstream direction. You don't need a hiking permit, though it's a good idea to talk beforehand with a ranger to find out current conditions.

Overnight camping within the monument is permitted only in the campground. Backpackers, however, can go up or down the canyons and camp outside the monument boundaries. Just be careful to choose high ground in case a flood comes rumbling through! Note that vehicles can't be parked overnight on the loop drive.

VICINITY OF NATURAL BRIDGES NATIONAL MONUMENT

Fry Canyon

The store here originally served uranium mining camps during the 1950s. Today the cafe and motel offer the only services on UT 95 between Blanding and Hite Marina. Rooms cost $33-49.50 s or d. Telephone service is not available in Fry Canyon. In winter, the cafe may be closed, but accommodations are usually still available. Two Anasazi ruins can be viewed nearby; a road goes to an overlook of one ruin and a short trail goes to the other. Ask for directions. Fry Canyon is 19 miles northwest of the Natural Bridges National Monument turnoff and 24 miles southeast of the Hite Marina turnoff.

Dark Canyon

This magnificent canyon system lies about 15 air miles north of Natural Bridges National Monument. Dark Canyon, with its many tributaries, begins in the high country of Elk Ridge and extends west to Lake Powell in lower Cataract Canyon. Steep cliffs and the isolated location have protected the relatively pristine environment. The upper canyons tend to be wide with open areas and groves of Douglas fir and ponderosa pine. Creeks dry up after spring snowmelt, leaving only widely scattered springs as water sources for most of the year. Farther downstream, the canyon walls close in and the desert trees of piñon pine, juniper, and cottonwood take over. At its lower end, Dark Canyon has a year-round stream and deep plunge pools; cliffs tower more than 1,400 feet above the canyon floor. Springs and running water attract wildlife, including bighorn sheep, black bear, deer, mountain lion, coyote, bobcat, ringtail cat, raccoon, fox, and spotted skunk. Experienced hikers enjoy the solitude, wildlife, Anasazi ruins, and varied canyon scenery. Although it's possible to visit Dark Canyon on a day-hike, you'll

need several days to get a feel for this area. To explore the entire canyon and its major tributaries would take weeks! Hiking through the canyons is mostly easy, though strenuous scrambles are needed to bypass a few pour-offs and other obstacles. Elevations of Dark Canyon range from 8,200 feet at its upper end to 3,700 feet at Lake Powell. Hikers must be extra cautious and self-sufficient, because outside help can be days away. Check with people at the BLM or U.S. Forest Service offices before a trip. Horses can do the trails in the upper (National Forest) section, but not in the constricted lower canyon. Topo maps available are the 7½-minute topo maps, the 1:100,000 Hite Crossing and Blanding maps, and Trails Illustrated's map of the Abajos and Dark Canyon. A new *Dark Canyon Trail Guide* is being published by the Canyonlands Natural History Association and should be available by spring, 1995. Check with the Monticello Multi-Agency Visitor Center or the Moab Information Center.

The upper half of the canyon system lies within Dark Canyon Wilderness, administered by the Manti-La Sal National Forest, Box 820, Monticello, UT 84535, tel. 587-2041. The Monticello office has information sheets on the 10 access trails to Dark Canyon and can advise on road conditions to the trailheads. A variety of loop hikes can be made in the tributary canyons. Woodenshoe Canyon is used by more than 50% of visitors to the area. Snow and mud usually block roads, all of which are unpaved, until mid-May to early June. When the roads are closed, hikers sometimes drive to Bears Ears Pass and hike to their trailhead. Spring through autumn are good hiking seasons in the higher country, though snowmelt sometimes causes spring flooding.

The lower half of Dark Canyon, currently designated a primitive area, lies mostly within BLM land; the area is a candidate for wilderness status. Trail notes describing hiking conditions, water sources, trailheads, and wilderness etiquette are available from BLM offices at Kane Gulch Ranger Station (trailhead for Grand Gulch) or Monticello (Box 7, Monticello, UT 84535, tel. 587-2141). Obtain a free permit from the BLM before visiting its lands.

The **Sundance Trail** is the most popular entry to lower Dark Canyon. The start of the trail can be reached on dirt roads that branch off UT 95 southeast of the Hite Marina turnoff; this approach can be used year-round in dry weather. Cairns mark the trail, which drops 1,200 feet in less than one mile on a steep talus slope. Boaters can reach the lower end of Dark Canyon in Glen Canyon National Recreation Area by going 14 miles up Lake Powell from Hite Marina. The lower canyon can be hiked year-round, with spring and autumn the best choices.

Grand Gulch Primitive Area

Within this twisting canyon system lie some of the most captivating scenery and largest concentrations of Anasazi ruins in all of southeastern Utah. The main canyon begins only about six miles southeast of Natural Bridges National Monument. From an elevation of 6,400 feet, Grand Gulch cuts deeply into Cedar Mesa on a tortuous path southwest to the San Juan River, dropping 2,700 feet in about 53 miles. Sheer cliffs, alcoves, pinnacles, Anasazi cliff dwellings, rock-art sites, arches, and a few natural bridges line Grand Gulch and its many tributaries. Canyon depths reach 600 feet. Nearly all of Grand Gulch has been cut out of Cedar Mesa Sandstone. The lower one and one half miles of canyon also reveal exposures of the older Cutler Formation (Halgaito Shale Member) and the Honaker Trail Formation. Wildlife to look for include mule deer, mountain lion, black bear, coyote, bobcat, fox, ringtail cat, spotted skunk, cottontail, white-tailed antelope squirrel, white-

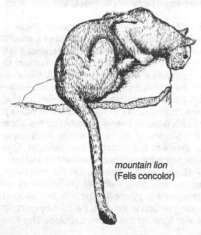

mountain lion
(Felis concolor)

throated wood rat, Ord kangaroo rat, piñon mouse, Great Basin gopher snake, Hopi rattlesnake, and midget faded rattlesnake. Some birds in the area are red-tailed hawk, great horned owl, peregrine falcon, mourning dove, titmouse, rock wren, and piñon jay. Vegetation includes piñon pine, juniper, cottonwood, Gambel oak, singleleaf ash, willow, sagebrush, blackbrush, rabbitbrush, prickly pear cactus, and flowering annuals. The Anasazi left behind hundreds of dwellings and thousands of pictographs and petroglyphs. They lived in Grand Gulch from A.D. 200 to 400 (Basketmaker II), 650-725 (late Basketmaker III), and 1060-1270 (Pueblo II-III); droughts may have caused all three departures. Mormon pioneers of the Hole-in-the-Rock expedition named the canyon in 1880, but the exhausted group was in no mood to enjoy the scenery.

Kane Gulch and Bullet Canyon provide access to the upper end of Grand Gulch from the east side. A popular loop hike using these canyons is 23 miles long (three to four days); you'll need a seven-and-one-half-mile car shuttle or you can hitch. Ask at the ranger station if a shuttle service is available. Collins Canyon, reached from Collins Spring Trailhead, leads into lower Grand Gulch from the west side. Hiking distance between Kane Gulch and Collins Spring trailheads is 38 miles one-way (five to seven days). A car shuttle of about 29 miles (including eight miles of dirt road) is needed. River runners can travel up the mouth from the San Juan River. The San Juan is 53 miles from Kane Gulch Trailhead and 19 miles from Collins Spring Trailhead. The lower third of Grand Gulch (below Collins Canyon) lacks the abundant Anasazi sites found in the middle and upper reaches and has few water sources.

The book *Wind in the Rock* by Ann Zwinger presents a personal account of the wonders of travel in Grand Gulch and nearby canyons. Spring and autumn are the choice times for hiking; it is also possible in summer, though you'll want to sit out the midday heat. Winter snow makes some of the slickrock sections hazardous. Be sure to visit the BLM's Kane Gulch Ranger Station or Monticello office for a permit and information. The BLM map of Grand Gulch Primitive Area ($2) shows the topography, mileages for each section of canyon, and major points of interest; it's good for both planning a

LOUISE FOOTE

trip and using while hiking. Other maps include the 7½-minute, 1:100,000 metric, and Trails Illustrated's Grand Gulch Plateau topos. Springs provide water in most parts of Grand Gulch but aren't always reliable, especially in summer; the BLM staff can give you an idea of what to expect. "Innocent vandalism" caused by visitors touching and climbing on the ruins and middens has caused serious damage. BLM staff will offer advice and literature on how to safely visit the ancient sites. Pot hunting has been another problem; report any suspicious behavior to the BLM. Grand Gulch receives heavy use, so respecting the ruins and camping without leaving ant traces are extra important.

Kane Gulch Ranger Station

The BLM provides permits, archaeological information, current hiking conditions, literature, and sales of maps and books. (Try to get maps in advance as rangers are sometimes out on patrol.) The station is at Kane Gulch Trailhead, four miles south on UT 261 from UT 95; open daily from early March to late November. No telephone, water, or trash collection is available. Normally this is the best place for first-hand information. You can also visit the BLM office at 435 N. Main in Monticello (Box 7, Monticello, UT 84535), tel. 587-2141. Open year-round Mon.-Fri. 7:45 a.m.-4:30 p.m. Everyone visiting the Cedar Mesa backcountry should drop in for the required permit and to get the latest information. Permits run $5 per person for overnight camping and are limited to no more than 12 persons. Note that groups of eight or more people with pack animals need to obtain permits at least three weeks beforehand from the ranger station or office. Help protect fragile desert soils by keeping all vehicles—including mountain bicycles—on established roads. Campfires are not permitted in the canyons.

Fish Creek And Owl Creek Loop Hike

Varied canyon scenery, year-round pools, Anasazi ruins, and a magnificent natural arch make this an excellent hike. Fish Creek and its tributary Owl Creek lie east of Grand Gulch on the other side of UT 261. A one-and-one-half-mile trail atop Cedar Mesa connects upper arms of the two creeks to make a 15.5-mile loop. From the trailhead (elev. 6,160 feet), you'll descend 1,400 feet to the junction of the two creeks. Opinions differ as to which direction to begin the loop, but either way is fine. Owl Creek might be the better choice for a day-hike because it's closer to the trailhead and has the added attractions of easily accessible ruins just a half mile away and Nevill's Arch three and one half miles farther (one-way). Contact the Kane Gulch or Monticello BLM offices for trail notes and current trail and water conditions. Maps are essential for navigation, because it's easy to get off the route in some places. The BLM trail notes have a topo map. Camping places are easy to locate; just avoid washes. You can always find at least intermittent water in the upper parts of both creeks.

The canyons have been carved in Cedar Mesa Sandstone, which forms many overhangs where the Anasazi Indians built cliff dwellings. Unfortunately, nearly all ruins sit high in the cliffs and can be hard to spot from the canyon bottoms (canyon depths average 500 feet). Binoculars come in handy for seeing the ruins, some of which are marked on the topo maps. Climbing equipment may not be used to reach the ruins.

The turnoff for the trailhead is between Mileposts 27 and 28 of UT 261, one mile south of Kane Gulch Ranger Station. Head east 5.2 miles on San Juan County 253, passable by cars when dry, to a parking area at the site of an old drill hole. A sign points the way north one and one half miles to Fish Creek and southeast a quarter mile to Owl Creek. Cairns show the way into the canyons, then you just follow the creekbeds. The route into Fish Creek goes north one and one half miles across the mesa from the trailhead (watch closely for cairns—it's easy to miss the trail where it climbs out of a wash), makes a steep descent into an arm of Fish Creek, and follows Fish Creek downstream to the confluence with Owl Creek; total distance from the trailhead to this point is nine miles one-way. Turn right two and one half miles up Owl Creek, normally dry in this section, to Nevill's Arch. It's possible to rockscramble up the slope to the window of the arch, where you'll enjoy fine views of the canyons and beyond. Owl Creek has water and becomes prettier and prettier as you head upstream. On the four miles from the arch to the trailhead, you'll need to circumvent three pour-offs: the first and second by going around to the right, the third by going to the left; look for the cairned routes. The first and second pour-offs have small waterfalls and idyllic pools. Above the third pour-off, you'll pass a well-preserved group of Anasazi ruins on the left. From here there's only a short but steep scramble to the rim, then a quarter mile across slickrock back to the trailhead.

Slickhorn Canyon

Adventurous hikers enjoy the Indian ruins and impressive scenery in this rugged canyon south of Grand Gulch. Canyon depths along Slickhorn's 12-mile length range from about 300 feet in the northern reaches to 800 feet near the confluence with the San Juan River. Boulders, talus slopes, and pour-offs in the streambed hamper travel and discourage casual visitors. Allow about four days to explore Slickhorn Canyon and some of its tributaries. A more ambitious trip is to go down Slickhorn to the San Juan River, hike downstream along a high, narrow ledge to the mouth of Grand Gulch, then travel up to one of the Grand Gulch trailheads in a week or more of hiking. The BLM offices at Kane Gulch and Monticello have information sheets, trailhead information, and a map. The BLM's Grand Gulch hiking map covers this area. Several trailheads can be reached by turning west on an unpaved road from UT 261 opposite the signed Cigarette Springs Road, 9.4 miles south of the Kane Gulch Ranger Station.

John's Canyon

This varied canyon lies southeast of Grand Gulch and Slickhorn canyons. A fingerlike network of deep narrow canyons in the upper drainages contrasts with a broad alluvial bottom downstream that's up to a mile wide. The main canyon is about 13 miles long and empties into the San Juan River. Canyon depths average about 1,000 feet. Experienced hikers will find the going relatively easy, as there are only a few boulder falls and small pour-offs in the upper canyons. High pour-offs in the lower canyon, however, effectively block access to the San Juan River. A map and information sheet available from the BLM offices have trailhead and spring information and a brief description of hiking in the canyon. Cliffs and overhangs on the rim in the north restrict access to only a few points; the BLM map shows one entry point, reached by a short dirt road off UT 261. In the south, a jeep road branches off UT

316 (the road to Goosenecks State Park), follows the rim of the San Juan River west, and then turns up into middle John's Canyon.

MEXICAN HAT

Spectacular geology surrounds this tiny community perched on the north bank of the San Juan River. Folded layers of red and gray rock stand out dramatically. Alhambra Rock, a jagged remnant of a volcano, marks the southern approach to Mexican Hat. Another rock, which looks just like an upside-down sombrero, gave Mexican Hat its name; you'll see this formation two miles north of town. The land has never proved good for much except its scenery. Farmers and ranchers thought it next to worthless. Stories of gold in the San Juan River brought a frenzy of prospecting in 1892-93, but the mining proved mostly a bust. Oil, first struck by drillers in 1908, has brought mostly modest profits. The uranium mill across the river at Halchita gave a boost to the economy from 1956 until it closed in 1965. Mexican Hat now serves as a modest trade and tourism center. Monument Valley, Valley of the Gods Scenic Drive, Goosenecks State Park, and Grand Gulch Primitive Area lie only short drives away. The shore near town can be a busy place in summer as river runners on the San Juan put in, take out, or just stop for ice and beer.

Practicalities

The **San Juan Inn** offers rooms ($52.32 s, $58.86 d), the **Olde Bridge Bar and Grill** (American, Mexican, and Navajo food daily for breakfast, lunch, and dinner), and the **San Juan Trading Post** (Indian crafts and groceries). Located on a ledge overlooking the river near the highway bridge, tel. 683-2220 or (800) 447-2022. **Canyonlands Motel**, tel. 683-2230, offers basic rooms for $32.40 s, $39.24 d; closed in winter. **Valle's Trading Post and RV Park**, tel. 683-2226, open all year, has tent and RV sites w/hookups for $12 s, $14 d. The trading post offers Indian crafts, groceries, showers, vehicle storage, and car shuttles. **Mexican Hat Lodge**, tel. 683-2222, offers rooms ($52.38 s or d), a pool, and a restaurant (American food daily for lunch and dinner). **Valley of the Gods Inn**, tel. 683-2221, has motel rooms ($56.18 and up), tent camping at $10.90, and RV at $16.35 w/hookups; it also has a cafe with American, Mexican, and Navajo food (open daily for breakfast, lunch, and dinner), Indian crafts, groceries, and car shuttles. **Burch's Cattle Co.** offers horseback riding. tel. 683-2221.

VICINITY OF MEXICAN HAT

Valley Of The Gods
Great sandstone monoliths, delicate spires, and long rock fins rise from the broad valley. This strange red-rock landscape resembles better-known Monument Valley but on a smaller scale. A 17-mile dirt road winds through the spectacular scenery. Cars can usually travel the road at low speeds if the weather is dry (washes are crossed). Allow one to one and one half hours for the drive. The east end of the road connects with US 163 at Milepost 29 (seven and one half miles northeast of Mexican Hat or 15 miles southwest of Bluff); the west end connects with UT 261 just below the Moki Dugway switch-

gold-mining operation at Mexican Hat, 1890s

backs (four miles north of Mexican Hat on US 163, then 6.6 miles northwest on UT 261).

Goosenecks State Park
The San Juan River winds through a series of incredibly tight bends 1,000 feet below. So closely spaced are the bends that the river takes six miles to cover an air distance of only one and one half miles! The bends and exposed rock layers form exquisitely graceful curves. Geologists know the site as a classic example of entrenched meanders, caused by gradual uplift of a formerly level plain. Signs at the overlook explain the geologic history and identify the rock formations. Goosenecks State Park is an undeveloped area with a few tables and vault toilets as the only facilities. Camping is available; no water or charge. From the junction of US 163 and UT 261, four miles north of Mexican Hat, go one mile northwest on UT 261, then turn left three miles on UT 316 to its end.

Muley Point Overlook
One of the great views in the Southwest lies just a short drive from Goosenecks State Park and more than 1,000 feet higher. Although the view of the Goosenecks below is less dramatic than at the state park, the 6,200-foot elevation provides a magnificent panorama across the Navajo Indian Reservation to Monument Valley and countless canyons and mountains. To get here, travel northwest nine miles on UT 261 from the Goosenecks turnoff. At the top of the Moki Dugway switchbacks (an 1,100-foot climb with sharp curves and 5-10% grades), turn left (southwest) 5.3 miles on a gravel road to the point. The turnoff may not be signed. This road is not suitable for wet-weather travel.

River Running On The San Juan
From the high San Juan Mountains in southern Colorado, this intriguing river wends its way into New Mexico, enters Utah near Four Corners, and twists through spectacular canyons before ending at Lake Powell. Sand waves spring up during flooding, usually in May and June. The waves can pop up out of flat water to heights of three feet and occasionally as much as seven or eight feet! Swift currents on the sandy bottom cause these harmless waves, which can migrate up or downstream before disappearing.

lazing down the lower San Juan River

Below the town of Bluff, the muddy river picks up speed and dives deep within its canyon walls. Most boaters put in at Sand Island Campground near Bluff and take out at the town of Mexican Hat, 30 river miles downstream, or continue another 56 river miles through the Goosenecks to Clay Hills Crossing or Paiute Farms (not always accessible) on Lake Powell. Allow at least four days for the full trip, though more time will allow exploration of side canyons and visits to Anasazi sites. Rafts, kayaks, and canoes can be used. The season now usually lasts all year, due to the Navajo Reservoir upstream.

Many commercial river-running companies offer San Juan trips. If you go on your own, you should have river-running experience or be with someone who has. Private groups need to obtain permits from the BLM San Juan Resource Area office well in advance; Box 7, Monticello, UT 84535, tel. 587-2141. The book *San Juan Canyons, A River Runner's Guide* by Don Baars and Gene Stevenson has a river log with detailed maps, practical advice, and background. Some people also like to run the river between Montezuma Creek and Sand Island, a leisurely trip of 20 river miles. The solitude often makes

up for the lack of scenery. It's easy to get a river permit for this section because no use limits or fees apply.

MONUMENT VALLEY

Towering buttes, jagged pinnacles, and rippled sand dunes make this an otherworldly landscape. Changing colors and shifting shadows during the day add to the enchantment. Most of the natural monuments are remnants of sandstone eroded by wind and water. Agathla Peak and some lesser summits are roots of ancient volcanoes, whose dark rock contrasts with the pale yellow sandstone of the other formations. The valley lies at an elevation of 5,564 feet in the Upper Sonoran Life Zone; annual rainfall averages about eight and one half inches.

In 1863-64, when Kit Carson was ravaging Canyon de Chelly in Arizona to round up the Navajo, Chief Hoskinini led his people to the safety and freedom of Monument Valley. Merrick Butte and Mitchell Mesa commemorate two miners who discovered rich silver deposits on their first trip to the valley in 1880. On their second trip both were killed, reportedly shot by

Paiute Indians. Hollywood movies made the splendor of Monument Valley known to the outside world. *Stagecoach,* filmed here in 1938 and directed by John Ford, became the first in a series of westerns that has continued to the present. John Wayne and many other movie greats rode across these sands.

The Navajo have preserved the valley as a tribal park with a scenic drive, visitor center, and campground. From Mexican Hat, drive 22 miles southwest on US 163 and turn left three and one half miles to the visitor center. From Kayenta, go 24 miles north on US 163 and turn right three and one half miles.

Visitor Center

An information desk, exhibits, and an Indian crafts shop are open daily about 7 a.m.-8 p.m. May-Sept., then daily 8 a.m.-5 p.m. the rest of the year, tel. (801) 727-3287. Visitors pay a $2.50 fee ($1 age 60 and over, free for six and under), collected on the entrance road.

Monument Valley Drive

A 17-mile, self-guided scenic drive begins at the visitor center and loops through the heart of the valley. Overlooks provide sweeping views from different vantage points. The dirt road is normally okay for cautiously driven cars. Avoid stopping and becoming stuck in the loose sand that sometimes blows across the road. Allow one and one half hours for the drive, open 7 a.m.-7 p.m. in summer, 8 a.m.-5 p.m. the rest of the year. No hiking or driving off the signed route is allowed. Water and restrooms are available only at the visitor center.

Valley Tours

Take one of the guided tours leaving daily year-round from the visitor center to visit a hogan, a cliff dwelling, and petroglyphs in areas beyond the self-guided drive. The trips last two and one half to three hours and cost $20 per person. Shorter trips of 90 minutes cost $15 per person. Guided horseback rides from near the visitor center cost $20 for one and one half hours; longer day and overnight trips can be arranged too. If you'd like to hike in Monument Valley, you must hire a guide; hiking tours of two hours to a day or more can be arranged at the visitor center.

Accommodations

Sites at **Mitten View Campground** near the Visitor Center cost $10; coin operated hot showers are available. The season is early mid-March to mid-October. Tenters should be prepared for winds in this exposed location. Goulding's Lodge (see below) has the nearest motel, restaurant, and store. Motels are also found at Kayenta in Arizona and at Mexican Hat and Bluff in Utah.

Goulding's Lodge And Trading Post

Harry Goulding and his wife Mike opened the trading post in 1924. It's located two miles west of the US 163 Monument Valley turnoff, just north of the Arizona-Utah border. **Goulding's Museum,** in the old trading post building, displays prehistoric and modern Indian artifacts, movie photos, and memorabilia of the Goulding family. Open daily, may close in winter; admission by donation. Motel rooms start at $111.80 s or d in summer, less off-season; guests can use a small indoor pool; meals are available in the dining room. A gift shop sells souvenirs, books, and high-quality Indian crafts. The nearby store has groceries and gas pumps. Monument Valley tours operate year-round; $30 half day, $62 full day with a six-person minimum, children under 12 go at half price. The lodge stays open all year. For accommodation and tour info, write Box 360001, Monument Valley, UT 84536, tel. (801) 727-3231.

Monument Valley Campground, tel. (801) 727-3235, offers tent and RV sites a short drive west; rates are $15 tent, $23.65 RV w/hookups. Open April 1 to November 1. The Seventh-day Adventist Church runs a hospital and mission nearby.

FOUR CORNERS MONUMENT

A concrete slab marks the point where Utah, Colorado, New Mexico, and Arizona meet. It's the only spot in the United States where you can put your finger on four states at once. Over 2,000 people a day are said to stop at the marker in the summer season. Average stay? Seven to 10 minutes. On the other hand, five national parks and 18 national monuments are within a radius of 150 miles from this point! Indians, mostly Navajo with perhaps some Ute and

Pueblo, set up dozens of craft and refreshment booths in summer. Navajo Parks and Recreation collects a $1 per vehicle (50 cents motorcycle) fee during the tourist season.

KAYENTA

The "Gateway to Monument Valley" is a town of 5,200 in a bleak, windswept valley (elev. 5,660 feet) in Arizona. Its name is loosely derived from the Navajo word Teehindeeh, meaning "bog hole," as there were once shallow lakes here. Kayenta, a handy stop for travelers, has two good motels and several restaurants.

Accommodations
Wetherill Inn is in the center of town on US 163, one mile north of US 160, tel. 697-3231. Its name honors John Wetherill, an early trader and rancher of the region who discovered Betatakin, Mesa Verde, and other major Anasazi sites. Rooms cost $77.66 s, $84.24 d in summer. The **Holiday Inn**, on US 160 at the turnoff for Kayenta, tel. 697-3221 or (800) HOLIDAY, has rooms ($117.72 s, $129.60 d in summer), restaurant, and pool. The **Coin-Op Laundry,** tel. 697-8282/3400, in town has tent and RV spaces at $9.50 w/hookups. Showers are available for noncampers at $2.25.

Food
The **Holiday Inn's** restaurant has good Navajo tacos and standard American fare; open daily for breakfast, lunch, and dinner. The **Blue Coffee Pot** is nearby on the other side of the highway; open daily for breakfast, lunch, and dinner. **Amigo Cafe** serves Mexican and American food; open daily for breakfast, lunch, and dinner; located on US 163 between the Kayenta turnoff and town. **Golden Sands Cafe,** near the Wetherill Inn, offers American food daily for breakfast, lunch, and dinner. **Pizza Edger** next to the Teehindeeh Shopping Center serves pizza. Buy **groceries** at the supermarket in the shopping center or at the Kayenta Supermarket (behind the Wetherill Inn).

Shopping And Services
Look for **Native American crafts** at both motels, Lee's Trading Co. (in shopping center), and Burch's Indian Room (near Wetherill Inn). **Tours** in 4WD vehicles to Monument Valley and surrounding country can be arranged from both motels; costs start at about $30 half day or $60 full day with a minimum of four or six persons.

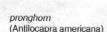

pronghorn
(Antilocapra americana)

LOUISE FOOTE

PAGE

Before 1957, only sand and desert vegetation lay atop Manson Mesa in far northern Arizona where Page now sits, 130 miles north of Flagstaff (AZ) and 72 miles east of Kanab, Utah. In that year the U.S. Bureau of Reclamation decided to build a giant reservoir in Glen Canyon on the Colorado River. Glen Canyon Dam was to become one of the largest construction projects ever undertaken. The 710-foot-high structure would create a lake covering 250 square miles with a shoreline of nearly 2,000 miles. Workmen hastily set up prefabricated metal buildings for barracks, dining hall, and offices. Trailers rolled in, one serving as Page's first bank. The Bureau of Reclamation named the construction camp for John C. Page, who served as the bureau's first commissioner from 1937 to 1943.

The remote desert spot gradually turned into a modern town as schools, businesses, and churches appeared. Streets were named and

prehistoric ruins on the brink of Glen Canyon

grass and trees planted, and Page took on the appearance of American suburbia. The town still has a new and clean look. Though small (pop. 7,000), it's the largest community close to Lake Powell, and offers travelers a good selection of places to stay and eat. Wedged between Glen Canyon National Recreation Area to the north, the Arizona Strip to the west, and the Navajo Reservation to the east and south, Page makes a useful base for visiting all these areas. The townsite (elev. 4,300 feet) overlooks Lake Powell and Glen Canyon Dam; the large Wahweap Resort and Marina are just six miles away. (Note: All telephone numbers below for Page and Wahweap Marina have the Arizona 602 prefix; however, sometime in 1995 all Arizona prefixes outside the Phoenix area will be changed to 520.)

John Wesley Powell Memorial Museum
The collection honors scientist and explorer John Wesley Powell. In 1869 he led the first expedition down the Green and Colorado River gorges, then ran the rivers a second time in 1871-72. It was Powell who named the most splendid section the "Grand Canyon." Old drawings and photographs illustrate his life and voyages. Fossil and mineral displays interpret the thick geologic section revealed by canyons of the Colorado River. Other exhibits contain pottery, baskets, weapons, tools of Southwestern Indian tribes, and memorabilia of early pioneers and the founding of Page. Related videos are shown on request. Travel info, Lake Powell boat tours, half-day river trips, jeep tours, flightseeing tours, and regional books are available. Summer hours (June-Sept.) are Sunday 10 a.m.-6 p.m. and Mon.-Sat. 8 a.m.-6 p.m.; May and October hours are Mon.-Sat. 8 a.m.-6 p.m.; March, April, and November hours are Mon.-Fri. 9 a.m.-5 p.m. Closed in winter. The museum is in downtown at the corner of Lake Powell Blvd. and North Navajo Drive, tel. 645-9496.

Diné Bí Keyah Museum
(Big Lake Trading Post)
This small collection of prehistoric and modern Indian artifacts is on the second floor; open daily

8 a.m.-7 p.m.; free admission. Big Lake Trading Post is 1.3 miles southeast on AZ 98, tel. 645-2404; Indian crafts and groceries are sold.

Corkscrew Canyon

This slot canyon twists and turns in beautifully layered sandstone just southeast of town. Light bouncing between the narrow walls gives off a warm glow, from the bright, sunlit orange at the rim to deep shadows near the floor. You've probably seen photos of Corkscrew Canyon's swirling patterns and deep hues. And you're likely to see photographers intently composing new photos when you enter the canyon. (A tripod is almost a "must" in the dim interior light.) The 3.6-mile road in has some spots of deep sand, so you'll need a 4WD vehicle; alternatively, you can take a tour (see "Tours" under "Practicalities," below) or just walk in. Because the canyon lies on Navajo land, you'll need a permit from them ($5 for the first person, $1.50 each additional); check hours with the Page/Lake Powell Chamber (tel. 645-2741) or Lechee Chapter House (tel. 698-3272/3316). From Business 89L in Page, turn southeast three miles on AZ 98, then turn right just past Milepost 299; a Navajo here issues permits from a vehicle. Follow the jeep road through Antelope Wash to Corkscrew Canyon. Corkscrew's sandy floor offers easy walking all the way through—about 600 feet—where it opens onto a broad wash.

PRACTICALITIES

Accommodations

All of Page's motels lie on or near Lake Powell Blvd., a three-and-one-quarter-mile loop designated US 89 L that branches off the main highway. More than two dozen bed and breakfasts offer accommodations too; contact the chamber office for a list. Most of the summer rates listed below drop substantially in winter. The new **Courtyard by Marriott,** 600 Country Club Dr., tel. 645-5000, offers a restaurant and exercise room and plans to have a golf course; $130.96 s or d. **EconoLodge** is at 121 S. Lake Powell Blvd., tel. 645-2488, $77.04 s, $88.04 d. **Empire House Motel,** 107 S. Lake Powell Blvd., tel. 645-2406, has a coffee shop and

swimming pool; $55.03 s, $68.23 d. **Super 8** is at 75 S. 7th Ave. (behind Taco Bell), tel. 645-2858, $59.75 s, $62.99 d. **Page Boy Motel,** 150 N. Lake Powell Blvd., tel. 645-2416, has a swimming pool; $39.62 s, $48.42 d. **Navajo Trail Motel** has rooms at 800 Bureau (behind Page Boy Motel), tel. 645-9508, for $43 s, $46 d; and nearby at 630 Vista (behind Glen Canyon Steak House), tel. 645-9508, for $54 s, $62.50 d. The **Weston Inn** (Best Western), 207 N. Lake Powell Blvd., tel. 645-2451 or (800) 528-1234, offers a swimming pool; $63.57 s, $69.05 d. **Best Western at Lake Powell,** 208 N. Lake Powell Blvd., tel. 645-5988 or (800) 528-1234, has a pool and spa; $101.25-108.95 s or d, $148.57 suites. **Holiday Inn,** 287 N. Lake Powell Blvd., tel. 645-8851 or (800) HOLIDAY, features a swimming pool, restaurant, and views over Lake Powell; $101.20 s or d. The **Inn at Lake Powell,** 716 Rim View Dr. and Lake Powell Blvd. (across from Holiday Inn), tel. 645-2466 or (800) 826-2718, has fine views, swimming pool, and an adjacent restaurant; $70.43-90.24 s, $75.93-101.24 d. **Bashful Bob's Motel,** 750 S. Navajo, tel. 645-3919, offers basic rooms; $37.90 s, $42.90 d.

Youth Hostel/Pension

The **Lake Powell International Youth Hostel,** 141 8th Ave., tel. 645-3898, does not require membership cards and is the most economical place to room in Page at $12-15 per person in dorm-style rooms. You will meet travelers from all over the world. Guests have access to laundry and kitchen facilities. The **Pension at Lake Powell,** 125 8th Ave., tel. 648-3898, is run by the same people as the hostel but offers individual rooms at $55-71.50 s or d ($27.50 off-season). Both facilities offer free airport shuttle service as well as shuttles to hiking and swimming areas.

Campgrounds

Page-Lake Powell Campground, Located 0.7 mile southeast of town on AZ 98, tel. 645-3374, offers sites for tents and RVs, $16.50 no hookups, $22 w/hookups; has indoor pool, spa, and showers; all rates come down in winter. Other campgrounds, an RV park, and motels are in the Wahweap area (see "Marinas" under "Glen Canyon National Recreation Area," below).

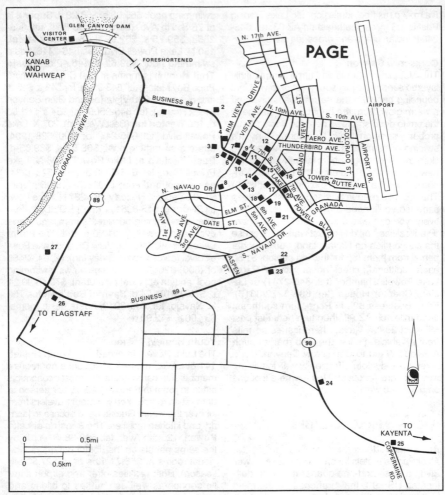

Food And Entertainment

Glen Canyon Steak House, 201 N. Lake Powell Blvd., tel. 645-3363, serves American food daily for breakfast, lunch, and dinner; specialties include steaks, seafood, ribs, and chicken; live country-rock bands perform evenings Tues.-Sunday. **Ken's Old West Restaurant,** 718 Vista Ave. (behind Best Western at Lake Powell), tel. 645-5160, has steak, prime rib, and seafood; open daily for dinner. Country-western bands provide music Mon.-Saturday. **Fami-** ly Tree Restaurant, 287 N. Lake Powell Blvd., tel. 645-8851, in the Holiday Inn, offers a varied menu and is open daily for breakfast, lunch, and dinner. **The Inn Restaurant,** 716 Rim View Dr. next to the Inn at Lake Powell, tel. 645-2467, serves American and Continental food daily for breakfast, lunch, and dinner. **M Bar H Cafe,** 819 N. Navajo, tel. 645-1420, serves American food daily for breakfast and lunch with dinner served Wednesday and Sunday.

Stop for Chinese/American food at **Starlite,** 46

PAGE

1. Courtyard by Marriott
2. McDonald's
3. Holiday Inn
4. Inn at Lake Powell
5. Weston Inn
6. Glen Canyon Steak House; Navajo Trail Motel #2
7. Best Western at Lake Powell; Ken's Old West Restaurant
8. Page Hospital
9. Page Boy Motel; Navajo Trail Motel #1
10. public library
11. Powell Museum
12. Bella Napoli
13. Zapata's Restaurant
14. Lakeview Shopping Center; Page Factory Stores
15. Strombolli's Pizza
16. Super 8 Motel
17. Starlite Restaurant; Pleasure Bound Bookstore; Wilderness River Adventures; Mesa Theatre
18. post office
19. Page Plaza; Page/Lake Powell Chamber of Commerce
20. Empire House Motel; EconoLodge
21. Page Memorial Park
22. Page High School
23. tennis courts
24. Page-Lake Powell Campground
25. Big Lake Trading Post
26. Gateway Plaza (Wal-Mart & Basha's); Chamber of Commerce Information Kiosk
27. Glen Canyon Golf & Country Club

S. Lake Powell Blvd., tel. 645-3620, open daily except Sunday for breakfast, lunch, and dinner. **Zapata's Mexican Restaurant,** 615 N. Navajo Dr., tel. 645-9006, is open Mon.-Sat. for lunch and daily for dinner; closed in winter. **Dos Amigos Mexican Restaurant,** 610 Elm St., tel. 645-3036, is open daily for lunch and dinner. **Bella Napoli,** 810 N. Navajo Dr., tel. 645-2706, offers fine Italian cuisine Mon.-Sat. for dinner in spring, then daily for dinner until mid-autumn; closed in winter. Pizza, spaghetti, and other Italian fare are served daily for lunch and dinner by **Strombolli's Pizza,** 711 N. Navajo Dr., tel. 645-2605; **Pizza Hut,** Lake View Shopping Center, tel. 645-

2455; and **Little Caesars,** Page Plaza, tel. 645-5565, carry-out only. Buy **groceries** at Safeway (Page Plaza at corner of Lake Powell Blvd. and Elm St.), Bashas' (Gateway Plaza), or at Mrs. C's Health Food Center (34 S. Lake Powell Boulevard). Catch movies at **Mesa Theatre,** 42 S. Lake Powell Blvd., tel. 645-9565.

Events
For more information about Lake Powell's events, contact **Lake Powell Resorts and Marinas,** tel. (800) 528-6154 (278-8888 in greater Phoenix). To learn about other events, contact **Page/Lake Powell Chamber of Commerce,** tel. 645-2741.

January: Hole-in-Rock Commemoration on Lake Powell celebrates the 1880 crossing of the Colorado River by Mormon pioneers; historic programs and tours take place at Wahweap and Bullfrog marinas. **Striper Derby** continues at Lake Powell (see November, below).

February: Striper Derby continues at Lake Powell.

March: Air Affair and Hot Air Balloon Regatta air show fly over the Page area on the last weekend. **Bullfrog Open** awards prizes for biggest largemouth bass.

April: Lake Powell Marathon on last weekend.

May: Cinco de Mayo (weekend close to the fifth). **Page Open Rodeo.**

July: Fourth of July Celebration with food, games, and dog show at Page Memorial Park and fireworks near the dam.

August: Halls Crossing-Bullfrog Swim is an early morning swimming race between the two marinas.

September: Lake Powell Triathlon takes place at Bullfrog Marina.

October: John Wesley Powell Days presents historic programs, storytelling, and a hilarious dry-land boat race.

November: Anglers compete for the biggest striped bass in the **Striper Derby,** lasting through February at Lake Powell. **Bullfrog's Festival of Lights Parade** on Thanksgiving weekend.

December: Here Comes Santa Parade in Page on first Friday and **Wahweap Festival of Lights Parade** on Lake Powell on the first Saturday. Striper Derby continues at Lake Powell.

Services And Recreation

The **post office,** is at 615 Elm St., tel. 645-2571. **Page Hospital** is at the corner of Vista Ave. and North Navajo Dr., tel. 645-2424. In **emergencies** (police, fire, medical), dial 911.

Page High School has an indoor **swimming pool** (open all year) near the corner of South Lake Powell Blvd. and AZ 98, tel. 645-4124. Play **tennis** at the courts on S. Lake Powell Blvd. (Church Row). **Glen Canyon Golf and Country Club** has a nine-hole golf course west of town on US 89., tel. 645-2715. They are building an additional 18-hole course across the street.

Information

Page/Lake Powell Chamber of Commerce has information about the sights and services of the area; staff also book lake and river tours, jeep tours, and scenic flights (plane and helicopter tours at the Grand Canyon can also be reserved); open daily 7 a.m.-7 p.m. from June 1 to September 30, daily 8 a.m.-6 p.m. in April, May, and October, then Mon.-Sat. 8 a.m.-5 p.m. Nov.-March; located in Page Plaza around the corner from Safeway (Box 727, Page, AZ 86040), tel. 645-2741. The **public library,** corner of 697 Vista Ave. and N. Lake Powell Blvd., tel. 645-2231, is open daily except Sunday. **Pleasure Bound Bookstore,** 48 S. Lake Powell Blvd. in Salsa Brava Mall, tel. 645-5333, has regional titles and general reading.

Tours

Lake Powell Overland Adventures, tel. 645-5501/3155, and **Duck Tours,** tel. 645-8881, then enter code 81, offer back-road drives to Corkscrew Canyon (in Antelope Wash) and other destinations in the area; tours normally don't operate in winter. Reservations can also be made through the John Wesley Powell Memorial Museum and Page/Lake Powell Chamber of Commerce. **Photographic Tours,** P. O. Box 2102, Page, AZ 86040, tel. 675-9109, provides transportation to scenic areas (specializing in slot canyons) with a professional photographer skilled in photographing such challenging scenery; starting at $26.50 for a one and one half hour session. **High Mesa Tours,** P. O. Box 5096 Page, AZ 86040, tel. 645-2266, offers luxury 4WD trips to scenic areas at $15-50 depending on number of passengers and destination. **Wilderness River Adventures,** 50 S. Lake Powell Blvd. in Lake View Shopping Center and at Wilderness Tours in the Gateway Plaza. Box 717, Page, AZ 86040, tel. 645-3279 or (800) 528-6154, offers half-day raft trips down the Colorado River from just below Glen Canyon Dam to Lees Ferry, 15 miles of smooth-flowing water; $41.60 adult, $33.35 children under 12. Trips leave once or twice daily February 15 to November 15, weather permitting. Grand Canyon raft trips of 3-12 days are offered too. **Lake Powell Air Service,** tel. 645-2494, has a long list of "flightseeing" trips, including Lake Powell and Rainbow Bridge (one-half hour, $55), Grand Canyon (90 minutes, $139), Monument Valley (90 minutes, $135; $175 with ground tour), and Bryce Canyon (90 minutes, $135); a two-person minimum applies to most tours. Children 12 and under get 20% off. Charter flights to Flagstaff, Phoenix, Las Vegas, Salt Lake City, and Grand Junction can also be arranged. Boat tours to Rainbow Bridge and other destinations leave from the nearby Wahweap Marina; see "Glen Canyon National Recreation Area," below.

Transportation

There was no bus service at press time. Wahweap Lodge operates **Page Shuttle** frequently to Page and the airport, tel. 645-2433. Most area motels also provide transportation for guests to and from the airport. Rent cars at the airport from **Avis,** tel. 645-2024, or **Budget,** tel. 645-3977. From Page's airport on the east edge of town, **Sky West Airlines,** tel. 645-9200 or (800) 453-9417, flies once daily (one-way fares) to Flagstaff ($89) and three times daily to Phoenix ($85 Saturday and Sunday, $119 weekdays) year-round; in summer, planes go daily to St. George ($80), Salt Lake City ($165), Las Vegas ($105), and other destinations.

GLEN CANYON
NATIONAL RECREATION AREA

This vast recreation area covers 1.25 million acres, most of which spreads northeast into Utah. Lake Powell stands as the centerpiece, surrounded by beautiful canyon country. Just a handful of roads approach the lake, so you'll need to do some boating or hiking to explore this unique land of water and rock. The recreation area also includes a beautiful remnant of Glen Canyon in a 15-mile section of the Colorado River from Glen Canyon Dam to Lees Ferry.

LAKE POWELL

Conservationists deplored the loss of remote and beautiful Glen Canyon of the Colorado River beneath Lake Powell. Today, we have only words, pictures, and memories to remind us of its wonders. On the other hand, the 186-mile-long lake now provides easy access to an area most had not even known existed. Lake Powell is the second largest man-made lake within the United States. Only Lake Mead, farther downstream, has a greater water storage capacity. Lake Powell, however, has three times more shoreline—1,960 miles—and holds enough water to cover the state of Pennsylvania a foot deep! Bays and coves offer nearly limitless opportunities for exploration by boaters. Nearly all of the lake lies within Utah. Only the lower part—Glen Canyon Dam, Wahweap Resort and Marina, Antelope and Navajo canyons, and the lower parts of Labyrinth, Face, and West canyons—extends into Arizona. The elevation of the surface fluctuates 20-30 feet through the year and peaks in July; Lake Powell reaches 3,700 feet when full. The Carl Hayden Visitor Center, perched beside the dam, has tours of the dam, related exhibits, and an information desk for all the Glen Canyon National Recreation Area.

Climate

Summer, when temperatures rise into the 90s and 100s F, is the busiest season for swimming, boating, and water-skiing. Visits during the rest of the year can be enjoyable too, though activities shift more to sightseeing, fishing, and hiking. Spring and autumn are the best times to enjoy the backcountry. Winter temperatures drop to highs in the 40s and 50s, with freezing nights and the possibility of snow. Lake surface temperatures range from a comfortable 80° in August to a chilly 45° in January. Chinook winds can blow day and night for periods from February to May. Thunderstorms in late summer bring strong, gusting winds with widely scattered rain showers. Annual precipitation averages about seven inches.

Geology, Flora, And Fauna

The colorful rock layers that rise above the lake's surface tell a story of ancient deserts, oceans, and rivers. An uplift of the Colorado Plateau beginning about 60 million years ago started a cycle of erosion that has carved canyons and created delicately balanced rocks and graceful natural arches and bridges.

The desert comes right to the edge of the water because fluctuating lake levels prevent plant growth along the shore. Common plants of this high-desert country include prickly pear and hedgehog cacti, rabbitbrush, sand sagebrush, blackbrush, cliffrose, mariposa and sego lilies, globemallow, Indian paintbrush, evening primrose, penstemon, and Indian rice grass. Piñon pine and juniper trees grow on the high plateaus. Springs and permanent streams support sandbar willow, tamarisk, cattail, willow, and cottonwood. Look for hanging gardens of maidenhair fern, columbine, and other water-loving plants in small alcoves high on the sandstone walls.

Most animals are secretive and nocturnal; you're more likely to see them in early morning or in the evening. Local mammals include pronghorn, mule deer, mountain lion, coyote, red and gray foxes, ringtail cat, spotted and striped skunks, bobcat, badger, river otter, beaver, prairie dog, Ord kangaroo rat, black-tailed jackrabbit, several species of squirrels and chipmunks, and many species of mice and bats. Some lizards you might see sunning on rocks are collared, side-blotched, desert horned, and chuckwalla. Snake species include common kingsnake, gopher, striped whipsnake, western rattlesnake, and western diamondback rattlesnake. Birds stopping by on their migrations include American avocet, Canada goose, and teal. Others, such as blue heron, snowy egret, and bald eagle, come for the winter. Birds you might spot any time of the year are American merganser, mallard, canyon wren, piñon jay, common raven, red-tailed and Swainson's hawks, great horned and long-eared owls, peregrine and prairie falcons, and golden eagle.

Recreation At Lake Powell

If you don't have your own craft, Wahweap and other marinas will rent a boat for fishing, skiing, or housebeating. Boat tours visit Rainbow Bridge (the world's largest natural bridge) and other destinations from Wahweap, Bullfrog, and Halls Crossing marinas. Sailboats find the steadiest breezes in Wahweap, Padre, Halls, and Bullfrog bays, where spring winds average 15-20 knots. Kayaks and canoes can be used in the more protected areas. All boaters need to be alert for approaching storms that can bring wind gusts up to 60 mph. Waves on open expanses of the lake are sometimes steeper than ocean waves and can exceed six feet from trough to crest.

Marinas and bookstores sell navigation maps of Lake Powell. You'll need an Arizona fishing license for the southern five miles of lake and a Utah license for the rest of Lake Powell. Licenses and information can be obtained from marinas on the water or sporting goods stores in Page. Fishermen catch largemouth, smallmouth, and striped bass, northern and walleye pike, catfish, crappie, and carp. Smaller fish include bluegill, perch, and sunfish. Wahweap has a swimming beach (no lifeguards), and boaters can find their own remote spots. Scuba divers can swim underwater with the sizable bass. Hikers have a choice of easy day-trips or long wilderness backpack treks. The canyons of the Escalante rate among America's premier hiking areas. Other good hiking areas within or adjacent to Glen Canyon N.R.A. include Rainbow Bridge National Monument, Paria Canyon, Dark Canyon, and Grand Gulch. National Park Service staff at the Carl Hayden Visitor Center can suggest trips and supply trail descriptions. Several guidebooks to Lake Powell have detailed hiking, camping, and boating information. Most of the canyon country near Lake Powell remains wild and little explored—hiking possibilities are limitless! Be sure to carry plenty of water.

GLEN CANYON DAM

Construction workers labored from 1956 to 1964 to build this giant concrete structure. It stands 710 feet high above bedrock, and its top measures 1,560 feet across. Thickness ranges from 300 feet at the base to just 25 feet at the top. As

skimming the waters of Lake Powell

part of the Upper Colorado River Storage Project, the dam provides water storage (its main purpose), hydroelectricity, flood control, and recreation on Lake Powell. Eight giant turbine generators churn out a total of 1,150,000 kilowatts at 13,800 volts. Vertigo sufferers shouldn't look down when driving across Glen Canyon Bridge; cold, green waters of the Colorado River glide 700 feet below.

Carl Hayden Visitor Center

Photos, paintings, movies, and slide presentations in the visitor center show features of Glen Canyon National Recreation Area, including Lake Powell and construction of the dam. A giant relief map helps you to visualize the rugged terrain surrounding the lake; look closely and you'll spot Rainbow Bridge. Guided tours inside the dam and generating room depart daily in summer every half-hour from 8:30 a.m.-5:30 p.m. You can begin a self guided tour daily 8 a.m.-4 p.m. (7 a.m.-6 p.m. in summer). National Park Service staff operates an Information desk where you can find out about boating, fishing, camping, and hiking in the immense Glen Canyon National Recreation Area (or write Box 1507, Page, AZ 86040), tel. 645-8404 or 645-2511. The Glen Canyon Natural History Association has a variety of books about the recreation area and its environs for sale next to the information desk. A Navajo rug exhibit illustrates the many different patterns used. Souvenirs, snacks, and postcards can be purchased at a gift shop in the visitor center building. The Carl Hayden Visitor Center is open daily 7 a.m.-7 p.m. in summer and 8 a.m.-5 p.m. the rest of the year. Tours, exhibits, and slide presentations are free. In summer, you can attend a campfire program several nights a week at nearby Wahweap Campground amphitheater.

MARINAS

The **National Park Service** provides public boat ramps, campgrounds, and ranger offices at most of the marinas. Rangers know current boating and back-road conditions, primitive camping areas, and good places to explore. **Lake Powell Resorts & Marinas** operates marina services, boat rentals, boat tours, accommodations, RV parks, and restaurants; contact

them for information and reservations (strongly recommended in summer) at Box 56909, Phoenix, AZ 85079, tel. (800) 528-6154 (278-8888 in greater Phoenix); fax (602) 331-5258. All the marinas stay open year-round; you can avoid crowds and peak prices by coming in autumn, winter, or spring. Private or chartered aircraft can fly to Page Airport, San Juan County Airport near Bullfrog, or to an airstrip near Halls Crossing.

Wahweap

The name means "Bitter Water" in the Ute Indian language. Wahweap Lodge and Marina, Lake Powell's biggest, offers complete boaters' services and rentals, guided tours, deluxe accommodations, an RV park, and fine dining. Wahweap is seven miles northwest of Page, five miles beyond the Visitor Center. **Wahweap Lodge** offers several types of rooms starting at $107.33 s or d from April 1 to October 31, then $69.75 s or d in winter; lake-view rooms cost about 10% more. Guests enjoy the scenery. Contact Lake Powell Resorts & Marinas for reservations at Box 56909, Phoenix, AZ 85079, tel. (800) 528-6154 (278-8888 in greater Phoenix); fax (602) 331-5258. Wahweap Lodge & Marina can also be reached at Box 1597, Page, AZ 86040, tel. 645-2433. **Lake Powell Motel** has less expensive rooms nearby at Wahweap Junction (four miles northwest of Glen Canyon Dam on US 89); $69.54 s or d April 1 to October 31, then $45.21 s or d in winter; call 645-2477 or contact Lake Powell Resorts & Marinas for reservations.

An **RV park** with coin showers and laundry costs $20.52 w/hookups ($13.34 in winter). **Wahweap Campground** is operated on a first-come, first-served basis by Lake Powell Resorts & Marinas; sites have drinking water but no showers or hookups; $8.50; campers may use the pay showers and laundry facilities at the RV park. The RV park, campground, and a picnic area are located between Wahweap Lodge and Stateline. Primitive camping (no water or fee) is available at **Lone Rock** in Utah, six miles northwest of Wahweap off US 89; cars need to be very careful not to stray into loose sand areas. Boaters may also camp along the lakeshore, but not within one mile of developed areas. A free picnic area and fish-cleaning station are located just west of Wahweap Lodge. Public boat ramps are located adjacent to the lodge and at Stateline, 1.3 miles northwest of the lodge and just into Utah. During summer (June 1 to September 30), you can also obtain recreation information from the **Wahweap Ranger Station** near the picnic area; at other times see the staff at Carl Hayden Visitor Center.

The marina offers six **lake tours,** ranging from an hour-long paddle-wheel cruise around Wahweap Bay ($9.63 adult, $6.90 children) to an all-day trip to Rainbow Bridge, 50 miles away ($69.18 adult, $36.92 children). Half-day trips to Rainbow Bridge cost $54.90 adult, $29.21 children. **Boat rentals,** at Stateline, include a 16-foot skiff with 25-h.p. motor ($66.25 per day), an 18-foot powerboat with 120-h.p. motor ($196.37 per day), 24-foot patio boat with 60-h.p. motor ($154.50), and three sizes of houseboats starting at $705.96 for three days. Water toys, fishing gear, and water skis can be rented too.

Dangling Rope

This floating marina lies 42 miles uplake from Glen Canyon Dam. The only access is by boat. Services include a ranger station, store, minor boat repairs, gas dock, and sanitary pump-out station. A dangling rope left behind in a nearby canyon, perhaps by uranium prospectors, prompted the name. The dock for Rainbow Bridge is seven miles farther uplake in Bridge Canyon, a tributary of Forbidding Canyon.

San Juan

Boats can be hand launched at **Clay Hills Crossing** at the upper end of the San Juan Arm. An unpaved road branches 11 miles southwest from UT 276 (road to Halls Crossing) to the lake; don't attempt the road after rains. River runners on the San Juan often take out here; no facilities.

Halls Crossing-Bullfrog Ferry

The *John Atlantic Burr* ferry can accommodate vehicles of all sizes and passengers for the short 20-minute crossing between these marinas. Halls Crossing and Bullfrog marinas lie on opposite sides of Lake Powell about 95 lake miles from Glen Canyon Dam, roughly midway up the length of the lake. Sections of paved Highway UT 276 connect each marina with UT 95. The ferry's daily schedule has six roundtrips from May 15 to September 30, then four roundtrips the rest of the year; no reservations needed. You can pick up a schedule from the marinas. Service is suspended for a brief time annually, usually in November, for maintenance; signs at the UT 276 turnoffs will warn you when the ferry is closed. Low water in late summer can also affect service; the ferry may have to use the boat ramps instead of ferry docks.

Halls Crossing

In 1880, Charles Hall built the ferry used by the Hole-in-the-Rock pioneers, who crossed the river to begin settlement in southeast Utah. The approach roads were so bad, however, that he moved the ferry 35 miles upstream to present-day Halls Crossing in the following year. Business continued to be slow, and Hall quit running the ferry in 1884.

Arriving at Halls Crossing by road, you'll first reach a small store offering **housekeeping units** (trailers: $117.85 d in summer, $89 d in winter), an **RV park** ($22.55 w/hookups in summer, $14.69 w/hookups in winter), and gas pumps; the store may close in winter, but services are still available (ask at the trailer office next door). Coin-operated showers and laundry at the RV park are also open to the public. The separate National Park Service **campground,** just beyond and to the left, has sites

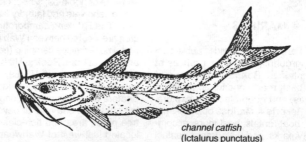

channel catfish
(Ictalurus punctatus)

LOUISE FOOTE

with a good view of the lake, drinking water, and restrooms; $8.50. Continue a half mile on the main road to the boat ramp and **Halls Crossing Marina.** The marina has a larger store (groceries and fishing and boating supplies), tours to Rainbow Bridge, a boat rental office (fishing, ski, and houseboat), gas dock, slips, and storage. The **ranger station** is nearby, though rangers are usually out on patrol; look for their vehicle in the area if the office is closed. Contact Lake Powell Resorts & Marinas for accommodation, boat rental, and tour reservations at Box 56909, Phoenix, AZ 85079, tel. (800) 528-6154 (278-8888 in greater Phoenix), fax (602) 331-5258. The marina can also be reached at Hwy. 276, Lake Powell, UT 84533, tel. (801) 684-2261.

Stabilized Anasazi ruins at **Defiance House** in Forgotten Canyon make a good boating destination 12 miles uplake; a sign marks the beginning of the trail to the ruins.

Bullfrog
Before the days of Lake Powell, Bullfrog Rapids gave boaters a fast and bumpy ride. Bullfrog Marina has the most extensive visitor facilities of Lake Powell's Utah marinas. If driving in on the highway, you'll come to the **visitor center,** on the right, tel. (801) 684-2243, open daily 8 a.m.-5 p.m. The **clinic,** tel. (801) 684-2288, is here too; open May 15 to September 30. A large **campground** lies on the left; sites have drinking water and restrooms for $8.50. Continue on the main road to a junction; a service station, store, and marine service here offer repairs and supplies. Continue straight at the junction for a picnic area and the boat ramp; turn right at the service station for Defiance House Lodge and Restaurant, Trailer Village, Bullfrog Painted Hills RV Park, and Bullfrog Marina.

Defiance House Lodge offers luxury accommodations and the **Anasazi Restaurant** (open daily for breakfast, lunch, and dinner). Rooms cost $96.36-105.71 s or d in summer (April 1 to October 31) and $62.65-68.70 s or d in winter; lake-view rooms go for the higher price listed. The front desk at the lodge also handles **housekeeping units** (trailers) and an **RV park** (both located nearby with the same rates as those at Halls Crossing) and **tours** to Rainbow Bridge and local canyons. Showers, laundry, a convenience store, and a post office

are at **Trailer Village.** The RV park has showers. Ask visitor center staff or rangers for directions to primitive camping areas with vehicle access elsewhere along Bullfrog Bay.

All-day **Rainbow Bridge tours** usually leave daily from April 15 to October 31 and stop on request to pick up passengers at Halls Crossing Marina; call for dates in winter; $69.18 adult, $36.92 children. **Canyon Explorer tours** depart in the evening for two hours in nearby canyons during the same season; $21.03 adult, $14 children. **Bullfrog Marina** has a store, snack bar, rentals (fishing, ski, and houseboat), gas dock, slips, and storage. Contact Lake Powell Resorts & Marinas for accommodation, boat rental, and tour reservations at Box 56909, Phoenix, AZ 85079, tel. (800) 528-6154 (278-8888 in greater Phoenix), fax (602) 331-5258. Bullfrog Resort & Marina can also be reached at Box 4055-Bullfrog, Lake Powell, UT 84533, tel. (801) 684-2233.

Hite
In 1883, Cass Hite came to Glen Canyon in search of gold. He found some at a place later named "Hite City" and set off a small gold rush. Cass and a few of his relatives operated a small store and post office, the only services for many miles. Travelers wishing to cross the Colorado River here had the difficult task of swimming their animals across. Arthur Chaffin, a later resident, put through the first road and opened a ferry service in 1946. The Chaffin Ferry served uranium prospectors and adventurous motorists until the lake backed up to the spot in 1964. A steel bridge now spans the Colorado River upstream from Hite Marina. Cass Hite's store and the ferry site are underwater about five miles downlake from Hite Marina.

The uppermost marina on Lake Powell, Hite lies 141 lake miles from Glen Canyon Dam. From here boats can continue uplake to the mouth of Dark Canyon in Cataract Canyon at low water or into Canyonlands National Park at high water. Hite tends to be quieter than the other marinas and is favored by some fishermen and families. The turnoff for the marina is from UT 95 between Blanding and Hanksville. On the way in, you'll find a small **store** with gas pumps, **housekeeping units** (trailers; same rates as at Halls Crossing), and a primitive **campground** (no drinking water; free). Primitive

camping is also available nearby off UT 95 at
Dirty Devil, Farley Canyon, White Canyon, Blue
Notch, and other locations. **Hite Marina,** at the
end of the access road, has a small store,
housekeeping units, gas dock, boat rentals (fishing, ski, and houseboat), slips, and storage.
Hikers can make arrangements with the marina
to be dropped off or picked up at Dark Canyon.

A **ranger station** is occasionally open; look for
the ranger's vehicle at other times. Contact Lake
Powell Resorts & Marinas for accommodation
and boat rental reservations at Box 56909,
Phoenix, AZ 85079, tel. (800) 528-6154 (278-
8888 in greater Phoenix), fax (602) 331-5258.
Hite Marina can also be contacted at Box 501,
Lake Powell, UT 84533, tel. (801) 684-2278.

BOOKLIST

DESCRIPTION AND TRAVEL

Abbey, Edward. "Slickrock." *Sierra Club Bulletin.* (July-Aug. 1971); page 12. Conflicts of wilderness values with politics and business interests.

Aitchison, Stewart. *Utah Wildlands.* Utah Geographic Series, Inc., no. 3, 1987; 110 pages, $17.95. Text and beautiful color photos reveal some of the wonders in Utah's backcountry. The author also presents thoughts on the value of wilderness and proposals by various groups for and against new wilderness areas.

Barnes, F.A., and M.M. Barnes. *Cameo Cliffs: Biking-Hiking-Four-Wheeling.* Canyon Country Publications, 1992; 160 pages, $7. Canyons, arches, and panoramas attract visitors to this little-known area east of US 191. Author Fran Barnes called it "Cameo Cliffs" because the pink cliffs reminded him of an old-fashioned pink-and-white cameo locket. You're not likely to see this unofficial name on maps, however. Barnes describes the area, divided by UT 46 into Cameo Cliffs North and South, in this small guidebook and separate map ($4.50) of the same name.

Barnes, F.A., and M.M. Barnes. *Canyon Country's Canyon Rims Recreation Area.* Canyon Country Publications, 1991; 216 pages, $13.50. Comprehensive, large-format guide to this vast area south and east of Canyonlands National Park. The author's subtitle explains "The rest of Canyonlands National Park. Park-quality land that was left out of Canyonlands National Park." You'll find good background information on geology, flora, fauna, archaeology, and history. Practical advice will help you prepare for this remote region and enjoy the viewpoints, scenic drives, hiking, and mountain biking. Well-illustrated with black-and-white photos, but you'll need the separate *Off-Road Vehicle Trail Map: Canyon Rims Recreation Area* to follow the road and trail descriptions.

Barnes, F.A. *Canyon Country Camping.* Wasatch Publishers, Inc., 1991; 128 pages, $6. The best of southeastern Utah's canyon country lies away from towns and other developments. This handy guide provides practical tips for finding a place to camp. Includes listings of public campgrounds and a chapter devoted to primitive camping.

Barnes, F.A. *Canyon Country Exploring.* Wasatch Publishers, Inc., 1978; 64 pages, $1.95. Introduction to the beautiful canyon country of southeastern Utah and how you can see it. Includes tips on travel by car, off-road vehicle, horseback, foot, powerboat, raft, canoe or kayak, air, and commercial tours.

Barnes, F.A. *Canyon Country Off-Road Vehicle Trails: Arches & La Sals.* Wasatch Publishers, Inc., 1978; 96 pages, $4.50. Backcountry driving guide to Arches National Park area north of Moab, and the La Sal Mountains southeast of Moab. You'll also want the accompanying *Arches & La Sals Areas Off-Road Vehicle Trail Map* ($4.50).

Barnes, F.A. *Canyon Country Off-Road Vehicle Trails: Canyon Rims & Needles Areas.* Wasatch Publishers, Inc., 1978; 96 pages, $4.50. Backcountry driving guide to Canyonlands National Park's Needles District and other canyon areas southwest of Moab. You'll also want the accompanying *Canyon Rims & Needles Areas Off-Road Vehicle Trail Map* ($4.50).

Barnes, F.A. *Canyon Country Off-Road Vehicle Trails: Canyon Rims Recreation Area.* Canyon Country Publications, 1991; 113 pages, $5. Backcountry driving guide to the areas south and east of Canyonlands National Park. This guide overlaps somewhat with Barnes's *Canyon Rims & Needles Area* book, but covers additional areas and has new trails. You'll also want the accompanying *Canyon Rims Recreation Area* map ($4.50).

Barnes, F.A. *Canyon Country Off-Road Vehicle Trails: Island Area.* Wasatch Publishers, Inc., 1978; 96 pages, $4.50. Backcountry driving guide to the back roads of Canyonlands National Park's Island in the Sky District area west of Moab. You'll also want the *Island Area Off-Road Vehicle Trail Map* ($4.50).

Barnes, F.A. *Utah Canyon Country.* Utah Geographic Series, Inc., no. 1, 1986; 120 pages, $17.95. Stunning color photos illustrate this book about the land, people, and natural history of southern Utah. The text also describes parks, monuments, and practicalities of travel in this fascinating region.

Bezy, John. *Bryce Canyon: The Story Behind the Scenery.* KC Publications, 1980; 48 pages, $5.95. Large color photos illustrate Bryce's creation, wonderful erosion forms, winter scenery, history, wildlife, and flora.

Bickers, Jack. *Canyon Country Off-Road Vehicle Trails: Maze Area.* Canyon Country Publications, 1988; 81 pages, $4.50. This guide will help you explore the remote western section of Canyonlands National Park and adjacent Glen Canyon National Recreation Area lands. You'll also want the *Canyon Country Off-Road Vehicle Trail Map-Maze Area* ($4.50).

Bickers, Jack. *The Labyrinth Rims: 60 Accesses to Green River Overlooks.* 4-WD Trailguide Publications, 1989; 80 pages, $4.50. Maps and descriptions lead you to more than 60 overlooks of this deep, meandering canyon between the town of Green River and the confluence with the Colorado River.

Carr, Stephen L. *The Historical Guide to Utah Ghost Towns.* Western Epics, 1987; 174 pages, $9.95. Excellent book about Utah's fading ghosts. The historic photos, well-written text, good directions, and maps will add to the pleasure of back-road travel.

Casey, Robert L. *A Journey to the High Southwest.* Globe Pequot, 1993; 464 pages, $19.95. Introduction, history, and travel in southern Utah and adjacent Arizona, New Mexico, and Colorado.

DeLorme. *Utah Atlas & Gazeteer.* DeLorme Mapping, 1993; 64 pages, $14.95. This atlas is composed of topographic maps covering the entire state. The small scale of the maps may limit some uses but the maps are helpful in understanding the terrain of places you may wish to travel.

Dunham, Dick, and Vivian Dunham. *Flaming Gorge Country: The Story of Daggett County, Utah.* Eastwood Printing and Publishing Co., 1978; 384 pages, $4.95. Tales and history of northeastern Utah.

Eardley, A.J., and James W. Schaack. *Zion: The Story Behind the Scenery.* KC Publications, 1979; 48 pages, $5.95. Large color photos illustrate descriptions of Zion's rock layers, canyons, prehistoric peoples, settlers, and ecology.

Gwynn, J. Wallace, ed. *Great Salt Lake: A Scientific, Historical, and Economic Overview.* Utah Geological and Mineral Survey Bulletin, no. 116, June 1980; 400 pages, $20. Comprehensive and well-illustrated articles on the lake's geological and historical past and its present life forms, chemistry, industries, and recreation.

Hagood, Allen. *Dinosaur: The Story Behind the Scenery.* KC Publications, 1990; 48 pages, $5.95. Introduction to the dinosaurs, fossil excavation, geology, and canyons of Dinosaur National Monument in northeastern Utah; has 65 color photos.

Hirsch, Bob, and Stan Jones. *Fishin' Lake Powell.* Sun Country Publications; 96 pages, $8.50. Helpful advice on where and how to catch Lake Powell's game fish.

Hoefer, Hans (and others). *American Southwest.* APA Insight Guides, 1984; 305 pages, $16.95. Outstanding color photography illustrates this travel guide of southern Utah and adjacent states. Many authors have contributed to the fine text.

Hoefer, Hans (and others). *The Rockies.* APA Insight Guides, 1985; 384 pages, $16.95. Impressive color photography illustrates this travel guide about the land, people, and history of the Rockies. Only the far north of Utah receives coverage, but this book provides good onward travel info for Wyoming and Colorado.

Hoffman, John F. *Arches National Park: An Illustrated Guide.* Western Recreational Publications, 1985; 128 pages, $9.95. Fine drawings and beautiful color photos illustrate descriptions of history, geology, flora, fauna, and touring the park.

Holdman, Floyd, and Nelson Wadsworth. *Utah.* Skyline Press, 1984. Eighty-eight color photos show the state's beauty and character in the towns, farms, mountains, and deserts.

James, George Wharton. *Utah, The Land of Blossoming Valleys.* The Page Company, 1922; 371 pages. Old-fashioned but comprehensive guidebook about Utah's prehistory, settlement, railways, Mormon religion, Salt Lake City, art, farming, mining, geology, national forests, canyons, natural bridges, and birds.

Klinck, Richard E. *Land of Room Enough and Time Enough.* Peregrine Smith Books, 1984; 136 pages, $10.95. The land, legends, and peoples of Monument Valley.

Kluckhohn, Clyde. *Beyond the Rainbow.* Christopher Publishing House, 1933; 271 pages. Tales of travel from 1926 to 1929 in the still-wild country of Rainbow Bridge and among the Navajo in southeastern Utah and adjacent Arizona.

Lohman, S W. *The Geologic Story of Arches National Park.* U.S. Geological Survey Bulletin, no. 1393, 1975; 113 pages. This well-illustrated guidebook summarizes geologic history and explains how forces have created the many rock arches.

McCarry, Charles. *The Great Southwest.* National Geographic, 1980; 199 pages. Fantastic color photography with text about history and travels in the region, including the canyon and plateau country of southern Utah.

McClenahan, Owen. *Utah's Scenic San Rafael.* Self-published (Box 892, Castle Dale, UT 84513), 1986; 128 pages, $8.95. The author, a local "desert rat," takes you on driving tours through the scenic San Rafael region of east-central Utah. About half the trips can be done by car; the others need high clearance or 4WD.

Porter, Eliot. *The Place No One Knew: Glen Canyon on the Colorado.* Sierra Club, 1963; 170 pages. Beautiful color photos show a world now lost to the waters of Lake Powell. Thoughtful quotations from many individuals accompany the illustrations.

Roylance, Ward J. *Seeing Capitol Reef National Park.* Wasatch Publishers, 1979; 112 pages. Handy guide introduces the park's history, geology, climate, and life. Road logs and hiking trail descriptions aid exploration.

Roylance, Ward J. *Utah: A Guide to the State.* Utah: A Guide to the State Foundation, 1982; 779 pages, $25. An updated version of the book published by the W.P.A. Writers Program in 1941. Much of the original material and format have been preserved. The comprehensive introduction of Utah's people and history is followed by 11 tours of the state. A paperback version containing only the tours is also sold (507 pages, $17.45).

Sierra Club. *Desert Southwest: The Sierra Club Guides to the National Parks.* Random House, 1991; 352 pages, $17.95. Beautiful color photos illustrate the wildlife and scenic beauties of Utah's five national parks. The other parks described are Mesa Verde in Colorado, Grand Canyon and Petrified Forest in Arizona, Carlsbad Caverns in New Mexico, and Guadalupe Mountains and Big Bend in Texas. The text tells of the history, geology, wildlife, and flora. Maps and trail descriptions show hiking possibilities.

Stegner, Wallace, ed. *This is Dinosaur: Echo Park Country and its Magic Rivers.* Roberts Rinehart, Inc., 1985; 128 pages, $8.95. Essays on this rugged land—its geology, dinosaurs, wildlife, Indians, explorers, river running, and visiting Dinosaur National Monument.

Thompson, George A. *Some Dreams Die: Utah's Ghost Towns and Lost Treasures.* Dream Garden Press, 1982; 194 pages, $12.95. Treasure tales and historic photos make this an entertaining book. Historical inaccuracies and poor directions are weak points.

Till, Tom. *Utah: Magnificent Wilderness.* Westcliff Publishers, Inc., 1989; 112 pages, $14.95. Outstanding color photos by Tom Till and thoughtful quotations by Wallace Stegner grace this large-format book.

Utah Division of Wildlife Resources. *Lakes of the High Uintas.* A series of 10 booklets available from the Utah Division of Wildlife Resources (1596 W. North Temple, Salt Lake City, UT 84116), 1981-1985; 14-45 pages each, $1 each plus postage. Anglers headed for the Uintas will find these detailed lake descriptions very useful. Also has practical advice on camping, hiking, and horse travel.

Utah Writers' Program of the Work Projects Administration. *Utah: A Guide to the State.* Hastings House, 1941; 595 pages. This classic guidebook to Utah still makes good reading. A lengthy introduction followed by detailed descriptions of towns and natural features provide rich historical background. The book offers a look at Utah before the postwar industrialization. Libraries usually have a copy. Much of the material has been incorporated in the 1982 guide of the same name by Ward J. Roylance.

West, Linda, and Dan Chure. *Dinosaur: The Dinosaur National Monument Quarry.* Dinosaur Nature Association, 1984; 40 pages, $4.95. A well-illustrated book about difficulties and triumphs of early quarry digging and current work. Explains about dinosaurs and how they lived.

Wharton, Tom. *Utah! A Family Travel Guide.* Wasatch Publishers, Inc., 1987; 224 pages, $8.50. How to enjoy Utah's great outdoors with the kids. Also suggests museums, parks, and ski areas that the younger set will like. The well-illustrated guide contains many clever bits of wisdom.

Wilson, Ted. *Utah's Wasatch Front.* Utah Geographic Series, Inc. no. 4, 1987; 118 pages; $17.95. Beautiful color photos join with informative text to portray the cities, mountains, Great Salt Lake, and vigorous people of this region in northern Utah. The author served as Salt Lake City's mayor for 10 years prior to writing this book.

Zwinger, Ann. *Wind in the Rock: The Canyonlands of Southeastern Utah.* University of Arizona Press, 1986; 258 pages, $9.50. Well-written accounts of hiking in the Grand Gulch and nearby canyons. The author tells of the area's history, archaeology, wildlife, and plants.

HIKING, BICYCLING, SKIING, AND CLIMBING

Adkinson, Ron. *Utah's National Parks: Hiking, Camping and Vacationing in Utah's Canyon Country.* Wilderness Press, 1991; 354 pages, $18.95. A wealth of information on exploring Zion, Bryce Canyon, Capitol Reef, Arches, and Canyonlands national parks. The guide devotes itself mostly to hiking descriptions—the best way to see the parks; good introduction material helps to make your visits enjoyable.

Allen, Steve. *Canyoneering the San Rafael Swell.* University of Utah Press, 1992; 256 pages, $14.95. Eight chapters each cover a different area of this exceptional, though little-known, canyon country. Trail and route descriptions cover adventures from easy rambles to challenging hikes. The author provides some climbing notes too. Detailed road logs help you get there, whether by mountain bike, car, or truck.

Barnes, F.A. *Canyon Country Hiking and Natural History.* Wasatch Publishers, Inc., 1977; 176 pages, $7. Introduction to the delights of hiking amongst the canyons and mountains in southeastern Utah.

Barnes, F.A., and Tom Kuehne. *Canyon Country Mountain Biking.* Canyon Country Publications, 1988; 145 pages, $8. Authors tell how to get the most out of bicycling the canyon country of southeastern Utah. Trail descriptions take you through Arches and Canyonlands national parks, La Sal Mountains, and Canyon Rims Recreation Area.

Barnes, F.A. *Canyon Country Slickrock Hiking and Biking.* Canyon Country Publications, 1990; 289 pages, $12. "An illustrated guide to a completely different kind of hiking and mountain biking in the canyon country of southeastern Utah." A good introduction, areas to explore, personal anecdotes, and many black and white photos make this book fun to read and use.

Barnes, F.A. *Hiking the Historic Route of the 1859 Macomb Expedition.* Canyon Country Publications, 1989; 49 pages, $4. Captain John Macomb led the first expedition to explore and write about what's now Canyonlands National Park. Adventurous hikers can retrace part of Macomb's route, thanks to the descriptions, maps, and photos of this little guide.

Bicycle Vacation Guides. *Bicycle Utah.* Bicycle Vacation Guides, Inc. This series of booklets describes 20 mountain bike routes, one booklet for each of Utah's nine travel districts. The booklets are: *Bridgerland, Canyonlands, Castle Country, Color Country, Dinosaurland, Golden Spike Empire, Great Salt Lake Country, Mountainland,* and *Panoramaland.* Each book gives locations of trails on a map, and gives full trail descriptions including a graph of the trail's vertical component. Booklets are found at many visitor centers and bookstores at $4.25 and can be ordered from Bicycle Vacation Guides, Inc., P.O. Box 738, Park City, UT 84060; tel. 649-5806.

Bjornstad, Eric. *Desert Rock: A Climber's Guide to the Canyon Country of the Southwest American Desert.* Chockstone Press, Inc., 1988; 464 pages, $25. Climbing routes on the towers, spires, buttes, and cliffs of the Four Corners region. Most of the book is devoted to Utah, including Canyonlands and Arches national parks, Fisher towers, Castle Valley, and Navajo lands.

Bromka, Gregg. *Mountain Biking Utah's Canyon & Plateau Country.* Off-Road Publications, 1992; 245 pages, $12.95. Covers central Utah's San Rafael Swell, Wasatch Plateau, and Fish Lake areas. The introduction has background on geology, geography, and history, as well as mountain biking advice.

Bromka, Gregg. *The Mountain Biker's Guide to Utah.* Falcon Press, 1994; 300 pages, $14.95. Eighty mountain bikes rides in Utah are described with photographs and maps.

Coello, Dennis. *Bicycle Touring in Utah.* Dream Garden Press, 1984; 118 pages, $11.95. Experience the beauty and varied landscapes of Utah on a bicycle. Tour descriptions and a section on getting started show the way.

Coello, Dennis. *The Mountain Bike Manual.* Dream Garden Press, 1985; 125 pages. Pedal away from the crowds and pavement with this book. Introduction explains how to choose and maintain a mountain bicycle. You'll also learn how to pack and plan for long-distance tours.

Davis, Mel, and John Veranth. *High Uinta Trails: A Hiking & Backpacking Guide to the High Uintas Wilderness.* Wasatch Publishers, Inc., 1993; 160 pages, $7.50. Guide to hiking, backpacking, camping, and fishing in the High Uintas Wilderness of northeastern Utah.

Gilson, Dale. *Alta Canyon Guidebook.* Redwood Coast Printers, 1977; 108 pages. A pocket-size guide to the hiking, rock-climbing, and skiing near Alta (southeast of Salt Lake City). Nearly half the book is devoted to the area's history, wildlife, and plants.

Hall, David. *The Hiker's Guide to Utah.* Falcon Press Publishing Co., Inc., 1992; 254 pages, $11.95. Good selection of 60 trips within Utah. The day and overnight hikes range from easy to difficult. An introduction will help you get started hiking.

Houk, Rose. *Trails to Explore in Great Basin National Park.* Great Basin Natural History Association, 1989; 46 pages, $5.95. Beautiful color photos and drawings illustrate the trail descriptions of Wheeler Peak and the Snake Range. Even the topo maps are in color. Trail background info makes for enjoyable reading too. The park, just west of Utah, offers easily accessible alpine scenery and tours of the famous Lehman Caves

Ingalls, Huntley. "We Climbed Utah's Skyscraper Rock." *National Geographic.* (Nov. 1962); page 705. Difficult first ascent of Titan Tower—the highest of the Fisher Towers near Moab.

Kals, W.S. *Land Navigation Handbook.* Sierra Club Books, 1983; 288 pages, $12. This handy pocket guide will enable you to confidently explore Utah's extensive backcountry. Not only explains how to use map and compass, but also other methods such as altimeter navigation and using the sun and stars.

Keilty, Maureen. *Best Hikes in Utah With Children.* The Mountaineers, 1993; 240 pages, $12.95. This guide describes 75 child-tested trails in all parts of Utah including hikes of easy, moderate, and difficult challenges, plus a few hikes that offer wheelchair access. Maps and photographs let readers know what to expect of hikes.

Kelner, Alexis, and David Hanscom. *Wasatch Tours.* Wasatch Publishers, Inc., 1976; 222 pages, $6.50. A guide to about 100 cross-country ski tours near Salt Lake City.

Kelsey, Michael R. *Canyon Hiking Guide to the Colorado Plateau.* Kelsey Publishing, 1991; 288 pages, $11.95. One of the best guides to hiking in southeastern Utah's canyon country. Geologic cross sections show the formations you'll be walking through. The book has descriptions and maps for 64 trips in Utah, 38 hikes in adjacent Arizona, 13 in Colorado, and 2 in New Mexico. The author is ahead of his time in using just the metric system, but the book is otherwise easy to follow.

Kelsey, Michael R. *Hiking and Exploring the Paria River.* Kelsey Publishing, 1991; 208 pages, $10.95. The classic Paria Canyon hike with info on the upper Paria Canyon, Bryce Canyon National Park, and other geologically colorful areas nearby. Includes histories of John D. Lee, ghost towns, ranches, and mining.

Kelsey, Michael R. *Hiking and Exploring Utah's Henry Mountains and Robbers Roost.* Kelsey Publishing, 1990; 224 pages, $9.95. You'll find adventure and scenic beauty in this little-known region of high mountains and rugged canyons. Descriptions and maps cover 37 destinations. The book provides an excellent background of the region's history, mining, geology, and wildlife. Fascinating stories relate the escapades of Butch Cassidy. Uses metric system.

Kelsey, Michael R. *Hiking, Biking and Exploring Canyonlands National Park and Vicinity.* Kelsey Publishing, 1992; 320 pages, $14.95. The author's newest guide emphasizes hiking and local history. He used his mountain bike and hiking boots to explore the backcountry, rather than a 4WD vehicle. Uses metric system.

Kelsey, Michael R. *Hiking Utah's San Rafael Swell.* Kelsey Publishing, 1990; 160 pages, $8.95. Motorists driving across I-70 in east-central Utah get just a glimpse at the massive rock fold called the San Rafael Swell. This book presents the area's fascinating history and shows the way to hidden canyons with 30 hikes. Good maps and geologic cross sections. Uses metric system.

Kelsey, Michael R. *River Guide to Canyonlands National Park.* Kelsey Publishing, 1991; 256 pages, $11.95. How to do a trip on the Green and Colorado rivers and the many hikes and things to see along the way. Lots of local lore too. Begins at the town of Green River on the Green and Moab on the Colorado; coverage ends at the confluence area (there's not much on Cataract Canyon). Uses metric system.

Kelsey, Michael R. *Utah Mountaineering Guide, and the Best Canyon Hikes.* Kelsey Publishing Co., 1986; 192 pages, $9.95. This guide points the way to Utah's highest peaks. The 74 hikes include some canyon treks in southern Utah. In the back are sections on old heliograph stations, Utah climates, bristlecone pines, geologic cross sections, and prehistoric Indians. Uses metric system.

Lambrechtse, Rudi. *Hiking the Escalante.* Wasatch Publishers, Inc., 1985; 189 pages,

$7.50. "A wilderness guide to an exciting land of buttes, arches, alcoves, amphitheaters and deep canyons." Introduction to history, geology, and natural history of the Escalante region in southern Utah. Contains descriptions and trailhead info for 42 hiking destinations. The hikes vary from easy outings suitable for children to a highly challenging four-day backpack trek.

Patterson, Thomas H. *Provo Area: Wasatch Hiking Map.* University of Utah Press, 1984, $5. Color topo map of trails on Mt. Timpanogos, Provo Peak, and Mt. Nebo.

Patterson, Thomas H. *Salt Lake City Area: Wasatch Hiking Map.* University of Utah Press, 1983, $5. Color topo map of trails southeast of Salt Lake City. Trails start from Mill, Big Cottonwood, and Little Cottonwood canyons.

Paxman, Shirley, Monroe Paxman, Gayle Taylor, and Weldon Taylor. *Utah Valley Trails.* Wasatch Publishers, Inc., 1978; 71 pages, $2.50. Handy hiking guide to mountains and canyons in the Provo area. Includes Timpanogos Peak, Provo Canyon, South Fork Provo Canyon, Hobble Creek Canyon, and Payson Canyon.

Ringholz, Raye Carleson. *Park City Trails.* Wasatch Publishers, Inc., 1984; 104 pages, $6.50. Hikes and cross-country ski tours in the mountains and canyons surrounding this old mining town. Includes a walking tour of Park City.

Schimpf, Ann, and Scot Datwyler. *Cache Tours.* Wasatch Publishers, Inc., 1977; 64 pages, $2.50. Thirty cross-country ski tours near Logan in northern Utah. Tour descriptions give distance, elevation change, and type of terrain; difficulty ranges from beginner to advanced.

Shelton, Peter. *The Insider's Guide to the Best Skiing in Utah.* Western Eye Press, Box 917, Telluride, CO 81435; 1989; 191 pages, $9.95. Good background and ski information.

Utesch, Peggy, and Bob Utesch. *Mountain Biking in Canyon Rims Recreation Area.* Canyon

Country Publications, 1992; 89 pages, $5. An illustrated mountain bikers' guide to exploring this vast and beautiful area south and east of Canyonlands National Park. You'll need the separate map *Canyon Country Off-Road Vehicle Trail: Canyon Rims Recreation Area* by F.A. Barnes.

Utesch, Peggy. *The Utah-Colorado Mountain Bike Trail System, Route I—Moab to Loma: Kokopelli's Trail.* Canyon Country Publications, 1990; 81 pages, $5. Learn about desert bicycling, then take off with the detailed descriptions of this well-illustrated guide. The 130-mile trail twists over spectacular terrain between Moab, Utah, and Loma, Colorado.

Veranth, John. *Hiking the Wasatch.* Wasatch Mountain Club and Wasatch Publishers, Inc., 1989; 202 pages, $9.95. Introduction and description of major trails and routes in the central Wasatch, near Salt Lake City.

Wasatch Mountain Club and Betty Bottcher. *Wasatch Trails: Volume One.* Wasatch Mountain Club, 1973; 77 pages, $2. Pocket-size guide to trails in the Wasatch Range southeast of Salt Lake City. Includes Parley's, Mill Creek, Big Cottonwood, and Little Cottonwood canyons.

Wasatch Mountain Club and Daniel Geery. *Wasatch Trails: Volume Two.* Wasatch Mountain Club, 1977; 112 pages, $2.50. This guide contains more difficult trails and routes in the Wasatch Range southeast of Salt Lake City. Many of these hikes link together for multi-day trips.

Waterman, Laura, and Guy Waterman. *Backwoods Ethics: Environmental Issues for Hikers and Campers.* Countryman, 1983; 280 pages, $13. Thoughtful commentaries on how the hiker can visit the wilderness with the least impact. Case histories dramatize the need to protect the environment.

Williams, Brooke. *Utah Ski Country.* Utah Geographic Series, Inc., no. 2, 1986; 126 pages, $17.95. Incredible color photos illustrate the resorts, backcountry, and skiers surrounded by Utah's "Greatest Snow on Earth."

Wood, John. *Cache Trails.* Wasatch Publishers, Inc., 1987; 78 pages, $3.50. Hiking trails in the mountains of northern Utah near Logan.

BOATING AND RIVER RUNNING

Abbey, Edward. *Down the River.* E.P. Dutton, 1991; 256 pages, $10. Abbey's love for the wilderness comes through in thoughtful descriptions of travels along rivers through deserts of the West.

Anderson, Fletcher, and Ann Hopkinson. *Rivers of the Southwest: A Boater's Guide to the Rivers of Colorado, New Mexico, Arizona, and Utah.* Pruett Publishing Co., 1987; 139 pages, $16.95. Find out about running both the famous and the rarely traveled rivers of the region. Descriptions, photos, and maps tell what it's like.

Baars, Don, and Gene Stevenson. *San Juan Canyons: A River Runner's Guide.* Canon Publishers Ltd., 1986; 64 pages, $12.95 (waterproof). Probably the best guide to the San Juan. Text and detailed maps take you from Bluff to Clay Hills.

Belknap, Bill, and Buzz Belknap. *Canyonlands River Guide.* Westwater Books, 1974; 63 pages, $8.95 ($12.95 waterproof). Topo maps show the river and points of interest along the Green and Colorado rivers in southeastern Utah. Includes the Green through Labyrinth and Stillwater canyons, and the Colorado through Westwater and Cataract canyons to Lake Powell. Notes and photos provide historical background.

Evans, Laura, and Buzz Belknap. *Desolation River Guide.* Westwater Books, 1974; 56 pages, $8.95 ($12.95 waterproof). Topo maps show the canyons and points of interest along the Green River through Desolation and Gray canyons. This 200-mile stretch connects Dinosaur National Monument and Green River, Utah. Notes and photos relate the river's history, Indians, geology, and wildlife.

Evans, Laura, and Buzz Belknap. *Dinosaur River Guide.* Westwater Books, 1973; 64 pages, $8.95 ($12.95 waterproof). Topo maps show the canyons and points of interest along the Green and Yampa rivers in Dinosaur National Monument of northeastern Utah and adjacent Colorado. Includes Lodore, Whirlpool, and Split Mountain canyons of the Green River. Notes and photos provide a historical background.

Goldwater, Barry M. *Delightful Journey: Down the Green & Colorado Rivers.* Arizona Historical Foundation, 1970; 209 pages, $21.95. Fewer than 100 people had run the entire Grand Canyon in 1940, when Goldwater joined a 47-day, 1,463-mile expedition from Green River, Wyoming, to Lake Mead in Arizona.

Hayes, Philip T., and George C. Simmons. *River Runner's Guide to Dinosaur National Monument and Vicinity, With Emphasis on Geologic Features.* Powell Society, 1973; 78 pages, $3. This river guide covers the Green and Yampa rivers in Dinosaur National Monument in northeastern Utah and adjacent Colorado. The Green River log goes from below Flaming Gorge Reservoir to Ouray, Utah; the Yampa River log runs from Deerlodge Park to Echo Park.

Huser, Vern. *Canyon Country Paddles.* Wasatch Publishers, Inc., 1978; 96 pages, $2.50. Introduction to river running in southeastern Utah by kayak, canoe, and raft. Has brief river descriptions of the Colorado, Green, San Juan, Muddy Creek, Dolores, Escalante, and Dirty Devil.

Jones, Stan. *Boating and Exploring Map: Lake Powell and Its 96 Canyons.* Sun Country Publications, 1985, $3.50. Information-packed map showing natural features, marinas, Indian sites, hiking trails, and 4WD tracks. Map text describes points of interest, navigation, history, fishing, and wildlife.

Kelsey, Michael R. *Boater's Guide to Lake Powell.* Kelsey Publishing, 1991; 288 pages, $12.95. Explore the hundreds of canyons accessible by boat. This handy guide covers boating, hiking, camping, geology, archaeology, and history. Uses metric system.

Mutschler, Felix E. *River Runners' Guide to the Canyons of the Green and Colorado Rivers, With Emphasis on Geologic Features; Volume 4.* Powell Society, 1972; 85 pages, $3. Guide to running the Green River from Ouray, Utah, to the town of Green River, passing through Desolation and Gray canyons.

Mutschler, Felix E. *River Runners' Guide to Canyonlands National Park and Vicinity, With Emphasis on Geologic Features.* Powell Society, 1977; 99 pages, $3. This guide covers the Green River from Green River, Utah, through Labyrinth and Stillwater canyons, and the Colorado River from Moab through Cataract Canyon to Lake Powell.

Nichols, Gary. *River Runners' Guide to Utah and Adjacent Areas.* University of Utah Press, 1986; 168 pages, $14.95. A comprehensive guidebook to running Utah's many rivers—the little-known ones as well as the popular Green and Colorado. Maps, photos, safety info, and difficulty ratings let you know the excitement and hazards of what you're getting into.

Stephens, Hal G., and Eugene M. Shoemaker. *In the Footsteps of John Wesley Powell: An Album of Comparative Photographs of the Green and Colorado Rivers, 1871-72 and 1968.* Johnson Books and the Powell Society, 1987; 286 pages, $34.95. Fascinating photo album of identical river views taken nearly 100 years apart. Photos show how little—and how much—the forces of erosion, plants, and man have changed the Green and Colorado river canyons. The text describes geologic features for each of the 110 pairs of photos. Maps show locations of camera stations.

Tejada-Flores, Lito. *Wildwater: the Sierra Club Guide to Kayaking and Whitewater Boating.* Sierra Club Books, 1978; 329 pages, $8.95. Comprehensive introduction to river running: choosing boats and equipment, river techniques, safety, practical advice on trip planning, overview of river possibilities in the U.S., and history of whitewater boating.

Zwinger, Ann. *Run, River, Run: A Naturalist's Journey Down One of the Great Rivers of the American West.* University of Arizona Press, 1975; 317 pages, $12.95. An excellent description of the author's experiences along the Green River from its source in the Wind River Range of Wyoming to the Colorado River in southeastern Utah. The author weaves geology, Indian ruins, plants, wildlife, and her personal feelings into the text and drawings.

HISTORY

Alexander, Thomas G., and James B. Allen. *Mormons & Gentiles: A History of Salt Lake City.* Pruett Publishing Co., 1984; 360 pages, $19.95. A detailed account of Salt Lake City's unique history.

Arrington, Leonard J. *Great Basin Kingdom: An Economic History of the Latter-day Saints.* University of Utah Press, 1993; 534 pages, $14.95. More than just a book about numbers, you'll find a wealth of information on Mormon history and organization between founding of the church in 1830 and adjustments to mainstream America by 1900.

Burton, Richard F. *The City of the Saints and Across the Rocky Mountains to California.* First published in 1861; reprinted in 1963 by Alfred A. Knopf. Burton's lively writing style, broad scholarly background, and curiosity put you amidst the Mormon promised land in its early years. Meet the pioneers and other colorful characters of the Old West, learn about the savage Indian tribes, and experience the dust and mosquitoes of 19th century travel.

Colbert, Edwin H. *The Great Dinosaur Hunters and Their Discoveries.* Dover Publications, 1984; 283 pages, $8.95. Discovery of the "terrible lizards" in England during the 1820s and the worldwide fossil searches that followed. Includes early digging in what's now

Dinosaur National Monument. Many photos and drawings illustrate the lively text.

Conrotto, Eugene L. "America's Last Indian War." *Desert Magazine.* (March 1961): page 32. An uprising of the Ute Indians in 1923 near Blanding.

Crampton, C. Gregory. *Land of Living Rock.* Alfred A. Knopf, Inc., 1972; 267 pages, $19.95. Story of the geology, early explorers, Indians, and settlers of the high plateaus in Arizona, Utah, and Nevada. Well illustrated with color and black and white photos, maps, and diagrams.

Crampton, C. Gregory. *Standing Up Country.* Alfred A. Knopf, Inc., 1964; 191 pages, $12.75. Illustrated historical account of the people who came to the canyonlands of Utah and Arizona—the Indians, explorers, outlaws, miners, settlers, and scientists.

Dellenbaugh, Frederick S. *A Canyon Voyage: The Narrative of the Second Powell Expedition.* Reprinted by The University of Arizona Press, 1984; 277 pages, $13.95. Well-written account of John Wesley Powell's second expedition down the Green and Colorado rivers, 1871-72. The members took the first Grand Canyon photographs and obtained much valuable scientific knowledge.

Gillmor, Frances, and Louisa Wetherill. *Traders to the Navajo.* University of New Mexico Press, 1983; 265 pages, $7.95. The Wetherill brothers began a trading operation in the Monument Valley region during the late 1800s and were among the first white men to explore this scenic land. Authors relate tales of lost mines, early travelers, and the Navajo people.

Lester, Margaret D. *Brigham Street.* Utah State Historical Society, 1979; 263 pages, $34. Though currently known as "South Temple Street," this broad thoroughfare took the prophet's name in the city's early decades. Church leaders, including Brigham Young, built their homes along this street close to the temple, while wealthy businessmen constructed fine mansions farther east. This illustrated volume tells the stories of many of the notable citizens who settled along the street, said to be the most beautiful between Denver and San Francisco.

McCormick, John S. *Salt Lake City: The Gathering Place.* Windsor Publications, Inc., 1980; 130 pages. Historic photos and drawings help tell the story of Salt Lake City. The text begins with Mormon leaders searching for their Zion, then relates the good times and bad as the pioneer settlement grew into a modern city. An excellent introduction to Salt Lake City's history.

Miller, David E. *Hole-in-the-Rock.* University of Utah Press, 1959; 229 pages, $10.95. Detailed account of pioneers struggling to build a 200-mile wagon road to the remote southeastern corner of Utah in 1879-80. A group of about 250 men, women, and children in 80 wagons navigated some of the West's most rugged country to become the first white settlers in San Juan County.

Morgan, Dale L. *The Great Salt Lake.* University of New Mexico Press, 1986 (first published in 1947); 432 pages, $10.95. Unusual, almost poetic history of what the author calls the mountain sea. Mountain men, explorers, and Mormon settlers march through the pages. Dale Morgan also served as the principal editor for the 1941 *Utah: A Guide to the State.*

Mortensen, A.R., ed. "Utah's Dixie . . . The Cotton Mission." *Utah Historical Quarterly.* July, 1961 (vol. 29, no. 3); 302 pages. Stories of the pioneers in the southwestern corner of Utah, known as Dixie.

Notarianni, Philip F. *Faith, Hope, and Prosperity: The Tintic Mining District.* Tintic Historical Society, 1982; 190 pages, $19.95. Fascinating picture book of Eureka and other early mining communities. Hundreds of photos reveal life of the miners and their families.

Peterson, Charles S. *Utah, a History.* W.W. Norton & Co., 1977; 213 pages, $14.95. Good popular history of Utah's exploration, Mormon settlements, economic changes, and politics through to modern times.

Poll, Richard D., ed. *Utah's History.* Brigham Young University Press, 1989; 757 pages, $27.95. This comprehensive account begins with the prehistoric peoples, then takes you through the eras of the Spanish, fur traders, government surveyors, Mormon colonization, modern Indian tribes, statehood, and present-day Utah. Maps, charts, and notes on the physical setting add to an understanding of this unusual state.

Powell, John Wesley. *The Exploration of the Colorado River and Its Canyons.* Dover Publications, reprinted 1961 (first published in 1895); 400 pages, $6.95. Powell's 1869 and 1871-72 expeditions down the Green and Colorado rivers. His was the first group to navigate through the Grand Canyon. A description of the 1879 Uinta expedition is included too.

Reay, Lee. *Incredible Passage Through the Hole-in-the-Rock.* Meadow Lane Publications, 1980; 128 pages, $7.95. Story of the determined Mormon pioneers who crossed extremely rugged canyon country to settle in Bluff in southeastern Utah. Includes descriptions of pioneer life and Indians.

Smart, William B. *Old Utah Trails.* Utah Geographic Series, Inc., no. 5, 1988; 136 pages, $17.95. Join the early explorers of the West on their treks across this vast land. Quotations, maps, and beautiful color photos rekindle their experiences.

Stansbury, Howard. *Exploration and Survey of the Valley of the Great Salt Lake of Utah, Including a Reconnaissance of a New Route Through the Rocky Mountains.* Robert Armstrong, Public Printer, 1853; 495 pages. (Reprinted in shorter form by Ann Arbor University Microfilms, Inc., 1966.) In this report of an early U.S. Army surveying expedition to Utah, Stansbury describes the Indians, geography, climate, pioneer travelers, Mormon settlements, and difficulties experienced on the way.

Utah Historical Quarterly. Utah State Historical Society, published quarterly. Book reviews and stories from Utah's past.

ARCHAEOLOGY

Ambler, J. Richard. *The Anasazi: Prehistoric Peoples of the Four Corners Region.* Museum of Northern Arizona, 1989; 64 pages, $6.95. Concise overview of this pueblo tribe.

Lister, Robert, and Florence Lister. *Those Who Came Before.* Southwest Parks and Monuments, 1983; 184 pages, $12.95. A well-illustrated guide to the history, artifacts, and ruins of prehistoric Southwest Indians. The author also describes parks and monuments containing archaeological sites.

McGregor, John C. *Southwestern Archaeology.* University of Illinois Press, 1982; 511 pages, $19.95. Curious why archaeologists like their work? Ever wonder how it's done? This book presents motivations and techniques of the scientists. It also describes cultures and artifacts from the earliest known peoples to recent times in a readable and useful form.

Mays, Buddy. *Ancient Cities of the Southwest: A Practical Guide to the Prehistoric Ruins of Arizona, New Mexico, Utah, and Colorado.* Chronicle Books, 1990; 132 pages, $9.95. A handy guide to visiting places of the Anasazi and other departed tribes.

Noble, David Grant. *Ancient Ruins of the Southwest.* Northland Press, 1991; 232 pages, $14.95. Well-illustrated guide to prehistoric ruins of Utah, Arizona, New Mexico, and Colorado. Contains practical info on getting to sites, nearby campgrounds, and services.

Oppelt, Norman T. *Guide to Prehistoric Ruins of the Southwest.* Pruett Publishing Co., 1981; 208 pages, $12.95. Introduction to ancient cultures with descriptions of more than 200 sites in southeastern Utah and adjacent states.

Smith, Gary, and Michael E. Long. "Utah Rock Art: Wilderness Louvre." *National Geographic.* (Jan. 1980): page 97. A photo essay.

Stokes, William Michael, and William Lee Stokes. *Messages on Stone.* Starstone Publishing Co., 1980; 57 pages, $2.50. A collection of petroglyphs and pictographs divided into related groups. The authors present ideas on how the rock art can be interpreted.

UTAH INDIANS OF TODAY

Dedera, Don. *Navajo Rugs: How to Find, Evaluate, Buy and Care for Them.* Northland Press, 1990; 128 pages, $12.95. Dedera gives the history of Navajo weaving, illustrates how it's done, shows regional styles, and offers practical advice on purchasing.

Dyk, Walter (recorded by). *Son of Old Man Hat, A Navajo Autobiography.* University of Nebraska Press, 1967 (1938 original copyright); 378 pages, $10.95. A Navajo relates growing up in the late 1800s. He was born during his family's return from four years of internment at Fort Sumner, New Mexico.

Gilpin, Laura. *The Enduring Navajo.* University of Texas Press, 1968; 505 pages, $37.50. Excellent book about the Navajo—their homes, land, ceremonies, crafts, tribal government, and trading posts.

Locke, Raymond F. *The Book of the Navajo.* Mankind Publishing, 1989; 512 pages, $5.95. Navajo legends, art, and history from early to modern times.

Looney, Ralph. "The Navajos." *National Geographic,* Dec. 1972; page 740. The Navajo people and how they've balanced their traditions with life in 20th-century America.

Luckert, Karl W. *Coyoteway: A Navajo Holyway Healing Ceremonial.* The University of Arizona Press and Museum of Northern Arizona Press, 1979; 243 pages, $13.95. A rare look at an important Navajo ceremony. The event requires nine days and involves chanting, fire making, sandpainting, and other rituals. Photos and translations of chants reveal some of the intricate Navajo beliefs.

Zolbrod, Paul G. *Diné bahane': The Navajo Creation Story.* University of New Mexico Press, 1984; 431 pages, $22.50. Deities, people, and animals come to life in this translation of Navajo mythology.

NATURAL SCIENCES

Arnberger, Leslie P., and Jeanne R. Janish. *Flowers of the Southwest Mountains.* Southwest Parks and Monuments Association, 1982; 139 pages, $9.95. Coverage includes common flowers and trees of southern Utah's high country above 7,000 feet.

Baars, Donald L. *The Colorado Plateau: A Geologic History.* University of New Mexico Press, 1983; 279 pages, $13.95. Written for the layperson, this book takes you on a tour of the Four Corners area geology from the ancient twisted rocks at the bottom of the Grand Canyon to the fiery volcanism and icy glaciations of the Pleistocene Epoch.

Barnes, F.A. *Canyon Country Geology for the Layman and Rockhound.* Wasatch Publishers, Inc., 1978; 157 pages, $5. Geologic history and a guide to rockhounding. Emphasis is on southeastern Utah and adjacent Arizona.

Craighead, John J. (and others). *A Field Guide to Rocky Mountain Wildflowers.* Houghton Mifflin Co., 1974; 275 pages, $14.95. Handy guide takes in Utah's high country. A plant key and detailed descriptions make identification easy. Illustrated with line drawings and color photos.

Dodge, Natt N. *100 Roadside Wildflowers of Southwest Uplands in Natural Color.* Southwest Parks and Monuments Association, 1980; 64 pages, $4.95. Introduction with a brief description and color photo for those flowers usually found in southern Utah above 4,500 feet.

Dodge, Natt, N. *Poisonous Dwellers of the Desert.* Southwest Parks and Monuments Association, 1981; 40 pages, $3.95. Creatures to watch out for include: poisonous insects, snakes, and Gila monsters. Advice is given on bite treatment and insecticides. Some nonvenomous animals often mistakenly thought poisonous are listed too.

Doolittle, Jerome. *Canyons and Mesas.* Time-Life Books (American Wilderness Series), 1974; 184 pages. Text and photos give a feel for the ruggedly beautiful country of southern Utah and adjacent states.

Elmore, Francis H., and Jeanne R. Janish. *Shrubs and Trees of the Southwest Uplands.* Southwest Parks and Monuments Association, 1976; 214 pages, $9.95. Color-coded pages help locate plants and trees above 4,500 feet (from the piñon-juniper belt to treeline).

Halfpenny, James, and Elizabeth Biesiot. *A Field Guide: Mammal Tracking in Western America.* Johnson Books, 1986; 163 pages, $13.95. No need to guess what animal passed by. This well-illustrated guide shows how to read trails of large and small wildlife. More determined detectives can study the scatology chapter.

Hamilton, Wayne L. *The Sculpturing of Zion; With Road Guide to the Geology of Zion National Park.* Zion Natural History Association 1984; 132 pages, $12.95. Outstanding book explaining geologic forces and history. Clear graphs, drawings, and beautiful color photography illustrate the nontechnical text.

Haywood, C. Lynn (and others). *Birds of Utah.* BYU Great Basin Naturalist memoirs, 1976; 229 pages, $10. Introduction tells of bird habitats, conservation, and early observations. Descriptions tell where and when sighted. Illustrated with color and black-and-white photos.

Haywood, C. Lynn. *The High Uintas: Utah's Land of Lake and Forest.* Monte L. Bean Life Science Museum, 1983; 101 pages, $6.95. This book will help you enjoy your travels in the Uintas. Introduction to the geology, plantlife, birds, and animals of Utah's loftiest lands. Well illustrated with color and black and white photos.

Lanner, Ronald M., and Christine Rasmuss. *Trees of the Great Basin: A Natural History.* University of Nevada Press, 1984; 256 pages, $31.95. Thoughtful and informative descriptions of 47 trees native to mountains of Nevada and western Utah. Author's enthusiasm for trees and their life cycles really comes across. Many of these trees occur in other parts of Utah too. The book has a color photo section.

Lindquist, Robert C. *The Geology of Bryce Canyon National Park.* Bryce Canyon Natural History Association, 1977; 52 pages, $1.99. A well-illustrated, nontechnical account of Bryce's geologic history and formation of the colorful erosional features.

McKee, Edwin D. *Ancient Landscapes of the Grand Canyon Region.* Northland Press, 1982; 52 pages, $3. Brief account of geologic forces that created Zion, Bryce, and the Grand Canyon.

MacMahon, James A. *Deserts.* Alfred A. Knopf, The Audubon Society Nature Guides, 1985; 638 pages, $19. Comprehensive naturalist's guide to the Great Basin, Colorado Plateau, and other arid regions of the West. Many color photos help identify the birds, mammals, fish, insects, reptiles, amphibians, and flora

Nelson, Ruth, and Tom Blaue. *Plants of Zion National Park: Wildflowers, Trees, Shrubs, and Ferns.* Zion Natural History Association, 1976; 333 pages, $9.95 Introduction to Zion's plants, habitats, and blooming seasons. A key, grouped according to families, aids identification. Many black and white drawings and color photos.

Olin, George, and Dale Thompson. *Mammals of the Southwest Deserts.* Southwest Parks and Monuments Association, 1982; 97 pages, $6.95. Well illustrated with black-and-white and color drawings.

Patraw, Pauline M., and Jeanne R. Janish. *Flowers of the Southwest Mesas.* Southwest Parks and Monuments Association, 1977; 112 pages, $9.95. Flowers and trees of the Upper Sonoran Zone (piñon-juniper belt) are illustrated and described.

Shaw, Richard J. *Wildflowers of the Wasatch and Uinta Mountains.* Wheelwright Press, 1983; 61 pages, $4.95. Compact guide with a color photo for each of the flowers described.

Sigler, William F., and Robert Rush Miller. *Fishes of Utah.* Utah State Dept. of Fish and Game, 1963; 203 pages. A handy guide for the fisherman who wants the inside story of his favorite fish. The book introduces Utah fishing and provides descriptions, illustrations, and life histories for many species.

Stokes, William L. *Geology of Utah.* Utah Museum of Natural History Occasional Paper, no. 6, 1986; 309 pages, $12. A comprehensive overview of Utah's geologic history, rock layers, fossils, and landscapes.

Stokes, William L. *Scenes of the Plateau Lands and How They Came to Be.* Starstone Publishing Co., 1969; 66 pages, $7.95. How mesas, canyons, volcanoes, and other geologic features were formed.

Sweet, Muriel. *Common Edible and Useful Plants of the West.* Naturegraph Publishers, 1976; 64 pages, $12.95. Nontechnical descriptions of plants and trees that have food, medicinal, and other uses. Most of these were first discovered by Indians and used later by pioneer settlers.

Taylor, Ronald J. *Rocky Mountain Wildflowers.* Mountaineers, 1986; 96 pages, $5.95. Pocket-size guide to high-country flowers, each with a description and color photo.

Welsh, Stanley L., and Bill Ratcliffe. *Flowers of the Canyon Country.* Canyonlands Natural History Association, 1986; 85 pages, $12.95. Beautiful color photography makes this book a pleasure to use while traveling in southern Utah. Each flower has a photo and nontechnical description.

Whitney, Stephen. *Western Forests.* Alfred A. Knopf, The Audubon Society Nature Guides, 1985; 670 pages, $31.95. Comprehensive guide to the woodlands, Rocky Mountain montane forests, and subalpine forests of Utah and other western states. The hundreds of color photos aid identification of wildflowers, trees, birds, mammals, reptiles, amphibians, and insects.

ONWARD TRAVEL

Castleman, Deke. *Nevada Handbook.* Moon Publications, 1991; 412 pages, $12.95. A lively guide to the cities, ghost towns, deserts, and mountains. Learn the inside story of the gambling centers and many other facets of this unusual state, the "Wildest in the West."

Loftus, Bill. *Idaho Handbook.* Moon Publications, 1994; 281 pages, $14.95. Like Utah, this northern neighbor offers vast wilderness areas of exceptional scenic beauty including the largest in the "lower 48"—the 2.3-million-acre Frank Church-River of No Return Wilderness. You'll find details for enjoying Idaho's skiing, hiking, mountain biking, river running, and culture.

Metzger, Stephen. *Colorado Handbook.* Moon Publications, 1992; 423 pages, $15.95. This handbook guides you to Mesa Verde National Park, beautiful canyon country, and the heart of the magnificent Rocky Mountains.

Metzger, Stephen. *New Mexico Handbook.* Moon Publications, 1994; 329 pages, $14.95. Magical landscapes, ancient Indian villages, and thriving art centers are just a few of the attractions here. This handy guide will help you get the most from your visit.

Pitcher, Don. *Wyoming Handbook.* Moon Publications, 1991; 429 pages, $12.95. Tales of Indians and pioneers provide a backdrop for exploring the steaming geysers of Yellowstone National Park, the precipitous peaks of the Tetons, and the majestic Wind River Mountains. The author gives practical tips on enjoying the resorts and cities, where to find rodeos and pow wows, and even how *not* to start a fight in a cowboy bar!

Weir, Bill, and Robert Blake. *Arizona Traveler's Handbook.* Moon Publications, 1994; 494 pages, $16.95. If you like the *Utah Hand-*

book, you'll enjoy using this one too! It's the most comprehensive guide to the Grand Canyon state's scenic wonders, cities, towns, history, outdoor recreation, and practicalities.

REFERENCE

Greer, Deon C. *Atlas of Utah.* Weber State College and Brigham Young University Press, 1981; 300 pages, $29.95. A comprehensive atlas of the state with excellent color maps. Good overview of Utah's geography, climate, geology, flora and fauna, history, social institutions, government, economy, and recreation.

Perry, John, and Jane Greverus Perry. *The Sierra Club Guide to the Natural Areas of Colorado and Utah.* Sierra Club Books, 1985; 317 pages, $9.95. A reference source with addresses, recreation possibilities, plant and animal checklists, and road directions for 189 different areas.

INDEX

Page numbers in **boldface** indicate the primary reference. Page numbers in *italics* indicate information in captions, charts, maps, or special topics.

ABOUT THE AUTHORS

BILL WEIR

Back in school, Bill Weir always figured he'd settle down to a career job and live happily ever after. Then he discovered travel. After graduating with a B.A. in physics from Berea College in 1972, Bill wound up as an electronic technician in Columbus, Ohio. But the very short vacation times just weren't enough for the trips he dreamed of. So in 1976 he took off with his trusty bicycle "Bessie" and rode across the United States from Virginia to Oregon with Bikecentennial '76. The following year he did an even longer bicycle trip—from Alaska to Baja California. Then the ultimate journey—a bicycle cruise around the world! That lasted from 1980 to 1984, with most of the time spent in the South Pacific and Asia. Naturally Bill used Moon's excellent *South Pacific Handbook* and *Indonesia Handbook*. Correspondence with the authors led to some text and photo contributions for their books and the idea of doing a guidebook of his own. From New Delhi in India, Bill returned to his home base of Flagstaff, Arizona, and set to work researching and writing the *Arizona Handbook*. The immense project took one and one half years of writing and nearly another year of production.

As soon as the writing of the Arizona book came to an end, Bill headed north across the Grand Canyon to the Beehive State. The *Utah Handbook* turned out to

be a big challenge, too, though the rewards of travel there matched his efforts. Now it's time for this fourth edition, thoroughly updated from the last one. The author and his new (to him) 4WD Isuzu Trooper II put on 7,500 Utah miles for this edition to bring you the best guidebook available!

Still free and single, Bill's major interests continue to be exploration of the inner and outer worlds along with writing and photography. The diverse worlds of the American West and Asia remain his favorites.

ROBERT BLAKE

Robert Blake was born at Pensacola Naval Air Station, the son of a U.S. Naval aviator. By the time he finished first grade, he'd lived in seven places—including all four corners of the country.

With a keen interest in astronomy, Robert attended Pensacola Junior College, University of Arizona, and Northern Arizona University in the mid- to late 1960s. Robert was drafted into the army in 1970. He served first as a guard in northern Italy, within sight of the Alps, then as an optical engineer at Night Vision Labs in Fort Belvoir, Virginia.

In the years since, Robert has taught college astronomy, physics, and math. He rose from teacher to lecturer, instructor, and finally assistant professor at Odessa College, where he directed the college planetarium.

Active in hiking, caving, and astronomy, Robert has enjoyed the Flagstaff area for 25 years. He met Bill Weir at a Flagstaff Hiking Club meeting; the two soon agreed to collaborate on future editions of the Arizona and Utah handbooks.

THE METRIC SYSTEM

1 inch = 2.54 centimeters (cm)
1 foot = .304 meters (m)
1 mile = 1.6093 kilometers (km)
1 km = .6124 miles
1 fathom = 1.8288 m
1 chain = 20.1168 m
1 furlong = 201.168 m
1 acre = .4047 hectares
1 sq km = 100 hectares
1 sq mile = 2.59 square km
1 ounce = 28.35 grams
1 pound = .4536 kilograms
1 short ton = .90718 metric ton
1 short ton = 2000 pounds
1 long ton = 1.016 metric tons
1 long ton = 2240 pounds
1 metric ton = 1000 kilograms
1 quart = .94635 liters
1 US gallon = 3.7854 liters
1 Imperial gallon = 4.5459 liters
1 nautical mile = 1.852 km

To compute centigrade temperatures, subtract 32 from Fahrenheit and divide by 1.8. To go the other way, multiply centigrade by 1.8 and add 32.

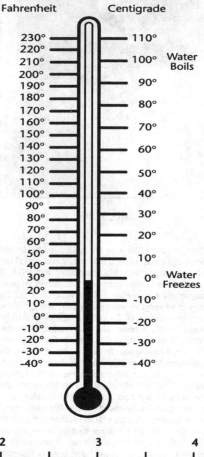

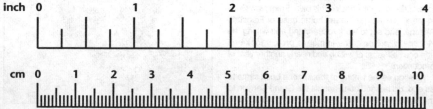

MOON HANDBOOKS—THE IDEAL TRAVELING COMPANIONS

Moon Handbooks provide travelers with all the background and practical information he or she will need on the road. Every Handbook begins with in-depth essays on the land, the people, their history, arts, politics, and social concerns—an entire bookshelf of introductory information squeezed into a one-volume encyclopedia. The Handbooks provide accurate, up-to-date coverage of all the practicalities: language, currency, transportation, accommodations, food and entertainment, and services, to name a few. Moon Handbooks are ideal traveling companions: informative, entertaining, and highly practical.

To locate the bookstore nearest you that carries Moon Travel Handbooks or to order directly from Moon Publications, call: (800) 345-5473, Monday-Friday, 9 a.m.-5 p.m. PST.

THE PACIFIC/ASIA SERIES

BALI HANDBOOK by Bill Dalton
Detailed travel information on the most famous island in the world. 428 pages. **$12.95**

BANGKOK HANDBOOK by Michael Buckley
Your tour guide through this exotic and dynamic city reveals the affordable and accessible possibilities. Thai phrasebook. 222 pages. **$13.95**

BLUEPRINT FOR PARADISE: How to Live on a Tropic Island by Ross Norgrove
This one-of-a-kind guide has everything you need to know about moving to and living comfortably on a tropical island. 212 pages. **$14.95**

FIJI ISLANDS HANDBOOK by David Stanley
The first and still the best source of information on travel around this 322-island archipelago. Fijian glossary. 198 pages. **$11.95**

INDONESIA HANDBOOK by Bill Dalton
This one-volume encyclopedia explores island by island the many facets of this sprawling, kaleidoscopic island nation. Extensive Indonesian vocabulary. 1,200 pages. **$25.00**

JAPAN HANDBOOK by J.D. Bisignani
In this comprehensive new edition, award-winning travel writer J.D. Bisignani offers to inveterate travelers, newcomers, and businesspeople alike a thoroughgoing presentation of Japan's many facets. 950 pages. **$22.50**

MICRONESIA HANDBOOK: Guide to the Caroline, Gilbert, Mariana, and Marshall Islands by David Stanley
Micronesia Handbook guides you on a real Pacific adventure all your own. 345 pages. **$11.95**

NEW ZEALAND HANDBOOK by Jane King
Introduces you to the people, places, history, and culture of this extraordinary land. 571 pages. **$18.95**

OUTBACK AUSTRALIA HANDBOOK by Marael Johnson
Australia is an endlessly fascinating, vast land, and *Outback Australia Handbook* explores the cities and towns, sheep stations, and wilderness areas of the Northern Territory, Western Australia, and South Australia. Full of travel tips and cultural information for adventuring, relaxing, or just getting away from it all. 355 pages. **$15.95**

PHILIPPINES HANDBOOK by Peter Harper and Evelyn Peplow
Crammed with detailed information, *Philippines Handbook* equips the escapist, hedonist, or business traveler with thorough coverage of the Philippines's colorful history, landscapes, and culture. 600 pages. **$17.95**

SOUTHEAST ASIA HANDBOOK by Carl Parkes
Helps the enlightened traveler discover the real Southeast Asia. 873 pages. **$21.95**

SOUTH KOREA HANDBOOK by Robert Nilsen
Whether you're visiting on business or searching for adventure, *South Korea Handbook* is an invaluable companion. Korean glossary with useful notes on speaking and reading the language. 548 pages. **$14.95**

SOUTH PACIFIC HANDBOOK by David Stanley
The original comprehensive guide to the 16 territories in the South Pacific. 740 pages. **$19.95**

TAHITI-POLYNESIA HANDBOOK by David Stanley
All five French-Polynesian archipelagoes are covered in this comprehensive guide by Oceania's best-known travel writer. 235 pages. **$11.95**

THAILAND HANDBOOK by Carl Parkes
Presents the richest source of information on travel in Thailand. 568 pages. **$16.95**

THE HAWAIIAN SERIES

BIG ISLAND OF HAWAII HANDBOOK by J.D. Bisignani
An entertaining yet informative text packed with insider tips on accommodations, dining, sports and outdoor activities, natural attractions, and must-see sights. 350 pages. **$13.95**

HAWAII HANDBOOK by J.D. Bisignani
Winner of the 1989 Hawaii Visitors Bureau's Best Guide Award and the Grand Award for Excellence in Travel Journalism, this guide takes you beyond the glitz and high-priced hype and leads you to a genuine Hawaiian experience. Covers all 8 Hawaiian Islands. 1,000 pages. **$19.95**

KAUAI HANDBOOK by J.D. Bisignani
Kauai is the island Hawaiians visit to get away from it all. 274 pages. **$13.95**

MAUI HANDBOOK by J.D. Bisignani
"No fool-'round" advice on accommodations, eateries, and recreation, plus a comprehensive introduction to island ways, geography, and history. Hawaiian and pidgin glossaries. 393 pages. **$14.95**

HONOLULU~WAIKIKI HANDBOOK: The Island of Oahu by J.D. Bisignani
A handy guide to Honolulu, renowned surfing beaches, and Oahu's countless other diversions. Hawaiian and pidgin glossaries. 354 pages. **$14.95**

THE AMERICAS SERIES

ALASKA-YUKON HANDBOOK   by Deke Castleman and Don Pitcher
Get the inside story, with plenty of well-seasoned advice to help you cover more miles on less money. 460 pages.   **$14.95**

ALBERTA AND THE NORTHWEST TERRITORIES HANDBOOK : Including Banff, Jasper, and the Canadian Rockies   by Andrew Hempstead and Nadina Purdon
Explore the rich history, rustic towns, and rugged wilderness of the pristine Canadian countryside. 450 pages.   **$17.95**

ARIZONA TRAVELER'S HANDBOOK   by Bill Weir
This meticulously researched guide contains everything necessary to make Arizona accessible and enjoyable. 445 pages.   **$16.95**

ATLANTIC CANADA HANDBOOK: New Brunswick, Nova Scotia, Labrador, Prince Edward Island, and Newfoundland   by Mark Morris and Nan Drosdick
Canada's eastern seaboard provinces boast a varied European heritage manifested in local cuisine, crafts, and architecture. 450 pages.   **$17.95**

BAJA HANDBOOK: Mexico's Western Peninsula including Cabo San Lucas   by Joe Cummings
A comprehensive guide with all the travel information and background on the land, history, and culture of this untamed thousand-mile-long peninsula. 362 pages.   **$15.95**

BELIZE HANDBOOK   by Chicki Mallan
Complete with detailed maps, practical information, and an overview of the area's flamboyant history, culture, and geographical features, *Belize Handbook* is the only comprehensive guide of its kind to this spectacular region. 263 pages.   **$14.95**

BRITISH COLUMBIA HANDBOOK   by Jane King
With an emphasis on outdoor adventures, this guide covers mainland British Columbia, Vancouver Island, the Queen Charlotte Islands, and the Canadian Rockies. 381 pages.
$15.95

CANCUN HANDBOOK   by Chicki Mallan
Covers the city's luxury scene as well as more modest attractions, plus many side trips to unspoiled beaches and Mayan ruins. Spanish glossary. 257 pages.   **$13.95**

CENTRAL MEXICO HANDBOOK: Mexico City, Guadalajara, and Other Colonial Cities   by Chicki Mallan
Retrace the footsteps of Cortés from the coast of Veracruz to the heart of Mexico City to discover archaeological and cultural wonders. 391 pages.   **$15.95**

CATALINA ISLAND HANDBOOK: A Guide to California's Channel Islands
by Chicki Mallan
A complete guide to these remarkable islands, from the windy solitude of the Channel Islands National Marine Sanctuary to bustling Avalon. 245 pages.   **$10.95**

COLORADO HANDBOOK   by Stephen Metzger
Essential details to the all-season possibilities in Colorado fill this guide. Practical travel tips combine with recreation—skiing, nightlife, and wilderness exploration—plus entertaining essays. 416 pages.   **$17.95**

COSTA RICA HANDBOOK by Christopher P. Baker
Experience the many wonders of the natural world as you explore this remarkable land. Spanish-English glossary. 574 pages. **$17.95**

GEORGIA HANDBOOK by Kap Stann
Discover the Old South of mint juleps and magnolia blossoms, and enjoy Georgia's legendary hospitality. Includes detailed information on the upcoming 1006 Summer Olympic Games. 350 pages. **$16.95**

IDAHO HANDBOOK by Bill Loftus
A year-round guide to everything in this outdoor wonderland, from whitewater adventures to rural hideaways. 282 pages. **$14.95**

JAMAICA HANDBOOK by Karl Luntta
From the sun and surf of Montego Bay and Ocho Rios to the cool slopes of the Blue Mountains, author Karl Luntta offers island-seekers a perceptive, personal view of Jamaica. 230 pages. **$14.95**

MONTANA HANDBOOK by W.C. McRae and Judy Jewell
The wild West is yours with this extensive guide to the Treasure State, complete with travel practicalities, history, and lively essays on Montana life. 427 pages. **$15.95**

NEVADA HANDBOOK by Deke Castleman
Nevada Handbook puts the Silver State into perspective and makes it manageable and affordable. 450 pages. **$16.95**

NEW MEXICO HANDBOOK by Stephen Metzger
A close-up and complete look at every aspect of this wondrous state. 375 pages. **$14.95**

NORTHERN CALIFORNIA HANDBOOK by Kim Weir
An outstanding companion for imaginative travel in the territory north of the Tehachapis. 765 pages. **$19.95**

NORTHERN MEXICO HANDBOOK: The Sea of Cortez to the Gulf of Mexico
by Joe Cummings
Directs travelers from the barrier islands of Sonora to the majestic cloud forests of the Sierra Madre Oriental to traditional villages and hidden waterfalls in San Luis Potosí. 500 pages. **$16.95**

OREGON HANDBOOK by Stuart Warren and Ted Long Ishikawa
Brimming with travel practicalities and insiders' views on Oregon's history, culture, arts, and activities. 461 pages. **$16.95**

PACIFIC MEXICO HANDBOOK by Bruce Whipperman
Explore 2,000 miles of gorgeous beaches, quiet resort towns, and famous archaeological sites along Mexico's Pacific coast. Spanish-English glossary. 428 pages. **$15.95**

TEXAS HANDBOOK by Joe Cummings
Seasoned travel writer Joe Cummings brings an insider's perspective to his home state. 483 pages. **$13.95**

UTAH HANDBOOK by Bill Weir
Weir gives you all the carefully researched facts and background to make your visit a success. 458 pages. **$16.95**

WASHINGTON HANDBOOK   by Archie Satterfield and Dianne J. Boulerice Lyons
Covers sights, shopping, services, transportation, and outdoor recreation, with complete
listings for restaurants and accommodations. 419 pages.   **$15.95**

WYOMING HANDBOOK   by Don Pitcher
All you need to know to open the doors to this wide and wild state. 495 pages.   **$14.95**

YUCATAN HANDBOOK   by Chicki Mallan
All the information you'll need to guide you into every corner of this exotic land. Mayan and
Spanish glossaries. 391 pages.   **$15.95**

THE INTERNATIONAL SERIES

EGYPT HANDBOOK   by Kathy Hansen
An invaluable resource for intelligent travel in Egypt. Arabic glossary. 522 pages.   **$18.95**

MOSCOW-ST. PETERSBURG HANDBOOK   by Masha Nordbye
Provides the visitor with an extensive introduction to the history, culture, and people of these
two great cities, as well as practical information on where to stay, eat, and shop. 260 pages.
$13.95

NEPAL HANDBOOK   by Kerry Moran
Whether you're planning a week in Kathmandu or months out on the trail, *Nepal Handbook* will
take you into the heart of this Himalayan jewel. 378 pages.   **$12.95**

NEPALI AAMA   by Broughton Coburn
A delightful photo-journey into the life of a Gurung tribeswoman of Central Nepal. Having lived
with Aama (translated, "mother") for two years, first as an outsider and later as an adopted
member of the family, Coburn presents an intimate glimpse into a culture alive with humor,
folklore, religion, and ancient rituals. 165 pages.   **$13.95**

STAYING HEALTHY IN ASIA, AFRICA, AND LATIN AMERICA
by Dirk G. Schroeder, Sc D, MPH
Don't leave home without it! Besides providing a complete overview of the health problems that
exist in these areas, this book will help you determine which immunizations you'll need
beforehand, what medications to take with you, and how to recognize and treat infections and
diseases. Includes extensively illustrated first-aid information and precautions for heat, cold,
and high altitude. 200 pages.   **$10.95**

TIBET HANDBOOK: A PILGRIMAGE GUIDE   by Victor Chan
This remarkable book is both a comprehensive trekking guide to mountain paths and plateau
trails, and a pilgrimage guide that draws on Tibetan literature and religious history. 1104 pages.
$30.00

MOONBELTS

Made of heavy-duty Cordura nylon, the Moonbelt offers maximum protection for your money
and important papers. This all-weather pouch slips under your shirt or waistband, rendering it
virtually undetectable and inaccessible to pickpockets. One-inch-wide nylon webbing, heavy-
duty zipper, one-inch quick-release buckle. Accommodates traveler's checks, passport, cash,
photos. Size 5 x 9 inches. Black.   **$8.95**

New travel handbooks may be available that are not on this list. To find out more
about current or upcoming titles, call us toll-free at (800) 345-5473.

IMPORTANT ORDERING INFORMATION

FOR FASTER SERVICE: Call to locate the bookstore nearest you that carries Moon Travel Handbooks or order directly from Moon Publications:

(800) 345-5473 • Monday-Friday • 9 a.m.-5 p.m. PST • fax (916) 345-6751

PRICES: All prices are subject to change. We always ship the most current edition. We will let you know if there is a price increase on the book you ordered.

SHIPPING & HANDLING OPTIONS: 1) Domestic UPS or USPS first class (allow 10 working days for delivery): $3.50 for the first item, 50 cents for each additional item.

Exceptions:
- **Moonbelt** shipping is $1.50 for one, 50 cents for each additional belt.
- Add $2.00 for same-day handling.
- UPS 2nd Day Air or Printed Airmail requires a special quote.
- International Surface Bookrate (8-12 weeks delivery):
  $3.00 for the first item, $1.00 for each additional item. Note: Moon Publications cannot guarantee international surface bookrate shipping.

FOREIGN ORDERS: All orders that originate outside the U.S.A. must be paid for with either an International Money Order or a check in U.S. currency drawn on a major U.S. bank based in the U.S.A.

TELEPHONE ORDERS: We accept Visa or MasterCard payments. Minimum order is US$15.00. Call in your order: (800) 345-5473, 9 a.m.-5 p.m. Pacific Standard Time.

ORDER FORM

Be sure to call (800) 345-5473 for current prices and editions or for the name of the bookstore nearest you that carries Moon Travel Handbooks • 9 a.m.–5 p.m. PST
(See important ordering information on preceding page)

Name: _____ Date: _____

Street: _____

City: _____ Daytime Phone: _____

State or Country: _____ Zip Code: _____

QUANTITY	TITLE	PRICE

Taxable Total _____

Sales Tax (7.25%) for California Residents _____

Shipping & Handling _____

TOTAL _____

Ship: ☐ UPS (no PO Boxes) ☐ 1st class ☐ International surface mail

Ship to: ☐ address above ☐ other _____

Make checks payable to: **MOON PUBLICATIONS, INC.** P.O. Box 3040, Chico, CA 95927-3040 U.S.A. We accept Visa and MasterCard. **To Order**: Call in your Visa or MasterCard number, or send a written order with your Visa or MasterCard number and expiration date clearly written.

Card Number: ☐ **Visa** ☐ **MasterCard**

☐ ☐ ☐ ☐ ☐ ☐ ☐ ☐ ☐ ☐ ☐ ☐ ☐ ☐ ☐ ☐

Exact Name on Card: _____

expiration date: _____

signature _____

S/95

WHERE TO BUY THIS BOOK

BOOKSTORES AND LIBRARIES:
Moon Publications Handbooks are sold worldwide. Please write our sales manager for a list of wholesalers and distributors in your area that stock our travel handbooks.

TRAVELERS:
We would like to have Moon Publications Handbooks available throughout the world. Please ask your bookstore to write or call us for ordering information. If your bookstore will not order our guides for you, please write or call for a free catalog.

MOON PUBLICATIONS, INC.
P.O. BOX 3040
CHICO, CA 95927-3040 U.S.A.
TEL: (800) 345-5473
FAX: (916) 345-6751

TRAVEL MATTERS

Travel Matters is Moon Publications' quarterly newsletter. It provides today's traveler with timely, informative travel news and articles.

You'll find resourceful coverage on:

- **Money**—What does it cost? Is it worth it?
- **Low impact travel**—tread lightly travel tips
- **Special interest travel**—cultural tours, environmental excursions, outdoor recreation, adventure treks, and more
- **Travel styles**—families, seniors, disabled travelers, package and theme tours
- **Consumer reviews**—books, language aids, travel gadgets, products, and services
- **Facts and opinions**—reader's letters and Moon Handbook author news
- **Moon Handbook booklist**—the latest titles and editions, and where and how to purchase them

To receive a free copy of *Travel Matters*, write Moon Publications Inc., P.O. Box 3040, Chico, CA 95927-3040, or call toll-free (800) 345-5473, Monday–Friday, 9 a.m. – 5 p.m. Pacific Standard Time.